Popular Educational Classics

This book is part of the Peter Lang Education list.
Every volume is peer reviewed and meets
the highest quality standards for content and production.

PETER LANG
New York • Bern • Frankfurt • Berlin
Brussels • Vienna • Oxford • Warsaw

Popular Educational Classics

A Reader

Edited by Joseph L. DeVitis

PETER LANG
New York • Bern • Frankfurt • Berlin
Brussels • Vienna • Oxford • Warsaw

Library of Congress Cataloging-in-Publication Data
Names: DeVitis, Joseph L., editor.
Title: Popular educational classics: a reader / edited by Joseph L. DeVitis.
Description: New York: Peter Lang, [2016]
Includes bibliographical references.
Identifiers: LCCN 2015033933 | ISBN 978-1-4331-2834-9 (hardcover: alk. paper)
ISBN 978-1-4331-2833-2 (paperback: alk. paper) | ISBN 978-1-4539-1735-0 (e-book)
Subjects: LCSH: Education—United States—Philosophy—History—20th century.
Education—United States—Philosophy—History—21st century.
Public schools—United States—History—20th century.
Public schools—United States—History—21st century.
Educational sociology—United States.
Classification: LCC LA209.2.P55 2016 | DDC 370.973 2 23
LC record available at http://lccn.loc.gov/2015033933

Bibliographic information published by **Die Deutsche Nationalbibliothek**.
Die Deutsche Nationalbibliothek lists this publication in the "Deutsche
Nationalbibliografie"; detailed bibliographic data are available
on the Internet at http://dnb.d-nb.de/.

Cover image: ©iStock.com/Kerstin Waurick

The paper in this book meets the guidelines for permanence and durability
of the Committee on Production Guidelines for Book Longevity
of the Council of Library Resources.

© 2016 Peter Lang Publishing, Inc., New York
29 Broadway, 18th floor, New York, NY 10006
www.peterlang.com

Printed in the United States of America

Dedication

To *Joe R. Burnett,*
For his staunch sense of fairness and abiding faith in democracy and education

Contents

Introduction

Joseph L. DeVitis

Popular Educational Classics: A Reader attempts to show how the last half century of school and society has dramatized deep tensions in how we analyze education and social change as students, teachers, administrators, scholars, policymakers, and concerned citizens. Competing belief systems have done battle with each other during the era covered in the text. One camp frames schooling within severe social constraints that need to be overcome—an ideology attuned to socially and politically progressive movements. The other, more conservative, perspective proposes educational policies and practices that move schools in a far different direction—one largely devoid of connection to wider social structures. That profound ideological struggle continues to this day. It is my hope that this book will be helpful in untangling the roots of the persistent debates that have divided the nation for so long. Moreover, my ultimate wish is to provide more clarity—and reflective action—on crucial public problems that have necessitated those heated conflicts. If we can make greater strides toward solving the "crisis in the classroom"—in fuller reality, the crisis in *society*—we will have better served our children and created a more humane community.

Some Stipulations and Caveats

This introduction will not discuss all 40 texts in the compendium. To do so would require a companion volume in itself, and my contributors have done exceptional work that I cannot improve upon. Instead, I will attempt to whet readers' appetites for what I would characterize as a kind of liberal education in contemporary educational studies. Nor will there be any images of ancient Greek or Roman columns. I use the words "popular" and "classic" loosely and in tandem to signify books that have been emblematic and memorable in educational circles from the 1960s to the present. It is no coincidence that the period chosen parallels my own journey as an educational theorist and practitioner. Indeed, I have assigned almost all of the books chosen for this volume in my college classes from 1969 to 2013. I have chosen them because they treat crucial questions in school and society in language and substance accessible not only to scholars but also to a wider public. I am less interested in undertaking an academic exercise than I am in motivating larger groups to seek educational change. Thus the book goes beyond rarefied jargon toward a more complete universe of discourse, policy, and practice. In a word, we need to augment our roles as public intellectuals who share knowledge and wisdom with a larger readership while foregoing any attempts to mystify, as if we were High Priests. To have a public, we must speak to its urgent interests by developing more generalizing vocabularies. Thus, for this compendium, I have purposely privileged books written by public intellectuals.

Similarly, I have largely excluded specific studies that speak in more specialist idioms and narratives or are solely rooted in earlier time periods. Many of the books chosen are indeed scholarly; all of them appeal to an extensive public rather than a small coterie of academic audiences. I want readers to *feel* the actual pulse and press of conflict in the particular decades represented in this book. Thus I have included only those works that deal, in whole or part, with the years under discussion. They are talked-about books that are read for what they offer for reform today and tomorrow, in and out of the classroom. In other words, they are socially and educationally relevant.

If we want to alter conditions in public schools and society, we will need to converse and act in more public terms. Armchair philosophizing will not be sufficient. A more concerted effort will be required to counter persistent posturing among politicians, policymakers, government officials, and even some school leaders who exert power over education. We should work with teachers to foster fuller control of their wider social, political, and economic destinies, including more substantial responsibility for participating in tough and tender dialogue and *action* on the contentious problems they face each and every day. I sincerely hope that the books in this text will aid in the struggle to actualize democratic schooling and a more democratic society. Granted, this will be extremely difficult in a culture of money, greed, power, and intensively lobbied laws and policies. The "haves" have been unwilling to give up even bird-like shares of what they hold, a sorry circumstance that leads seamlessly to the next section.

The books surveyed in this collection draw upon significant issues related to several interwoven themes: the critical impact of politics on education, the actual possibility of harm in schooling, and the search for meaning in education. Of course, none of those subjects can really be evaluated separately. This introduction recognizes that false dichotomy. I compose such a rhetorical structure to focus readers' attention on key propositions that run throughout the book, whether distinctly articulated or implied.

Education *Is* Political

Readers will find that this text is strewn with outright and veiled *political* premises and assumptions. In some 40 years of teaching teachers, I have often been surprised after repeating the words, "Education is political." That claim tends to draw some raised eyebrows, especially among undergraduates. It is a truism that is not always taken as a rule of the profession, especially among beginning teachers. Indeed, it is congruent with Dan C. Lortie's findings in *Schoolteacher: A Sociological Inquiry* (1975) that teachers have traditionally tended to be conservative culturally and politically. That circumstance was particularly the case during my years as a professor in the South. However, the National Education Association (NEA) has been credited with helping Jimmy Carter win the presidency in 1976 (the first time the NEA endorsed a national campaign). Carter came through on his promise to establish the federal Department of Education and appointed Ernest L. Boyer, who is discussed in this book, as the Commissioner of Education in 1977. Since then, both the American Federation of Teachers (AFT) and the NEA have continued to be active in national, state, and local politics during decades of waning unionization.

It is wise to take care in analyzing political language about education and to be wary of sloganeering. Words such as "excellence," "rigor," "world class," "No Child Left Behind," "Race to the Top," and the like are typically used to persuade when they more realistically proffer empty bromides and public relations offenses. Naturally, both rightist and leftist recommendations seek to win us over. No matter what one's political viewpoints, education is too important to be left to undiscerning policymaking—a fact of life that, if ignored, has usually been harmful and sometimes ruinous.

Some strange stirrings occur when analyzing the politics of education. Throughout the period covered in this book, there has been a persisting struggle between the right and the left to draw rhetorical blood while zigzagging toward school reform. At times I have been compelled to admit that the right has spoken more directly and clearly to public audiences. (The political left could learn from the lucid speech of Senators Bernie Sanders and Elizabeth Warren.) Meanwhile, the academic left has spoken too often in obtuse, esoteric forms and tones while ironically urging an awakening of the public through liberationist means. Less clouded communication would seem to offer a good start. Here is an admittedly extreme scholarly example of the opposite in *one* sentence:

> A politics presuming the ontological indifference of all minority social identities as defining oppressed or dominated groups, a politics in which differences are sublimated in the constitution of a minority identity…can recover the differences between social identities only on the basis of common and therefore commensurable experiences of marginalization, which experiences in turn yield a political practice that consists largely of *affirming* the identities specific to those experiences. (Guillory, 1993, p. 12)

As we take a breath, we realize that the elephant in the schoolhouse has long been evident: education cannot really be transformed until our society has the courage and will to face poverty head-on. Ray Bradbury (1997), who knew how to separate social reality from science fiction, perhaps put it best: "Poverty made a sound like a wet cough in the shadows of the room" (p. 82). The right does not admit noticing the elephant's walk, and the left does not appear to be adept at riding the animal more vigorously with wider publics. With any luck, maybe even Democrats will begin to mention "the poor," and not just the middle class. Rather than skirting around the edges and often using public schools as scapegoats, we would gain more traction by attacking structural economic problems endemic to American society. Some of the writers in this book offer glimmers of hope in that they recognize poverty as *the* basic issue to be tackled. One need look no further than the career of Diane Ravitch (2000, 2010, 2013) to see that major reversals can occur. She spent several decades as a conservative critic of public schools but is now a vocal opponent of right-wing apostles who bash teachers, extol massive testing, and neglect the social, economic, and political condition of the poor:

> The fact is that poverty does matter. No matter what standardized test you look at, the results portray the influence of socioeconomic status on test scores. Despite outliers, the kids with the most advantages are at the top, the kids with the fewest advantages are at the bottom. This is true of international tests, state tests, federal tests, the ACT, the SAT. Standardized tests are the means by which privilege is distributed. The outcomes are predictable. (Ravitch, 2014, p. 1)

In recent years, Ravitch has shed the thin cloak of such conservative concepts as "choice," "vouchers," "markets," "deregulation," and "privatization." These are some of the same notions adopted by neoliberals who champion an individualistic culture that calls for cutbacks in basic human services and largely disavow communitarian concerns (Lipman, 2007). They prize an essentially corporate approach to public schooling; the public good seems to have escaped their attention. Conversely, Ravitch grants that she has studied the evidence anew and discarded many of her past allegiances. She would now doubtless concur with this characterization of a nation steeped in a present-day version of social Darwinism and a blame-the-victim mentality: "Obsessed with success and wealth and despising failure and poverty, our society is systematically dividing the population into winners and losers" (Taibbi, 2014, pp. 12–13).

For further examination of the consequences of politics in education, see additional books analyzed in this volume by the following: Raymond E. Callahan, Dan C. Lortie, Samuel Bowles and Herbert Gintis, John E. Chubb and Terry M. Moe, Michael W. Apple, Henry A. Giroux, Peter McLaren, David C. Berliner and Bruce J. Biddle, Jean Anyon, John Ogbu, David Tyack and Larry Cuban, Richard Rothstein, Linda Darling-Hammond, David F. Labaree, and David L. Kirp.

Schools and Society *Can* Be Harmful

Yes, schooling can indeed be injurious to mind, body, and soul. That theme is at least as old as Jean-Jacques Rousseau's *Emile* (1762), in which he proclaimed that human beings, by nature, are good but become corrupted by society. One of the foremost proponents of anti-schooling has been Ivan Illich, whose *Deschooling Society* (1971/2000) is reviewed in this collection. He argues that institutional structures—most assuredly including schools—bear the baggage of "hell paved with good intentions" in human lives. School personnel, Illich claims, transmit an oppressive culture of certainties, social expectations, myths of "progress," and false hope to students (especially those in depressed circumstances). Furthermore, compulsory schooling compels them (particularly those in the middle class and above) to accept societal adjustment to ever-growing patterns of consumption. In Illich's view, schooling tames our freer spirit, calcifying our "habits of the heart."

Other writers, such as Jonathan Kozol in *Savage Inequalities: Children in America's Schools* (1991), have grittily described the noxious conditions in which many urban school districts are forced to struggle and cope. They are often left behind to deal with decaying walls, raw sewage, poisonous drinking water, and the like. Their students are packed like sardines into ramshackle structures, and teachers are hard to find because of gross underfunding. The per capita funding for these districts, as compared to their more affluent suburban neighbors, should make us cringe about the inequalities between rich and poor in the world's richest nation:

> We are children only once; and after those years are gone, there is no second chance to make amends. In this respect, the consequences of unequal education have a terrible finality.... The

winners in this race *feel* meritorious. Since they also are, in large part, those who govern the discussion of this issue, they are not disposed to cast a cloud upon the means of their ascent. (Kozol, 1991, p. 217)

(It should be noted that Kozol's narrative is a prime example of how the themes in this book are often interrelated. His work is, of course, highly influenced by the effects of social reproduction and the politics of education in sustaining inequality.)

More recently, Kenneth Teitelbaum (2013) has hammered home a similar message:

Maybe we would be better off spending less money on improving standards and accountability and more on the underlying conditions that adversely affect learning, including the fact that one in five children in this country come from families in poverty, an increase of 40 percent in the last decade. Some of these children are literally traumatized by the stresses they face and yet are expected to learn the same curriculum and pass the same state exams as children from wealthy families. (Teitelbaum, 2013, p. 2)

In fact, a 2015 report by the Children's Defense Fund (Giannarelli, Lippold, Minton, & Wheaton) shows that our society has not mustered the political will to rightfully be called a caring nation: if the United States authorized an extra 2% of its budget to raise employment, produce viable jobs, and provide for children's vital needs, it would reduce child poverty by 60%. If such fervent and rational critiques are taken seriously, decent men and women—especially politicians, policymakers, and educators among them—should be ashamed and enraged. Yet the elephant still sits at the classroom door, and it has not moved since Kozol wrote his challenging book. It has actually become more elephantine.

The theme of "schooling can be harmful" is also discussed in other books in this text by Paul Goodman, Herbert Kohl, Jeannie Oakes, Michelle Fine, Lisa Delpit, and Alfie Kohn.

Education *Should Be* Meaningful

A number of the authors in this volume speak to the quest for meaning through education. The philosopher Nel Noddings (1992) applies moral education to actualize "attitudes and skills required to sustain caring relations and the desire to do so" among students and teachers in *The Challenge to Care in Schools: An Alternative Approach to Education* (1992). She incorporates concerns for humane pedagogical dispositions, classroom environment, and careful curriculum planning. Teachers should motivate through dialogue, modeling, and "confirmation" (affirming pupils' distinctive strengths) and ask them overarching questions about themselves and the world around them:

Who am I? What sort of person should I be? What is my place in the universe? How should I treat other human beings?… How shall I make a living? What do I owe nonhuman animals? Are there objects I should cherish? What does it mean to be a parent, friend, or citizen in today's world? (Noddings, 1992, pp. xxiii–xxiv)

And no one combines critical pedagogy and existential yearning for meaning more exquisitely than Maxine Greene in *The Dialectic of Freedom* (1988). Her notion of freedom is "the capacity to surpass the given and look at things as if they could be" (p. 3). She *does* recognize that freedom is not easily won; oppressive cultural and social walls block fuller human fulfillment in all ages. Yet Greene beseeches teachers to provoke students to the point that they "reach beyond themselves, to wonder, to imagine, to pose their own questions" in an often senseless world (p. 14). Citing, among others, Fyodor Dostoevsky, John-Paul Sartre, and John Dewey throughout her masterful work, she pushes each of us to believe that meaning can be created in our individual lives and in concert with other human beings. With needed persistence, Greene prods us "to break with the 'cotton wool' of habit, of mere routine…to seek alternative ways of being, to look for openings…to discover new possibilities" (p. 2).

Other authors of books in this anthology offer diverse perspectives on the creation of meaning in education: Jerome S. Bruner, Neil Postman and Charles Weingartner, Charles E. Silberman, John I. Goodlad, Mortimer J. Adler, Ernest L. Boyer, Theodore R. Sizer, E.D. Hirsch, Jane Roland Martin, Gloria Ladson-Billings, C.A. Bowers, and Yong Zhao.

In closing, it is my profound hope that readers will find either new or renewed ways of viewing schools and society through deep reflection on all these books. They are meant to stir our consciences, to disorder our certainties, and to force us to treat education and culture with both reason and passion. None of our authors or contributors writes from canned scripts or required rubrics. Each *does* write so that education and its world can still be sustained—and made better—throughout and beyond our current struggles.

References

Bradbury, R. (1997). *The golden apples of the sun.* New York: Morrow.

Giannarelli, L., Lippold, K., Minton, S., & Wheaton, L. (2015). *Reducing child poverty in the United States: Costs and impacts of policies proposed by the Children's Defense Fund.* Washington, DC: Urban Institute.

Greene, M. (1988). *The dialectic of freedom.* New York: Teachers College Press.

Guillory, J. (1993). *Cultural capital: The problem of literary canon formation.* Chicago: University of Chicago Press.

Illich, I. (2000). *Deschooling society.* London: Marion Boyars. (Original work published 1971).

Kozol, J. (1991). *Savage inequalities: Children in America's schools.* New York: Harper Perennial.

Lipman, P. (2007). No child left behind: Globalization, privatization, and the politics of inequality. In E.W. Ross & R. Gibson (Eds.), *Neoliberalism and education reform.* Cresskill, NJ: Hampton Press.

Lortie, D.C. (1975). *Schoolteacher: A sociological inquiry.* Chicago: University of Chicago Press.

Noddings, N. (1992). *The challenge to care in schools: An alternative approach to education.* New York: Teachers College Press.

Ravitch, D. (2000). *Left behind: A century of battles over school reform.* New York: Simon & Schuster.

Ravitch, D. (2011). *The death and life of the great American school system: How testing and choice are undermining education.* New York: Basic Books.

Ravitch, D. (2013). *Reign of error: The hoax of the privatization movement and the danger to America's public schools.* New York: Vintage.

Ravitch, D. (2014, March 2). *Poverty matters. Diane Ravitch's blog.* Retrieved from http://www.dianeravitch.net/2014/03/02/poverty

Rousseau, J.J. (1979). *Emile: Or on education* (A. Bloom, Trans.). New York: Basic Books. (Original work published 1762).

Taibbi, M. (2014). *The divide: American injustice in the age of the wealth gap.* New York: Speigel & Grau.

Teitelbaum, K. (2010, April 10). Poverty, children, and schooling. *Wilmington* [NC] *Star News.* Retrieved from http://starnewsonlline.com/articles/20130410/ARTICLES/130419976

PART ONE

The 1960s

ONE

Jerome S. Bruner, *The Process of Education* (1960)

Timothy Glander

Jerome Bruner's classic 1960 text, *The Process of Education*, pivots on the now well-known aphorism: "…any subject can be taught effectively in some intellectually honest form to any child at any stage of development."[1] Simple, elegant, profound: as a hypothesis it would remain largely untestable empirically. (Just what, exactly, would intellectual honesty mean here?) Nevertheless, as commonsense understanding, or perhaps as wishful thinking, the axiom resonated with readers in the early 1960s who felt the full brunt of the social alienation and intellectual fragmentation of the age and longed to find some structural coherence and unity between the learner and the world.

An early reviewer gushed about Bruner's book: "There are some rare and wondrous occasions in reading when one has a tremendous sense of the presence of power, the feeling that there is some very special significance in the pages. The book that calls forth such a response is not always a great or near perfect work, but in it something has been said in such a way that for you, some views of the world will never quite be the same."[2] Even the always critical, and usually prescient, Paul Goodman could not subdue his enthusiasm for the book: "In my opinion it will be a classic, comparable for its philosophical centrality and humane concreteness to some of the essays of Dewey."[3] Goodman went on to identify that Bruner's main goal was "to develop not test-passers and technicians, but discovers and inventors," and he accurately noted that Bruner did so by laying "stress on heuristic principles, on the encouragement of intuition, on adaptation to the child's developing world, on the importance of initiative, fantasy, and practical experience of the subject matter." For Goodman, Bruner's book embodied the best part of the humanist tradition, and whether he "knew it or not," Bruner was "breathing the spirit of Mary Boole, (Alfred North) Whitehead, and classical progressive education."[4]

Goodman was right. *The Process of Education* made a compelling argument, yet for all its profound insight, it offered little that was strikingly new or novel in thinking about education. The book restates questions that have perennially framed educational theory and responds with proposals that are highly reflective of the constellation of progressive educational ideas that we associate with John Dewey from earlier in the twentieth century.[5] Like Dewey, Bruner placed primacy on the role of the child as engaged in a meaningful encounter with the world. In so doing, he offered a perspective on teaching and learning that was sharply at odds with the prevailing didactic and conformist style of most American schooling then and now. Written in a highly engaging manner, and cast as an expression of a new cognitive science, the book quickly caught fire for Harvard University Press, selling 83,000 copies in its first edition and launching a major school reform movement, the effects of which still linger with us.[6]

Strangely, however, Bruner did not reference Dewey and progressive education at all in his text, nor did he express any understanding of how his proposal fit within the context of educational history.[7] His approach was largely ahistorical, and the upshot was that he and his collaborators were presenting something new and fresh and potentially revolutionary. While this may have been in part a consequence of Bruner's ignorance of educational history (a deficit he acknowledged in later years), a more probable explanation is that any demonstrable congruence with Dewey and progressive education would have been a difficult sell from a public relations standpoint.[8] The Progressive Education Association had been dissolved by 1955, and in 1961 Lawrence Cremin published his widely read postmortem on progressive education, *The Transformation of the School*.[9] What had been labeled and caricatured as "progressive education," including John Dewey's work in particular, came to be viewed in the 1950s as the source for much that was wrong with American education by an increasingly vocal group of mostly right-wing critics. Any direct or indirect association of his ideas to John Dewey would not have been in Bruner's political or professional interests—nor, for that matter, would it help to advance the larger political agenda of those who funded Bruner's work. Thus, one way to read *The Process of Education* is as an advocacy for the continuation of some of the best of Dewey's progressive educational ideas, but one safely shielded from the image of the bogeyman that Dewey and progressive education had come to possess.[10]

Yet another way to read the book is as a carefully crafted proposal for further educational research funding from the nexus of military institutions, national security agencies, and corporate foundations dominant during the Cold War. By one count, Bruner makes no fewer than thirty-one appeals to support further specific research questions generated in his text. Again, it is not surprising that, in making his case for further funding, Bruner would distance himself from Dewey, whose social and economic views were regarded as quite radical by 1950s standards. Moreover, Dewey's democratic ethos was seen as subversive and dangerous to the Cold War ideologues who, through the distribution of research monies, set the social science research agendas of the time.

If the strength of *The Process of Education* can be found in its unacknowledged fidelity to some of Dewey's key progressive educational ideas, the book's shortcomings can be found in its failure to consider and extend other key aspects of Dewey's educational philosophy. I am referring here primarily to Dewey's emphasis on the critical examination of educational aims and social purposes, as well as his democratic orientation, which emphasizes the teacher's creative role in "psychologizing" the curriculum. The top-down approach of Bruner's book abjures these Deweyan themes and is weaker as a result. This chapter will further consider Bruner's book and explore some of the reasons for, and some of the consequences of, these omissions.

II

The Process of Education was the outgrowth of the now-famous conference at Woods Hole, Massachusetts, in September 1959. There gathered, wrote Bruner, "some thirty-five scientists, scholars, and educators to discuss how education in science might be improved in our primary and secondary schools."[11] The participants reflected a largely homogeneous group, as most of them were drawn from large U.S. research universities, and most reflected training in mathematics, the physical sciences, and psychology, although two historians and a classicist also joined the group. Bärbel Inhelder, Jean Piaget's collaborator from the University of Geneva, was the lone woman in the group and represented its only international perspective. Bruner served as chair of the conference and prepared the chairman's report, which was published as *The Process of Education.*

There should be no doubt, however, that the educational ideas expressed in the text were essentially Bruner's. While all the participants were encouraged to provide critique and comment on the draft report, Bruner wrote in his preface that he made "no effort…to reach a consensus of the Conference as a whole."[12] Several participants were apparently offended by what they regarded as Bruner's autocratic approach. "I had thought, incorrectly," wrote one participant, "that *The Process of Education* was a report of work done collectively by a group of people thinking collectively.… But now I read Dr. Bruner's book five years later, I see how much of the pattern was really his own." Another participant was even more dismayed: "It seems to me that Dr. Bruner ignored the opinions of almost everyone at the conference.… [H]e gave us the 'back of his hand' by emasculating what we had worked so hard to draft."[13]

Despite these objections to the final narrative, it is clear that the work emerged most distinctively from the Cold War context of the time and that the Woods Hole participants shared deeply held beliefs about the national security value of their work. The participants were responding to what they envisioned "to be a long term crisis in national security," itself a consequence of the Central Intelligence Agency (CIA) manpower studies that imagined the United States to be falling behind the Soviet Union in the creation of scientists and engineers with expertise in weapons development. The conference was funded by interconnected foundations and agencies, including the National Science Foundation, the Rand Corporation, the United States Air Force, and others, which were primarily motivated by war-related values.

Many of the conference participants, including Massachusetts Institute of Technology physicist and conference organizer Jerrold Zacharias, had cut their teeth doing such work during World War II and had made their professional careers engaged in highly classified research for the national security apparatus during the Cold War. What emerged from the Woods Hole Conference, argues historian Ronald W. Evans, "was a manufactured consensus, paid for by stakeholders with an interest in education conducted on behalf of national security. It was a direct outgrowth of the cold war, and of persistent attacks on progressive education. As such, it represented the United States of America, or at least a significant selection of its national intellectual leadership, in concerted action against progressive education."[14]

The Process of Education should also be seen as an early iteration of the enduring national obsession with the so-called STEM (Science, Technology, Engineering, Mathematics) disciplines. It represented a manifestation of "Big Science," a model for scientific inquiry that grew out of large-scale, war-related projects developed during World War II.[15] And it advanced an ideological orientation to science that emphasized an accumulative and centralizing view of knowledge in the hands of experts, driven by the values of efficiency and control. The military culture in which the work was embedded was decidedly undemocratic, and the abounding Cold War fears and surveillance forced constraint and conformity on the activity of science that, by its very nature, requires openness and independence.

Social and educational research during this period was treated with suspicion, seen as "unscientific," or both. Many social and educational researchers attempted to ape the approach of the dominant physical sciences in an effort to secure funding from the interlocking national security agencies and corporate foundations.[16] By mid-century most social and educational research had gravitated toward a narrow scientism that relied on quantitative analysis and rejected normative, interpretive, and critical perspectives. Had Bruner's book simply echoed this prevalent scientism, it would have drawn little attention, would have done little to solidify and advance the enduring national mantra for the STEM disciplines, and would have been quickly forgotten. Instead, bolstered by the cadre of physicists and mathematicians who participated in the conference, whose scientific stature tacitly legitimated the conference proceedings and whose Cold War credentials provided appropriate cover, Bruner was free to craft a provocative narrative that engaged the imagination of the general reader even as it stayed within the undemocratic boundaries of the Cold War culture.

It is important to note here that Bruner mastered this kind of sleight of hand through his own war-related work before, during, and after World War II. Bruner was—to use the most accurate descriptor—a propagandist. He was among those social scientists in the first half of the twentieth century whose scholarly interests in understanding opinion management dovetailed with the interests of a corporate-military state seeking to fund and apply such understanding to shaping the opinions of an emerging mass society.[17] Even before the outbreak of World War II, Bruner was involved in propaganda-related work, writing his dissertation at Harvard on "A Psychological Analysis of International Radio Broadcasts of Belligerent Nations" and working at state-sponsored foreign-broadcast monitoring services, first at Princeton in 1940 and then in Washington, D.C., in 1941.[18] By 1942 Bruner had shifted his attention to a study of domestic opinions through the Office of Facts and Figures, the organizational precursor to the Office of War Information. Working for the U.S. wartime propaganda agency, he wrote his first book, *The Mandate from the People*, on domestic wartime public opinion.[19] From there he continued to engage in propaganda-related work for the Psychological Warfare Division of Supreme Headquarters Allied Expeditionary Force (PWD-SHAEF) in England and France during the war. In the postwar period Bruner remained a highly sought-after expert on propaganda matters, participating in such programs of Cold War opinion management as the highly classified Project Troy study and the CIA's Center for International Studies (CENIS) at MIT, among other related activities in the 1950s.[20] While the full story of Bruner's propaganda work with these and other agencies has yet to be told, it is clear that such work occupied much of his focus throughout at least the 1940s and 1950s; and this experience would have—at the very least—shaped his thinking about the need for opinion management as a necessary ingredient of educational policy formation and implementation. As he sat down with the Woods Hole Conference notes to write his first book on educational theory, crafting a message that would positively resonate with key segments of American public opinion would have likely been foremost on his mind.

III

And what a carefully crafted and marvelous message *The Process of Education* would turn out to be. Only 92 pages in length, Bruner's book consists of an introduction and five thematic chapters, reflecting many Deweyan progressive educational ideas, while still subtly advancing Cold War educational aims: The Importance of Structure, Readiness for Learning, Intuitive and Analytic Thinking, Motives for Learning, and Aids to Teaching. In "Chapter 1 – Introduction" and "Chapter 2 – The Importance of Structure," Bruner insightfully explores the important role of understanding the underlying structure and fundamental principles of disciplinary knowledge. All subject matter possesses a coherent and identifiable structure, according to Bruner. This structure can, and should, make up the centerpiece of the curriculum and the primary focus of instruction. The teaching of specific skills and topics should be regarded as secondary and subordinate to the teaching of this underlying structure. Such an understanding of underlying structure makes it easier for students to relate what is learned to other learning experiences. "Grasping the structure of a subject is understanding it in a way that permits many other things to be related to it meaningfully," according to Bruner. "To learn structure, in short, is to learn how things are related."[21] Without such an understanding, Bruner argues, knowledge is inefficient to convey and difficult to remember. Finally, and most importantly, understanding the inherent structure of a discipline makes the learning meaningful, generates intellectual excitement, and compels further learning. In a passage that sounds almost as if it were lifted directly from John Dewey, Bruner writes: "The best way to create interest in a subject is to render it worth knowing, which means to make the knowledge gained usable in one's thinking beyond the situation in which the learning has occurred."[22]

In "Chapter 3 – Readiness for Learning," Bruner considers this inherent structure in relation to the Piagetian stages of cognitive development. He argues for the readiness of elementary school-aged children to access this structural knowledge in ways that are in keeping with their developmental stage, and makes the case for the now-famous "spiral curriculum." His primary focus is on learning in the so-called concrete operations stage, roughly the beginning school-age years of about five or six, until the child passes into the formal operations stage between ten and fourteen years of age. Bruner suggests that giving children access to structural knowledge during the concrete operations stage will facilitate future learning and make it occur more efficiently and more deeply during later stages of cognitive development. He contends that during the concrete operations stage children are able to use symbolic representations of reality in the service of solving problems, and they are able to understand structural relationships provided that they are exposed to them in ways that are commensurate with their way of seeing the world. Again sounding much like Dewey, Bruner writes: "What is most important for teaching basic concepts is that the child be helped to pass progressively from concrete thinking to the utilization of more conceptually adequate modes of thought. But it is futile to attempt this by presenting formal explanations based on a logic that is distant from the child's manner of thinking and sterile in its implications for him. Much teaching in mathematics is of this sort. The child learns not to understand mathematical order, but rather to apply certain devices, or recipes, without understanding their significance and connectedness. They are not translated into his way of thinking."[23] When learning is presented in such a sterile and distant way, teachers tend to compel learning through either extrinsic rewards or punishments. Both miss the point for Bruner, as they did for Dewey, and they do not provide the conditions conducive to further independent learning. Rather, the intrinsic rewards of "interest and curiosity and the lure of discovery" must be summoned through an ongoing engagement of the child with an authentic and meaningful problem. "One of the least discussed ways of carrying a student through a hard unit of material is to challenge him with a chance to exercise his full powers, so that he may discover the pleasure of full and effective functioning," writes Bruner. "Good teachers know the power of this lure. Students should know what it feels like to be completely absorbed in a problem. They seldom experience this feeling in school."[24]

In "Chapter 4 – Intuitive and Analytical Thinking," Bruner makes perhaps his most original and timely contribution. When our schools emphasize intellectual achievement, it is typically analytical thinking, which is prized and rewarded. This is understandable, according to Bruner, because the use of analytical approaches leads to much success in problem solving. Moreover, the successful application of an algorithm can be evaluated directly and, more or less, easily. Nevertheless, the primary emphasis on analytical thinking has led to a formalism that devalues intuitive thinking, which, Bruner argues, is a necessary component of all serious inquiry in the various disciplines. Mathematicians, physicists, and biologists have especially recognized the centrality of intuitive thinking to their work, seeing it variously as the ability to make good guesses or of having the capacity to suddenly and inexplicably reach a solution to a perplexing problem. Analytical and intuitive thinking must be seen as complementary, and our schools should value both and provide experiences that encourage the development of both.

Bruner admits to not being exactly sure what constitutes intuitive thinking. And he makes multiple calls for further research into identifying the nature of intuitive thinking as well as research into determining the necessary conditions for its growth and maintenance. He holds, however, that having an understanding of structural knowledge provides fertile ground for productive intuitive thinking, enabling students to draw connections among phenomena previously thought to be unrelated. Students must also be encouraged to develop a strong self-confidence, warranted by their structural knowledge, in order to approach their intuitive inquiry with confidence. For Bruner, however, there is also the sense of the primacy of intuitive experience, that it must somehow be cultivated as an antecedent to, and in anticipation of, further curricular learning. Echoing Dewey's synthesis of child-centered perspective and curriculum-centered perspective, Bruner concludes that "it may be of first importance to establish an intuitive understanding of materials before we expose our students to more traditional and formal methods of deduction and proof."[25]

In "Chapter 5 – Motives for Learning," Bruner considers with great sensitivity some of the psychological and social circumstances that compel and thwart intrinsic rewards for learning, and provides some suggestions on ways to soften the impact of the competitiveness associated with our meritocracy. In the final chapter, "Aids to Teaching," he offers some tentative thoughts on how these observations might assist classroom teachers. Here he makes some broad-stroke policy recommendations as well about the teaching profession, some of which are fairly well worn (e.g., raising the status of the teaching profession, better teacher recruitment and training, etc.). But some of his recommendations (for instance, those having to do with the teacher as a "communicator, model and identification figure") are quite rich and remain worthy of further consideration today. The teacher is generally cast in a positive light throughout the text, although it is clear that, for Bruner, the teacher is to play only a minor role in determining what to teach. Curriculum is best left in the hands of the subject-matter experts, and the teacher's job is largely to translate expert knowledge into developmentally appropriate learning experiences.

Throughout the text Bruner repeatedly attempts to qualify statements and perspectives about which he might reasonably anticipate sharp disagreement. Despite his primary focus on the physical sciences and mathematics, he bends over backward to be inclusive of the humanities—sometimes to the point of silliness. His insistence on the application of his structural orientation to understanding the humanities evinces little understanding of these disciplines, as, for instance, when he argues that "if a student is led further to understand that there are a relatively limited number of human plights about which novels are written, he understands literature the better for it."[26]

Bruner nevertheless recognizes that the national obsession with the STEM disciplines has the potential to marginalize teaching and learning in the humanities, an observation that seems oddly prescient given our circumstances today: "We can ill afford an alienated group of literacy intellectuals who feel that advances in science, which they may fail to understand out of a sense of being shunned by the system of rewards for technical and scientific achievement, betoken the destruction of traditional culture. It is certainly plain that at the very least there will have to be energy devoted to improving curricula and teaching in the humanities and social sciences comparable to what is now being devoted to science and mathematics."[27] Despite being surrounded by colleagues at the Woods Hole Conference who were enthusiastic about new teaching technologies—including some colleagues who would likely stand to profit from their widespread adoption—Bruner struck a contrarian position. He offered a pointed rebuff to those technophiles who believed machines should simply replace teachers, and he worried instead about the passivity and intellectual lethargy these new media seem to engender in students as it turned them into spectators. Again, more research on this and related topics is needed, he assured the reader. His narrative throughout the text is marked by a degree of equanimity that would be disarming to anyone who might be predisposed to a critical perspective on the dominant Cold War aims of American education at that time.

IV

The publication of *The Process of Education* made Bruner a star. It was quickly translated into nineteen languages and distributed widely over areas of American influence. By 1961 Bruner was invited to join the Education Panel of President John F. Kennedy's Science Advisory Committee and participated with others in making recommendations on the direction of American educational policy.[28] The popularity of Bruner's book implicitly demonstrated the enduring value, efficacy, and viability of some key Deweyan progressive educational ideas. Indeed, one might say that it was precisely in repackaging these ideas that Bruner was able to tap into a deeply and widely held belief among American educators (if not also among the general population) in the importance of attending first and foremost to the child as meaningfully engaged with the world. In the Cold War battle for the hearts and minds of people at home and abroad, this was a key belief to underscore.

And yet *The Process of Education* carefully avoided attending to some other central Deweyan progressive ideas, potentially more transformative, having to do with the empowerment of teachers and the democratization of educational and social goals. Dewey explicitly rejected the view of the teacher as someone who simply translated and reduced expert knowledge to the child's developmental level. Instead he argued for a view that distinguished the teacher's knowledge of the subject matter from that of the subject-matter expert, and he elevated this teacher knowledge to a much more profound and intellectually demanding and complex level. For Dewey, in "psychologizing the curriculum," the teacher "is concerned with the subject-matter of the science as *representing a given stage and phase of the development of experience.* His problem is that of inducing a vital and personal experiencing. Hence, what concerns him, as a teacher, is the ways in which that subject may become part of experience: what there is in the child's present that is usable with reference to it; how such elements are to be used; how his own knowledge of the subject-matter may assist in interpreting the child's needs and doings and determine the medium in which the child should be placed in order that his growth may be properly directed. He is concerned, not with the subject matter as such, but with the subject matter as a related factor in a total and growing experience."[29]

Unlike Bruner, who was content to see the teacher as a mere conduit for the expert knowledge developed far away from the classroom, Dewey placed the onus on the teacher to continuously create and recreate curricula and method in responding to the needs of the learning child. In our own time, as we witness the further marginalization and disempowerment of teachers, it is important to remember what has been lost as Bruner's view of the teacher came to overshadow and replace Dewey's.

Perhaps even more troublesome is Bruner's complete abandonment of Dewey's emphasis on the need to continuously refine and articulate the social purposes for schooling. For Dewey, schools represented the primary means by which a democratic "society can formulate its own purposes, can organize its own means and resources, and thus shape itself with definiteness and economy in the direction it wishes to move."[30] For Dewey, the foundational questions about the purpose of education can never be separated from the practical questions of educational process, pedagogical method, or curricular content. Bruner, however, was either oblivious to, or silent on, this critical Deweyan point. So while in the book's opening paragraph Bruner acknowledges an increasing tendency among Americans to engage the question of "What shall we teach and to what end?" his analysis avoids posing this question seriously. He defers instead to the undemocratic educational aims of the Cold War interests for which he worked: the efficient preparation of scientists and engineers for a nation at war and that would presumably remain at war for many years to come.

Today we have done little to modify this shallow purpose for schooling. We continue to orient our educational institutions around an obsessive focus on the STEM disciplines and to otherwise provide narrow forms of standardized vocational training. This has had a destructive impact on our culture and has damaged our ability to act as a democratic society.[31] Again, we would do well to look past Bruner to Dewey in order to recover more humane, democratic, and hopeful educational purposes.

As a major cultural artifact of the Cold War, *The Process of Education* provides important clues to understanding the educational and social worlds we have inherited. Written at a time of increased awareness of the need to manage public opinion as a means of policy implementation, the book appropriated some effective and widely supported Deweyan progressive educational ideas and carried them into the second half of the twentieth century. In doing so, Bruner helped to keep part of the progressive educational tradition alive during a time of its significant retrenchment. On the other hand, Bruner's book may also have helped to further entrench some of the undemocratic educational practices and policies of the Cold War with which we remain saddled. For this primary reason the book, and the cultural context from which it came, deserves our continued careful and critical study.

Notes

1 Jerome Bruner, *The Process of Education* (1960; repr, Cambridge, MA: Harvard University Press, 1977), 33.

2 Frank G. Jennings, "A Friend of the Learning Child," *Saturday Review*, October 16, 1960, 94.

3 Paul Goodman, "Enlightened Teaching for the Young," *The New York Herald Tribune*, December 23, 1960, 28.

4 Ibid.

5 See especially John Dewey's 1902 essay "The Child and the Curriculum," in *The Essential Dewey, Volume 1: Pragmatism, Education and Democracy*, ed. Larry A. Hickman and Thomas Alexander (Bloomington: University of Indiana Press, 1998). Others have also recognized the parallels between Dewey's ideas and *The Process of Education*. See, for instance, Neil Postman and Charles Weingartner, *The School Book: For People Who Want to Know What All the Hollering Is About* (New York: Delacorte Press, 1973) and, more recently, David Olson, *Jerome Bruner: The Cognitive Revolution in Educational Theory* (New York: Continuum, 2007).

6 Elizabeth Knoll, "The Process of Education, 1960," Harvard University Press Blog, March 4, 2013. http://harvardpress.typepad.com/hup_publicity/2013/03/the-process-of-education-jerome-bruner-1960.html#more (accessed August 18, 2015).

7 Bruner did acknowledge in the book's preface that "many of the ideas that emerged at the Conference and after have long and honorable lineages in the history of educational thought." Nevertheless, Bruner does not provide any citations or references that would recognize and acknowledge these lineages. See Bruner, *The Process of Education*, xxv.

8 Jerome Bruner, *In Search of Mind: Essays in Autobiography* (New York: Harper and Row, 1983), 178.

9 Lawrence A. Cremin, *The Transformation of the School: Progressivism in American Education, 1876–1957* (New York: Alfred A. Knopf, 1961).

10 A year after the publication of *The Process of Education*, one finds Bruner actually repeating some of the negative caricatures of Dewey and Progressive Education in the essay "After John Dewey, What?," which appeared in *Saturday Review* (Suppl., June 17, 1961) and was republished in his *On Knowing: Essays for the Left Hand* (Cambridge, MA: Belknap Press of Harvard University Press, 1962).

11 Bruner, *The Process of Education*, xvii.

12 Ibid., xxii.

13 As quoted in John L. Rudolph, "From World War to Woods Hole: The Use of Wartime Research Models for Curriculum Reform," *Teachers College Record* 104, no. 2 (March 2002): 232.

14 Ronald W. Evans, *The Hope for American School Reform: The Cold War Pursuit of Inquiry Learning in Social Studies* (New York: Palgrave, 2011), 73.

15 For an insightful analysis of this model, see John L. Rudolph, *Scientists in the Classroom: The Cold War Reconstruction of American Science* (New York: Palgrave, 2002).

16 For a helpful discussion of the manifestation of this scientism, see Mark Solovey's *Shaky Foundations: The Politics-Patronage-Social Science Nexus in Cold War America* (New Brunswick, NJ: Rutgers University Press, 2013).

17 For an analysis of the term "propaganda," as well as the confluence of these interests at mid-century, see Timothy Glander, *Origins of Mass Communications Research During the American Cold War: Educational Effects and Contemporary Implications* (Mahwah, NJ: Lawrence Erlbaum Associates, 2000).

18 Bruner recounts some of this experience in his 1983 autobiography, *In Search of Mind*, 38–39.

19 Jerome S. Bruner, *Mandate from the People* (New York: Duell, Sloan and Pearce, 1944).

20 For an analysis of Project Troy, see Allan A. Needle, "Project Troy and the Cold War Annexation of the Social Sciences," in *Universities and Empire: Money and Politics in the Social Sciences During the Cold War*, ed. Christopher Simpson (New York: The New Press, 1998), 3–38. For an analysis of CENIS, see Christopher Simpson, *Science of Coercion: Communication Research & Psychological Warfare, 1945–1960* (New York: Oxford University Press, 1994).

21 Bruner, *The Process of Education*, 7.

22 Ibid., 31.

23 Ibid., 38–39. One might compare Bruner's position here to Dewey's in his 1902 essay "The Child and the Curriculum": "There is a sense in which it is impossible to value too highly the formal and symbolic. The genuine form, the real symbol, serve as methods in the holding and discovery of truth. They are tools by which the individual pushes out most surely and widely into unexplored areas. They are means by which he brings to bear whatever of reality he has succeeded in gaining in past searchings. But this happens only when the symbol really symbolizes—when it stands for and sums up in shorthand actual experiences which the individual has already gone through. A symbol which is induced from without, which has not been led up to in preliminary activities, is, as we say, a *bare* or *mere* symbol; it is dead and barren. Now, any fact, whether of arithmetic, or geography, or grammar, which is not led up to and into out of something which has previously occupied a significant position in the child's life for its own sake, is forced into this position. It is not a reality, but just the sign of a reality which *might* be experienced if certain conditions were fulfilled. But the abrupt presentation of the fact as something known by others, and requiring only to be studied and learned by the child, rules out such conditions of fulfillment. It condemns the fact to be a hieroglyph: it would mean something if one only had the key. The clue being lacking, it remains an idle curiosity, to fret and obstruct the mind, a dead weight to burden it." From: *The Essential Dewey, Volume 1: Pragmatism, Education and Democracy*, 243.

24 Bruner, *The Process of Education*, 50.

25 Ibid., 59.

26 Ibid., 24.

27 Ibid., 79.

28 Bruner recalls the book's reception and the changes it brought to his life in his *In Search of Mind*, 184–187.

29 John Dewey, "The Child and the Curriculum," in *The Essential Dewey, Volume 1: Pragmatism, Education and Democracy*, 242–243.

30 John Dewey, "My Pedagogic Creed," in *The Essential Dewey, Volume 1: Pragmatism, Education and Democracy*, 234. Originally published in 1897.

31 For an excellent elaboration of this point, see Martha Nussbaum, *Not for Profit: Why Democracy Needs the Humanities* (Princeton, NJ: Princeton University Press, 2010).

Two

Raymond Callahan, *Education and the Cult of Efficiency: A Study of the Social Forces That Have Shaped the Administration of the Public Schools* (1962)

Gary K. Clabaugh

Introduction

Here, in brief, is why *Education and the Cult of Efficiency* is a classic: it remains embedded in memory long after it has been read; it can be reread with a sense of discovery; it explains the present by describing the past; and it adds a vital perspective to public schooling's historic narrative.[1]

Focus on Efficiency

Broadly speaking, today's school reformers misuse and overemphasize high-stakes testing, are preoccupied with narrow vocational objectives, proceed as if privatization is necessarily superior, bully teachers instead of eliciting their cooperation, and fault public education for the inevitable academic consequences of festering social and economic injustices. Many wonder how such a misbegotten agenda ever became so dominant.[2] Callahan describes its beginnings.

Education and the Cult of Efficiency focuses on that critical period (1900–1930) when the general social and economic climate pushed public schooling into a long-lasting embrace of what Callahan labels "the cult of efficiency."

Until Congress sharply restricted immigration in the mid-1920s, an unprecedented flood of foreigners poured into the United States. Combined with the simultaneous mass movement of millions from farm to city, this influx ballooned urban school enrollment and created unprecedented funding challenges. Between 1906 and 1917, for example, the School District of Philadelphia was forced to build 44 new elementary and 6 new high schools.[3] That's 50 new schools in just 11 years.

Temple, Town Meeting, and Factory

What people wanted from these schools varied from person to person. But we can make sense of their expectations if we recast complex priorities in terms of three ideal types. Every school incorporates all three of these types to a greater or lesser degree, although one is typically dominant.

The most time-honored ideal type is the school as temple. Its origin can be traced back some 6,000 years to the very first schools. Here the focus is on tradition, values, and proper behavior. The United States Military Academy at West Point is an excellent example of a temple-dominant school.

The school as temple contrasts sharply with the ideal type—the town meeting. Here the focus is on accommodating individual differences through civility, bargaining, and compromise. Quaker (Society of Friends) schools typically exemplify town meeting–dominant education.

The most modern ideal type originated in the 1900–1930 time period that Callahan describes. It is the school as factory. Here the dominant concern is efficiency and productivity. This focus was the consequence of the explosive growth of urban school populations just described, along with prevailing inflation at the time. This combination generated intense funding pressure—so intense, in fact, that school administrators could hardly avoid industrial-style management. Efficiency—defined as low per-pupil cost—became their top priority, and the school as factory was born.[4]

Largely absent from these factory-dominant schools were concerns about tradition, pride of work, personal happiness, life fulfillment, depth of character, abiding values, group membership, and "proper" behavior—all manifestations of the now largely ignored school as temple.

Similarly absent was a focus on democratic decision-making, individual differences, concern for others, civility, and willingness to compromise, all key elements of the school as town meeting and of a functioning democracy.

The first public schools, usually one-room affairs, were a combination of temple and town meeting. But with the explosive growth of urban public schooling, these priorities were largely left to elite private schools. Ordinary people's children now ended up in factory-dominant schools.[5]

Despite some waxing and waning, the school as factory remained dominant throughout the twentieth century. And today's reformers are insuring its continued dominance thus far this century. Like their early twentieth-century predecessors, for instance, they still proceed with a top-down style of management that imperiously disregards teacher knowledge and experience. And they waste educators' irreplaceable time and energy on over-emphasized (and badly misused) high-stakes, quality-control testing that foolishly applies a single proficiency standard to all and sundry.

As a matter of fact, taken together, their contemporary school as factory "reforms" exceed anything that the early twentieth-century cult of efficiency evangelists imagined. They impose things like vouchers; the contracting out of ancillary and auxiliary school services; privatized school district management; and privately operated, publicly financed charter schools—including for-profit corporate chains. Worse, they offer big bags of federal money to states and/or school districts that join in this celebration of the school as factory with greatest—often bogus—enthusiasm.

The New Breed

In the Callahan era, business-style school management fit the spirit of the time. President Coolidge famously captured that spirit with this statement: "The chief business of the American people is business."[6] Callahan emphasizes that the public school's unique organization, support, and voter control made it especially susceptible to this *zeitgeist*. Meanwhile, however, elite private schooling scoffed at industrialization.

In this era, "experts" began preaching the virtues of "scientific" business methods and practices. They sermonized that modern schools should be run like the most up-to-date industrial corporations, using cost accounting and cost management as their guides.[7] They promised that running the schools like a business would, by improving efficiency, solve the public school funding crises.

Most of these scientific management experts were professors who, in addition to advising industry, wrote influential school administration texts, acted as consultants to major city school systems, and trained industrial-style school administrators in newly minted departments of educational administration.[8]

Business-oriented school boards, elected by cost-conscious voters, eagerly hired these new industrial-style managers. The expectation was that they would put the school district in the black by focusing on per-pupil costs. Callahan explains that if budget restrictions meant, say, offering only one foreign language, these business-trained managers were expected to choose the cheapest per-pupil option.

Callahan unambiguously disapproves of business methods and industrial values for school management. He charges that it debases schooling, and he offers plentiful evidence that these allegedly superior management methods were often based on scientifically primitive studies of heavy industry—the production of pig iron being one example.

Callahan charges that this new breed of "scientific" managers was uneducated and unscholarly. No liberal arts were included in their training, and they were rarely required to study things like educational philosophy, teaching methodology, or child development. Hence, says Callahan, school leaders trained in this manner were not equipped to ask the basic questions in education. Moreover, they had no real understanding of what being educated actually meant. Worse still, they no longer identified with educators, but with business executives.[9]

Callahan notes further that America's habitual anti-intellectualism legitimized their ignorance. Their supposedly pragmatic style of leadership often appealed to the businessmen who increasingly dominated local boards of education. But this contempt for mere book learning badly damaged public education.[10]

A Nation at Risk and the Muckrakers

The present wave of school reform was touched off by the Reagan administration's release of *A Nation at Risk*. This jeremiad set off a deluge of criticism that has yet to abate. It is now more or less taken for granted by the media that our public schools are substandard and that something must be done.

During the cult-of-efficiency era, something similar happened. The early 1900s saw the rise of investigative journalists and novelists who came to be called muckrakers. Their detailing of business abuses and government corruption proved both popular and profitable. Soon a formidable cluster of popular journals such as *McClure's*, *Colliers*, and *The Saturday Evening Post* were shocking the public with lurid revelations.

It wasn't long before public schooling was added to the muckrakers' target list. Just as with *A Nation at Risk*, alarmed readers were repeatedly told that their public schools were horribly managed and that reform was urgently needed. And the remedy that the muckrakers most often recommended was "scientific management."[11]

The "Cult of Efficiency"

Callahan details how business values, muckraking journalism, public cost concerns, and the "scientific" management movement combined to form what he calls the "cult of efficiency." And he explains that public schooling's susceptibility to pressure, fads, and fancies meant that this cult spread like metastasizing cancer.

One of the more interesting features of Callahan's book is his detailed description of the cult's major evangelists. John Franklin Bobbitt, a University of Chicago professor, for instance, was one of the new faith's most prominent "preachers." Bobbitt's lectures and publications brashly reduced public education to industrial proportions, transformed schools into factories, and urged American educators to make efficiency their master. Callahan documents the extremity of Bobbitt's pro-business bias with numerous quotes and examples, and he demonstrates how Bobbitt's recommendations were based on his background as an advisor to heavy industry.

In an era without much job security, only a few educators had the gumption to openly reject this new vision. One was Thomas J. McCormick, a high school principal from La Salle, Illinois. He informed the Bobbitt-embracing National Education Association's Department of Secondary Education that the word "practical" required a much deeper meaning than was being ascribed to it by the scientific management crowd. Then he informed these NEA officials[12] that in their "inordinate zeal to 'practicalize' and popularize education," they were forgetting that its purpose was "to make men and women as well as engineers and 'rope-stretchers.'"[13]

"Scientific Management," or the Taylor Method

"Scientific management" played such a key role in the cult of efficiency that Callahan devotes an entire chapter to it. He describes how it first captured national attention in 1910 when the method played a pivotal role in an Interstate Commerce Commission hearing on railroad freight rates. A number of witnesses testified that if the railroads would only adopt scientific management, they could increase wages and still lower costs. One "expert" even testified that scientific management could revolutionize the whole of industry to the same degree, as had the introduction of machinery.

These ICC hearings vaulted scientific management, along with its chief architect, mechanical engineer Frederick W. Taylor, from obscurity to national prominence.[14] Taylor was certain that there was one best way to do any job, and scientific investigation could reveal what that was. Apply it, he promised, and costs will fall as productivity soars.

Taylor assured all and sundry that his method could cancel out "the innate laziness of men," save money, and dramatically improve production.[15] The workers' role was simply to do exactly as they were told because, according to Taylor, they were incapable of understanding the scientific basis of the procedure.[16] Should they refuse to cooperate fully, they should be sacked.[17]

Taylor's ideas were soon applied to public schools. Callahan writes: "His ideas were adopted, interpreted and applied chiefly by administrators: and while the greatest impact was upon administration, the administrator, and the professional training programs of administration, the influence extended to all of American education from the elementary schools to the universities."[18]

In case the reader is unfamiliar with the contemporary rebirth of Taylor's system, here is the website teacherbiz's description of what is going on right now in Camden, New Jersey's, public schools: "*Professional educators with decades of experience are being provided with canned, scripted curricular units that even go so far as to tell teachers what to say and what to write on the board* [emphasis in original] *in virtually every lesson; these units must be followed to the day, without diversions to accommodate for struggling students, etc.*"[19] Numerous traditional public schools, charter schools, and charter school chains (for example, KIPP, the largest corporate charter school chain in the United States) generally follow such a procedure.[20]

To any skilled teacher this system is plainly ridiculous. He or she has spent a professional lifetime learning how to properly adjust instruction. But some contemporary reformers, school administrators, and school corporate heads seem to think that scripted lessons are the latest thing.

Scripted lessons do have the "advantage" of encouraging experienced, more expensive, and independent-minded teachers to quit—or, as was the case in New Orleans, simply be fired as charter schools took over. Then underqualified but less expensive and more compliant replacements can be recruited from "alternative" sources, such as Teach for America.[21]

"Scientific management" was supposedly based on precise measurement—typically, time and motion studies. School managers were to use the resultant data to tell teachers precisely what to do, when to do it, and how long it must take. And underlying this lockstep approach was one of Taylor's key assumptions: "Most of us remain, through the great part of our lives, in this respect, grown-up children, and do our best only under pressure of a task of comparatively short duration."[22] The goal was to get the absolute most out of the teacher/workers without, as Taylor solicitously puts it, "injuring their health."[23]

Taylor also recommended paying efficient workers bonuses. He said his experiments disclosed that people would not work at a higher rate of speed unless they were paid more and assured that the pay increase was permanent.[24] Teachers seldom benefitted from this aspect of Taylor's system.

Other Evangelists

Frank Spaulding, chairman of the newly formed Department of Education at Yale University, was another leading light in the "scientific" management of schools. It was Spaulding, Callahan explains, who introduced "costs per pupils," "investment per pupil," and references to students as "products" of the "school plant."[25] Spaulding stated flatly that what is to be taught must ultimately be determined not on educational, but financial grounds.[26]

While Spaulding's influence was growing, other advocates of "scientific" management also came to prominence. One was Franklin Bobbitt, as mentioned above. Callahan recounts that

Bobbitt regarded teachers as mere "workers" ("more mechanics than philosophers," as Bobbitt disdainfully put it). He also asserted that they require a top-down style of management and detailed instruction in the methods to be employed. Regarding overall goals, Bobbitt recommended that a clear-cut set of exact standards be supplied by the business and industrial world—as a public service.[27]

One might think that Spaulding, Bobbitt, and company outdid all contemporary reformers in transforming public schools into factories. But neither they nor any other early twentieth-century reformers ever advocated anything like replacing traditional schools with privately managed, publicly financed charter schools—many of them operated by for-profit corporate chains.

High-Stakes Tests and Teacher Ratings

Like today's reformers, cult-of-efficiency advocates depended heavily on high-stakes tests. And Callahan reports that many educators thought this unwise, though most voiced no opposition—perhaps because their jobs were at stake. Once in a while, though, one would speak out. Here is what William E. Maxwell, the school superintendent of New York City, had to say:

> When I read that…after shedding lakes of ink and using up untold reams of paper and consuming the time of un-numbered teachers in administering and scoring the Courtis standard tests in addition, subtraction, multiplication and division, the learned director reached the conclusion that "29% of the pupils in the eighth grade could exchange places with a like number of students in the fourth grade," I am inclined to exclaim: "My dear sir, what do you expect? That all the children in a grade would show equal ability in adding, subtracting, multiplying and dividing? Any teacher of experience could have told you that they would not. You should have known it yourself. One flash of Horace Mann's insight would be worth a thousand miles of your statistics."[28]

Current efforts to reform public schooling also are dependent on high-stakes testing.[29] Outcomes are widely disseminated to pressure educators…and it works. A suburban Philadelphia newspaper, for example, features the following headline: "Board Addresses Decrease in Test Scores." And the first line of the story reads: "A number of lower scores on standardized tests left officials in the Wissahickon School District with a lot of explaining to do."[30]

This kind of press is a key reason why more and more educators give short shrift to everything that isn't tested. They are so intimidated that they just teach to the test. Others, finding it impossible to legitimately raise scores to the demanded level, resort to cheating. But despite these difficulties, it is a rare school administrator who has the guts to question this priority.

Teacher Accountability

Early twentieth-century reformers also set out to hold teachers accountable. In 1913 the *American School Board Journal* reported that urban administrators were "almost without exception" working out "elaborate plans for rating the work of instructors."[31] Sometimes these evaluations included all school personnel, even the janitor.[32]

One particularly disturbing element of some rating schemes was crediting the teacher with the percentage of children promoted. Higher promotion rates resulted in substantial dollar savings.[33] This encouraged teachers to pass students regardless. Cost accounting, notes Callahan, superseded instruction.

Callahan also reports that the difficulty of including relevant social, economic, and educational factors in the ratings caused many teachers to ultimately be assessed on general impressions.[34] And it seems unlikely that those developing these ratings considered that classrooms were often vastly overcrowded, and that underpaid and overworked teachers were not only expected to successfully instruct, but to comfort the afflicted; inspire the defeated; rein in bullies; correct disruptive behavior; observe the children for signs of abuse and/or neglect; instill a love of learning, patriotism, good citizenship, sportsmanship, and fair play; check heads for lice; teach students manners; cope with kids (and parents) who spoke little or no English; and do all of this with nothing more than some chalk, a blackboard, a bulletin board, and a few books.[35]

The Timid, Docile Teacher

Callahan reports that many administrators doubted they could rate teachers fairly. But most rated them anyway. He attributes this to self-defense.[36] Teachers also regarded these ratings as odious and unfair. Yet they meekly, if resentfully, accepted them. Callahan remarks that "the teacher had been, and was expected to be, timid."[37]

He attributes this timidity to teacher powerlessness and vulnerability. Most worked without tenure and could easily be fired.[38] He adds, however, that the teachers of this era generally were timid, unassertive individuals to begin with. In fact, he quotes John Dewey on this: "In the main the most docile of the young are the ones who become teachers when they are adults. Consequently they still listen docilely to the voice of authority."[39]

Both Callahan and Dewey fail to recognize that this docility might have been largely attributable to the fact that the teaching force was overwhelmingly female in a male-dominated world.[40]

School Quality Surveys

"Scientific management" also featured school-quality surveys similar in intent to the ratings required by No Child Left Behind and Race to the Top. The "experts" conducting these surveys typically were professors from the newly established and rapidly expanding university-based programs in educational administration. Focusing on price and product and uncritically embracing business-style management, they provoked prestigious opposition.

John Dewey, for instance, strongly opposed the application of business procedures and industrial values to schooling. He recognized the power and place of genuine science in education, but he repeatedly criticized as oversimplified and unscientific the supposedly "scientific" management then being conducted. [41]

Dewey wryly observed that most of the "scientific" initiatives in the works at that time were really the same old education masquerading as science. He also stated that while testing can be valuable, it was being put to exactly the wrong purposes. Instead of being used to gain a better understanding of children, it was being misused to classify and standardize them.[42] Dewey's concerns, along with those of other prestigious critics, were largely ignored.

The Platoon School

Callahan also describes the birth, growth, and incomplete decline of the platoon school. It was, in essence, a pedagogical assembly line, splitting students into platoons that moved from one specialist teacher to another according to a rigid schedule. One platoon might be studying arithmetic with that specialist teacher; another might be working on art or physical education with these specialist teachers; still another might be completing a science assignment in the back of an English classroom while a basic grammar lesson was going on.

The core idea was to make maximum use of the "school plant" and its facilities. Even six-year-olds had six or seven teachers a day—sometimes more. In this system dollar values largely replaced educational values in decision making. Callahan describes, for instance, how the retention of children in a grade was balanced by making an equal number of double promotions. But the essential problem with it was, and is, that students are human beings, not industrial products.

The platoon school is still around. Secondary schools with their tight schedules, specialist teachers, and lockstep schedules are direct descendants. But until it began to fall out of favor around 1930, the platoon system also was widely used in elementary schools.[43]

Climate of the Times in Which the Work Was Written

Callahan began working on this book in 1957. The Cold War was intense. The Soviet Union had just launched the first-ever human-made satellite. This kindled broad fears that the United States had fallen behind the Soviets in both science and education. Congress subsequently approved, and President Eisenhower signed into law the National Defense Education Act, the most comprehensive education legislation in the nation's history. It increased federal spending on education fivefold.[44]

While Callahan continued his research and writing, ever-increasing numbers of U.S. advisors were being sent to South Vietnam. African Americans conducted a historic sit-in at a segregated Woolworth's lunch counter in Greensboro, North Carolina. The Berlin Wall was erected. The Soviet Union launched the first man into space. A U.S.-backed invasion of Cuba failed. And the Food and Drug Administration approved "the Pill."

In 1962—the year Callahan's work was actually published—the Cuban Missile Crisis brought the United States and the U.S.S.R. to the brink of mutual annihilation. U.S. involvement in Vietnam grew ever more intense. James Meredith, an African American, was admitted to the racially segregated University of Mississippi (but only because he was protected by a court order and truckloads of steel-helmeted U.S. Marshals). And Rachel Carson's best-selling book *Silent Spring* warned of an impending worldwide environmental catastrophe.

Strengths and Weaknesses of Callahan's Book

Callahan details a historic period in which three major developments were occurring simultaneously: industrialization, immigration, and urbanization. The interplay among these forces makes any causal analysis complex. Fortunately, Callahan's specific concern—the transformation of public schooling to an essentially industrial model—is relatively limited in scope, as are his causal claims. Anything more ambitious would have required multiple volumes. So he gets a "pass" on this one.

The most salient strength of *Education and the Cult of Efficiency* is its contemporary relevance. Time and again one can see connections with what is happening today.

Another strength is the care and industry that went into its writing. Clearly it was painstakingly researched and carefully written.

A weakness is Callahan's failure to grant full consideration to the need for efficiency. He doesn't ignore that need, but at times he underplays it. Public schooling is very expensive. In the school year 2012–2013, for instance, it cost U.S. taxpayers $632 billion. But, as Callahan emphasizes, we must not allow too intense a focus on efficiency to distort—even destroy—schooling's ultimate purposes.

A greater weakness is Callahan's failure to consider how a predominantly female teaching force influenced the events he describes. During the period 1900 to 1930, female teachers outnumbered men by about 5 to 1. This dominance, combined with the sexism of the age, surely encouraged the condescending and dismissive view of teachers that Callahan emphasizes.

By 1930, when Callahan's book closes, the number of male public school teachers began inching upward. By 1986 males in teaching reached a peak of 31%—nearly double that of 1930. During Reagan's presidency, however, the percentage of male teachers began a steady decline to the present low of 23.7%.[4]

Do today's reformers shrug off teacher knowledge because the teaching force is still overwhelmingly female? Would they pay more attention if it were 76.3% male? Perhaps.

Significance and Influence When Written and Its Relevance Today

Education and the Cult of Efficiency attracted considerable attention when it was first published. There were numerous reviews, and they were generally favorable. *The Clearing House*'s review, for instance, stated: "This volume should provide both layman and educator with knowledge which may be helpful in directing the future of American education."[46]

But the book did have detractors. One was the sociologist David Street who, in the *American Journal of Sociology*, wrote:

> Educators pressing for an enlarged professional mandate over the affairs of the public schools keep stumbling over the hard fact that…their claims to a monopoly of expert knowledge are weak. Thus, while it is clear that the intrusions into the schools made by businessmen, veterans' groups, and other outside interests have often been detrimental to American education. It is also apparent that educators have had little in the way of a solid defense against these intrusions.[47]

Street seems to think that veteran teachers possess little or no hard-won knowledge. But an experienced educator knows a great deal more about teaching than the typical sociologist, school board member, businessman, politician, or school reform–minded billionaire. Why, then, don't would-be school reformers work cooperatively with veteran teachers? Would expert accountants, veterinarians, lawyers, or physicians be similarly ignored?

Street also comments:

> [T]he author's line of argument itself reflects to some extent the weakness of the education pro-
> fession's ideological position. He is certain that the efficiency-seekers were wrong, but his reply
> is only the oblique one that quality should be more important. The analysis and the educa-
> tional philosophy underlying it do not seem to come to terms with the realities that education
> is involved in the local political process, that resources are never what the educator "needs,"
> that the superintendent must act as mediator between values of education and economy, and
> that he must use whatever managerial knowledge he can find. There can be no utopian concern
> for quality alone.[48]

Of course public school policy is political, and there can be no utopian concern for quality
alone. And Callahan clearly knows that. But school funding too often falls flagrantly short of
what is needed. For instance, teachers—particularly those in revenue-starved big-city or rural
schools—are often so short on vital supplies that they pay for them out of their own pockets.
This was certainly going on at the time in question, yet Street fails to acknowledge anything of
the sort. Plus, one wonders if he would be so sanguine about compromised educational quality
if a child he loved were being short-changed.

It certainly is true, as Street asserts, that the superintendent is caught in the middle and
must use whatever knowledge is at hand. But Callahan clearly agrees with that. What he
condemns are administrators who, for the sake of their careers, throw youngsters under the
cost-cutting bus.

William Cartwright of Duke University wrote a more thoughtful critique. He praises Callahan's effort, but only as a "useful caricature." He writes that the book is not really "a study of
the social forces that have shaped the administration of the public schools. It is a study of only
one of those forces. And even that study is incomplete. It does not give adequate recognition
to the fact that school superintendents are required to be business administrators."[49]

Cartwright offers fair criticism. Callahan's subtitle is too ambitious. And perhaps his account is something of a caricature, but one that artfully captures the essence of the age.

Conclusions

Early on we noted that Callahan's style is polemical. Perhaps this quote from *Education and the
Cult of Efficiency* explains what set him on edge:

> In the end, the American people got what they deserved for forcing their educators to spend
> their time on accounting rather than on the education of children. Until every child has part
> of his work in small classes or seminars with fine teachers who have a reasonable teaching load,
> we will not have given the American high school, or democracy for that matter, a fair trial.
> To do this, America will need to break with its traditional practice, strengthened so much in
> the age of efficiency, of asking how our schools can be operated most economically and begin
> asking instead what steps need to be taken to provide an excellent education for our children.
> We must face the fact there is no cheap, easy way to educate a man; and (without) that a free
> society cannot endure.[50]

At its conclusion Callahan offers this hope for his book:

> [I hope it] will provide both laymen and educators with knowledge which may be helpful in directing the future of American education.… Beyond this, it is hoped that the American people will see that the introduction into education of concepts and practices from fields such as business and industry can be a serious error. Efficiency and economy—important as they are—must be considered in the light of the quality of education being provided. Equally important is the inefficiency and false economy of forcing educators to devote their time and energy to cost accounting.[51]

At the moment Callahan's hopes seem misbegotten. In many financially distressed districts, cost accounting still reigns; only now it is joined by the overuse, misuse, and abuse of standardized testing and the most intense expressions of the school as factory yet devised.

Should would-be reformers actually want to improve public education, not just rearrange things to suit their own selfish purposes, they must first address those core issues that destroy academic achievement at its very roots. Things like grossly unequal school funding, the 2.7 million American children with an incarcerated parent,[52] the steady erosion of the middle class, and the concentrated poverty that is failed schooling's prime breeding ground.[53]

Notes

1   Rush Welter, *Popular Education and Democratic Thought in America* (New York: Columbia University Press, 1962); Vernon Mallinson, review of *Education and the Cult of Efficiency* by Raymond E. Callahan, *British Journal of Educational Studies*, 12, no. 1 (November 1963), 87–88.

2   Private schools have generally escaped the standardized testing requirements. For instance, in Pennsylvania they are exempt from the recently imposed Keystone tests that public school students must pass to qualify for a diploma.

3   Peter Williams, *Philadelphia: The World War I Years* (Charleston, SC: Arcadia Publishing, 2013), 27.

4   Raymond Callahan, *Education and the Cult of Efficiency* (Chicago and London: University of Chicago Press, 1962), 14–15.

5   Cost concerns mean that diocesan-controlled Roman Catholic schools typically were and are factories, too. Wealthier Catholics, however, can send their children to non-diocesan Roman Catholic academies that adopt the school as temple model.

6   Often misquoted as "The business of America is business." Actually, in January 1925, Coolidge told the Society of American Newspaper Editors: "The chief business of the American people is business." See http://www.thisdayinquotes.com/2010/01/business-of-america-is-business.html for the full story.

7   Callahan, 158–161.

8   The formal training of school administrators was just getting under way.

9   Callahan, 247.

10 Ibid.

11 Callahan, 245.

12 At this time school administrators, not classroom teachers, dominated the NEA.

13 Quoted in Callahan, 11.

14 Callahan, 19–22.

15 Callahan, 27.

16 Callahan quotes Taylor at length on this. See Callahan, 27.

17 Quoted in Callahan, 32.

18 Callahan, 41.

19 *Predictable reform tactics in Camden, Part 2: Layoffs and Scripted Lessons.* teacherbiz. https://teacherbiz.wordpress.com/2014/05/15/predictable-reform-tactics-in-camden-part-2-layoffs-and-scripted-lessons/

20 *Schools Matter: Full Interview with Former Charter Teacher.* http://www.schoolsmatter.info/2014/01/full-interview-with-former-charter.html

21 *The Great Charter School Tryout: Are New Orleans Schools a Model for the Nation or a Cautionary Tale?* http://newwf.org/the-great-charter-tryout-are-new-orleans-schools-a-model-for-the-nation-or-a-cautionary-tale/

22 Taylor, quoted in Callahan, 29.

23 Taylor, quoted in Callahan, 31.
24 Callahan, 31.
25 Callahan, 70.
26 Callahan, 73.
27 Callahan, 83.
28 Maxwell, quoted in Callahan, 122.
29 This contemporary development had its origin in the 1980s with the publication of *A Nation at Risk* (Washington, DC: U.S. Department of Education, National Commission on Excellence in Education, 1983).
30 Eric Devlin, "Board Addresses Decrease in Test Scores," *The Ambler Gazette*, December 14, 2014, 1.
31 Callahan, 104.
32 Callahan, 108.
33 Callahan, 169.
34 Callahan, 105.
35 Some time ago I came across a form of this list on the web but cannot relocate it.
36 Callahan, 111.
37 Callahan, 66.
38 Callahan, 111.
39 Quoted in Callahan, 121.
40 Vintee Sawhney, *The Women's Liberation Movement of the 1960's*. The CWLU History Website GrrlSmarts. http://www.uic.edu/orgs/cwluherstory/_notes/GrrlSmarts/sawhney.html
41 Callahan, 124–125.
42 Idem.
43 Callahan, 145.
44 Thomas D. Snyder, ed., *120 Years of American Education: A Statistical Portrait* (Washington, DC: Center for Education Statistics, 1993), 34.
45 *Profile of Teachers in the U.S. 2011*. http://www.edweek.org/media/pot2011final-blog.pdf
46 Howard F. Bolden, review of *Education and the Cult of Efficiency*, by Raymond E. Callahan. *The Clearing House*, 37, no. 7 (March 1963), 441–442.
47 David Street, review of *Education and the Cult of Efficiency*, by Raymond E. Callahan. *American Journal of Sociology*, 69, no. 6 (May 1964), 673–674.
48 Idem.
49 William H. Cartwright, review of *Education and the Cult of Efficiency*, by Raymond E. Callahan. *Mississippi Valley Historical Review*, 49, no. 4 (March 1963), 722–723.
50 Callahan, 120.
51 Callahan, 263.
52 Katie Riley, *Sesame Street Reaches Out to 2.7 Million American Children with an Incarcerated Parent*. Factank: New in the Numbers, Pew Research Center, June 21, 2013. http://www.pewresearch.org/fact-tank/2013/06/21/sesame-street-reaches-out-to-2-7-million-american-children-with-an-incarcerated-parent/
53 See, for example, Hope Yen, "4 in 5 in USA Face Near-Poverty, No Work." *USA Today*, July 28, 2013. http://www.usatoday.com/story/money/business/2013/07/28/americans-poverty-no-work/2594203/

THREE

Paul Goodman, *Compulsory Mis-education* (1962) and *The Community of Scholars* (1964)

David Hursh

Paul Goodman, New York Jewish intellectual, married bisexual father of three children, essayist, anarchist, and Aristotelian scholar, was one of the most influential writers of the 1960s. Regrettably, he is now largely forgotten. But for many of us who entered adulthood in the 1960s and sensed something amiss in society, Goodman gave us a vision and a voice. He relentlessly criticized schools and society for promoting docility and conformity and called for a society in which people engaged in learning to improve their own lives and the world around them. I read *Compulsory Mis-education* (1962), *The Community of Scholars* (1964), and their companion, *Growing Up Absurd* (1960), a few years after they were published, and shortly after beginning my undergraduate studies in 1966. It has been almost 50 years since I read them. A recent film on Goodman's life is appropriately titled *Paul Goodman Changed My Life* (2008). In re-reading these two books, it is clear to me that Goodman's ideas still resonate with me today.

The Context of This Character

Goodman, born in New York City in 1911, lived at various times as a classic New York intellectual sought after by the media for his critique of society, and at other times as an outcast marginalized for that same critique. Similarly, those who knew him, such as Susan Sontag; Grace Paley (1959, 1985); Vera Williams (1981, 1984), author of wonderful children's books; Michael Rossman (1971, 1972), activist in the Berkeley Free Speech Movement; Allen Graubard (1972), whose 1960s critiques of the free school movement from a Deweyan perspective are still the best introduction to Dewey and George Dennison, author of *The Lives of Children: The Story of the First Street School*

(1972), all longed to be around and in conversation with Goodman while at the same time grappling with his verbal aggressiveness and his swings between self-importance and whining.

Not surprisingly, given that his father left the family just after Goodman's birth, never to be heard from again, and Goodman's concern with youth, he was (most of the time) a devoted father. Unfortunately, to his great sadness, his only son, Matthew, died in a mountain climbing accident in 1967. Goodman's writing and health declined after the incident, and he died in 1972.

Existentialism, Education, and Schools

The impetus for Goodman's critique of school and society resides in his concern that we as a society fail to provide people in general and adolescents in particular with a way to make sense of the world. Goodman's views reflected the 1960s interest in existential philosophy and personal meaning (particularly Albert Camus [1946, 1951] and John Paul Sartre [1969], in the poetry of The Beats,[1] and in Salinger's (1951) *The Catcher in the Rye*, with Holden Caulfield's distain for phonies. Like his colleague Edgar Friedenberg, who wrote *The Vanishing Adolescent* (1959), Goodman felt that schools hindered the process by which adolescents came to define themselves as people. Friedenberg wrote that

> growth is seriously blocked by anything that keeps youngsters from responding specifically to one another. Our cultural insistence on generalized patterns of response that ignore the significance of subtle but vital human differences is one of the things that most seriously impedes adolescence. (p. 64)

Goodman had little good to say about formal elementary and secondary education, describing schools as controlling and breaking students' spirits. He stated that schools are engaged in "progressive regimentation and brainwashing" (1962, p. 10) and that "mental illness is caused by powerlessness" brought on by institutions such as schools (p. 12). Goodman concluded that because students had little or nothing say about what they learned and lacked opportunities to connect their learning with larger issues, their motivation was undermined. Students had to adjust to the schools rather than schools adjusting to them. School, he contended, "reduces the young to ciphers, and the teachers to a martinet" (p. 56). In the end, school provided not merely a poor education, but mis-education.

In response, Goodman argued not for merely reforming schools but reconstructing education and society. He claimed that we needed to envision how education could occur in many places and times. Since much of what schools taught focused on disseminating content—much of which would be soon forgotten or was simply wrong—we should aim to teach children how to ask questions and solve problems. He wrote that we need to ask "Education how? Where? For what? And under whose administration?"

Goodman agreed with Dewey's educational goals and argued for a progressive approach. But he thought Dewey too optimistic in that Dewey believed that schools could demonstrate how democracy could work. "In fact," wrote Goodman, "our schools reflect our society closely, except that they emphasize many of its worst features, as well as having the characteristic defects of academic institutions of all times and places" (p. 24).

Adolescence

Goodman's concerns for and insights about adolescents formed the basis of his personal and political efforts. For Goodman, post–World War II America utterly failed to provide adolescents with existential meaning. In fact, for adolescents, as reflected in the title of his best-known book (1960), growing up was indeed absurd. He argued that society caused many of our difficulties with adolescents. He noted that schools offered adolescents few "worthwhile experiences" (1962). Further, he deplored the postwar culture of production and consumption that "dried up the spontaneous imagination of ends and the capacity to invent ingenious expedients" that "disintegrated communities" and "destroyed human scale" (p. 10). Such a view made it difficult to offer proposals to change schools and society, and proposing alternatives thus became increasingly difficult: "The structures and folkways of our society are absurd, but [most people feel] they can no longer be changed. Any hint of changing them disturbs our resignation and rouses anxiety" (p. 6). He added:

> It is in schools and from the mass media, rather than at home or from their friends, that the mass of our citizens in all classes learn that life is inevitably routine, depersonalized, venally graded; that it is best to toe the mark and shut up; that there is no place for spontaneity, open sexuality, free spirit. Trained in the schools, they go on to the same quality of jobs, culture, politics. This is education, mis-education, socializing to the national norms and regimenting to the national "needs." (p. 23)

Elsewhere he stated that "our schools have become petty-bourgeois, bureaucratic, time-serving, Gradgrind-practical, timid, and nouveau riche climbing. In the upper grades and college, they often exude a cynicism that belongs to rotten aristocrats" (p. 22). He clearly had little hope that schools could become places that supplied a meaningful education.

Goodman's concern with adolescence and his reluctance to blame adolescents for their problems reflect the thinking of another social critic of his time, C. Wright Mills (1959), who described doing sociology as embracing the sociological imagination: the process through which we examine the larger structural forces that affect our lives and make sense of our experience as not idiosyncratic but societal. It is the way in which we come to understand our personal troubles as public issues.

It is clear that Goodman uses writing and speaking to sort out how he makes sense of the world. Reading Goodman as a late teenager, I began to connect my "personal troubles" with "social structures" to ask questions about the structure of society, where society stands in human history, and who holds power in society. I began to raise questions about my high school and university education, feeling that I was expected to only memorize curricular content. But I could not expect the university to assist me in sorting out the important issues we faced then and continue to face now regarding environmental sustainability, American imperialism in Asia, and racial, gender, and economic inequality. I began to think about how to change society and schools to support people in making sense of the world around them.

Perhaps not surprisingly, my first research project examined adolescents involved in the drug culture. My chapter "The Crucible of Adolescence" in Jaffee and Clark's *Worlds Apart: Young People and Drug Programs* (1974) examined how society, often through the commercial media, used scare tactics rather than more objective information to persuade adolescents not to use illicit drugs. However, my interviews revealed that youth felt that the tactics misrepresented the dangers and only increased their mistrust of social services, authorities, and the police. Instead, adolescents needed to be taken seriously as they attempted to sort out their experiences.

Education Alternatives: Education Beyond Schools

As described above, Goodman (1962) had largely given up on formal education. He wrote that schools needed to teach students how to analyze and change the world, but they were instead primarily interested in "guaranteeing the right character" (p. 21). It is in schools, he wrote, that

> our citizens learn that life is inevitably routine, depersonalized, venally graded; that it is best to toe the mark and shut up; that there is no place for spontaneity, open sexuality, free spirit. Trained in the school, they go on to the same quality of jobs, culture, politics. This is education, mis-education, socializing to the national norms and regimenting to the national "needs." (p. 23)

Goodman echoed Dewey's (1915) criticism that education focused on the needs of business and provided narrow job training in the vocational track and a narrow academic focus in the college prep track (Weltman, 2000). Goodman (1964) criticized the New York Commissioner of Education at the time for stating that "The educational role is, by and large, to provide—at public and parents' expense—apprentice-training for corporations, government, and the teaching professions itself. And also to train the young to handle constructively their problems of adjustment to authority" (p. 18). Goodman (1960) detested the idea that education should be preparation for the needs of corporations and government, for fitting "people wherever they are needed in the production system" (p. 4).

Goodman was not optimistic that schools could be reformed to provide a meaningful education. They were too bureaucratic and believed too much in standards and standardization. In *The Community of Scholars* (1964), he proposed numerous reforms, most emphasizing, like his friend Ivan Illich (1971), de-schooling society. He often described himself as an anarchist, writing: "This book is a little treatise on anarchist theory" (1964, p. 162) and that "the most useful arrangement is free-association and federation rather than top down management and administration" (p. 163).

For Goodman, learning required that children and adults trust and get to know one another and that they build on one another's interests. This required reorganizing the education system, including closing down large schools and creating storefront and freedom schools.

The best example of Goodman's ideal of what schools should be like is Dennison's First Street School, described in *The Lives of Children* (1972). Goodman advocated that schools' enrollment be no more than 25 students, with one certified teacher and other adults from the community. The First Street School had 23 children, all low-income, Black, White, and Puerto Rican.

Goodman also advocated that elementary and secondary education be broadened to include the whole community, an idea taken up by some public schools, including the School Without Walls in Rochester, New York, and the Parkway School in Philadelphia. He encouraged university faculty and students to secede from a university to establish their own learning communities, meeting informally and charging only enough tuition to pay the faculty.

Alternative Education Structures

De-schooling and other alternatives were taken up in the 1960s as universities and educational foundations began to experiment with other structures. In 1968 the Ford Foundation funded an experimental program at the University of California, Davis, where 45 college students lived together for a summer in a fraternity house, planned and prepared communal meals (because no one else offered, I was in charge of planning meals and purchasing food), and had conversations and informal classes with faculty from UC Davis and the University of California, Berkeley. I was selected to participate based on my having organized, as an undergraduate, conferences on educational reform. The 45 students had numerous opportunities to learn from one another and the faculty. Two members of the faculty influenced me profoundly: Sim Van der Ryn (2005, 2007) and Michael Rossman (1971, 1972).

Van der Ryn, who is now emeritus professor of architecture at UC Berkeley, introduced me to rethinking the relationship between built structures and sustainability. He pioneered sustainable design, founding in the 1970s the Farallones Institute in Petaluma, California, to develop "ecologically integrated living design." He also taught us "pressure point design," which is a useful technique for building temporary dormitory and classroom furniture.

Michael Rossman was active in the Berkeley Free Speech Movement (1964), critiqued the authoritarian and mindless nature of U.S. society, and, as I learned from the film *Paul Goodman Changed My Life*, was Paul Goodman's friend. I admired Rossman's critical, accessible writing and hoped that someday I might write him. The politics of the Berkeley Free Speech Movement, which protested UC Berkeley's regulations banning political speech on campus, is chronicled in his book *The Wedding Within the War* (1971). His central critique of education is published in *On Learning and Social Change* (1972).

That summer experience epitomizes Goodman's notion of teachers and students coming together, raising questions, and seeking answers without formal grading or assessments, motivated only by their desire to learn from one another.

After the summer ended I returned to Manhattan, Kansas, the home of Kansas State University, to become the assistant director of the alternative university initially named University for Man and then later simply UFM. UFM reflected Goodman's anarchic vision in that it offered hundreds of free classes every semester on any topic that anyone could teach and anyone could take. We trusted that those who offered to teach would do what they said and that the "students" who enrolled did so because they cared about learning. We had only a few instances when this was not so.

Among the semester-long courses were "Black-White Relations," "The World in the Year 2000" (at the time it seemed so far away), and my course, "Existential Philosophy," which I taught twice. Among the readings for the course was Maxine Greene's first book, *Existential Encounters for Teachers* (1967). She begins the book by noting that "to teach in the American school today is to undertake a profoundly human as well as professional responsibility" (p. 3).

UFM, which was initially funded in the 1960s by Kansas State University, is now funded through a variety of sources, including nominal fees charged to students. Teachers still are not paid, and students receive no grades.

Elementary and Secondary Education

Goodman focused on adolescents and schools in part because he perceived how we chose to educate children as key to how we understand the nature of freedom and the relationship between the individual and society. Like Dewey, Goodman felt that the crucial philosophical questions about knowledge and society were played out in schools. Dewey valued working out the practical aspects of pedagogy because it made real his more abstract philosophical questions. Dewey (1894), in a rare instance of philosophical and personal clarity, wrote to Alice, his wife: "I think I'm in a fair way to become an educational crank. I sometimes think I will drop teaching philosophy directly, and teach it via pedagogy."

Dewey's and Goodman's notions about education convinced me that I should become an "educational crank." In *High-Stakes Testing and the Decline of Teaching and Learning* (2008), I describe my decision to become an elementary teacher in 1972:

> Like Dewey, I realized that it is in education that the perennial social and philosophical questions regarding how we are to live in the world are put into practice. It is in teaching that we can raise questions about which knowledge is most worth knowing and how we learn. We can investigate how to organize social institutes so as to develop the knowledge, skills, and attitudes necessary for democratic citizenship. (p. 28)

I taught elementary and middle school for 8 years, first in an alternative private school in Omaha, Nebraska, and then in a school I started in Manhattan, Kansas. In both schools I was guided by Goodman's commitment that schools should be places that emphasize the development of meaningful relations and the creation of knowledge, as well as Dewey's notions of how schools might be structured.

While Goodman valued Dewey, he agreed more with A.S. Neill, the founder and director of Summerhill, because Neill never required students to go to class. This should not be surprising, given that it was the compulsory nature of schooling that, in his view, caused the most damage. Because students had to be there, he felt, educators did not have to connect to the student but merely deliver content.

Goodman's Impact

In the film of Goodman's life, he is referred to as "the most influential person you've never heard of." Few remember what he wrote, and when he is remembered he is often dismissed as a critic who offered no solutions. But as I have tried to describe here, while he didn't specify solutions—he was too much an anarchist for that—he suggested how we might think about things and what we might do.

He was a moralist who sought a society that reflected his Jeffersonian ideals of a radical, educative community. Martin Luther King, Jr., citing Goodman, concurred that society was "spiritually empty." And, like Goodman, King connected his moral goals to his goals for society. King stated that in 1967 we suffered not from, as Goodman described, "spiritual emptiness that is terrifying[,] but spiritual evil.... [Y]oung men of America are dying, fighting and killing in Asian jungles in a war whose purposes are so ambiguous that a whole nation is seized with dissent" (Lee, 2011).

Goodman focused much of his writing on adolescence because he felt it was in that crucible that we worked out who we are and our relationship to one another and society. He also argued against restricting learning to formal educational institutions such as schools and, indeed, because schools were compulsory, argued that schools were places least likely to contribute to genuine learning. Instead, he contributed to the literature on de-schooling and other alternative approaches. Goodman imagined reconstructing society to support people in questioning one another and society.

Goodman was cantankerous, contradictory, and someone people both wanted to be around and to avoid. From all accounts he was not always easy to get along with. (See Susan Sontag's [1972] comments upon learning of Goodman's death.) But his writing challenges our basic assumptions about schools, society, and ourselves, and pushes us to consider other possibilities.

I realize that this review is about Goodman and not me, but Goodman understood the political as the personal (and vice versa), so it would be important not to leave his work "out there" but to incorporate his ideas into our own lives. His was a voice that encouraged the reader and listener to take risks in engaging in both serious intellectual work and political action. Finally, writing this review has revealed how Paul Goodman's work changed my life.

Note

1   For example, Allen Ginsberg's line in *Howl* (1956): "I saw the best minds of my generation…who passed through universities with radiant cool eyes hallucinating Arkansas and Blake-light tragedy among the scholars of war, who were expelled from the academies for crazy & publishing obscene odes on the windows of the skull."

References

Camus, A. (1946). *The stranger.* New York: Alfred A Knopf.

Camus, A. (1951). *The rebel.* New York: Alfred A Knopf.

Dennison, G. (1972). *The lives of children: The story of the First Street School.* New York: Random House.

Dewey, J. (1894, August 25–26). John Dewey to Alice Chipman Dewey and children. Letter. John Dewey Papers, Special Collections, Morris Library, Southern Illinois University.

Dewey, J. (1915, May 5). Untitled. *The New Republic,* p. 42.

Friedenberg, E. (1959). *The vanishing adolescent.* New York: Dell.

Ginsberg, A. (1956). *Howl and other poems.* San Francisco, CA: City Lights.

Goodman, P. (1960). *Growing up absurd.* New York: Vintage.

Goodman, P. (1962). *Compulsory mis-education.* New York: Vintage.

Goodman, P. (1964). *The community of scholars.* New York: Vintage.

Graubard, A. (1972). *Free the children: Radical school reform and the free school movement.* New York: Pantheon.

Greene, M. (1967). *Existential encounters for teachers.* New York: Random House.

Hursh, D. (1974). The crucible of adolescence. In D.T. Jaffee & T. Clark (Eds.), *Worlds apart: Young people and drug programs* (pp. 20–45). New York: Vintage.

Hursh, D. (2008). *High-stakes testing and the decline of teaching and learning: The real crisis in education.* Lanham, MD: Rowman & Littlefield.

Illich, I. (1971). *Deschooling society.* New York: Harper & Row.

Lee, J. (Producer & Director). (2011). *Paul Goodman changed my life.* Motion Picture. New York: Zeitgeist Films.

Mills. C.W. (1959). *The sociological imagination.* Oxford, UK: Oxford University Press.

Neill, A.S. (1960). *Summerhill: A radical approach to childrearing.* New York: Pocket Books.

Paley, G. (1959). *The little disturbances of man*. New York: Doubleday.

Paley, G. (1985). *Later the same day*. New York: HarperCollins.

Rossman, M. (1971). *The wedding within the war*. New York: Doubleday.

Rossman, M. (1972). *On learning and social change*. New York: Random House.

Salinger, J.D. (1951). *The catcher in the rye*. Boston, MA: Little, Brown and Company.

Sartre, J.P. (1969). *Nausea*. San Francisco, CA: New Directions.

Sontag, S. (1972, September 21). On Paul Goodman. *New York Review of Books*. http://www.nybooks.com/articles/archives/1972/sep/21/on-paul-goodman/

Van der Ryn, S. (2005). *Design for life: The architecture of Sim Van der Ryn*. Layton, UT: Gibbs Smith.

Van der Ryn, S., & Cowan, S. (2007). *Ecological design*. Washington, DC: The Island Press.

Weltman, B. (2000). Revisiting Paul Goodman: Anarcho-syndicalism as the American way of life. *Educational Theory*, *50*(2), 179–199.

Williams, V. (1981). *Three days on a river in a red canoe*. New York: Mulberry Books.

Williams, V. (1984). *A chair for my mother*. New York: Greenwillow Books.

FOUR

Herbert Kohl, *36 Children* (1967)

Barbara J. Thayer-Bacon

Born in 1937, Herbert Kohl began a 6-year teaching assignment in Harlem in 1962, just 2 years before the Civil Rights Act of 1964 required public schools in the United States to desegregate or risk losing their federal funding. He wrote about that teaching experience in *36 Children* (1967). Growing up in a Jewish family in the Bronx and attending the Bronx High School of Science, Kohl's childhood dream was to become a teacher, and he was sorely disappointed when he learned, after enrolling at Harvard, that the university did not offer teaching degrees. (He detailed that disappointment in a later publication, *Growing Minds* [1984]].) Kohl graduated from Harvard in 1958 with a philosophy and mathematics degree, attended University College, Oxford on a Henry Fellowship (1958–1959), and studied philosophy at Columbia University on a Woodrow Wilson Fellowship (1959–1960). However, he never gave up his dream to become a teacher, and in 1961 he enrolled in Teachers College, Columbia University, to earn his K–8 teaching credential. He has been teaching and writing ever since ("Herbert Kohl," 2014).

Synopsis

In *Growing Minds* and other publications, Kohl tells us that, while seeking a teaching credential at Teachers College, Columbia University, he was removed from his student teaching assignment because he stood up for three students he had been tutoring when a substitute teacher disrespected those students. He was also removed from his next teaching assignment for asking too many questions and giving honest, critical feedback on the school's reading program (or lack thereof) when invited to do so at the end of the school year. *36 Children* is the story of his "third time is a charm" chance to teach "regular children" in a public school system that assigned him to teach in Harlem as punishment for his previous indiscretions.

36 Children is not a scholarly book. It is written as a novel/journal and is mainly an account of Kohl's first full year of teaching in Harlem, although some attention is also paid to the second year and to his later efforts to stay in touch with the students from the first year's class. The book not only contains Kohl's writing, but also a number of contributions from his students.

36 Children is written as a firsthand report from the classroom of an "inner city" school, as such schools were called then. (Today we would call Kohl's school an "urban" school.) At the time of Kohl's writing, it was also referred to as a "ghetto" school, as the entire student body was African American. ("Negro" was the term used then, before the Civil Rights Movement and the affirmation of "Black" as a term.) It is important to understand the context of the times in which Kohl wrote *36 Children*, for it can be used in teacher education programs today not only for its lessons about "qualities of a good teacher," but also for its rich description of a particular time in the history of education in the United States. As such it can help today's teachers and those of tomorrow to understand where we have made significant progress and where we have not.

Climate of the Times

I was born in 1953, one year before the Supreme Court ruled in *Brown v Board of Education of Topeka, Kansas*, 347 U.S. 483 (1954) that the provision of separate public schools for Black and White students was unconstitutional. The case was argued in 1952, reargued in 1953, and decided in 1954, officially overturning the *Plessy v Ferguson* (1896) ruling that allowed state-sponsored, segregated schools. However, *Brown* did not spell out specifically when desegregation had to take place, so in 1955 the Supreme Court considered arguments by schools requesting relief concerning the task of desegregation. *Brown II* is the court's decision to delegate the task of carrying out school desegregation to district courts "with all deliberate speed." In many parts of the United States, particularly the deep South, this ambiguous language was used to delay and avoid desegregation, with school districts using such tactics as closing down school systems, using state money to finance segregated "private" schools, or admitting only a few "token" Black students, leaving most enrolled in underfunded, unequal Black schools. It should be noted that while Black schools were inferior in terms of physical conditions and lack of resources (such as science labs, current textbooks, or even enough textbooks), more recent research has confirmed that there were many talented teachers working in Black schools who lost their jobs with desegregation (Fultz, 1995; Morris & Morris, 2000; Walker, 1996).

At the time Kohl wrote *36 Children*, Harlem was a segregated New York City community. Its residents experienced issues associated with discrimination in a racist society, including poverty, high crime rates, high rates of alcohol and drug abuse, and families struggling to stay together and care for their children and elders. There were no White children in Kohl's classroom, nor were there any Latino/a, Native American, or Asian American students. The classroom was entirely African American. In today's world, Herbert Kohl and others such as Jonathan Kozol (another 1958 Harvard graduate who became a teacher in Boston during the 1960s), have brought to our attention the fact that public schools in the United States, as a result of White flight to the suburbs and the proliferation of private schools, have re-segregated and are currently more segregated in many urban areas than they were prior to *Brown*. The promise of desegregated, equally resourced schools with a diverse, highly qualified, professional corps of teachers and administrators capable of insuring that *all* children in America receive a high-quality education has yet to be fulfilled in America's public school systems (Kozol, 1991, 2005).

Although Kohl does not mention it in *36 Children*, at the time of his teaching in Harlem the United States was involved in the post–World War II Cold War between the allies who had fought together against Germany, Italy, and Japan. Historians do not all agree on the dates of the Cold War, but the range is generally stated to be roughly 1947 to 1991. The Cold War began in earnest with the occupation of Berlin by the allies and Russia's refusal to leave the eastern sector of the city and, indeed, the eastern segment of a partitioned Germany after World War II. It is called the "Cold War" because there were no actual battles between the Western Bloc (the United States and its NATO allies) and the Eastern Bloc (the U.S.S.R. and the Warsaw Pact nations), but there was a significant build up of militaries during this period, along with a sizable expenditure of federal funds on military equipment and development. There were also regional wars that took place during the Cold War, with both sides providing military support: the Korean War (1950–1953), the Vietnam War (1955–1975), and Russia's war with Afghanistan (fought from 1979 to the mid-1980s). Most historians mark the end of the Cold War as the tearing down of the Berlin Wall in 1989, a barrier that was built to separate East Berlin from West Berlin.

For military families like mine, the Cold War was a time of tension, fear, and the buildup of the U.S. war machine. For the children in Kohl's classroom, the Cold War was more distant in their lives, unless they had friends and family members serving in the military. But for poor communities in the United States, the impact of the Cold War was felt in other areas as well, for Congress had chosen to fund the building of a nuclear arsenal and collateral wartime weapons over the funding of our public school system.

What led the nation into the social unrest of the 1960s was the Civil Rights Movement and its concomitant efforts not only to desegregate public school systems, but also to protest segregation in all public arenas, including restaurants, stores, movie theaters, and sporting events. While Kohl does not discuss the feminist movement in *36 Children*, Judy Kohl, whom he married during the period covered in the book, is an excellent example of what women were doing in the 1960s to address social injustice in the United States. Judy was very important to Kohl's ability to sustain himself through this period. He credits her as a person he could talk to about the stresses he was experiencing in teaching. Judy worked in education as well—as a special education teacher with a tremendous amount of patience, as Kohl later tells us (*Growing Minds*, 1984). Her presence in the 36 children's lives is a warm, caring one, and they grow very fond of her, just as their teacher grows very fond of her. In fact, when Judy and Herbert Kohl married during the school year, the children in the classroom, with help from their families, threw them a surprise party. Judy wrote books with her husband, and with him co edited Myles Horton's autobiographical *The Long Haul* (published in 1990, the year Horton passed away), about Highlander, an adult learning center in Tennessee. Highlander was founded by Myles Horton in 1932 and still exists. It offers activist adults a place to learn how to lead social justice movements to eradicate of oppressive conditions in their communities (Adams & Horton, 1975; A. Horton, 1989; M. Horton, 1990; Horton & Freire, 1990). *The Long Haul* received the Robert F. Kennedy Book Award in 1991.

Main Themes

In *36 Children* Kohl tells us that he spent the summer of 1962 preparing to teach a fifth-grade class, only to find out the first week of school that he will be teaching 6–1, the highest-level sixth-grade class, at PS XXX. He has 20 girls and 16 boys in his class, all of whose names and ages are given at the beginning of the book. As he begins to know who these 11- and 12-year-old children are, we are introduced to them as well. Kohl learns how to be a good teacher during the year, and he passes these lessons on to his readers. For me, reading *36 Children* in the 1980s served as a wonderful affirmation of lessons I was learning on my own as an elementary teacher at Montessori schools in the artist communities of the Poconos (Pennsylvania) and Santa Barbara (California), and the Catholic community of the San Luis Rey mission area in Oceanside (California). Kohl is a good storyteller, and I still remember some of his stories many years later. I used to share the lessons he offers in *36 Children* in my undergraduate teacher education courses, and I still share them in my graduate education classes. There is a timeless quality to what he experienced in the school year 1962–1963.

Kohl gives an honest description of his lack of preparation, his fears, and his exhaustion as he tries to engage 36 children who are already tired of school. Anyone who has been a teacher can relate to those fears and to the exhaustion felt at the end of each day. Who are the students I will be working with, how well will they get along with each other, and am I ready for them? Do I know the curriculum inside out, and am I prepared to present it in multiple ways? Will I be able to interest the students in the curriculum I am required to teach? Kohl tells us: "I was afraid that if one child got out of my control the whole class would quickly follow, and I would be overwhelmed by chaos" (p. 30). That is a fear shared by virtually all beginning teachers. The children in his class taught him to let go of "ranting and carping" at them, to not take everything they said so seriously, and to allow them the space to occasionally "blow off some steam." Children have bad days, just like adults, and children living in poverty often have to deal with adult-type stress in their lives (parents who lose their jobs, electricity that is turned off because of missed payments, landlords who evict their families for not paying the rent on time, parents who don't come home or come home drunk and start taking their frustrations out on their children, single-parent homes, and so on).

One of Kohl's first lessons is that he needs to get to know his students. He decides he needs to do this on his own terms, so he does not read their student "record cards" that tell him about their pasts. He wants them to have the chance to start with a clean slate and to tell him who they are *now*. That is a good way to allow children a chance to reinvent themselves each school year and to avoid the labels of "lazy" or "defiant." However, for children with special needs that previous teachers and care-providers have worked hard to identify, not being able to pass on that vital information to the child's next teacher is a handicap.

When the children in Kohl's sixth-grade class show no interest in the lessons he tries to teach, he decides he needs to find out what they *are* interested in learning more about. He begins by listening to his students and learning to be a good observer. He gives them 10-minute breaks between lessons, and he listens to what they talk about. He begins to supplement the curriculum with books he brings in that speak to their interests. After listening to them discuss their neighborhoods and realizing that he doesn't know what their home situations are like, he seeks to get to know them by giving them homework assignments such as "draw where you live," "draw what your home looks like." He realizes he has never experienced what they live with daily.

Kohl learns to share with the students who he is, too. He shares with them his interest in Greek mythology and the roots of words, and he watches the class become "word hungry." He says he "overwhelmed them with books" but didn't require them to write reports or read a set number of pages (p. 40). He lets them discover what they like to read and watches as some devour all the books he brings in, while others hardly read at all. The children introduce him to books he hasn't read as well, such as the Nancy Drew books (which were my favorites at their age, too). Kohl brings in chess and checkers for the students to learn to play and watches who is drawn to them. Eventually he begins to invite them to his home, something that today is considered risky and dangerous for a teacher, as the children and teacher are both vulnerable to charges of harm. I risked having my own students and their friends came to our home to play, as I was one of three elementary teachers in our only elementary class in one school, and I was the head teacher in the only upper elementary class in two other schools.

Kohl also tells stories about taking the children on field trips, including an overnight trip to Cambridge to see Harvard University, to the Upper West Side to see Columbia University and Teachers College, and to attractions like the Metropolitan Museum. He shared with them places he loves. My co-teachers and I took our students on annual camping trips in California and on museum trips to New York City and Philadelphia from the Poconos. Parents were always invited to join us, as were the parents of Kohl's students. Like Kohl, I learned a lot about my students by being with them in other settings, and we all learned that children who may be struggling with reading or math skills can be excellent swimmers and tent builders, for example. Again, Kohl confirmed for me something I found so valuable: get to know your students outside of the classroom. What you learn about them will surprise you!

Kohl starts out the school year with not enough books or supplies but, with the children's help, slowly discovers closets full of science material. The children bring in their own records to share with him and show him where the record player is stored at the school, as "they knew the exact distribution of all the hidden and hoarded supplies in the school," and that begins a daily pattern of sharing the latest records at the end of the morning or afternoon (p. 43). In order to get his hands on the school's science equipment, Kohl volunteers to take care of it for the school. He tells us how he learned that it was "useless to fight with the administration over their irresponsibility" (p. 42). He had learned from his previous teaching experiences that fighting with the administration got him fired or transferred. Since he wanted to stay with his 6–1 class, he "learned to keep quiet, keep the door of my classroom shut, and make believe the class and I functioned in a vacuum, that the school around us didn't exist" (p. 42). He learned to pick his battles and to make compromises when necessary. He was surprised to find out that the children understood very well the concept of adults having to make compromises, since their parents had to do this on a daily basis. Kohl feared that admitting his limits would hurt his relationships with his students, but instead it strengthened them.

The children in Kohl's class begin writing and sharing their stories with him and each other. Some write sporadically, others continually. Kohl shares many of their stories with us in *36 Children*. I also used writing as an important part of the curriculum in my elementary classroom, mainly journaling, and I still use journaling in my university classes. Like Kohl, I have learned much about my students and their daily lives through their writing.

Kohl learned to find something his students could be expert at, and to allow them to share their expertise with other students. Positioning students as teachers helps them find ways to shine. Kohl learned to trust that his students *do* want to learn, just maybe not the deadly dull curriculum he was required to teach them. The Montessori method taught me this important lesson, too, as in a Montessori classroom students are allowed to choose their own work (Montessori, 1912). Even those students who came to me hating school after having had bad experiences elsewhere stopped resisting learning once they understood that they could choose to do nothing as long as they were not distracting other students.

Kohl learned that all students need to feel included in the classroom community, and that it is important to draw students in and help them make friends. I found that I could not look forward to teaching children for 3 years in our multiage class unless I found ways to befriend them and help them develop friendships with others as well. I still rely on this lesson today, even in graduate-level classes, where I continue to seek to establish caring learning communities (Thayer-Bacon, 2008, 2013; Thayer-Bacon & Bacon, 1998).

Kohl also learned that it was important to get to know his students' families and to position himself as an ally seeking to advocate for the students—and, by extension, their families. I remember his stories of sneaking food into hospital rooms for family members who were sick and could not eat the hospital food being served to them, and stories of eating meals at families' homes (*Growing Minds*, 1984). I also had several children with serious family problems that came to light only after I had gained their trust, which can take more than a year. I found it so much healthier to start from a place of assuming parents love their children and want the best for them, just as I, a single parent, wanted the best for my three children. Just as Kohl started each school year offering his students a "clean slate," it is important to offer parents a "clean slate," too. Teacher and parents then are positioned as a team working together to help their children thrive.

Kohl describes in *36 Children* the heartaches he experiences—even heartbreaks, as he watches his students in that first class move on to other teachers and other schools and struggle. He also tells us about the children who did not make it through the year because of family relocations and of being difficult to control (specifically, a student named John).

> The next year I had a class of Johns, and seeing how easily they responded to adult confidence and trust, I have always regretted my lack of effort with John. Yet I have to admit that I did not have the necessary confidence as a teacher and as a human being the year I taught the thirty-six children. It took the thirty-six children to give me that. (pp. 178–179)

Every teacher carries within her or him feelings of regret that they didn't try hard enough or find the right approach for particular children with whom they have worked. Every teacher thinks back on times they wish they had had more energy, patience, knowledge, or time to help a child in need.

Kohl taught me that it is okay to take breaks from teaching in order to avoid burnout. For me, this meant living on a teacher's 9-month salary for 12 months so that I could have the summers off and spend them playing with my children. I still follow this practice today, and I give myself summer sabbaticals. The year after he teaches the 36 children in 6-1, Kohl is given a class in a new school in Harlem, 6-7, "the bottom." He tells us he was a much better listener, and the children seemed to talk more. Together they redesign the curriculum, and the children win over his focus and efforts. But Kohl begins to experience the heartbreak of "watching the other teachers, being abused by the administration, seeing the children fail and nobody care" (p. 188). The 36 children Kohl first taught begin to visit and hint to him "of their failure and despair" (p. 189). He begins to feel as though he set the children up for subsequent disappointment and bitterness: "they all came back discouraged and demoralized" (p. 190). After the second year of teaching, Kohl takes a year off and goes to Europe, where he is able to live on royalty earnings from his writing. This break helps him to stay in teaching. He shares with us letters he received from students in *36 Children*, giving him updates on their lives. He learns to pace himself and find other avenues for helping the children, such as starting summer reading programs and alternative schools. Kohl leaves Harlem after 6 years to teach in Berkeley, California. He ends *36 Children* this way:

> Without hope and without cynicism, I try to make myself available to my pupils. I believe neither that they will succeed nor that they will fail. I know they will fight, falter, and rise again and again, and that if I have the strength I will be there to rejoice and cry with them, and to add my little weight to easing the burden of being alive in the United States today. (p. 224)

Strengths and Weaknesses

Herbert Kohl's *36 Children* represents one teacher's desire to help improve the quality of education for targeted, minority children in America's school systems. As a White teacher and a graduate of some of America's most prestigious universities, he accepted the challenge of teaching in an all-Black, low-income school, with the desire to challenge his own—as well as others'—racist beliefs about Black children, as well as classist beliefs about poor children. Kohl strongly believed that all children deserve a chance to receive a good education. When we read *36 Children* today, it is shocking to learn of the level of neglect, abuse, and teacher bias the children encountered in America's public schools in 1962. We can praise Kohl for his courage and desire to advocate for children whom others were woefully mistreating and/or neglecting, but we can also hold him accountable for his lack of an in-depth critique of the social systems that caused his students' community so much stress, and his subtle acceptance of deficit theories that justified racist policies.

At times Kohl positions the students and their families as tragic victims, and he leans toward sentimentality—with himself, the caring White teacher, coming to their rescue as their ally. His story is one of heroic teachers and their unintended roles in perpetuating racism; he does not offer a sociological or political analysis of the school systems and the policies they must address. In today's world, the ally role can be a dangerous position that opens a teacher to much criticism if he or she is positioned as a shepherd or savior (Rancière, 1991, 2006). Today we find that educational policies place blame on our teachers working in public schools, while the teachers feel powerless, defeated, overwhelmed, and exhausted by their individual efforts (Villa & Buese, 2007). Teachers today are leaving their jobs in droves because our current efforts to standardize the curriculum and evaluate teachers through students' test scores are punishing the Herbert Kohls of the United States—that is, the teachers willing to work with children in serious need and to tap into their backgrounds and interests to engage them in their learning, instead of following a scripted curriculum.

Significance and Influence, Then and Now

Herbert Kohl is credited with being a strong voice for progressive alternative education, founding the Open Schools Movement (in the 1960s)—open classrooms in particular—and with writing over 30 books ("Hebert Kohl," 2014). Writing a firsthand report from the classroom in an inner-city school has become something of a new literary genre, thanks to Kohl's influence. Other books cut from the same cloth are Sylvia Ashton-Warner's *Teacher* (1963), Jonathan Kozol's *Death at an Early Age* (1967), Peter McLaren's *Cries from the Corridor* (1980), and Samuel Freedman's *Small Victories* (1991), the story of Jessica Siegel's year as a high school English teacher on the Lower East Side of Manhattan.

Kohl's writing significantly influenced many other famous educators such as John Holt, Jonathan Kozol, Ivan Illich, Peter McLaren, and Neil Postman, to name a few. In the 1980s he worked with his wife, Judith Kohl (who has worked with him on many collaborative projects), to help Myles Horton put together his autobiography, as noted earlier in this chapter.

Kohl inspired a generation of us, many of whom were students in public schools during the years of desegregation in the 1960s when he began teaching, to embrace a career in education and consider teaching the noblest profession there is. He inspired us to get out of our comfort zones and work to help *all* children receive a quality education. For Kohl, this is a social justice issue, and a pedagogical imperative.

Conclusion

36 Children is still relevant today, as I have sought to demonstrate through the lessons about what it means to be a good teacher that Kohl describes for us. Since the publication of *36 Children*, the United States has desegregated and resegregated schools in our urban spaces, due to "White flight" to the suburbs during the 1960s and 1970s, and then White flight to charter schools and private schools beginning in the 1980s. It is a good description of "how things were" prior to the Civil Rights Act and an important measuring stick to mark our progress and to show where there is still plenty of work to do.

References

Adams, F., & Horton, M. (1975). *Unearthing seeds of fire: The idea of Highlander.* Winston-Salem, NC: John F. Blair.

Ashton-Warner, S. (1963). *Teacher.* New York: Simon & Schuster.

Freedman, S.G. (1991). *Small victories.* New York: Harper Perennial.

Fultz, M. (1995, Spring). Teacher training and African-American education in the South, 1900–1940. *Journal of Negro Education, 64*(2), 196–214.

Herbert Kohl (educator). (2014, November 21). Wikipedia. http://en.wikipedia.org/wiki/Herbert_Kohl_(educator)

Horton, A.I. (1989). *The Highlander Folk School: A history of its major programs, 1932–1961.* Brooklyn, NY: Carlson Publishing, Inc. (Original work published 1971.)

Horton, M. (1990). *The long haul: An autobiography* (H. & J. Kohl, Eds.). New York: Teachers College Press.

Horton, M., & Freire, P. (1990). *We make the road by walking* (B. Bell, J. Gaventa, & J. Peters, Eds.). Philadelphia, PA: Temple University Press.

Kohl, H. (1967). *36 children.* New York: New American Library.

Kohl, H. (1984). *Growing minds: On becoming a teacher.* New York: Harper & Row.

Kozol, J. (1967). *Death at an early age.* Boston, MA: Houghton Mifflin.

Kozol, J. (1991). *Savage inequalities.* New York: Crown Publishers.

Kozol, J. (2005). *The shame of the nation: The restoration of apartheid schooling in America.* New York: Crown Publishers.

McLaren, P. (1980). *Cries from the corridor.* Toronto, Canada: Methuen.

Montessori, M. (1912). *The Montessori method.* New York: Random House.

Morris, V.G., & Morris, C.L. (2000). *Creating caring and nurturing educational environments for African American children.* Westport, CT: Bergin and Garvey.

Rancière, J. (1991). *The ignorant schoolmaster* (K. Ross, Trans.). Stanford, CA: Stanford University Press.

Rancière, J. (2006). *Hatred of democracy* (S. Corcoran, Trans.). London & New York: Verso.

Thayer-Bacon, B. (2008). *Beyond liberal democracy in schools: The power of pluralism.* New York: Teachers College Press.

Thayer-Bacon, B. (2013). *Democracies always in the making: Historical and current philosophical issues for education.* Lanham, MD: Rowman & Littlefield.

Thayer-Bacon, B., & Bacon, C. (1998). *Philosophy applied to education: Nurturing a democratic community in the classroom.* Upper Saddle River, NJ: Prentice Hall. *36 Children.* (2014, November 21). Wikipedia. http://en.wikipedia.org/wiki/36_Children

Valli, L., & Buese, D. (2007, September). The changing roles of teachers in an era of high-stakes accountability. *American Educational Research Journal, 44*(3), 519–558.

Walker, V.S. (1996). *Their highest potential: An African American school community in the segregated South.* Chapel Hill: University of North Carolina Press.

FIVE

Paulo Freire, *Pedagogy of the Oppressed* (1969)

Roberto H. Bahruth and Donaldo Macedo

> I consider the fundamental theme of our epoch to be that of *domination*—which implies its op-
> posite, the theme of *liberation*, as the objective to be achieved. It is this tormenting theme which
> gives our epoch the anthropological character mentioned earlier. In order to achieve humanization,
> which presupposes the elimination of dehumanizing oppression, it is absolutely necessary to sur-
> mount the limit-situations in which people are reduced to things. (Freire, 2000, p. 103)

As the quotation above illustrates, Paulo Freire is timelier today than when *Pedagogy of the Oppressed* was first published in 1970, given the draconian inequalities created by neoliberalism, the
cruel manufactured wars worldwide, and the savage human misery that is dehumanizing both
its perpetrators and its victims. While violence, dire poverty, and a dehumanizing ruling class are
significantly more pernicious today due to both the weakening of nation-states and a sophisticated
world-wide surveillance apparatus made possible through technology, new forms of hegemons
increasingly replicate historical elements that provided the context in which the *Pedagogy of the
Oppressed* was written.

Paulo Freire was born in 1921 in Recife, Pernambuco, Brazil, into a middle-class family that
had lost its economic and class position during the Depression years of the 1930s. Because of its
modest economic means, Freire's family moved to Morro de Saúde, a very poor town on the out-
skirts of Recife, where he occasionally experienced hunger and witnessed the almost-permanent
hunger of others on a daily basis. As Freire recounted:

> It was a real and concrete hunger that had no specific date of departure. Even though it never
> reached the rigor of the hunger experienced by some people I know, it was not the hunger experi-
> enced by those who undergo a tonsil operation or are dieting. On the contrary, our hunger was of

the type that arrives unannounced and unauthorized, making itself at home without an end in sight. (Freire, 1996, p. 63)

It was this painful experience of hunger that fueled a constant rebelliousness that made Freire actively participate as a maker of history for most of his life, and leave behind a legacy of unquestionable value to humanity at his death on May 2, 1997. Following this untimely loss of Freire as our teacher-scholar, a plethora of eulogies appeared from around the world as a testimony to the importance of his life's work. *Pedagogy of the Oppressed* represents the coherence of his seminal understanding of what it means to implement a humanizing pedagogy for educators and learners working together through dialogical encounters.

Overview

When Paulo Freire went to work *with* peasants to teach them literacy, he did not bring with him a deficit orientation, a toolbox of "save the peasants from themselves" techniques, or the myths of superiority of the dominant culture. He knew the peasants were the holders of knowledge not legitimized by the ruling class. Rather than starting with the written word, he began with a dialogical praxis to reveal to the peasants the intelligence they used daily as a means of survival. Once the myths of inferiority were surmounted through these conversations, the internalized oppression of the peasants began to break down, and a major obstacle was removed from the work. Then, using organic vocabulary and generative themes from the everyday lives of the peasants, he began to teach them how to encode their worlds with the written word. Out of this praxis *Pedagogy of the Oppressed* was born, generated by Freire's work *with* his students—mostly peasants who, due to unjust policies of a quasi-oligarch society, were denied access to literacy. By literacy, he meant not only the reading of the word, but also the reading of the world.

It is important not to underestimate his scholarship before his arrival that enabled Freire to implement this pedagogy, as well as the ongoing reflection upon the collaborations in word-world exchanges informing his continued and deepening understanding of his cultural work—what Frei Betto (1997) called "praxis, theory, praxis." Finally, in writing *Pedagogy of the Oppressed*, the ultimate use of literacy was put into service by Freire, the scholar, to solidify his ideas and to write upon the world. It is evident that his work has reached around the globe and has contributed to revolutionary changes in educational settings prompted by teachers who care enough about their vocation to study it thoughtfully. It would be easy to fall into a tone of eulogizing Paulo Freire; but in many ways, through the corpus of his work, he lives on through the lives of those he touched personally, and those who were only touched by his words. One need only Google his name to see the enormous scope of attention world scholars continue to pay to his work.

To transform sterile, contrived basal texts into profound discussions of the relationships between word and world represents the alchemy of theory and praxis (Betto, 1997). The vocation of teaching requires caring, not coddling, as Freire so clearly points out, and scholarship is an expression of that caring (Bahruth, 2005). Revolution is an act that requires great love of humanity and of all life. *Pedagogy of the Oppressed* presents theoretical foundations of a revolutionary, transformative praxis to humanize education.

Historical Context for Freire

To understand oppression and to get to its roots, it is essential to understand, for example, patriarchy. Women have historically been treated as objects (Lerner, 1986; Minnich, 1990; Fehr, 1993), even ridiculed for being emotional. In *Pedagogy of the Oppressed*, Freire provides an analysis of the human conditions of oppressor and oppressed and outlines ways in which humanity never achieves its full potential. He also delineates a pedagogical response to oppression, demonstrating through his work, as well as cultural work done elsewhere, how educators and the oppressed can work together to take agency into their own hands. What Freire names here—the culture of silence, false generosity, generative words, the dialogical and anti-dialogical, banking, internalized oppression, conscientization—makes visible and helps to develop a consciousness for the oppressed to refuse to be treated as objects of history and power as they move into their roles as historical subjects. The ultimate means of the pedagogy of the oppressed is humanization by working *with* the exploited masses through literacy projects whereby the word becomes a means of liberation. However, it is important to point out that Freire's legacy should not be reduced only to his contributions to the development of a revolutionary literacy. Freire used literacy as a tool that would enable the oppressed to achieve a higher, critical awareness of their condition, to understand that the dire poverty to which they had been relegated was not destiny but part and parcel of a social construction that could be deconstructed and, in the process, unveil both the ideology and its mechanisms designed for the production and reproduction of human misery. That is, Freire used literacy not as an end in itself but as a means to conscientization, which is an emancipatory pedagogical process designed to teach students through critical literacies (reading the word and the world). It is a pedagogy meant to help them to negotiate the world in a thoughtful way that exposes and engages the relations between the oppressor and the oppressed. Its central educational objective is to awaken in the oppressed to knowledge, creativity, and constant critical reflexive capacities necessary to demystify and understand the power relations responsible for their marginalization and, through this recognition, begin a project of liberation.

Its commitment to critical reflection and transformative action makes conscientization central, for example, to action research and liberation pedagogy, as they both require that the researcher and the liberation pedagogue perform the critical questioning inherent to conscientization. This is done to ensure that due consideration is given to important social, economic, and cultural contributors to social justice in designing the research and the critical pedagogical space that lead to liberation and emancipation (Hostetler, 2005). Freire's use and development of conscientization articulates the history of conscientization and the principles that undergird this process as a liberating pedagogy. It functions as an antidote to the detrimental pedagogies of what Freire termed "banking education" and emphasizes the vital role conscientization plays in both critical reflection and action. In other words, conscientization becomes, in Freire's pedagogy, the soul of praxis. While this seminal work is critical, the continuation of his scholarship provides witness to his own "unfinishedness" (Freire, 1998b), as he used literacy to expand his ideas while continuing to hone his pedagogical arguments. In essence, Paulo Freire was a humanist who learned as he taught, reflected upon his encounters, and grew pedagogically over the course of his life's work.

In *Letters to Cristina* (1996), Freire provides an autobiographical account of his own conscientization and the purpose of his struggles to contest exploitation as he elaborated upon the different contexts of his work around the world due to exile, and his gravitation to countries where the promise of democratization was taking place. Chile in the early 1970s is one example. While writing these letters, he makes new meanings of old memories—one of the dangerous effects of literacy that motivates the oppressor to withhold it from the oppressed. (One need only recall that it was once illegal to teach slaves to read in the United States.)

One memory specific to language is related to Freire's adventures with the poorer children of his neighborhood. They would crawl under fences to take mangos from other people's gardens. The other boys were called thieves, but he was called a mischievous boy. He related this to social class, since his father wore a necktie every day, even after moving to the poorer neighborhood when he lost his job. We see this linguistic gerrymandering throughout history. One government has an administration while another has a regime. In Israel, Jewish people are "massacred" by suicide bombers, while Palestinians who are shot by the IDF "find death along the road to Bethlehem." Macedo (1994) discusses these "negatively charged" words (migrants as opposed to settlers), and Johnson and Lakoff (1980) make it clear that we never mix metaphors across social classes or political lines. This naming is one of the acts of power readily seen in government terms such as "Hispanic," a generic term for a diverse population of Spanish speakers and their descendants. Naming also includes euphemisms to hide the truth and to whitewash (pun intended) state-sponsored crimes against humanity, for example, "ethnic cleansing" as a reframing of genocide. *Pedagogy of the Oppressed* opposes banking (where learners are empty vessels treated as objects) and endorses dialogical engagement *with* learners, where this naming is called into question as a tool of oppression. Language becomes a tool of renaming, and therefore liberation, as learners develop a language of criticity and assert their roles as agents of history.

Through his travels, Freire came into contact and communion with other great scholars joined in the work of revolutionary pedagogy. Pérez Cruz (2009) elaborates on several fruitful encounters with Raul Ferrer, the Cuban scholar and architect of the renowned Cuban Literacy Campaign of 1961 (Murphy, 2012). He makes clear the conversations and collaborations between these two pedagogues and the connections between the Cuban project and Freire's work in Brazil. Pérez Cruz connects Freire to José Martí, Amilcar Cabral, and Ché (as Freire cited in his work). Freire's work took him to Africa, Nicaragua, Cuba, and other politically volatile terrains of engagement, and he gained knowledge from each of these contexts.

The historical context for *Pedagogy of the Oppressed* worldwide is one of anti-colonialism in the Third World, civil rights in the United States, with accompanying anti-war efforts and feminist consciousness, and anti-imperialism as witnessed by the Cuban experiment. His work is surrounded and influenced by progressive publications such as Postman and Weingartner's *Teaching as a Subversive Activity* (1969), Ivan Illich's *Deschooling Society* (1971), and Bowles and Gintis's *Schooling in Capitalist America* (1976). Freire went on to co author a book with Myles Horton (1990) of Highlander School, attended by Rosa Parks and Martin Luther King, Jr., just two short weeks before Rosa Parks refused to give up her seat, thereby launching a popular movement for civil rights and changing the course of history. Paulo Freire worked in a climate of social upheaval, and more than once his literacy projects were uprooted by coup d'états where harsh fascism replaced popular and progressive governments.

How deep are Freire's pedagogical roots? Gil Antón (2003) asserts that we do not need students (estudiantes); we need estudiosos (studious people). Rhetoric abounds about lifelong learners, but the prescriptive fascism of corporate schooling, including high-stakes testing and textbook publishers, prevents most students from developing scholarly dispositions. What distinguishes Freire from other "educationalists" is what he referred to as "una pedagogía inquieta" (a restless pedagogy), never content with a lesson and always looking for deeper layers of meaning and method. Freire was a scholar who concerned himself not just with the mechanics of reading, but also with the sociopolitical contexts of his day and the history of prior scholars' attempts and ruminations upon their pedagogies. He made clear the connections between education and social injustice. He understood the complex dialectical relationships between reading the word and the world in ways necessary to transform dehumanizing conditions for oppressor and oppressed. As Carlos Fuentes (1992) so eloquently stated, "If we do not recognize our humanity in others, we shall not recognize it in ourselves."

Given this scholarly disposition, it is safe to assume that Paulo Freire read far and wide across the geopolitical/historical spectrum. He must have known that Tolstoy set up his own school to teach the children of his peasant laborers. Closer to home, he knew about the pedagogical work of Simón Rodriguez, José Martí, and José Mariátegui. He referenced scholars such as Hegel, Marx, Gramsci, and Kosík, and was deeply influenced by their work. It's clear he studied the Frankfurt School scholars and was influenced by European schools of thought. The Cubans make the connection—while recognizing the genius of Freire's work—that some of the roots of his methodology came from their revolutionary literacy project of which he was aware through his exchanges with Raul Ferrer in Cuba, as well as the work of Cuban educators in Africa (Pérez, 2004; Pérez-Cruz, 2009). He knew the work of John Dewey and Maxine Greene in America, especially their discussion of aesthetic education and anesthetic schooling, the latter being synonymous with Freire's concept of banking.

Relevance of Freire Today

Freire's work has had a tremendous impact upon teachers and the children in their care around the world. Testimonies abound of his transformative influence over teachers (see Chávez Chávez, 1997; Hayes, Bahruth, & Kessler, 1998) when classrooms designated as doomed became sites of dramatic successes in literacy and learning.

The pedagogy of the oppressed is suggesting a deeper understanding of the dialectical relationships between subject and object realities. This is why compensatory programs to "save" the oppressed and the national organizations designed to work in their favor were easily co-opted into the status quo. This lack of understanding—perhaps it is naïve to think this is born out of misunderstanding by the powerbrokers—led to numerous compromises over the years that ended up doing the exact opposite of what seemed to be intended, and the status quo gained financial control over the movement through federal programs. Over the course of 4 decades, we watched federal programs dwindle away from bilingual education, the usurping of OBEMLA into an English-language impetus, and eventually even the disappearance of funds altogether. TESOL as an organization played an instrumental role in undermining the stronger elements of NABE by competing for funding. Eventually, even the funding available to TESOL was removed, and it now depends upon membership, for-profit conferences, and the support of publishing companies (Goodman, 1989) that represent the "literacy and poverty pimps" (Macedo, 1994, 2001) who build empires that do anything but promote progressive pedagogy. The continued commodification and privatization of education itself is a force instrumental in undermining the Jeffersonian vision of an educated citizenry. Hedges (2009) denounces the mechanisms of an "empire of illusion" that work deliberately to lead the masses toward the abyss. According to Herman and Chomsky (1988):

> The bewildered herd is a problem. We've got to prevent their roar and trampling. We've got to distract them. They should be watching the Superbowl or sitcoms or violent movies. Every once in a while you call on them to chant meaningless slogans like "Support our troops." You've got to keep them pretty scared, because unless they're properly scared and frightened of all kinds of devils that are going to destroy them from outside or inside or somewhere, they may start to think, which is very dangerous, because they're not competent to think. Therefore it's important to distract them and marginalize them. (p. 27)

In the context of higher education, numerous scholars condemn trends in funding and grants and the emergence of the corporate university, which is often awarded major financial support for conducting research that has direct military and industrial benefits (Schmidt, 2000; Aronowitz, 2000; Giroux, 2007). Even the eager rush to fund STEM programs demonstrates a shrinking away from the humanities (Villaverde, 2000), where alternative discourse might have been a part of the development of consciousness through the voices of poets, novelists, artists, and so on.

Managed populations respond to the ringing of bells and other conditioned prompts and produce predictable, desired behaviors. Lawtoo (2013) argues that behavior is contrived through subtle hypnotic processes that become a "mimetic unconscious," governing and limiting our human potential. Leaders, on the other hand, are wise enough to work *with* the people and not apart from them. As a result, their struggle resonates with the populations they work with in solidarity and produces a collective, generative, transformative praxis. It explains why Cesar Chávez and Martin Luther King, Jr., successfully motivated people to act with resolve for the collective good and commitment to a humanizing ideal.

Institutions announce lofty ideals in their mission statements but work in ways to ensure that those ideals will never be accomplished. This is one reason why Freire's eloquent notion of word-world ("palabramundo") holds so much power and meaning. It provides a barometer to critically examine the dialectical relationships between the flowery discourse of these proclamations and the realities that either work toward ideals or prevent their emergence. Some basic examples from the framers of our Constitution demonstrate dialectical relationships as they expose the dissonance. For example, "general welfare" is not separate from "domestic tranquility," as these two work dynamically in the social and economic contexts of reality.

The usefulness of Freire's arguments remains timeless and timely because, as a society becomes more and more an administered population through distractions, ineffective educational policies (again the euphemistic No Child Left Behind comes to mind), the media, technology, and other mechanisms of oppression become normalized, invisible, and immobilizing. Through acceptance of "the way things are," a form of subtle fatalism results as people are swept away at the speed of the microchip, resigning themselves to the treadmill of consumerism as objects of history. Agency requires consciousness and a commitment to the "greater good."

Pedagogy of the Oppressed pivots upon the shift from anti-dialogical to dialogical engagements to problematize hegemony and its accompanying myths, and uses literacy to move beyond dehumanizing practices into fuller human relationships for the oppressor and the oppressed. It is always a praxis of working *with* and learning from students in every encounter. According to Freire:

> It is as self-contradictory for true humanists to use the banking method as it would be for rightists to engage in problem-posing education. (The latter are always consistent—they never use a problem posing pedagogy. (1970, p. 85)

It is also a pedagogy of the oppressor, as Freire points out, in that the heavy lifting of the democratic struggle will have to come from the oppressed, even though the oppressor stands to gain from the humanizing effects of conscientization. The dialectical relationship between the dehumanization of the oppressed and the dehumanization of the oppressor as a consequence becomes clear.

With access to education by more and more students who were previously denied and left out, the corporatization of higher education, through the persistence of banking as a mechanism to deny dialogue—despite all of the research on learning that demonstrates the ineffectiveness of lectures and power point delivery systems—has as one of its purposes to neuter the wider scope of knowledge and human conditions available through the influx of diversity.

Conferences continue to be arranged in formats that make dialogical engagements all but impossible, except in the cafés and bars after the presentations. Freire's pedagogical innovation promoting critical encounters, his shift from authoritarian to authority, and his practice of patient impatience as he helps learners to move from natural curiosity into an epistemological curiosity (Freire, 1998a) all demonstrate a recognition and celebration of learners as subjects, whereas traditional schooling only treats them as objects. This is the necrophilia he decries when he states: "From the first, the act of conquest, which reduces persons to the status of things, is necrophilic" (p. 119).

With the increasing diversity of university populations, nothing is harvested from the wide variety of experiential richness learners bring with them, because the knowledge is predetermined, static, superimposed, and centered upon a bias in favor of the ruling class. We all have blind spots, and it is through dialectical encounters that we discover the many lenses through which the world can be understood from lived experiences different from our own. It is the contemplation and compilation of the collective meaning-making where learning is most fruitful and useful toward the education of learned individuals. With the increasing corporatization of education, the humanities are under siege precisely because of their potential to contribute to the "well-rounded" individual. As Pearl S. Buck observed:

> Meanwhile, I like very much to be in the company of the learned, deservedly or not. They are truly learned men and therefore without conceit or bombast. They are simple in manner, kind and mildly humorous, and they are careful not to wound one another. This is because they are civilized as learning alone can civilize the human being. (1954, p. 388)

In place of the humanities, we see the emphasis and financial support going to STEM projects that do little to question the delivery systems within institutions. If they did, funding would dry up quickly. Notice how foreign-language programs are continuously funded despite the dreadful plague of resigned monolingualism they produce. Conversely, bilingual education programs are targeted for defunding precisely when they demonstrate effectiveness.

Perhaps the most blind are the "normalized intellectuals" (Honneth, 2009) who have been colonized into the system without questioning the internal "logic" of institutions of higher learning. They are well versed in the rhetoric of elitist myths denounced by Freire as mechanisms to justify the superiority of one group and the inferiority of another. Lawtoo (2013) warns of the dulling effects: "To accede to power via education corresponds to a submission to the hegemonic order which produces a passive, empty subject." Those who do question, who make a serious effort to transcend the "stupidification" (Macedo, 1994) of their own schooling in order to promote a more humanistic praxis through their teaching, often find themselves relegated to the "internal abroad." They may as well be speaking a foreign language, not only because the shift represents such a dramatic departure from banking, but also because those who have been normalized are enjoying the support of the institution and have settled into a cozy arrangement with anti-dialogical lecturing. Gabbard's analysis in *Silencing Ivan Illich* (1993) demonstrates how normalized academicians censor alternative discourse. The dominant, quantitative orientation clings to the myth of objectivity, and a practice of what Freire described as scientism rather than science. Yet, as Macedo points out:

> Although many educators, particularly those who blindly embrace a positivistic mode of inquiry, would outright deny the role of ideology in their work, nonetheless, they ideologically attempt to prevent the development of any counterdiscourse within their institution. (2001, p. xii)

It is undeniable that practicing critical pedagogy is a tremendous amount of work, but it is also significantly more rewarding and satisfying than conforming to the status quo. Once students have the opportunity to participate in a critical pedagogical space, they bemoan going to other classes based upon banking. Experiences in genuine learning through dialogical encounters whet the appetite for more and augment the frustrations of the anti-dialogical coursework they must endure to earn a degree. It is clear that students are hungry to know once they discover the illusion of learning they were conditioned to prior to dialogical encounters. Not all students embrace these opportunities, because the rules have changed and they prefer a system they can game to a system where they have to think. Chomsky and Macedo (2000) claim this disposition is the result of schooling as "the social construction of not seeing." Schmidt (2000) correctly describes what is at stake: "We do not lose our identity by confronting the system, we lose it by conforming to it." As Dykstra asserts:

> If there is a key to reinventing our educational system, it lies in what our teachers believe about the nature of knowing. Without a reexamination and change in beliefs about the nature of knowing, there will be no substantial change in the enterprise of education. (1996, p. 202)

Freire is prophetic in addressing the development of technology with a warning that it can be a tool of freedom as long as its uses promote humanization. Ellul (1965) warns us that the exact opposite is occurring and that neoliberalism is not about the globalization of capitalism, but of "technique," which he explains as the shift whereby humans are conditioned to be at the service of machines, rather than machines being at the service of humanity. (A comprehensive review of this dilemma is provided by Beatham, 2000, 2008.)

Conclusion

The reductionists, pedants of piecemeal, got it right if the goal is to reproduce hegemony through a system of reading instruction that appears logical yet serves the purpose of withholding literacy from would-be learners. Fragmentation is a mechanism of oppression, and behaviorism is the scientism of manipulation. Freire and Macedo (1998) refer to the "false dichotomies" that separate thinking and feeling, word and world, reading and writing, teacher and learner, theory and practice, which lead to anti-dialogical practices. Integration is the pedagogical response to such theories and systems, and Freire's "word world" (1983) is the most eloquent representation of literacy, since it expresses so much so simply.

It is undeniable that the world we live in is in crisis—morally, economically, socially, environmentally, and attitudinally. We are living in an age of narcissism, nihilism, fatalism, and distraction. As Postman (1986) notes, we are "amusing ourselves to death" (Giroux, 2001; Hedges, 2009; Jackson, 2008; Barber, 2007). The dominant paradigm of hegemony is behaviorism. It appears in the discourse of schools where labels announce a deficit orientation that justifies the continuation of pedagogical negligence. Since problems are located in the students and their families, the violence (Stuckey, 1991) of the dominant paradigm goes unquestioned and unchallenged. Standardization controls the curriculum and represses teachers who know better. Teacher preparation often reflects a domestication process wherein students are indoctrinated into the faulty logic of oppressive practices. Giroux thus implores critical pedagogues:

> Against the encroaching forces of militarization, corporatism, and ideological intolerance, educators have the difficult task of matching their sense of engaged scholarship with a meaningful and critical pedagogy, one that enables students to engage in debate and dialogue about pressing social problems and to believe not only that civic life matters but that they can make a difference in shaping it. (Giroux, 2007, p. 5)

Teaching is not a technique; it is an art anchored in scholarship, and history tells us an artist rejects colonization and demands self-determination.

Never in the history of humanity has a pedagogy offered through Freire's work been so promising and so vital. As long as oppression exists, *Pedagogy of the Oppressed* will be relevant. While it is evident what strengths and groundbreaking insights come through the experiences he was able to contemplate and connect with theory, weaknesses are mainly what he addressed through the evolution of his theories in later books. His emerging clarifications and deepening of insights demonstrate his openness to a scholarly path. The core of ideas presented in *Pedagogy of the Oppressed* is sound and well thought out. That this book has resonated continuously around the world in so many languages is evidence of its importance.

Another indication of the precise nature of Freire's analysis of mechanisms of oppression and pedagogical ways to overcome it is provided by the ways in which his work has been consistently ignored, rejected, and dismissed by oppressors and anti-intellectuals. In the context of the United States, for many years it was claimed that Freire was only relevant in Third World contexts. To this Macedo (1992) comments, " Have you been to East LA, Camden, or East St. Louis lately?" He points to the work of Jonathan Kozol (2005), elaborated upon in Chapter 18 of this volume. The Third World-ization of the extremely poor in the United States makes Freire's work most relevant in ghettos and cultures of poverty (Kohl, 1994). White (2003) captures the postmodern dilemma:

From Adorno's perspective, the meaning of the Information Economy is the final victory of the organization of "facts" over truth. The brutal consequence of this victory is suffering and death for certain "administered populations" and, at best in the First World, a great diminishment of what it means to be human…. The "end of history" that conservatives have celebrated becomes the end of hope for justice and universal wellbeing. (p. 176)

Paulo Freire has left behind a legacy of hope and ontological clarity for cultural workers who continue to engage in the ceaseless struggle for social justice and humanization. The paradigm shift from well-behaved technicist to a praxis of critical pedagogy has salvaged the vocation of teaching and filled the lives of so many with the joy and satisfaction gained through the celebration of human intelligence. We owe a debt of gratitude to the humble teacher from Pernambuco who took the trouble to care. He used literacy to pen a pedagogical response to oppression through a language of critique infused with a pedagogy of love as taught to him by his second wife, Nita Freire. According to Paulo Freire, it was from her pedagogy of love that he learned that to love again is always possible, since her presence in his life prevented him from losing what characterized Freire and his work most: hope. In his last writings, perhaps as a tribute to Nita, Freire continually returned to the theme of hope, challenging us to embrace it as an essential part of our human condition:

In truth, from the point of view of the human condition, hope is an essential component and not an intruder. It would be a serious contradiction of what we are if, aware of our unfinishedness, we were not disposed to participate in a constant movement of search, which in its very nature is an expression of hope. Hope is a natural, possible, and necessary impetus in the context of our unfinishedness. Hope is an indispensable seasoning in our human, historical experience. History exists only where time is problematized and not simply a given. A future that is inexorable is a denial of history. (Freire, 1998b, p. 69)

References

Aronowitz, S. (2000). *The knowledge factory.* Boston, MA: Beacon Press.

Bahruth, R. (2005). Critical literacy versus reading programs: Schooling as a form of control. *International Journal of Learning* (RMIT University, Australia).

Barber, B. (2007). *Consumed: How markets corrupt children, infantilize adults and swallow citizens whole.* New York: W.W. Norton.

Beatham, M. (2000/2008). Technological literacy. In D. Gabbard (Ed.), *Knowledge and power in the global economy* (2nd ed.). Mahwah, NJ: Lawrence Erlbaum.

Betto, F. (1997, Fall). Paulo Freire: Reading of the world. *Taboo: The Journal of Culture and Education*, 127–128.

Bowles, S., & Gintis, H. (1976). *Schooling in capitalist America: Educational reform and the contradictions of economic life.* New York: Basic Books.

Buck, P.S. (1954). *My several worlds.* New York: John Day.

Chávez Chávez, R. (1997, Fall). To my teacher—Paulo, humbly I thank you. *Taboo: The Journal of Culture and Education, 2.*

Chomsky, N., & Macedo, D. (2000). *Chomsky on miseducation.* Lanham, MD: Rowman & Littlefield.

Dykstra, D. (1996). Teaching introductory physics to college students. In C. Fosnot (Ed.), *Constructivism.* New York: Teachers College Press.

Ellul, J. (1965). *The technological society.* New York: Knopf.

Fehr, D. (1993). *Dogs playing cards: Powerbrokers of prejudice in education, art and culture.* New York: Peter Lang.

Freire, P. (1970). *Pedagogy of the oppressed.* New York: Continuum.

Freire, P. (1983). The importance of the act of reading. *Journal of Education, 165,* 5–11.

Freire, P. (1996). *Letters to Cristina.* New York: Routledge.

Freire, P. (1998a). *Teachers as cultural workers: Letters to those who dare teach.* Boulder, CO: Westview Press.

Freire, P. (1998b). *Pedagogy of freedom.* Lanham, MD: Rowman & Littlefield.

Freire, P. (2000). *Pedagogy of the oppressed: 30 anniversary edition.* New York: Continuum.

Freire, P., & Macedo, D. (1998). Foreword. In C. Hayes, R. Bahruth, & C. Kessler (Eds.), *Literacy con cariño* (rev. ed.). Portsmouth, NH: Heinemann.

Fuentes, C. (1992, March 30). The mirror of the other. *The Nation,* p. 411.

Gabbard, D. (1993). *Silencing Ivan Illich: A Foucauldian analysis of intellectual exclusion.* San Francisco, CA: Austin & Winfield.

Gil Antón, M. (2003). *Segundo Congreso Internacional de Educación para la Vida.* Universidad Autónoma de Nuevo León, Monterrey, México.

Giroux, H. (2001). *Stealing innocence: Corporate culture's war on children.* New York: Palgrave Macmillan.

Giroux, H. (2007). *The university in chains: Confronting the military-industrial-academic complex.* Boulder, CO: Paradigm.

Goodman, Y. (1989). *Keynote address.* TESOL Conference, San Antonio, Texas.

Greene, M. (2001). *Variations on a blue guitar: The Lincoln Center lectures on aesthetic education.* New York: Teachers College Press.

Hayes, C., Bahruth, R., & Kessler, C. (1998). *Literacy con cariño.* Foreword by Paulo Freire and Donaldo Macedo. Portsmouth, NH: Heinemann.

Hedges, C. (2009). *Empire of illusion: The end of literacy and the triumph of spectacle.* New York: Nation Books.

Herman, E., & Chomsky, N. (1988). *Manufacturing consent: The political economy of the mass media.* New York: Pantheon.

Honneth, A. (2009). *Pathologies of reason.* New York: Columbia University Press.

Horton, M., & Freire, P. (1990). *We make the road by walking: Conversations on education and social change.* Philadelphia, PA: Temple University Press.

Hostetler, K. (2005, August). What is "good" educational research? *Educational Researcher, 34*(6), 16–21.

Illich, I. (1971). *Deschooling society.* London: Calder & Boyers.

Jackson, M. (2008). *Distracted.* Amherst, NY: Prometheus Books.

Johnson, M. & Lakoff, G. (1980). *Metaphors we live by.* Chicago: University of Chicago Press.

Kohl, H. (1994). *I won't learn from you: And other thoughts on creative maladjustment.* New York: The New Press.

Kozol, J. (2005). *The shame of the nation: The restoration of apartheid schooling in America.* New York: Crown.

Lawtoo, N. (2006). Dissonant voices in Richard Rodriguez's *Hunger of memory* and Luce Irigaray's *This sex which is not one. Texas Studies of Literature and Language, 48*(3), 220–249.

Lawtoo, N. (2013). *The phantom of the ego: Modernism and the mimetic unconscious.* East Lansing: Michigan State University Press.

Lerner, G. (1986). *The creation of patriarchy.* New York: Oxford University Press.

Macedo, D. (1992). Personal communication. Boise State University, Boise, ID.

Macedo, D. (1994). *Literacies of power: What Americans are not allowed to know.* Boulder, CO: Westview Press.

Macedo, D. (2001). Foreword. In P. Freire, *Pedagogy of freedom.* Lanham, MD: Rowman & Littlefield.

Minnich, E. (1990). *Transforming knowledge.* Philadelphia, PA: Temple University Press.

Murphy, C. (2012). *Maestra.* www.maestrathefilm.org. USA/Cuba.

Pérez, E. (2004). *Freire entre nosotros.* Havana, Cuba: Editorial Caminos.

Pérez Cruz, F. (2009, June). *Paulo Freire y la revolución cubana: Reflexiones para las urgencias de la praxis.* XXVIII International Congress of the Latin American Studies Association (EDU-5083), Rio de Janeiro.

Postman, N. (1986). *Amusing ourselves to death: Public discourse in the age of show business.* London: Penguin Books.

Postman, N., & Weingartner, C. (1969). *Teaching as a subversive activity.* New York: Delacorte.

Schmidt, J. (2000). *Disciplined minds: A critical look at salaried professionals and the soul-battering system that shapes their lives.* Lanham, MD: Rowman & Littlefield.

Stuckey, J.E. (1991). *The violence of literacy.* Portsmouth, NH: Heinemann.

Villaverde, L.E. (2000). Arts education. In D. Gabbard (Ed.), *Knowledge and power in the global economy: Politics and the rhetoric of school reform.* Mahwah, NJ: Lawrence Erlbaum.

White, C. (2003). *The middle mind: Why Americans don't think for themselves.* San Francisco, CA: HarperCollins.

SIX

Neil Postman and Charles Weingartner, *Teaching as a Subversive Activity* (1969)

Richard Ognibene

It is surprising and disappointing that so much of what has been written about the history and impact of the 1960s fails to include anything about education (Brokaw, 2007; Cavallo, 1999; Gitlin, 1999). It's an unfortunate omission. An institution whose emerging ideology and practice during that decade was framed by books by Jerome Bruner (1960) and A.S. Neill (1960) at one end and by Carl Rogers (1969) and Neil Postman and Charles Weingartner (1969) at the other was making a contribution to a new emphasis on respect and care for individuals regardless of their academic ability, gender, race, disability, or impoverishment. This chapter will highlight one of those texts, Postman and Weingartner's *Teaching as a Subversive Activity*, a book whose primary focus addressed teaching and learning processes and alienation issues that affected students across the board. The chapter begins with an examination of educational developments in the prior decades that provide the context for the subversive proposals in Neil Postman and Charles Weingartner's book.

The Non-Subversive Background

The goal and practice of progressive education as envisioned by John Dewey was modified almost from the beginning. Two years after the publication of his *Democracy and Education* (1916), a National Education Association report delineated a list of educational goals that were practical and non-intellectual, a trend that continued until the post–World War II period, culminating in an educational movement known as life adjustment education. For Dewey, the role of the teacher was to develop creative activities that took advantage of student interests nurtured by environments with which they were familiar. These group activities would stimulate natural thought processes that led to the acquisition of traditional subject matter and simultaneously promote the social and cooperative skills necessary to maintain our democratic civic culture (Dworkin, 1967). In contrast, the primary curricular emphases of life adjustment education were home economics, business education, and common learnings—a course that replaced history and English with one that emphasized participation in community affairs, human relations, and personal problem solving (Broder, 1976; Tanner & Tanner, 1990).

Two factors combined to put an end to life adjustment education, one of which was the emergence of the Cold War with the Soviet Union in the late 1940s, a tension-filled development that was intensified by the Soviets' successful test of an atomic bomb in 1949 (Mazuzan, 1994). The other factor was the public attack against life adjustment by prominent critics such as the historian Arthur Bestor and James Bryant Conant, the scientist who was president of Harvard.

Bestor's books *Educational Wastelands* (1953) and *The Restoration of Learning* (1955) severely criticized the "educationists" whose trivial curriculum replaced traditional liberal arts courses. His critique set the stage for educational assessments such as James Conant's *The American High School Today* (1959), an influential book that asserted that the high school needed no radical change and affirmed the value of the basic secondary liberal arts and science curriculum for all students. As Conant well knew by the late 1950s, concerted efforts to improve high school math and science had begun shortly after the end of World War II.

After several years of Congressional debate, one American response to threats posed by the Soviet Union was to create a National Science Foundation (NSF) in 1950, whose purpose was to fund scientific explorations, award fellowships to graduate and undergraduate students doing research, and raise the standards of science education in public schools (Spring, 2011, pp. 360–362).

To achieve the latter goal, the NSF funded curriculum study groups dominated by college teachers whose task was to create new curricula in math, physics, and biology. Between 1956 and 1975, the NFS provided funding for 43 projects in mathematics and science, money that was used to cover the expenses of the study groups and the new materials they produced and to organize summer teacher-training institutes on college campuses across the country (Gutek, 2000, pp. 191–196). Although this was an impressive effort, by 1970 there was a near consensus that curriculum reform had not taken hold, primarily because teachers had little input in developing the new material (Silberman, 1970). When Postman and Weingartner published *Teaching as a Subversive Activity* in 1969, it was evident that curriculum reform had not yet been satisfactorily achieved.

Even if the "new" curricula did not last in the actual form in which they were developed, the reasoning behind them remained intact. A summary statement of the intentions of the makers of the new curricula was provided in Jerome Bruner's *The Process of Education* (1960). As Bruner repeatedly noted, learning was a process of inquiry and discovery. Teachers must find ways to entice students to connect creatively and intuitively with the material at hand. If the students were successful, those lessons would be learned deeply and serve as the basis for more advanced study when students are at the right age and stage of psychological development. Bruner was the most influential spokesperson of the new education in the 1960s. *Teaching as a Subversive Activity* also promoted the inquiry method without reservation. Nevertheless, Postman and Weingartner had an insurmountable disagreement with Bruner:

[He] has done much to answer the question "How do people come to know?," but, curiously, he has not addressed himself to the question "What's worth knowing?," at least from the point of view of the learner. It is almost impossible to find in Bruner's explications of inquiry learning one illustration of children's solving problems that are of deep concern to children. (Postman & Weingartner, 1969, p. 53)

Progressive Education: Vintage 1969

Throughout the 1960s, observers and participants in schools serving minority populations published books that provided horrifying descriptions of some of those schools. Nat Hentoff's *Our Children Are Dying* (1966) and Jonathan Kozol's *Death at an Early Age* (1967) are two such examples. The "death" in Hentoff's and Kozol's titles described the despair and sense of hopelessness that killed children's spirit and any belief that they could make a better life for themselves. On the other hand, there were books published in 1969 by Herbert Kohl, George Dennison, Carl Rogers, and Neil Postman and Charles Weingartner that were intended to provide information about how to create educational experiences that would enable students to blossom rather than wither and die.

In 1969 Herbert Kohl and George Dennison wrote books based on their teaching experiences—Kohl in a public school in Harlem and Dennison in a small free school on New York's Lower East Side. Kohl's book *The Open Classroom* (1969) was an instructional companion to *36 Children* (1967), his inspirational account of his first full year of teaching in which he learned how to connect to his students. He consciously created a non-hierarchical classroom community using interesting magazines, fables, music, field trips, and their life stories as the basis for writing and artwork that yielded academic achievements they had never experienced and which no one in the school expected from them. Kohl (1969) tells us in his introduction that the purpose of *The Open Classroom* was straightforward: "This book is a handbook for teachers who want to work in an open environment" (p. 15). An open classroom is a communal environment in which the teacher and students are authentically themselves and solve problems together.

In several respects, George Dennison's *The Lives of Children* and Carl Rogers's *Freedom to Learn*, both published in 1969, share views that are compatible, though different in origin. Dennison had studied gestalt therapy under the direction of Paul Goodman (himself a well-known educational critic), and Rogers, a psychotherapist, was singularly famous as the creator of client-centered therapy. Like Kohl's *36 Children*, Dennison's *The Lives of Children* is filled with examples of students who emerged from failure and despair to become young people who were, to use a Rogerian term, more fully functional.

The key to these successes was the ability of the teacher to step back and relate to the children in the present moment and not dwell on their past failures. The presence of an adult who was non-judgmental but who subtly expressed confidence in them produced results. Dennison was more in tune with the idea of student freedom as practiced at A.S. Neill's (1960) Summerhill school, while Rogers was more comfortable laying out an array of strategies to promote free-choice classroom options that could be motivational.

In 1971 Dennison, Goodman, Hentoff, Kozol, and John Holt wrote a letter to the editor of *The New York Review of Books* describing the work of experimental alternative schools that incorporated many of the principles found in their own work. The purpose of the letter was to solicit money to be sent to a newly created fund to subsidize some of those schools, many of which had serious financial problems. Although *Teaching as a Subversive Activity* used a different approach to promote educational change, Postman and Weingartner were supportive and aware of the contributions those authors made to the 1960s educational reform movement. In their next book, *The Soft Revolution* (1971), Postman and Weingartner told their readers:

> If you think we need new kinds of schools that are good for kids, and you would like to help guys like George Dennison, Paul Goodman, Nat Hentoff, John Holt, and Jonathan Kozol to get such schools started, send one dollar to…. (p. 181)

Although there is no bibliography in *Teaching as a Subversive Activity*, one book frequently referred to in that text was Carl Rogers's *On Becoming a Person* (1961). Postman and Weingartner were clearly in sync with, and part of, the neo-progressive educational renaissance that reached a crescendo as the decade of the 1960s was coming to a close.

Teaching as a Subversive Activity: The Essential Concepts

Like other social and educational critics, Postman and Weingartner viewed the 1960s as a period of rapid change, not all of which was positive. As was true of all their books—as well as those that Postman later wrote alone—they had faith that education could improve conditions that were negative, but not the way in which education was being practiced.

> It is the thesis of this book that change—constant, accelerating, and ubiquitous—is the most striking characteristic of the world we live in, and that our educational system has not yet recognized this fact…. It is not beyond our ingenuity to design school environments which can help young people to master concepts necessary to survival in a rapidly changing world. (1969, p. xiii)

In both the first and concluding chapters of *Teaching as a Subversive Activity*, Postman and Weingartner use the term "crap detecting" to describe the need for students to recognize, and respond to, social change. Schools should help students reexamine the culture and institutions in which they were brought up and encourage them to participate in transforming them as necessary. Schools and teachers can foster crap detecting by helping students understand that their views of the world are shaped by the medium sending them (McLuhan), and that institutions and cultural norms are not inviolate, but open to interpretation and change (1969, Chapter 2).

The way this can be accomplished in schools is to use the inquiry method, a style of teaching that is "not designed to do better what older environments try to do…. It activates different senses, attitudes and perceptions [and] generates a different, bolder, and more potent kind of intelligence" (p. 27). This approach requires "the most important intellectual ability man has yet developed—the art and science of asking questions—[but, unbelievably!] it is not taught in school" (p. 23). Teachers are the key to creating successful inquiry environments, and in order to do that they must (1) refrain from telling; (2) communicate via questions; (3) accept multiple answers; (4) promote student-to-student dialogue; (5) not summarize responses; (6) develop lessons from problem-based student responses; and (7) measure success in terms of behavioral changes in students (pp. 34–37).

Postman and Weingartner's disdain for irrelevant traditional curriculum and its accompanying authoritarian methodology is clear. They cite H.L. Mencken's line that the main thing children learn in school is how to lie, and G.B. Shaw's comment that the only time his education was interrupted was when he was in school. They assert that children know that school is a game. "The game is called 'Let's Pretend'; and if its name were chiseled into the front of every school building in America, we would, at least, have an honest announcement of what takes place there" (p. 49).

The consequence of the game is profound student alienation, and we have already noted some of the ways Kohl and Dennison overcame that. For Postman and Weingartner, the solution to alienation is the use of a questions-based curriculum. They give four pages of sample questions (illustrations, not requirements), some of which are personal, others of which are language-based, or historical, or scientific or math-related, and so on (pp. 62–65). The questions posed must deal with problems that are perceived as useful and realistic to the learners (p. 81). They must be divergent, or open-ended, which leads to additional questions that probe issues more deeply. Indirectly criticizing Bruner once more, they write that "we will need to start talking more about the 'structure of the learner and his learning' and less about 'the structure of the subject'" (p. 80).

For Postman and Weingartner, an additional crucial consideration is the reality derived from perception studies that things are what we make of them; we are meaning-makers in the sense that our naming and understanding things is shaped by our past experiences. The stuff out there (like school subjects) is not static and grasped by everyone in the same way. Since we acquire and transmit meaning through language, "the new education, in addition to being student-centered and question-centered must also be language-centered" (p. 102). *Teaching as a Subversive Activity* is replete with explanations, examples, and thought-provoking lists that flesh out the general ideas presented above.

One such list addresses questions about how to be subversive if you are a teacher and buy into the general themes of the book. The suggestions fill a chapter (XII, pp. 193–206), and the first one provides a flavor of many parts of the text. To become more subversive, Postman and Weingartner propose that teachers tape a piece of paper with these questions on the mirror they use every morning: "What am I going to have my students do today? What's it good for? How do I know?" (p. 193). Next come suggestions about the value of not telling, but listening to students as described in several of Carl Rogers's publications related to communication theory. Another asks, what would happen if you walked into class with a noticeable assumption that you thought all the students were brilliant? Teachers could make parts of their course outlines and tests concerned with future issues and not just those of the past. There are others, but the chapter ends with these words: "There is nothing in what we have said in this book that precludes the use, *at one time or another*, of any of the conventional methods and materials of learning" (p. 205; italics in original). This conclusion aligns with what others thought of Postman's educational writings: "[H]e scrutinized every aspect of schooling…[but] his own conclusions were an invitation, an insistence that we figure things out for ourselves" (Kavanagh, 2003, p. 12).

In *The School Book* (1973), Postman and Weingartner include a chapter entitled "What Is a Good School?" The chapter fleshes out ideas presented in *Teaching as a Subversive Activity* and contains statements on ways in which a good school can operate more subversively. The statements fill 15 pages (pp. 30–44); only a few can be cited here in abridged form to provide some insight about their ideas. A school is good when:

> time sequences are not arbitrary;
> students are not all required to do the same activity at the same time;
> question asking is more valued than memorization;
> individual judgments replace standardized evaluation processes;
> collaborative relationships are established rather than authoritarian ones;
> teachers act as facilitators rather than authority figures;
> community participation is valued more than bureaucratic paternalism; and
> knowledge, attitudes, and skills being cultivated are future oriented.

Perhaps 75 such statements, much elaborated, fill those 15 pages.

Responses to *Teaching as a Subversive Activity* Then and Now

Teaching as a Subversive Activity is a timeless book. The 1971 paperback version is still in print, and an online citizen journal in northern India published a positive review of it in 2014, with no mention that it was a 45-year-old book (Kishore, 2014). In the 1960s Postman (New York University) and Weingartner (Queens College) were English education professors and members of the National Council of Teachers of English (NCTE), where some of their earlier work on the "new" English curriculum and linguistics was previewed and discussed. In 1965 they were part of a small cabal of NCTE members who were trying to influence their staid organization, and to do so they created a fictitious special interest group in which they would serve as "secretaries in charge of questioning assumptions." The group met for 3 years and, humorously, even put out an occasional newsletter. "Something happened after the publication of *Teaching as a Subversive Activity*," one member of the group noted, and "over the next two decades Postman and Weingartner made a number of major addresses at NCTE conventions" (Karl, 2004, p. 23). That's understandable, since these authors proposed that education should be "language-centered"; still, it must have been a little difficult for some members to sit though Postman's 1969 address entitled "Bullshit and the Art of Crap-Detection."

Teaching as a Subversive Activity was widely used in foundation courses in teacher education programs and enthusiastically read by prospective teachers who grew up in an era of social protest. It was "the leading education prep book of the time," notes one professor who was in a teacher-training program when the book was published (Dodge, 2014). Another age-related professorial colleague describes the book as a "manifesto...for those of us who were committed to changing the backward-looking public education system of the day" (Hatch, 2007). The book is still used in some education courses (Johnson, n.d.).

Teaching as a Subversive Activity served as the philosophical starting point for an experimental public high school program in New Rochelle, New York, identified as the Three I Program (Inquiry, Involvement, and Independent Study). It featured community experiences—so as to allow students' special interests to flourish—and in-school seminars designed to do the same thing. The critique of traditional curriculum and the description of the desired alternative program outcomes were taken directly from Postman and Weingartner's text (*Shapiro Gaddy Presentation*, 1970). At a religiously affiliated middle school in Rochester, New York, two teachers who had participated in a workshop related to *Teaching as a Subversive Activity* conceptualized a play entitled *The Carnival of Life*, which was a critique of the alienation present in modern schools and society. "Men go to the moon to wonder," the program cover stated, but "children go to the circus to understand." The carnival framework enabled a runaway girl to meet a magical clown who took her around the circus. There they met performers who sang, danced, and read literary selections and poetry—all of which were related to living an authentic life and creating a world where "you cannot lie." Clearly, this was not a school that needed a "let's pretend" sign (E. Ognibene, personal communication, September 16, 2013; M. Weis, personal communication, September 18, 2013). These brief examples only hint at the larger sphere of influence the book had. Jay Rosen, a student and then a colleague of Postman, offered this reflection when Postman died in 2003:

> His original and core readership remained teachers, and I witnessed it numerous times, the ritual: a woman in her 40s or 50s would approach after a speech. "Professor Postman, I just want to tell you, I read your book, *Teaching as a Subversive Activity*. That book changed my life." Often she would have the book with her, and he would sign it...with a felt tip pen. (Rosen, 2003)

There are two themes that run through much of the contemporary commentary (including my own) about the pedagogical aspects of *Teaching as a Subversive Activity:* (1) I read the book before, and it still influences how I teach, or (2); I just discovered this 1969 book and I am amazed how relevant its classroom recommendations still are (Snell, 2011). As I will note later, Postman and Weingartner's relevance to the social purpose of education may be even more important now.

Beyond the earlier reference to the book review published in a pro-democracy, online newspaper in India, *Teaching as a Subversive Activity* has had some international significance. In England, after much debate, the subject "Citizenship Education" became a requirement in the country's National Curriculum in 2002. Since evaluation of this addition was the next step, explanations and interpretations of the subject have been ongoing. One example is Ralph Leighton's 2006 article revisiting Postman and Weingartner's 1969 book and asking, "Is teaching Citizenship Education a subversive activity?" His short answer is yes, and the article tells us why. According to Leighton, prevailing practices in typical English classrooms produce passive students who are taught to accept their place in society and not question authority. Leighton's solution is crap detection, meaning-making, and the questions-oriented curriculum sections cited at length from *Teaching as a Subversive Activity*. Reading the article is like reading a summary of the book.

A real-world application of the essential components of Postman and Weingartner's text can be found in the activities of The Philosophy Club, headquartered in Melbourne, Australia. This organization's purpose is to engage in "collaborative philosophical enquiry with children," and that is accomplished through co-curricular and extra-curricular workshops for students ages 8 to 14. The longest section of the club's website (Philosophy Club, n.d.) has the heading "Teaching as a Subversive Activity Redux," and the information presented is almost entirely paraphrased from the text. The activities described are clearly derived from the same source.

If They Were Alive Today

Postman and Weingartner co authored five books between 1966 and 1973, a publication partnership that ended when Weingartner moved to the University of South Florida, where he became a professor emeritus in 1982. He died in 2007. They were obviously in philosophical agreement about the purpose and practice of education, but the remainder of this analysis is related to Postman and some subsequent material he wrote.

As one commentator noted, Postman wrote some 20 books addressing diverse topics but which "in fact centre on a core of recurring themes dealing with the intersection of technology, language, and education" (Rose, 1996). Postman's last book, *Building a Bridge to the 18th Century* (1999), affirms that perspective and again demonstrates his role as teacher and social critic. In the last chapter of the book (pp. 155–174), he reminds us that one of the contributions of the Enlightenment was the promotion of skepticism as an intellectual virtue. Postman earlier called that quality "crap detecting" and commented that modern educators label that ability "critical thinking," but do little to encourage it. So once again he calls for question-asking and the study of the role of language as the basis of school curriculum, to which he added science and technology education as sources of inquiry, not content to be mastered, and comparative religion as a way to better understand the aspects of culture and society informed by different faiths.

Postman died in 2003, at a time when corporate involvement in public education was becoming increasingly devastating. Corporate educational priorities include the privatization of public schooling; the destruction of teacher unions, enabling entry-level teachers to be hired and resulting in cost savings and lower taxes; and unfettered access to an education marketplace worth $700 billion. Their methods of destruction are the use of evaluation systems devoid of sound measurement principles, mass funding of alternative schools through corporate foundations whose money is directed to private charter school organizations, and financial support of politicians who would pass laws and create policies that enable all of this to happen.

In 2009 Diane Ravitch published a book whose title, *The Death and Life of the Great American School System*, explains corporate educational goals and outlines how it is done and who is doing it. Ravitch, a research professor at New York University, is a powerful voice in the resistance to corporate educational dominance. One can only speculate how much Neil Postman, once her NYU colleague, could have contributed to the mobilization of forces needed to stop the corporate takeover of American education. One suspects he would have been an invaluable ally. An essay Postman published in his *Conscientious Objections* (1988) suggests why.

The essay was a fictitious commencement speech in which Postman contrasts the Athenians with the Visigoths (pp. 185–190). We remember the Athenians, Postman says, because they gave us literacy, philosophy, political democracy, science, poetry, and plays that still touch us, and a reverence for beauty and excellence. In comparison, the Visigoths were marauders who overran the Roman Empire. They did not contribute to culture; rather, they destroyed much of what had been created and ushered in the long period of Western history known as the Dark Ages. There are modern-day Athenians and Visigoths, and Postman points out their many differences, of which this is the first:

> To be an Athenian is to hold knowledge and, especially, the quest for knowledge in high esteem—these are, to an Athenian, the most exulted activities a person can perform. To a Visigoth, the quest for knowledge is useless unless it can help you to earn money or to gain power over other people. (p. 188)

Postman died just at the beginning of the age of insane overemphasis on compulsory stan-dardized testing that results in reduced time for creative, engaging, and experimental activities in order to make graduates "career ready." In 1982 Postman penned this sentiment: "Children are the living messages we send to a time we will not see" (p. xi). We can be sure that, if they were alive today, Neil Postman and Charles Weingartner would reject the messages being sent and urge more insistently than ever that teaching become a subversive activity. They would be proud, I think, of the ways teachers are doing this now and enlisting the support of parents and community members to help them.

References

Bestor, A. (1953). *Educational wastelands*. Urbana: University of Illinois Press.

Bestor, A. (1955). *The restoration of learning*. New York: Alfred A. Knopf.

Broder, D.E. (1976). *Life adjustment education: An historical study of a program of the United States Office of Educa-tion*. Unpublished doctoral dissertation, Columbia University, New York, NY.

Brokaw, T. (2007). *Boom! Voices of the sixties*. New York: Random House.

Bruner, J. (1960). *The process of education*. Cambridge, MA: Harvard University Press.

Cavallo, D. (1999). *A fiction of the past: The sixties in American history*. New York: Palgrave.

Conant, J.B. (1959). *The American high school today*. New York: McGraw-Hill.

Dennison, G. (1969). *The lives of children*. New York: Random House.

Dennison, G., Goodman, P., Hentoff, N., Holt, J., & Kozol, J. (1971, February 11). New nation seed fund. *New York Review of Books*. Retrieved from http://www.nybooks.com/articles/archives/1971/feb/11/new-nation-seed-fund/

Dodge, A. (2014, October 27). Teaching as a subversive activity. *HuffpostEducation*. Retrieved from http//:www.huffingtonpost.com/arnold-dodge/teaching-as-a-subversive-_b_5724706.html

Dworkin, M. (Ed.). (1967). *Dewey on education: Selections*. New York: Teachers College Press.

Gitlin, T. (1993). *The sixties: Years of hope, days of rage*. New York: Bantam Books.

Gutek, G. (2000). *American education: 1945–2000*. Prospect Heights, IL: Waveland Press.

Hatch, J.A. (2007). Learning as a subversive activity. *Phi Delta Kappan, 89*(4), 310–311.

Hentoff, N. (1966). *Our children are dying*. New York: Viking Press.

Johnson, R. (n.d.). Neil Postman and Charles Weingartner. Kirkwood Community College. Retrieved from http://faculty.kirkwood.edu/site/index.php?p=28139

Karl, H. (2004). Of questioning assumptions, crap detecting, and splinters of ice in the heart. *English Journal, 94*(2), 20–24.

Kavanagh, P. (2003, November 21). Why Postman matters. *Commentary*, pp. 12–13.

Kishore, L. (2014, September 4). Book review: *Teaching as a subversive activity*. U4Uvoice. Retrieved from http://u4uvoice.com/jammu-kashmir-news/book-review-teaching-subversive-activity/

Kohl, H.R. (1967). *36 children*. New York: New American Library.

Kohl, H.R. (1969). *The open classroom*. New York: New York Review.

Kozol, J. (1967). *Death at an early age*. Boston, MA: Houghton Mifflin.

Leighton, R. (2006). Revisiting Postman and Weingartner's "new education": Is teaching citizenship education a subversive activity? *Citizen Teaching and Learning, 2*(1), 79–89.

Mazuzan, G. (1994). *The National Science Foundation: A brief history*. Retrieved from http://www.nsf.gov/about/history/nsf50/nsf8816.jsp

Neill, A.S. (1960). *Summerhill: A radical approach to child rearing*. New York: Hart Publishing Company.

Philosophy Club. (n.d.). Retrieved from www.thephilosophyclub.com.au

Postman, N. (1969). Neil Postman—Bullshit and the art of crap-detection. *Critical Thinking Snippets*. Retrieved from https://criticalsnips.wordpress.com/2007/07/22/neil-postman-bullshit-and-the-art-of-crap-detection/

Postman, N. (1982). *The disappearance of childhood*. New York: Delacorte Press.

Postman, N. (1988). *Conscientious objections*. New York: Vintage Books.

Postman, N. (1999). *Building a bridge to the 18th century*. New York: Vintage Books.

Postman, N., & Weingartner, C. (1969). *Teaching as a subversive activity*. New York: Delacorte Press.

Postman, N., & Weingartner, C. (1971). *The soft revolution*. New York: Dell Publishing.

Postman, N., & Weingartner, C. (1973). *The school book*. New York: Delacorte Press.

Ravitch, D. (2009). *The death and life of the great American school system*. New York: Basic Books.

Rogers, C. (1961). *On becoming a person.* Boston, MA: Houghton Mifflin.

Rogers, C. (1969). *Freedom to learn.* Columbus, OH: Merrill.

Rose, E. (1996). Review of *The End of Education: Redefining the Value of School. Journal of Technology Education,* *8*(1). Retrieved from http://scholar.lib.vt.edu/ejournals/JTE/v8n1/Rose.html

Rosen, J. (2003, October 10). Neil Postman: A civilized man in a century of barbarism. *Salon.* Retrieved from http://www.salon.com/2003/10/10/postman/

Shapiro Gaddy presentation to the board of education: The Three I Program proposal. (1970). Retrieved from http://www.joshkarf.com/3i/proposal1970

Silberman, C. (1970). *Crisis in the classroom.* New York: Random House.

Snell, R. (2011, January 25). Teaching as a subversive activity. *Information and Access.* Retrieved from http://informationandaccess.blogspot.com/2011/01/teaching-as-subversive-activity-by-neil.html

Spring, J. (2011). *The American school: A global context from the Puritans to the Obama era* (8th ed.). New York: McGraw-Hill.

Tanner, D., & Tanner, L. (1990). *The history of school curriculum.* New York: Macmillan.

Part Two

The 1970s

Charles E. Silberman, *Crisis in the Classroom: The Remaking of American Education* (1970)

William M. Reynolds

My motive is political, in the broadest sense of the term—as George Orwell defined it, "to push the world in a certain direction, to alter other people's ideas of the kind of society that we should strive after." (Silberman, 1970, p. vii)

It is not possible to spend any prolonged period visiting public school classrooms without being appalled by the mutilation of spontaneity, of joy in learning, of pleasure creating, of sense of self. (Silberman, 1970, p. 10)

Introduction

When Charles E. Silberman (1925–2011) wrote *Crisis in the Classroom: The Remaking of American Education* (1970), he was not faced with public schools and university teacher education classrooms that were saturated with the corporate, neoliberal agenda of standardization, high-stakes testing, accountability, pay-for-performance, and scripted lesson plans. He was appalled for different reasons, but his sentiments certainly echo through the years and have some relevance for the current historical moment. He would, no doubt, be absolutely horrified by the state of public education 45 years later. He was concerned, as were many educational critics, curriculum theorists, and others of that period, by the lack of meaning in public school and university classrooms.

Silberman was not an educator but rather a journalist and sociologist (see Pinar, Reynolds, Slattery, & Taubman, 2004). In the late 1960s Silberman was a member of the editorial board of *Fortune* magazine. *Crisis in the Classroom* was supported by a $300,000 grant from the Carnegie Corporation and appeared in the *Atlantic Monthly* in a pre-publication serial that included sensation-causing titles such as "Murder in the School Room" and "How the Public Schools Kill Dreams and Mutilate Minds" (Pinar et al., 2004). Both the articles and the book were widely read not only by educators but also by the public in general. Silberman also edited a volume in 1973 entitled *The Open Classroom Reader* in which he maintained a consistency with the humanistic reform-mindedness of *Crisis in the Classroom*: "The public schools, those 'killers of the dream,' to use a phrase of Lillian Smith's—are the kind of institution one cannot really dislike until one gets to know them" (Silberman, 1970, p. 10).

Unlike the twenty-first-century fixation with accountability and test scores, in the 1970s the crisis was one of meaning. Education was in need of "remaking." Silberman wrote the book not only for the scholarly community, but for teachers, administrators, school board members, and the general public as well. In 1971 it reached number 9 on *The New York Times* best-seller list for non-fiction, quite an accomplishment for a book on education.

Humanism

The pervasive emphasis on cognition and its separation from affect poses a threat to our society in that our educational institutions may produce cold, detached individuals uncommitted to humanitarian goals. (Weinstein & Fantini, 1970, p. 27)

The cumulative effect of the schooling experience is devastating. We graduate credential but crazed, erudite but fragmented shells of human possibility. (Pinar, 1976, p. 27)

The spirit of humanism was alive and well in the 1970s. Again, the focus of educational discussion was not on improving the technical arena, such as test scores, but on meaning and the human condition. Silberman was shocked by the instrumentalism that governed schools. He wanted them to be remade with a Deweyan concern for the education of the whole child. Education was not only for cognition but for the self as well and thus should be an education for the head and the heart.

Dewey argued in theory: that a deep and genuine concern for individual growth and fulfillment not only is compatible with but indeed demands an equally genuine concern for cognitive growth and intellectual discipline, for transmitting the cultural heritage of society. (Silberman, 1970, p. 220)

This reflects the spirit of 1970s discussions on humanism and education, an orientation that many publications, educators, and educational associations would emphasize in the decade. The Association for Supervision and Curriculum Development (ASCD), in particular, took up the mantra of humanistic endeavors. ASCD was, at the time, the central organization focusing on curriculum theory, and much of the innovative work done in the 1970s in curriculum, and education in general, came from the writings that it published. (This was before its main emphasis shifted to educational administration.) ASCD gave its 1970 yearbook the title *To Nurture Humanness*. In this volume, editors M.M. Scobey and G. Graham called for tranquility and self-actualization—the latter concept having been made famous by humanistic psychologist Abraham Maslow (1968). In it are several elements of the humanistic position: persons as holistic and in a state of becoming or growing, the necessity of interaction with the environment for learning and knowledge creation, the importance of dialogue for both the exchange and growth of knowledge, and the centrality of acknowledging and fostering individuality (Schubert, 2002).[1] These issues would also concern Silberman. Even though Silberman in many ways defies classification, it would be safe to say that his work fit well with the humanistic tradition—if, indeed, a humanistic tradition does exist.

The Book

Quixotic? Perhaps. Utopian? Maybe so. Nevertheless, we think Charles Silberman has performed a great service, if only because his book may stimulate individuals to effect some changes in their own classrooms. At this moment in our history, that may be all we can expect (Greene, 1970, p. 141).

One of the ways in which Silberman's book was able to reach such a broad audience was that, though well-researched and copiously documented, it is not filled with sociological or educational jargon. Since Silberman was a journalist, it is not surprising that *Crisis in the Classroom* is written in that style, —one that makes even his most complex arguments comprehensible to the general reading public. He also uses the journalistic technique of firsthand observations.

Silberman's book is divided into four parts: "The Educating Society," "What's Wrong with the Schools," "How the Schools Should Be Changed," and "The Education of Educators." Let us take a brief look at each section. This chapter cannot possibly offer an exhaustive study of Silberman's book; rather, it will point out portions of the book that seem relevant, lasting, and important to this author, as well as areas that may have been weak in Silberman's analysis.

The Educating Society

In the two chapters in Section 1 ("Introduction: Education for What?" and "American Education: Success or Failure"), Silberman addresses some crucial topics. He discusses the problem of mindlessness in public schools but expands that criticism not only to the schools but to the entire educational system and society as well. What did Silberman consider mindlessness? In schools and in society, it is the lack of a sustained effort to question the purposes of education. Why are we doing what we are doing? He does suggest that most public school personnel (teachers, principals, and superintendents) are smart and caring people. But he describes how they "botch" it up: "it is because it simply never occurs to more than a handful to ask *why* they are doing what they are doing—to think seriously or deeply about the purposes or consequences of education" (Silberman, 1970, p. 11). Silberman claims that we confuse the means with the ends in education. Getting through the day with lesson plans, organization, control, and management constitute the means, but he contends that they are seen as the ends. Silberman uses the example of the "tyranny of the lesson plan":

> [The lesson plan] in turn encourages an obsession with routine for the sake of routine. School is filled with countless examples of teachers and administrators confusing the means with the ends, thereby making it impossible to reach the end for which the means were devised. (p. 125)

This led Silberman to conclude that all in our society could benefit from consistently asking questions about what we are doing, and why we are doing it.

In Chapter 2, Silberman questions whether or not American education is a success or a failure. His answer is that there is a great paradox regarding education and its "pervasive sense of crisis" (p. 19). He suggests that the crisis is not exclusively an educational problem, but one of the larger society as well. Despite the amazing improvements in many areas of life by 1970, those improvements did not generally produce happiness or contentment, but instead dissatisfaction. The problem is that, as good as things are—and they are better than they were—they are not as good as they could be. Silberman says that the media are in part responsible for making people aware of poverty and violence. He uses as an illustration the nightly coverage of the war in Vietnam. He expands his ideas about the media and education that in many ways foreshadow cultural studies, including the study of popular culture. Silberman argues that youth learn just as much from media as they do in school:

> Students probably learn more about certain subjects from television than from schools; moreover, as the sociologist Herbert J. Gans of Columbia University has suggested, television and to a lesser extent the other mass media play a major role in "bringing the news"[2] about how to live in contemporary society. (p. 32)

Silberman indicates that other professionals (doctors, lawyers, and social workers, for example) need to view themselves as educators as well in order to make improvements in how we educate the entire society, and that the field of education itself requires philosophical professionals.

What's Wrong with the Schools?

In the second section of the book, Silberman discusses education and equality, docility and reform. Schools are not "the great equalizer," and if they are to fulfill that role, they must go about the task of educating youth from "minority-group and lower-class homes" (p. 54). He critiques a rather famous 1969 article from the *Harvard Educational Review* by Arthur Jensen of the University of California, Berkeley. Jensen argued that genetic factors were responsible for African American students' lower IQ scores and poor achievement, and he suggested that schools that educate African American students should concentrate on rote learning. Much to his credit, Silberman writes that Jensen's whole argument "that black-white IQ differences are largely genetic in origin simply does not stand" (Silberman, 1970, p. 77). He follows with a detailed explanation of the cultural factors that must be considered when judging poor children's development. Regarding Jensen's argument concerning the environment, Silberman concludes that "Jensen's whole treatment of environment, in fact, is simplistic almost to the point of caricature" (p. 77). Silberman concludes that the failure of "slum" schools should be placed at the door of societal and school conditions, not on any elaboration of poor children's inadequacies.

Education, according to Silberman, produces docile students. Education in the late 1960s and early 1970s was (and continues to be in the twenty-first century) about control and compliance. All schools share a number of characteristics that foster this mindless docility. Silberman elaborates on such characteristics as compulsion (the fact that children must be in school), length of the school day, crowded classrooms, and the evaluative condition (Silberman, 1970). This behaviorist orientation, together with a rigid adherence to timetables, schedules, and the like—not only cuts learning short but establishes a rather factory-like obedience to the clock. Children learn to follow schedules in a routinized manner and in shabby classrooms. For Silberman, the fragmentation in subjects and the consequent lack of interest in the subject matter characterize the public schools from the elementary level through high school. Children are not allowed to explore their own curiosity but are compelled to follow the regimentation of the school day. This time management was exacerbated by rigid codes of behavior, dress, and discipline.

Silberman also tackles the formidable issue of educational reform, describing of the failures of educational reform "sketchily but well" (Greene, 1970, p. 136). He says that the reform movement(s) of the post-Sputnik era promised significant transformation, but nothing much has changed. The efforts at incorporating programmed instruction, technology in the classroom, teacher-proof materials, team-teaching, and so on did not fundamentally change the schools. Much of the reform was ignored by teachers or only tacitly engaged. Silberman quotes Goodlad (1969): "We are forced to conclude that much of the so-called educational reform movement has been blunted at the classroom door" (p. 60). It is interesting that Silberman, once a supporter of the structures of the disciplines,[3] at this point changed his mind and continued throughout the book to distance himself from those previously held ideas.

How the Schools Should Be Changed

In Silberman's third chapter, "How the Schools Should Be Changed," he outlines his vision of the remaking of public schools. In the case of the elementary school, the "open classroom" is recommended. Silberman refers to the primary schools in England and the Plowden Report (1963) on their status. This report, named after the committee chair, endorsed "informal education" or "open education" (Barth, 1972; Featherstone, 1968) and promoted the "open classroom" concept. Informal education was also known as "schools without walls." One facet of the concept is that there are no walls separating one classroom from another, giving students more freedom to move around the school. Silberman is strong in his support for this concept. In 1973 he published *The Open Classroom Reader*. In it he offers a sense of "informal education," which he contrasted (in this volume and in *Crisis in the Classroom*) with the heavy-handed, stultifying, teacher-proofed schools. He tells his readers that "open education," "informal education, "and "the open classroom" are all terms that could be used for this progressive concept:

> It is rather an approach to teaching and learning—a set of shared attitudes and convictions about the nature and purposes of teaching and learning, about the nature of childhood and adolescence and ultimately about the nature of man. (Silberman, 1973, p. xix)

With the advocacy of the "open classroom" concept, Silberman was echoing Dewey's notion that childhood should be treasured for its own sake and not simply as a preparation for later life. His echoing of Dewey received praise from many of his contemporary critics. Silberman states in the book that this "informal education" can happen in the United States (*It Can Happen Here*). He does not focus solely on young children but also discusses secondary schools as well in his advocacy for a less restrictive, dehumanizing education. He reminds us that, in 1970, there appeared to be a growing movement for a less restrictive environment in high schools. Indicators of this change were more liberal regulations on everything from dress codes to toilet passes (Pinar et al., pp. 188–189). As Silberman writes:

> Somewhat bolder attempts to humanize the schools as a whole—for example, by cutting the number of required classes, leaving students with a third or more of their time unscheduled, to be used for independent study, for taking more elective courses, for fulfilling some course requirements outside the classroom or for relaxation and leisure. (Silberman, 1970, p. 337)

Silberman was for reforming the entire public school system. But his critique and ideas for reform did not end with public schools; rather, they moved to teacher education and universities as well.

The Education of Educators

> The remaking of American public education requires, and indeed will not be possible without, fundamental changes in the education of teachers—without, in a sense, the creation of a new breed of teacher-educator, educated to self-scrutiny and to serious thought about purpose. (Silberman, 1970, p. 374)

In his section on the education of educators, Silberman treats the issue of teacher education. Interestingly, many of his same criticisms could be leveled at teacher education in the twenty-first century. Like education in general, education for prospective teachers needs to progress toward a more informal and less technical/instrumental orientation. Prospective teachers need to be given alternative ideas about what teaching and learning can be and what different strategies might be employed to implement those new ideas. Otherwise, according to Silberman, they will teach much in the same way that the teachers before them taught.

After a lengthy discussion of the "Liberal Education of Teachers," in which the whole notion of just what a liberal education was/is, Silberman seems to indicate that the age-old curriculum question of what kind of knowledge is of most worth, or whose knowledge is of most worth, applies mainly to the liberal arts curriculum in colleges and universities. But Silberman also maintains that the dialogue and cultivation of liberal education is just as crucial for the education of teachers. Accordingly, prospective teachers and teacher educators should think about and focus on the purposes of education—just as he had earlier advocated for continual questioning about public schools. In order for prospective teachers to engage in this kind of self-scrutiny, Silberman proposes that teacher education must emphasize the history and philosophy of education and the study of psychology, sociology, and anthropology. In addition, teachers should enhance their own self-understanding; therefore a liberal arts education enhances teacher education. He also declares that teachers can never read too many books. At the same time, teacher education requires both liberal education and professional education. Silberman felt that good pre-service teacher education should be taught by excellent professors who are excellent teachers—not by pedagogues engaged in "do as I say and not as I do." One of the issues in the 1970s that interfered with this notion of the professor as teacher was in one sense caused by the shift in colleges and universities to a research rather than a teaching focus. In the competition among universities, even "the second-echelon universities among them, some of the largest producers of teachers" (Silberman, 1970, p. 405), were pushed to become first-echelon. This shift placed a premium on research instead teaching. When that competition heated up, the emphasis was also placed on graduate education and not undergraduate education, and research further trumped teaching:

> The process is cumulative: attracting academic "stars" makes it easier to attract able students, and able students make it easier to attract the academic stars. The result is a tremendous pressure toward uniformity and conventionality in undergraduate programs. (p. 405)

Finally, there is a Deweyan penchant in *Crisis in the Classroom* for dialogue in teacher education programs. Silberman argues that teacher education programs should be "centers of inquiry rather than buildings for the one-way transmission of information" (p. 522).

Critique

Silberman's book elicited a plethora of reviews and critiques upon its publication (see Etzioni, 1970; Greene, 1970; McCracken, 1971; & Smith, 1971). Among them, Etzioni's was perhaps the most searing. One of his major criticisms of Silberman was based on Silberman's use of exaggerated journalistic observations, coupled with a lack of empirical evidence: "As Silberman's reporting is loaded with such adjectives, I cannot but start wondering about the reliability of all his first-hand observations" (Etzioni, 1970, p. 94). Among several other criticisms of Silberman's book, the review included a critique of a lack of specificity on informal schooling, questions about humanizing teacher education, and a lack of clarity in regard to the benefit of these informal schools for working-class or lower-middle-class students:

> It may seem ungrateful to a book which raises many provocative issues to conclude by saying the best we can hope to do is outgrow it rapidly—both as a policy guide for educational reforms and as a form of educational research. (Etzioni, 1970, p. 98)

Another negative appraisal, written by Robert Dreeben of the University of Chicago, appeared in the *American Journal of Sociology* in 1971. Dreeben's assault centered on Silberman's research, which Dreeben felt lacked substance. He indicated that many of Silberman's footnotes were "irrelevant." Again, Silberman's shortcoming was felt to be his scholarship. Dreeben characterized it as "scholarship light": "Most disappointing, Silberman fails to indicate systematically what schools look like, how they work, and how they are connected to surrounding social conditions" (Dreeben, 1971, p. 596).

Rodney P. Smith of Yale University (1971) and Samuel McCracken of Boston University (1971) also critiqued Silberman's book. Although these evaluations were more forgiving, they presented some thoughtful reflections. Smith believed that Silberman's book, despite the criticisms of others about his lackluster research, was the most scholarly, knowledgeable, and current "compared to all the critics of education in the past two decades" (Smith, 1971, p. 845). Smith's criticism focused on Silberman's failure to ask questions about the connections between the reform of schools and the renewal of society.

> What is the place of education in a renewal of society? No, Silberman does not ask this question, though he might have. In this respect, on careful reading of *Crisis in the Classroom*, one sees that Silberman is not so much the harsh critic of education as he is the Dutch uncle of society in general. Thus, the blame for the present crisis in American education is to be shared by the educational establishment and the rest of the country. (Smith, 1971, p. 847)

McCracken faulted Silberman for being "longer on diagnosis than on prescription" (McCracken, 1971, p. 86). He indicated that Silberman's book could lead to conflicting and unhelpful reforms, yet he found the book to be "useful to the discerning reader" (McCracken, 1971, p. 86).

The most insightful essay review of *Crisis in the Classroom* was written by Maxine Greene of Teachers College, Columbia University. Greene stated that it was difficult to agree with Silberman's optimism, given the state of the nation in 1970, but that he had provided some "positive assertions about a humane education for all" (Greene, 1970, p. 136). Greene writes that it is a fine, if flawed book. She also makes clear that Silberman was influenced by the work of John Dewey. Although the successes and failures of progressive education in the 1920s and 1930s are discussed, Silberman succeeds in "defining present situations in which Dewey's relevance is being newly recognized" (p. 133). She also indicated that Silberman did an excellent job of presenting recent educational history. Greene's closing paragraph is perhaps the most poignant commentary on the book.

> We share his hopes for a humane society. We are pleased and impressed by his Deweyan af-
> firmations. We also believe that free days, open classrooms, and carefully structured learning
> environments will save the lives of many schoolchildren and help them learn to learn. But
> we are much afraid the "mindlessness" so effectively challenged by Charles Silberman is not
> the only obstacle to a transformation of the schools. There may be an entire civilization to be
> remade. (p. 141)

Finally, those that were working and studying in the critical tradition in education in graduate schools in the mid-1970s particularly critiqued Silberman for not taking into consideration the Marxist/neo-Marxist reproduction theory of schooling in his analysis of education in the United States. This was and remains a valid criticism.

Many of the critical assessments of Silberman's work are correct: he did not produce a dense "scholarly" treatise on education, and it did lack a sustained critical political analysis. However, if the purpose of Silberman's endeavor was to reach a wider audience or open the conversation about education and society in the early 1970s, the book was successful. A journalistic style might have been—and might still be—a way to accomplish those goals. *Crisis in the Classroom* (1970), despite the criticisms it received, helped the American public to recognize significant issues and dilemmas in American education, and it raised awareness about the hope of humanistic reforms rather than the over-emphasis on instrumentalist reform (see Pinar et al., 2004, p. 189)—both in schooling and the larger sociopolitical context. As I read this book, there was an eerie sense that many of the problems that Silberman discusses are questions we are still debating in 2015. Given the present state of American education, which is producing consumer citizens for the corporate economy through high-stakes testing, accountability, core curriculum, exclusive job focus, and the like, perhaps the author of a best seller from 45 years ago just might have some ideas worth listening to once again. At the very least, we might well consider his call for a more humane society.

Notes

1 Pinar et al., p. 190.
2 See Gans, 1966.
3 For a discussion of the structures of the discipline notion of curriculum theory, see Bruner (1960).

References

Barth, R. (1972). Open education. In D. Purpel & M. Belanger (Eds.), *Curriculum and cultural revolution* (pp. 424–454). Berkeley, CA: McCutchan.

Bruner, J.S. (1960). *The process of education*. New York: Vantage.

Dreeben, R. (1971). Review of *Crisis in the classroom: The remaking of American education,* by Charles E. Silberman. *American Journal of Sociology, 77*(3), 595–597.

Etzioni, A. (1970). Review of *Crisis in the classroom: The remaking of American education*, by Charles E. Silberman. *Harvard Educational Review, 41*, 87–98.

Featherstone, J. (1968, March 2). A new kind of schooling. *The New Republic, 158*(9).

Gans, H.J. (1966). Popular culture in America: Social problems in a mass society or social asset in a pluralistic society? In H. Becker (Ed.), *Social problems: A modern approach*. New York: John Wiley & Sons.

Goodlad, J. (1969, April 19). The schools vs. education. *Saturday Review*. Retrieved from http://www.unz.org/Pub/SaturdayRev-1969apr19-00059?View=PDF

Greene, M. (1970, September). The crisis of mindlessness. Review of *Crisis in the classroom,* by Charles E. Silberman. *Teachers College Record, 72*(1), 133–141.

Jensen, A.R. (1969). How much can we boost IQ and scholastic achievement? *Harvard Educational Review, 39*(1), 1–123.

Maslow, A. (1968). *Toward a psychology of being*. New York: Van Nostrand Reinhold.

McCracken, S. (1971, March). The school problem. Review of *Crisis in the classroom*, by Charles E. Silberman. *Commentary*, pp. 84–86. *The New York Times*. (1971, January, 31). Best-seller list. Retrieved from http://www.hawes.com/1971/1971-01-31.pdf

Orwell, G. (2005). *Why I write*. New York: Penguin Books. (Original work published 1945).

Pinar, W.F. (1976). *Sanity, madness and the school*. Meerut, India: Sadhna Prakashan.

Pinar, W.F., Reynolds, W.M., Slattery, P., & Taubman, P.M. (2004*). Understanding curriculum: An introduction to the study of historical and contemporary discourses* (pp. 187–197). New York: Peter Lang.

Schubert, W.H. (2002). *Curriculum books: The first hundred years* (2nd ed.). New York: Peter Lang.

Scobey, M., & Graham, G. (Eds.). (1970). *To nurture humanness: A commitment for the 70's*. Washington, DC: ASCD.

Silberman, C.E. (1970). *Crisis in the classroom: The remaking of America education*. New York: Random House.

Silberman, C.E. (Ed.). (1973). *The open classroom reader*. New York: Random House.

Smith, R.P. (1971). *Crisis in the classroom*: A critique. *Educational Leadership: Journal of the Department of Supervision and Curriculum Development, N.E.A., 28*(8), 845–847. Retrieved from http://www.ascd.org/ASCD/pdf/journals/ed_lead/el_197105_smith.pdf

Weinstein, G., & Fantini, M. (1970). *Toward a humanistic education: A curriculum of affect*. New York: Praeger.

EIGHT

Ivan Illich, *Deschooling Society* (1971)

David Gabbard

I. Synopsis

Deschooling Society (Illich, 1971) should begin where it ends, with the story of Pandora. In what Illich describes as the prehistoric telling of her tale from matriarchal Greece, Pandora was an Earth goddess, sent to Earth with an amphora or pythos—what we would recognize today as a lidded urn made of clay. Within this urn dwelt every variety of evil. It contained only one good, and that was hope. One day, Pandora accidently allowed all of the evils to escape, but she replaced the lid before hope could follow.

Pandora's story intertwines with that of two brothers, Prometheus and Epimetheus. Both are central to our understanding of what Illich means by our "schooled" society and what "deschooling" that society would look like. What he does not mean is a society in which people have created schools. The presence of schools does not define a schooled society. Schooling signifies something far different, something Illich associates with the figure of Prometheus and how his story, as the bearer of foresight and the god of technological innovation, mirrors the story of modern man.

Through his trickery of the gods, Prometheus brought fire to humans, granting them the power to forge iron, enhancing their capacity to produce tools, and giving rise to the inseparable ideas: that first, with the right tools, humans can plan and control the world because, second, the world is in need of planning and control. Illich locates the origins of these ideas not in the matriarchal society of prehistoric Greece, where we find our original Pandora, but in classical Greece, which had grown into a rational, authoritarian patriarchy that degraded Pandora's myth. In its misogyny, classical Greece attributed the release of all the evils not to accident, but to Pandora's deliberate disobedience of the gods' order not to lift the lid of her urn. This moment marks, for Illich, the origins of modern man. Her willful transgression released every evil into the world, creating the demand for planning that would bring order to the chaos she'd unleashed.

Illich characterizes this demand as "the Promethean endeavor to forge institutions in order to corral each of the rampant ills" (Illich, 1971, p. 105) released from Pandora's urn. It leads to what he describes as the Promethean ethos—the notion that human beings must plan and control predictable processes that produce results upon which they can rely and "have a right to claim" (p. 105). Under these conditions, expectations displace the hope that pre-classical Pandora retained in her urn a hope defined by Illich as "faith in the goodness of nature" (p. 105) and "dependence on personal good will" (p. 111) that "centers desire on a person from whom we await a gift" (p. 105). Stated more simply, the Promethean ethos proclaims that human beings must plan and control predictable processes that produce expectations that these processes will satisfy the demands created by those same processes.

Compulsory schooling functions as one of those processes to be planned and controlled in order to produce predictable results—expectations. Illich defines it as "the age specific, teacher-related process requiring full time attendance at an obligatory curriculum" (Illich, 1971, pp. 25–26). It takes on special meaning for Illich, however, because of the centrality of compulsory schooling's role as the primary social ritual for conditioning people into the larger Promethean ethos. Illich's background as a Catholic priest for over 20 years prior to the publication of *Deschooling Society* provided him with a unique vantage point from which to discuss the ritualistic role of compulsory schooling. Within theology there is a field of study known as ecclesiology. Illich viewed ecclesiology as a precursor to sociology. It concerns itself with the origin, development, and structure of that community known as the church, studying the corporatization of individuals into that more or less unified community. This leads us to understand Illich most literally when he makes claims such as "school has become the world religion of a modernized proletariat, and makes futile promises of secular salvation to the poor of the technological age" (p. 10). Or, "The school system today performs the threefold function common to powerful churches throughout history" (p. 37). Compulsory schooling serves an ecclesiastical role by preparing children for a society dominated by the Promethean ethos.

Relatedly, liturgy forms a field of academic specialization within ecclesiology that examines how the church uses multiple series of rituals for socializing people to recognize and judge their own status as members of the church. Schooling teaches children to need school, but they will remain unfit for society until they learn to consume school. The more school you consume, the more power you gain as a consumer—more power to consume more. More power translates into more status, which explains why Illich identifies the college graduate as setting the standards for consumption in a schooled society. Everyone aspires to consume at the level or standard set by the college graduate.

Schooling, then, takes on the form of a commodity, and education becomes its fetish, which helps to explain the opening lines of Chapter 1 in *Deschooling Society*: "Many students, especially those who are poor, intuitively know what the schools do for them. They school them to confuse process with substance. Once these become blurred, a new logic is assumed: the more treatment there is, the better are the results; escalation leads to success" (p. 1).

Returning to the "threefold function" that it shares in common with "powerful churches throughout history" (p. 37), compulsory schooling serves as "the repository of society's myth" (p. 37)—the Promethean ethos. Children are born unfit for society. They must be made fit, and can only be made fit through the planned and predictable process of schooling. If they internalize the myth, they, along with their parents, come to claim a right to this process because of the value it purports to hold for them.

It seems odd to think that people can be made to claim a right to something that is, in fact, compulsory. However, Illich argues that the second function served by schools and powerful churches entails the "institutionalization of that myth's contradictions" (p. 37). Finally, and relatedly, the third function relates to the school as "the locus of the ritual that reproduces and veils the disparities between myth and reality." Students become "schooled to confuse teaching with learning, grade advancement with education, a diploma with competence, and fluency with the ability to say something new" (p. 1). No reforms to compulsory schooling will succeed in lifting the veil that disguises these disparities. We must demythologize schooling.

Doing this, Illich suggests, demands that we recognize ourselves, not in the heroic figure of Prometheus that fuels this myth, but in his fate. As punishment for his trickery of them that allowed him to bring fire to humanity that gave them the power to forge iron, the gods condemned the god of foresight and technological advancement to spend eternity bound to a rock by iron chains. Every day, a huge eagle would come to eat his liver, which the ancient Greeks viewed as the seat of the human soul and intelligence. They also may have known something of its regenerative power, for Prometheus's liver would heal every day only to be eaten again by the eagle, which symbolized Zeus taking his vengeance upon him.

For Illich, this scene mirrors compulsory schooling's reproduction of the contradictions and disparities inherent within the Promethean ethos. It should reveal to us the futility of compulsory schooling as central to society's larger "Promethean endeavor to forge institutions in order to corral each of the rampant ills" (Illich, 1971, p. 105) unleashed from Pandora's urn. Illich captures this futility with the image of a small metal casket or box that he saw in a New York toyshop. To open the box, you must push a button. When it opens, you expect to be able to take something out of it. Instead, a mechanical hand reaches out, recloses the lid, and locks it from the inside. "This contraption," he says, "is the opposite of Pandora's 'box'" (p. 105). We find no satisfaction or hope in that box. We have become slaves to our technologies, our tools, and our institutions. Our delusions otherwise chain us to them, like Prometheus at the rock. This is why we must, as Illich argues, deschool society by disestablishing school. Because they are the repository and reproductive engine of society's myth, creating a constitutional-level separation of school and state requires a demythologizing of society. We must bring the Promethean Age of expanding expectations to an end.

The transformation of society called for by Illich entails a rejection of Promethean expectations and a return to hope that he sees as characteristic of more primitive times in our species' history. Remember, Prometheus had a brother, Epimetheus. Prometheus was known for foresight, which understands the past and the present solely in terms of the future. When this notion of foresight becomes wedded to rituals of progress, expectations expand endlessly. Our ever-expanding list of perceived needs that can only be served by planned processes can, simultaneously, never be satisfied. We render ourselves insatiable, and society unsustainable. Epimetheus, on the other hand, was known for hindsight, which, as I will explore more fully below, suggests the capacity to know the present and contemplate the future through the lens of the past. While Prometheus abandoned her, Epimetheus married Pandora, whose amphora contained hope. The social transformation made possible by deschooling society would signify a shift from Promethean expectations to Epimethean hope. Again, Illich defines hope in terms of "faith in the goodness of nature" (p. 105) and "dependence on personal good will" (p. 111) that "centers desire on a person from whom we await a gift" (p. 105). "Children," he says,

> phantasize flying their spacecrafts away from a crepuscular earth. From the perspectives of the Man on the Moon, Prometheus could recognize sparkling blue Gaia as the planet of Hope and as the Arc of Mankind. A new sense of the finiteness of the Earth and a new nostalgia now can open man's eyes to the choice of his brother Epimetheus to wed the Earth with Pandora.
>
> At this point the Greek myth turns into hopeful prophecy because it tells us that the son of Prometheus was Deucalion, the Helmsman of the Ark who like Noah outrode the flood to become the father of a new mankind which he made from the earth with Pyrra, the daughter of Epimetheus and Pandora. We are gaining insight into the meaning of the Pythos (Amphora/urn), which Pandora brought from the gods as being the inverse of the box: our vessel and Ark. (Illich, 1971, p. 115)

Illich titles his final chapter of *Deschooling Society* "The Rebirth of Epimethean Man," because this level of social transformation could only be made possible by a transformation of human consciousness. And only this transformation of consciousness, marked by hope and "dependence on personal good will" rather than institutional expectations, can make his inversion of compulsory schooling into "learning webs" possible.

II. An Epimethean Man Living in a Promethean Age

In many ways, Illich personified the hindsight associated with Epimetheus, tempting us to view him as an Epimethean man living in a Promethean Age. As previously stated, hindsight entails more than the ability to look in our rearview mirrors at the objects disappearing behind us at ever-increasing speed. Illich valued hindsight because of the value he placed on history. In his view, the study of history enhances what I think he means by hindsight: our capacity to know the present and contemplate the future through the lens of the past.

In the introduction to what amounts to his first volume of a collection of dialogues with and monologues by Illich, David Cayley (1992) emphasizes the importance of this understanding of Illich as a "radical traditionalist" whose obedience to virtues long forgotten made him "'very consciously a remainder of the past, one who still survives from another time'" (Cayley, 1992, p. 3). This "other timeliness" of Illich's laid the foundations of the vantage point from which he questioned, understood, and evaluated that present and its certainties. Any commentary on the context and time period of *Deschooling Society*, then, must address his hindsight on that present.

Illich cultivated much of his hindsight from his family's deep roots in their European past and their centuries-long relationship with the Roman Church. The family home, built during the Middle Ages and the time of the crusades, stands on an island off the coast of Dalmatia. "The very same olive-wood rafters," Illich told Cayley, "supported the roof of my grandfather's house. Water was still gathered from the same stone slabs on the roof. The wine was pressed in the same vats, the fish caught from the same kind of boat…. For people who lived off the main routes, history still flowed slowly, imperceptibly" (pp. 2–3). Born in 1926, Illich spent his early years between his grandfather's house in Dalmatia and his grandmother's house in Vienna. According to Cayley,

> By 1938 Illich already knew in his bones that that the world into which he had been born was vanishing. Soon he would become a wanderer…but he took this fading world within himself where it would nourish a stance so radically traditional that for a few years in the late 1960s and early 1970s excited North American audiences though it was vanguard. (p. 2)

Because of his mother's Jewish ancestry, Illich was forced to leave Austria in 1941, when he began his pre-university studies in chemistry and crystallography in Italy. He would later earn degrees in theology and philosophy at the Gregorian University in Rome, rounding off his studies with a Ph.D. in history from the University of Salzburg in 1951. Soon after completing this final degree, Illich, having already taken his vows in Rome, began his work as a priest in New York City, where he requested assignment to a parish comprised of a growing population of Puerto Rican immigrants. There he developed many of the most important foundations of his thought on institutions, the Catholic Church in particular.

Puerto Rican immigrants presented a problem for the institutional church, or what Illich called the Church as IT. In the eyes of IT, the Puerto Rican problem stemmed from the immigrants' never having learned to need the institutional church. Most of the Puerto Rican parishioners had come from rural areas of the island where the institutional church had not established any physical or social presence. They had never experienced the Church as an institution demanding compulsory attendance. Furthermore, they were experiencing increasing levels of discrimination as immigrants. This led Illich to work with them and Cardinal Spellman to establish San Juan Day in celebration of Puerto Rico's patron saint.

In 1956, 5 years after arriving in New York, Illich received a new assignment as vice rector of the Catholic University at Ponce in Puerto Rico. It was during that time that he met Everett Reimer, with whom he began a series of long conversations on the topic of schooling. Early on, Illich recognized the polarizing effects of compulsory schooling on the island. Schooling tied equal economic opportunity to equal educational opportunity, but making the latter equally accessible to all was not economically feasible. What upset him most, however, was hearing people blame themselves for "failing to achieve the impossible" (Illich, 1971, p. 7), which only compounded the effects of poverty.

Illich also understood the promises of schooling as part of a larger Promethean endeavor. They began surfacing in Puerto Rico by the 1950s as part of what President Harry S. Truman had called "the Development Decade." Having emerged victorious from World War II—not only militarily, but also economically and politically—the United States confronted only one opponent: the Soviet Union. The face-off between the United States as the economic, political, and military center of the capitalist world and Russia as the leading force behind the only competing ideology defined the Cold War. World War II signified the culmination of 300 years of imperialism on the part of the capitalist powers. As a tactic in the ensuing ideological battle of Cold War politics, the Development Decade offered what would prove to be a false promise to non-industrialized nations around the world. The United States wanted those nations to see their future as a path to development.

The United States would provide financial and technical assistance in helping realize its presumed aspirations to model itself in its Promethean image. As the last point in his Four Point Plan, Truman proclaimed during his inaugural speech in 1949, "We must embark on a bold new program for making the benefits of our scientific advances and industrial progress available for the improvement and growth of underdeveloped areas" (Truman, 1949). We must understand *Deschooling Society*, then, as a warning to those "underdeveloped areas," urging them to be cautious about adopting the certainties of this Promethean worldview. In doing so, Illich helped many of us born into this worldview question many of our most sacred certainties, including the institution of compulsory schooling.

The Epimethean qualities of his character that made him such a radical traditionalist must have helped Illich relate to and forge powerful connections with peoples deemed "underdeveloped" by the Promethean powers. He was ordered to leave Puerto Rico by Bishop James McManus for denouncing the Church's involvement in the politics surrounding birth control on the island. Before leaving, he began a series of workshops on the question of development and the emergent practice on the part of rich nations of sending volunteers to poor countries to assist with the Promethean development programs. At the request of American priest John Considine, Pope John XXIII signed a letter ordering the North American Church to send 10% of its personnel to South America to assist with those projects. Through his workshops and seminars, Illich wanted

> to point out the damage, the damage done by volunteerism, the damage to the person who went there through the establishment of a sense of superiority, a savior complex, and the damage to the image in the U.S. of what poor countries are.... I wanted...[people] to reflect on the cultural reality of the country to which they were going, and to look back on the United States from outside its own borders, often for the first time. (Cayley, 1992, p. 94)

A year after leaving Puerto Rico in 1960, Illich continued this program of "de-Yankeefication" in Cuernavaca, Mexico, where he established the Center for Intercultural Documentation, or CIDOC.

III. Reading Illich

Due to the depth and duration of my relationship with *Deschooling Society*, I cannot write any detached evaluation of the strengths and weaknesses of Illich's classic work. Instead, I want to offer my reflections on how we should read him. Properly understood and appreciated, *Deschooling Society* defies a simple, single reading. It demands more, just as it rewards more for any of us willing to accept its invitation to lead us toward a fuller and more critical awareness, however painful, of our most sacred modern certainties and their hideous consequences. In this sense, *Deschooling Society* offers us entrée to a world where "the habits of the heart are as crucial to scholarship as the habits of the head" (Cayley, p. 4). In this world, the act of reading takes on the qualities of a feast, where we take ideas into our mouths, taste and chew them, spit or swallow and allow them to nourish the organs of our senses. It becomes possible to embody the spirit of what stays with us from a text. This redefines the purpose of study or disciplined learning. One learns not merely to cultivate a different view of the world, but a different way of being and living in the world. We become the words we allow ourselves to consume incarnate. Rereading becomes an act of refreshment.

You should not expect one reading of *Deschooling Society* to instantly transform your life, though one reading might be enough to commit you to that process over the course of your lifetime. Even then, I would not guarantee that a single reading would lead to any such commitment. My relationship with this work and others from Illich spans more than 30 years and dates back to my time in Germany, where I was stationed as an infantryman in the U.S. Army. It happened to be the first book that I found while searching the English-language bookstores in and around Frankfurt for books on education. Its perspective, however, was still too foreign to me. I lacked the frame of reference and background knowledge required for understanding, let alone appreciating, its meanings. I had no idea who Illich was or that *Deschooling Society* had, already by 1988 when I discovered it, achieved the status of a "classic" in educational thought. Again, it was the first book I ever read on education, and I was totally unprepared for the experience of it.

In spite of the challenges it presented me, I sensed something deeply important about *Deschooling Society*, enough to return to it once I'd come back to the United States and finished sufficient graduate coursework in the Department of Educational Foundations at the University of Cincinnati with Joel Spring. Spring was among many educational theorists and scholars who spent time with Illich at the Center for Intercultural Documentation (CIDOC) in Cuernavaca, Mexico. Illich had helped establish CIDOC and conducted a series of seminars there during the early 1970s on deschooling and related issues.

My doctoral studies expanded my frame of reference for understanding works in educational theory. For my dissertation, I used Michel Foucault's *Archeology of Knowledge* to devise a method for explaining what I described as the "silencing" of Illich in educational discourse—why his ideas, in spite of his early success (as evidenced by the number of significant figures in educational thought who flocked to CIDOC), did not spawn the same following as Paulo Freire's *Pedagogy of the Oppressed* (published just a year earlier). Still, as I would later learn from my personal encounters with Illich during my post-doctoral studies in the Science, Technology, and Society program at Penn State, my efforts failed to capture the depth of *Deschooling Society* and what it represented.

Graciously, both Illich and his close friend Lee Hoinacki read my dissertation, and it was Hoinacki who told me that Illich had taken moral offense at my treatment of his ideas. In his view, I had detached them from his person. Illich himself reinforced this message when he made me promise that I would not "deconstruct" Jacques Ellul before he would guide me through a study of his works. What I had missed, and what is far from obvious to any reader, was the deep intimacy of Illich's words and his relationship to his own writing as a product of his approach to learning. Again, Illich adhered to a tradition of scholarship that placed the heart on a par with the head.

Illich calls the cultivation of the organs of inner senses that root in the heart by its traditional name, *ascesis*, and says that it is the indispensable complement to critical habits of the mind. "For a full millennium," Illich has written, "the Church cultivated a balanced tradition of study and reflection…. The habits of the heart and the cultivation of its virtues are peripherals to the pursuit of higher learning today…. I want to argue for a new complementarity between critical and ascetical learning. I want to reclaim for ascetical theory, method, and discipline a status equal to that the University now assigns to critical and technical disciplines" (Cayley, 1992, p. 4).

One should consider these aspects of Illich before approaching or deciding to enter into a relationship with *Deschooling Society*. It will help you gain a fuller appreciation of one of his favorite phrases—*Corruptio opitmae qu'est pessima* (the corruption of the best becomes the worst) and its significance for understanding his critique of compulsory schooling.

IV. Deschooling Today

Owing in some measure to the appearance of his writings on schooling in *The New York Review of Books* in the months leading up to the publication of *Deschooling Society*, Illich's ideas attracted a great deal of attention during the early 1970s. Some of that attention came from some of the leading leftists who made the trek to Cuernavaca to participate in Illich workshops at CIDOC. Though he followed *Deschooling Society* with a number of other important and related books (*Tools for Conviviality* [1973], *Medical Nemesis* [1975], and *Toward a History of Needs* [1978]), by the 1980s interest in his ideas had waned, particularly in education-related fields. Illich, however, never sought a following. I think he was too busy following and living his own Epimethean vision. He did welcome friendship, though, and most of the people today who continue finding relevance in his ideas were, indeed, his friends. Many of them remain actively engaged in the publication of works meant to carry his ideas forward. Dana Stuchul, for example, edits *The International Journal of Illich Studies*.

Popularity, however, is not the most important measure of relevance. Are Illich's ideas still relevant? In speaking about university students, he remarked that today's university system creates "students who have gotten utterly used to the fact that what they learn must be taught, and nothing they are taught must really be taken seriously" (p. 70). We tell ourselves that the university is not compulsory schooling. However, returning to Illich's thoughts on the ritualization of progress and endlessly expanding expectations, we see where it is compulsory for those who can find the means to afford it, even if it requires graduating with tremendous debt from college loans. Somehow, it remains compulsory for those who seek entrance to the middle class. So, we can continue telling ourselves that the university is not compulsory. But how many of today's university students can tell you what they came to the university to study? How many of them know why they're there? How many of them came with a desire to learn? Certainly, there are many, but are they in the majority? The challenges of Ivan Illich remain open.

References

Cayley, D. (1992). *Ivan Illich in conversation.* Concord, Ontario: Anansi.

Gabbard, D. (1994). *Silencing Ivan Illich: A Foucauldian analysis of intellectual exclusion.* San Francisco, CA: Austin and Winfield.

Illich, I. (1971). *Deschooling society.* London: Calder & Boyars.

Illich, I. (1973). *Tools for conviviality.* London: Calder & Boyars.

Illich, I. (1975). *Medical nemesis.* London: Calder & Boyars.

Illich, I. (1978). *Toward a History of Needs.* New York: Pantheon.

Truman, H. (1949, January 20). Inauguration speech. Retrieved from http://www.presidency.ucsb.edu/ws/index.php?pid=13282

NINE

Dan Lortie, *Schoolteacher: A Sociological Study* (1975)

Jean Ann Foley and Joseph C. Wegwert

Introduction

Dan Lortie's *Schoolteacher* (1975) presents a sociological study of teachers' socialization into the profession and the nature of teachers' thinking and work. The book builds on Waller's discussion in *The Sociology of Teaching* (1932) of what the occupation of teaching does to teachers and Jackson's *Life in Classrooms* (1968), which describes the nature of teachers' working lives and the pressures of decision making within the classroom. Lortie examines the teaching profession with the intention of revealing pervasive patterns and themes that drive the occupation. His study compares the themes rooted in the history of the American schoolteacher with his research of 94 teacher interviews (the sample he called "Five Towns") and in comparison with other occupations. The major argument from Lortie's study is that three orientations of the teaching profession—Presentism, Individualism, and Conservatism—form a *teacher ethos* that binds the occupation and impedes change and improvement.

Synopsis

The nine chapters of Lortie's *Schoolteacher* are divided into four themes: American Education History; Occupational Perpetuations; Teacher Meanings Associated with Their Work; and Forecasts for the Future. In our synopsis of the book, we briefly describe the arguments associated with each theme and link them to the three orientations that form Lortie's teacher ethos.

American Education History (Chapter 1)

Chapter 1 of *Schoolteacher* examines historically based social patterns of the teaching occupation over 3 centuries and identifies tensions held between the poles of change and continuity. The cellular structure of teaching, the administrative hierarchy, and the social status of teachers, marked by easy entry into the profession, highlight the historical contexts embedded in becoming a teacher. Lortie identifies the one-room schoolhouse that gave a single teacher the responsibility for educating a diverse group of students ranging in age, aptitude, and ability as the beginning of the cellular tradition of education. Teachers' isolation from one another precluded shared work experiences. As the school system grew and then became mandatory, more cells were added to keep the structure of the school independent, flexible, and interchangeable in order to accommodate growth. Lortie argues that the cellular structure contributes to continuity, since independent cells prohibit discussion and common language development.

Historically, schools have been governed by a third party. "In public education," writes Lortie, "that party has consisted of a school board composed of elected or appointed citizens" (p. 2). An administrative structure that utilizes non-teachers to evaluate and direct teachers and the school organization sets up a tension regarding the low status of teaching and the lack of power to investigate change from within the teaching profession. The governing body can intrude on the cellular classroom at will. When ideas for reform are initiated from outside the teaching profession, tension is created between the need for change and the need for teachers to conserve the status quo.

Lortie describes the social position of teachers as "special but shadowed" (p. 10). The shadowed notion is derived from colonial times, when clergy "took on teaching duties along the way" (p. 11). The shadowed position stigmatizes teaching and creates strain between teachers' desired identities and their actual conditions of work. Low status in teaching is also guaranteed by easy entry. Lortie writes, "It is as if the society, acting through governmental agencies, sought to offset the limited incentives of teaching by making access easier" (p. 18).

These historically based occupational social patterns create categorical binaries that reflect ongoing tensions for the teaching profession: cellular vs. interdependence, autonomy vs. collegiality, and easy entry vs. higher status. Lortie argues that an occupational culture loaded with such tensions makes change difficult and focuses efforts toward continuity and conserving the status quo.

Occupational Perpetuations (Chapters 2, 3, and 4)

After examining the prevailing patterns of the teaching occupation over 3 centuries of American history, Lortie moves to a discussion of the "process of occupational perpetuation" (p. viii). Here he begins to test the historical patterns of the profession against how the teachers of Five Towns describe themselves and their work. A major argument regarding the recruitment of teachers is framed by the notion of "apprenticeship of observation" (p. 61). Since all teachers have been students and have had the opportunity to observe over 10,000 classroom hours, they enter the teaching profession with many preconceived notions about how they intend to teach. Their methods of teaching are biased by their lengthy observation experience. Also, evidenced by their choice to become teachers, these students are "favorably disposed toward the existing system of schools" (p. 54). This form of recruitment, from the ranks of students, supports Lortie's argument of continuity and conservation. The concept of individual experiences and their effects on how teachers perform also reinforces the autonomy theme.

When Lortie compares the general and specialized schooling of teachers with the schooling of other professionals (doctors, lawyers, engineers), he finds that there is relatively little special schooling required for teachers. The interviews gathered from Five Towns revealed that "experience was their major means of learning how to teach" (p. 77). This lack of special schooling and reliance on trial and error for successful teaching lays the basis for an intuitive approach to teaching that precludes the development of a common technical language. Teachers' doubts about possessing a common technical culture affect their collective status in two ways: they are less ready to assert their authority on educational matters and less able to respond to demands from society (p. 80).

According to Lortie, the teaching profession is career-less, unstaged, flat, front-loaded, and disjunctive in terms of effort and net satisfaction. Career-less is defined as "less opportunity for the movement upward which is the essence of career" (p. 84). Lortie hypothesizes that the lack of stages in the teaching career results in "the dominance of present versus future orientation among teachers" (p. 86). The nature of teacher rewards echoes a present orientation. The dominant rewards for teachers are psychic in nature and relate to reaching the student. "Psychic rewards," Lortie writes, "consist entirely of subjective valuations made in the course of work engagement; their subjectivity means that they can vary from person to person" (p. 101). This system of rewards sustains the concepts of independence and isolationism, as the teacher's focus is on enlightening students one-on-one in the confines of their classroom at some point in each day.

Teacher Meanings Associated with Their Work (Chapters 5, 6, 7, and 8)

When referring to the purpose of teachers' work, Lortie reveals that there are enormous tensions between what teachers hold as an ideal purpose or goal, "exerting moral influence, 'soldering' students to learning and achieving general impact" (pp. 102–103), and their ability to achieve this goal. At the root of the tension is the "endemic uncertainty" that is at the core of the teacher reward system. The teacher lives in a non-causal world. There is no cause and effect found in the classroom. If a student progresses or learns, the teacher can never be certain that she can take credit for the change. The lack of cause and effect in the classroom reflects a lack of causal thinking on the part of the teacher. Teachers typically do not engage in research and do not read research in an effort to address teaching problems. Their world is one filled with pedagogical accidents and mystery.

When Lortie discusses the sentiments teachers attach to their tasks, we begin to see the nature of the sociological argument. Teachers operate under the belief that the classroom must be bounded in order for them to do their job; however, the classroom is permeable. When outsiders (parents, administrators, other teachers) are continually allowed to interrupt the teacher, a message of not valuing what the teacher values most (teaching in an undisturbed classroom) is communicated to the students as well as to the teacher. Lortie argues that the teacher's sense of devaluation strengthens individualism and a victim mentality that weakens the ability to effect change or implement reform.

Forecasts for the Future (Chapter 9)

In his final chapter, Lortie connects the analyses of his study with practical action by looking at three scenarios. The first focuses on "cultural change—on alterations in thought about practice" (p. 215). In order to attack the problems of the occupation from this viewpoint, teachers would have to develop a common language. The second scenario proposed by Lortie is related to collective bargaining. In order to bargain effectively and create an environment of give and take, teachers must be able to agree on issues other than salary. The third scenario points to the contradictions of education centralization. Lortie identifies one important issue on how centralization would affect the classroom teacher: "teachers would find themselves confronted with a crisis in the definition of their employment status…as bureaucrats within the governmental structure" (p. 227). The framework within which Lortie forecasts an application of his findings to the future of education provides a link to the context for his work. The scenarios are used as examples for "how to" destabilize the three orientations of the teaching profession. This is a technical ideology that fits neatly with the context of the time period.

Cultural and Educational Contexts

Lortie's *Schoolteacher*, published in 1975, emerged just prior to the onslaught of the accountability and standardization movement that today so potently and dysfunctionally shapes the educational lives of children, parents, and teachers—and just after the eclipse of significant social movements that had worked to disrupt the stable cultural and political terrains of American society. In other words, *Schoolteacher* arrived as the unfolding effects of the anti-war and Civil Rights Movements of the 1960s and early 1970s increased the cultural and political visibility of youth, women, gays, lesbians, and workers. These shifts manifested in unprecedented status anxieties felt throughout the hegemonic frameworks of corporate capitalism. These anxieties were further fueled by global economic shifts and domestic political crises that, by 1975, were evident in a perceived (from "below") crisis of political and institutional legitimacy and a perceived (from "above") crisis of excess democracy. In the early 1950s, with the issue of Sputnik and the resultant "race for space," American elites turned to the schools as sources of both panic and panacea; in the early 1970s, with a sluggish economy, a political "credibility gap," and cultural challenges to dominant values, schools once again were offered up at the altar of blame and redemption (Kaye, 1991).

By the mid-1970s the relatively stable domestic political "accord" or "settlement" that successfully reframed American capitalist hegemony out of the economic and political instability of the 1930s and World War II and into a period of economic growth and middle-class complacency was seriously unraveled. The postwar consensus, rooted in the social welfare and stabilization measures of the New Deal and the Keynesian economics on which it rested, provided increased status and economic opportunities for White, largely male, middle-class workers. Yet the 1960s and 1970s witnessed growing unrest and resistance from those identity and economic groups not fully included in the postwar bargain, and their voices were raised in challenge to the official dominating refrains of "freedom," "opportunity," and "democracy" (Kaye, 1991).

An increasing democratization of the American economy and polity coming out of the postwar "consensus" had, by the early 1970s, combined with increasing competition from technologically revitalized Japanese and German economies and an emerging solidarity of

Middle Eastern oil-producing nations to challenge the unquestioned American market domination that defined the 25 years following World War II. American elites began to clearly articulate a two-pronged response—economic and cultural—to these counter-hegemonic conditions (Kaye, 1991).

First, American elites began to lay the groundwork for the neoliberal economic policies we see all around us today. With its origins in the deep recession of the 1970s, neoliberalism was born out of the "stagflation" (economic stagnation in combination with monetary and price inflation) that characterized emergent and previously unseen recessionary features, including "very slow growth, increasing unemployment *and* rising inflation" (Kaye, 1991, p. 56). Kaye (1991) describes the cause of the recession as "nothing less than a world crisis of the capitalist accumulation process entailing a 'massive restructuring of capital and the international division of labour'" (p. 56). In short, capitalist elites in Western nations, led by Great Britain and the United States, recognized a crisis of capitalism that required a revision of the postwar social contract and undertook this task unilaterally and with hegemonic vigor. It can be argued that corporate elites advocated policies designed to deepen the recession of the 1970s as a disciplinary response to the hegemonic challenges from marginalized elements in American society (Hursh, 2001). Toward this end, elites abandoned the Keynesian economic strategies that had been embraced and utilized since the Great Depression and, instead, deployed neoliberal policies, including "the deregulation of the economy, trade liberalization, the dismantling of the public sector [such as education, health, and social welfare], and the predominance of the financial sector of the economy over production and commerce" (quoted in Hursh, 2001, p. 353). Kaye (1991) writes:

> It is even arguable that it was capital's determination to wage "class war from above" which finally brought an end to the post-war settlements…. Stated bluntly, the emphasis given to combating inflation instead of unemployment, and the steps taken to accomplish it, were in deference to the effectively mobilized interests of business-capital. (p. 57)

The second response by American elites to the counter-hegemonic pressures arising out of the social and cultural dislocations of the 1960s and early 1970s came as a cultural counterattack, precipitating what has been called the "culture war." Often framing it as a cultural and moral crisis of values, elites lamented what they saw as a move away from the "truth" of American exceptionalism—an exceptionalism rooted in a long-standing unity and ideological consensus— and toward a cultural disintegration and decay engendered by a radical multiculturalism lacking a cultural center (Cheney, 1995; Schlesinger, 1992). One powerful artifact that illuminates the thinking by elites in their efforts to re-establish ideological hegemony comes in the form of a report by the Trilateral Commission in 1975 entitled *The Crisis of Democracy* and co authored by the Harvard political scientist Samuel Huntington (1975). The report presented an argument about the question of "governability" in American society, concluding that the United States was experiencing the repercussions of an "excess of democracy." Kaye's (1991) treatment of this report and the hegemonic perspective embedded in its assumptions are revealing:

> Referring to the heightened political consciousness, participation and activism of "public-interest groups, minorities, students and women" along with the growth of "white-collar unionism," all of which are seen as assaults on existing patterns of authority…[the report] speaks of how these movements were challenging, nay, threatening, democracy itself! Indeed, Huntington writes that "some of the problems of governance in the United States today stem

from an 'excess of democracy'…." Informing us that "democracy is only one way of consti-
tuting authority" and that in the 1960s it was implemented in institutional settings where it
ought not to have been, he proceeds to restate the Cold War, essentially anti-working-class,
proposition that "the effective operation of a democratic political system usually requires some
measure of apathy and noninvolvement on the part of some individuals and groups." (pp.
79–80)

Decades earlier, Walter Lippmann helped to provide the philosophical scaffolding for the
"power elite" view of liberal democracy drawn upon by the Tri-Lateralists. Representing the
philosophical antithesis of John Dewey, Lippmann eschewed civic participation by the masses
and embraced instead a government of "experts"—those properly trained in largely technical
fields:

> According to Lippmann, in a properly running democracy the large majority of the population
> (whom Lippmann labeled "the bewildered herd") is protected from itself by the specialized
> class's management of the political, economic, and ideological systems and, in particular, by
> the manufacturing of consent—bring about agreement on the part of the public for things that
> they do not want. (Ross, 2000, pp. 57–58)

By the mid-1970s the response by dominant elites to the cultural and economic transformations of the decade and a half was to "capture" (once again) the reform discourse of
schools so as to interrupt the threatened cultural attack on a traditional curriculum and stem
the tide of democratization that threatened corporate hegemony. It is within this context that
Lortie's study rests. Beginning in the mid-1970s, schools operated as institutional and curricular sites of both a conservative cultural restoration and the institutionalization of a pervasive
neoliberalism (Apple, 2001). Lortie's notion of a professional teacher ethos embedded in *presentism*, *individualism*, and *conservatism* offers insights into the enabling—and dysfunctionally complicit—role of teachers as schools have served as *hospitable hosts* for this conservative
cultural restoration and economic restructuring.

The neoliberal corporate educational reform movement, along with its attendant conservative cultural restoration that emerged in tandem with Lortie's volume, seemingly offered
teachers alternatives to the disempowering aspects of their professional lives. Over time, the
accountability and testing regime that originated in the 1970s offered teachers an illusory
empirical certainty over the subjective and isolated understandings of success—the "psychic rewards" noted by Lortie. Similarly, the discourses of standardization and metrics since the 1970s
have provided a common technical language found in law and medicine but notably absent
in teaching. Finally, the emergent corporate educational reform agenda provided standardized
curricula that eschewed revisionist controversy and offered teachers both a way out of the oft-
disparaged merry-go-round of curricular "fads" and greater connection to colleagues working
from the same corporate agenda and accountable to the same mechanisms of measurement.

The neoliberal corporate educational reform movement, along with its attendant conser-
Through Lortie's lens, we can see how the discourse of accountability framing the movement for standardization and testing resonated with the unrequited desire of teachers to *know*
the results of their pedagogical efforts, offering a "research-based" accounting that served to
replace the intangible, "psychic rewards" of the profession. Yet the *presentism* of psychic rewards has only given way to the *presentism* of test scores. While the development of a common
technical language and collaboration around standardized curriculum may well have reduced
the isolating *individualism* inherent in Lortie's teacher ethos, it has likely reinforced both *pre-*

sentism and *conservatism* as teachers look no further than the next round of testing and search only for ways to increase those test scores. In short, it appears that the teacher ethos that Lortie described in 1975 positioned teachers to not only uncritically consume corporate educational reform mechanisms and the culturally conservative restoration via corporate curriculum and testing, but also to deepen the *conservatism* and *presentism* embedded in the teacher ethos.

Strengths and Weaknesses

Upon its publication in 1975, *Schoolteacher* was heralded as "some of the most trenchant, unique, and helpful research ever done on teaching" (Larson, 1976, p. 642). A major strength of the book is the careful and creative analysis of Lortie's data. He uses symbolic interactionism as the lens for examining the teaching profession. From the symbolic perspective, behavior is an open-ended process linked to agreed-upon meanings within a community. The open-ended process relates to the continuous interaction between individual and society and implies that social life is improvised and can be transformed as the group modifies its symbolic meanings.

Geertz (1973) suggests that an analysis of culture from the symbolic view is not an experimental science in search of law but an interpretative one in search of meaning. Lortie's analysis is not prescriptive, with admonitions on what teachers should do. Rather, he mines the teachers' interviews for understanding. Through this careful inquiry, a bounded culture emerges that provokes more questions for research as well as suggestions for intruding on an oppressive ethos that resists change and fetters teachers. The analysis captures the complexity of the teaching profession and, by uncovering its culture, reveals a brutal triad of orientations that chain teachers to a compliant and anti-intellectual profession. Hargreaves (2009) termed the three orientations—presentism, conservatism, and individualism—"The Unholy Trinity" (p. 146). Neufeld (2009) asserts: "A completely redefined school culture must become the medium of reform" (p. 33). Neufeld (2009) also claims: "*Schoolteacher* opened the book for analyses of a profession and revealed it to be lacking as an occupation for promoting education inquiry or building the 'intellectual capital' of its occupants" (p. 35).

Acland (1976) reviewed Lortie's book and came away with the message "that teachers are caught in self-defeating, anxiety-provoking traps" (p. 139). His critique of the book addressed "the articulation of these guiding ideas and the data" (p. 140). In addition, he argued that Lortie's study drew more from a psychological spectrum than from a sociological lens. Acland's final assessment contends that Lortie does not comment on the position expressed by literature of the time that the purpose of schools and teachers "is to reproduce the division of labor... and sort students" (p. 141). This omission, according to Acland, may be "laying yet another self-defeating trap for teachers to fall into" (p.142).

Pederson and Fleming (1979) raised a number of critiques, but the most potent has to do with the absence of political, social, and economic factors in Lortie's analysis. While symbolic interactionism provided a cultural lens for understanding the teacher profession, it lacked a political and social context. Without this context, the frame for understanding Lortie's arguments is a conservative one that does not connect social and political issues to findings and interpretations. As Hargreaves (2009) suggests, "Lortie in particular and the perspective he largely adopted of symbolic interactionism in general, never really undertook a political or critical analysis of the macro system of society" (p. 152).

We concur with Pederson and Fleming (1979) and support Hargreaves's (2009) argument that the failure to include a critical lens privileged a penchant for reducing Lortie's findings to recipe-based approaches for improving schools, especially in the context of the neoliberal corporate reform agenda of standardization and testing. This impact is reflected in what we refer to as the *professional reformers*—school leaders, organizational consultants, and mainstream academics—working at the school/classroom/programmatic (or micro) level to "fine-tune" school structures, teachers' skill sets, and the culture of schools in efforts to disrupt the dysfunctional relationships between individualism, presentism, and conservatism. The 1980s and 1990s, in particular, saw rapid growth in professional development programs. Teachers were encouraged to attend professional development meetings, to reflect on their teaching, to learn new strategies, and to plan for the future. Hargreaves (2009) suggests that in many cases these attempts to bring teachers together for improvement and change resulted in a "contrived collegiality" (p. 148) that developed into resentment toward mandatory meetings and a desire to collaborate less. Hargreaves concludes: "Only by moving outside the Anglo American assumptions of Lortie's work and educational scholarship, can we grasp that the prime enemy of educational change, is actually social and political conservatism" (p. 153).

In the second edition of *Schoolteacher* (2002), Lortie writes in the preface: "I sought to write as objectively as I could to avoid confusion with advocacy for a particular program of reform" (p. vii). The "objective" position relies on a structural-functional approach that builds upon a "positivist sociological model" (Giroux & Penna, 1979, p. 24). Such a model reflects "an apolitical posture that sees as unproblematic the basic beliefs, values, and structural socioeconomic arrangements characteristic of American society" (p. 24). It is somewhat ironic to realize that Lortie's formidable contribution to research in education is tangled within a conservative and instrumental hegemonic web. Yet, as Lortie's work takes the reader past the schoolhouse door and into the classroom lives of teachers, it builds on the earlier work of Waller (1932) and Jackson (1968) and foregrounds a new wave of ethnographic research. These studies reveal the complex web of school culture and the ideologies and social relations that shape the experiences and lives of students and teachers (e.g., Willis, 1977; McLaren, 1986; McNeil, 1986). In sum, Lortie's uncovering of "the unholy trinity" (Hargreaves, 2009, p. 146)—presentism, conservatism, and individualism—is a powerful insight, but one that is most transformative through a critical lens.

Significance

Understanding the economic and cultural context of schools and society in the 1960s and 1970s is crucial to understanding both Lortie's analytical framework and the impact of his analysis on the trajectory of school improvement efforts by both *professional reformers* (micro level) and the elements of *neoliberal corporate reform* (macro level) over the past 40 years. We find that Lortie's work offers two points of relevance for today's educational context. First, Lortie's analysis of the teacher ethos suggests how schools have operated and continue to operate as *hospitable hosts* that allow the neoliberal wedge of corporate reform and a pervasive and disempowering instrumental professionalism to infiltrate school reform efforts. Second, Lortie's analysis of the teacher ethos and the "apprenticeship of observation" (p. 61) provides potentially powerful insights regarding the challenges facing teacher preparation programs. Colleges of education are increasingly pushed into an anti-intellectual and anti-democratic instrumentalism endemic to *professional reform* and *neoliberal corporate reform* efforts such as those promoted by the National Council for Accreditation of Teacher Education (NCATE), the Council for the Accreditation of Educator Preparation (CAEP), and the national accreditation process.

Lortie's framework helps us to see why schools are such easy political targets and, further, why the series of corporate reforms imposed on schools from the 1980s into the 2000s—the *Nation at Risk* report (1983), Goals 2000 (1994), No Child Left Behind (2001), and Race to the Top (2009)—have seamlessly mapped onto the teacher ethos. As Lortie's teacher ethos has intersected with the efforts by *professional reformers* to promote collegiality and collaboration, the "push to create data-driven, networked professional learning communities has certainly brought about less individualism but it has also increased the amount of presentism. In turn, this has led to a new conservatism where collaborative interactions are pleasurable, but also hurried, technical, uncritical, and narrow" (Hargreaves, 2009, p. 150). Placed in the context of the high-stakes testing and the accountability fetish of neoliberal corporate school reform, this "new conservatism," argues Hargreaves, is "different and deeper" than that offered by Lortie:

> The conservatism that accompanies addictive presentism is a deeper one of purpose as well as practice; of ends as well as means. The means hurry interaction, and focus around data-driven improvements and just-in-time interventions to accelerate progress in narrowly defined basics of literacy and numeracy. The ends are concerned with improved achievement scores in narrowly conceived areas of curriculum, or in the slick and speedy world of 21st century corporate skills such as teamwork, flexibility, and adaptability…. This is conservatism of ends by narrowing and exclusion, reinforced by a conservatism (and presentism) of hurried and unreflective means that inhibit professional engagement with these deeper and wider questions of teaching and learning. (Hargreaves, 2009, pp. 150–151)

Further, this same instrumental rationality permeates the culture of teacher education as many colleges of education move through the accreditation process of NCATE/CAEP and, along the way, embrace a "deeper presentism" that elides "deeper and wider questions of teaching and learning" (Hargreaves, 2009, pp. 150–151). In teacher education contexts, students are not as deeply immersed in the *teacher ethos* as Lortie's classroom teachers. However, as colleges of education increasingly turn to clinical professors and site-based instruction, teacher candidates are likely to encounter heavy doses of *presentism*, *individualism*, and *conservatism* without the benefit of critical theoretical perspectives. Indeed, teachers' professional identities are deeply embedded in a rejection of theory and an attachment to (false) constructs of neutrality (Hargreaves, 1984). For students themselves, Lortie's notion of an *apprenticeship of observation*—the over 10,000 hours of classroom experience nearly all students bring to teacher preparation—already positions teacher candidates to claim a strong sense of certainty regarding the realities of classroom teaching. It is this *apprenticeship of observation* that students bring into their teacher education programs and that so powerfully communicates, and often mis-educates, about teaching and learning.

Elementary teacher education programs are especially at the epicenter of a teacher identity formation process deeply steeped in White-ness, middle-class-ness, female-ness, and heteronormativity. These privileged positionalities operate to normalize the family contexts and educational experiences of most teacher candidates. Whether teaching in their home-like (middle-class) communities, where the familiar will comfortably define and bound encounters with their students, or in communities of poverty, the normalizing dynamic and the privileged positionalities of many elementary teacher education candidates are at play. They portend careers reproductive of dominant structures, cultures, and ideologies. The economic and racial privilege that advantages many teacher education students is misinterpreted by them as the deserved rewards reasonably accrued in a system based on *meritocracy* (Saltman, 2014).

Lortie's insights into the ethos of the teaching profession offer teacher educators insights into the false consciousness that many teacher candidates carry with them into the college of education. *Presentism*, *conservatism*, and *individualism*, and their connections to students' long *apprenticeship of observation* provide a starting place for a curriculum of critical teacher education. This curriculum can position teacher candidates to reflexively deconstruct their own experiences and position them to critically consume the curriculum of proceduralism and instrumentality increasingly imposed on colleges of education and, of course, schools themselves.

References

Acland, H. (1976, Spring). Book reviews. *American Educational Research Journal, 13*(20), 139–153.

Apple, M. (2001). *Educating the "right" way: Markets, standards, God, and inequality.* New York: RoutledgeFalmer.

Cheney, L. (1995). *Telling the truth: Why our culture and our country have stopped making sense and what we can do about it.* New York: Simon & Schuster.

Geertz, C. (1973). *The interpretation of cultures.* New York: Basic Books.

Giroux, H., & Penna, A. (1979). Social education in the classroom: The dynamics of the hidden curriculum. *Theory and Research in Social Education, 7*(1), 21–42.

Hargreaves, A. (1984). Experience counts, theory doesn't: How teachers talk about their work. *Sociology of Education, 57,* 44–54.

Hargreaves, A. (2009). Presentism, individualism and conservatism: The legacy of Dan Lortie's schoolteacher: A sociological study. *Curriculum Inquiry, 40*(1), 143–154.

Huntington, S., et al. (1975). *The crisis of democracy.* New York: New York University Press.

Hursh, D. (2001). Social studies with the neo-liberal state: The commodification of knowledge and the end of imagination. *Theory and Research in Social Education, 29*(2), 349–356.

Jackson, P.W. (1968). *Life in classrooms.* New York: Holt, Rinehart and Winston.

Kaye, H. (1991). *Powers of the past: Reflections on the crisis and the promise of history.* Minneapolis: University of Minnesota Press.

Larson, R. (1976). Review of *Schoolteacher: A sociological study. Teachers College Record, 77*(4), 642–645.

Lortie, D. (1975). *Schoolteacher: A sociological study.* Chicago: University of Chicago Press.

McLaren, P. (1986). *Schooling as ritual performance.* New York: Routledge & Kegan Paul.

McNeil, L. (1986). *Contradictions of control: School structure and school knowledge.* New York: Routledge & Kegan Paul.

Neufeld, J. (2009). *Redefining teacher development.* London: Routledge.

Pederson, G., & Fleming, T. (1979). Review of *Schoolteacher: A sociological study,* by Dan C. Lortie. *Canadian Journal of Education, 4*(4), 103–110. Retrieved from http://www.jstor.org/stable/1494755

Ross, E.W. (2000). Redrawing the lines: The case against traditional social studies instruction. In D.W. Hursh & E.W. Ross (Eds.), *Democratic social education: Social studies for social change* (pp. 43–63). New York: RoutledgeFalmer.

Saltman, K. (2014). *The politics of education: A critical introduction.* Boulder, CO: Paradigm.

Schlesinger, A. (1992). *The disuniting of America.* New York: Norton.

Waller, W. (1932). *The sociology of teaching.* New York: Wiley.

Willis, P. (1977). *Learning to labor.* New York: Columbia University Press.

Ten

Samuel Bowles and Herbert Gintis, *Schooling in Capitalist America: Educational Reform and the Contradictions of Economic Life* (1976)[1]

James M. Giarelli

Introduction

Schooling in Capitalist America grows out of a long tradition of classical and contemporary educational thought that focuses on the relationship between educational institutions and social justice. The first portion of this chapter presents a brief summary of some of this tradition, since it is an essential context for understanding the origins and importance of *Schooling in Capitalist America*. The second part of the chapter provides a very brief synopsis of the book's argument and theoretical stance. The chapter concludes with a reference to some of the critical literature and Bowles and Gintis's reflections on their own work.

History and Context

In Plato's treatment of education and justice in *The Republic*,[2] Socrates and his colleagues devote the first several dialogues to a detailed plan for preparing different social groups for their separate—but complementary—roles in Athenian society through distinctively different educational experiences and curricula. This same concern with the relationship between education and social justice, albeit from very different perspectives, occurs within the American experience. Thomas Jefferson argued that the creation of a system of public education for the common people was the best defense against the tyranny of dynastic elites. Horace Mann argued that common schools could be a force for both social mobility and social stability and serve as the "balance wheel of the social machinery." W.E.B. Du Bois, in *The Souls of Black Folk*,[3] argued that the problem of the twentieth century and the "two worlds" created by the "color line" raised "the central problem of training men for life."

As a fully developed school system flourished in the early years of the twentieth century in the context of the rise of industrialism, metropolitan culture, and capitalist economic and social relationships, these questions about the relationship between educational institutions and social justice increasingly focused on issues of social class differences grounded in economic status and power. John Dewey, the foremost educational theorist of the first half of the twentieth century, was well aware of the miseducative and undemocratic consequences of schools and a social order segregated by social-class divisions. As Dewey wrote, "the objective precondition for the complete and free use of the method of intelligence is a society in which class interests that recoil from social experimentation are abolished."[4]

These philosophical views were given sociological support by Dewey's colleague George S. Counts in a series of studies of American schools and social inequality. In *The Selective Character of American Secondary Education* (1922), *The Social Composition of Boards of Education* (1927), and *School and Society in Chicago* (1928), Counts convincingly demonstrated the domination of the Chicago school system by economic and corporate elites and the failure of public schools to counter the perpetuation of social and economic inequalities.[5] These works set the stage for Counts's *Dare the School Build a New Social Order?*, first delivered as speeches to the Progressive Education Association in 1932.[6] In these speeches, Counts specifically and directly locates the source for the worldwide depression of the 1930s and the

> extreme material insecurity; dire poverty…privation, misery, and even starvation…severe physical suffering; breakfastless children…an exhaustion of hope in the ranks of the damned… to a system which exploits pitilessly and without thought of the morrow the natural and human resources of the nation and of the world.[7]

For Counts, progressive education and organized teachers must consciously and intentionally use their educational and social positions to promote a new social order in which "all… resources must be dedicated to the promotion of the great masses of the people."[8] As Counts writes,

> with the present concentration of economic power in the hands of a small class…the survival…of a society that could in any sense be called democratic is unthinkable. America is the scene of an irreconcilable conflict between two opposing forces. On the one hand is the democratic tradition…, [and] on the other is a system of economic arrangements that increasingly partakes of the nature of industrial feudalism. Both of these forces cannot survive…. Unless the democratic tradition is able to organize and conduct a successful attack on the economic system, its complete destruction is inevitable.[9]

Schooling in Capitalist America is deeply informed by and sympathetic to this tradition that directly links educational practices and policies to the creation and extension of political, social, and economic equality. However, despite Counts's jeremiad, by the 1960s and 1970s the dismally disappointing evidence of the failure of schooling to mitigate social inequality necessitated a radically different theoretical approach to the problem of education and social justice. Bowles and Gintis look closely at two "strands" of modern educational literature linking schooling to social justice, what they call the idea of "education as panacea."[10]

Bowles and Gintis call the first the "democratic school," associated most closely with the philosopher John Dewey.[11] In *Democracy and Education*,[12] Dewey argued that schools must (1) integrate youth into the various roles of adult life (the integrative function), (2) mitigate extremes of wealth and poverty by expanding equality of opportunity (the egalitarian function), and (3) promote human potential (the developmental function). For Bowles and Gintis, while "Dewey's overall framework seems eminently correct,"[13] his error was in failing to recognize that under capitalism, social systems are autocratic, not democratic, and work and personal development are alienated and coerced, not intrinsically motivated and fulfilling. Thus, the hopes of progressive educators such as Dewey and Counts for an educational system in which schools would lead toward a just and democratic social order never had a chance in a capitalist society. As Bowles and Gintis write, "the failure of progressive educational reform stems from the contradictory nature of the objectives of its integrative, egalitarian, and developmental functions in a society whose economic life is governed by the institutions of corporate capitalism."[14]

Bowles and Gintis call the second "education as panacea" view the "techno-meritocratic school" or the "standard view."[15] From this perspective, the relationship between schooling, social mobility, and economic success is based on the following logic:

(1) People are hired and promoted on the basis of how well and how much they produce.
(2) The quality and quantity of production are a function of the level of skills one has (i.e., technical-cognitive competence).
(3) Technical-cognitive competence is acquired through education.
(4) Everyone has an equal opportunity for formal education and thus to acquire technical-cognitive competence.
(5) Thus, schools play a major role in determining future social and economic success by transmitting technical-cognitive competencies that are then bought and sold in an open free market.

This standard view of a meritocracy, with schools providing an equal opportunity to acquire competencies required for social mobility and economic success, was the foundation for most of the 1960s and 1970s school reforms efforts. For example, many of the "Great Society" programs focused on (4) the assumption that social inequality was a result of unequal educational opportunity. Another set of educational reform strategies focused on (3) the assumption that lower-class, working-class, and minority students were "disadvantaged" from the start by their "negative" or "culture-of-poverty" home environments. Thus, these programs, such as Head Start and other compensatory education efforts, focused on interventions before the onset of formal education to equalize competencies and allow for "fair competition."

As the data on these efforts were analyzed, it became clear that the programs grounded in the techno-meritocratic model were not working. The Coleman Report[16] data showed that school success was still powerfully associated with family socioeconomic status and position in class structure, that compensatory and Head Start gains were lost quickly once children were in school, and that economic inequality persisted and in fact increased, despite apparent successes in equalizing educational opportunity. In a re-working of much of this data in *Inequality: A Reassessment of the Effect of Family and Schooling in America*,[17] Christopher Jencks and his colleagues, including Herbert Gintis, concluded that schooling played a relatively insignificant role in redistributing income and improving future economic success. Their findings showed that improving what goes on inside schools (e.g., better teachers, better facilities) had little effect on school and social outcomes. The largest effect on these outcomes was associated with "non-measurable" variables such as norms, attitudes, beliefs, and cognitive style, but these were not part of the empirical analysis. On the very last page of the book, after a tedious summary of the inexplicability of all the data, Jencks concludes:

> As long as egalitarians assume that public policy cannot contribute to economic equality directly but must proceed by ingenious manipulation of marginal institutions like the schools, progress will remain glacial. If we want to move beyond this tradition, we will have to establish political control over the economic institutions that shape our society. This is what other countries call socialism. Anything less will end in the same disappointment as the reform of the 1960s.[18]

Finally, in *Who Gets Ahead?: The Determinants of Economic Success in America*,[19] Jencks and his fellow researchers confirm and extend their earlier findings that the variables associated with economic success are completely divorced from the standard view that schools are the primary agency for social mobility, economic success, and the amelioration of inequality.

Schooling in Capitalist America must be understood within this history. Indeed, in the first several chapters, Bowles and Gintis provide a fair-minded account of this context to explain their turn to a fundamentally different theoretical lens drawn from the Marxist tradition. The logic is simple. If there is a perennial assumption that education plays a central role in creating and extending the conditions for social justice, and if there are two perspectives that offer an account of how this occurs, and if it does not occur and neither perspective can explain this failure, then a fundamentally new perspective is needed. *Schooling in Capitalist America* arises not out of some ideological interest in partisan politics, but rather primarily as an intellectual response to the utter failure of mainstream views to provide a rigorous theoretical foundation for understanding the complicated relationships of social and economic life or a practical foundation for productive political, pedagogical, and policy initiatives.

The next section will briefly summarize the main elements of Bowles and Gintis's alternative theoretical and practical foundations.

The Root of the Problem

The theoretical core of *Schooling in Capitalist America* is Part II, "Education and the Structure of Economic Life," including Chapter 3, "At the Root of the Problem: The Capitalist Economy," by far the longest chapter in the book. An all-too-brief synopsis of Marxism and of Bowles and Gintis's Marxist analysis of education are all that is possible here.[20]

The motivating force in a capitalist economy is the employer's quest for profits. Paying less to workers in wages than what the goods they produce can be sold for results in profit. The difference between wages and value of goods is surplus value or profits. The production of profit requires that workers have nothing to sell except their labor. Thus, capitalism requires the separation of two distinct and antagonistic classes defined by their relationship to the means of production: those who own or control the means of production and those who work or labor. One class tries to maximize wages; the other tries to maximize profit. However, this is not merely a technical or economic process, but—more important—a social process. Workers are not simply trying to produce goods and make wages, but also trying to satisfy personal and social needs. Employers are attempting to convince workers that their social and personal interests are identical to the production of surplus value for the owner's expropriation. Schooling in capitalist society plays a dual role in this social process by (1) providing workers with skills and motivation to increase their productive capacity, and (2) perpetuating inequality by defusing class antagonisms arising from the inequality of the social process. Thus, schooling in capitalist society does not add or subtract from overall inequality and repressive personal development. Instead, capitalist schooling is best understood as an institution and social process that perpetuates and produces the social relationships required to sustain capitalist economic life by legitimating inequality through the ideological myth of a meritocracy, creating and reinforcing patterns of social conflict between workers to defuse dissent, fostering personality types compatible with relationships of domination and subordination in the economic sphere, and creating a surplus of skilled labor to drive down wages and discipline the workforce. Schooling does not do this directly through the conscious intent of school administrators and teachers, but rather through a close correspondence between the social interactions that govern interactions in the workplace and the social relationships of the educational system. School social relations replicate workplace relations, and motivational systems of schools mirror the role of wages and fear of unemployment in the economic sphere. This "correspondence principle" is at the heart of Bowles and Gintis's understanding of Marxism and schooling. Schools, in their curricula, norms, forms of relationships, assessment procedures, and motivational structures, reproduce the social relations of a capitalist economic system not by conscious intent, but rather by structural determination. Nonetheless, while school serves the interests of profit and elite political stability, the consequences of schooling create a contested terrain. The same education that produces skilled workers to increase profits is often ill suited for the perpetuation of institutions whose sole purpose is the exploitation of labor. An education—even an education under capitalism—is a potential threat to the status quo. Thus, for Bowles and Gintis, educational change is best understood as a response to the changes in the capitalist economy and the cracks and spaces in the deterministic structure opened by uneven development in the capitalist economy, the shift from industrial to corporate capitalism, and the transition to a global market system. As Bowles and Gintis argue, while the central role of capitalist schools is to preserve the capitalist social order, there is often a lag between the incessant change within the economic system and the inertia and resistance to change within the educational system that is designed to reproduce it. Thus, the principle of correspondence is never static, and the structures of determination are never totalizing.

For Bowles and Gintis, genuine attempts at educational change cannot simply repeat the failed slogans and programs of the past. The schools by themselves cannot build a new social order, create authentic democracy, or become leaders for social justice. However, the possibilities created by the contradictions within the capitalist economy do open up opportunities for radical educational and social programs and change. As Bowles and Gintis write, such a program of educational reform

> would have as its overriding objective the ultimate dismantling of the capitalist system and its replacement by a more progressive social order…. The unifying theme of a program of revolutionary reforms is that short-run successes yield concrete gains for those participating in the struggle and, at the same time, strengthen the movement for further change…. [I]f these alternatives are to contribute to a better social order, they must be part of a more general

revolutionary movement—a movement which is not confined to schooling, but embraces all spheres of life.[21]

For Bowles and Gintis, the most significant role of the school would be *after* an economic revolution as the institution charged with a democratic re-education of substantive social relations. That is, the school will play the same role, but for the different purpose of legitimizing and reproducing social relations of equality. The post-revolutionary school will teach the norms, foster the personality characteristics, and develop pedagogies that correspond and are conducive to the maintenance and extension of a socialist economic sphere and democratic social arrangements. The final section of *Schooling in Capitalist America* considers some of the "educational alternatives" that might play a role in the larger struggle for revolutionary social change.

Alternatives and Criticisms

There is extensive critical literature and commentary on *Schooling in Capitalist America*. Many problems may arise if it is read as a work in educational theory. Bowles and Gintis's inclusion and consideration of educational alternatives such as open enrollment in higher education, free schools, de-schooling, and local control initiatives is hardly revolutionary. More substantively, J.J. Chambliss has argued convincingly that Bowles and Gintis fundamentally confuse Dewey's discussion of a democratic ideal with his more persistent critical views on existing institutions.[22] Dewey offers a democratic ideal as a starting point for experimentation with concrete educational change. Bowles and Gintis's discussion of educational alternatives does the same thing. They offer socialism as an ideal and then consider programs and ideas as hypothetical experiments that might advance a larger program of revolutionary change. Indeed, it turns out that their program of revolutionary education is thoroughly Deweyan in its emphasis on problem-centered curricula, dialectical models of development, and close interactions between the schools and other forms of active community life.

In 1977 an entire issue of *History of Education Quarterly* was devoted to a symposium on *Schooling in Capitalist America*. The contributors raised a variety of criticisms directed at Bowles and Gintis's reliance on "functional" analysis, their failure to maintain a consistent Marxist mode of analysis, their over-reliance on the "orthodox" Marxist principle of correspondence between economic "base" structures and culture "superstructure" institutions, and their misreading of the history of American education, among others.[23] Of course, there has been extensive debate about the empirical basis of their work in light of the research literature developed over the last almost 40 years.

In brief—and typical of specialized academic debate—Bowles and Gintis have been criticized for misinterpretations in their readings of philosophy of education, inaccuracies in their analyses of the history of American education, their failure to be consistently Marxist, their failure in being too consistently Marxist, their reliance on sociological models, and their failure for not basing their work sufficiently in social science models. All of these specialized criticisms have been addressed and explored in the research and scholarly literature since the publication of *Schooling in Capitalist America*.

Perhaps more important for the purpose of this chapter are the authors' own thoughts on *Schooling in Capitalist America*. In 2002 Bowles and Gintis published a detailed summary of the main findings of more contemporary research studies on education and inequality and their relationship to their original work in *Schooling in Capitalist America*.[24] While they report that much of their empirical work has been supported by more recent research, this article summarizes the main change in their thinking since 1976. As they write:

> We took it as obvious that a system of democratically run and employee-owned enterprises coordinated by both markets and governmental policies was both politically and economically viable as an alternative to capitalism. We remain convinced of the attractiveness of such a system, but we are less sanguine about its feasibility, and more convinced that reforms of capitalism may be the most likely way to pursue the objectives we embraced at the outset.[25]

Thus, some 35 years after the publication of *Schooling in Capitalist America*, and while satisfied with the evidence for and cogency of Bowles and Gintis's basic argument, it is important to note the shift from the 1976 view that the entire capitalist system had to be replaced by revolutionary change to the 2002 view that a reform of capitalism might be the most likely way to accomplish their objectives for social justice.

Conclusion

This is not a criticism of Bowles and Gintis. It is essential that the exchange of ideas over time include a critical examination of deeply held beliefs. However, one thing is certain. Social and economic inequalities are increasing at a dramatic rate, and there is no evidence that schooling is a significant factor in countering this inequality.[26] The fundamental classical and contemporary inquiry about the relationship between educational institutions and social justice is not only still current, but more urgent than ever. *Schooling in Capitalist America* stands as a pivotal text in this tradition of thought and research and is surely a modern educational classic.

Notes

1   Samuel Bowles and Herbert Gintis, *Schooling in Capitalist America: Educational Reform and the Contradictions of Economic Life* (New York: Basic Books, 1976). All page citations are to this text.
2   *The Republic of Plato*, trans. Allan Bloom, 2nd ed. (New York: Basic Books, 1991).
3   W.E.B. Du Bois, *The Souls of Black Folk* (1903; repr. New York: W.W. Norton and Company, 1999).
4   John Dewey, "The Underlying Philosophy of Education," in *John Dewey: The Later Works 1925–1953*, ed. Jo Ann Boydston, (Carbondale: Southern Illinois University Press, 1986), 8:101.
5   George S. Counts, *The Selective Character of American Secondary Education* (Chicago: University of Chicago Press, 1922); *The Social Composition of Boards of Education* (Chicago: University of Chicago Press, 1927); *School and Society in Chicago* (New York: Harcourt Brace, 1928).
6   George S. Counts, *Dare the Schools Build a New Social Order?* (Carbondale: Southern Illinois University Press, 1932.
7   Counts, *The Selective Character of American Secondary Education*, 30–31.
8   Counts, *The Selective Character of American Secondary Education*, 40.
9   Counts, *The Selective Character of American Secondary Education*, 41.
10 Bowles and Gintis, *Schooling in Capitalist America*, 20.
11 Bowles and Gintis, *Schooling in Capitalist America*, 21.
12 John Dewey, *Democracy and Education* (1916; repr. New York: Free Press Reprint, 1997).
13 Bowles and Gintis, *Schooling in Capitalist America*, 46.
14 Bowles and Gintis, *Schooling in Capitalist America*, 45.
15 Bowles and Gintis, *Schooling in Capitalist America*, 20.
16 Coleman, James S., *Equality of Educational Opportunity* (Ann Arbor, MI: Inter-university Consortium for Political and Social Research, 1966). Available at http://doi.org/10.3886/ICPSR06389.v3
17 Christopher Jencks et al., *Inequality: A Reassessment of Effect of Family and Schooling in America* (New York: Basic Books, 1972).
18 Jencks et al., *Inequality*, 265.

19 Christopher Jencks et al., *Who Gets Ahead?: The Determinants of Economic Success in America* (New York: Basic Books, 1979).

20 An excellent primer on Marxism and reading Marx is "Reading Marx's Capital with David Harvey," available at http://david-harvey.org/reading-capital/

21 Bowles and Gintis, *Schooling in Capitalist America*, 246.

22 J.J. Chambliss, "How to Read John Dewey," *The Gadfly* 1 (May 1978): 16–20.

23 See, in *History of Education Quarterly*, 17, no. 3 (1977): David K. Cohen and Bella H. Rosenberg, "Functions and Fantasies: Understanding Schools in Capitalist America," 113–137; "Commentaries" by Joseph Featherstone, 139–149; David Hogan, 149–153; and Mark Stern, 154–158; and "Replies" by Herbert Gintis, 159–164.

24 Samuel Bowles and Herbert Gintis, "Schooling in Capitalist America Revisited," *Sociology of Education* 75, no. 1 (2002): 1–18.

25 Bowles and Gintis, "Schooling in Capitalist America Revisited," 15.

26 For example, see Emmanuel Saez and Gabriel Zucman, "Exploding Wealth Inequality in the United States," Washington Center for Equitable Growth. Posted October 20, 2014. Available at http://equitablegrowth.org/research/exploding-wealth-inequality-united-states/

Eleven

Michael W. Apple, *Ideology and Curriculum* (1979)

Steven P. Camicia and Barry M. Franklin

Introduction

Michael Apple graduated from Teachers College, Columbia University, and worked with Dwayne Huebner and a number of major curriculum scholars who, during the first half of the twentieth century, established Teacher's College's Department of Curriculum and Teaching as a major center of research in that area. Apple developed his initial approach to curriculum by considering the role that the sociology of knowledge plays in our understanding of curriculum and schools. At the time he launched his scholarship, curriculum was undergoing a transition from a positivistic and "politically neutral" form of schooling that was primarily focused on the most effective ways of explaining human development, charting human progress, and reforming schools and society, to an arena that was directed toward overtly political ends. One way to frame Apple's contribution to educational scholarship is in the way he directed his scholarship to advance a social agenda designed to promote equity.

The Context

Ideology and Curriculum (Apple, 1979) was instrumental in making complex neo-Marxist concepts accessible to an audience unfamiliar with these concepts and their relationship to education. Apple combines lenses of social reproduction, selective tradition, hegemony, ideology, and curriculum to examine the role of schools in perpetuating social inequalities. He was influenced by the critical theorists Jürgen Habermas and Alvin Gouldner, as well as by scholars from Britain such as Michael

F.D. Young, Basil Bernstein, Geoff Whitty, and others (Gottesman, 2012). The influence of the "new sociology of education" on the work of Apple and others is detailed in an edited collection of essays entitled *Ideology, Curriculum, and the New Sociology of Education* (Weis, McCarthy, & Dimitriadis, 2006b). We will examine this volume in more detail toward the end of this chapter when we discuss the relevance of *Ideology and Curriculum* for today.

The first edition of *Ideology and Curriculum* provided for many their first encounter with the notion that curriculum is never a neutral expression of knowledge. This type of first encounter was especially true at the time of the book's publication, when the field of curriculum studies was relatively uncritical of dominant understandings of knowledge. Rather than questioning the nature of the knowledge taught in schools, dominant curriculum scholars were preoccupied with how best to teach and learn such knowledge. In this regard, the book's turn toward the sociology of knowledge was groundbreaking in its ability to open new conversations regarding schooling and society.

The Book

Apple (1979) observes that school knowledge is not "neutral," as was either assumed or left unexamined by much of the prior work in the curriculum field. Because schools have limited time and resources, certain choices must be made about what knowledge is taught and what procedures are followed. For example, in the subject of history, there is a limited amount of time within the curriculum, and certain narratives will be taught while others are not. The chances are great that narratives of dominant social groups will be taught more often than narratives of marginalized groups. As another example, is the school day organized in a way similar to that of the floor of a factory or a corporate headquarters? Some examples of such questions illustrate overarching questions posed in the book. Related to overt curriculum, "Whose vision of economic, racial, and sexual reality, whose principles of economic reality, whose principles of social justice are embedded in the content of schools?" (p. 157). In terms of the hidden curriculum, how do "the basic day to day regularities of schools contribute to students' learning" ideologies that favor the interest of dominant social groups? (p. 14).

In his introductory chapter, Apple (1979) writes: "The knowledge that now gets into school is already a choice from a much larger universe of possible social knowledge and principles…. [I]t is repeatedly filtered through ideological and economic commitments" (p. 8). Rather than neutral endeavors, curriculum development and implementation are a reflection both of society and society's inequitable power relations. Apple continues: "Social and economic values, hence, are already embedded in the design of the institutions we work in, in the 'formal corpus of school knowledge' we preserve in our curricula, in our modes of teaching, and in our principles, standards, and forms of evaluation" (pp. 8–9). *Ideology and Curriculum* provides a powerful discourse to readers who are unfamiliar with the ways in which inequitable power relations within society structure *what* and *how* knowledge is taught in schools. Because the knowledge of dominant social groups is seen as more legitimate than the knowledge of marginalized social groups, schools reproduce social capital by selecting a form of knowledge that favors dominant groups.

By applying Antonio Gramsci's concept of hegemony to education, Apple (1979) is able to illustrate the total, ubiquitous, and invisible influence of hegemony in schools and society. Apple writes that hegemony "refers to an organized assemblage of meanings and practices, the central effective and dominant system of meanings, values and actions which are *lived*" (p. 5; emphasis in original). As such an all-encompassing phenomenon, hegemony is not confined to a world of abstract meanings and symbols; rather it is embedded in social relationships and actions. Because of this totalizing quality of hegemony, it is almost inconceivable to think or act outside of its sphere. This privileges dominant thoughts, relationships, and actions as "commonsense" and "neutral." Other ways of thinking, relating, and acting are seen as irregular— even dangerous. Apple writes: "Ideological and social stability rests in part on the internalization at the very bottom of our brains, of the principles and commonsense rules which govern the existing social order" (p. 43). In other words, it is "common sense" to think, relate, and act in certain ways. To step outside of these structures renders a person, or his or her perspective, unrecognizable.

The ways in which people construct reality are set within certain opportunities and constraints that perpetuate dominant social and cultural meanings in the curriculum. In *Ideology and Curriculum*, Apple (1979) extends the concept of hegemony to better understand how social reproduction operates. Hegemony makes it possible to examine the mechanisms by which social, cultural, and economic reproduction operate in schools. A seemingly neutral apparatus that favors certain ways of understanding and relating within the world reproduces inequalities. Citing such theorists as Samuel Bowles, Herbert Gintis, Pierre Bourdieu, and Michael Young, Apple illustrates how schools reproduce an inequitable distribution of power within society. He writes: "For Bourdieu, to understand completely what schools do, who succeeds and who fails, one must not see culture as neutral…rather one sees the culture tacitly preserved in and expected by schools as contributing to inequality outside of these institutions" (p. 33). This is partially accomplished through the curriculum by portraying social inequalities as non-controversial and inevitable.

In Chapter 3 of *Ideology and Curriculum* (Apple, 1979), written with Nancy King, examples from a kindergarten classroom provide illustrations of the types of claims that Apple makes throughout the book. Schools function as instruments of social control, a viewpoint described by Apple and Franklin in more detail in Chapter 4. As Apple points out, viewing schools as instruments of social control is not a new observation. Neither is the reality that schools that function this way are confined to conservative, humanist, or liberal orientations. Historically, conservative-oriented stakeholders in education have used the social control function of schools to explicitly construct and maintain social and economic hierarchies.

The case of a kindergarten class highlights the encounter that most students have when they transition from family to work. In Apple (1979) and King's example, kindergarten students enter the classroom in September with a stronger concept of play than work. By October the concept of work is more prevalent in student responses during interviews. In addition, students begin to internalize procedures, rules, and norms (and the concept of abnormality). Apple and King are careful to point out that this is not because the students are in a bad school or have a bad teacher. In fact, the school and teacher in question are highly regarded. The main purpose of the example is to show how schools function as instruments of social control that are largely hidden. They exist in instruments such as schedules and routines. However, as illustrated in the remainder of the book, both the explicit and hidden curricula of the schools are embedded in a larger societal structure of social, cultural, and economic relations.

The cultural capital that stratifies society at large is reproduced in classrooms. Another way to say this is that schools and society have a dialectical relationship. This is accomplished through everything from the type of knowledge that is valued to the procedures and norms that are at the level of "common sense" in a classroom. As such, schools should be examined as things to be improved, in that they point to a society that needs to ameliorate inequitable power relations. If schools are a reflection of social relations, then changing the social relations within society would change the social relations reproduced in schools. In this respect, the lens that Apple (1979) places on schools highlights a change in conversation outside of schools rather than focusing all of our efforts on school reform.

Apple (1979) wrote Chapter Four of *Ideology and Curriculum* with Barry Franklin. The two authors describe the early foundations of the field of curriculum, starting from the late nineteenth century. Early curriculum theorists explain the roots of a conservative movement that saw schools as mechanisms for maintaining social control. Conformity to a notion of the proper functioning of society was at the heart of the movement. The history of the curriculum field illustrates how dominant economic and cultural groups remain illusively hidden in both curriculum and the assumptions that foster its creation.

Conceptions of community are central to how early curriculum theorists constructed curriculum. At the time of transition from an agrarian to an industrial society, these theorists feared urban centers as chaotic places populated by immigrants and people of color that needed to be assimilated into dominant White, middle-class culture. The initial conception of the type of community that theorists sought to construct was modeled on small-town community. They believed that the imposition of small-town "values" and "beliefs" on all levels of community would preserve dominant notions of the "best" community. This was also a reaction to theorists' fears that corporations would dictate values and beliefs that were contrary to those of the middle class.

Curriculum theorists later moved toward scientific and efficiency-based models that used intelligence and a differentiated curriculum as a way to construct an ideal community. This functioned to create a curriculum that maintained a dominant managerial class that was educated to understand society as a whole, as well as a working class that would be trained toward specific functions in the job market. Apple (1979) and Franklin write that the formative members of the curriculum field "undoubtedly felt secure in their belief that a 'real' community could be built through education, one with 'natural' leaders and 'natural' followers, and one in which people like 'us' could define what 'they' should be like" (p. 78). This observation serves as a background for the ways in which classrooms, such as the kindergarten classroom examined in Chapter 3, mirror the interests of dominant economic and cultural groups. This also explains the hegemonic role of the intellectual in keeping economic and cultural capital within the hands of the dominant class and culture.

In Chapter 5, Apple (1979) examines the ways that consensus and avoidance of conflict function in the curriculum to maintain hegemony. As mentioned in other chapters, the influence of the ideological structures within the curriculum remains relatively hidden. The knowledge and procedures contained in the curriculum are selective, but endure at the level of "common sense" and remain unexamined by educators or students. Apple focuses this inquiry upon the disciplines of science and social studies. Both function in similar ways to present knowledge as apolitical and decontextualized. Rather than examine the controversies and political interests that position dominant scientific theories to be seen as "legitimate," the curriculum encourages students to be uncritical of scientific knowledge. Similarly, the social studies curriculum emphasizes rules and consensus rather than conflict. The combination of consensus, selective tradition, and hidden curriculum serves to perpetuate the function of schools as maintaining social inequality while appearing to be democratic.

In contrast, curriculum that includes an examination of conflict and the selective tradition has the potential to disrupt the mechanisms of hegemony that portray the public school curriculum as "common sense" or "neutral." For example, by including an analysis of the benefits of social movements and revolutions, the curriculum could provide space for understanding how knowledge and society change in relation to the kinds of choices that communities have. An examination of the ways in which marginalized groups have been excluded by dominant groups from the selective tradition provides an important insight into the political nature of knowledge and schools. Knowledge is constructed and maintained by dominant groups through systemic oppressions such as racism, sexism, homophobia, transphobia, classism, ablism, and nationalism. A curriculum that examines these oppressions and privileges the perspectives of marginalized groups could show that legal and economic rights movements are an integral part of any movement toward social justice. Apple (1979) writes: "The fact that laws *had* to be broken and were then struck down by the courts later is not usually focused upon in social studies curricula. Yet, it was through these types of activities that a good deal of progress was and is made" (p. 100; emphasis in original). Without such a curriculum, schools function to legitimate an unjust social order.

In Chapter 6, Apple (1979) returns to his discussion of hegemony by exploring the use of systems analysis as a management technique in schools. The logic of systems analysis emphasizes consensus and legitimacy while deemphasizing the political and value-laden context of schooling. An overemphasis on consensus, as Apple details in Chapter 5, functions to push marginalized people and perspectives out of conversations. This process is rooted in the very language of consensus, where the assumption of consensus predetermines the outcome of a conversation. Systems analysis intensifies a system of hegemony by locating goals and assessments as predetermined. Through hegemony, the selective tradition, and ideology, these predetermined goals are necessarily a reflection of the social injustices found in society at large. Apple writes: "Systems approaches attempt to bring about a technical solution to political and value problems" (p. 119). An appeal to science also gains much traction in a society where science and technology are highly valued instruments of societal improvement.

Unfortunately, an emphasis on measurement, standardization, and order often obscures an understanding of the complex environments of schools. One of the first steps toward understanding these environments and addressing social inequalities is to understand the history and ideology that established systems management as a manifestation of hegemony. That kind of thought and practice originated with industries and corporations' attempts to increase and perpetuate the economic and cultural capital of dominant groups. The system appears on the surface as value-free, technical, and neutral; however, the ideology that supports the system is built on assumptions that are in the interest of dominant groups. In order to truly shift the conversation about education toward one of social justice, educators, curriculum developers, administrators, students, and community members must be able to see the system as political and value-laden. This requires a political stance and a moral commitment to change—one that a conflict-free system built upon consensus nullifies.

Chapter 7 turns to the processes of categorizing and labeling as forms of hegemony in schools. While the stated goals of these processes and outcomes might be ameliorative, therapeutic, or moral, they share the attribute of consensus with other forms of social control. Apple

(1979) points to critical theory as a way to understand how to increase critical consciousness of the ways that the language of categorizing and labeling functions to perpetuate economic and cultural reproduction. Although categories and labels are legitimized under systems management and technical ideologies as "neutral" and "taken for granted," these categories and labels are social constructs that emanate from institutions.

The effect of this "neutral" stance is to decontextualize individuals and institutions and, as a result, shift culpability for social inequalities from the institution to abstract individuals. Apple (1979) writes: "Usually the 'deviant' label has an *essentializing* quality in that a person's (here, a student's) entire relationship to an institution is conditioned by the category applied to him. He or she *is* this and only this" (p. 135; emphasis in original). For example, by labeling a student "deficient," institutions reduce their culpability regarding the social injustices that marginalize students. Rather than looking at the institution or inequitable economic and cultural relations, the individual student is abstract, decontextualized, and in need of repair. Students of low socioeconomic status and students of color are labeled in these ways to a much larger degree than other students. Rather than placing culpability on institutions and society, the labels function to place it on the students themselves. The injustice of these labels only intensifies as students who are assigned pejorative labels enter other spheres (e.g., work), because the stratification that these labels impose follows students outside of the schools. Once understood in this light, it is difficult to maintain the stance that the explicit and hidden curriculum of schools is "neutral." Instead, schools function as ideological and hegemonic mechanisms that ossify economic and cultural reproduction.

Educators, psychologists, school administrators, curriculum developers, and educational researchers rely on this system of classification and labeling for their stake in the managerial system. Apple (1979) writes: "The 'professional helpers' who employ the supposedly diagnostic and therapeutic terminologies *must* find (and hence create) individuals who fit the categories, otherwise the expertise is useless" (p. 145; emphasis in original). The intentions of these experts might be therapeutic or moral, but the results of their intentions, categorizations, and interventions serve to mirror the social inequalities found in society at large. The effects of the ideological underpinnings of this system in stratifying knowledge are illustrated in the ways that schools sort students into categories with access to different types of school knowledge.

In his final chapter, Apple (1979) suggests ways to build coalitions that better understand the relationships between power and knowledge, with the goal of acting upon that understanding. Apple writes: "Throughout this volume my point has been that such inquiry provides one area through which we can examine the cultural and economic reproduction of class relations in unequal societies" (p. 156). This involves examining the dialectical relationships that schools have with the larger society in order to create new possibilities for social justice.

Referring to Habermas's notion of knowledge and human interest, Apple notes that there is a connection between the types of knowledge generated and the needs and interests of those generating it. If the purpose is to control and bureaucratize, technical knowledge is generated. If the purpose is to address social injustices within society, emancipatory knowledge is generated. This latter goal promotes research methodologies of advocacy such as those based on critical theory. These methodologies challenge "models that serve as excuses to change the individual child rather than the social and intellectual structure of the school to make it more responsive and responsible" (p. 164). Rather than viewing students as deficient, emancipatory methodologies view society and institutions as systemically deficient and unjust.

Finally, this project involves constant reflection upon actions and the ways in which actions, even within the critical paradigms, might lead to unintentional consequences (e.g., their role in a hegemonic system). Because hegemony is all-encompassing, the critical paradigms are embedded within hegemonic systems and subject to the same effects of these systems as other paradigms. This and related concerns, however, should not inhibit action aimed at increasing social justice. Rather, we should develop projects that are always mindful of the inequalities of hegemony and our relationships to it and others in our society.

Critiques of the Concepts and Book

The critics of the concepts presented in *Ideology and Curriculum* cover a range of worldviews. (We use the term "worldviews" rather than ideologies to avoid confusion.) Those of a conservative worldview criticize Apple's work concerning, among other things, the nature and role of pedagogy and curriculum. As an illustration, one of the more publicized encounters for which Apple received criticism stemmed from his examination of 9/11 and patriotism in schools (Apple, 2002). He discusses this in one of the chapters of the third edition of *Ideology and Curriculum* (Apple, 2004). He writes:

> No analysis of the effects of 9/11 on schools can go on without an understanding of the ways in which the global is dynamically linked to the local. Such an analysis must more fully understand the larger ideological work and history of the neo-liberal and neo-conservative project and its effects on the discourses that circulate and become common sense in our society. (p. 170)

Apple (2004) applies concepts from *Ideology and Curriculum* to the ways in which 9/11 has influenced schools and curriculum. In particular, he examines the role of "common sense" in the construction of an uncritical examination of the causes of 9/11. Conservative groups view such critical analysis as unpatriotic and antithetical to the purposes of school and curriculum. Those with a conservative worldview promote an uncritical version of patriotism, and when an event such as 9/11 takes place, the "ideological ground" (p. 158) is in place to legitimate unequal power relations.

In response to Apple, his conservative critics claim that his views are unpatriotic. For example, Finn (2003) writes:

> Apple believes that "social criticism is the ultimate act of patriotism." Where but on a university campus would the act of criticizing trump the need to ensure that young people have a firm grasp upon that which they are examining? Where else would patriotism commence with negative rather than positive attitudes? (p. 8)

Apple (1979) draws our attention to "common sense" beliefs and practices, such as those related to patriotism, and how they bolster hegemonic structures that serve the interests of dominant groups. This examination encourages a greater understanding of events and their causes from multiple perspectives. It is only by adopting such global perspectives that we can begin to understand inequality.

Others criticize Apple's (1979) use of concepts in areas such as the sociology of knowledge (Pinar, 2011; Young, 2008) and neo-Marxism (Farahmandpur, 2004; Whitty, 1985). As part of his critique of Apple, Pinar quotes recent writing by Young, whose work serves as a basis for much of the conceptual framework in *Ideology and Curriculum*. In a book section entitled "Social constructivism in the sociology of education: what went wrong?" (p. 200), Young examines the contractions of critically oriented curriculum work from the 1970s on. He writes: "The double-bind that combined emancipation and its impossibility was particularly problematic in education" (p. 204). While curriculum has the potential to be emancipatory through the deconstruction of hierarchies (counter-hegemonic in terms of *Ideology and Curriculum*), how can curriculum avoid re-inscribing another truth that is itself a social construct and subject to power relations? Pinar expands this critique by asking:

> If the "forms" that power assumes have shifted, would not the relationship (e.g., reproduction) between power and education (as one of its forms) change as well? If "power" is not only economic, political, and cultural (if it is also, for instance, semiotic and psychic), is its medium of hegemony—ideology—likewise recast? (p. 26)

Because societies are constantly subject to changing contexts and circumstances—such as those related to globalization, media, and communication—the connection between power and knowledge becomes increasingly fragmented, varied, and dispersed. As Pinar asks, "How do those who conduct ideological critique escape misrecognition of themselves and others?" (p. 26).

Relevance for Today

Ideology and Curriculum is in its third edition, and its ideas are as relevant today as at the time of its initial publication. The strength of the book has been to dramatically change conversations in education. The critical conversations that Apple sought to initiate have been evident. In the third edition of the book, he points to feminist, postcolonial, critical race, and queer theories as examples of the conversations that examine and challenge hegemony in its various forms. The language and concepts introduced through *Ideology and Curriculum* have had a transformational effect on our understanding of the relationships between culture, knowledge, power, and inequalities in schools. Much of the critical work that has changed conversations and transformed schooling and society has been influenced by the concepts presented in *Ideology and Curriculum*.

Weis, McCarthy, and Dimitriadis (2006a) point out that a lot has changed in the last 25 years due to changing symbolic and economic systems. Globalization has rapidly changed the way that self, "other," and economy are understood and instantiated. The authors write: "Apple's earliest work was written against a backdrop where the links between schools, the economy, and identity were more certain than they are today. Yet, given its dynamism, his project has never been more valuable for researchers, critics, and activists" (p. 9). Other prominent scholars explore the current relevance and importance of *Ideology and Curriculum* in relation to gender and schooling (Arnot, 2006), social and economic roles of education (Anyon, 2006), globalization (Torres, 2006), power and knowledge (Nozaki, 2006), the increase of administrative logics (Carlson, 2006), deskilling of teachers (Luke, 2006), critical agency of youth (Fine, 2006), the role of "common sense" in limiting possibilities (Gitlin, 2006), and Apple's commitment to social movements and critical curriculum (Gandin, 2006). As this list of topics and authors illustrates, *Ideology and Curriculum* has impacted a vast array of topics related to the field of education. Although some of the ideas that Apple (1979) presents in *Ideology and Curriculum* have been transformed to respond to changing times and contexts, they have served as a basis for much of the critical work in education.

The climate of systems management, categories, and labels has intensified, as evidenced by policies in the United States related to No Child Left Behind, Race to the Top, and exit exams (Carlson, 2006). While they are described as interventions (note the title No Child Left Behind), the implementation of these policies has served to intensify standardization, accountability, and the related abstraction of individual students and the decoupling of school and society. The events of September 11, 2001, also magnify neoliberal and neoconservative ideologies that have a dialectical relationship with schools. The combination of these hegemonic ideologies has made the themes related to power and knowledge in *Ideology and Curriculum* more relevant today than ever.

References

Anyon, J. (2006). Social class, school knowledge, and the hidden curriculum: Retheorizing reproduction. In L. Weis, C. McCarthy, & G. Dimitriadis (Eds.), *Ideology, curriculum, and the new sociology of education* (pp. 37–45). New York: Routledge.

Apple, M.W. (1979). *Ideology and curriculum*. Boston, MA: Routledge & Kegan Paul.

Apple, M.W. (2002). Patriotism, pedagogy, and freedom: On the educational meanings of September 11. *Teachers College Record*, *104*(8), 1760–1772.

Apple, M.W. (2004). *Ideology and curriculum* (3rd ed.). New York: RoutledgeFalmer.

Arnot, M. (2006). Retrieving the ideological past: Critical sociology, gender theory, and the school curriculum. In L. Weis, C. McCarthy, & G. Dimitriadis (Eds.), *Ideology, curriculum, and the new sociology of education* (pp. 17–36). New York: Routledge.

Carlson, D. (2006). Are we making progress? Ideology and curriculum in the age of No Child Left Behind. In L. Weis, C. McCarthy, & G. Dimitriadis (Eds.), *Ideology, curriculum, and the new sociology of education* (pp. 91–114). New York: Routledge.

Farahmandpur, R. (2004). Essay review: A Marxist critique of Michael Apple's neo-Marxist approach to educational reform. *Journal for Critical Education Policy Studies*, *2*(1).

Fine, M. (2006). Contesting research rearticulation and "thick democracy" as political projects of method. In L. Weis, C. McCarthy, & G. Dimitriadis (Eds.), *Ideology, curriculum, and the new sociology of education* (pp. 145–165). New York: Routledge.

Finn, C. (2003). Why this report? In Thomas B. Fordham Foundation (Ed.), *Terrorists, despots, and democracy—What our children need to know* (pp. 5–15). Washingpton, DC: Thomas B. Fordham Foundation.

Gandin, L.A. (2006). Situating education: Michael Apple's scholarship and political commitment in the Brazilian context. In L. Weis, C. McCarthy, & G. Dimitriadis (Eds.), *Ideology, curriculum, and the new sociology of education* (pp. 185–202). New York: Routledge.

Gitlin, A. (2006). (Re)visioning knowlege, politics, and change: Educational poetics. In L. Weis, C. McCarthy, & G. Dimitriadis (Eds.), *Ideology, curriculum, and the new sociology of education* (pp. 167–184). New York: Routledge.

Gottesman, I. (2012). From Gouldner to Gramsci: The making of Michael Apple's *Ideology and curriculum*. *Curriculum Inquiry*, *42*(5), 571–596.

Luke, A. (2006). Teaching after the market: From commodity to cosmopolitan. In L. Weis, C. McCarthy, & G. Dimitriadis (Eds.), *Ideology, curriculum, and the new sociology of education* (pp. 115–141). New York: Routledge.

Nozaki, Y. (2006). Riding tensions critically: Ideology, power/knowlege, and curriculum making. In L. Weis, C. McCarthy, & G. Dimitriadis (Eds.), *Ideology, curriculum, and the new sociology of education* (pp. 69–89). New York: Routledge.

Pinar, W.F. (2011). *The character of curruiculum studies: Bildung, currere, and the recurring question of the subject*. New York: Palgrave Macmillan.

Torres, C.A. (2006). Schooling, power, and the exile of the soul. In L. Weis, C. McCarthy, & G. Dimitriadis (Eds.), *Ideology, curriculum, and the new sociology of education* (pp. 47–65). New York: Routledge.

Weis, L., McCarthy, C., & Dimitriadis, G. (2006a). Introduction. In L. Weis, C. McCarthy, & G. Dimitriadis (Eds.), *Ideology, curriculum, and the new sociology of education*. New York: Routledge.

Weis, L., McCarthy, C., & Dimitriadis, G. (Eds.). (2006b). *Ideology, curriculum, and the new sociology of education*. New York: Routledge.

Whitty, G. (1985). *Sociology and school knowledge: Curriculum theory, research and politics*. London: Methuen.

Young, M.F.D. (2008). *Bringing knowldge back in: From social constructivism to social realism in the sociology of education*. New York: Routledge.

PART THREE

The 1980s

TWELVE

Mortimer J. Adler, *The Paideia Proposal: An Educational Manifesto* (1982)

Joseph Watras

When Mortimer Adler published the first volume of *The Paideia Proposal* in 1982, he told his readers that the term *paideia* was from the ancient Greek and referred to the general learning that was appropriate for all people in the society. Subtitled "an educational manifesto," Adler's *The Paideia Proposal* was a declaration of aims for school reform. Accordingly, it was more a political document than a reasoned philosophical treatise.

By reputation, Adler was a philosopher, yet he had not been trained in philosophy. Lacking a high school diploma, Adler entered Columbia University in 1921 after taking extension courses. The university granted him standing as a sophomore and extended a scholarship. He chose psychology as his area of study and, for his Ph.D., wrote his dissertation on ways to measure appreciation of music. Nonetheless, Robert Maynard Hutchins, then president of the University of Chicago, asked Adler to join the philosophy department. When the faculty members complained that Adler lacked the proper training and background, Hutchins created a position for Adler in the law school as professor of philosophy of law.[1]

Synopsis and Climate of the Times

In the course of his career, Adler wrote several books in which he tried to make philosophy popular. His *The Paideia Proposal* took the same direction with what might be called general education. Adler claimed that the programs of the comprehensive high school were misguided, and he considered the solution to be the adoption of a liberal arts course of study in every high school. Although he simplified this program for many students, he contended that comprehensive high schools harmed some students with a mixture of vocational and general education. Adler's background lent itself to such an interpretation, as did the backgrounds and educational interests of the members of what Adler called the Paideia Group. They were people who had graduated from or led schools that followed liberal arts programs. Many of them served publishers who followed a similar line. For example, the group included such figures as Jacques Barzun, former provost of Columbia University; Ernest Boyer, president of the Carnegie Foundation for the Advancement of Teaching; and Theodore Sizer, former headmaster of Phillips Academy. Of 22 members, the group included three superintendents of public schools who could act as representatives for grades K–12.[2]

In addition, some members had close personal associations with Adler. Charles Van Doren was such a member. Van Doren's father had been a popular professor of literature at Columbia. According to *The New York Times*, Van Doren achieved notoriety in 1959 when he confessed to having been part of a rigged, but widely publicized, television quiz show. When the U.S. Congress investigated the allegations, Van Doren compounded his problems by lying. The scandal cost Van Doren both his job as a professor at Columbia and his reputation. In a newspaper article, he thanked Adler for coming to his rescue by offering him a job.[3]

When the *Paideia Proposal* was published, Van Doren was the editorial vice president of the *Encyclopedia Britannica* and associate director of the Institute for Philosophical Research. Adler served as chairman of the Board of Editors of the *Encyclopedia Britannica* and was the founder and director of the Institute for Philosophical Research. Geraldine Van Doren, Charles's wife, was a member of the Paideia Group and a senior fellow of the Institute, as was James Van Doren.[4]

In addition to selecting like-minded individuals to serve on the Paideia Group, Adler seemed to be aware of political opportunities that made his educational ideas attractive. He acknowledged that *The Paideia Proposal* was a good fit with public attitudes of the time. While Adler praised American schools for offering twelve years of free public schooling to all children, he criticized the schools for failing to provide equal educational opportunity to all students. He asserted that the country was ready to fulfill this promise because people realized that schools offered different courses of study for different groups of students and that the quality of education was not equal in these various tracks. Adler claimed that such differentiation contradicted the ideas of John Dewey and Robert Maynard Hutchins, who wanted every child to receive the best education. Although Adler did not explain Dewey's or Hutchins's ideas of what comprises the best education, he defined it as one in which students learned about things that were essential to a human's life. While some students had opportunities to learn about the life of the mind, other students underwent various types of vocational training. For Adler, training for an occupation was not an appropriate education for free men and women.[5]

Adler was correct in claiming that public opinion among Americans in 1982 favored encouraging all students to learn the same information and skills. This followed a general shift among Americans to the right on federal policies. During the 1960s, Americans expressed concern for civil rights and sought to use schools to produce economic prosperity. For example, in 1964, the U.S. Congress passed the Civil Rights Act, which sought to reduce racial segregation in schools, and in 1965 it passed the Elementary and Secondary Education Act, which sought to improve the instruction of children from low-income families. Opinion polls showed that the public supported these measures. In 1965 polls showed that 90% of Americans approved of voting rights bills, and more than 70% supported antipoverty legislation.

But things changed rapidly. One year later, President Lyndon Johnson was unable to obtain approval of a fair housing bill, and his approval rating fell to 44%.[6]

In part, this swing to the conservative viewpoint may have been normal. According to James L. Sundquist, in recent times the political attitudes of Americans have changed every 25 years. In this case, the war in Vietnam, the riots in the cities, and the rise of Black Power may have contributed to the voters' turnaround in their previous attitudes. To add to the disappointment of liberal voices, nationwide evaluations revealed that programs relying on education to end poverty had failed. One of the most promising was Head Start. In 1965 Sargent Shriver, then director of the Office of Economic Opportunity, had begun this project with money budgeted for Community Action Programs but not spent. The first large-scale study of Head Start took place in 1969. Unfortunately, the results indicated that it did not improve children's cognitive abilities.[7]

In his campaign for the presidency in 1980, Ronald Reagan built on conservative attitudes. He claimed that antipoverty programs hurt the nation's economy. When the Reagan Administration reduced those expenses, the economy did not rebound. Thus, needing another cause, Reagan blamed inadequate instruction in public schools, and his administration formed the National Commission on Excellence in Education. When it issued its report in 1983, it claimed that all students should take more classes in the basic subjects of English, mathematics, science, social studies, and computer science. College-bound students should take two years of a foreign language. The NCEE members agreed that such a program of five basic studies would end the decline of student performance on standardized tests and increase students' level of knowledge. They predicted that this would enable students to become productive workers who could make the nation's industries more competitive.[8]

Adler's Main Themes and Arguments

Within this political context, Adler made his *Paideia Proposal*. It accommodated the political attitudes of the times by following the lines that the federal government was pursuing—with one exception. Instead of recommending a limited list of required subjects, Adler claimed that all schools should meet the same three objectives: enable the students to grow throughout their lives, prepare them for intelligent citizenship, and give them the basic skills common to all work in American society. To Adler, this meant that their education had to be general and liberal, because he believed such training would turn into a benefit as students graduated and sought jobs. Unlike specific vocational training, such general preparation would help young people learn new trades when situations demanded it, because it taught students to think rather than to master skills that had narrow applications.[9]

Adler proposed the same course of study for all children for all twelve grades, and he removed all electives or variations, except that students could choose which second language they wanted to learn. While English was to be the language of instruction, students could learn any of the ancient or modern foreign languages they wished. They were to become fluent in this second language, because such facility would enlarge their understanding of Western culture.[10]

The *Paideia Proposal* divided the subject matter that the students learned into three combinations, which he assigned to three separate columns. The first column had the goal of acquisition of organized knowledge. It required didactic instruction through texts and lectures.

The areas of study in this column included language, literature, fine arts, mathematics, history, geography, and social studies. The second column focused on intellectual learning skills, to be achieved through coaching and supervised practice. It included reading, writing, calculating, problem solving, and critical judgment. The third column consisted of things that would enlarge the students' understanding of ideas and values, to be accomplished through Socratic questioning and active participation. The activities included discussion of books and works of art as well as involvement with artistic activities. Adler claimed that the innovative aspect of his curriculum was that it offered students the opportunity to persist in the study of various subjects from an early age until they left school. He believed that they would thus acquire a fuller understanding of the subjects than if they took one course here and another course there.[11]

Adler argued that his proposal built on student activity. With the exception of lectures, the dominant method of teaching was a requirement that the students do something. For example, Adler preferred what he called the "Socratic mode" to expand their understanding of ideas or values. He called the method "maieutic" because it helped students give birth to ideas. In this maieutic method, Adler wanted the teacher to coach students by asking questions and encouraging them to probe each other's views about subjects at hand. This made the classroom a setting for discussions, debates, and performances of music and poetry.[12]

Although critics complained that all children could not profit from the same type of education, Adler believed that they shared the same human nature, and this made it possible to design a program that could cater to the basic humanness of each person. On the one hand, his program would eliminate vocational training and some programs that are not academic. On the other, he acknowledged that programs might vary in the speed with which teachers move through the material or in the type of help the teachers offer students to help them master the subject matter or the skills required. Adler did not think the program should be altered or made overly simple for some students, because such changes would deny those students the benefit of the enriched curriculum and the appropriate instruction.[13]

Adler agreed that he had to overcome the uneven preparation that children experienced before entering school. To mitigate the disparities, he suggested that there should be early childhood programs for two or three years to prepare children for school. In fact, Adler compared his suggestion to the rationale behind the creation of the earlier Head Start Program. He did not make any comments about the difficulties that Head Start had encountered, nor did he offer any suggestions to improve the Head Start model. Instead, he expressed his faith that early education could influence students' chances of later success.[14]

As for the problem of individual differences, Adler claimed that children shared similar human qualities through which they expressed their unique talents and interests. More important, they had a right to learn the information and skills that permitted them to make a good life for themselves by participating successfully in the economy. Nonetheless, he believed that remedial help could overcome any resistance to his program that might appear to result from the individual differences among students.[15]

Adler recognized that the program would not succeed unless teachers could guide learning in the classroom and motivate learning acquired through homework. Although teachers' abilities were central to the process, students had to learn through their own activities. Adler thought that teachers could overcome this paradox by taking advantage of the natural functions of students' minds. These included acquiring knowledge, developing intellectual skills, and enlarging understanding. The teacher could advance these with a method of instruction appropriate to each one. For example, drills, exercises, and tests helped students acquire knowledge. Students acquired intellectual skills when a teacher coached them individually as they engaged in activities that required reading, writing, or figuring. Finally, enlarging understanding came from discussions in which the students explored topics with the teacher and with each other.[16]

Adler acknowledged that teachers in contemporary schools received too little pay and lacked the sort of status that would compensate for the investment this proposal required. To remedy the imbalance, Adler called for increases in teachers' salary and improvements in the social status they enjoyed. At the same time, he claimed that teacher preparation programs had to increase the intellectual development of teachers. The solution Adler recommended was that teachers complete an academic program as undergraduates and pursue teacher education as graduate students. As for school principals, he thought they should be drawn from the ranks of successful teachers and should have the authority to select teachers for their schools and enforce standards of conduct among the students.[17]

In 1983 Adler published a sequel to *The Paideia Proposal* entitled *Paideia Problems and Possibilities.* Adler claimed that he wrote the second volume to address the national response that the first volume had elicited. To help readers who had not read the first volume, he devoted two chapters to repeating the recommendations of *The Paideia Proposal.* He organized the new material around questions that he said came from educational conferences at which members of the Paideia Group had participated in discussions. The questions concerned the following four areas: curricular framework, applicability of the program to all students, methods of instruction, and matters of administration. For example, the concerns about the curriculum sought to distinguish the Paideia from a back-to-basics movement. Adler answered that the Paideia program was basic to all learning, but it was not simply the teaching of reading, writing, and arithmetic. Questions about the applicability for all students were rooted in fears that the program would eliminate special education classes. Adler acknowledged that some children with learning disabilities needed special attention; however, he felt it was unnecessary to have separate classes for gifted students, because the improved quality of his program would develop their abilities. As for the teachers, Adler expected them to be generalists, as he felt that this made them competent in each of the three methods of instruction. Although he seemed to accept the notion that teachers might concentrate on specific subject areas (such as mathematics), he did not think they needed to specialize in a method of instruction or type of student. In discussing administration, Adler did not think the size of the school made a significant difference in how things should operate.[18]

The section on possibilities had a two-and-one-half page chapter explaining how to begin a Paideia program and a three-and-one-half page chapter listing the things that could prevent schools from adopting it. To begin a program, Adler thought that schools could introduce opportunities for students to discuss books, works of art, and music. At the same time, teachers could begin coaching students in the skills of listening, speaking, and reading. He contended that these two steps should be enough to introduce other aspects of the Paideia Proposal. In the chapter on possibilities, Adler warned against allowing practical problems to overshadow general principles. In addition, he asked educators not to reject theoretical principles when practical issues arose. To assuage any concerns, Adler repeated that there was no evidence that the Paideia Proposal would not work. He repeated that once educators accepted the basic validity of the goals, they would implement the program.[19]

Adler's third volume appeared in 1984. It was entitled *The Paideia Program: An Educational Syllabus,* and it contained 16 essays written by members of the Paideia Group. Although two additional members had joined, only 11 members contributed essays. The public school administrators were not represented. The Van Dorens contributed four essays and Adler wrote three essays. An 11-page introduction repeated the program's design. The remaining essays fell into three categories. Three chapters discussed how teachers could conduct seminars, how they could coach students, and how they might manage didactic instruction. The next nine chapters considered ways of teaching specific subject matter, such as English language and literature, mathematics, and science. The last section had three chapters that considered the structure of a Paideia school, its important characteristics, and methods of grading.[20]

The suggestions in each section were a mix of the traditional and the unusual. For example, to lead a seminar, teachers should ask questions that will define the discussion and provide direction. They should ask students to explain the reasons for their answers, and they should encourage students to examine the responses of other students. The instruction of history should begin with matters close to the students' experiences and move outward from there. The structure of a Paideia school should allow for about twenty-five students to work as a group with a seminar leader. The schedule had to be flexible, since the methods of instruction varied from didactic lectures to intensive coaching to seminar discussions. Grading posed a problem because Adler believed that typical tests measured how much information students had acquired. This was a meaningless measure because they quickly forgot the many facts they had memorized. Instead of depending on formal tests, he recommended that teachers supplement objective scores with estimates of a student's understanding that came from experiences in coaching and discussions.[21]

Strengths and Weaknesses

Although Adler presented the *Paideia Proposal* as a manifesto, educational philosophers argued against the logic on which it was based. For example, Nel Noddings lodged three important complaints. First, she noted that Adler linked together two opposing but prominent educators and presented them as supporters of his views. She argued that Hutchins had very different ideas of what constituted the best education than did Dewey, and that the extent of their disagreement indicated that they could not agree with Adler's views. Second, she took issue with Adler's view that the best education for the best students is best for everyone. To her, it appeared that Adler wanted all children to learn what the best students have always learned. Noddings claimed that such a policy would make it difficult for children with talents for things such as farming, repairing electronics, or dancing to realize that they can contribute to society in those areas. Thus she thought the way to provide an equal education to children with different talents is to advance those interests in schools. Third, Noddings claimed that Adler made a logical error when he asserted that the Paideia Proposal offered a general and liberal education. She contended that because it was exclusively intellectual, it was narrow and specialized.[22]

Whether the views of philosophers of education such as Noddings made any difference, Adler had become pessimistic about the progress of the Paideia Program by 1988. In a letter to his colleagues, he explained that two factors stood in the way of educational reform. One was the training that teachers received, and the other was the dominance of achievement tests.

These factors reinforced each other. Teachers had to prepare students for tests. To enable them to score well on the tests, the teachers had to present the material in a way that prepared them to answer questions on tests. Adler suggested that things would improve if teachers measured students according to the capacities they brought to learning. If they had learned as well as their individual capacities allowed, they had performed admirably. Their understandings should not be compared to each other. [23]

In his letter, Adler told the members of the Paideia program that they would have to change the prevailing views of testing and grading in order to improve schools. He suggested that the way to approach this task was to make educators at all levels realize the difference between information and knowledge and between memorizing facts for tests and understanding knowledge as a way to advance thought. Since these were the types of changes the *Paideia Proposal* sought, reform did not require curricular change. Adler wanted teachers to change their methods of teaching. Although he accepted that didactic instruction had to exist, he wanted it to accompany coaching and discussion. The problem was that this had not happened. After eight years of effort, he could not find any schools that had completely adopted the Paideia model. About one hundred of them used the model, and they were elementary schools. Even so, these schools rarely used it. For example, Adler estimated that they employed coaching and discussions for about one-tenth of teaching time. High schools ignored his ideas because they had to prepare students for college, and this meant passing tests. And because few schools embraced the Paideia model, Adler could not convince charitable foundations to provide adequate funds to advance his organization.[24]

Shortly after writing his letter, Adler met with his colleagues in the Paideia Group. At the time, its council was supported by Adler's Institute for Philosophical Research; however, Adler had not been able raise funds to keep the programs alive. Fortunately, a member of the group was the dean of the School of Education of the University of North Carolina at Chapel Hill. When it was clear that the National Center for the Paideia Program could become an agency of the school, Adler relinquished his role in the effort and returned to his position at the Institute for Philosophical Research, which he called his ivory tower.[25]

When the Paideia program became part of the University of North Carolina, the members of the Paideia Council (as the Paideia Group was now called) adopted a declaration of principles that listed twelve doctrines affirming the following beliefs: all children can learn; they deserve the same quality of education; the primary cause of learning is the activity of the student's mind; and student achievement should be measured by the student's individual capacities—and not solely by comparison with other students. In addition, they simplified Adler's original diagram of the curricular framework, though they retained its general content and meaning.[26]

If Adler's view that the *Paideia Proposal* had failed to change schools was correct, Ronald Reagan's National Commission on Excellence in Education seemed to share the same fate. They had begun at about the same time. Twenty years later, Maris Vinovskis reported that there was no objective evidence that the NCEE's effort had enabled students to learn more, even though they had to enroll in more courses to graduate from high school. The younger children had fewer students in their classes, and teachers were subjected to more careful supervision. According to Vinovskis, the problem was that the effort relied on teachers working harder. This simplistic solution was all that was available, because the federal government had not supported efforts to improve teaching.[27] It may well be that Adler's proposal failed for the same reason.

Notes

1   Ann T. Keene, "Mortimer J. Adler," *American National Biography Online*, www.anb.org/articles/20/20-01889.html. Accessed November 28, 2014.

2   Adler, *The Paideia Proposal: An Educational Manifesto* (New York: Macmillan, 1982), vii–viii.

3   Alex Brown, "After 49 Years, Charles Van Doren Talks," *The New York Times*, July 21, 2008. www.nytimes.com/...21iht-edbeam.1. 14660467ht. Accessed November 9, 2014.

4   Adler, *The Paideia Proposal*, vii–viii.

5   Adler, *The Paideia Proposal*, 3–8.

6   James L. Sundquist, *Politics and Policy: The Eisenhower, Kennedy, and Johnson Years* (Washington, DC: Brookings Institution, 1968), 181–199.

7   Sundquist, *Politics and Policy*, 498–499; Edward Zigler and Susan Muenchow, *Head Start: The Inside Story of America's Most Successful Experiment* (New York: Basic Books, 1992).

8   National Commission on Excellence in Education, *A Nation at Risk: The Imperative for Educational Reform* (Washington, DC: U.S. Government Printing Office, 1983).

9   Adler, *The Paideia Proposal*, 9–20.

10 Adler, *The Paideia Proposal*, 21, 28.

11 Adler, *The Paideia Proposal*, 22–25.

12 Adler, *The Paideia Proposal*, 28–31.

13 Adler, *The Paideia Proposal*, 33–36.

14 Adler, *The Paideia Proposal*, 37–39.

15 Adler, *The Paideia Proposal*, 41–45.

16 Adler, *The Paideia Proposal*, 49–56.

17 Adler, *The Paideia Proposal*, 57–65.

18 Mortimer J. Adler, *Paideia Problems and Possibilities* (New York: Macmillan, 1983), 25–64.

19 Adler, *Paideia Problems*, 79–82.

20 Mortimer J. Adler, *The Paideia Program: An Educational Syllabus* (New York: Macmillan, 1984).

21 Adler, *The Paideia Program*, 23, 111, 169–171, 180–183.

22 Nel Noddings, "The False Promise of the Paideia: A Critical Review of *The Paideia Proposal*," in *The Curriculum Studies Reader*, ed. David J. Flinders and Stephen J. Thornton (1983; repr. New York: RoutledgeFalmer, 2004), 163–170.

23 Mortimer J. Adler, *A Second Look in the Rearview Mirror: Further Reflections of a Philosopher at Large* (New York: Macmillan, 1992), 93–98.

24 Ibid.

25 Adler, *A Second Look*, 103–107.

26 Adler, *A Second Look*, 107–110.

27 Maris Vinovskis, "Missed Opportunities," in *A Nation Reformed? American Education Twenty Years After A Nation at Risk*, ed. David T. Gordon (Cambridge, MA: Harvard Education Press, 2003), 115–130.

THIRTEEN

Ernest L. Boyer, High School: A Report on Secondary Education in America (1983)

John A. Beineke

Introduction

Ernest L. Boyer (1928–1995) was an innovative higher education administrator and national educational leader who focused on systemic change in teaching and learning. He was chancellor of the State University of New York system and advisor to Presidents Richard Nixon and Gerald Ford. In 1977 President Jimmy Carter named Boyer Commissioner of Education, a position that, at the time (prior to the creation of the Department of Education), was the chief federal education office in the nation. Boyer went on to head the Carnegie Foundation for the Advancement of Teaching in 1979, a position he held until his death in 1995.

High School: A Report on Secondary Education in America was published in 1983. Using data from two large studies of the American high school—one by John Goodlad and the other by James Coleman—it was a call for educational reform at the secondary school level. Boyer also collaborated with two dozen school, community, and university professionals,whom he termed "observers," to fashion his report.

Cultural and Educational Context

The early years of the 1980s were colored by the events of the preceding decade. The Watergate affair and the fall of a president; the American withdrawal from Vietnam; two other truncated presidencies accompanied by inflation, high oil prices, and interest rates—all combined to create what President Jimmy Carter labeled a "crisis of confidence." The failure of the United States to gain the release of dozens of American citizens held hostage by the Iranian government added to the malaise. The election of Ronald Reagan in 1980 brought with it a new tide of conservative economic and cultural thought.

As the 1980s dawned, the business of America appeared to be business, and the prototype for success was Japan. The Japanese economic model was built, as many believed, on its educational system. If the United States was unable to compete with Japan and other emerging Asian nations, then the cause was believed to be the failure of its schools. At the same time, the idea of "leadership" emerged as an area of study and practice. John Gardner's *On Leadership* (1990) was published, and the historian James MacGregor Burns also focused on that topic in his book *Leadership* (1978). New programs appeared in leadership development, such as the W.K. Kellogg Foundation's National Fellowship Program, the Center for Servant Leadership, and the Center for Creative Leadership. Courses in colleges of education that were once titled "educational administration" were now labeled "educational leadership," and school leaders became part of the solution to the perceived problems in the schools.

There had been, at the time of *High School*'s publication in 1983, 25-year cycles of educational reform. The first decade of the twentieth century witnessed the introduction of scientific approaches to education led by Edward L. Thorndike, who emphasized student assessment and measurement. By the early 1930s progressive education was at the forefront of the nation's educational agenda, with both child-centered advocates such as William Heard Kilpatrick and social reconstructionists, led by George S. Counts's guiding practices in American schools. In 1957, prompted by the scientific successes of the Soviet Union, most notably in the launching of its orbiting satellite "Sputnik," the nation once again directed serious attention to education. Progressive education was dismissed as too permissive and unstructured, while science and math, in addition to an overall "back-to-basics" curricular approach, gained dominance in the educational thinking of the time.

After the Soviet success, another quarter century passed before the United States again turned its attention to the educational arena and the role that schools played in America's social, economic, and cultural arenas. The early 1980s saw a renewed interest in education, and a raft of discussions and reports on K–12 education appeared. The most influential report (though not entirely accurate), was the U.S. Department of Education's *A Nation at Risk: The Imperative for Educational Reform* (National Commission on Excellence in Education, 1983). The document warned—often in militaristic language—that if U.S. schools did not improve, the very security and economic well-being of the nation was "at risk." Other titles critical of the schools included Mortimer Adler's *The Paideia Proposal: An Educational Manifesto* (1982) and *Against Mediocrity: The Humanities in America's High Schools* (Finn, Ravitch, & Fancher, 1984). Both of these works took an essentialist point of view, advocating the study of the "basics" (read: the humanities) and greater academic rigor in the schools.

Other studies and recommendations appeared in the early 1980s. Theodore Sizer, former headmaster of Phillips Academy and dean of Harvard's Graduate School of Education, wrote *Horace's Compromise: The Dilemma of the American High School* (1992), which offered a pragmatic view on how to improve schools. *A Place Called School: Prospects for the Future* (1984), by John Goodlad, former dean of education at the University of California, Los Angeles, used massive sets of data to describe the status of schools and made a variety of recommendations across the educational landscape. A plethora of studies, reports, and attendant proposals on how to improve education continued to appear as the decade progressed.

The Book

Ernest Boyer began *High School* (1983)—his contribution to the national dialogue on educational reform—with two simple sentences: "Education is in the headlines once again. After years of shameful neglect, educators and politicians have taken the pulse of the public school and found it faint" (p. 1). His working thesis was that a "report card on public education is a report card on the nation" (p. 6). *High School* was both a status report on secondary public education and an enumeration of recommendations. The findings included the centrality of language in the education of students, the need to strengthen the teaching profession, the introduction of service learning, the linking of technology to the schools, a call for schools to collaborate more with higher education and the corporate world, and a renewed commitment to education by parents, school boards, and government (p. 7).

Noting a decade-long decline in SAT and ACT scores, Boyer perceived the causes to be a combination of both the educational and the social—from high absenteeism and decreased emphasis on writing to changes in family structure and television viewing. While assessments are used in *High School*, Boyer endorses the view that statistical averages from standardized examinations are an incomplete measure of education in examining the purpose of schooling. The "report card" using test scores was mixed, and Boyer saw improvement on the horizon. Evidence pointed to a leveling off of the decline in test scores, the tightening of college admission standards, and the shaping of a core curriculum. Most important, though, was the "revival of interest in the nation's schools" (p. 39).

High School provided an overview of the history of education by describing the Progressive Era, the misinterpretation of John Dewey on progressivism, the growth of high school enrollment in the twentieth century, and the lessons offered (and quickly forgotten) from the 1942 *Eight Year Study*. (That project, founded by the Progressive Education Association, explored curricular connections between secondary and post-secondary education and concluded that the traditional high school course of study was not crucial for achievement in college, and that experimental and interdisciplinary paths should be encouraged. However, the effects of the report were negligible.) Boyer also outlined the essentialist backlash of the 1950s and the back-to-basics movement. He contended that the history of education had asked the question, "What do Americans want high schools to accomplish?" and answered, "Quite simply, we want it all" (p. 57).

Predating Goals 2000 (the George H.W. Bush and Bill Clinton school reform agenda), *High School* stressed the need for aims and objectives in education. The volume presents four of these: (1) the capacity for students to think critically and communicate effectively, (2) a core curriculum based on the human heritage and an interdependent world, (3) the preparation of all students for the world of work, and (4) the need to help all students fulfill their social and civic obligations (pp. 66–67). *High School* was critical of the growth of "nonacademic" courses such as physical education, music, driver education, and cooperative education programs, to name a few. While valuable, these courses and programs had been provided to students at the expense of English, social studies, mathematics, and science. To remedy this imbalance, Boyer endorsed the 1983 National Commission on Excellence in Education's call for "The New Basics," which proposed a core curriculum tilted toward the "academic" courses he viewed as having been overlooked or ignored (pp. 73–77).

While not prescribing exactly what each of the "core" courses should contain, *High School* returned to the theme of the critical nature of writing and communication. Dismissing the difficulty in measuring robust student writing, Boyer maintained that the root cause was the limitations placed on teachers to assess a large amount of student work. The standard five- or six-course teacher load, with 25 to 30 students in each class, should be replaced with two sections of 20 students for each teacher (pp. 90–91). In the chapter titled "The Curriculum Has a Core," the "core of common learning" is outlined in broad strokes with limited specificity. The disciplines and areas recommended include literature, the arts, foreign language, and United States history, as well as world civilization, non-Western studies, civics, science and math, technology, health, and vocations. A culminating seminar or project was proposed as a capstone in the senior year (pp. 94–117).

Lest *High School* be viewed as a menu of courses for the college-bound student, the study observed that, at the time (the early 1980s), 40% of high school graduates did not continue on to post-secondary institutions. The students who directly entered the "world of work" were addressed in the chapter titled "Transition: To Work and Learning." Race and family background, as well high school work experience, were listed as factors that impact those who enter the workforce rather than go on to study in a higher education setting. Calling vocational education "an unfulfilled promise," Boyer was concerned about the low academic standards and stigma that often accompanied vocational studies. The 1980s were still a time of "tracking," which often led to vocational students pursuing less rigorous and challenging coursework. On this point, Boyer called for the elimination of tracking altogether (pp. 118–127).

Boyer did not totally dismiss assessment and testing. He concluded his chapter on vocational education by recommending a new assessment instrument to replace the SAT. Labeling it a Student Achievement and Advisement Test (SAAT), the instrument would provide guidance to those students not planning to move on to higher education. *High School* also advocated for a more comprehensive student evaluation system that would include written teacher evaluations, student-prepared portfolios, and a senior project. An additional suggestion regarding evaluation was for high schools to follow and survey students after graduation in order to better inform future program and curricular offerings (pp. 134–136).

A number of ideas were tendered in the area of instruction. Fundamental was the need for more involvement by teachers in the way that curriculum, scheduling, and school rules were implemented. An example was the selection of textbooks. Boyer believed that states needed to relax their control over the selection process, thereby allowing teachers a greater voice in the materials they would be using in their classrooms. (The use of primary sources in history was strongly encouraged.) Time on task was also viewed as critical to student learning. The endless interruptions to the instructional day and non-academic activities that take up precious student/teacher time had one teacher stating, "the first step to improving the American high school is to unplug the PA [public address] system" (pp. 141–143).

The centrality of renewing the teaching profession was given a prominent place within the pages of *High School*. This critique and its attendant solutions remain familiar today, over 3 decades since the volume's publication. Teachers were viewed as isolated, with little time to interact professionally with their colleagues. Recommendations included the recognition of good teachers with tangible rewards and public acknowledgment. The issue of low teacher salaries was allotted significant space in the book. Working conditions should be improved, including the provision of adequate supplies, more attractive lounges and work areas, and time to discuss professional issues within the workday. Sabbaticals, study leaves, and teacher exchanges were all endorsed (Boyer, 154–173).

The preparation of teachers was closely tethered to renewing the profession. John Goodlad would more fully address this issue in his book *Teachers for Our Nation's Schools* (Goodlad, 1990). According to Boyer, quality teacher education students should be recruited with the same diligence as athletes were by recruited by universities. He argued that the selection of teacher education candidates required greater rigor. Each prospective teacher should have a major in an academic discipline during the junior and senior years, with a fifth year of study devoted to pedagogy and an internship. (The 5-year teacher preparation concept embodied in the Holmes Group, a consortium of research universities, was only in a rudimentary stage at that time.) *High School* did specifically list a four-course "core" for teacher education students that would include Schooling in America, Learning Theory and Research, the Teaching of Writing, and the Use of Technology. Following initial teacher preparation, "staff development" or "continuing education"—what today is known as professional development—should be incorporated into every school for every teacher. And a teacher "ladder" was presented as a way to differentiate and affirm the various levels and responsibilities of the teaching profession (pp. 171–185).

An eponymously titled film based on Boyer's *High School* (Guggenheim, 1983) was produced soon after the book's publication. It was carried by the Public Broadcasting Service and sponsored by the petroleum company Atlantic Richfield. The hour-long documentary tracked the book by referencing the major points through a day at a typical urban/suburban high school. The need for a strong English/communication component in the high school led the film's narrative, but it was also student-centered, illustrating the wide range of academic and behavioral challenges that educators face.

Perspectives from Contemporary Critics and Historians

What critics wrote about *High School* when it was published—both in professional education journals and mainstream journals of opinion—affords another lens through which the book can be assessed. In addition, the treatment of the volume in history of education works can place *High School* in a larger context over the past 3 decades.

High School was often included within multiple reviews of education reform books that appeared at the time. Andrew Hacker examined eight of these studies for the *New York Review of Books*. His extended essay, rather harshly titled "The Schools Flunk Out," found *High School* less a "research project than Boyer's own book" (Hacker, 1987). Hacker wrote that Boyer takes learning seriously, as evidenced by the fact that *High School's* strongest recommendation was that schools teach students how to write. While Hacker questioned whether good writing could be taught, he admitted that teachers who carefully read and give thoughtful feedback to students can only serve to advance that critical skill. Compared to the seven other volumes under review, Hacker found that Boyer's was the only one that discussed education as contributing to the life of the mind rather than serving solely as a tool to meet the needs of economic competitiveness.

The Catholic journal *Commonweal* also looked at a number of volumes related to educational reform, noting the "general surge of interest in schools in general, and in the high school in particular" (Ratte, 1984). Reviewer John Ratte placed the high school in the problematic sociocultural context of having to transform the family, the economy, and race relations in an attempt to solve overall social problems. Pedagogically, Ratte noted Boyer's advocacy of Socratic dialogue in the high school classroom and less lecturing by teachers in the front of the room. Ratte found *High School* "remarkably clear and well written for a commission report."

Timothy Healy, who was president of Georgetown University at the time he wrote his review for *The New York Times*, grouped *High School* with three other books that focused on school reform. Along with *High School*, Healy saw much commonality among *A Nation at Risk* (NCEE, 1983), Sizer's *Horace's Compromise* (1992), and Finn, Ravitch, and Fancher's *Against Mediocrity* (1984). This unanimity was found in the idea of equal access to secondary education for all Americans, a commitment to improve teachers while not bashing the profession or those who educate teachers, the need for building-level leadership, and, finally, the indictment that institutions of higher education had shown distaste and disinterest in the nation's public high schools. Healy called Boyer "an experienced observer" and made the connection of education and politics at both the state and federal levels.

In *The New Republic*, a moderately left-of-center journal of opinion, David Owen found *High School* light on evidence, yet succinct on ideas. Owen thought it paradoxical that, while adamant about the elimination of academic tracking of students in classrooms, Boyer appealed for residential math and science academies for gifted students, which would be moving "white kids into federally funded prep schools."

In the *Phi Delta Kappan*, curriculum historian Laurel Tanner pointed out that Boyer's major goal was to examine the current condition of American secondary education as an educational institution by looking at teachers, students, and the curriculum. Yet for such a broad mission, Tanner noted that Boyer depended on vignettes from a limited number of schools rather than in-depth case studies. Nonetheless, the *Kappan* review made clear that *High School* was a "constructive report" (Tanner, 1984). As a curriculum theorist, Tanner also observed that Boyer suggested a common core that is appropriate to contemporary needs. Tanner was heartened that, after years of focusing on young children, attention was now being turned to the secondary school. She concluded that Boyer and the Carnegie study were excellent starting places for finding new documentation in that venture.

While *High School* gained national attention in 1983 and 1984 that included fairly uniform, positive commentary on its methods and findings, the *Harvard Educational Review (HER)* provided the most detailed and critical analysis of the book. Devoting eight journal pages to their review, a group of high school teachers "dialogued" about the study and then had Paula Evans compose an essay based on those discussions (Evans, 1984). The teachers found *High School* to be positive in tone, encouraging in its outlook, and jargon-free—thus appropriate for a wider audience than professional educators. The teachers also acknowledged the challenging agenda that high schools were tasked with, and its optimistic approach to "renewing" the institution.

But Evans and her colleagues believed the study to be deficient in a number of areas. The superficiality of the recommendations made in *High School* was the overriding concern of the educators in the *HER*. The study is "bland, prosaic, ingenuous, and laundered" (Evans, 1984). It avoided a thorough examination of important topics, especially the changing, diverse demographics of schools. Other concerns were the absence of new insights or considerations as to organization and purposes of schools; insufficient plans to implement the recommendations; and Boyer's limiting his observations to the gifted and at-risk populations rather than all students.

Boyer's recommendation of a single track for academic and vocational programs of study was criticized as unrealistic, given the diverse student population found in the modern high school.

The teachers in the *HER* review concluded that *High School* "paints a dismal scene of boredom, information overload, routinization, passivity, and joylessness," while offering only "lofty ideals" as solutions. The consensus of the group was that Boyer avoided difficult questions such as: How do we engage students? How do we teach students to ask meaningful questions? How do we help students tolerate ambiguity and grapple with knowledge? A final criticism was the book's apparent lack of constraining social context. Boyer basically discounted the sociocultural dimension of schools and students, Evans claims, and quoted him thusly: "The school has little influence over the home and family environment." The teachers indicated this area could not be ignored. The review's final word on *High School* was "disappointment" (Evans, 1984).

Book reviews provide for an immediate analysis of a work's impact. In their longer view, what historians of education ascertain as a book's influence can provide alternative perspectives. Since *High School's* publication 30 years ago, such insights have been diverse. Writing less than a decade after the appearance of *High School*, Laurel Tanner and Daniel Tanner, in their history of curriculum, coupled Boyer's work with that of John Goodlad, calling them both "moderate" in tone and pointing "to the need for a coherent curriculum to meet the function of general education in a free society." They contrasted these books to the more radical back-to-basics agenda that did not attune the curriculum to the child and adolescent (Tanner & Tanner, 1990).

Henry J. Perkinson's *The Imperfect Panacea: American Faith in Education, 1865–1990* was also a look back at *High School* after less than a decade. Mildly skeptical of the plethora of reform reports that were "spewing out from the word processors of educational theorists," Perkinson lumped Boyer in with Sizer, Goodlad, and Adler. He concluded in his epilogue that these works were somewhat limited, as they "all focused on the restructuring and reorganization of the local school" (Perkinson, 1991).

Two decades out, Gerald L. Gutek (2000) was more specific as to Boyer's historical contribution to educational reform. For Gutek, Boyer's work was representative of the other reports, especially in its emphasis on basic subjects such as English, science, mathematics, and history, which would form a "common curricular core" along with the notions of technological training and community service (Gutek, 2000). Almost 30 years after the publication of *High School*, another educational historian, John Rury, in his *Education and Social Change: Contours in the History of American Schooling* (2012), noted Boyer's attention to the size of high schools in terms of enrollment and the vocational needs of students circa 1980 (Rury, 2012).

Analysis and Relevance of *High School* for Modern Educational Practice

What resonates most to a current reader of *High School* is its emphasis on curriculum. While the term "common curriculum" is used, it does not carry the same meaning that the Common Core State Standards (CCSS) hold for educators today. For Boyer, the curriculum was a series of courses—boxes, one might say—that were to be filled with subjects. *High School* is silent on what is to be taught within those boxes. By contrast, the Common Core State Standards are quite prescriptive—through assessments—as to what teachers are to teach, especially in the areas of literacy and mathematics. Other than writing and communication, there is a lack of specificity on Boyer's part in the areas of math, science, and even history. Because of Boyer's strong support for teachers, one might infer that the autonomy of the classroom educator would allow them to be the curricular leaders.

Boyer did strike upon a number of topics and issues that were prescient. He opened up the discussion on "big schools versus small schools" and the idea of creating "schools within schools" when the number of students in one building reached a certain level. While concluding that smaller schools might be preferable, he did hedge his sanction of the comprehensive high school by noting the variety of curricular offerings available in larger schools (Boyer, 1983, p. 235). *High School* drew attention to meeting the needs of the gifted student with the term "accelerated learning." One thought by Boyer was to allow gifted students access to the business world in areas such as technology. The high-risk student was also given significant space. There was a passion on Boyer's part in his narrative for "dropouts" and their future in America. The increasing need for remedial education at the college level, along with the possibility of "middle colleges" that combine grades 11 and 12 with freshman- and sophomore-level collegiate courses in one school, still seems an idea worth pursuing (pp. 236–248, 251–259).

Other areas that *High School* foresaw included the increased emphasis on what students needed to know—a thesis that would be proclaimed by E.D. Hirsch (1987) as well as Finn, Ravitch, and Fancher (1984) in the mid-1980s. The professionalization of teaching and the centrality and value of the classroom teacher, a theme that John Goodlad would trumpet, was seen in Boyer's book. The critical need for vocational education anticipated the "linking movement" in California and the "Ready for Work and College" movements—both of which were programs that connected high schools to the world of work for those students not transitioning to the higher education setting.

While Boyer was prophetic on a number of points in *High School*, he also missed or failed to see other trends that would transform public schools in the near future. These included technology, which was viewed with mild suspicion. *High School* acknowledged the emerging role of the computer but could not predict its ubiquitous place not only in the schools but also in society in the twenty-first century. His guarded comments now seem limited in vision. The standards/assessment movement was absent in *High School*. Still 20 years in the future, this homogenization of education represented by No Child Left Behind and the Common Core State Standards was not signaled as a major future educational trend by Boyer and his colleagues.

With the recent advent of leadership as a discipline of study unto itself, it is probably unfair to criticize Boyer's chapter on the role of the building-level principal. It is now a given that leadership at the school and district level can have a pronounced impact on student success. Boyer focused on building level leadership while seeming to ignore the district-level office of superintendent or the influential state-level education departments and their personnel (Boyer, 1983, pp. 199–229).

Ernest Boyer's *High School* was neither the best nor the worst of the numerous studies and reports on educational reform that emerged in the 1980s. Its paramount contribution may have been that it came from one of the period's foremost educators and was sponsored by a prestigious foundation. Several foundations today—as among them the Bill and Melinda Gates Foundation and the Walton Family Foundation—have become intimately engaged in educational reform. While the Carnegie Foundation was viewed as non-partisan in its funding of Boyer's work, there has been criticism of both the Gates and Walton Foundations for being highly political in nature. The Gates Foundation has been seen as using its resources to advance the Common Core State Standards movement, while the Walton Family Foundation has aggressively supported charter schools.

High School was a part of the larger panoply of educational reports that made sure education would no longer be an issue examined only every "quarter-century" or so. President George H.W. Bush, in fact, wanted to be the "education president." His successor in the White House, Bill Clinton, had made education the keystone of his political portfolio as governor of Arkansas. He kept it at the forefront during his 8 years as president with Goals 2000, which was a bipartisan approach built on his predecessor's ideas. Education reform was now on the nation's agenda and has remained there. No Child Left Behind and Race to the Top became virtual banners that George W. Bush and Barack Obama displayed in the White House when education could no longer be relegated to second- or third-tier status on political agendas.

At the conclusion of the film *High School*, the narrator paraphrases Boyer: "For over 150 years we have given to the high schools the hopes for our democracy—the unfulfilled agenda of our nation. More than any other American institution we depend on what happens here [in the high school]. Our schools are a reflection of ourselves. They are no more than we have made them, they will become no more than what we wish them to be" (Guggenheim, 1983).

References

Adler, M.J. (1982). *The Paideia proposal: An educational manifesto*. New York: Macmillan.

Boyer, E.L. (1983). *High school: A report on secondary education in America*. New York: Harper & Row.

Burns, J.M. (1978). *Leadership*. New York: Harper & Row.

Evans, P.M. (1984). A dialogue among teachers. *Harvard Educational Review*, *54*(3), 364–371.

Finn, C.E., Ravitch, D., & Fancher, R.T. (1984). *Against mediocrity: The humanities in America's high schools*. New York: Holmes & Meier.

Gardner, J.W. (1990). *On leadership*. New York: Free Press.

Goodlad, J.I. (1984). *A place called school: Prospects for the future*. New York: McGraw-Hill.

Goodlad, J.I. (1990). *Teachers for our nation's schools*. San Francisco, CA: Jossey-Bass.

Guggenheim, C. (Director). (1983). *High school* (Motion Picture). Washington, DC: Guggenheim Productions, Inc.

Gutek, G.L. (2000). *American education 1945–2000: A history and commentary*. Prospect Heights, IL: Waveland Press.

Hacker, A. (1987, April 12). The schools flunk out. *New York Review of Books*, *31*(35), p. 39.

Healy, T. (1984, May 13). High schools on the brink. *New York Times Book Review*, pp. 14–15.

Hirsch, E.D. (1987). *Cultural literacy: What every American needs to know*. New York: Houghton Mifflin.

National Commission on Excellence in Education. (1983). *A nation at risk: The imperative for educational reform*. Washington, DC: U.S. Government Printing Office.

Perkinson, H.J. (1991). *The imperfect panacea: American faith in education, 1865–1990*. New York: McGraw-Hill.

Ratte, J. (1984, April 20). The American high school. *Commonweal*, *111*, pp. 244–246.

Rury, J. (2012). *Education and social change: Contours in the history of American schooling*. New York: Routledge.

Sizer, T.R. (1992). *Horace's compromise: The dilemma of the American high school*. Boston, MA: Houghton Mifflin.

Tanner, L.N. (1984, January). Despite weaknesses, new Carnegie Report offers valuable support for school improvement. *Phi Delta Kappan*, *65*, pp. 369–370.

Tanner, D., & Tanner, L.N. (1990). *History of the school curriculum*. New York: Macmillan.

FOURTEEN

John Goodlad, *A Place Called School: Prospects for the Future* (1984)

Jessica A. Heybach

Schools have the critical responsibility to enculturate young people into our social and political democracy. They [schools] succeed only with constant educational renewal, both because each group of students brings new challenges and because social and political shifts create corresponding changes in priorities for learning. The needed renewal is neither simple nor easy; it requires simultaneous changes inside schools and the education of educators as well as active engagement by a caring public.1

Introduction

The life and work of John I. Goodlad (1920–2014) cannot easily be captured and summarized in a single book chapter, but the above quote comes close to crystallizing Goodlad's scholarship and its impact on the discipline of education. So much has already been written about Goodlad and his work that I fear this chapter may be redundant; however, the complex contextualized image of schools as outlined by Goodlad over decades of serious investigation should never be allowed to fade from the educator's consciousness. He stands as a giant in the field of educational thought and research, and his text *A Place Called School* should be required reading for all who seek to understand *from where* today's fervor regarding educational change came—and *to where* we might go if we listen closely to the quieter, more philosophical lessons of this text. In the strange world of metrics we now occupy, *A Place Called School* has been cited over 6,550 times, according to Google Scholar. This seminal text details Goodlad's interpretation of the findings from the most extensive empirical study ever conducted in American schools and offers a description of the essential components needed to understand and properly renew individual schools as well as the overall aim of public schools in a democracy. The analysis provided in this chapter begins by situating *A Place*

Called School in both time and space, goes on to offer a brief examination of the main assertions in the text, and finally interrogates how this text has come to be understood with the luxury of hindsight.

A Brief History of John Goodlad and the Promise of Educational Renewal

John Goodlad, educational theorist, practitioner, and researcher, witnessed an era of intense change in the social fabric of American life, but famously noted how little the educational system had moved over that same span of years. He authored and co authored over 30 books, 80 book chapters, and more than 200 journal articles—a corpus that certainly places him in the categories of "prolific" and "seminal." Goodlad's work has been at the heart of progressive thought predicated on a humanist philosophy—a philosophy that positions the learner's needs at the center of the educational enterprise. The increasing discontent of neoliberal educational reformers surely could not have been predicted, but Goodlad's work, often described as that of educational reform, diverges radically from the mainstream assumptions that lay dormant in most of the educational reform literature. Although Goodlad is often labeled a "reformer," this characterization will be challenged later in this section. In any case, his ideas have been central for many who desire to make schools more humane, more democratic, and more just for those who occupy them most—students and teachers alike.

A summary of Goodlad's life begins with the humble story of a boy raised by parents who were not formally educated beyond elementary school, but whose ambition quickly outpaced what was considered possible in those years for the working class in North Vancouver, British Columbia. He entered the teaching profession in a rather informal manner and without all the overly credentialed titles one would need today, but rather as a young teacher in a one-room schoolhouse. This experience, followed by other grade school teaching positions in Canada, appears to have been a rather formidable determinant of his philosophical assumptions and concerns. In later years, he spoke of his time as a teacher in a one-room schoolhouse in terms that would be considered innovative and downright radical even today: children engaged with other children across age groups and ability groups, participating in an integrated curriculum they themselves had deemed important, while never earning a single formal grade. In this setting, he comes to outline the questions that become the animating force of his career: What does it mean to prepare young people for a meaningful life within a democracy? What would it mean to consider the cultural implications of schooling? How best should we prepare teachers for the intellectual and moral work they participate in daily? How should schools embark on continual renewal efforts as the world around the school shifts and evolves?

After his experiences in the one-room schoolhouse and prior to his arrival at the University of Chicago, Goodlad came to work at a "reform" school for boys. This experience appears to have colored much of his later scholarship and ethos regarding why "reform" can be a dangerous idea if imposed from afar and infused with unwieldy power. He wrote in a 2010 *Washington Post* three-part blog series:

> Reform, however, is commonly regarded as coming from the outside, imposed, and frequently regarded on the inside as noxious. In the dictionary in front of me, reform as a verb is "to put an end to [an evil] by enforcing or introducing a better method or course of action." The far

less palatable definition of the noun is "amendment of what is defective, vicious, corrupt, or depraved." Because, early in my career, I taught in and directed the education component of the British Columbia Industrial School for Boys (a.k.a. reform school), I always cringe with our careless use of "school reform," which I have endeavored, unsuccessfully, to get at least school principals and teachers to eschew.[2]

It becomes clear from this rendering that Goodlad's use of the word "renewal" is deliberate and should not be conflated with "reform." Thus, the labeling of Goodlad as an educational reformer should be refuted not only on semantical grounds, but on philosophical ones as well. Moreover, important connections arise among Goodlad's commitment to a cultural analysis of schooling, his belief in the power of the environment to shape youth, and his experiences in a variety of alternative educational settings. These connections lay the foundation for a lifetime of work inquiring into the moral, as well as what he described as the spiritual dimension of schools often ignored in most educational reform efforts—particularly today's reforms.

Goodlad earned his Ph.D. from the University of Chicago, a degree he finished in three years under the mentorship of Ralph Tyler, and held professorships at Agnes Scott College, Emory University, the University of Chicago, and the University of California, Los Angeles (UCLA). While at UCLA, he held the post of dean of the Graduate School of Education from 1967 to 1983 and helped UCLA gain prominence in the field. His books on education include the highly acclaimed *A Place Called School* (1984)—named American Educational Research Association's Outstanding Book for 1985 and the Distinguished Book of the Year Award from Kappa Delta Pi—*Teachers for Our Nation's Schools* (1990), *In Praise of Education* (1997), and *Romances with Schools* (2004). Goodlad has received numerous national awards in recognition of his work and was president of the American Association of Colleges for Teacher Education and the American Educational Research Association.

John Goodlad's final stop in a long and prolific career was as emeritus professor at the University of Washington, where he was a co-founder of the Center for Educational Renewal and president of the Institute for Educational Inquiry (IEI). His work in these two venues centered on a broad range of educational matters and the professional development of teachers and school leaders. In particular, the work of these two groups is described by the IEI as dedicated to "Foster[ing] in the nation's young the skills, attitudes, and knowledge necessary for effective participation in a social and political democracy."[3] These ideals were, and continue to be, further developed and expanded upon through the work of a variety of other organizations that Goodlad developed and inspired: namely, the National Network for Educational Renewal, the Agenda for Education in a Democracy, the Center for Educational Renewal, and the Goodlad Institute for Educational Renewal. All of these organizations are dedicated to what can be characterized as the grassroots, local renewal of educational spaces rather than the reform of our institutions through distant mandates that typically homogenize and serve the corporate interests of profit and efficiency.

An Overview of *A Place Called School*

A Place Called School reports the findings of "A Study of Schooling," in which Goodlad and numerous colleagues conducted what was generally described as a qualitative study of 7 geographical areas, 13 communities, 38 schools, 1,350 teachers, 8,624 parents, and 17,163 students over a period of 4 years. The overall purpose of the study was to "provide some insight into the schools studied and to raise thoughtful questions about what they appear to be doing, as well as, perhaps, *why* they do what they seem to be doing" (my emphasis).[4] The comprehensive view of school life offered was described as centered around three domains: the personal (self), the instructional (classroom), and the societal (school). To fully understand each domain, comprehensive data were collected through surveys, observations, interviews, and curriculum documents, out of which relevant variable clusters were defined as 16 "commonplaces" (i.e., teaching practices, content or subject matter, instructional materials, physical environment, activities, human resources, evaluation, time, organization, communications, decision making, leadership, goals, issues and problems, implicit (or "hidden") curriculum, and controls or restraints). The argument is made repeatedly that the study did not test hypotheses; rather, the multi-faceted interests of the researchers were incorporated for "wholly descriptive purposes, and to formulate heuristic interpretations about schooling in the particular locations under investigation."[5]

Goodlad acknowledges the painstaking difficulty of writing up the findings of the study and notes that he abandoned two other versions of the text but finally settled on a third. The recurring themes outlined by Goodlad in the immense collection of data include "school functions, relevance, how teachers teach, circumstances surrounding teaching, the curriculum, distribution of resources for learning, equity, implicit curriculum, satisfaction, and the need for data."[6] From the collected data, he names two "pervasive themes" that must be considered when improving schools: the school as a unit for improvement and caring. Goodlad reminds the readers that "Schools will improve slowly, if at all, if reforms are thrust upon them. Rather, the approach having most promise, in my judgment, is one that will seek to cultivate the capacity of schools to deal with their own problems, to become largely self-renewing."[7] Further, he frames "caring" as the concern of the public for its schools: "our schools will get better and have continuing good health only to the degree that a significant proportion of our people, not just parents, care about them."[8] Here it becomes clear why his commitment to a local school's internal renewal processes and the thoughtful commitment of the public in caring for its schools are more than simply his personal convictions, but rather ideals that emerge out of his exhaustive work within schools themselves.

The one measure that was omitted from the study was student achievement data. This choice has troubled many critics of the study, and I sense that this omission is the reason Goodlad's work is often overlooked in non-academic educational policy circles.[9] However, Goodlad and his research team defend the decision by explaining that the goal of the study was not to look at schools through the narrow lens of inputs and outputs: "Studying what goes on in schools holds more promise for understanding schools than what comes out of schools."[10] Achievement data focuses only on the output of schooling and thus flattens the contextual experience of schooling that occurs in the life of teachers, students, administrators, and parents. In the preface to the text he notes that "persons seeking 'a quick fix' will be bored and, at best, will flip the pages in search of a laundry list of recommendations. I have avoided such."[11] Yet in the final two chapters Goodlad does discuss some areas of interest for school improvement and imagines how Americans might "move" the ever-so-immutable institution of schooling. Before turning to these assertions, I want to complicate some of Goodlad's findings, given contemporary school initiatives, teacher education, and educational policy.

Interestingly, today's educators and observers frantically wring their hands over the "achievement gap," yet Goodlad framed such a problem as an "education gap" and defined it as "the distance between man's most noble visions of what he might become and present levels of functioning."[12] He argued that *had* this "gap" pervaded educational discourse at the state level, then we would have seen many citizens willing to participate in educational reform rather than waiting for a national movement to fix such a complex problem as schooling. However, today's Common Core movement *did* originate in the states (the location Goodlad had hoped for), with the Council of Chief State School Officers (CCSSO) and the National Governors Association Center for Best Practices (NGA) taking the lead and orchestrating the national dialogue around standards, curriculum, and refocusing the aim of schooling on a clear path to career and college readiness. Although I hesitate to speak for Goodlad, I am left to wonder if, like other progressive ideas, his have been hijacked by neoliberal private entities. This reality echoes the appropriation of Horace Mann's common school movement by the "robber barons" of the late nineteenth and early twentieth century's industrial revolution, which similarly exploited progressive ideals for private gain, and has left historians to debate the genuine success of the common school movement in America. In other words, what began as a progressive state-initiated movement was quickly and suddenly subsumed by corporate profiteers and the like.

The phrase "We want it all" is central to understanding the main thrust of *A Place Called School*. In general, parents feel that *their* child's school is doing a fairly good job, and when asked about the following four board goals—academic, vocational, social and civic, and personal—they rate all of them as "very important" on average.[13] Slight variations in the data occur depending on what level of education one is analyzing; thus, the key word in this sentence is "on average." The use of averages throughout Goodlad's text was a source of contention in a well-articulated review of the book written by Jo Anne Pagano. She argues that the use of averages and composites obscures the data and leads to a "thin-description" rather than the "thick-description" desired by most qualitative researchers.[14] Regardless of this methodological concern, Goodlad reveals that parents and students alike are keenly aware that schools do more than simply attend to the intellectual and academic parts of a student's life, and hence this is the reason why all the above areas are of equal importance to the public. Furthermore, schools and educators offer daily custodial care of youth whether they see themselves in this capacity or not. Goodlad crystallizes these findings and suggests two phrases that should appear on every classroom's bulletin board: "Teach my children with tender loving care" and "Knowledge sets the human spirit free."[15] However, there is the small caveat that *if* the academic aims are ill attended to, the public does become angered and disheartened about the ability of schools to prepare youth for adult life in a democracy.

The chapters titled "Inside Classrooms," "Access to Knowledge," "Teachers and the Circumstances of Teaching," and "What Schools and Classrooms Teach" offer an in-depth view of the instructional practices of teachers and the curriculum. Although there is always some variability, on average, the classrooms that were observed were shockingly similar in character—heavily teacher-directed, pedagogically flat spaces where students passively received information in a variety of adult-determined content areas and activities. In terms of inherent interest, students of all levels repeatedly ranked the core subjects of math, English, science, and social studies at the bottom of their interest list, but the arts, physical education, and vocational education were consistently at the top. Moreover, students preferred subjects where they were involved in "drawing, making, shaping, moving, and interacting."[16] However, these subjects were simultaneously regarded as the "easiest" and "least important," especially for those who were college bound (a notion Goodlad avidly refutes by stating that *all* students should engage with the arts and vocational education, not just those who will not attend college). The contemporary over-reliance on instructional "methods" in teacher education may, in fact, be the profession's attempt to correct this critique. However, when "methods" are coupled with an increase in "behavior management strategies" and the persistent call for the "assessment" of learning, the teacher is still positioned to be the orchestrator of learning, and I doubt that Goodlad's concerns have been—or will be—overcome through only subtle shifts in emphasis.

Regarding time spent on learning actual content, Goodlad found the public's fear that we must "return to the basics" to be relatively unsupported by the data he collected. In the 13 elementary schools studied, the overwhelming majority of the classroom day was spent on the basics—math and English. At the junior and senior high levels, English and math still occupied the largest part of the school day, but overall the curriculum appeared to be well balanced. However, the type (or level) of curriculum and instruction a student received was emblematic of the socioeconomic level of the community and whether or not the students were college bound. Not surprisingly, these differences appeared to be tied to social inequalities related to wealth, race, language, and ability. In other words, macro- and micro-tracking practices were alive and well in the classrooms that Goodlad observed. Consequently, the seminal work on tracking by Jeannie Oaks grew out of the large body of data collected and analyzed in "A Study of Schooling."[17]

The complexity and fine details of this study are impossible to summarize in this brief section. However, I hope that, by this point, the reader understands the overall outline of the work. On many counts, the details of the text were met with affirmation by the educational community, and many who were already philosophically aligned to Goodlad's work took notice of the call for the local renewal of schools. The thoughtful narrative gave noteworthy substance to what many educators already sensed and understood about school culture. Goodlad writes: "Pedagogy is not like painting, an art that begins and builds from an uncluttered canvas. The place we call school imposes a variety of restraints." These restraints are the complex cultural work that teachers must at times counteract and at other times build upon to succeed in educating America's diverse youth. Even the more controversial findings of the text were reasonably articulated without oversimplifying the complexity of the educational endeavor. However, to better understand why this text does not capture the larger public's attention and that of policymakers, I offer a brief reminder of the era in which *A Place Called School* was conceived that will help in the understanding of this historically essential book.

The 1980s—A Birthplace of "Crisis"

A Place Called School was written in an era of increased scrutiny regarding the outcomes of the American educational system. The national political scene was organizing itself around a movement dubbed "back to the basics." Conservative politics were ascending to a proper place where they could defend the "shining city on the hill" narrative and restore American "values." The linchpin to this aim was the positioning of schools at the center of the great struggle to create in our young an allegiance to the American dream through a model of citizenry conceived only as an economic a priori in the global marketplace.[18] The early 1980s can be seen as the birthplace of many of the educational "reforms" of today. From Common Core Standards to the over-reliance on standardized test scores, from the corporate takeover of public schooling to the erosion of teacher unions, the 1980s set in motion a paradigm shift in regard to educational policy and practice. This shift, I believe, echoes what Thomas Kuhn theorizes regarding paradigm shifts in the scientific world.[19]

Sifting through the early 1980s educational rhetoric has been somewhat challenging—if not downright enraging—in light of the realities many educators now occupy. Writing this chapter has been an arduous task due to the recent conflation of neoconservative and neoliberal forces in educational policy that defy all known renderings of public schools in a democracy.[20] I also characterize this experience as difficult because I am of the generation that is under investigation. At the time of *A Place Called School*'s publication, I was in elementary school in what Goodlad characterized as a "B"-rated classroom: White, middle-class, suburban, boring, passive, occupied by teachers who felt they were adequately prepared for the task at hand, and cared for by parents who felt that their children's schools were doing an "all right" job. My older sisters were the recent high school graduates who were cast as ill prepared for the global job market and disaffected from the demands of citizenship in *A Nation at Risk* (1983).

Unsuspecting, my peers and I were oblivious to any level of mis-education taking place within the walls of our classrooms. In 1984 I was about to be told for the first time by a teacher in front of my peers that I had "good" reading comprehension, and was on the verge of answering the brain-teaser written on the chalkboard for an extra credit point: "How many birthdays does the average man have?" As a cohort, my peers and I were about to learn about sex and our changing bodies—the year after the virus responsible for AIDS was discovered. We were the last generation to grow up entirely "off-line," as the first cell phone had just been approved by the U.S. Federal Communications Commission (September 21, 1983), and Steve Jobs had just released the first personal computer (January 24, 1984)—neither of which I actually owned until I went off to college in the early 1990s. Many of us were unaware that we were in the midst of the highest unemployment rate since 1941, or that our parents were struggling to pay the bills as a result. The famine in Ethiopia was about to capture our imaginations, and we would soon learn the lyrics to the song "We Are the World." The iconic McDonald's franchise was about to suffer a mass shooting that left 21 dead and 19 injured in San Diego. And through all of this, we were completely oblivious to the fact that our *schooling* was what would make our lives and our democratic society difficult and troublesome in the very near future.

The most infamous document of the era was certainly *A Nation at Risk*,[21] whose authors claimed:

> If an unfriendly foreign power had attempted to impose on America the mediocre educational performance that exists today, we might well have viewed it as an act of war. As it stands, we have allowed this to happen to ourselves. We have even squandered the gains in student achievement made in the wake of the Sputnik challenge. Moreover, we have dismantled essential support systems which helped make those gains possible. We have, in effect, been committing an act of unthinking, unilateral educational disarmament. [22]

One might assume that rhetoric of this kind was seen as outlandish. The difficulties and failures of the education system were akin to an act of *war*? Certainly this narrative has become so deeply ingrained in the psyche of educational reformers, who often lack experience in actual classrooms, that this exact language was echoed (almost verbatim) in a 2012 document penned by the Council on Foreign Relations.[23] Adding to the doomsday narrative, *A Nation at Risk* proclaimed: "For the first time in the history of our country, the educational skills of one generation will not surpass, will not equal, will not even approach, those of their parents."[24] Such claims, I hope, will always be met with a healthy dose of skepticism, but for some reason such skepticism was missing from the common rhetoric of the era.

Still, the education world of the early 1980s was abuzz with various reports and declarations, demands and desires for change. *A Nation at Risk, High School, The Paedeia Proposal, Academic Preparation for College, A Place Called School*—all of these texts supported the notion that something was amiss, and gravely so, in American schools.[25] Unfortunately, it appears that the public and educational policymakers took to heart and put into action the recommendations of only one of these documents—*A Nation at Risk.* Theodore Sizer reminds readers of this era that Goodlad's work was 361 pages long, with 19 pages of references and notes, and provided a rich discussion of why schools were the way they were, while *A Nation at Risk,* by comparison, was 36 pages long, with 25 pages of appendices, and succeeded in offering a crisp, bulleted, easy-to-read analysis of various outcome data, tidy recommendations, and a thoughtless call to action.[26] Overt fear-mongering in *A Nation at Risk* is found in phrases such as "history is not kind to idlers," reminding educators that fear is a powerful motivator in convincing Americans to respond to a threat akin to an act of *war.* However, this action might be seen as a call to reaction. I suspect that Goodlad would be sympathetic to my phrasing "a call to reaction" because he often distinguished between *behavior* and *action,* noting: "There is a considerable distinction between behavior and action. To act takes courage, risks failure, and often stirs contrary views and actions."[27] Reactions seen as behaviors, on the other hand, can be thought of as thoughtless responses to stimuli. Goodlad took seriously the intellectual demands of deliberate action, and history has shown that others of this era did not have time for such messiness.[28]

Regardless of the particularities, the stage was set for decades of crisis narrative, reform plans, a subtle but now rapid dismantling of the social contract that rested at the center of the American public schooling ideal—and the scapegoating of an entire profession. Although some of these documents invite readers into the complexities of a classroom and life in a school, many of them operate as usefully as a grenade launcher in the town square. Hyperbole aside, what has been the operational function of this narrative of educational failure on a system, and on generations of young people who will inherit the world whether or not they are adequately educated? Are schools *really* solely responsible for the outcomes of their graduates when they occupy a living, breathing zeitgeist of macroeconomic transnational capitalism that seems far more influential on their life prospects than state academic standards, the SAT, and lesson plans? Returning to my personal narrative for a moment, I would suggest that my schooling has been the least of my problems; instead, events such as September 11, 2001, the war in Iraq, the collapse of the housing market, the cost of health care, record unemployment rates (even among the well-educated), and crippling student loan debt—these are surely more significant in the algorithm that will determine if my generation has achieved, or will achieve, more than our parents.

Concluding Thoughts: Or, Why More "Data" Will Not Save Schools

The strengths of *A Place Called School* are significant, then and now. First, this text is surely a methodological achievement in size and complexity; also, the intense collaborative nature of the research design, analysis, and various write-ups leave educational researchers in awe. The comprehensive nature of the book inspires the educational researcher to move beyond the narrow trappings of quantitative and qualitative methodologies, which today seem to embody the language of fetish and result in myopic views of schooling. Furthermore, today the academy has made a spectacle of methodology—leaving my doctoral students to earnestly look up from their methods textbooks and ask, "What is the difference between the purpose statement and the problem statement?"—as if the words *purpose* and *problem* have suddenly taken on some new and illusive meaning they must now learn in order to conduct quality research. Goodlad restores the tradition of inquiry to its rightful place in educational research and resists the seductive language of methods, technique, and the hypothetico-deductive model of inquiry. The decision to move the language of the text toward a broader audience by omitting the specialized jargon of methods should be seen as a bold, conscious action, not an oversight.

However, I do see a need to critique Goodlad's call for more data regarding the place we call school. My critique is sourced in the zeitgeist of today's educational fervor (with the advantage of hindsight) and posits that more complex, comprehensive forms of data will not, and currently do not, matter in the case of schools, because this assumes a certain sophistication and political care on the part of those involved in analyzing the data and bringing such claims to educational reform and policy. Further, the call for "more data" assumes that the system is not, in fact, already doing the work it was intended to do to keep in place the imperatives of social reproduction, meritocracy, and Whiteness. I say this not simply to be contrarian, or because this collection's editor has asked each author to offer some sort of critique, but because I am downright serious in this observation. Goodlad's writing has done significant work in shaping the hearts and minds of those already in the proverbial choir, and has helped the educational researcher to rethink how we come to see education as a cultural endeavor within a democracy. But it has unfortunately done little to shape the beliefs of those with actual "active" power over the institution of schooling (i.e., state and federal government officials), and, in particular, it has done little to stop the forces that subject schooling to the logic of efficiency, technocratic rationality, and capitalistic aims.

A concern that flows from this text unfortunately arrives at the contemporary reality that educators need more data to solve our educational problems. An unsuspected weakness in this book is that it indulges our desire for data absent a radical critique of data. I fear that Goodlad's words unknowingly lend tacit support to the heavy-handed overreach of the state and federal government into the minutiae of life inside classrooms. In the 30 years since *A Place Called School* was released, education has only seen an escalation in a "survival of the fittest" outputs reality, and I have little faith that more data—even more complex, culturally sensitive data—can undo or ward off this pervasive vision of schooling. Thus, I believe strongly that what schooling in America needs is a *philosophical* revolution—one that will protect schools, classrooms, teachers, and students from the co-opting forces of progressive ideals for economic gain.

Finally, I want to return to Thomas Kuhn's notion of paradigm shifts within the scientific community to illuminate why the recommendations of Goodlad will remain difficult to achieve within our contemporary historical moment. Kuhn describes what I would loosely characterize as hegemony, the role of paradigms within different professional specializations of science, and why revolutionary forces of change are not universally felt by all specializations— what he labeled the "specialization's effect."[29] Although sub-specializations are aware of such changes (e.g., the arrival of quantum mechanics), each individual stakeholder experiences these changes through his or her own disciplinary assumptions: "Undoubtedly their experiences had had much in common, but they did not, in this case, tell the two specialists the same thing."[30] Given the non-universal experience with significant changes within disciplines, Kuhn goes on to explain that crisis tends to be the prelude to paradigm shifts. However, "though they [scientists] may begin to lose faith and then to consider alternatives, they do not renounce the paradigm that has led them into crisis."[31] Unfortunately, "once it has achieved the status of paradigm, a scientific theory is declared invalid only if an alternate candidate is available to take its place."[32] Thus, if education borrows Kuhn's understandings, it becomes clear that until the institution of schooling is able to be conceived of from within an alternative dimension that rises to that of a paradigm, it is unlikely that subtle shifts will transform the reality of schooling. Finally, the expansion of professional specializations, which keeps us arguing with each other over the very experience of schooling, does the field of education no favors in warding off the aggressive appropriation of progressive ideals for pecuniary gain. In this light, Goodlad's book is indispensable for a continuing thoughtful critique of schooling as an institution—if only such a text could become paradigmatically powerful in shifting the ground beneath the school.

Notes

1   "Honoring John I. Goodlad," Goodlad Institute for Educational Renewal, http://www.bothell.washington.edu/research/centers/goodladinstitute/about/johngoodlad (accessed January 10, 2015).

2   Valerie Straus, "Goodlad on School Reform: Are We Ignoring Lessons of the Last 50 Years?" *The Answer Sheet* (April 27, 2010), http://voices.washingtonpost.com/answer-sheet/john-goodlad/goodlad-straight-talk-about-ou.html (accessed November 1, 2014).

3   Institute for Educational Inquiry, http://www.ieiseattle.org (accessed November 1, 2014).

4   John I. Goodlad, Kenneth A. Sirotnik, and Bette C. Overman, "An Overview of a Study of Schooling," *The Phi Delta Kappan* 61, no. 3 (1979): 174.

5   Goodlad et al., "An Overview," 177.

6   John I. Goodlad, *A Place Called School: Prospects for the Future* (New York: McGraw-Hill, 1984), 28–31.

7   Goodlad, *A Place Called School*, 31.

8   Goodlad, *A Place Called School*, 32.

9   National Commission on Excellence in Education, *A Nation at Risk: The Imperative for Educational Reform* (Washington, DC: U.S. Government Printing Office, 1983), https://www2.ed.gov/pubs/NatAtRisk/risk.html; Ernest L. Boyer, *High School: A Report on Secondary Education in America* (New York: Joanna Cotler Books, 1983); Mortimer J. Adler, *The Paideia Proposal: An Educational Manifesto* (New York: Touchstone, 1982); College Board through the Educational Equality Project, *Academic Preparation for College: What Students Need to Know and Be Able to Do* (New York: College Entrance Examination Board, 1983).

10   Goodlad et al., "An Overview," 178.

11   Goodlad, *A Place Called School*, xix.

12   John I. Goodlad, *What Schools Are For* (Bloomington, IN: Phi Delta Kappa Educational Foundation, 1979), 16.

13   Goodlad, *A Place Called School*, 37; Jo Anne Pagano, "The Schools We Deserve," *Curriculum Inquiry* 17, no. 1 (1987): 107–122.

14   Pagano, "The Schools We Deserve."

15   Goodlad, *A Place Called School*, 88.

16   Goodlad, *A Place Called School*, 124.

17   Jeannie Oaks was a professional staff member of the project who wrote multiple technical reports regarding the data of "A Study of Schooling." See Jeannie Oaks, *Keeping Track: How Schools Structure Inequality* (New Haven, CT: Yale University Press, 1986).

18   Heybach and Sheffield explore this in the following chapter, Jessica A. Heybach and Eric C. Sheffield, "Creating Citizens in a Capitalistic Democracy: A Struggle for the Soul of American Citizenship Education," in *Citizenship Education Around the World: Global Perspectives, Local Practices*, ed. J. Petrovic and A. Kuntz (New York: Routledge, 2014), 66–86.

19   Thomas Kuhn, *The Structure of Scientific Revolutions* (1962; repr. Chicago: University of Chicago Press, 2012).

20   Heybach and Sheffield, 66–86.

21   Theodore R. Sizer, "Back to *A Place Called School*," in *The Beat of a Different Drummer: Essays on Educational Renewal in Honor of John I. Goodlad*, ed. Kenneth A. Sirotnik and Roger Soder (New York: Peter Lang, 1999), 103–104. Sizer offers a description of the relationship between Goodlad's work and *A Nation at Risk*. The National Commission on Excellence in Education, led by David Gardner (president-elect of the University of California), published the report *A Nation at Risk* and "turned to Professor Goodlad for help. The Study [*A Study of Schooling*] staff met with the Commission and offered access to all of its then-gathered material. Contact thereafter apparently was fleeting."

22   National Commission on Excellence in Education, *A Nation at Risk: The Imperative for Educational Reform* (Washington, DC: U.S. Government Printing Office, 1983), https://www2.ed.gov/pubs/NatAtRisk/risk.html

23 Council on Foreign Relations, "U.S. Education Reform and National Security," http://www.cfr.org/united-states/us-education-reform-national-security/p27618, 3.
24 *A Nation at Risk.*
25 *A Nation at Risk*; Boyer, *High School*; Adler, *The Paideia Proposal*; College Board, *Academic Preparation for College.*
26 Sizer, "Back to *A Place Called School.*"
27 Straus, "Goodlad on School Reform."
28 Straus, "Goodlad on School Reform." Goodlad states: "The prospect of sweeping change was gaining attention and conversation. Of course, as philosopher Hannah Arendt makes clear in her classic book *The Human Condition*, there is a considerable distinction between behavior and action. To act takes courage, risks failure, and often stirs contrary views and actions."
29 Kuhn, *The Structure of Scientific Revolutions*, 50.
30 Kuhn, *The Structure of Scientific Revolutions*, 51.
31 Kuhn, *The Structure of Scientific Revolutions*, 77.
32 Kuhn, *The Structure of Scientific Revolutions*, 77.

Fifteen

Theodore R. Sizer, *Horace's Compromise: The Dilemma of the American High School* (1984)

Brett Elizabeth Blake and Robert W. Blake, Jr.

Introduction

Theodore Sizer's *Horace's Compromise* was the first of a trilogy of books that helped to place Sizer's name alongside other famous school reformers, including John Dewey, whose work influenced him profoundly. Professor Sizer founded the Coalition of Essential Schools (CES) the same year he published *Horace's Compromise.* He believed that schools could be more egalitarian and more focused on the needs of students, emphasizing standards over standardization. However, they had to follow a set of principles that he saw as not only "largely general" but, more important, as "insistent." Among these guiding principles were such overarching ideas as "sustenance" and "integrity," embedded in a "tone of decency and trust" among all participants. Sizer would no doubt contend that these principles are no less important today as U.S. schools face an increasing barrage of tests, standards, and accountability measures that continue to "compromise" teachers' teaching and students' learning.

Data for *Horace's Compromise* came from a longitudinal ethnographic study of American high schools that was co-sponsored by the National Association of Secondary School Principals and the Commission on Educational Issues of the National Association of Independent Schools.

Ted Sizer was dean of the Harvard Graduate School of Education and professor and chair of the Education Department at Brown University. Dr. Sizer died in 2009.

Cultural and Educational Context

As Beineke (2015) discusses briefly in his essay on Ernest Boyer (Chapter 13 of this collection), Sizer was writing at a time of renewed interest in the American educational system and the role that schools played in society. As the progressive movement(s) of the late 1960s and 1970s fell into disfavor and Ronald Reagan, a conservative Republican, was elected president, society, too, turned toward economic systems (think: Reagan's "trickle-down" economics), singling out Japan as a business (and educational) model that the United States should emulate.

This feeling was powerfully echoed in the National Commission on Excellence in Education's publication *A Nation at Risk: The Imperative for Educational Reform* (1983), which outlined steps that schools needed to take to ensure our nation's security. Written in what Rich and DeVitis (1987) deemed "a strident, urgent style employing military metaphors reminiscent of the Sputnik era" (p. 222), *A Nation at Risk* stood in direct opposition to Sizer's "less is more" principle by decreeing that both a longer school day and a longer school year were needed. *Horace's Compromise* was part of the blizzard of reports and manifestos on education that swirled through America from April 1983 through the end of 1984, causing leading conservative educators to jump on the bandwagon, while books such as *Cultural Literacy: What Every American Needs to Know* (Hirsch, 1984) were published to great acclaim.

Synopsis

Sizer begins his book with an introduction on the complexity and diversity of "adolescence," juxtaposing this complexity with the fact that, regardless of such diversity, most high schools are strikingly similar. "Horace" is the main "character" (a composite of the many teachers Sizer had met and observed over the years who situated in this context, working long hours and extra jobs to keep his mission as a teacher intact). High schools, after all, were designed to keep adolescents "in line" and were constructed so that teachers could accomplish this goal by teaching or "covering" the curriculum and then testing to "ensure" learning. And yet, like other school reformers who came after him (see Ayers, 1998; Blake, 2004), Sizer implied the importance of the *nature* of adolescents—not only the "tumultuous time [they experienced] in the best of circumstances" (Ayers, in Blake, 1997, p. 3), but also as a "critical period involving dramatic transitions in one's physical as well as one's social environment" (Blake, 2010, p. 3). He emphasized how society, in 1984, tended to underrate and misunderstand the "complicated issues that require careful reasoning" (p. 4), including complex choices that adolescents undertake on a daily basis. High schools are crucial in the development of adolescents and must, Sizer recommended, restore to teachers the "largest share of responsibility" in reaching them.

Following the introduction is the prologue, aptly titled "Horace's Compromise." It is here that Sizer clearly outlines a day in the life of a fictitious (and yet very real) teacher, Horace, and the details of his "compromise." Understanding this "compromise" is essential to the book as a whole.

Horace "arises at 5:45 AM" (p. 9), wanting to arrive at school by 7:00 to begin his day of teaching at 7:30. If he could afford to live closer to school, even in the same district, he would. (In the next half-dozen pages, Sizer describes the events in Horace's five-and-one-half hour, seven-period teaching day, five of which are spent actually teaching). Horace leaves at 2:30 p.m. and proceeds to his second job, the liquor store his wife and brother-in-law own and operate. Working there until early evening, Horace has dinner around 7:45 and afterward returns to his teacher duties: papers, planning, and phone calls to students who have missed class. By 10:45 or so, Horace calls it a night and falls asleep watching the 11 o'clock news. Such is the daily life of Horace. Though busy, it seems unfulfilled. The fundamental question in this book is Why? What is *the* "compromise" so essential to Horace's teaching life? What is "it" that, while going against his high standards and better judgment, becomes so necessary in his teaching?

Let's do the numbers. Horace "teaches" a total of 120 students per day (45 fewer than in the major metropolitan areas of New York City, St. Louis, or Detroit). As an English teacher, he believes in the necessity of writing and the written expression to organize thoughts and ideas. Thus he wants his students to write "something for criticism at least twice a week—but he is realistic" (p. 17). He compromises and settles for "once a week." With most of his students being juniors and seniors, Horace believes that they should be writing "beyond sentences and paragraph exercises" and working on pieces that involve more critical analyses: "short essays, written arguments, and moderately complex sequencing…" (p. 17). Sizer states that Horace's ideal is "a page or two…minimum—but Horace is realistic" (p. 17). Instead he assigns "one or two paragraphs." As a veteran teacher, Horace also believes in the need for critical feedback to his students—thoroughly reading, critiquing, and commenting on their writing. Normally, however, "Horace takes only fifteen to twenty minutes to check over each student's daily homework, to read the week's theme, and to write an analysis of it" (p. 17). Consequently, "he compromises, averaging five minutes for each student's work by cutting all but the most essential corners" (pp. 7–8).

In the next few pages (17–19) Sizer continues to detail Horace's workload and the "compromises" he must take to get it all done. These duties—some required and some chosen— include preparation, assignment reading, actual teaching, administrative duties, extra duties (Theater Club), writing student recommendations (over 50 per year), and working a second job that adds roughly 7% to his low base salary of $27,300 (1980 dollars). Thus, before he

> assigns his one or two paragraphs per week, he is committed for over thirty-two hours of teaching, administration, class preparation, and extracurricular drama work. Collecting one short piece of writing per week from students and spending a bare five minutes per week on each student's week work adds ten hours, yielding a forty-two hour work week. (p. 19)

Anything else he does (commuting, breaks, "biological necessities") is extra. As Sizer summarizes:

> Most jobs in the real world have a gap between what would be nice and what is possible…. Even after adroit accommodations and devastating compromises—only *five minutes per week* of attention on the written work of each student and an average of ten minutes of planning for each fifty-odd-minute class—the task is already crushing, in reality a sixty-hour work week. (p. 20)

Even so, Sizer explains that the general public seemingly couldn't care less if Horace does not assign an extra paragraph per week, or if he does not engage students in active learning, instead relying on lectures and the use of the overhead projector. As long as his classes are orderly, which they are, and as long as his students get into college, which most do, all are happy. Complaining would "find no seriously empathetic audience…no one blames the system; everyone blames him" (p. 21); and if he happened to share his views with someone conducting a study on high schools, "he will be portrayed as a whining hypocrite" (p. 21). Thus are the essential pieces of the compromise of Horace.

The remainder of the book (reminiscent of Schwab's "The Practical 3: Translation into Curriculum" [1973]) is divided into four sections, each dealing with a component of the 1980s high school. The sections are *The Students, The Program, The Teachers,* and *The Structure.* We will summarize them in order.

The Students

> We all work best for people we respect, we study well in school for teachers we admire, we admire and respect those teachers who know us as individual, worthwhile people. (p. 66)

Indeed, adolescence is a tumultuous period in life. As Sizer takes us into three different high schools, we catch a glimpse of how each school's expectations and treatment of students differ. This difference in discourse, he insists, is not based solely on race, but falls more squarely on social class. As we are taken through an upper-class school, a low-income urban school, and an urban Catholic school, we see how adults pay little attention to (and do not speak to) those students in the urban, so-called "lower-class" schools. In all of these schools, however, we notice how almost everything the students do is underrated, and we vividly view classroom vignettes of the "separateness," "complacency," and "docility" of most of the students. Yet Sizer shows us the "hunger" that many of the students he observed demonstrated—a hunger that often goes unnoticed.

The Program

> Should there be a common learning…a set of skills and beliefs? If mandatory, [it] is an abuse of state power, an excessive reach of political authority…less is more. (pp. 86–88)

In this section, Sizer reminds us how rigidly compartmentalized high schools are. He returns to the "factory model" metaphor (originally coined by Dewey) by stating that students' schedules are a "series of units," much like a "conveyor belt" on the factory line. However, rather than an orderly, quiet factory line, he describes the often "frenetic" nature of high schools: rushing between classes, gulping down lunches, and sitting through (too often large) classes in which students are just an "audience" (think: factory line worker). They busy themselves with mundane activities such as copying notes from interconnecting chalkboards that seem to swallow entire rooms.

What Sizer suggests one *should* see in high school classrooms is students "doing": collaborating, observing, presenting, and demonstrating mastery through inference, critical thinking, and, above all, writing. Indeed, Sizer envisions writing as "not only an end in itself; it is a means by which a person can delve into his or her mind" (p. 104). He concludes by reminding us that the word "principal," by definition, means "first, foremost, or lead," or "principal" teacher, and therefore every principal should play the role. After all, one "goes to school to change" (p. 122). Leaders can help adolescents to learn, grow, and change in this world.

The Teachers

Good teachers can inspire powerful learning, especially in adolescents. (p. 180)

As we meet three very different teachers here, we are reminded again that good teaching involves not only sound judgment, but a bit of theater. We "watch" as a Catholic nun teaches 39 students in an urban classroom and are astounded that, even with such high numbers, teaching cannot be done "at arm's length" (p. 122). These teachers show us the art of negotiation, of turning the concrete into the abstract (and vice versa), and the joy of success. Good teachers, indeed, inspire.

Sizer claims that "learning is complex, effortful, and often painful" (p. 151). However, he adds that it might be less so if American society were to pay more sustained attention to teachers—if, for example, both parents and policymakers advocated and pushed for more engaging work environments, demanded salary increases and smaller class sizes, understood that tracking is dangerous, allowed teachers to be in charge of (and test from) one's own curriculum, and agreed that "some success…is better than no success at all" (p. 165). Most critically, however, society needs to understand that teaching must rest in the hands of teachers, much like the work of other professionals (e.g., that of physicians and attorneys). Teachers need to be the decision makers, the power wielders, and the collaborators. As Sizer points out succinctly: "*Horace* is the key" (p. 201; emphasis added).

The Structure

Bureaucracy depends on the specific, the measurable. Large, complex units need simple ways of describing themselves, so those aspects of school keeping which can be readily quantified often become the only forms of representation (p. 207)…. [The] particular needs of each student should be the only measure. (p. 214)

Most of us dislike change, Sizer claims, so high schools remain bastions of top-down, quantifiable, measurable, licensed, regulated settings that stifle initiative and creativity. In fact, society places too much of its belief in systems that can be "scientifically managed," essentially rendering American education "paralyzed" (p. 206) in terms of change.

Because reformers are usually not teachers—teachers, after all, are really only viewed as "semi-competent" (p. 219)—-this top-down approach is allowed to remain out of reach of the very people who work so closely every day in schools, as well as the more powerless students who hunger to learn from them. And teachers do have the power to demand better schools. According to Sizer, then, this vision of a better school includes the centrality of the teacher and students, a variety of school settings (depending on who the students are), a flexible structure, and the use of the mind—every minute of every school day. We are reminded that the "unchallenging mindlessness…of the status quo…doesn't make waves" (p. 237). Only a continuing conversation, both practical and political in nature, can do that—a conversation that has at its core our high school students and their learning, one that can lead to real and sustained change.

Weaknesses/Early Critiques

Early critiques of Sizer's work came in many forms. Most commonly, researchers and educators alike seemed to confuse Sizer's message of the necessity of a "student-centered" curriculum, reminiscent of failed progressivism, or one of "puzzling humanism" (Rich & DeVitis, 1987), with his general vision for a more egalitarian system with "vague" (Westheimer, 1993) specifics. Indeed, this first book of the trilogy did not lay out specific changes. In fact (and Sizer claims that doing so would be a detriment to real reform in education), it claims that "models and programs, to have sustenance and integrity, must arise independently out of the communities and schools" (p. 225). He immediately followed with a listing of nine common principles that could guide school reform—principles that are "as insistent as they are largely general" (p. 225). Even so, the criticism that he offered no specific formula or recipe for addressing failing schools was an early target. And yet it is clear from reading the 2004 preface and afterword (which appeared in the 2004 published version of the original 1984 copyright) Sizer *understood* that to be a problem, albeit in retrospect.

More important, we believe that two major omissions/misunderstandings in the original 1984 publication were a lack of the knowledge of the importance of simultaneous second-language instruction as a crucial cognitive and linguistic tool for adolescents' learning, and a tacit—seemingly cursory—review of the real issues of "low resource" schools. These urban schools, with underperforming teachers and students, violence-ridden campuses, and segregated systems, rivaled those of pre-*Brown v. Board of Education* in 1954. (To be fair, Sizer returned to both of these issues in his later work, and those who worked alongside him in the 1980s and 1990s didn't see these issues as omissions at all. Indeed, one had to know him to realize that he understood clearly the inherent institutionalized racism that pervaded poor urban school systems. The first Essential Schools were themselves located in then-crumbling downtown Providence, Rhode Island. But for those reading the 1984 book, these two issues do not stand out as painfully ignored by choice (or ignorance), as they would if he were writing today.

Less important, but certainly worth mentioning, is Sizer's disdain for "vocational education," reflected in his statement that they "are often cruel social dumping grounds" (p. 35). (In fact, a short 4 years after *Horace's Compromise* was published, Oakes's [1985] groundbreaking study on tracking clearly supported Sizer's contempt for such practices. Oakes [1988] went even further in describing the lower-track class structure as one of less experienced teachers, poor curriculum that emphasizes low-level worksheet learning, and classes often made up of students of color, linguistic diversity, and low social status.) So, while we largely agree with Sizer's description of the so-called "lower track," vocational education—then and now—has been the only option for poor, under-counseled, under-taught students of color. There are, however, some current programs—for example, the Thomas A. Edison Career & Technical Education High School in Queens, New York—that have incorporated literacy and numeracy-based courses into their curricula in line with the push for a "career-ready" workforce of the twenty-first century. Perhaps Sizer's statement on vocational education was more an indictment of vocational programs of the 1980s that might not be as appropriate today.

Later Critiques

When Sizer's last book in the "Horace" trilogy, *Horace's Hope: What Works for the American High School* (1996) was published, critics returned to *Horace's Compromise* to reframe their arguments for a national standardized curriculum. Calling Professor Sizer "a left-leaning radical," Mosle (1996) wrote in *The New York Times*:

> The bigger problem with the progressive movement has less to do with its methods per se than with the great difficulty of replicating its successes on a larger scale…there's something ultimately impractical about a reform program that is so difficult to implement. Even Horace, Mr. Sizer's fictional composite character, introduced in 1984 in *Horace's Compromise*, his landmark study of the American high school, has been at his reforms for quite a while. Mr. Sizer created Horace to express the collective frustrations of many high school teachers in "factory model" schools, and at first Horace seemed like an inspired device…. Horace [now] seems a little worn out. Isn't it time that he collected his pension and retired?

Other critics believed that Sizer's recommendations for better schools—the elements of The Essential School Movement—were simply far better "articulated on paper than in practice." In a review of *The Students Are Watching* (1999), which Sizer co authored with his wife, *New York Times* critic James Traub claimed:

> The coalition schools illustrate a vexing problem for progressives, for while the best of them are inspiring, most of them, as Sizer himself has acknowledged, fall far short of the founding principles. (Traub, cited in Fox, 2009)

Strengths

Still, amid the current wave of reform initiatives, Sizer's approach and sensibilities appear strikingly sound. If anyone can do more than expel disengaged kids from high school or award just certificates of attendance to one-third of our seniors, this book suggests that it will be Theodore Sizer (Sedlack, 1985).

Founded as a group of 12 schools in 1984 and based on 10 common principles outlined by Sizer (9 in the original book), the Coalition of Essential Schools now numbers over 600 affiliates nationwide, "with many schools still using the 10 common principles but not being affiliates" (Darlene Hart, Coalition of Essential Schools, email communication, February 19, 2015). Even within the context of the time, Mosle's statements seem quite perplexing. With simple research, she could have found that, by 1992,

> 120 Coalition schools were in existence and another 172 were either planning on becoming members or were discussing the common principles (and presumably exploring the eventual possibility of Coalition membership). In less than ten years, Sizer's reform effort had spread to almost three hundred schools across the country. Today, the Coalition is involved with over nine hundred private, parochial, public, urban, suburban, and rural schools across the United States. (Muncey & McQuillan, 1996)

It would appear that one's definition of "large scale" would need defining, but even an impact on 300 schools seems substantial. In fact, Mosle—or anyone, for that matter—would be hard pressed to find a single reform effort that not only had such longevity but also impacted hundreds of schools (and thousands of students) nationwide.

In additional to longevity, another strength of "Horace's compromise" is its focus on students, faculty, and the climate in which they work. In the second book in the trilogy, *Horace's School* (1992), Sizer states:

> Good schools are thoughtful places. The people in them are known…. There are quiet places available as well as places for socializing. No one is ridiculed. No one is the servant of another. The work is shared. The entire place is thoughtful: everything in its routine meets a standard of common sense and civility. At such places do adolescents learn about the thoughtful life. (p. 128)

Like Dewey (1902/1990), his contemporary Kozol (1991), and later Ayers and Ayers (2011), Sizer's emphasis on the student, common decency, and active learning is refreshing. With the composite, fictitious Horace at its center, "Horace's compromise" makes one feel as if he or she were actually in the school, experiencing not only Horace's working conditions, but also his students' frustrations, reflections, and their small successes. That is what good ethnography is supposed to do: give us entry into a culture previously unknown to the outside world—in this case, the American high school.

As for the curriculum (again, see Schwab, 1973, as well as Blake, 2002), William Schubert (1986) often challenged his students with this fundamental question: "What is most worthwhile to learn and experience?" The strength of *Horace's Compromise* echoes this sentiment through the insistence of pushing teachers and students to constantly ask what is *essential* within the learning process. Posing that question so eloquently is a fundamental key and lasting legacy of *Horace's Compromise* and the Coalition of Essential Schools. One only needs to follow the career of Grant Wiggins, Sizer's former colleague at Brown and to read *Wiggins and McTighe*'s *Understanding by Design* (1998, 2005) and *Essential Questions* (McTighe & Wiggins, 2013) to see the lasting impact that *Horace* had on teaching and learning.

One of Sizer's prime perspectives is that a crucial part of schooling should be a focus on the student and her application of understanding through a true demonstration of learning: an *Exhibition of Mastery*. The notion of showing by doing is not unique but is particularly difficult given today's push for more standards and testing (see Common Core State Standards and the *PARCC* assessment). One contemporary area that seems to promote the concept of an *Exhibition*, at least on the surface, is the edTPA, a pre-service teacher performance assessment initiated by Stanford's Center for Assessment, Learning and Equity (SCALE). Strongly supported by Linda Darling-Hammond (keynote speaker at the edTPA national conference, 2012), edTPA is an example of an *Exhibition of Mastery*, where students have to show, through writing and the use of a video clip, their mastery of the complexities of teaching. (In fact, a video of a science lesson displayed by Darling-Hammond at the 2012 conference—one that modeled good teaching—could have been recorded 10, 20, or even 30 years ago in any number of Essential Schools.)

In a 1996 review of an ethnographic study of the impact of the Coalition of Schools, Muncey and McQuillan stated:

There are no quick fixes or miracle panaceas for American education. We urge ongoing and future reform efforts to study closely and learn from the experiences of these Coalition schools—including those some might consider disappointments—rather than dismissing them on the way to catching the next wave of educational change. (p. 295)

Interestingly enough, we believe that if you remove the copyright date from *Horace's Compromise*, the text and ideas could now be presented as a "new and bold" perspective in education reform. Yet again, we believe that the legacy of Sizer is the longevity of Horace's ideas and the humanist spirit that discerns what is essential to learning is…after all…essential.

References

Ayers, R., & Ayers, W. (2011). *Teaching the taboo: Courage and imagination in the classroom.* New York: Teachers College Press.

Ayers, W. (1998). *A kind and just parent: The children of juvenile court.* Boston, MA: Beacon Press.

Beineke, J.A. (2016). Ernest L. Boyer, *High school: A report on secondary education in America*, 1983. In J.L. DeVitis (Ed.), *Popular educational classics: A reader.* New York: Peter Lang.

Blake, B.E. (1997). *She say, he say: Urban girls write their lives.* Albany: State University of New York Press.

Blake, B.E. (2004). *A culture of refusal: The lives and literacies of out of school adolescents.* New York: Peter Lang.

Blake, B.E. (2010). Theoretical overview: Adolescent culture and the culture of refusal. In J.L. DeVitis & L. Irwin-DeVitis (Eds.), *Adolescent education: A reader.* New York: Peter Lang.

Blake, R.W., Jr. (2002). *An enactment of science: A dynamic balance among teacher beliefs, curriculum, and context.* New York: Peter Lang.

Dewey, J. (1938). *Experience and education.* New York: Macmillan.

Dewey, J. (1990). *The school and society. The child and curriculum.* Chicago: University of Chicago Press. (Original work published 1902).

Fox, M. (2009, October 22). Theodore R. Sizer, leading education-reform advocate, dies at 77. *The New York Times.* Retrieved September 3, 2015, from http://www.nytimes.com/2009/10/23/education/23sizer.html?_r=0

Kozol, J. (1991). *Savage inequalities: Children in America's schools.* New York: HarperCollins.

McTighe, J., & Wiggins, G. (2013). *Essential questions: Opening doors to student understanding.* Alexandria, VA: Association for Supervision and Curriculum Development.

Mosle, S. (1996, September 29). Doing our homework. [Review of *Horace's hope: What works for the American high school*, by Theodore Sizer, 1996.] *The New York Times.*

Muncey, D.E., & McQuillan, P.J. (1996). *Reform and resistance in schools and classrooms: An ethnographic view of the coalition of essential schools.* New Haven, CT: Yale University Press.

National Commission on Excellence in Education. (1983). *A nation at risk: The imperative for educational reform.* Washington, DC: U.S. Government Printing Office.

Oakes, J. (1985). *Keeping track: How schools structure inequality.* New Haven, CT: Yale University Press.

Rich, J.M., & DeVitis, J.L. (1987). An evaluation of the aims and curriculum proposals in Sizer's "Horace's Compromise." *Clearing House, 60*, 219–222.

Schubert, W. (1986). *Curriculum: Perspective, paradigm, and possibility.* New York: Macmillan.

Schwab, J. (1973). The practical 3: A language for curriculum. *School Review, 78*(1), 1–23.

Sedlak, M.W. (1985, May). Review of *Horace's compromise: The dilemma of the American high school. American Journal of Education, 3*(3), 437–440.

Sizer, N.F., & Sizer, T.R. (1999). *The students are watching: Schools and the moral contract.* Boston, MA: Beacon Press.

Sizer, T.R. (1984). *Horace's compromise: The dilemma of the American high school.* Boston, MA: Houghton Mifflin.

Sizer, T. R. (1992). *Horace's school: Redesigning the American high school.* Boston, MA: Houghton Mifflin.

Sizer, T.R. (1996). *Horace's hope: What works for the American high school.* Boston, MA: Houghton Mifflin.

Westheimer, J. (1993). America's house of cards: Rethinking the high-school curriculum. *Curriculum Inquiry, 23*, 351–357.

Wiggins, G., & McTighe, J. (1998). *Understanding by design.* Alexandria, VA: Association for Supervision and Curriculum Development.

Wiggins, G., & McTighe, J. (2005). *Understanding by design* (expanded 2nd ed.). Alexandria, VA: Association for Supervision and Curriculum Development.

Sixteen

Jeannie Oakes, *Keeping Track: How Schools Structure Inequality* (1985)

Susan Schramm-Pate and Kenneth Vogler

Synopsis: Themes and Arguments in *Keeping Track*

In her 1985 book *Keeping Track: How Schools Structure Inequality*, social scientist Jeannie Oakes argues that tracking exaggerates initial differences among students and contributes to mediocre schooling for many who are placed in middle or lower tracks. She makes a strong case that these stigmas, influenced by the sorting and labeling of students, follow us from elementary school to secondary school. Oakes presents the results of her analysis of a comprehensive range of tracking studies. She finds that there is little evidence that homogeneous grouping improves the achievement levels of any group. She argues that students of the working-class poor and people of color are often placed in lower tracks, where they are given a less demanding and less rewarding set of curricular experiences. As a result, they suffer a loss of self-esteem and develop negative self-concepts.

Oakes's book is characterized by issues of equity and accusations of racism in the face of both a degradation of educational opportunities for students identified as gifted and talented, and a lack of concern for students identified as needing extra assistance. Oakes argues that equity is a noble goal but should not be pursued at the expense of students who lie at either end of the normal curve. For her, this is especially relevant at this juncture in the early twenty-first century, when schooling is characterized by political rhetoric and a heightened concern for educational accountability.

Oakes (1985) defines tracking, examines its underlying assumptions, and summarizes what she judges to be the disappointing effects of the practice of sorting and labeling students. She maintains that, even as educational policy in the United States gives voice to a commitment of equity and excellence, schools continue to be organized in ways that segregate and re-segregate, and deliver educational experiences in ways that are far from progressive. Today, while much as been done to equalize opportunities for all students regardless of race, class, gender, and/or sexual orientation, institutionalized practices that involve tracking and other sorting functions still serve to assure the success of some at the expense of others.

In *Keeping Track*, Oakes (1985) examines the underlying assumptions and summarizes what she judges to be the disappointing effects of the practice of dividing students into instructional groups based on an assumed similarity in ability or attainment. She writes:

> This book is about schools and what students experience in them. More precisely, it is about twenty-five junior and senior high schools and about some of the experiences of 13,719 teenagers who attended those schools. A sameness permeated those experiences. Yet underneath this cloak of sameness the day-to-day lives of these students were quite different in some very important ways.... This book is about some of these differences in the experiences of the students and what the differences have to tell us about how secondary schooling operates in American society. The schools themselves were different: some were large, some very small; some in the middle of cities, some in nearly uninhabited farm country; some in the far West, the South, the urban North, and the Midwest. But the differences in what students experienced each day in the schools stemmed not so much from where they happen to live and which of the schools they happen to attend but, rather, from differences *within* each of the schools. (Oakes, 1985, p. 2)

Today, various terms are used to describe these sorting practices: *ability grouping, tracking, leveling, streaming, and homogenous grouping* (Welner & Yettick, 2010). Typically, in a tracking system, the entire school population is assigned to classes according to whether the student's overall achievement is above average, normal, or below average. Students attend academic classes only with students whose overall academic achievement is the same as their own. Among older students, tracking systems usually diverge according to what students are taught. Students in academically advanced tracks study higher mathematics, more foreign languages, and literature. Students in less academic tracks acquire vocational skills, such as welding or cosmetology, or business skills, such as typing or bookkeeping. Students are usually not offered the opportunity to take classes deemed more appropriate for another track, even if the student has a demonstrated interest and ability in the subject.

Tracking's close cousin, ability grouping, is the practice of dividing students into instructional groups based on the criterion of assumed similarity in ability or attainment. The difference between ability grouping and tracking is that ability groups are often small, informal groups formed within a single classroom. Assignment to an ability group is often short-term (usually lasting no longer than one school year), and often varies by subject. Assignment to an ability group is made (and can be changed at any time) by the individual teacher and is usually not noted in student records. For example, a teacher may divide a typical mixed-ability classroom into three groups for a language arts lesson: those who need to review basic facts before proceeding, those who are ready to learn new material, and those who need a more challenging assignment. For the next lesson, the teacher may revert to whole-class, mixed-ability instruction, or may assign students to different groups.

Oakes (1985) argues that secondary teachers in higher-track classes often use advanced course materials and teach concepts that require extensive critical thinking skills, whereas those in lower-track classes tend to draw heavily from worksheets and workbooks, rarely assigning work that requires critical thinking. Oakes's claim that the curricula of higher-track courses are much more rigorous and comprehensive than those of lower-track courses is grounded in evidence by teachers who report spending less time addressing disciplinary issues in higher-track classes than in lower-track classes. Teachers in her study suggest that more time is required to promote "proper" student behavior than the development of critical thinking and independent learning skills.

Oakes (1985) admits that the practice of tracking tends to arouse strong feelings among parents and educators. Some parents, confident that their child is among the brightest, believe that s/he will be slowed down in classes enrolling less able students. Some teachers view tracking and ability grouping as a means of reducing student variability so that managing and teaching a group of students becomes a more reasonable task. Some parents and educators worry about self-perceptions associated with students' enrollment in either the highest or the lowest tracks, or their assignment to certain high- and low-ability groups.

According to Oakes (1985), the differences in viewpoint revolve around whether it is advantageous to seek homogeneity in groups and classes or to let placement occur randomly. She argues the pros and cons of tracking and ability grouping from the perspective of their impact on students' academic, social, emotional, or personal development (or some combination of these), as well as the relationship of ability grouping and tracking to egalitarian and democratic beliefs (1985). Oakes explores the ways that tracking exaggerates initial differences among students and contributes to mediocre schooling for many who are placed in middle or lower tracks.

In a later work, Oakes and Lipton (1990) note that school policies determine three structural qualities of the tracking system: *extensiveness* (the number of subjects tracked and the type of distinct curricula offered); *specificity* (the number of track levels offered); and *flexibility* (whether students move from one track to another). Although track assignment, in theory, is based on academic ability, other factors such as class, race, and gender often influence placement. When students are tracked, they often end up being inadvertently placed in classrooms with students of similar raced, classed, and gendered backgrounds. Children of working-class poor people, women, and people of color are often tracked into low-track courses that may be labeled "tech" or "tech prep," while students in higher SES groups are tracked into high-track courses labeled "honors," "advanced placement," or "international baccalaureate."

In *Beyond Tracking: Multiple Pathways to College, Career, and Civic Participation*, Oakes and Saunders (2008), as editors, enter the long-standing debate about improving high schools from a hybrid standpoint that seeks to prepare all students for college and careers. Their Multiple Pathways (MP) approach is a response to the changing relationship between schooling and work that emerged as a result of the global marketplace. In the new economy, the majority of well-paying jobs require a postsecondary education or preparation. The editors argue that today's students can better prepare for these economic and vocational realities in high school programs that educate them in content areas as well as in the technical and dispositional skills needed for their workplaces. The MP approach, they contend, bridges the gap between academic and vocational education and gives new meaning and definition to college prep and vocational experiences.

Significance and Influence of *Keeping Track*

Jeannie Oakes was on the research team for John Goodlad's "A Study of Schooling" for his seminal book, *A Place Called School* (1984), which included 16 students at the Graduate School of Education at the University of California, Los Angeles (UCLA). Goodlad credits Oakes with participating in "almost everything along the way" (Goodlad, 1984, p. xii). According to him, "Jeannie Oakes worked with me in editing successive drafts; her insightful suggestions for both substance and style are woven into the fabric of the manuscript" (p. xii).

The "Study" included 38 schools ranging from elementary to middle to high school and concluded that, overall, "the curricula were reasonably well-balanced" (p. 157). Tracking and ability grouping were a major part of the study, and the researchers raised some serious questions about the educational benefits claimed for tracking and suggested some negative side effects. Goodlad and his team found that ability grouping and tracking did not appear to produce the expected gains in student achievement as had been previously purported (see, for example, Goodlad & Klein and Associates, 1974; Rosenbaum, 1976; Sirotnik, 1981). They found that by the time students progressed to middle and high school (i.e., secondary school), there were marked differences between higher- and lower-track classes. Goodlad writes:

> Consistently, the differences in curricular content, pedagogy, and class climate favored the former. Consistently, the practices and atmosphere of the low track classes conveyed lower academic and, indeed, more modest expectations generally, as well as greater teacher reinforcement of behaving, following rules, and conforming. Consistently, students of low economic status and from minorities were disproportionately represented: high frequency of membership in low track classes; low membership in high track classes. Almost without exception, classes is not tracked into levels by containing a heterogeneous mixture of students achieving at all levels were more like high than low-track classes in regard to what students were studying, how teachers were teaching, and how teachers and students were interacting in the classroom. (p. 159)

Goodlad and his researchers challenged the teaching practices and school organizational structures associated with tracking. Oakes's focus was on the secondary schools in the study (i.e., junior high schools and senior high schools), including curricular content, instructional practices, and social relationships and interactions. The team's findings suggested marked inequalities among students in regard to access to knowledge and pedagogical practices in the varying tracks, and as a consequence of these findings, further extension of federal, state, and local interest in equality of educational opportunity came about.

After completing her dissertation at UCLA, Oakes published *Keeping Track* (1985), which included a foreword written by her mentor, Goodlad:

> Dr. Oakes' penetrating analysis of findings resulted in several technical reports and the present book. Ernest Boyer's discussion of tracking in *High School* (Harper & Row, 1983) drew upon her work. The distinctive contribution in what follows lies in its description and discussion of the hundreds of classes that composed the junior and senior high school sample in A Study of Schooling. Most of these were tracked; some were not. We can take little comfort from her conclusions. (1984, p. xi)

Within *Keeping Track's* 10 chapters, Oakes presents data and analysis regarding the way

tracking resegregates students in racially desegregated schools. Minority students were overrepresented in the lower tracks, as were white children of low income families. That is, the proportion of poor and minority students in low track classes was substantially greater than the proportion of poor and minority students in the population of the schools studied. The data reveal, also, the tendency of vocational programs to serve as a form of tracking in which poor and minority children once again were overrepresented. (p. xi)

Oakes found that there is little evidence that tracking improves the achievement levels of *any* group. She also found that students from disadvantaged backgrounds are given a less demanding and less rewarding set of curricular experiences and that children in the low tracks suffer a loss of self-esteem and develop negative self-concepts.

Ten years after Oakes's innovative text on tracking and ability grouping, economists Dominic Brewer, Daniel Rees, and Laura Argys (1995) argued that their research showed negative effects of tracking on students who are currently in the higher-level tracks. The researchers thus contended that the costs in student performance raise questions about the wisdom of eliminating tracking. Brewer and fellow researchers (1995) did not believe that tracking and ability grouping is universally bad for low-ability students and neutral for other students. Instead, they argued that the conventional wisdom on which detracking policy is based (i.e., students in low tracks are drawn disproportionately from working-class poor families and minority groups) was unsupported in their research. In other words, they argued that they found little evidence to support Goodlad's (1984) and Oakes's (1985) claims.

The Brewer team (1995) argued that the picture is more complex than Goodlad (1984) and Oakes (1985) suggested, and that the statistics they examined show that there is an overall gain in efficiency associated with tracking and ability grouping. Brewer and colleagues do not deny that there is an equity issue associated with tracking and ability grouping, but they feel that students in upper-tracked classes will suffer a loss in achievement test scores if they are heterogeneously grouped with students of varying abilities. However, they do agree with Oakes (1985) that detracking creates "winners and losers," since students in lower tracks realize achievement gains by being placed in heterogeneous classes at the expense of higher-level tracked students.

Educational and Cultural Context

In the early twentieth century, one of John Franklin Bobbitt's scientific management principles designed for public schools was simply this: work up the raw material into that finished product for which it is best adapted (Spring, 1986). The "raw material" and "finished product" refers to students who were to be molded by the school and fitted into the cogs of the capitalist wheel (1986). During the first four decades of the twentieth century, various educators argued for efficiency in public schooling. One can insert the word "economical" for efficiency here, since these educators were concerned with educating the most students for the least amount of money. In *Justice, Ideology, and Education* (1994), Stevens and Wood argued that "the idea of a unified curriculum gave way to the ideal of differentiating students for predetermined places in the work force" (cited in Spring, 1986, p. 2). The application of these principles of management resulted in a tracking system in schools that tended to reproduce the divisions of the social class system.

Conservative political and educational patterns in the United States in the 1970s and 1980s crushed the "dream of nineteenth-century common school reformers—an educational system providing the same education for all students—[and] gave way to a system of highly specific curricula" (Spring, 1986, p. 313). "Highly specific curricula" belies the ideal of a unified curriculum for *all* and gives way to the ideal of differentiating students for predetermined places in the workforce. The Nixon administration's educational policies set the stage for educational programs designed to prepare students for specific careers, a return to basic education, and an expansion of vocational education. According to Spring (1986), the Reagan administration's 1983 manifesto *A Nation at Risk* prompted an increased role for the federal government in education and a new wave of criticism that accused schools of causing an imbalance in international trade because of low academic standards. "A new cry was raised for high educational standards as a means of graduating students capable of improving American technology and thus winning the international trade war with West Germany and Japan" (Spring, 1986, p. 314). Tracking systems in schools were the result of business management philosophies that were applied to schooling, and this sorting and labeling reproduced the divisions of the social class system (Apple, 1982; Bourdieu & Passeron, 1977; Spring, 1989).

Borrowed from the European school system, tracking and ability grouping are among the predominant organizing practices of U.S. public schools, and have been an accepted feature of the country's school systems for more than a century. Coming into use at a time when schools were enrolling growing numbers of immigrant children as the result of compulsory schooling laws, tracking was adopted as a means of sorting those children viewed as having limited preparation or capacity for schooling. Unfortunately, however, tracking quickly took on the appearance of internal segregation (Spring, 1986, 1989).

The types of tracks have changed over the years. Traditionally there were academic, general, and vocational tracks, identified by the kind of preparation they provide. By the early twentieth century, some schools had developed up to eight distinctly labeled tracks that represented particular curricular programs that reflected an assessment of students' probable social and vocational futures. John Dewey (1916, 1997) and his progressivist educational followers challenged the lockstep curriculum: traditional grade-level divisions, subject matter divisions of classroom time and resources, and a sequential model that has the teacher introducing a new lesson, followed in rapid succession by recitation or group practice, additional seatwork, and, finally, homework to allow students to practice the skill on their own. Dewey (1916, 1997) argued that in order to enhance higher-level thinking skills, we needed heterogeneous, multi-aged groupings of students and that we needed to combine content-based and problem-based instructional strategies with a constructivist pedagogy to improve student achievement and promote student inquiry. (Despite Dewey's impact on progressive education in America, his curricular recommendations have largely been reserved for the elite.) We still grapple with classroom teaching in school organization that has not evolved much from its infancy in the early twentieth century.

Indeed, many American public secondary schools today base track levels on course difficulty, with tracks that have names such as basic, honors, college preparatory, International Baccalaureate (IB), and/or advanced placement. Similarly, early childhood and elementary schools might segregate children in terms of high, average, or low ability. History has shown that, by and large, progressive schooling experiences have not been enjoyed by the masses. Rather, it has been much more common for schoolteachers to arrange their classrooms homogeneously and by ability, placing the highest-achieving students in one cluster and the lowest in another and to focus on the 3Rs, as back-to-basics educators called for efficiency and accountability. The

Brown Center Report on American Education (2013) noted that 61% of fourth-grade math teachers practiced ability grouping in 2011, up from 40% in 1996.

From a personal standpoint, as a child in an Ohio elementary school in the 1960s, I clearly recall being specifically sorted and labeled in the third grade. Reading groups were popular, and my teacher, Mrs. Cornice, decided she would have three reading groups—the *Corvettes* (for the high-achieving students—my good and smart friend, Angie, was one of those); the *Fords* (for the medium-achieving students—that was me); and the *Dump Trucks* (for the low-achieving students—thank heavens I wasn't in that group!). Even as an 8-year-old, I understood the implication and signification of Mrs. Cornice's reading group names. Our teacher implied that we could move "up"; however, I don't think I ever made it into the *Corvettes* but remained a *Ford* that year *and* pretty much the rest of my K–12 public school career. At least I wasn't a *Dump Truck*, I assured myself.

In the 1960s a new tracking system was born (see James Conant, 1959). It was designed to provide a range of curricular opportunities for high-achieving, college-bound students who would be placed in academic tracks. In contrast, vocational courses were populated with those considered intellectually less able—a practice that disadvantages students of color and low-income children (Oakes, 1985). Getting out of the *Dump Truck*s is no easy task; indeed, it's almost impossible.

Strengths of *Keeping Track*

The notion of a self-fulfilling prophecy and the concept of hidden curriculum and the process of hegemony undergirds Oakes's seminal text. Tracking and ability grouping, according to Melissa Weiner (2014), "perpetuates inequality both in the educational system and society at large" (p. 43). Clearly, students self-identify when they are surrounded by peers of similar raced, classed, and gendered backgrounds in their courses. Not only does this result in a lack of cultural capital; it also leads to a self-fulfilling prophecy by which students' expectations about themselves eventually lead them to behave in ways that confirm these expectations (Weiner, 2014).

Oakes, in *Keeping Track*, enables us to better understand the ways in which students who are placed in lower-track courses accept as the norm, as common sense, their place in schools. They participate in this cycle of oppression perpetuated by the hidden curriculum and accept as logical the views of the dominant culture, which labels and separates them. The exclusion of people of color, women, and poor people from college preparatory, advanced placement, and IB courses continues—and will continue until we question the assumption that these children need remediation and eradicate the overt acts of racism, sexism, and classism that perpetuate the oppression of these individuals and supports the social order that oppresses and disempowers them.

Preceding texts such as Willard Waller's *The Sociology of Teaching* (1961), Paulo Freire's *Pedagogy of the Oppressed* (1970), and *Schooling in Capitalist America* by Samuel Bowles and Herbert Gintis (1976) framed a sharp criticism of tracking, labeling, and sorting children within the institution of school. These opponents of tracking argued that tracking or sorting students into homogeneous groups affects such educational outcomes as self-esteem, dropout rate (also known as "leaving school early"), and the likelihood of going to postsecondary institutions. Following these scholars' strong arguments criticizing the prevailing practice of tracking, Oakes (1985) argued that students in the low tracks are often drawn disproportionately from poor families or from minority groups. Gamoran and Mare (1988) found that the graduation rates for non-college-tracked students are 10% lower than for their college-tracked peers. They equate this difference to tracking.

> In theory, the process of tracking children is supposed to facilitate learning by separating them into groups, so that they are taught alongside peers of similar ability and partners with higher or lower abilities. In practice, however, even researchers who favor tracking as a theory generally acknowledge that it lacks consistency, effectiveness, and equity. (Welner & Yettick, 2010, p. 885)

Proponents of tracking contend that detracking students who are in higher-level tracks will cause them to suffer negative effects. In *The Paideia Proposal* (1982), Mortimer Adler argues that all students in the public schools, regardless of ability level, must be given access to the same basic curriculum. According to Adler, the pace would be slower for some than others, and in some cases the depth and extent of study in a given area of the curriculum will vary, but there will be no separation into vocational or business or basic tracks. For him, it is commonsensical to separate students on the basis of ability. Furthermore, Adler (1982) posits that the Western canon of literature, science, art, history, and mathematics should be foundational for all students. In other words, he and his perennialist followers abhor vocational education but claim that tracking is necessary in group instruction, which is the way schools are organized. However, according to Goodlad (1984):

> Tracking, on the surface, is the organizational arrangement by means of which students observed to be making buried progress in school are grouped so as to reduce the apparent range of achievement and performance in any one group.... For many people tracking appears to be such a rational commonsense solution to a vexing problem that arguments against it often are ridiculed as soft, progressive, fuzzyheaded thinking. (pp. 150–151)

Keeping Track (1985) makes clear to us the dichotomy between tracking advocates and detracking proponents, and, in this text, Oakes calls for a compromise. Subsequent policies such as No Child Left Behind (2002) claimed to make a conscious effort to equalize opportunities for all students, regardless of their backgrounds. However, as Stevens and Wood (1994) argued over 20 years ago, the very structure of the school, particularly its sorting and tracking function, is designed to ensure the success of some at the expense of others. In *Crossing the Tracks: How "Untracking" Can Save America's Schools* (1992), Anne Wheelock details several detracking experiments and concludes that detracking is a necessary component of successful school reform. Robert Slavin, in *Achievement Effects of Ability Grouping in Secondary Schools: A Best-Evidence Synthesis* (1990), argues that a decision to assign a child to an ability group or track at one point in that child's school experience will greatly influence later grouping decisions; therefore, the practice should be used only when there is a clear justification and an absence of other alternatives.

Weaknesses of *Keeping Track*

It is impossible to read *Keeping Track* without thinking about the feminist landscape and the role of the job market in shaping secondary education. While Oakes touches upon several liberal principles, she makes no direct mention of feminism (AAUW, 1992, 2010), globalization

(Stromquist, 2002), or neoliberalism (Brown, 2003) in *Keeping Track*. Focusing on race and class, Oakes (1985) avoids a discussion of both the centrality of the marketplace in terms of vocational schooling for working-class poor students and students of color, and the impact of tracking and ability grouping on girls and young women. But because the research and scholarship on feminism and schooling (AAUW, 1992, 2010) was in its infancy when *Keeping Track* was written, as was neo-Marxist educational theory (Apple, 1982), it would be somewhat unfair to criticize the book through a feminist lens.

Oakes's major concern in *Keeping Track* is that tracking is used to segregate students on the basis of socioeconomic class status (SES) and race, as well as ability. As she puts it:

> Tracking is the process whereby students are divided into categories so that they can be assigned in groups to various kinds of classes. Sometimes students are classified as fast, average, or slow learners and placed in too fast, average, or slow classes on the basis of their scores on achievement or ability tests. Often teachers' estimates of what students have already learned or their potential for learning more determine how students are identified and placed. Sometimes students are classified according to what seems most appropriate to their future lives. Sometimes, but rarely in any genuine sense, students themselves choose to be in "vocational," "general," or "academic" programs. (p. 3)

Hindsight enables us to view and critique *Keeping Track* through a feminist lens that provides another way of thinking about the proposed reforms and policy in schooling. For example, the Association of American University Women (1992) focused on the quality and quantity of science and mathematics education that girls and young women receive in secondary schooling and college. In *How Schools Shortchange Girls* (1992), the AAUW revealed that most girls in American secondary public schools were not taking higher-level science and mathematics classes such as physics and chemistry. In the more than 20 years since that study was published, the number of girls taking and succeeding in higher-level mathematics and science classes has increased (AAUW, 2010). In *Why So Few?* (2010), the AAUW reports that girls who take higher-level mathematics and science classes in high school and college do not necessarily pursue mathematics and science careers. Though they may be taking mathematics and science courses with increased frequency in secondary and post-secondary schooling, they are not breaking into Science, Technology, Engineering, and Mathematics (STEM) careers with the same frequency. The AAUW reports that while girls and young women are taking higher-level math and science courses today, they still are not on a par with their male counterparts in higher-level STEM careers.

Beyond contemporary neoliberal stances, Dewey (1916, 1997) argued that schools should attend to student experiences and learning rather than production. Similarly, a retrospective critique of *Keeping Track* in 2015 enables us to access the scholarly literature on neoliberalism (Stromquist, 2002) that relies on competition and avoids discussions of power asymmetries, thus affording alternative viewpoints about the proposed reforms to tracking and ability grouping.

Relevance of *Keeping Track* Today

We are still grappling with the vocational/academic split that was articulated in Goodlad's "Study" (1984) and followed up in Oakes's dissertation and seminal text, *Keeping Track* (1985). Beginning with the Harvard University report entitled *General Education in a Free Society*

(Harvard University, 1945), high schools in the United States required three units in English, three in science and mathematics, and two in social studies. Students were required to complete this common core, which now occupies over two-thirds of every student's curriculum in high school. Students' general education in high school is still rounded out by the choice of an elective; however, the consistent theme of the Harvard report that still resonates today is the binding experience of the "common core and the infusion of everything else with the claims of a common culture, citizenship, and standards of human good" (Harvard University, 1945, p. 102).

Today, as public school educators are faced with Common Core State Standards (CCSS) that are federally and state mandated and tied to funding, there is much to learn and admire from *Keeping Track* (Oakes, 1985). Especially within the context of CCSS, Oakes's pioneering text is required reading for teachers and school administrators, scholars, and community leaders who are new to the tracking and ability grouping literature. Indeed, Oakes's text lays the foundation for the ways in which K–12 educators can implement policy and programs that impact the labeling and sorting of students within capitalist schooling. They can use this groundbreaking book to carefully articulate the potential roadblocks that prevent students from connecting to academic topics and disciplines and information technologies that might help them gain access to further education and experience. In particular, working-class poor people, women, and people of color are impacted by the cultural challenges of tracking—some of which are almost impossible to overcome. Let us think about spaces in schools and arrangements that are progressive and democratic, reimagining them to include not only workshops and on-the-job internships, but also vital places where students can actively construct knowledge and where they have the potential to disrupt the social system and level unequal economic playing fields.

References

Adler, M.J. (1982). *The paideia proposal: An educational manifesto.* New York: Simon & Schuster.
American Association of University Women. (1992). *How schools shortchange girls: A study of major findings on girls and education.* Washington, DC: AAUW Educational Foundation.
American Association of University Women. (2010). *Why so few? Women in science, technology, engineering, and mathematics.* Washington, DC: AAUW Educational Foundation.
Apple, M.W. (1982). *Education and power.* Boston, MA: Routledge and Kegan Paul.
Bourdieu, P., & Passeron, J. (1977). *Reproduction in education, society and culture* (R. Nice, Trans.). Beverly Hills, CA: Sage Publications.
Bowles, S., & Gintis, H. (1976). *Schooling in capitalist America.* New York: Basic Books.
Brewer, D.J., Rees, D.I., & Argys, L.M. (1995). Detracking America's schools: The reform without cost? *Phi Delta Kappan, 77*(3), 210–214.
Brown, W. (2003). Neo-liberalism and the end of liberal democracy. *Theory & Event, 7*(1), 1–43.
Brown Center Report on American Education. *How well are American students learning?* Washington, DC: Brookings Institution.
Conant, J.B. (1959). *The American high school today.* New York: McGraw-Hill.
Dewey, J. (1916). *Democracy and education.* New York: The Free Press.
Dewey, J. (1997). *Experience and education.* New York: Touchstone Books.
Freire, P. (1970). *Pedagogy of the oppressed.* New York: The Free Press.
Gamoran, A., & Mare, R.D. (1988). *Secondary school tracking and educational inequality: Compensation, reinforcement, or neutrality?* University of Wisconsin-Madison. Retrieved from www.ssc.wisc.educde/cdewp87-39. pdf
Goodlad, J.I. (1984). *A place called school: Prospects for the future.* New York: McGraw-Hill.
Goodlad, J.I., & Klein, M.F. and associates. (1974). *Looking behind the classroom door.* Worthington, OH: Charles A. Jones.

Harvard University. Committee on the Objectives of a General Education in a Free Society. (1945). *General education in a free society: Report of the Harvard committee.* Cambridge, MA: Harvard University Press.

Oakes, J. (1985). *Keeping track: How schools structure inequality.* New Haven, CT: Yale University Press.

Oakes, J., & Saunders, M. (Eds.). (2008). *Beyond tracking: Multiple pathways to college, career, and civic participation.* Cambridge, MA: Harvard Education Press.

Rosenbaum, J. (1976). *Making inequality: The hidden curriculum of high school tracking.* New York: John Wiley & Sons.

Sirotnik, K.A. (1981). What you see is what you get: A summary of observations in over 1000 elementary and secondary classrooms. *A Study of Schooling Technical Report Number 29.* Los Angeles: Laboratory in School and Community Education, Graduate School of Education, University of California.

Slavin, R. (1990). *Achievement effects of ability grouping in secondary schools: A best-evidence synthesis.* Madison, WI: National Center on Effective Secondary Schools.

Spring, J. (1986). *The American school, 1642–1985.* New York: Longman.

Spring, J. (1989). *The sorting machine revisited: National educational policy since 1945.* New York: Longman.

Stevens, E., Jr., & Wood, G. (1994). *Justice, ideology, and education: An introduction to the social foundations of education* (3rd ed.). New York: McGraw-Hill.

Stromquist, N. (2002). *Education in a globalized world.* Lanham, MD: Rowman & Littlefield.

Waller, W. (1961). *The sociology of teaching.* New York: Russell and Russell.

Weiner, M.F. (2014). *Teaching race and anti-racism in contemporary America.* New York: Springer.

Welner, K.G., & Yettick, R.H. (2010). Tracking. In C. Kridel (Ed.), *Encyclopedia of curriculum studies* (pp. 885–886). Los Angeles, CA: Sage.

Wheelock, A. (1992). *Crossing the tracks: How "untracking" can save America's schools.* New York: The New Press.

Seventeen

E.D. Hirsch, Jr., *Cultural Literacy: What Every American Needs to Know* (1987)

Emily Nemeth and Karen Graves

Synopsis

"Of course it's cultural imperialism. Cultural imperialism has gotten a bad rap." That's how a seminar participant recalls hearing E.D. Hirsch, Jr., defend his argument at the core of *Cultural Literacy: What Every American Needs to Know* a few years after the book was published.[1] In 1987 the celebrated Professor of English at the University of Virginia had weighed in on the national concern regarding illiteracy. He posited that cultural literacy—the "traditional literate knowledge, the information, attitudes, and assumptions that literate Americans share"—was the only sure remedy for interrupting and disrupting the relationship between illiteracy and poverty.[2] It was a bold claim, with clear ramifications for public schools. Hirsch traced a decline in literacy to a favorite punching bag in American politics: colleges of education. Condensing the diverse mix of philosophies and curricula that characterized teacher preparation programs into a pappy concoction of Jean-Jacques Rousseau and John Dewey, and operating on the assumption that whatever is taught in college finds its way directly to school practice, Hirsch claimed that teachers' emphasis on the processes of learning had displaced content knowledge in the nation's schools. His analysis of the literacy problem relied on a transmission model of schooling, one that holds that the school's primary purpose is to introduce students to a shared culture that enables the communication required for society to function.

Hirsch laid out a clear trajectory in the six chapters that constitute his argument. He began by connecting literacy to cultural literacy, taking care to acknowledge and then dismiss multicultural education from his system. His thesis was based on the premise that the "acculturative responsibility of the schools is primary and fundamental." However, Hirsch charged that schools have failed in this basic mission of ensuring students' "mastery of national culture" and subsequent "mastery of the standard language" because educators had come to take cultural literacy for granted.[3] He worried that in a decentralized school system that circumstance led to disaster—students were not learning essential information. Hirsch wanted students to acquire a set of background knowledge and facts representing the core of mainstream culture so that they might act as empowered citizens. He clarified that it was not necessary for students to know much about these concepts; they simply needed to be able to follow the rhetoric of writers and speakers. Hirsch grounded this claim in an overview of schema theory, introducing readers to psychological research highlighting the role of background knowledge in reading comprehension. Here he staked his claim to a widely acknowledged pedagogical principle: learning requires the integration of facts and cognitive skills. Hirsch finished the first half of his book by reinforcing the link forged in the modern era between national language and national culture. He acknowledged that these are human constructs, arbitrarily designed with little concern for the efficiency of grammatical structure. Still, Hirsch recognized them as powerful constructs, demanding a privileged place in schools.

Hirsch then turned to the question at the center of his educational philosophy: In a diverse nation, who has the right to determine what every citizen needs to know? He did not completely dismiss localism or pluralism, but pointed to the "brute fact of history," that is, that national culture has increasingly dominated ethnic cultures in modern times. In the case of the United States, Hirsch explained, the national culture is defined by the English language; national legal codes; a civil religion based on the principles of altruism and self-help, equality, freedom, truth telling, and respect for law; and myths relating to practicality, ingenuity, inventiveness, independent thinking, the frontier, and world beneficence.[4] Returning to the belief that school is the primary site of acculturation, Hirsch insisted that "we must be traditionalists about content."[5] In other words, Hirsch ostensibly invited a compromise that holds the end goal of a common core of cultural information constant while allowing for various methods and resources for learning. Nevertheless, he made it clear that he was opposed to the critical thinking movement, which he described as ineffectual. Differences between conservatives and critical theorists became more obvious in the final chapter, where Hirsch made the case for defining the contents of cultural literacy. Feeling an obligation to make implied knowledge explicit, Hirsch worked with historian Joseph Kett and physicist James Trefil to compile "The List" of what literate Americans know. Sponsored by the Exxon Education Foundation, they described The List as a provisional, objective description of contemporary American literate culture. They rejected the notion of using The List to influence what Americans *should* know, hoping to distance their project from cultural politics. The rationale exposed, yet again, Hirsch's fundamental assumption regarding education: "Although our public schools have a duty to teach widely accepted cultural values, they have a duty *not* to take political stands on matters that are subjects of continuing debate."[6] Hirsch then provided a detailed blueprint of how to normalize cultural literacy in American schools. He called for a transformation of the K–8 curriculum by identifying core knowledge and designing a sequence for teaching it, establishing blue-ribbon panels to sidestep resistance from school administrators at the state and local levels, and instituting a series of standardized tests geared to the new curriculum.

Context

One critic began his review of *Cultural Literacy* by noting that "Professor Hirsch has a good idea, plays with it in an engaging and stimulating manner, and ends up with a bad book. And yet it is one of those bad books that has made it big…because it has a catchy title, raises timely questions, does so in a provocative way, and supplies a cure-all for our educational ills."[7] There is no doubt that Hirsch was tackling an important question: What role does education play in a democracy? In a sense, this is a perennial question to be considered by each generation of citizens. But viewed from another angle, Hirsch's work was striking a chord fit for the time. *Cultural Literacy* became a strategic call to arms in the culture wars of the late twentieth century.

Historians point to a shift in the American political economy beginning in the 1970s, when conservatives regrouped to challenge liberal policies established by the federal government in the 1960s. Hard-won legislation supporting voting rights, equal employment opportunities, access to education, and women's rights provoked a conservative backlash in many sectors. In 1971 future Supreme Court Justice Lewis Powell warned of a liberal attack on the American free enterprise system and traced its "most dynamic source" to college campuses where professors lectured and wrote on the failings of capitalism. He called for an evaluation of textbooks to ensure that students encountered balanced perspectives that would include "fair and factual treatment of our system of government and our enterprise system."[8] Powell argued that this sort of review was necessary in light of emerging scholarship on the civil rights and labor movements and noted similar trends concerning what he perceived as an unbalanced, liberal hold on the curriculum in secondary schools. He outlined short- and long-term steps that conservatives should take to contest the establishment of left-leaning polices, including institutional support for scholars, writers, and speakers who would present conservative points of view, and a stepped-up emphasis on the effective use of public media.

Appointed to the Supreme Court by President Nixon later that year, Powell cast the deciding vote in the 1973 school funding case *San Antonio v. Rodriguez*. In the 5–4 decision, the majority ruled that education was not a fundamental right of citizens of the United States and left it to the individual states to sort out funding inequities among school districts. Scholars point to this decision as a watershed moment when the trend in education policy turned back toward an emphasis on efficiency over equity.[9] Supporters of economic equity in education faced additional challenges in 1978, when California voters passed Proposition 13, which reduced property taxes. The measure ignited a tax revolt across the country that further exacerbated the school funding crisis and shifted the gaze away from inequitable funding formulas. The other educational issue that reverberated across the nation in 1978 was affirmative action. Yet again, Powell found himself at the center of a divided court. His opinion in *Bakke v. Davis* set guidelines for affirmative action policy that would stand for decades, but it did little to quell disputes over the consideration of race in college admission decisions.

Although the political terrain was contested, liberal victories mounted. Congress passed Title IX in 1972, as well as the Education for All Handicapped Children Act in 1975. The Supreme Court's decision in *Lau v. Nichols* (1974) supported bilingual education by ruling that simply providing the same resources for children in schools does not meet the non-discrimination standard of the 1964 Civil Rights Act. The emerging gay rights movement experienced victory (California) and defeat (Florida, Oklahoma), with the employment rights of lesbian and gay schoolteachers at the center of debate as the decade came to an end.

These relatively moderate efforts toward social justice gave rise to the Moral Majority, a coalition of conservative and Christian fundamentalist voters established in 1979, and the landslide election of President Reagan in 1980. Reagan's administration produced the 1983 report that is recognized as the origin of a school reform movement that has grown increasingly powerful, careening along a bipartisan path through the last five presidential administrations. *A Nation at Risk* sounded an alarm similar to the one Hirsch would strike in *Cultural Literacy*; both highlighted utilitarian goals for schooling and dealt in sweeping claims.[10]

Hirsch contributed to the first phase of the late-twentieth-century school reform movement, which aimed at a national consensus on the elements of reform. The second phase of reform focused on decentralizing implementation, as seen in the details of George H.W. Bush's America 2000, Bill Clinton's Goals 2000, George W. Bush's No Child Left Behind, and Barack Obama's Race to the Top initiatives. Four themes ran through both phases of this reform movement: (1) defining academic excellence chiefly in terms of standardized achievement tests based on traditional academic curricula; (2) pitting concerns for diversity and equity against rigid definitions of academic excellence; (3) increasing options for school choice; and (4) restructuring aspects of schooling such as the locus of decision making and teacher preparation.[11]

The same year that Hirsch founded the Core Knowledge Foundation, Reagan's Secretary of Education, William Bennett, delivered his lecture on *Moral Literacy and the Formation of Character*, drawing an explicit parallel to Hirsch's advocacy for cultural literacy. Other books followed in the wake of *A Nation at Risk*, with 1987 proving to be a banner year. Allan Bloom's *The Closing of the American Mind* addressed intellectual deficiencies in higher education, while Diane Ravitch and Chester Finn delivered distressing news regarding how little 17-year-olds knew about history and literature as traditionally taught. National Endowment for the Humanities Chair Lynne Cheney published *American Memory: A Report on the Humanities in the Nation's Public Schools*.[12]

The reform period following *A Nation at Risk* was awash in educational manifestos, which piled up on the shores of the Left and the Right. Walter Feinberg observed that authors working in this genre "exploit scholarly disagreements and interpretative ambiguities" and write "their own narratives in vivid colors with little doubt expressed about how things are and still less about how they ought to be."[13] Research standards differ from traditional academic scholarship in that manifestos are rated less on their truth value and more on their "capacity to mobilize collective discontent and to channel collective understanding toward their vision of education."[14] On that score, *Cultural Literacy* earned a place on the A List.

Strengths and Weaknesses

Hirsch's study of *Cultural Literacy* is at its strongest when he occupies common ground with other scholars. The problem is, he doesn't recognize this commonality often enough. Hirsch notes, in line with criticisms of basal readers at the time, that reading programs should not focus too narrowly on the developmental process at the expense of content. This tension between process and content is not lost on literacy educators who have argued for a holistic approach to the reading process—an approach that recognizes the importance of rich content and a sophisticated narrative structure, but one that also emphasizes reading as a complex cognitive, linguistic, sociocultural, and developmental process.[15] Hirsch's case for content stood in the 1980s' tug-of-war between policymakers and literacy educators after *Becoming a Nation of*

Readers was released in 1985.[16] The stable place basal readers had secured in reading education was being questioned, specifically by Ken Goodman, who was charged by the National Council of Teachers of English's Commission on Reading to explore current approaches to reading instruction. Goodman ultimately exposed significant shortcomings in the exclusive use of basal readers for reading instruction, such as the way they "limited the text available to readers" and "underestimated what children know about language and text."[17] Like Hirsch, Goodman did not think the reading process would be inhibited by rich content.

Hirsch's push for content, however, focuses too narrowly on content for what he assumed was a universal American culture. It falls short of accounting for the lives and experiences of the diverse young people who were attending K–12 schools at the time he was writing, or those in our schools today. Scholars of culturally relevant and culturally sustaining pedagogies capture the way that such narrow approaches have served to marginalize the cultures and languages of youth of color and the way that such an exclusionary approach hinders learning. English language learners also face tensions as they learn how to read and write in English. If the content of the text is as new for the language learner as the language itself, the reading process becomes more difficult. However, if given familiar or culturally relevant material, the student can rely on predictability and familiarity of the story and then make good use of the graphophonemic code that leads to being able to learn additional content while reading.[18]

Hirsch allows for some flexibility by way of the intensive curriculum: one can go deeply into particular areas of study "appropriate for their diverse temperaments and aims," allowing for both variety and choice.[19] In an ironic fashion, Hirsch uses Shakespeare as his example— a White, male, English playwright. His examples still fall within what has long represented White, middle-class values versus the diverse and rich traditions that students bring from their homes and communities.

One might read Hirsch's call for an extensive curriculum—the "traditional literate knowledge, the information, attitudes, and assumptions that literate Americans share"[20]—as a defense of a liberal arts education. There is much to be appreciated here regarding the aim to help students develop a degree of intellectual flexibility so that they might better respond to change, and to prepare informed citizens to engage meaningfully in public discourse. But Hirsch tends to overreach in his advocacy for *Cultural Literacy*. From the beginning, he insists that his theoretical model "constitutes the *only* sure avenue of opportunity for disadvantaged children…."[21] Hirsch claims too much efficacy for schools, ignoring both the larger sociopolitical context and institutional restrictions within American schooling. As Feinberg observes, Hirsch "writes as if every district, every school, and, indeed, every classroom teacher is free to interpret and teach the subject matter as their wills dictate and there are insufficient pressures promoting uniformity."[22] Hirsch's argument relies on assertion more than evidence and is marked by an unwillingness to engage counterarguments of prominent sociologists of education on the ways in which social class, gender, and race operate to reproduce class positions, even when the same knowledge content is being delivered in schools.[23]

Hirsch does a bit better with historians, relying on the guidance of his friend and colleague, Diane Ravitch. His critique of the twentieth-century practice of tracking, for instance, accurately notes the way it lowered academic standards for many students. In many instances, however, Hirsch employs historical references in a careless way, paying little mind to the complexities of historical research and the ways that differing perspectives can complicate interpretations. This is especially noticeable in regard to his assumptions about the rationale behind the rise of universal schooling, the parallel that he implies between the 1918 *Cardinal Principles* report and contemporary theories on critical thinking, and the absence of any awareness of critiques of the Coleman Report.[24]

The most critical lapse in Hirsch's historical analysis, however, concerns his attack on progressive education. He offers a facile reading of Rousseau and Dewey and sets the pair up in a straw man proposal to explain the failings of twentieth-century schooling. He misses the mark twice, both in his characterization of progressive education and its influence on contemporary school practice. As historian Wayne Urban points out, "Hirsch is at best half correct.... His argument is pure presentism, viewing past actors and positions in terms of present problems."[25] Hirsch distorts—and then appropriates—parts of Dewey's philosophy, such as the well-known critique of either-or thinking in *Experience and Education*.[26] He reads historical scholarship selectively, steering clear of the standard interpretation that accounts of progressive education taking over American schools are overblown. He simply assumes "that the dead hand of William H. Kilpatrick is still on the wheel of American education."[27]

Hirsch anticipates challenges from critical theorists who object to schooling that presses a class-bound, patriarchal, Eurocentric curriculum onto a pluralistic society, but he never really engages the points of critique. Summing them up as ideological objections, Hirsch dispenses with the criticism in the space of a few paragraphs. He gives more credence to those who worry that The List will encourage a trivial pursuit of cultural knowledge.[28]

Mindful but uninhibited by the controversial nature of proposing a list of information that *all* Americans should know, Hirsch's methods did little to curb the controversy. He and his colleagues drew upon academic vocabulary, invited peer debriefing and review, referenced popular sources of information, and, finally, relied on their own experience and judgment to identify "5000 essential names, phrases, dates, and concepts" that a "common reader" or a "literate person" might know.[29] Aware of the debate that could surface with this kind of proposal, Hirsch was explicit about the boundaries of The List, aiming to reflect its fleeting temporal location. Through the use of cardinal directions, Hirsch stated that the northern border marked knowledge that was too discipline-specific; the southern border knowledge that was too general; to the east, knowledge that was too new; and in the west, knowledge that was too old. Anticipating pushback from readers regarding the guise of neutrality, Hirsch attempted to quash debate by pointing to "consensus" or "wide agreement" among the public.[30] But he failed to recognize the sociocultural, sociopolitical, and sociohistorical context in which The List was generated. He was also silent about how disagreements were handled and whether or not he welcomed suggestions from the public in terms of what might be missing.[31] Moreover, certain details of the process remain unclear, including how Hirsch went about selecting members of the public to serve as consultants—and whether or not they accounted for, or attempted to mitigate, the institutional power and cultural capital he and his colleagues embodied as White, male faculty from an elite university. Were there steps taken to remain anonymous to the public—or a more active move, to shed their academic affiliations during their encounters with these individuals? What language was used to introduce the survey to the public? Was it in any way framed as a list of terms for the "educated" or "literate" person—and if so, did such a framing allow for disagreement? Making the claim that such a compilation of terms, dates, and phrases would equate to cultural literacy obligated the authors to acknowledge their own positionalities as cultural beings.

Hirsch's proposal for cultural literacy was in some ways a rejoinder to the more recent social turn in literacy studies; literacy is, in fact, cultural.[32] Hirsch's proposal stands in stark contrast to more recent New Literacy Studies, which recognize literacy as a social practice among people informed by the context, cultures, languages, and histories in which it is used. Reading and writing are used for specific purposes across social domains and reflect particular values, beliefs, and ideologies embodied in those spaces.[33]

The social turn in literacy would have us look at Hirsch's work through a sociocultural and sociohistorical lens to acknowledge that his list, too, was ideological. There was nothing neutral about generating a list of terms, events, and historical figures and calling it "cultural literacy"—nor was there anything neutral about setting the bounds in the north, south, east, and west to narrow the focus of The List. Brian Street proposed that literacy—or, more appropriately, literacies—have been narrowly conceived as an autonomous set of discrete skills developed over time. He challenged the notion of "autonomous" literacy—a literacy that is value neutral—proposing "ideological" literacy as a more appropriate framework.[34] Such a proposal fractures Hirsch's claim that he has managed to avoid cultural politics.

Hirsch asserted that there was a difference between "cultural politics" and "cultural literacy," claiming that their inherent aims were "fundamentally different." The aim of cultural politics was to "change the content and values of culture," whereas the aim of cultural literacy was simply to shed light on "widely accepted cultural values."[35] However, as Luke argued, the dominant culture has long operated under the guise of neutrality and has long been embedded by its proponents within texts and, more specifically, school textbooks. Critical literacy scholars have collectively demonstrated the ideological nature of literacy, its connection to power and privilege, and the ways in which it has been used as a means to control the distribution of knowledge.[36] While Hirsch noted that his list might not be entirely neutral, he simultaneously argued for its merit, claiming it would allow for more fluid conversation among Americans and enhance experiences of readers. But we wonder: Which Americans and which readers would be inculcated with the "standardized linguistic medium and script," at the expense of what, and to accommodate whom?[37] Such a proposal contrasts with what Nel Noddings maintains is necessary in a democratic society: "It isn't that we need a common body of knowledge in order to communicate; it is that we need to communicate in order to build a common body of knowledge."[38]

Influence and Relevance

Crusading for cultural literacy launched a new phase in Hirsch's career. He founded the Core Knowledge Foundation the year before *Cultural Literacy* was published and followed up with books on school policy in 1996, 2006, and 2009.[39] He began publishing the core knowledge series aimed at parents in 1992, and by 1999 over 800 schools in 44 states had adopted the Core Knowledge curriculum.[40] In the meantime, the English professor with little regard for education scholarship became University Professor of Education and Humanities at the University of Virginia, his work was featured on National Public Radio and in newspapers of record, and he had the ear of prominent liberals as well as conservatives. By all accounts, Hirsch's brand of cultural literacy was having a significant impact on what Americans thought about school curricula.

Hirsch rejected the notion that the position he advanced in *Cultural Literacy* was political. But Feinberg countered that the attempt to depoliticize issues that result in "making the meaning and identity of the dominant group the norm" was itself "a highly political act."[41] As Hirsch's reputation as educational consultant to the nation continued to grow, he was more forthcoming about the political influence of his educational ideas. He defined himself as an "educational pragmatist," a combination of political liberalism and educational conservatism. Grandiose claims continued to mark Hirsch's rhetoric as he explained the connection he drew between politics and educational policy: "The only practical way to achieve liberalism's aim of greater social justice is to pursue conservative educational policies."[42] In one of the most insightful critiques of Hirsch's work, Feinberg emphasized the importance of digging down to the root of Hirsch's educational theory in order to understand the particular kind of democracy Hirsch was promoting. It all began and ended with the need to control meaning.[43]

Critics have pointed to the sleight of hand Hirsch employs in his work. This is perhaps most significant in terms of his distinction between description and prescription in the cultural literacy project. In the book and in earlier interviews, he clearly indicated that the extensive curriculum was descriptive in nature, and he explicitly rejected the notion of a core curriculum. But in the last chapter of *Cultural Literacy* and in subsequent interviews, Hirsch made the case for creating demand for the curriculum he was promoting; and he laid out a series of steps to see that cultural literacy was adopted in public schools throughout the nation.[44] His blueprint for curriculum reform has been realized in the years since, to a remarkable degree for a supposedly non-prescriptive agenda. Along the way Hirsch disparaged educational scholarship of all stripes, cutting educators out of the policy arena. Hirsch believed that "Both educational traditionalists and progressivists have tended to be far too dogmatic, polemical, and theory-ridden to be reliable beacons for public policy."[45]

In 1997 Hirsch argued that "there has been a movement in [his] direction," suggesting a shared desire for a national curriculum.[46] In light of states' recent adoption of the Common Core State Standards (CCSS), a nationally unified, regulated educational system with explicit, universal benchmarks for student learning, perhaps Hirsch was right. According to the Core Knowledge Foundation website, "the standards echo and support the work of the Core Knowledge Foundation."[47] The standards have come under close scrutiny, especially with regard to their accompanying assessments. Given the state of the CCSS, would a national curriculum be feasible? There is little wonder why people gravitate to the certainty and stability offered by a shared list of terms, dates, phrases, and events. Lists simplify curricular decisions and make teaching and learning—a socially complex, politically nuanced, and historically embedded practice—seem more manageable and even predictable. The desire is rational, but what then happens to the "ambiguous realities" or those realities outside the mainstream?[48]

The debate around what to include and exclude is an eternal question for practitioners, scholars, and policymakers working in the field of education as we experience tension in timescales: time marches on, events continue to accumulate, and students continue to encounter the world and the people in it. Yet the time to cover these materials and acknowledge the funds of knowledge our students bring to the classroom remains relatively the same.[49] Given the diversity within our schools, we're prompted to pose questions similar to those raised by Jennifer Walsh-Marr—for example, do we have a shared definition of culture? If not, whose culture will be included and whose will be excluded?[50] Hirsch assembled a "multicultural committee" in 1988 and has since continued to move toward embracing a more diverse understanding of culture. Yet he claims that "the body of assumed knowledge in American public discourse has remained stable for many decades."[51] Is he referencing hegemonic perspectives of the majority or the curricular strongholds of the elite? If the ultimate goal of Hirsch's proposal is to make communication easier among Americans, must he also account for homeschooled children where states are loosening their regulatory grip? What about students in private schools? And the young people in American Indian Schools? Would unifying the curriculum under a shared cultural guise also insist on the unifying of language? And if so, what happens to English language learners whose primary language differs from Dominant Academic English?[52]

Hirsch has continued to express concern about student learning, with a particular focus on student mobility and the lack of curricular continuity that students experience as they move from one district to another, or from one classroom to another within the same school. His goal of stabilizing students' lives is not likely to be attained through a national curriculum, given the multitude of factors facing young people in terms of their economic, social, and emotional well-being. Controlling for social factors goes beyond the "swarm of students who move from school to school."[53] The move to equip all students with the mastery of shared background knowledge as *the* social justice issue is too simplistic. Students' learning experiences are transpiring within a complicated nexus of family circumstances, community relations, and ideological divides, not to mention educational inequities and the inequalities embedded within these social settings.

We return to Hirsch's 1987 resolution regarding *Cultural Literacy*. As in tetherball, the ontological claim comes swinging around to be smacked back by scholars in rival camps, who are more certain of the complex nature of culture than they are comforted by the idea that any given "list" could cultivate democracy. Being too entrenched in either camp has profound consequences for curricula and even more dire consequences for the lives and literacy engagements of youth. Hirsch's work and its reception remind us of the critical balance between providing students with sufficient background knowledge to deal with institutional expectations and helping them explore their own rich cultural identities, histories, and languages. Curricular design, however well intended, should not supplant the actual identities, histories, and languages of the people who give life to democracy.

Notes

1 The authors thank Valerie Kinloch and Lyn Robertson for their insightful comments on a draft of this chapter. In 1993 E.D. Hirsch was a guest lecturer at a National Endowment for the Humanities summer institute, "Educating a Citizenry: School and Society in the World of Thomas Jefferson." In 1999 Hirsch defended the "imposition by American public schools of mainstream Anglo culture on black and Hispanic children" by emphasizing what he meant by cultural and linguistic imperialism: "the internal imposition of a school-based culture and language within the public schools of a nation." He described the practice as a benign and necessary part of schooling. See E.D. Hirsch, "Americanization and the Schools," *Clearing House* 72, no. 3 (January/February 1999): 136–139, doi: 10.1080/00098659909599613 (accessed January 6, 2015).

2 E.D. Hirsch, Jr., *Cultural Literacy: What Every American Needs to Know* (Boston, MA: Houghton Mifflin, 1987), 127.

3 Ibid., 18.

4 Ibid., 97–99.

5 Ibid., 126.

6 Ibid., 137. The compilers made an exception to the guideline that items on the list reflect current knowledge for scientific items because they deemed Americans' knowledge of science to be sub-par. Some of the scientific items on the list are included for the purpose of shaping knowledge. The list is included in an appendix, 146–215.

7 Peter H. Rohn, review of *Cultural Literacy: What Every American Needs to Know*, *Educational Studies* 19 (Winter 1988): 361.

8 Lewis F. Powell, Jr., Memorandum to Eugene B. Sydnor, Jr., August 23, 1971, pp. 4–5, Lewis F. Powell, Jr. Papers, Box 29, Lewis F. Powell Jr. Papers, 1921–1998, Ms 001, Lewis F. Powell, Jr. Archives, Washington and Lee University, Lexington, VA, http://ead.lib.virginia.edu/vivaxtf/view?docId=wl-law/vilxwl00013.xml (accessed January 9, 2015).

9   Jonathan Kozol, *Savage Inequalities: Children in America's Schools* (New York: HarperPerennial, 1991), 213–214.

10   National Commission on Excellence in Education, *A Nation at Risk: The Imperative for Educational Reform* (Washington, DC: Government Printing Office, 1983).

11   Steven E. Tozer, Guy Senese, and Paul C. Violas, *School and Society: Historical and Contemporary Perspectives*, 5th ed. (Boston, MA: McGraw-Hill, 2006), 442–450.

12   William J. Bennett and Washington, DC, Department of Education, *Moral Literacy and the Formation of Character* (n.p.: 1986). *ERIC*, EBSCO*host* (accessed January 9, 2015); Allan Bloom, *The Closing of the American Mind* (New York: Simon and Schuster, 1987); Diane Ravitch and Chester E. Finn, Jr., *What Do Our 17-Year-Olds Know? A Report on the First National Assessment of History and Literature* (New York: Harper & Row, 1987); Lynne V. Cheney, *American Memory: A Report on the Humanities in the Nation's Public Schools* (Washington, DC: National Endowment for the Humanities, 1987); Gary B. Nash, "Lynne Cheney's Attack on the History Standards, 10 Years Later," *History News Network*, http://historynewsnetwork.org/article/8418 (accessed January 9, 2015).

13   Walter Feinberg, "Educational Manifestos and the New Fundamentalism," *Educational Researcher* 26, no. 8 (November 1997): 34.

14   Ibid., 35.

15   Stephen B. Kucer, "What We Know about the Nature of Reading," in *What Research Really Says about Teaching and Learning to Read*, ed. Stephen B. Kucer (Urbana, IL: National Council of Teachers of English, 2008), 29–61.

16   Richard Anderson, Elfrieda H. Heibert, Judith A. Scott, and Ian A.G. Wilkinson, *Becoming a Nation of Readers: The Report of the Commission on Reading* (Washington, DC: National Academy of Education, 1985).

17   Patrick Shannon, "Resistance Is Futile?" in *What Research Really Says about Teaching and Learning to Read*, ed. Stephen B. Kucer (Urbana, IL: National Council of Teachers of English, 2008), 5.

18   Gloria Ladson-Billings, *The Dreamkeepers: Successful Teachers of African American Children*, 2nd ed. (San Francisco, CA: Jossey-Bass, 2009); Gloria Ladson-Billings, "Culturally Relevant Pedagogy 2.0: a.k.a. the Remix," *Harvard Educational Review* 84 no. 1 (2014): 74–84; Marylou M. Matouch and Danling Fu, "The Paradoxical Situation Created by Test-Driven Schooling for Multilingual Children," in *What Research Really Says about Teaching and Learning to Read*, ed. Stephen B. Kucer (Urbana, IL: National Council of Teachers of English, 2008), 176–197; Django Paris, "Culturally Sustaining Pedagogy: A Needed Change in Stance, Terminology, and Practice," *Educational Researcher* 41, no. 3 (2012): 93–97.

19   Hirsch, *Cultural Literacy*, 128.

20   Ibid., 127.

21   Ibid., xiii; emphasis added.

22   Feinberg, "Educational Manifestos," 28.

23   Ibid., 32.

24   Hirsch, *Cultural Literacy*, 108, 113–124, 133. James Coleman's 1966 national survey of schools indicated that most students in the United States attended segregated schools that, he determined, provided relatively equal educational opportunity in terms of resources. Coleman attributed differences in academic achievement to student background and socioeconomic status. Although critics pointed to methodological flaws, the Coleman Report proved influential in directing educational policy.

25   Wayne J. Urban, review of *The Closing of the American Mind: How Higher Education Has Failed Democracy and Impoverished the Souls of Today's Students*; *Cultural Literacy: What Every American Needs to Know*; and *What Do Our 17-Year-Olds Know? A Report on the First National Assessment of History and Literature*, *Journal of American History* 75, no. 3 (December 1988): 872.

26   John Dewey, *Experience and Education* (New York: Collier Books, 1938).

27   Feinberg, "Educational Manifestos," 29; Urban, book review, 872.

28   Hirsch, *Cultural Literacy*, xiv–xv, 18–19, 31, 59, 118–119, 142–144. Hirsch paid more attention to his multicultural critics over the course of the next decade. Following the 1996 publication of *The Schools We Need and Why We Don't Have Them*, Hirsch charged that the "militant bilingualism and multiculturalism of the 1980s made American schools even more confused and rudderless places than they had already been," "Americanization and the Schools."

29   Hirsch, *Cultural Literacy*, 135.

30   Ibid., 136–137.

31   Ibid., 137.

32   James Paul Gee, "Literacy, Discourse, and Linguistics: Introduction and What Is Literacy? in *Literacy: A Critical Sourcebook*, eds. Ellen Cushman, Eugene R. Kintgen, Barry M. Kroll, and Mike Rose (Boston, MA: Bedford/St. Martin's, 2001), 525–544; Valerie Kinloch, *Harlem on Our Minds* (New York: Teachers College Press, 2010); Brian Street, *Literacy in Theory and Practice* (London: Cambridge University Press, 1984).

33   David Barton and Mary Hamilton, *Local Literacies: Reading and Writing in One Community* (New York: Routledge, 1998).

34   Street, *Literacy in Theory and Practice*.

35   Hirsch, *Cultural Literacy*, 137.

36   Allen Luke, "Critical Literacy: Foundational Notes," *Theory into Practice* 51, no. 1 (2012): 4–11; Stephanie Jones, *Girls, Social Class and Literacy: What Teachers Can Do to Make a Difference* (Portsmouth, NH: Heinemann, 2006); Peter L. McLaren and Colin Lankshear, "Critical Literacy and the Postmodern Turn," in *Critical Literacy: Politics, Praxis, and the Postmodern*, eds. Colin Lankshear and Peter L. McLaren (Albany: State University of New York Press, 1993), 379–419.

37   Ernest Gellner, quoted in Hirsch, *Cultural Literacy*, 74.

38   Nel Noddings, *Education and Democracy in the 21st Century* (New York: Teachers College Press, 2013), 30.

39   "E.D. Hirsch, Jr.," *Core Knowledge*, http://www.coreknowledge.org/ed-hirsch-jr (accessed January 7, 2015); E.D. Hirsch, Jr., *The Schools We Need and Why We Don't Have Them* (New York: Doubleday, 1996); E.D. Hirsch, Jr., *The Knowledge Deficit: Closing the Shocking Education Gap for American Children* (Boston, MA: Houghton Mifflin, 2006); E.D. Hirsch, Jr., *The Making of Americans: Democracy and Our Schools* (New Haven, CT: Yale University Press, 2009).

40 John O'Neil, "Core Knowledge & Standards: A Conversation with E.D. Hirsch, Jr.," *Educational Leadership* 56, no. 6 (March 1999): 28–31. *Education Full Text (H.W. Wilson)*, EBSCO*host* (accessed January 7, 2015).

41 Feinberg, "Educational Manifestos," 33.

42 E.D. Hirsch, "Why Traditional Education Is More Progressive," *American Enterprise* 8 (March/April 1997): 42–45.

43 Feinberg, "Educational Manifestos," 33. See also p. 28.

44 Hirsch, *Cultural Literacy*, xiv, 127–145; E.D. Hirsch, Jr., "'Cultural Literacy' Doesn't Mean 'Core Curriculum,'" *English Journal* 74 (October 1985): 48–49; Charles J. Shields, "E.D. Hirsch Follows His Cultural Literacy with a New Core Curriculum," *Curriculum Review* 31 (January 1992): 11–15, *Education Full Text (H.W. Wilson)*, EBSCO*host* (accessed January 10, 2015); Mark F. Goldberg, "Doing What Works: An Interview with E.D. Hirsch, Jr.," *Phi Delta Kappan* 79 (September 1997): 83–85. *Education Full Text (H.W. Wilson)*, EBSCO*host* (accessed January 10, 2015). Also see Rohn, review of *Cultural Literacy*, 362–363; Edgar Schuster, "In Pursuit of Cultural Literacy," *Phi Delta Kappan* 70 (March 1989): 540; Feinberg, "Educational Manifestos," 28, 31.

45 E.D. Hirsch, "Reality's Revenge: Research and Ideology," *Arts Education Policy Review* 99, no. 4 (March/April 1998): 3–15. *Education Full Text (H.W. Wilson)*, EBSCO*host* (accessed January 10, 2015); Walter Feinberg, "Rejoinder: Meaning, Pedagogy and Curriculum Development: Feinberg Answers Hirsch," *Educational Researcher* 27, no. 7 (October 1998): 30.

46 Goldberg, "An Interview," 85.

47 "Common Core State Standards," *Core Knowledge*, http://www.coreknowledge.org/ccss (accessed January 20, 2015).

48 Jennifer Walsh-Marr, "Keeping Up the Conversation on Culture: A Response to Robert Courchêne and Others," *TESL Canada Journal* 29, no. 1 (2011): 113–120.

49 L.C. Moll, C. Amanti, D. Neff, and N. Gonzalez, "Funds of Knowledge for Teaching: Using a Qualitative Approach to Connect Homes and Classrooms," *Theory into Practice* 31, no. 2 (1992): 132–141.

50 Walsh-Marr, "Keeping Up the Conversation on Culture."

51 Goldberg, "An Interview," 84; E.D. Hirsch, "Beyond Comprehension: We Have Yet to Adopt a Common Core Curriculum that Builds Knowledge Grade by Grade—But We Need To," *American Educator* 34, no. 4 (Winter 2010–2011): 32.

52 Kris D. Gutiérrez, Jolynn Asato, Mariana Pacheco, Luis C. Moll, Kathryn Olson, Eileen L. Horng, Richard Ruiz, Eugene García, and Teresa L. McCarty, "Conversations: 'Sounding American': The Consequences of New Reforms on English Language Learners," *Reading Research Quarterly* 37, no. 3 (2002): 328–343.

53 E.D. Hirsch, Jr., "Not to Worry?" *Daedalus* 131, no. 3 (2002): 31; Hirsch, "Beyond Comprehension"; Goldberg, "An Interview."

EIGHTEEN

Maxine Greene, *The Dialectic of Freedom* (1988)

Wendy Kohli

Introduction

The kernel of *The Dialectic of Freedom* was delivered as the annual John Dewey Lecture in 1988 and developed for publication later that year by Teachers College Press. This "classic" represents one of Maxine Greene's most coherent philosophical accounts of her stance on democracy, freedom, education, and the social imagination. But the unique strength of the book lies in its interdisciplinarity, drawing on history, literature, the arts, and multiculturalism to embody and contextualize Greene's philosophical insights.

This chapter will first situate the book in the cultural and political context in which it was written. A retrospective of Greene's prior work to that point follows, including a review of the philosophical traditions that inform it. Then a brief synopsis of the book will be provided that includes the salient themes and arguments with which she grapples. Finally, a reflection on the book is offered that illuminates its relevance for today.

Situating Maxine Greene: Her Educational, Political, and Cultural Context

The 1980s, when Greene wrote *The Dialectic of Freedom*, were known as "the Reagan years," beginning with the inauguration of Ronald Reagan in January of 1981. This decade was understood by those on the political left as a conservative era—even reactionary—in that it was characterized by *reactions* to the more progressive years of the 1960s and 1970s. Those on the right, however, including those comprising the rising "new right," thought the 1980s were a *revolutionary* time. They viewed Reagan's policies as a defining break from the status quo, from what they viewed as the expansive "liberal agenda" of the Democrats. This was true in educational circles as well as more broadly in national politics and culture.

From the start, Reagan's signature intent was to reduce the role of the federal government in all sectors of society, including education. When he appointed Terrel Bell to run the fledgling Department of Education begun by Jimmy Carter, Reagan wanted to shut it down. Things did not go quite as his political rhetoric exhorted. Secretary Bell, a former educator with his own ideas, was concerned about the quality of K–12 education in the United States, particularly as it impacted our economic competitiveness internationally—which at the time was focused primarily on Japan. Bell proceeded to develop a National Commission to study the teaching and learning in K–12 public education. The resulting report, known henceforth as *A Nation at Risk*, warned: "The educational foundations of our society are presently being eroded by *a rising tide of mediocrity* that threatens our very future as a Nation and a people" (emphasis added).[1] Similar to the effects of the Sputnik launch in 1957, this report propelled education to the forefront of a national conversation over needed changes in educational policy and practices.

Within a short time, President Reagan grasped the *political* value of education and proceeded to endorse the commission's recommendations. These included strengthening high school graduation requirements, especially in the "five new basics" of English, math, social studies, computer science, and foreign language; "more rigorous and measurable standards" for schools and colleges, which included more standardized testing; lengthening the school day and/or school year; improving teacher education; and supporting educational reform at the state and national levels with the necessary financial support and political leadership.

This last recommendation was interesting in that, although state and local governments were recognized as the entities historically responsible for education, the report made it clear that the *federal government* had an important role: "The Federal Government has *the primary responsibility* to identify *the national interest in education*. It should also help fund and support efforts to protect and promote that interest" (emphasis added).[2] It was clear from the report that "the national interest" really meant the national *economic* interest.

At the same time, a cadre of "conservative" intellectuals contributed their voices to this national conversation.[3] They provided Reagan with the cultural "capital," if you will, to support particular changes in the curriculum—especially ones that called for a more unified, common set of texts and standards. Some of the more powerful proponents of this perspective included E. D. Hirsch, Allan Bloom, and William Bennett.

Hirsch wrote *Cultural Literacy: What Every American Needs to Know* in an effort to re-establish a common curriculum and attain some semblance of "shared knowledge" across U.S. society.[4] Cultural literacy, he argued, was a "national vocabulary [that] functions, or should function, as our broadly shared instrument of communication."[5] Hirsch made an attempt to codify this "national vocabulary" in the provocative and infamous "A Preliminary List,"[6] and it was this list that was to serve as a beginning for school districts to "devise an *extensive* curriculum based on the national vocabulary and arranged in a definite sequence."[7] To his credit, Hirsch was not arguing for the development of a "national core curriculum"; he thought that approach was "neither desirable nor feasible."[8]

Although Hirsch's primary goal to raise the literacy rates of all Americans was an *educational* one, he did make an *economic* connection to literacy not unlike that at the foundation of *A Nation at Risk*. Hirsch says early on in his book:

> The standard of literacy required by modern society has been rising through the developed world, but American literacy rates have not risen to meet this standard. What seemed an acceptable level in the 1950s is no longer acceptable in the late 1980s, when only highly literate societies can prosper economically. Much of Japan's industrial efficiency has been credited to its almost universal high level of literacy.[9]

So whether he liked it or not, whether intentional or not, Hirsch's work was co-opted by the (Republican) political establishment of the time.

Allan Bloom, a renowned classicist and philosopher known for his translations of two classics in the philosophy of education, Plato's *Republic* and Rousseau's *Emile*, was disturbed by the changes he saw in the American educational landscape, especially in higher education. The demographics of the 1980s pointed to a more diverse, pluralistic, and multicultural environment. For Bloom, these demographic changes, as well as the curricular changes influenced by the political and social movements of the 1960s, prompted him to write a critique of contemporary colleges and universities.

Bloom's book *The Closing of the American Mind* indicted universities for losing their traditional moral compass and coherence. He attributed this "decomposition of the university"[10] to many factors, including the inculcation—even indoctrination—of relativism and openness.[11] As Bloom sardonically quipped: "Openness—and the relativism that makes it the only plausible stance in the face of various claims to truth and various ways of life and kinds of human beings—is the great insight of our times."[12] To be fair to Bloom, he had a classicist view of the university and of the liberal arts and believed that the moral and political goals of education should be directed toward the formation of "good" citizens who can think critically and act in the public sphere.[13] Unfortunately, in his critique of progressive social and educational goals for the university (a critique of what has come to be known as "political correctness"), Bloom did not employ *his own critical thinking* skills to examine the values he held and how they, too, are infused by a particular political ideology and cultural framework.

William Bennett, who served as Reagan's secretary of education after Bell from 1985 to 1988, echoed the calls for a return to the traditional liberal arts and humanities. In 1984 he convened "A Study Group on the State of Learning in the Humanities in Higher Education."[14] Bennett granted that "the solution is not a return to an earlier time when the classical curriculum *was the only* curriculum…[and that] ours is not, of course, the only great cultural tradition the world has seen…[but] *the core of the American college curriculum…should be the civilization of the West*" (emphasis added).[15]

Clearly, all three of these intellectuals were grappling with the changing demographics of the college population and the development of a multicultural commitment on the part of K–12 and university educators. And Bennett, more than Hirsch or Bloom, understood the *political* message attached to his calls for educational reform. As someone immersed in the political milieu of Washington, he was able to leverage the academic arguments made by Hirsch and Bloom to serve Reagan's political and economic agenda.

In this conservative context of the 1980s, Maxine Greene resisted the technocratic calls for more standardization, accountability, and technological "innovation" to improve our academic and economic competitiveness. Instead, she argued for more attention to the fundamental purposes of education and schooling, including the formation of critical thinkers who are informed, democratic citizens. To accomplish this, she continued to promote an inclusive, humanities-based curriculum that decentered the traditional "White-man's canon" of literature, one that would educate citizens for a *multicultural* democracy.

These foundational values were non-existent in the commission's stance, which took for granted that the primary purpose of education was to serve the *economic interests* of the country. Developing critically informed citizens for a democracy was not high on their list. However, fundamental values and purposes *were embedded* in the calls for change from Hirsch, Bloom, and Bennett. Greene's embrace of the humanities as essential to a liberally educated person overlapped that of these intellectual critics. They all shared and valued, in the abstract at least, a commitment to the moral, ethical, and political purposes of education. However, Greene would disagree strongly with them on the means to achieve these ends and on what knowledge and experience would be privileged in any curriculum.

In looking back over Greene's lifetime of scholarly accomplishments, we can see that she addressed recurring themes related to the individual in the community, the education of citizens in a democracy, and the place of the arts and imagination in creating a public sphere. As one of the preeminent philosophers of education in the twentieth century, Greene used her powerful intellect and imagination to speak passionately about the failings that she saw in society, particularly as they impacted the lives of women, people of color, immigrants, and other marginalized members. And she remained a forceful advocate for public schools, and for equity in funding those schools, so that *all members of society*, regardless of class, race, ethnicity, or gender, could achieve their dreams.

The primary philosophical traditions that inform Greene's work are existential phenomenology, critical theory, pragmatism, and aesthetics.[16] Across her extensive writings over decades, fundamental existential, political, and ethical themes recur and re-animate critical questions in contemporary contexts.

Greene's first book, *The Public School and the Private Vision: A Search for America in Education and Literature*,[17] signals the themes that she will pursue for the remainder of her life. Certainly, they find their way into *The Dialectic of Freedom*, as she traces the connections between education and democracy through American literature and history. Always "searching," Greene demonstrates from the start her interdisciplinary range and depth as she probes the roots of the American Dream, our founding commitment to democracy, and how they connect to the formation of public schools in the nineteenth century. Unlike her contemporaries in philosophy of education at the time, Greene had the courage of her convictions to utilize literary texts as a means to grasp enduring philosophical and social issues. Hawthorne, Thoreau, Melville, Whitman, and Twain illuminate the "predicaments of freedom" that foreshadow her 1988 classic.[18]

Two years later, in *Existential Encounters for Teachers*,[19] Greene unites two of her passions: education and existential identity. In this groundbreaking work, arguably the first education text to address existentialism so directly, Greene challenges teachers to reflect critically on their relationship with students and the responsibilities that come from "choosing" themselves as authentic educators. She invites them to do this through "encounters" with existential philosophers, and by doing so, instantiates her respect for teachers as thinkers—not just technocratic functionaries submerged in bureaucracy.

Greene's admiration for and commitment to teachers, as well as her critique of bureaucracy, is developed more fully in *Teacher as Stranger: Educational Philosophy for the Modern Age.*[20] This philosophy of education text ran counter to the dominant paradigm of the time (Anglo-analytic philosophy) and offered an alternative narrative to the very conception of what it means to "do philosophy." For Greene, the existential phenomenologist, thinking is an *embodied* act grounded in an embodied consciousness—not an abstract, disembodied logical process. Lived situations, contemporary educational issues, and resonant literary examples were infused in her educational philosophy. Greene put it well: "To do educational philosophy… is to become critically conscious of what is involved in the complex business of teaching and learning…. If he [sic] can learn to do philosophy, he may liberate himself for understanding and choosing."[21] It is this existential preoccupation with choosing, with acting, with meaning making that is a signature aspect of Greene's critique of the status quo in educational theory and practice.

In 1978 Greene published her first book of essays, *Landscapes of Learning*, which was "based on lectures written between 1974 and 1977 and originally read before various professional audiences."[22] By then she was well established at Teachers College, Columbia University, and had been named the William F. Russell Chair in the Foundations of Education in 1975. These essays continue to develop the existential and political questions that would shape her lifelong intellectual search. In her preface to the volume Greene says: "My primary interest has been to draw attention to the multiple realities of our culture in such a way as to arouse readers to pose critical questions of their own."[23] Throughout, Greene draws on critical theory, existentialism, and literary texts to provoke educators to "wide-awakeness."

In her respect for the capacity of teachers to be actively engaged in determining their professional lives, Greene tells us that "I am interested in trying to awaken educators to a realization that transformations are conceivable, that learning is stimulated by a sense of future possibility and by a sense of what might be."[24] She refuses to accede to the taken-for-granted of educational bureaucracies and positivistic scientism that defined much of schooling and teacher education at the time. Her commitment to demystification, to emancipation, to critical *praxis*, to the transformative power of the imagination, permeates these essays. She incites us to think about the "predicaments" in which we find ourselves and offers compelling examples through history, literature, and philosophy to move us to choosing, to imagining, to acting on our freedom in order create a more equitable democratic world.

Synopsis of Greene's Themes and Arguments in *The Dialectic of Freedom*

Maxine Greene the existentialist, Maxine Greene the critical theorist, and Maxine Greene the Deweyan democratic pragmatist are all concerned with the question of freedom. As she says in the introduction to *The Dialectic of Freedom*, when describing the William F. Russell Chair at Teachers College, "The chair was endowed for the sake of advancing inquiry into the connections between education and freedom, and my various explorations in my various disciplines… have all centered around what has become *the main theme of this book*—and, perhaps, the *main theme of my life*" (emphasis added).[25]

Greene opens her inquiry in Chapter 1 with an exploration of the concept of freedom, especially in the context of contemporary American society. Freedom for many Americans is informed by the power of the American Dream and the individualism that permeates that myth. Historically, the individual embedded in this powerful cultural trope has been identified with "self-dependence and self-determination," as opposed to being "connected...together in community."[26]

As mentioned earlier, for Greene, freedom is not an abstract condition into which one is born; one *obtains* freedom through *choosing*, through *acting*. Here we see the strong existentialist influences of Sartre and others as Greene challenges us to take responsibility for our freedom, for our own being in the world: "the person who chooses himself/herself in his/her freedom cannot place the onus on outside forces...."[27]

Yet, at the same time, as someone influenced by the dialectical theory of Marx and Dewey, Greene resists the "either/or" thinking that dominates much of American political, economic, and educational thought. Greene is very cognizant of the material conditions in the world that shape (if not determine) our existence. It is this tension between the subjective and objective world that informs Greene's notion of "the dialectic of freedom," a "dialectic that can[not]... be resolved in perfect synthesis or harmony."[28] Greene argues that we live within a plethora of dialectics—that "there is...a dialectical relation marking every human situation."[29]

For Greene, one continually makes and remakes oneself through naming, choosing, resisting, and acting. By developing a critical consciousness, an individual is able to see and to name her world, and consequently develop "the capacity to surpass the given and look at things as if they could be otherwise."[30] It is this capacity that Greene defines as "human freedom."[31] Drawing on Dewey here, Greene develops her understanding of the social imagination in order "to think forward into a future...to reach beyond...to becom[e] different from what we have been."[32]

Greene places this capacity to imagine that the world can be different in the context of education and schooling and implores teachers "to reach beyond themselves, to wonder, to imagine, to pose their own questions" in order to help children become empowered persons as well.[33] One way Greene helps us all find our freedom is through the imaginative acts required to understand the arts. It is through literature, in particular, that Greene helps us interpret the complexities of freedom and education in American history.

And so it is to American history and literature that we now turn in order to grasp the key ideas in Chapter 2 of her book, "American Paradox, American Quest." Greene helps us understand the multiple and divergent meanings attached to the concept of freedom: that "it becomes increasingly difficult to make universal claims about the human desire for freedom."[34] She takes us back to the early years of our country to contrast the founding view of freedom and liberty with contemporary notions of the self-reliant individual embedded in *laissez-faire* capitalism. This latter notion, a *negative* freedom, a freedom from constraints, speaks of "the absence of all state interventions and controls."[35] Greene, however, is not content with this meaning of freedom. Once again turning to Dewey, she reminds us that Thomas Jefferson drew on the political discourse of Locke and Rousseau, as well as the Greeks, who understood that "freedom would be achieved and maintained to the extent that rational and autonomous men would *come together in speech and action*" (emphasis added).[36] Greene goes on to argue: "As Jefferson saw it, the concept of freedom was associated with a concept of action. It was neither privatist nor subjective; it could only be maintained out in the open among self-directing (and self-supporting) persons."[37]

Through literary works from the nineteenth century, Greene brings to life the "underside of American freedom" that is "the consequence of a *laissez-faire* system"[38] as well as "the relationship between human connection and the desire for freedom."[39] Herman Melville, F. Scott Fitzgerald, Nathaniel Hawthorne, Henry David Thoreau, and Walt Whitman are all deployed by Greene to illuminate the complexities and contradictions of freedom at the individual, community, and societal levels. She underscores the importance of the free individual *within* community and privileges the value of the public sphere as the site for free persons to come together to converse and act together. Like Dewey before her, Greene laments the increase in privatism and the gradual decline of "the public" and searches for ways to interrupt this decline through education. She asks:

> What is left for us in this positivist, media-dominated, and self-centered time?… How, given the emphasis on preparing the young for a society of high technology, are we to move them to perceive alternatives, to look at things as if they could be otherwise? And why? And to what ends?[40]

Greene, ever the philosopher of education, asks the perennial question: To what ends are we preparing the young in our schools? She reminds us that one of Horace Mann's arguments for establishing public schools was to develop "independence and self-control…and giv[e] people the means to resist the selfishness of others."[41] Later on, Dewey would elaborate on the role of education and schools in developing the capacity for achieving freedom through cooperative experiences and interactions in democratic classrooms. Like Dewey, Greene thought of freedom as a condition to be achieved through association with others. It is not an individually "endowed" quality to be passively taken for granted. Freedom is continually made and remade, through thought and action in community.

At the same time, the critical theorist in Greene understands that not everyone has the capacity to act on her own freedom in the same ways, with the same power. Understanding that we are all "thrown into the world" in particular places, in unique situations, Greene is sensitive to the barriers, the "walls," that certain individuals and groups faced at any given time in their history because of oppression and prejudice. It is through these people and their stories that Greene situates and embodies her concept of freedom.

Chapter 3, "Reaching from Private to Public: The Work of Women," and Chapter 4, "Multiplicities, Pluralities and a Common World," address the "walls" faced by marginalized people and how they have challenged them. Greene once again demonstrates the power of the literary imagination to bring to life those "who have acted to make a space for themselves in the presence of others."[42] One powerful example is that of Ralph Ellison's novel, *Invisible Man.* After Greene offers an interpretation of the story, in the context of societal racism and oppression, she goes on to make a more general point:

> The novel, then, may shed a new kind of light on the problem of freedom, especially in our time. It may be a light from without…since an "invisible man" cannot be absorbed in what is taken to be "normal" or real. He cannot fully "belong," and so his vision remains that of the critical stranger, who always sees more (and differently) than the one habituated to the everyday world.[43]

Greene, as well as many of us who engage in critical pedagogy, might adopt a stance of the "critical stranger" in order to gain a different perspective on a situation; to see the possibilities that may obtain through our actions; to move out of our "submerged," habituated positions *in order to act on our freedom*. At the same time, Greene asks: "How, in a society like ours, a society of contesting interests and submerged voices, an individualist society…can we educate for freedom? And in educating for freedom, how can we create and maintain a common world?"[44]

The arts provide an answer to this profound question. In Chapter 5, the last in the book ("Education, Art and Mastery: Toward the Spheres of Freedom"), Greene reviews some of the limiting understandings of freedom to clear the way for a more engaged concept—an embodied concept that lives and breathes in our diverse classrooms. In an impassioned plea, Greene says: "The challenge is to engage as many young people as possible in the thought that is freedom—the mode of thought that moved Sarah Grimke, Elizabeth Cady Stanton, Septima Clark…and so many others into action."[45] It is in echoing Freire and Dewey that she speaks about education for freedom. Invoking Dewey's concept of "the 'anaesthetic' experience [that] numbs people and prevents them…from launching inquiries," Greene connects her concept of education to "the imaginative capacity" and "conscious thinking" that can move us out of our sedimented existences. For Greene, the arts and the social imagination form the bulwark against "the technicist and behaviorist emphases…in American schools."[46]

The Relevance of *The Dialectic of Freedom* for Us Today

Greene's powerful critique of the technocratic, bureaucratic, anti-democratic forces in educational policy and practice were prescient in 1988, and her words continue to be as relevant today as they were then. If we look back at the national trends begun by *A Nation at Risk* (1983), we see that education was going to be a "bipartisan" political issue supported by all of the administrations following Reagan. Every president since Reagan maintained that he was the "education President." The first President Bush "convened a first-ever education summit of the nation's governors."[47] President Clinton, who had attended the Bush summit as governor of Arkansas, focused his educational reform as a response to corporate and private-sector needs and developed his policy, Goals 2000, as a direct call for national standards. Not to be outdone by his father, President G. W. Bush, with bipartisan support—particularly that of Senator Ted Kennedy—passed the reauthorization of the ESEA, known as No Child Left Behind.[48] And we can see how Race to the Top,[49] a continuation of NCLB, promoted by President Obama and his Secretary of Education, Arne Duncan, can be traced back to the 1983 report. Quite a legacy: over 30 years later we are still immersed in the conversations begun by this "wake-up" call to the nation, especially the call for a more "rigorous common curriculum," "national standards," and an emphasis on technology to improve our competitiveness.[50]

Maxine Greene grasped early on the insidious power of this technocratic thinking and spent her life in resistance to it.

Notes

1   National Commission on Excellence in Education, *A Nation at Risk: The Imperative for Educational Reform* (Washington, DC: U.S. Government Printing Office, 1983), http://www2.ed.gov/pubs/NatAtRisk/recomm.html (accessed February 15, 2015).
2   *A Nation at Risk.*
3   They themselves might eschew that label if understood primarily in political terms.

4 E.D. Hirsch, *Cultural Literacy: What Every American Needs to Know* (New York: Houghton Mifflin, 1987), 5.
5 Hirsch, 103.
6 Hirsch, 146–215.
7 Hirsch, 139.
8 Hirsch, 139.
9 Hirsch, 1–2.
10 Allan Bloom, *The Closing of the American Mind* (New York: Simon & Schuster, 1987), 347.
11 Bloom, 26.
12 Bloom, 26.
13 Bloom, 268.
14 William J. Bennett, *To Reclaim a Legacy: A Report on the Humanities in Higher Education* (Washington, DC: National Endowment for the Humanities, 1984), i.
15 Bennett, 29–30.
16 To name a few, she relied heavily on Jean-Paul Sartre, Maurice Merleau-Ponty, Albert Camus, John Dewey, Hannah Arendt, and Paulo Freire.
17 Maxine Greene, *The Public School and the Private Vision: A Search for America in Education and Literature* (New York: Random House, 1965).
18 Greene, *The Public School*, 122.
19 Maxine Greene, *Existential Encounters for Teachers* (New York: Random House, 1967).
20 Maxine Greene, *Teacher as Stranger: Educational Philosophy for the Modern Age* (Belmont, CA: Wadsworth Publishing Company, 1973).
21 Greene, *Teacher as Stranger*, 7.
22 Maxine Greene, *Landscapes of Learning* (New York: Teachers College Press, 1978), 1.
23 Greene, *Landscapes of Learning*, 2.
24 Greene, *Landscapes of Learning*, 3–4.
25 Maxine Greene, *The Dialectic of Freedom* (New York: Teachers College Press, 1988), xii.
26 Greene, *The Dialectic of Freedom*, 1.
27 Greene, *The Dialectic of Freedom*, 5.
28 Greene, *The Dialectic of Freedom*, 8.
29 Greene, *The Dialectic of Freedom*, 8.
30 Greene, *The Dialectic of Freedom*, 3.
31 Greene, *The Dialectic of Freedom*, 3.
32 Greene, *The Dialectic of Freedom*, 3.
33 Greene, *The Dialectic of Freedom*, 14.
34 Greene, *The Dialectic of Freedom*, 25.
35 Greene, *The Dialectic of Freedom*, 26.
36 Greene, *The Dialectic of Freedom*, 27.
37 Greene, *The Dialectic of Freedom*, 28.
38 Greene, *The Dialectic of Freedom*, 32.
39 Greene, *The Dialectic of Freedom*, 36.
40 Greene, *The Dialectic of Freedom*, 55.
41 Greene, *The Dialectic of Freedom*, 33.
42 Greene, *The Dialectic of Freedom*, 56.
43 Greene, *The Dialectic of Freedom*, 99.
44 Greene, *The Dialectic of Freedom*, 176.
45 Greene, *The Dialectic of Freedom*, 125.
46 Greene, *The Dialectic of Freedom*, 126.
47 Diane Ravitch, Education in the 1980's: A Concern for Quality. *Education Week*, http://www.edweek.org/ew/articles/1990/01/10/09200009.h09.html (accessed February 15, 2015).
48 No Child Left Behind, http://www2.ed.gov/policy/elsec/leg/esea02/index.html
49 Race to the Top, http://www2.ed.gov/programs/racetothetop/index.html (accessed February 15, 2015).
50 Philip Elliott, *A Nation at Risk*, 30 Years Later. *Huffington Post*, http://www.huffingtonpost.com/2013/04/24/a-nation-at-risk-30-years-report-schools_n_3147535.html (accessed February 15, 2015).

NINETEEN

Peter McLaren, *Life in Schools: An Introduction to Critical Pedagogy in the Foundations of Education* (1988)

E. Wayne Ross

Prologue to *Life in Schools*

In 1980 Peter McLaren's *Cries from the Corridor* was a bestseller in Canada, making the year-end notable books lists from *Maclean's* and the *Toronto Sun*. The book, McLaren's journal of his teaching experiences in an elementary school in the Jane-Finch Corridor of North York, an "inner-city suburb" of Toronto, sparked heated public debate on urban education. McLaren describes the initial purpose of the book as simply to draw attention to the terribly oppressive conditions of his students, who lived in nearby public housing projects, and to address the concerns of urban schoolteachers who felt helpless in their overcrowded and underfunded classrooms. He hoped the powers that be might provide more resources to urban schools to decrease class size, develop programs relevant to students' needs, and implement culturally responsive curriculum and pedagogy.

The Canadian Journal of Education described *Cries from the Corridor* as a

> day-to-day, diary-style narrative, [in which] short classroom episodes are recounted in chronological fashion…interspersed [with] occasional references to pedagogical concerns, such as McLaren's realization that standardized methods or curricula had little impact, and instead "free," "open," or "progressive" styles were required with more "relevant" topics…. But almost the entire book consists of raw reports of an even more raw reality as almost every conceivable classroom horror show is recounted. (West, 1981, p. 81)

The book succeeded in drawing attention to the conditions of urban students' lives in and out of schools, with media coverage pressuring the Board of Education to make some short-lived gestures of reform. But the educational establishment was generally not impressed.

The *CJE* review declared the book to be of "limited academic utility," noting that "while it raises important issues, and presents the underside of classroom life, it isn't good ethnography" and lacks "almost any analysis" (West, p. 82). It seems remarkable, then, that *Life in Schools*, now in its sixth edition, and having been named one of the twelve most significant books in education (Engle, 2004), devotes nearly one-third of its pages to reprinting McLaren's journal. How can this be?

From the publication of *Cries from the Corridor* in 1980 to the latest edition of *Life in Schools*, McLaren's thought has continuously evolved, and he has been remarkably responsive to what in many cases has been severe criticism from fellow academics. For example, the crucial part of Gordon West's review in the *CJE* presents the book as symptomatic of a deficit that plagued the entire field:

> Problems remain individualized in isolated students, even when there is a whole classroom or school full of them.... The analysis arbitrarily stops at families, bad housing, or neighborhoods, and resists going behind these even to ask how they become that way.... Given the obvious problems and inhumane conditions which are undeniably part of working class life, one might begin to ask who has an interest in their persistence and what functions they fulfil [*sic*]. To what extent is the unpopularity of such a class analysis among Canadian educators a result of the lack of working class organization and consciousness in this country? And how could such an organization contribute to progress in education? *Cries from the Corridor* is typical of the Canadian education literature in failing to address or to offer answers to such questions. It is nonetheless to its credit that it does succeed in presenting the raw data of the problem. (pp. 82–83)

Cries from the Corridors ends with McLaren leaving for graduate school after 5 years in the classroom, and his subsequent scholarly work on critical pedagogy can be understood as a direct response to the unanswered questions that West raises. Critical pedagogy asks who has an interest in the persistence of poverty and inequality. More generally, it goes beyond surface meanings and received wisdom to understand root causes and social contexts as well as the personal consequences of actions, processes, practices, and discourses.

In the preface to *Life in Schools*, McLaren agrees with West's criticism that "my journal was primarily description, without theoretical framework that could help the reader better understand the conditions I was attempting to portray":

> By failing to set my classroom journal within a critical theoretical context, I could not adequately reveal how power and knowledge work in the interests of the capitalist class over the working class. Consequently, I ran the risk of allowing readers to reinforce their stereotypes of what schooling was like in the "blackboard jungle" and what constituted the behavior of economically disadvantaged students. I also was in danger of portraying impoverished communities as crucibles of violence and hatred, devoid of humanity and dignity. (2015, p. xxv)

McLaren describes *Life in Schools* as the story of his reinvention as an educator, from a liberal humanist who focused on social and educational reform to a Marxist humanist advocating revolutionary praxis, that is, educating for social revolution through critical pedagogy. While McLaren now believes it was a "grave mistake" to publish his diaries without providing critical analysis of the social and economic conditions that shaped the lives of his students and their families, he has turned this mistake into a compelling pedagogical moment. The book invites readers to read, critique, and deconstruct his early teaching practice; it also prompts readers to begin to analyze the assumptions that inform their teaching practices and, more generally, the liberal humanist discourse of contemporary progressive and well-intentioned teachers.

Synopsis of the Book

Life in Schools was first published in 1989, and across its six editions the basic structure of the book remained relatively consistent, although the content has changed and expanded in notable ways. The progressive radicalization of McLaren's thought can be traced across each edition of the book. In the fifth edition, McLaren introduced revolutionary critical pedagogy, and the book's publisher, Pearson PLC, subsequently dropped it from its list. It did not take long for Paradigm to pick up the rights. *Life in Schools* has always reflected an emancipatory politics, critiquing the abuses of capitalism, racism, sexism, homophobia, cultural imperialism, and asymmetrical power relations, but the left-leaning postmodernism and politics of reform that informs parts of the earlier editions has been swept away. It seems the new publishing home for *Life in Schools* allowed the full force of McLaren's revolutionary thought to come through as he unabashedly argues for "total social revolution."

With a combination of rhetorical flair, literary allusion, polemic, and empirical analysis that unmistakably characterizes much of McLaren's work, the opening section of the book presents the sociopolitical context for (e.g., G. W. Bush and Obama administration education policies) and introduction to revolutionary critical pedagogy.

McLaren acknowledges the diversity of perspectives represented in the field of critical pedagogy, but unifying commitments include creating engaging and vibrant spaces wherein students are encouraged to question dominant epistemological, axiological, and political assumptions that are taken for granted and often prop up the dominant social class. Critical pedagogy is based on the proposition that education is not a neutral activity, "that all knowledge is a form of ideological production. Critical pedagogy…possesses many vocabularies of self and social formation, but is essentially a Freirean approach to reading the word and the world dialectically" (p. 8).

Following from John Dewey's (1916) analysis of the social function of education, and perhaps as an oblique response to Ellsworth's (1989) criticism of the field, McLaren argues that critical pedagogy as an "empowering" or "transforming" pedagogy carries little meaning without first answering the question "empowering for whom and for what purpose? To what end is such transformation directed, whose interests will be served, and who will benefit from such transformation?" (p. 9).

Revolutionary critical educators are described as those who "work from a Marxist humanist perspective" and argue for

> a dialectical reasoning that involves becoming conscious of and transcending the limits within which we can make ourselves; it calls for externalizing, historicizing, and objectifying our vision of liberation, in treating theory as a form of practice and practice as form of theory as we contest the psychopathology of everyday life incarnate in capitalism's social division of labor. (p. 9)

The tension in critical pedagogy is describing it in practical concrete terms without representing it as a practice that follows a recipe or blueprint. McLaren identifies "some talking points for approaching the nuts and bolts of "revolutionary critical pedagogy" (p. 10). These points include:

- Revolutionary critical pedagogy makes no claim to political neutrality;
- Critical pedagogy eschews any approach to pedagogy that reduces teaching to narrow thinking skills in isolation from the debates and contexts in which the skills are employed; all thoughts, acts, and relations are political in the ideological sense;
- Dialogue is critical, but getting all the opposing positions out on the table is not the same thing as a coherent argument; ideological differences do not resolve themselves when placed in the "correct organizational framework";
- A dialectical approach to understanding the world is critical; students need to learn how social relations in a capitalist society are internally or dialectically related;
- Teachers need methodological approaches that help them reconstruct the social and historical conditions surrounding the production, circulation, and reception of symbolic forms;
- A narrow focus on stratification and social inequality leads to an abandonment of working-class struggle; class struggle has to be linked to the relation internal to labor;
- Recognition of the "class character" of education in capitalist schooling and advocating for "socialist reorganization of capitalist society";
- Theoretical knowledge is seldom linked to labor practices; revolutionary critical pedagogy, in contrast, consists of teaching students how knowledge is related historically, culturally, and institutionally to production and consumption; and
- Revolutionary praxis is brought about by approaching Marxism not as an inert body of ideas for contemplation, but as a motive focus for remaking society, as a way to give material force to ideas through collective action; that is, praxis is the locus of synthesizing form and content, thought and action.

Part II, "Cries from the Corridor," consists of McLaren's diary of a day-to-day struggle as a teacher in an urban school, along with a brief afterword. The shift in content and tone from the introduction to this section of the book is dramatic. After the conceptually dense and broadly sweeping introduction, the reader is presented with a compelling account of life in schools that is journalistic in style and often darkly comedic. McLaren writes that it is painful for him to read these vignettes because the journal illustrates he was not immune to many of the criticisms that he now lays "at the feet of unjust schooling practices and the workings of a racist, sexist, and culturally imperialistic social formation…" (p. 33). The vignettes are painfully honest descriptions whose power, I believe, is in capturing, without generalization, the hopes, fears, failures, and small successes that many novice teachers experience. This section is the "raw data of the problem" that McLaren asks readers to critically engage with after their introduction to critical pedagogy in the "theory" sections that follow in Parts III, IV, and V.

Part III, "Critical Pedagogy: An Overview," sets out the foundational principles of critical pedagogy. This is an introductory text, and there is no effort to advance complex theoretical arguments in the theory sections of the book. The starting assumption is that people are "essentially unfree and inhabit a world rife with contradictions and asymmetries of power and privilege" (p. 131) and that critical educators work with theories that are dialectical—that is, they recognize that "the problems of society are more than simply isolated events of individuals or deficiencies in the social structure." These "problems" are part of an interactive context in which the individual and society are inextricably interwoven "so that reference to one must by implication mean reference to the other" (p. 131).

Arguing for and illustrating the relevance of theory and its relation to practice, McLaren uses clear, accessible language to describe the relationships between critical pedagogy and (1) social construction of knowledge (e.g., forms of knowledge, class, culture, hegemony, and ideology); (2) power/knowledge relation (e.g., discourse); (3) curriculum (e.g., hidden curriculum, cultural politics, and the Common Core); and (4) resistance theory (e.g., cultural capital). This group of admittedly incomplete categories provides the theoretical framework for readers to examine McLaren's, as well as their own, experiences in schools. The section ends with questions that build on the concepts central to critical pedagogy. For example:

> Should teachers be answerable for the larger social consequences of their collective individual acts? Should a consistent failure of teachers to act on the obligations incurred at the social level—i.e., to redress social injustice, racism, and sexism—be legitimate grounds for challenging their personal actions in the classroom? What are the moral variants against which we shall construct ourselves as social agents of change? (p. 155)

Part IV, "Analysis," explores specific processes of schooling in more detail, with brief and richly sourced chapters devoted to race, class, and gender; myths of education; and teachers and students. A key theme in this section is that the needs and problems of students are the starting point for critical pedagogy, and issues of voice and conversation are highlighted.

In Chapter 9, the conclusion of Parts III and IV of the book, McLaren argues that for critical pedagogy to become viable in schools, teachers need to employ both critical analyses and utopian thinking, combining the language of critique with the language of possibility in an effort to "recapture the idea of democracy as a social movement grounded in a fundamental respect for *individual freedom* and *social justice*" (p. 187; italics in original). Recalling Aronowitz and Giroux (1985), he identifies two crucial directions for reforming contemporary school practices: first, viewing schools as democratic public spheres (i.e., regarding schools as sites of self- and social empowerment); and second, viewing teachers as transformative intellectuals. To these McLaren adds a third: viewing teachers as social and moral agents (i.e., there is no neutral sphere into which teachers can retreat to engage student experience).

McLaren makes it clear that he is not advocating "radical democracy" along the lines of Laclau and Mouffe (1985), hooks (1996), and, one might presume, Giroux (1996) and even Freire (2004), but rather an "authentic democracy" beyond the bounds of capitalism:

> Teachers must function as more than agents of social critique. They must attempt to fashion a language of hope that points to new forms of social and material relations that break free from the material conditions of everyday life with their unequal distributions of wealth, power, and privilege based on the appropriation and exploitation of surplus labor…. Only in this engagement can we, as agents of transformation and hope, begin to both feel and understand the suffering and alienation of the world and also be provided with the will, the purpose, and the understanding to overcome it. Overcoming it cannot be achieved by trying to make capitalism adjust itself to human needs but by abolishing the capitalist system itself. (p. 191)

Chapter 9 also contains excellent, but all too brief, descriptions of schools engaged in "liberating education." The book, and the field in general, would benefit from more extended accounts of enacted critical pedagogy.[1]

Part V, "Looking Back, Looking Forward," extends the analyses of race with a chapter on unthinking Whiteness; the book's "closing" chapter, "The Hope and Struggle Ahead," situates

200

critical education geopolitically. In the introduction to Part V, McLaren reasons that this new section provides space for him to explore ideas that were only tangentially addressed in earlier editions of the book. Chapter 10, "Unthinking Whiteness, Rethinking Cultural Contact as Interculturality," could not be more relevant in light of the recent racial violence in the United States and worldwide (Polgreen, 2015; Dees & Cohen, 2015). McLaren frames this chapter with an analysis of the fatal shooting of Trayvon Martin in 2012 and the 2009 execution-style murder of Oscar Grant by a police officer in Oakland, California. Exploring so-called colorblindness, the school-to-prison pipeline, and the construction of race and Whiteness, this chapter offers a trenchant exploration of critical race theory and decolonial pedagogy.

The book concludes with an epilogue reflecting on the 25 years of *Life in Schools* and an appendix reprinting a 2013 interview with McLaren from *Global Education Magazine*. While both of the chapters in Part V, as well as the epilogue and appendix, include some of the most important insights in the book, the repeated closing crescendos in the final 100 pages dampen the dramatic power of the book.

Critical Reception

Any book that is published in six editions across 25 years by several publishers has had a broad and receptive audience. But *Life in Schools*, like any work that stakes out decidedly contrarian positions, certainly has had it critics. Below I sample a range of perspectives from scholarly critics.

One of the first reviews of the book to appear was written by Walter Werner (1989) for *Pedagogy + Phenomenology*. Werner's review focuses on the needs and problems of his students, who were practicing teachers taking a course in critical pedagogy. Werner is supportive of McLaren's aims and writes a rather favorable review, concluding that it is through books such as *Life in Schools* that teachers can "recover their sense of efficacy" and formulate collective counter-responses to social and economic injustices. But Werner makes three pointed criticisms of the book as an introductory textbook. First, the book often assumes too much on the part of readers and should more carefully develop the language that gives readers access to theorizing. According to Werner, the book clearly argues that knowledge is historically and socially rooted, that knowledge is an ongoing construction by groups of people who live in particular times and places, and that some forms of knowledge have more legitimacy and status than others:

> These claims are communicated well to anyone who does not have a background in the sociology of knowledge. What can be confusing to teachers, though, is that the boundaries of knowledge are not clarified. There is little distinction made among knowledge, beliefs, customs, everyday "constructions of reality," commonsense understandings, and even consciousness itself. (pp. 274–275)

After presenting a number of illustrative excerpts from the book, Werner says:

> Claims such as these are so encompassing and general that readers could benefit considerably from more definition and careful analysis than is given in the book. Glossed over is much of the legitimate debate about knowledge, ideology, and objectivity. If all descriptions, meaning, ideas, and knowledge are ideological—and this would have to include McLaren's

book—then the category is empty, ceases to be useful in analysis, and leaves the reader mystified. There would be little sense in engaging in any serious critique if power is the major criterion for determining the truth and worth of ideas. (p. 276)

Werner's second observation is a question: "Would discourse in the field of critical pedagogy be possible without the use of in-house jargon?" Werner laments that such specialized language limits accessibility to "outsiders." Yes, students in any area of study often experience frustration when confronted with new kinds of language, but to my mind this criticism is a paradox. How do we develop a new language without the introduction of "new" concepts (e.g., hegemony, ideology, dialectical, etc.)?

Last, Werner raises the issue of teachers' responses to the deconstruction of the myths of schooling and education that are central to critical pedagogy:

> They initially feel over whelmed by the magnitude of the question concerning how schools are shaped by and so thoroughly embody the inequalities of the larger society, and they are frustrated by the seeming hopelessness of their being able to effect any meaningful change. There often is considerable pessimism as they come to see that the problems and issues that critical pedagogy illuminates are rooted outside the microworld of each unique classroom. (p. 277)

Werner's concern is that the language of possibility is much less developed than the language of critique in the first edition of the book. Over the course of subsequent editions, and particularly in the two most recent editions, which emphasize revolutionary critical pedagogy, McLaren has addressed this concern in depth. While many readers will reject a language of possibility that begins with the premise that capitalism must be destroyed, there is no denying that revolutionary critical pedagogy engages both critical analysis and utopian thought in ways that open up more possibilities than ever.

In a long review article for *Educational Theory*, John Smyth (1990) engages *Life in Schools* as a critical ethnography and, in comparison to the flood of studies and reports on schooling that were produced in the 1980s, Smyth finds McLaren's book "both intellectually informed about the debate [on schooling] as well as having a compelling evidential basis" (p. 267). McLaren's journal accounts are compared favorably with those of Kohl (1961), Kozol (1967), Willis (1977), Herndon (1985), and other prominent teaching narratives and ethnographies as a "searing and compellingly authentic personal account of what the struggle for life was like both for himself as a teacher and for the students in his…school" (p. 268).

McLaren's critical pedagogy was not a coherent blueprint or a "quick fix" for the way schools ought to be, but goes "a long way toward dispelling the often-made but rarely substantiated claim of inaction ascribed to all critical theorists" (p. 272):

> McLaren's work is replete with the practical, but not as an end in itself; he has a profoundly philosophical, ethical, and humane view of the egalitarian ends toward which school practice ought to be directed. (p. 272)

Smyth argues that the unexpurgated journal narratives work to immerse readers in the lived experiences of the classroom and allow them to vicariously experience what it was like to have undergone such an evolution in thought about teaching. Praising the honesty of McLaren's political project, Smyth argues:

In describing his practices as a teacher and the experiences of his students McLaren goes to considerable lengths…to describe both "real and present conditions, and certain conditions still to come which [he] is trying to bring into being." His overwhelming concern in undertaking this critical ethnography is with sketching out the way in which people are implicated in simultaneously regulating and altering the terms and conditions under which they live and work together and how they "define what is possible and desirable for themselves and others." (p. 279)

In the concluding paragraphs of his review, Smyth, drawing on the work of Brodkey (1987) and Simon and Dippo (1986), describes the fundamental conditions that critical ethnography must meet:

> (1) the work must employ an organizing problematic that defines one's data and analytical procedures in a way that is consistent with its project; (2) the work must be situated, in part, within a public sphere that allows it to become the starting point for the critique and the transformation of the conditions of oppressive and inequitable moral and social regulation; and (3) the work must address the limits of its own claims by a consideration of how, as a form of social practice, it too is constituted and regulated through historical relations of power and existing material conditions. (Simon & Dippo, 1985; quoted in Smyth, 1990, p. 279)

Smyth then declares that, in *Life in Schools*, McLaren has done all of these things, making it a model critical ethnography.

The *Educational Researcher* published an essay review by Mary Ann Doyle (1996) of four books by McLaren, including two editions of *Life in Schools*. In contrast to the reviews by Werner and Smyth, her review sees *Life in Schools* as an entirely different book. The review begins by calling McLaren a "strident and prolific" critical theorist. Oddly enough, Doyle criticizes McLaren for the honesty of his teaching journal, which Smyth and other reviewers made specific points of praise:

> The journal entries are brutally frank and detailed, and McLaren did not delete vulgar language, accounts of violence and abuse, or even his own failed attempt to engage his students equitably. (p. 28)

Without acknowledging McLaren's self-criticism of his own teaching or highlighting the book's strategic use of the journal entries as source material for critique and deconstruction, Doyle adopts an accusatory tone in her judgment that

> McLaren's efforts to build solidarity with some of the most active and resistant students often lead him into the contradictory behavior supporting some student at the expense of the emotional and sometimes physical security of others. (p. 28)

Without elaboration or analysis, Doyle posits that McLaren's critique of school curricula and teacher education programs reduces teachers to "clerks of the empire" and is "fraught with difficulties"; she declares critical theory to be a "regime of truth" (p. 28). Doyle echoes the complaints of others that the book is weak on issues of gender. She contends that McLaren's claims of reflexivity seem more rhetorical than actual and that his reference list and suggested reading are composed of mostly male critical theorists. All of these are, of course, legitimate criticisms. What is notable is that most of Doyle's references are to reviews of the book that are reprinted in the second edition of *Life in Schools*. The reviews of Ursula Kelly and John Portelli appear, along with a response by McLaren, which Doyle labels a "missed opportunity," because "he defended himself" against specific challenges by the reviewers.

Doyle does, however, acknowledge the shifts in emphasis in the second edition of the book:

> What McLaren accomplished in his essay response, however, is a rearticulation of the shifts in emphasis that have characterized his work since completing the first edition of *Life in Schools*. He identified these areas as identity and race, gender and sexuality, language and the production of desire, and the politics of popular culture and popular pleasures. He elaborated on the work of Teresa Ebert in the area of "resistance postmodernism" and distanced himself from ludic postmodernism, which had been characterized as a kind of "epistemological relativism." (pp. 29–30)

Doyle musters only begrudging credit for what others would see as extraordinary openness to the criticism and reflexivity McLaren demonstrates in the second edition of *Life in Schools*:

> Although McLaren recognized a wider scholarly influence on his writing in the second edition of *Life in Schools*, I believe he continued to under theorize the inherently contradictory effects of advocating a politics of resistance based on productive agency, particularly the production of rupture, refusal, and forms of the unacceptable…. He suggested: "We can achieve a pedagogy of transformation if we turn our teaching into an outrageous practice and a practice of outrage" (1994, p. 299). This appeal to the outrageous misapprehended the complexity of resistance. Particularly ignored were those contradictions associated with being different by being female and differences amplified by social markers such as race, class, age, and nationality. (p. 30)

Doyle concludes her review of *Life in Schools* and other McLaren books by acknowledging that McLaren has articulated a vision drawn from a "more complex set of relations of solidarity among feminist, diverse social theorists and other historically marginalized peoples" (p. 32).

Influence and Relevance for Today

Social justice is one of the chief concepts driving contemporary educational research and teacher education. Inequities in wealth, opportunity, and privilege are often situated in relation to issues of schooling, but typically are treated in isolation from one another and are neither historicized nor politicized. In *Life in Schools*, McLaren takes up questions many others have ignored and presents a worldview that begins with the whole—the system of capitalism—and then proceeds to an examination of the parts (e.g., inequalities) to see where each fits and functions. His dialectical approach to investigating schools, education, and society allows us to see Marxism as (1) a science (describing how capitalism functions); (2) as critique (the deleterious effects of capitalism); (3) as vision (utopian images of a post-capitalist world); and (4) as strategy (moving from here to there, "what is to be done?"). As Ollman (2003) points out, most interpreters of Marx only emphasize one or a few of these themes, but *Life in Schools*, and revolutionary critical pedagogy in particular, illustrates how each of these elements can inform and contribute to others.

Marxist analysis of schools and education has long flourished in England and India, but North American education literature has seemingly been immune to Marxist analysis since Bowles and Gintis's *Schooling in Capitalist America* (1976). In the wake of the global financial crisis of 2008, there has been a renewed interest in Marx and his analyses (e.g., Eagleton,

2011), and there has been a slowly growing interest in Marxist analysis of education in North America, which is in no small part due to the influence of McLaren—particularly his *Life in Schools*.[2] There is no doubt that critical pedagogy today has been profoundly influenced by McLaren's scholarship, and his political activism has been firmly focused on fostering class consciousness and organizing for revolutionary transformation.

Ollman (2003) writes that most people who reject a Marxist analysis of capitalism don't simply disagree with it, but instead "treat the capitalism Marx is speaking about as if it isn't there" (p. 3). Capitalism is not invisible, but, as Ollman points out, neither is it immediately apparent:

> For it to be noticed, let alone understood, people's attention has to be drawn to certain relations the elements of which are not always obvious. But if most of its inhabitants don't even see capitalism, the system, any effort to explain how it works must be accompanied by an equally strenuous effort at displaying it, simply showing that it exists and what kind of entity it is. Widely ignored in the literature on Marx, revelation, therefore, is as crucial to Marxism as explanation, and indeed the latter is impossible without the former. (Ollman, 2003, pp. 3–4)

Life in Schools is an enduring and evolving revelation of capitalism and the systems of education and schooling that serve its needs.

Notes

1   Extended descriptions of dialectical Marxist approaches to classroom teaching can be found in the work of teacher Greg Queen. See, for example, Queen (2014).
2   Evidence of growing interest in North American Marxist educational analysis can be found in the work of young and mid-career scholars such as Faith Agostinone-Wilson, John Elmore, Derek Ford, Shelia Macrine, and Curry Malott, among others, and in the unlikely creation of the Marxian Analysis of Society, Schools and Education SIG in the American Educational Research Association.

References

Aronowitz, S., & Giroux, H.A. (1985). *Education under siege: The conservative and radical debate over schooling.* South Hadley, MA: Bergin & Garvey.
Bowles, S., & Gintis, H. (1976). *Schooling in capitalist America.* New York: Basic Books.
Brodkey, L. (1987). Writing critical ethnography narratives. *Anthropology and Education Quarterly, 18*(2), 67–76.
Dees, M., & Cohen, J.R. (2015, June 22). White supremacists without borders. *The New York Times.* Retrieved from http://www.nytimes.com/2015/06/22/opinion/white-supremacists-without-borders.html
Dewey, J. (1916). *Democracy and education.* New York: Macmillan.
Doyle, M.A. (1996). Peter McLaren and the field of critical pedagogy. *Educational Researcher, 25*(4), 28–32.
Eagleton, T. (2011). *Marx was right.* New Haven, CT: Yale University Press.
Ellsworth, E. (1989). Why doesn't this feel empowering? Working through the repressive myths of critical pedagogy. *Harvard Educational Review, 59*(3), 297–324.
Engle, S. (2004, February 12). UCLA education professor Peter McLaren's *Life in Schools* ranked in top 12 significant writings of foreign authors. *UCLA Newsroom.* Retrieved from http://newsroom.ucla.edu/releases/UCLA-Education-Professor-Peter-4934
Freire, P. (2004). *Pedagogy of hope: Reliving Pedagogy of the Oppressed.* New York: Continuum.
Giroux, H. (1996). Pedagogy and radical democracy in the age of "political correctness." In D. Trend (Ed.), *Radical democracy: Identity, citizenship, and the state* (pp. 179–194). New York: Routledge.
Herndon, J. (1985). *Notes from a school teacher.* New York: Simon & Schuster.
hooks, b. (1996). Representation and democracy: An interview. In D. Trend (Ed.), *Radical democracy: Identity, citizenship, and the state* (pp. 228–236). New York: Routledge.
Kohl, H. (1961). *36 children.* New York: Signet.
Kozol, J. (1967). *Death at an early age.* New York: Signet.

Laclau, E., & Mouffe, C. (1985). *Hegemony and socialist strategy: Towards a radical democratic politics*. London: Verso.

McLaren, P. (1980). *Cries from the corridor: The suburban ghettos*. Agincourt, ON: Methuen.

McLaren, P. (1994). *Life in schools: An introduction to critical pedagogy in the foundations of education* (2nd ed.). New York: Longman.

McLaren, P. (2015). *Life in schools: An introduction to critical pedagogy in the foundations of education* (6th ed.). Boulder, CO: Paradigm.

Ollman, B. (2003). *Dance of the dialectic: Steps in Marx's method*. Urbana: University of Illinois Press.

Polgreen, L. (2015, June 20). From Ferguson to Charleston and beyond, anguish about race keeps building. *The New York Times*. Retrieved from http://www.nytimes.com/2015/06/21/us/from-ferguson-to-charleston-and-beyond-anguish-about-race-keeps-building.html

Queen, G. (2014). Class struggle in the classroom. In E.W. Ross (Ed.), *The social studies curriculum: Purposes, problems, and possibilities* (4th ed., pp. 313–334). Albany: State University of New York Press.

Simon, R., & Dippo, D. (1986). On critical ethnographic work. *Anthropology and Education Quarterly, 17*(4), 195–202.

Smyth, J. (1990). Review of *Life in schools: An introduction to critical pedagogy in the foundations of education*. *Educational Theory, 40*(2), 267–280.

Werner, W. (1989). Review of *Life in schools: An introduction to critical pedagogy in the foundations of education*. *Phenomenology + Pedagogy, 7*, 271–277. Retrieved from http://ejournals.library.ualberta.ca/index.php/pandp/article/view/15105/11926

West, G. (1981). Review of *Cries from the corridor: The new suburban ghetto*. *Canadian Journal of Education, 6*(1), 81–83.

Willis, P. (1977). *Learning to labor*. New York: Columbia University Press.

PART FOUR

The 1990s

TWENTY

John E. Chubb and Terry M. Moe, *Politics, Markets, and America's Schools* (1990)

John F. Covaleskie

I. Synopsis

In *Politics, Markets, and America's Schools*, John Chubb and Terry Moe[1] put forth a simple and very direct thesis: Our system of public schools is a failure for reasons that make reform impossible. The system of public schooling can only be replaced by a marketplace of mostly private schools and those public schools fit enough to compete (but liberated from democratic governance). The thesis is twofold: in the first place, public schools, as institutions of democratic politics, are intrinsically unreformable; second, a market in which individuals choose schools for their children is the only means of reforming education in the United States.

The reason the public system cannot be reformed but must be replaced is that public schools are governed democratically, an approach that is inherently unstable and subject to change and uncertainty. This makes it difficult to do long-term planning to make schools better. Government schools, according to Chubb and Moe, are failures precisely because they are governed democratically, and democracy is an inefficient and unstable way to make decisions. Thus, they argue that reform efforts have left "the institutions of educational governance unchanged.… [T]hese institutions are more than simply the democratic means by which policy solutions are formulated and administered. They are also the fundamental causes of the very problems they are supposed to be solving" (p. 18).

At the same time, the fact that government schools are a monopoly makes them inherently inefficient, with no real incentive to improve. So the second prong of their argument is the positive statement of this inherent inefficiency: only the discipline of the marketplace can lead to best practices, more efficient education, and more effective teaching and learning—and only autonomy from democratic control will allow these things to happen.

The assumption that schools must be *forced* to improve is central to the rhetoric of choice and markets. The claim is consistently made that, under the current regime, schools (that is, the people who work in them) have no desire to do their jobs well. Public schools, the argument goes, have guaranteed enrollments (teachers have guaranteed jobs), and so there is no need to excel, and no desire to do so.

More directly, Chubb and Moe state: "Our analysis shows that the system's familiar arrangements for direct democratic control do indeed impose a distinctive structure on [schools and districts]…and that this structure tends to promote organizational characteristics that are ill-suited to the effective performance of American public schools" (p. 21). Democratic control of school districts serves "to limit and undermine school autonomy" (p. 23). The problem with this, according to Chubb and Moe, is twofold: (1) "democracy is essentially coercive. The winners get to use public authority to impose their policies on the losers" (p. 28); and (2) "The schools are agencies of society as a whole, and everyone has a right to participate in their governance. Parents have a right to participate too. But they have no right to win" (p. 32). This latter point—that in a democratic regime all citizens have a right to participate—is a problem to be solved: parents *should* "win."

Parents should win because the education of children is properly the domain of parents, not society; and it is a fundamental right of parents to choose the *kind* of education their own children receive. In contrast, the operation and theory of democratic education is rooted in the belief that educating the citizens of the next generation is, while undeniably the primary responsibility of the parents, also the responsibility of the society as a whole (see, for example, Dewey,[2] Meier,[3] and Kozol[4]).

More fundamentally, Chubb and Moe point out that democratic decisions are always up for revision and reconsideration, and here they have a point. The difficulties this presents for schools are real: How can district administrators, teachers, and school boards plan for the future when the expectations are unstable and at least potentially constantly in flux?

The solution that Chubb and Moe offer is elegant in its simplicity: remove public schools from the vicissitudes of democratic life. This will effect school improvement in that it will (1) remove the regulatory regime that disallows schools to experiment and innovate (grant schools "autonomy") and (2) simultaneously create a private market of schools that will virtually force improvement. This last point goes to the heart of the argument—the connection between marketization and school improvement. Since democratic control of schools is, *ex hypotheo*, rigid, controlling, hegemonizing, and stifling of creativity and experimentation; and since markets, also *ex hypotheo*, are liberating, dynamic, innovative, and conducive to excellence, removing democratic control and submitting schools to the discipline of the marketplace is the best—and the only—way to achieve educational excellence:

> Bureaucratic autonomy and effective school organization are natural products of the basic institutional forces at work on schools in a marketplace. They are products of school competition and parental choice. Success is built into the institutional structure of private education. As public education is now structured, institutions make success almost unnatural…. In the private sector, where schools are controlled by markets…autonomy is generally high. In the public sector, where schools are controlled by politics…autonomy is generally low. (p. 183)

However, Chubb and Moe also recognize that "in nonurban systems with good students and able parents, autonomy can be high in the public sector too" (p. 184). It is interesting to note here that their measure of success has nothing to do with the quality of education or outcomes; rather, freedom from democratic accountability ("autonomy") is the measure, in and of itself, of "reform."

The magic combination, then, is autonomy and competition. Given autonomy, schools that can shape themselves to the market will draw students, and schools that do not attract consumers will be closed. The parents' voices are the only ones that matter in deciding the kind of education that will be offered. The parents "win"—always and by definition.

The policy recommendation at the end of the argument is summed up by the title of the final chapter: "Better Schools Through New Institutions: Giving Americans Choice" (p. 185). As Chubb and Moe argue throughout the book, "reformers would do well to entertain the notion that choice *is* a panacea…. Choice is a self-contained reform with its own rationale and justification. It has the capacity *all by itself* to bring about the kind of transformation that, for years, reformers have been seeking to engineer in myriad other ways" (p. 217; emphasis in original). Their position is that an effective regime of true parental school choice is not only *necessary* for school reform, but *sufficient* as well. Not only are no other reforms necessary to create an excellent national education system, but choice indeed "must be adopted *without* these other reforms" (curricular, pedagogical, organizational, or otherwise), since any truly systemic reforms will, by definition, interfere with local school autonomy: "A true choice system strikes at the foundation of democratic control" (p. 216). As far as Chubb and Moe are concerned, this is a good thing.

That fact notwithstanding, they claim that "The choice system we have outlined here would be a truly public system—and a democratic one" (p. 225). It is worth reflecting on how this claim redefines both "public" and "democratic." First, they mean that the "usual processes of democratic governance" would be the way that the system of choice would be created. The tax system and rate, the kind of schools included in the program (including religious or not), whether to provide supplemental programs for the disadvantaged, "and other controversial issues of public concern" would all be decided democratically, but then the schools themselves would be removed from democratic control (p. 225). Democratic governance would be ended by democratic means. The democratic public would still fund education, approve the creation of new schools within the system, arrange transportation to schools and other administrative and financial tasks, and then provide neither oversight nor regulation over how the money is used. Schools would, independently and individually, "be legally autonomous: free to govern themselves as they want, specify their own programs and methods, design their own organizations, select their own student bodies, and make their own personnel decisions" (p. 226).

Finally, while Chubb and Moe claim to reject vouchers as a way to fund the new market in schools, their recommendation amounts to implementing a voucher system and calling it something else. What they recommend is that money be paid directly to schools through a "Choice Office in each district…. At no point will it [money] go to parents or students" (p. 219). They leave open the question of whether private schools are to be included, but we see in retrospect—and, in fact, understood at the time—that they likely would be. Of course, what they have described is a voucher program: funding attaches to students and is paid out of public money to schools—public or private—in which the children are enrolled.

II. Cultural and Educational Context

Voucher plans have been part of educational discourse, albeit marginally at first, since Milton Friedman's seminal article, "The Role of Government in Education,"[5] which criticized the idea of public education not as ineffective, but as totalitarian. The state should not be in the business of educating citizens, Friedman claimed, since that would allow the state to exercise a pervasive and pernicious mind control over future citizens. As Chubb and Moe did later, Friedman would grant that authority to parents, who properly have the authority and right to decide what and how their children should be taught. The underlying premise is that, as Rand Paul recently said in the context of vaccinations, "The state does not own your children. Parents own the children."[6]

This notion of ownership is an interesting one. Those who advocate for public education usually write about children in terms of (1) membership, and (2) the fact that the community has a responsibility for all its children. To put this another way, advocates of public education speak of children "belonging to" the community in the sense of *being members of that community*; in contrast, when advocates of school choice couch their arguments in terms of children belonging to the parents, they mean *as in ownership*. This is a significant difference in the meaning of a democratic society and the nature of children, as well as the meaning of *belonging*.

Politics, Markets, and America's Schools was published in 1990 by the Brookings Institution, a center/left-of-center Washington think tank. This is significant, because it suggests how the culture had accepted the movement toward educational privatization, and how taken for granted the failure of public schools was. Chubb and Moe did not need to argue that public schools have failed, or that private schools are better than public ones. That work had already been done for them by the National Commission on Excellence in Education in its widely distributed *A Nation at Risk*.[7] The report's opening sentence is: "Our Nation is at risk." It goes on: "If an unfriendly foreign power had attempted to impose on America the mediocre educational performance that exists today, we might well have viewed it as an act of war…. We have, in effect, been committing an act of unthinking, unilateral disarmament." That much of the rhetoric around public school failure lacks a factual basis[8] has not made it less influential in shaping the debate.

The effort to replace public school reform with a market system of competition and privatization was taking place within a larger movement in which, as President Reagan had said, government could not be the solution to our problems because government was itself the problem. This, as we have seen, is the thesis that Chubb and Moe develop. We can see the competition/privatization argument around schooling as part of a neoliberal effort to privatize, monetize, and profitize pretty much everything from prisons to public highways, water, and even war, with much of the supply, security, and intelligence in our extended Middle East wars being carried out by private firms such as Blackwater and Halliburton and their subsidiaries.

The view that government is the problem is at the heart of the privatization movement in all its guises, and it is fundamentally anti-democratic. The premise of the American democratic experiment has been until recently that government is the means by which "We the people" make decisions and implement them on behalf of the common good. This changed radically with the recent rise of the radical libertarian right, which has rejected democratic governance in favor of a libertarianism that rejects the very idea of a common good and replaces the democratic public with a marketplace. We should, in principle, reject the notion of making decisions in common, as befits a democratic polity, in favor of individual decisions in pursuit of individual benefit.[9]

The autonomy that Chubb and Moe point to as the panacea for school improvement is, unambiguously, the release from democratic governance. Many so-called "public charters" are public only in the sense that they exist under the nominal supervision of a charter-granting agency that is public: the schools themselves are corporate entities that organize and operate independently of democratic control, often for profit. To replace democratic governance with a market is simply to give up on the democratic experiment in which government is the means by which "We the people" institutionalize and implement our collective judgment about the common good.

III. Strengths and Weaknesses of the Book

Politics, Markets, and America's Schools is well written and accessible, as befits a work designed to shape public discourse and change attitudes toward public education. Specifically, Chubb and Moe divert the public conversation about education away from equity and the consequences of inequality.

We fund schools in such a way that the *average* per-child expenditure in the state of Utah was $6,688 in 2012 (which means many schools received less than that), while the state of Vermont in that year spent *on average* $18,882 per child (which means many schools spent more than that).[10] To attend a school at the top end of this range is not the same as going to one of the schools at the bottom of the range. Availability of course offerings (Advanced Placement, for example), educational resources (e.g., library holdings, computers, and up-to-date textbooks), and extracurricular activities create very different schools for children of different states, types of community (rural, suburban, or urban), social classes, and races.

As Chubb and Moe admit, problems of quality do not trouble schools in wealthy suburbs (p. 184), nor is autonomy an issue in those schools. That is to say, in communities that enjoy the advantages that wealth provides, real public schools, democratically governed, are doing just fine. What plagues our low-performing schools is not that they are public, but that so many of them have been systematically underfunded and under-resourced by a public that has chosen to consider large numbers of students to be disposable. If we end the experiment in common school education—in education for democratic life—we simply declare that we are no longer interested in issues of equity or equality: we are only concerned with obtaining a good education for our own individual children, where "good" means "preparation for a high-salary job." The most likely parents to succeed in this new game, of course, are the same parents winning at the old game. The difference is that we will no longer have to feel any guilt about the children denied a good education. It will be their (or their parents') choice that dooms them, not the neglect of the public.

At the same time, Chubb and Moe accurately point to a problem of democratic governance that we often ignore: it does make governance inherently unstable and challenging. In several of our large cities, for example, governance in recent history has gone from citywide school boards to local district control by neighborhood school boards and back again to citywide governance. Many mayors have recently begun to experiment with appointed school chief executives apart from the city or neighborhood school boards. As state school board elections bring different views to the board, evolution and comprehensive sex education can come and go from state standards every time the majority shifts on the state board. (In my state, Oklahoma, there is—as I write this—a bill before the legislature, voted out of committee with a solid majority, to eliminate funding for AP History, since it teaches American history with insufficient patriotic hagiography.)

On the other hand, there are those who see this tentativeness as a strength of democracy properly understood, and who see schools in particular as an opportunity for significant adults to model democratic life for our children. For example, Deborah Meier[11] makes the argument that this democratic give-and-take makes schools effective incubators of democratic citizens. If children see their elders, both within the school community and the broader political world, debating and discussing educational policy and content, they will learn something important about the function and operation of democracy. Alternatively, Meier asks, where are our children more likely to learn the skills of democratic life if not in school?

While Chubb and Moe argue that they are not, in fact, pushing for privatization, this claim is at best naïve, and at worst disingenuous. One of the things that makes public schools *public* is that they are governed by the democratic process and in the public interest. In their place, Chubb and Moe would have schools governed as private corporations and in the interest of the individuals who run and attend them. The schools they advocate would be funded by taxpayer money, but governed and structured as private entities. In fact, their recommendation is even more extreme than that of most voucher advocates, who mostly recommend that voucher programs would include both private and truly public schools. Chubb and Moe, in contrast, specifically seek to eliminate truly public schools, leaving only publicly funded, privately governed, schools.

Further, the passage of time has definitively disproved their prescriptions and predictions. After many years of voucher programs, school-choice programs, and the creation and multiplication of charter schools, there is simply no evidence that, on average, the varieties of schools independent from their school boards and largely exempt from school regulation by the state are any different in their academic performance than comparable public schools from which they draw students. Some charter schools, private schools, and public schools are excellent, drawing the very best from their students. Some are terrible, producing low rates of achievement and high rates of incompletion. Most are average, and academic performance is unrelated to governance, a finding that is in direct contradiction to the predictions of Chubb and Moe.[12]

However, there is one measure by which schools of choice clearly outscore their public counterparts—namely, if we let parents choose their children's school, they are more likely to be satisfied with the school they choose. And this is precisely where we see something of the ideology at work in this issue: parent satisfaction, in a market regime where schooling is a commodity to be consumed, becomes a reasonable facsimile for school quality. However, this is not at all the case if the measure of school quality has to do with preparation for corporate and/or professional success, and even less if schools have anything to do with formation of democratic citizens.

And this is where we see the real influence of the attacks on public education. In the minds of the general population, education has been transformed through political discourse from a democratic good to be distributed to all for the general welfare of all and the effective functioning of democratic life (which is far more complex than mere governance).[13]

IV. Influence and Relevance

Chubb and Moe had the good fortune to be writing their book at a time when the ground had been prepared for their argument, that is, when the attack on government had undermined public support for public institutions, and schools were objects of particular assault after the publication of *A Nation at Risk*.

It is difficult to identify precisely how much *Politics, Markets, and America's Schools* directly contributed to the shift to school choice through vouchers and charter schools, and how much it benefitted from being published after years of well-funded and persistent criticism of public education as a practice and as an idea. What is clear, in retrospect, is that the erosion of the common school ideal has proceeded at a rapid pace in recent decades. According to the National Center for Educational Statistics,[14] the number of students in charter schools increased from 300,000 to 2,100,000 between 1999 and 2011.

Another development has been the growth of private organizations, both for-profit and non-profit, that run charter schools. In the 2011–2012 school year, 1,206 public schools (mostly individual charter schools) were operated by non-profit educational management organizations (EMOs), including schools in 28 states and the District of Columbia, with almost half a million students enrolled. An additional 800 schools with an enrollment of 460,000 students were run by EMOs that are operated for profit.[15] What all these schools, with all these students, have in common is that they are governed by the discipline of the marketplace, not the collaborative and cooperative processes of the democratic polity. Yes, they are autonomous—that is, from the democratic polity, but not from corporate economic power.

It is important to emphasize that private schools (secular or sectarian) and charter schools (for-profit and non-profit), as well as true public schools, can and do serve the public good. However, two caveats are necessary. First, there is no check on schools that do not, in fact, serve the public good. And, since one premise of the school choice movement is precisely that there is no real public to be considered, we might be justified in suspecting that many do not, in fact, serve the public good. More fundamentally, we must note that even in those cases where private or charter schools do serve the public good, *they are always serving some individual's or group's version of the public good, not the public's version*.

This shift makes two tremendous differences in the way we talk about public education. One difference is alluded to above: We no longer view education as a public good to be provided to citizens for public reasons. Education is no longer connected to civic purposes of citizenship formation.

Significantly, we find it difficult to discuss the gross inequalities embedded in our system as a moral issue. There was a time when the public, *as a public*, was *morally* responsible for making certain that all children, regardless of race, class, gender, or any other condition, were given an education that prepared them for full democratic citizenship. This was an ideal that was violated in as many ways as it was fulfilled, but it was always a ground for critique.

So when critics such as Jonathan Kozol[16] point out that we betray our own ideals when we send children to public schools that lack staff, funds, and resources, that are inadequate to the civic and economic tasks assigned to them, his challenge is that we are not, in fact, what we say we are. However, when education changes from a civic good that citizens deserve into to a commodity provided to consumers through choice, we are free to reject Kozol's critique as having any real claim on us. Kozol reminds us that we are a people committed to the ideal that we provide free public education to all children as a consequence of their membership in our society: the education of children is a shared responsibility.

But suppose that we make education a commodity to be sought and obtained through a market. Now, the proper response to Kozol's challenge is to point out that he is mistaken, that we do not claim to be that kind of people, that the education of the next generation is the responsibility not of the public (of which there is no such thing) nor of the community (which has been redefined as merely a collection of individuals), but of the individual parents of each individual child. In an educational market (as in any other market), I do not have a responsibility to my neighbor or my neighbor's children; parents choose the education they want for their children individually, and the children get what their parents have chosen, which becomes what they deserve by virtue of having chosen it. This fits comfortably with the notion that children *belong* to their parents and the corollary that there is no communal responsibility for the well-being of those children; it fits very badly with the idea that democracy is a shared way of life.[17] This is part of the reason why the project of privatization had to systematically undercut the sense of a common good in favor of championing the untrammeled pursuit of one's own advantage (and that of one's children).

This strikes me as a serious impoverishment of the civic polity. Even if public schools were as bad as critics say (they are not), and even if the economic consequences of low-performing schools were as great as supposed (they are not[18]), and even if a mix of private schools and charter schools would improve some (relatively unimportant) measured outcomes as much as advocates claim (they do not); even if all the above were not either ideological acts of faith or sheer misrepresentations of reality—even then the goal of a decent democratic society would be to fix the public system so that every child would be provided with a high-quality education in a first-rate public school committed to the fostering of democratic citizenship. We would not abandon our collective responsibility to children in favor of a marketplace designed to distribute consumer goods efficiently, not civil good equally.

Notes

1   John E. Chubb and Terry M. Moe, *Politics, Markets, and America's Schools* (Washington, DC: Brookings Institution, 1990). Subsequent references to this text will simply supply page number(s).
2   John Dewey, *Democracy and Education: An Introduction to the Philosophy of Education* (New York: The Free Press, 1918).
3   Deborah Meier, *The Power of Their Ideas: Lessons for America from a Small School in Harlem* (Boston, MA: Beacon Press, 1995).
4   Jonathan Kozol, *Shame of the Nation: The Restoration of Apartheid Schooling in America* (New York: Crown, 2005).
5   Milton Friedman, "The Role of Government in Education." In *Economics and the Public Interest*, ed. Robert A. Solo (New Brunswick, NJ: Rutgers University Press, 1955), http://www.edchoice.org/The-Friedmans/The-Friedmans-on-School-Choice/The-Role-of-Government-in-Education-(1995).aspx
6   Rand Paul, "Rand Paul: Parents 'Own' Children, Not the State," *The Hill*, February 2, 2015, http://thehill.com/policy/healthcare/231501-rand-paul-the-state-doesnt-own-your-children
7   National Commission on Excellence in Education, *A Nation at Risk* (Washington, DC: U.S. Government Printing Office, 1983), http://www2.ed.gov/pubs/NatAtRisk/index.html
8   David C. Berliner and Bruce J. Biddle, *The Manufactured Crisis: Myths, Fraud, and the Attack on America's Public Schools* (New York: Basic Books, 1996).
9   And it is important to note that, as I write this (in February 2015), the thinning idea of a public, and of a public good, is no longer an artifact only of far-right libertarian-anarchists. We see this also in the refusal of mostly well-educated, left-of-center parents to vaccinate their children against dangerous and highly contagious diseases such as the measles, despite the fact that their decision puts other children in the community at risk for infection, as "herd immunity" is weakened by their decisions.
10 Kids Count Data Center, Per-Pupil Expenditures Adjusted for Regional Cost Differences. Updated January 2015, http://www.datacenter.kidscount.org/data/tables/5199-per-pupil-educational-expenditures-adjusted-for-regional-cost-di#detailed/2/2-52/false/868,867,133,38,35/any/11678
11 Meier, *The Power of Their Ideas.*

12 Diane Ravitch, *Reign of Error: The Hoax of the Privatization Movement and the Danger to America's Public Schools* (New York: Alfred A. Knopf, 2013).

13 Dewey, *Democracy and Education: An Introduction to the Philosophy of Education* (New York: Macmillan, 1916).

14 National Center for Educational Statistics, Fast Facts: Charter Schools (Washington, DC: U.S. Department of Education, 2014), http://nces.ed.gov/fastfacts/display.asp?id=30

15 Nora Kern, *Report Shows Continued Growth of Charter School Management Organizations* (Washington, DC: National Alliance for Public Charter Schools, December 2, 2013), http://www.publiccharters.org/2013/12/report-shows-continued-growth-charter-school-management-organizations/

16 Jonathan Kozol, *Savage Inequalities* (New York: HarperPerennial, 1992); *Shame of the Nation.*

17 Dewey, *Democracy and Education.*

18 John F. Covaleskie, "Educational Attainment and Economic Inequality: What Schools Cannot Do," *Journal of Thought* 44, no. 1/2 (2010): 83–96.

TWENTY-ONE

Jonathan Kozol, *Savage Inequalities: Children in America's Schools* (1991)

Sue Books

With the publication of *Savage Inequalities: Children in America's Schools* in 1991, Jonathan Kozol brought to public attention the devastating inequalities that permeate U.S. classrooms, given our heavy reliance on property taxes to fund public schools and given the racism, scorn of the poor, and callous indifference that sustain this destructive situation. More than anyone before him—and, arguably, since—Kozol set out to educate the public on the hows and whys of school finance—its tax levies and foundation formulas—as well as its consequences and moral import. Students in sub-par schools (almost always poor and disproportionately Black and Latino) get less of everything that money can buy for schools: good teachers, skilled administrators, buildings in good repair, books, technology, and engaging extracurricular activities. Chronically receiving less than others takes a harsh toll on children, educationally and existentially. As one middle-school student in East St. Louis, Illinois, told Kozol, "It does not take long for little kids to learn they are not wanted" (Kozol, 1991, p. 35).

Kozol's work in education began in the 1960s, in the heat of the civil rights struggle, when he accepted a job as a fourth-grade teacher in a poor Black neighborhood in Boston. He did not last long, as he was fired after assigning reading not on the school's approved list: the poetry of Langston Hughes. Nevertheless, deeply affected by what he had seen and heard, Kozol went on to publish *Savage Inequalities*, one of the most influential of his 13 books documenting poverty and educational inequality in the United States. A *New York Times* bestseller and 1992 finalist for the National Book Critics Circle Award, *Savage Inequalities* is cited throughout the school finance literature, has been assigned to thousands of college students, and, a Google search suggests, was a book club favorite for several years. *Publishers Weekly*, for the first time in its history, endorsed the book on its cover and urged President George H.W. Bush to read it (Applebome, 1995).

As part of his research, Kozol visited schools and spoke with teachers and principals, community activists, parents, and students over a period of 3 years, beginning in 1988, in 30 largely Black and Latino neighborhoods in East St. Louis, Chicago, New York City, Camden and Cherry Hill in New Jersey, Washington, D.C., San Antonio, and Cincinnati. Many of the children and teenagers shared their hopes, dreams, and perceptions, and in this way bore witness to the consequences of inequitable and inadequate schooling, as well as poverty, environmental racism, and dangerously deficient health.

In high-poverty neighborhoods with few, if any, White people, Kozol found shocking rates of asthma and lead poisoning, along with schools with leaky roofs, cracked windows, broken toilets, closets "repurposed" as classrooms, and demoralized teachers and principals. Many parents, thwarted by a system oblivious to their concerns, were outraged, and young people, both sharply insightful and woefully uneducated, knew they were being cheated. Kozol also visited well-funded schools, often just a few miles away, where students—mostly White—were not distracted by excessive heat or cold, were not taught by a succession of substitute teachers, and were not told, in so many words: *You don't matter.*

Through such juxtapositions, Kozol fleshed out qualitative pictures of injustice with students' and teachers' insights and observations as well as his own. A walk around a public housing project in East St. Louis, for example, revealed confusion among 7- and 9-year-olds about the most basic school structures:

> None of the children can tell me the approximate time that school begins. One says five o'clock. One says six. Another says that school begins at noon.
>
> When I ask what song they sing after the flag pledge, one says, "Jingle Bells."
> Smokey cannot decide if he is in second or third grade.
> Seven-year-old Mickey sucks his thumb during the walk. (pp. 12–13)

Through such recountings, Kozol put names and faces on the damning statistics that can more easily be forgotten. Kozol has been criticized for his journalistic methodology; "the power of the anecdotes piles up" (Fowler Morse, 2012, p. 39). Yet letting children speak for themselves also allowed Kozol to challenge anticipated rationalizations—for example, that school differences are the sad but predictable result of "cultural differences" or that some students just don't care. Sharing the voices of children who are unable to "care" or "not care" about an education they never receive helps to undercut such victim blaming.

Savage Inequalities was published 37 years after the U.S. Supreme Court declared that "separate educational facilities are inherently unequal" (*Brown v. Board of Education*, 1954), a hard-fought affirmation of the centrality of equal educational opportunity to democratic life as well as individual psychological development—a ruling that was largely undermined by subsequent courts. Two decades after *Brown*, the court concluded that gross disparities in funding do not violate the U.S. Constitution, as long as some semblance of public schooling is provided (*San Antonio Independent School District v. Rodriguez*, 1973). Furthermore, suburban districts need not participate in school desegregation plans in the absence of evidence of intentional segregation (*Milliken v. Bradley*, 1974). As Philadelphia mayor Richardson Dilworth warned in the early 1950s, *Milliken* set the stage for the now-familiar development of a "white noose" of small suburban school districts around large, overwhelmingly poor, Black and Latino city districts (Beers, 2001, p. 197). Furthermore, the 1980s saw "the celebration of individualism raised to the level of public policy"—with disastrous results for education (Freedman, 1991). Reduced federal support during the Reagan years (Verstegen, 1990) strengthened a view of public schooling as a zero-sum game.

Initial reception: Praise, Anger, and Resignation

Upon its publication, *Savage Inequalities* received mixed reviews. The book is "accusatory" (Mitgang, 1991), and readers tend to respond emotionally with either strong support for the message or strong objection. Herbert Mitgang (1991), writing in *The New York Times*, framed the book as a much-needed exposé that points out the obvious, shows the national crisis inherent in local school problems, and tells the human story behind the mechanics of school finance. Mitgang's colleague Andrew Hacker (1991) similarly described the book as "important" and thoroughly "in the American grain," as Kozol calls for no more than the provision of equal opportunity, a principle enshrined in widely affirmed civic and religious ideals.

Hacker (1991) also pointed out one of the ideological barriers to fairer funding: "Poor children…are increasingly looked upon as surplus baggage, mistakes that should never have happened," and so as hardly worth more generous educational investment. Further, the affluent would protest any limitation on their spending on their own children, as "all they want is for New Trier to beat out Rye when it comes to Ivy League admissions" (Hacker, 1991). This air of resignation (it's sad, but…) continues to shape much of the commentary on the book: acknowledgment, on the one hand, that Kozol's advocacy rests in putatively shared ideals, but warning, on the other, that taking those ideals seriously would come at a cost—and offered as an explanation of why, of course, they cannot be.

In general, commentators variously (1) have praised and lent their own voices to Kozol's fiery social criticism, (2) have objected to its policy implications, (3) have complained that Kozol offers "no solution" or useful analysis, or (4) have critiqued his depictions of urban poverty as one-sided. Let me say more about each of these four broad critical responses.

Policy disagreements have sometimes degenerated into character assassination and sarcasm. Marcus Winters (2006), for example, in a sharply critical review of *Savage Inequalities* and four other books by Kozol, construed his research as self-serving poverty tourism and mocked Kozol's "Ahab-like pursuit of more money" for education. Students in poorly funded urban schools, Winters (2006) argued, suffer less from large disparities in funding than from the "incentive structure" of the education system. More choice and voucher plans presumably would allow parents to pull their children out of unsatisfactory schools, thereby creating an incentive for schools "to use their resources wisely" (Winters, 2006). Other critics (e.g., Applebome, 1995; Freedman, 1991; and Tager, 1993) found fault more generally with Kozol's failure, as they see it, to suggest solutions or to provide a solid analysis of the fundamental problem.

Both strands of critique, in my view, misunderstand Kozol's project. Although Winters (2006) reads Kozol through a narrow policy framework, Kozol is not making an instrumental argument about how, most efficiently, to raise test scores in urban public schools. Rather, he is crying out in a prophetic voice about the injustices that flourish when wealth and self-interest drive education policy. Behind the complaint that Kozol provides no solution, I suspect, is recognition that educational fairness would cost something—namely, eradication of the privilege institutionalized in the current funding system. The objection is not really that Kozol provides no solution, but that he fails to provide a cost-free and easy-to-implement "fix." In fact, Kozol speaks quite directly about what he believes needs to happen: jettison an inherently unjust system of decentralized funding and fund schools the way almost every other developed nation does—namely, through national coffers. This would create, at the least, the possibility of equality or—better yet—equity, by linking resources with educational need. It is not that there is no conceivable way to provide a better education for the urban poor, but rather that doing so would require changing a structure in which others are invested.

As Hacker (1991) suggested in a more sophisticated version of the "no solution" argument, all parents want what they believe is best for their children. However, as Kozol makes painfully clear, support of a *system* of school funding that enables parents who can afford million-dollar homes to buy essentially million-dollar educations for their children ensures that other people's children will end up with low-cost "ghetto schooling." Laundering school quality through an irrational system of school funding (with no logical link between educational need and property value) guarantees this outcome.

More recently, Raquel Farmer-Hinton, Joi Lewis, Lori Patton, and Ishwnzya Rivers (2013), all of whom attended school in East St. Louis, have criticized Kozol's writing as reductionistic in its portrayal of poor Black communities as bleak—and only bleak—places of despair. In their neighborhoods, they recall, "families, teachers, community centers, churches, and extracurricular programs were sources of familial, aspirational, resistant, navigational, and social capital" (Farmer-Hinton et al., 2013, p. 2). In failing to highlight community strengths, Kozol offers a one-sided view of complex neighborhoods and in this way adds credence to the popular picture of "urban students and families as subjects who need to be saved" (Farmer-Hinton et al., 2013, p. 2). Kozol's (1991) description of East St. Louis as "a scar of sorts, an ugly metaphor of filth and overspill and chemical effusions, a place for blacks to live and die within, a place for other people to avoid when they are heading to St. Louis" (p. 39), for example, fails to convey the rich human relationships that empower young people.

Some of my students who grew up in the South Bronx have said essentially the same thing: Kozol's representation of urban poverty is not inaccurate, just incomplete. Certainly, like any social critic, Kozol wrote purposefully and made decisions about which conversations and descriptions to include. Yet I think there is more to this critique than failure to appreciate the artistry implicit in social criticism. Too often, Kozol's subjects evoke pity, but not necessarily respect.

That said, it is important to recognize that Kozol was not trying to capture the complexity of urban poverty so much as to highlight—largely for White and middle-class readers—the depth and pervasiveness of social injustice. I recall a discussion of *Savage Inequalities* shortly after it was published at a public library in Greensboro, North Carolina. "We already knew all this," several African American participants said. Kozol did not write for those who "already knew," but rather for those who, if better informed, might throw their weight into the struggle for more justice and equal opportunity. As Kozol noted in an interview with Marge Scherer (1992):

> Even very conservative businessmen out in rich suburbs have in weak moments looked at me and said, "Well, you're right, we would never play Little League baseball this way." They wouldn't dream of sending their kids out with baseball mitts to play ball against a team that had to field the ball with bare hands. They'd regard that as being without honor. I say to them, "It's interesting. You wouldn't play baseball that way but you run the school system that way."

School funding matters, Kozol argued, because children who get markedly less than others end up sitting in cramped classrooms, freezing in winter and sweltering in summer, with one substitute teacher after another, and so often do not learn very much. In this regard, silence about the tangible damage wrought by poverty and injustice is not helpful. As William Julius Wilson (1990) argued, social justice-oriented scholars who eschew "unflattering" descriptions of inner-city ghettos, including this terminology, too often have ceded serious discussion of "the dreadful economic condition of poor blacks" to those happy to recycle versions of the discredited culture-of-poverty thesis (p. 9). Although caricatures are never helpful, writing that links cause and effect, however damaging, in words, images, and arguments accessible to a public audience is sorely needed.

Festering Inequalities Became Even More Savage

The "ghetto education" Kozol railed against is now even more accepted "as a permanent American reality" (Kozol, 1991, p. 4). Children still suffer from gross disparities in school funding that create deplorable conditions for teaching and learning, and now attend schools in communities so segregated by race, ethnicity, and class that they are "without precedent in the U.S." (Orfield & Frankenberg, 2014, p. 5). Since the 1980s, education policymakers have increasingly ignored segregation in schooling and focused instead on issues of accountability, seemingly assuming that equal opportunity can be achieved in separate and unequal schools, provided that uniform standards for academic achievement are doggedly enforced.

A cascade of Supreme Court rulings throughout the 1990s and continuing into the early 2000s gave school districts a judicial green light to return to "separate and unequal" schooling. Released from court-enforced integration plans, hundreds of them resegregated. Between 1991 and 2011, the percentage of Black and Latino students in schools with very few White students (fewer than 10%) increased in every region of the country, with one exception: whereas more than 44% of Latino students attended such schools in 2011, 47% attended them in 1991. In the Northeast, where by this measure the schools are now more segregated than in any other region, *more than half* of all Black students and more than two-fifths of all Latinos attend schools with these demographics (Orfield & Frankenberg, 2014).

The number of "apartheid schools" with virtually no White students (less than 1%) has increased as well—from 2,762 such schools nationwide in 1988 (when integration was at its peak) to 2.5 times as many (6,727) in 2011 (Zamora, 2014). Racial/ethnic segregation matters so much in part because it overlaps so neatly with poverty. Schools that serve all or almost all Black and Latino students are almost always high-poverty schools as well. Half of all students in intensely segregated schools are also in schools where more than 90% of their classmates live in low-income families, which means they are isolated from middle-class as well as White and Asian peers (Orfield & Frankenberg, 2014).

Racial achievement gaps overall have narrowed substantially over the last four decades, but nevertheless remain large, and income-based gaps have widened significantly.[1] Also, although the gap in high school graduation rates among White students and students of color has also narrowed, gaps in college graduation rates are growing, and students of color and low-income students who make it to college are dramatically under-represented in selective schools (Reardon, 2014).[2]

As a case study of sorts of the pernicious ways in which racism, disdain of the poor, disin-genuous "accountability," and inequitable school funding interact today, consider the educa-tion of Michael Brown, the Black 18-year-old whose fatal shooting by a White police officer on August 9, 2014, was the catalyst for protests across the nation. Michael was shot in Ferguson, Missouri, a suburb of St. Louis and one of the most racially segregated areas in the country. Today, a network of school districts sort students into segregated schools "as effectively as any Jim Crow law" (Hannah-Jones, 2014). Michael attended the Normandy schools, which rank dead last in overall academic performance in the state. By the time Brown graduated, the district had lost its state accreditation after years of dismal test scores. Only about half of the Black male students at Normandy High graduate, and just one in four graduates enroll in a 4-year college. However,

> Just five miles down the road from Normandy lies Clayton, the wealthy county seat where a grand jury recently deliberated the fate of Darren Wilson, the officer who killed Mr. Brown. Success there looks very different. The Clayton public schools are predominantly white, with almost no poverty…. The district is regularly ranked in the top 10% in the state. More than 96% of its students graduate. Eighty-four percent head to four-year universities. (Hannah-Jones, 2014)

In the absence of law and policy designed to alter such patterns, racial isolation has intensified and poverty has become more concentrated.

Even when population shifts provide seemingly golden opportunities to promote school integration, too often "educational gerrymandering" occurs instead (Siegel-Hawley, 2013). The Henrico County (Virginia) public schools are a case in point. Population growth required the county in 2008–2009 to build a new high school and redraw attendance lines. However, instead of using the opportunity to reduce racial isolation, school officials adopted a plan that assigned 17% of all high school–age Black students and almost 10% of all Latinos to intensely segregated schools (90% or more Black or Latino)—even more than had been the case be-fore—while preserving several virtually all-White school zones.

Meanwhile, despite decades of school finance litigation, no movement to fund schools out of the national wealth has gained political traction, nor have patterns of resource distribution been altered. All but five states[3] have been sued over their systems of school funding, and in a majority of these cases plaintiffs have prevailed (National Education Access Network, 2014). Nevertheless, despite these "paper victories," legislative foot-dragging and fiscal maneuvering have preserved a property-tax-based system that fails to fund public schools equitably or ad-equately across the board.

Consider just one example among countless others: patterns in funding, demographics, and achievement at two elementary schools in California. Based on state assessments, Stone Corral Elementary, about 30 miles from Sequoia National Park in the farmland near Visalia, ranks as one of the worst schools in the state. William Faria Elementary in Cupertino (home to Apple, Inc.) ranks as one of the best. All the students at Stone Corral live in poverty, and 60% are learning English; the average family income is about $14,000 a year. At William Faria, none of the students are poor; only 4% are learning English; and the average family income is more than 10 times as great: $160,000 a year. Consequently, with a much smaller tax effort, parents in the William Faria district can raise significantly more money for their children's schools (Baines, 2014).

An 1,800-square-foot home in the William Faria school district likely will cost well over a million dollars while an 1,800-square-foot home in Stone Corral's district can be had…for under $200,000. The property value differential means that William Faria generates approximately 500% more money in taxes per student than Stone Corral…. There are no water fountains at Stone Corral because the water in the area has been polluted by unregulated disposal of livestock waste. On the other hand, in addition to receiving more money from the state through higher property taxes, William Faria's parents are willing and able to fund a dizzying array of social events, such as First Day Tea, Dinner on the Green, and Ice Cream Socials. (Baines, 2014)

Since Kozol wrote *Savage Inequalities*, the Great Recession and slow recovery from the economic trauma, along with growing and widespread resentment about the shared costs of public schooling, have constrained funding for education. At least 30 states provided less funding per student for 2014–2015 than they did before the recession, including 14 that cut per-student funding by more than 10% (Leachman & Mai, 2014). Hardest hit have been high-poverty schools unable to draw on local revenue to compensate for shortfalls in state funding. In New York State, for example, budget cuts for schools in poor and middle-class communities, per pupil, have been double or triple those in wealthy areas (Easton, 2012). A proliferation of tax caps and credits that siphon funds from public schools directly or indirectly have made matters worse. State property tax caps,[4] tax breaks for corporate "job creators" or for individual "donors" to private school scholarship funds, and other putative school reform initiatives all drain resources from public schools and exacerbate inequalities (Books, 2014).

In a national study designed to bring more conceptual clarity to the question of fairness in school funding, Baker, Sciarra, and Farrie (2014) asked whether it is, in fact, fair—and concluded, essentially, that it is not. Acknowledging the well-documented correlation between student and school poverty, they used as a key measure of fairness whether states are providing school districts with adequate funding to meet educational needs linked to poverty. States differ markedly on this measure both because some fund schools far more generously than others and because some weigh poverty in the distribution more heavily than others. The third iteration of the funding study, based on 2011 data, shows that per-pupil funding in Wyoming, the highest-spending state, was 2.5 times greater than in Idaho, the lowest spending state ($17,399 per pupil versus $6,753), and that within-state disparities compounded gaps among states. In 2011 in only 14 states was funding (state and local resources) linked with poverty-related educational need. In 15 states, the funding-poverty correlation was neutral, and in 19 states, it was regressive—meaning that high-poverty districts received less funding.

Although the fundamental unfairness Kozol documented is still with us, new questions and more sophisticated research methodologies have shed more light on the mechanics (the how and why) of unfairness. For example, in a recent report for the Center for American Progress, Baker (2014) used Kozol's language to build a typology of conditions that create severe fiscal disadvantage for schools with below-average state and local resources but above-average student need. The typology includes both "savage inequalities" resulting from large disparities in local taxable property wealth and "stealth inequalities" resulting from state school finance formulas that fail to correct, and sometimes exacerbate, local disparities. The result: "Affluent suburbs with big houses on tree-lined streets, palatial high schools, top-notch lacrosse and fencing teams, and elite orchestras" exist alongside "nearby urban ghettos replete with overcrowded and crumbling schools, high crime and considerable dropout rates" (Baker, 2014).

Finally, let me say more about the education of Michael Brown, whose short life bore witness to many of the injustices Kozol documented a quarter-century ago. In 1999 the St. Louis, Missouri, metropolitan area was released from a school desegregation order, and the struggling schools rapidly resegregated. Ten years later, the state ordered the Normandy schools (98% black, very poor, and with the worst achievement record in the state) to absorb the Wellston schools, another high-poverty district that was 100% Black. Conditions in the Wellston schools, according to state officials, were "deplorable" and "academically abusive." So why were the Wellston students not sent instead to some of the high-performing, mostly White districts nearby? Because, a state board of education official explained, "You'd have had a civil war" (Hannah-Jones, 2014).

When the Normandy schools lost state accreditation, students were permitted to transfer to schools in other districts. Many parents in Normandy were elated. However,

> Parents in the school district that had to take Normandy's students—Francis Howell, an 85% white district 26 miles away—were not. Officials there held a public forum to address community concerns. More than 2,500 parents packed into the high school gym.

> Would the district install metal detectors? What about the violence their children would be subjected to, an elementary school parent asked. Wouldn't test scores plummet? The issue wasn't about race, one parent said, "but trash." (Hannah-Jones, 2014)

Despite such fears and prejudices, in the fall of 2013, more than 400 Normandy students enrolled in Francis Howell. Test scores did not plummet, but the influx did precipitate further crisis in the Normandy schools. By law, "failing" school districts whose students opt to leave must pay the costs of their education in the new district. Unable to afford this, Normandy closed a school and laid off 40% of its staff.

The state then took over the Normandy schools, reaccredited them, and announced that the transfer law no longer applied. Shortly thereafter, "one by one, transfer districts announced that Normandy children were no longer welcome" (Hannah-Jones, 2014). Parents of the routed children sued and won a temporary injunction allowing them to enroll their children in the transfer districts. However, the ruling came on August 15, 2014, after classes had already begun in some districts, and is now being contested by the state. Hannah-Jones (2014), who pieced together this story for *ProPublica* and *The New York Times,* asked the (now former) state commissioner of education whether Black children in Missouri are receiving an equal education today:

> Commissioner Chris Nicastro…paused, then inhaled deeply. "Do I think black children in Missouri are getting in all cases the same education as their white counterparts?" Ms. Nicastro said. "I'd have to say no."

Michael Brown's school experience stands as a sad epilogue to Kozol's plea to allow "all our children…a stake in the enormous richness of America" (p. 233). Today's public schools, still separate and unequal, are also undermined by state and federal policies that hold schools accountable for test scores without holding the broader society accountable for the education of all our children. The lines drawn in *Rodriguez* (1973) and *Milliken* (1974), permitting grossly unequal funding and resegregation, are now etched even more deeply into the soil and soul of our educational system. The "haves" need not share very much with the "have-nots" in a nation, in Kozol's words, "hardly 'indivisible' where education is concerned" (p. 212).

Conclusion: Reckoning with Shame

Mitgang (1991) called *Savage Inequalities* "accusatory," and I would agree in the sense that Kozol forces readers to reckon with the shameful gap between avowed ideals and commitments and the reality of injustice suffered by children who in no way deserve it. There are only so many ways to try to reconcile this conflict: (1) discredit the messenger (e.g., Kozol as "poverty tourist"); (2) qualify the message (What Kozol says is fine, but where's the solution, the analysis, and/or the fuller picture?); or (3) own up, perhaps in shame, to the uncomfortable truth. In her discussion of moral emotions, Taylor (1987) contrasts this emotion—shame—with guilt, related but different in their effect on one's sense of self:

> When feeling guilty…the view I take of myself is entirely different from the view I take of myself when feeling shame: in the latter case I see myself as being all of a piece, what I have just done, I now see, fits only too well what I really am. But when feeling guilty I think of myself as having brought about a forbidden state of affairs and thereby in this respect disfigured a self which otherwise remains the same. (p. 92)

In other words, in shame, we must own up to the fact that perhaps we are not who we thought we were, even though we may have believed or hoped we were better.

This is not easy to do. The message that we, as a society, have failed miserably to live up to our own avowed ideals—and maybe never intended to at all—is a far cry from Reagan's "morning in America" reassurance that was still ringing in the air when Kozol wrote *Savage Inequalities*. However, it is a message for which Kozol deserves thanks. In the absence of a societal change of heart and owning up to its shame, neither quick-and-easy "solutions," ever-more-nuanced analyses, nor market-oriented education "reforms" will help us become who we still perhaps hope we are: guardians of ideals, including the provision of equal educational opportunity for of all our children. The only good news is that this ideal may still remain within reach.

Notes

1   To calculate the income achievement gap, Reardon (2014) drew on 13 nationally representative studies, 1960–2010, and reported the difference in average test scores among students at the 90th and 10th percentiles in the family income distribution.
2   Only 15% of Hispanic and 23% of Black young adults (aged 25–29) had B.A. degrees in 2012, compared with 40% of their White peers. Among the students of color and low-income students in college, only 5% to 6%, respectively, are in selective schools (Reardon, 2014).
3   The five states are Hawaii, Iowa, Mississippi, Nevada, and Utah.
4   New York is instructive here. Citing budgetary exigencies, the state cut education resources each year from 2009 to 2013, despite a promise 2 years earlier to invest $5.5 billion more in classrooms, with 72% going to the highest-need schools (Easton, 2012). In 2011, over the objections of educators, school district officials, and unions, the state passed a 2% property tax cap. Because the allowed increase raises much less revenue for schools in low-wealth communities than in high-wealth communities, poor communities suffer most.

References

Applebome, P. (1995, October 25). At lunch with Jonathan Kozol: Listening to the South Bronx. *The New York Times*. Retrieved January 9, 2015, from http://www.nytimes.com/1995/10/25/garden/at-lunch-with-jonathan-kozol-listening-to-the-south-bronx.html

Baines, L. (2014). Public education: For richer, for poorer. *Teachers College Record*. Retrieved January 11, 2015, from http://www.tcrecord.org/PrintContent.asp?ContentID=17707

Baker, B.D. (2014, July). *America's most financially disadvantaged school districts and how they got that way: How state and local governance causes school funding disparities*. Center for American Progress. Retrieved January 11, 2015, from http://cdn.americanprogress.org/wp-content/uploads/2014/07/BakerSchoolDistricts.pdf

Baker, B.D., Sciarra, D.G., & Farrie, D. (2014, January). *Is school funding fair? A national report card* (3rd ed.). Education Law Center, Rutgers Graduate School of Education. Retrieved January 10, 2015, from http://www.schoolfundingfairness.org/National_Report_Card_2014.pdf

Beers, P. (2001). *Pennsylvania politics today and yesterday: The tolerable accommodation*. University Park: Pennsylvania State University Press.

Books, S. (2014). Disparity, austerity, and public schooling in the U.S.: Why Quentin can't read. In H.R. Hall, C.C. Robinson, and A. Kohli (Eds.), *Uprooting urban America: Multidisciplinary perspectives on race, class and gentrification* (pp. 207–225). New York: Peter Lang.

Brown v. Board of Education, 347 U.S. 483 (1954).

Easton, B. (2012, May 25). Albany's unkindest cut of all. *The New York Times*. Retrieved January 11, 2015, from http://www.nytimes.com/2012/05/26/opinion/the-danger-in-school-spending-cuts.html?_r=0

Farmer-Hinton, R.L., Lewis, J.D., Patton, L.D., & Rivers, I.D. (2013). Dear Mr. Kozol…. Four African American women scholars and the re-authoring of *Savage Inequalities*. *Teachers College Record*, 115(5), 1–38.

Fowler Morse, J. (2012). Still savage, still unequal. In R. Ognibene (Ed.), *A persistent reformer: Jonathan Kozol's work to promote equality in America* (pp. 37–60). New York: Peter Lang.

Freedman, S. (1991, October 6). Separate and unequal: *Savage inequalities: Children in America's schools*, by Jonathan Kozol. *The Los Angeles Times*. Retrieved January 9, 2015, from http://articles.latimes.com/1991-10-06/books/bk-35_1_savage-inequalities

Hacker, A. (1991, October 6). Why the rich get smarter. *The New York Times*. Retrieved January 11, 2015, from http://www.nytimes.com/books/00/06/04/specials/kozol-savage.html

Hannah-Jones, N. (2014, December 19). How school segregation divides Ferguson—and the United States. *The New York Times*. Retrieved January 11, 2015, from http://www.nytimes.com/2014/12/21/sunday-review/why-are-our-schools-still-segregated.html

Kozol, J. (1991). *Savage inequalities: Children in America's schools*. New York: Crown.

Leachman, M., & Mai, C. (2014, October 16). *Most states still funding schools less than before the recession*. Washington, DC: Center on Budget and Policy Priorities. Retrieved January 10, 2015, from http://www.cbpp.org/files/10-16-14sfp.pdf

Milliken v. Bradley, 418 U.S. 717 (1974).

Mitgang, H. (1991, September 25). Books of the Times: Shortchanging the nation's children. *The New York Times*. Retrieved January 9, 2015, from http://www.nytimes.com/1991/09/25/books/books-of-the-times-shortchanging-the-nation-s-children.html

National Education Access Network. (2014, December). *Litigations challenging constitutionality of K–12 funding in the 50 states*. Retrieved January 12, 2015, from http://schoolfunding.info/

Orfield, G., & Frankenberg, E. (2014, May 15). *Brown at 60: Great progress, a long retreat and an uncertain future*. The Civil Rights Project/Proyecto Derechos Civiles. Retrieved January 9, 2015, from http://civilrightsproject.ucla.edu/research/k-12-education/integration-and-diversity/brown-at-60-great-progress-a-long-retreat-and-an-uncertain-future

Reardon, S. (2014, January). Education. *State of the union: The poverty and inequality report, 2014* (pp. 53–58). The Stanford Center on Poverty and Inequality. Retrieved December 30, 2014, from http://web.stanford.edu/group/scspi/sotu/SOTU_2014_CPI.pdf

San Antonio Independent School District v. Rodriguez, 411 U.S. 1 (1973).

Scherer, M. (1992, December). On *Savage Inequalities*: A conversation with Jonathan Kozol. *Educational Leadership*, 50(4), 4–9. Retrieved December 28, 2014, from http://www.ascd.org/publications/educational-leadership/dec92/vol50/num04/On-Savage-Inequalities@-A-Conversation-with-Jonathan-Kozol.aspx

Siegel-Hawley, G. (2013). Educational gerrymandering? Race and attendance boundaries in a demographically changing suburb. *Harvard Educational Review*, 83(4), 580–612.

Tager, F. (1993). Kozol's Moral Outrage: *Savage Inequalities: Children in America's Schools*. *Radical Teacher*, 43(46).

Taylor, G. (1987). *Pride, shame, and guilt: Emotions of self-assessment*. New York: Oxford University Press.

Verstegen, D.A. (1990). Education fiscal policy in the Reagan administration. *Educational Evaluation and Policy Analysis, 12*(4), 355–373.

Wilson, W. J. (1990). *The truly disadvantaged: The inner city, the underclass, and public policy.* Chicago: University of Chicago Press.

Winters, M.A. (2006). Savage exaggerations. *EducationNext.* Retrieved January 11, 2015, from http://educationnext. org/savage-exaggerations/

Zamora, A. (2014, May 13). Discussion: School resegregation 60 years after *Brown v. Board. ProPublica.* Retrieved January 9, 2015, from http://www.propublica.org/getinvolved/item/revisitingbrown-resegregating-u.s.-schools-60-years-after-brown-v.-board

Michelle Fine, *Framing Dropouts: Notes on the Politics of an Urban Public High School* (1991)

Melissa M. Jones

Synopsis and Context

In the mid-1980s researcher and feminist scholar Michelle Fine undertook an in-depth investigation into the culture of urban schools "to unearth those institutional policies and practices that enable, obscure, and legitimate" (Fine, 1991, p. 8) the undeniable mass exodus of low-income urban students of color who drop out of high school. At the time Fine's study began, the reported dropout rates of African American and Latino students from low-income urban communities was 40–60%, a staggering statistic with unpalatable consequences for students. The bulk of the dropout literature at the time concentrated on the characteristics of students who drop out of school, which is how Fine began her study. Once she became immersed in the school system, however, she shifted her focus away from *these kids* to *this institution* as the traditions, policies, and practices of schooling came into question. Her research question evolved from why someone would drop out of high school to "why so many would stay in a school committed to majority failure" (Fine, 1991, p. 7). Instead of seeking to know why a student would choose to leave, she began to ask, why not?

With the understanding that dropping out of school ultimately limits the opportunities and choices for adolescents and young adults, Fine (1991) was concerned with the way in which perceived equal opportunities led to very real unequal outcomes, with educators rationalizing the exile of low-income, minority students from school. Her investigation led her to the halls, offices, and classrooms of a comprehensive public high school in New York City, as well as to teacher and parent meetings, and even into the neighborhoods and homes of the students. Through the use of critical ethnography, she explored attitudes, perceptions, traditions, communications, resources, and instructional practices, as well as the structures and funding policies that perpetuate student and teacher disempowerment.

Contributing Factors for Dropping Out

Fine (1991) uncovered these primary contributing factors to students' dropping out of high school: (1) racism and colliding cultures, (2) teacher disempowerment, (3) retention and educational despair, (4) false promises, and (5) critical consciousness and resistance. Since they have ramifications for educational systems today, a brief overview of each is warranted.

Racism and colliding cultures. Racism appeared to be the foundation of the students' plight, with teachers teaching from a narrowly defined and advantaged perspective and disregarding students' experiences. The teachers' privileged way of knowing the world was presented as the only way of knowing, with students left to make any tenuous connections they could to the content being presented. Fine observed that the teachers appeared to be anesthetized to the realities of students who lived in poverty, which involved watching their mothers grapple with needing welfare versus protecting their pride; witnessing violence and drug use at home, in the community, and in school; and observing families struggling without the bare necessities to survive. For some families, dropping out of school had morphed into a tradition, with generations having similar experiences despite the hope each had when beginning their school careers. Whether this anesthetizing of student experiences was a survival mechanism adopted by the teachers, or an intentional attempt to ignore student experiences, it resulted in neglectful educational practices that made students feel unwelcome, disconnected, misunderstood, and inferior. Why a student would not remain in school under such circumstances became obvious through Fine's research.

Teacher disempowerment. Underlying the numb demeanor of teachers toward the plight of students living in poverty was the war being waged between teachers and administrators. Experiencing disempowerment themselves left teachers feeling undervalued and uninspired to teach. Reeling from active silencing by the administration and handicapped by the notorious lack of materials available in urban settings, the teachers often saw their best efforts undermined. As one teacher explained, "They keep us from imagining what could be" (Fine, 1991, p. 155).

This disempowerment filtered into the classroom as Fine (1991) witnessed a direct connection between the disempowered teacher and the disempowered student. Teachers who felt respected and valued engaged students in meaningful ways, but teachers who felt disenfranchised from the school community and were denied meaningful involvement in decision making and policy planning became so immersed in their own oppression that they often had nothing left to share with their students. This cycle of educational neglect had devastating consequences, since disempowered students more often than not dropped out of school. Educators had some culpability in the exodus of these students.

Retention and educational despair. Students who struggled academically or behaviorally were often left to their own devices, resulting in feelings of alienation, fear, inability, and discouragement. These feelings were compounded by retention practices that proliferated throughout the school district. As Fine noted, retention may have offered students "the final justification to give in, to acknowledge defeat, and to surrender to the pressures of poverty and family need" (Fine, 1991, p. 74). Students expressed less fear of peer and community violence than they did of the mental slaughter that occurred when teachers ignored student learning problems and failed them in devastating ways. Students often became the casualties of retention, giving up on the path to learning through school, with some seeking alternative routes to achievement while others simply faded from the school scene.

False promises. In the New York urban school in which Fine (1991) conducted her research, students were routinely seduced into alternative programs promising success and opportunity, including the General Educational Development (GED) test, enrollment in private training programs, and the military. Fine found the GED programs to be a dumping ground, with students counseled out of school and into GED programs they could not or would not complete. The private training programs were often expensive and led to abysmal outcomes, and the military resulted in depressing outcomes for far too many students, including a "less than honorable discharge, low skills, and poor pay" (Fine, 1991, p. 100). Yet the "transfer of bodies" (p. 88) from a public school education to an alternative route was routine in the inner-city school that was the focus of her research, with "the margins of society, exported to the sidelines" (p. 105) on a consistent basis. Although these alternatives resulted in limited success for the students who took them, they provided educators with a rationale for removal, as bodies were simply relocated from one failing program to another. Fine referred to these programs as "optimistic fictions of second chances" (p. 100), with no counter perspective provided for the promises and rhetoric offered by the alternatives.

Critical consciousness and resistance. Not all students blindly accepted the alternatives suggested by educators. Fine met many young men and women who worried "about the discrepancies between what is promised and what they witness" (Fine, 1991, p. 105). She referred to this as a complicated, contradictory consciousness in that students actually waged war against the status quo. Unfortunately, their resistance may have contributed to further alienation from the educational community. As students mobilized against and resisted oppressive forces (including uncaring educators, irrelevant instruction, and policies and practices that encouraged student disengagement), their only form of agency was quashed through discipline referrals and their resulting removal from learning. This systematic purging of students who resisted these inequities and unfair practices resulted in huge numbers of students exiled to the margins. Practices such as those exposed in *Framing Dropouts* generate serious questions about the maintenance of power and control, unveiling both social and political forces that maintain unequal power hierarchies.

Characteristics of Effective Teachers in Urban Settings

Even with the debilitating and unequal conditions exposed by Fine (1991), there was a message of hope as effective instructional strategies were also unearthed in her research. Fine discovered what she referred to as an "expression of community" (Fine, 1991, p. 57) generated by teachers who demonstrated that they genuinely cared about their students. Characteristics of effective teachers included flexibility, being willing to listen to students' stories, being willing to engage in personal storytelling, and providing a sense of community and intellectual safety in the classroom. In classrooms where students felt valued, "expertise, understanding, critique, and knowing were shared, negotiated, and considered the stuff of education" (Fine, 1991, p. 59). Teachers engaged students in conversations concerning racism, solidarity, and community in ways that fostered beneficial critique and analysis. The need for critical conversations in the classroom became apparent to Fine, acknowledging that educators have the power to choose to construct either "classrooms of silencing or community" (Fine, 1991, p. 59). When teachers ignored or redirected conversations and critiques of the school or community, they effectively partitioned the students' reality from the curriculum, trivializing student experiences and alienating them from the learning experience.

Strengths and Critiques of *Framing Dropouts*

Recognized Strengths

The strength of Fine's (1991) research is the in-depth collection of voices she compiled to bring credibility to her work. She spent a school year (1984–1985) with students, teachers, administrators, and families, listening to and learning from those who were living the experience under study. Her focus on the political aspects of schooling provokes critical conversation about the inequalities of education in America. Online reviews, both historical and contemporary, were highly favorable, calling the text a classic and a must-read, although concern was expressed about the sad inequalities unearthed throughout the text ("Good Reads," n.d.). In a scholarly review of Fine's work, Grannis (1992) exclaimed: "*Framing Dropouts* is by far the most close-in examination of the interactive processes of students' dropping out or being dropped out of schools that has been published" (p. 31), and I would venture to say that is true even today. He suggested that the "proactive, sociopolitical framework" (p. 31) used by Fine to provoke conversation about the inequalities of urban public schooling was indeed effective. Grannis's primary concern, however, was that we cannot stop with the research highlighted in *Framing Dropouts*. It is clear that more needs to be done, specifically regarding issues of racism and classism in schools.

Voiced Criticisms

Fine's (1991) work did incite some criticism, especially a particularly provocative critique by Page (1994). Through her in-depth analysis of Fine's research, Page uncovered discrepancies that called into question the credibility of *Framing Dropouts* as generalizable research. She noted the significance of the title, as Fine framed the result of her research around a political agenda, with an obvious goal of interrupting and unpacking the traditional discourse about high school dropouts. Page pointed out that Fine redirected the dialogue toward the policies and practices of schools and away from the students themselves. As an educational ethnographer, Fine intended to unfold the story of an urban public high school, asserting that it has relevance across other urban educational settings. However, Page found these contentions too broad and biased to be used as a standard for measuring the effectiveness of other comprehensive high schools.

The bulk of Page's criticism is directed at the methodology used to collect, analyze, and report the data, claiming bias on the part of the researcher. According to Page, Fine's "moral conviction" (Page, 1994, p. 485) to expose inequalities clouded her vision; thus she presented an unfair picture of the environment under study. Specific discrepancies, misquotes, and misrepresentations were identified by Page to accentuate her point. By misrepresenting certain encounters, Page argued that Fine's ethnographic account was not credible. Through her political activism and subjectivity, Fine had effectively upstaged the participants and their stories, that is, she "obscure[d] evidence" (Page, 1994, p. 491) instead of describing reality. In place of illuminating a situation, as ethnographers are charged to do, Fine cloaked it, shining a spotlight only on the realities she felt important to enhance.

Page (1994) claimed that Fine incriminated the school system and administrators by not giving them voice, thereby demonstrating the same oppressive practices she had charged the school culture of perpetuating. She used Fine's own words to describe the "asymmetric power relations" (Fine, 1991, p. 45; Page, 1994, p. 491) of "the university expert explaining what is 'really' going on, with little consideration of what the locals know and can teach" (p. 491).

A counterpoint. Page's (1994) critique is one with which most ethnographers, including Fine, are seriously concerned. In *Framing Dropouts*, Fine (1991) questions her own act of silencing, just as Page suggests: "Have I merely reversed the traditions of privilege, now privileging the voices of those silenced rather than the voices of those already privileged?" (p. 7). Fine's outright problematizing of the matter helps the reader to keep the data in perspective. Since it is often difficult to remain objective when conducting ethnographic research (as researchers become members of, and active participants in, the environments under study), constant and open reflexivity on the part of the researcher is paramount (Ellis & Bochner, 2000). Doing so allows the reader of the research to recognize the potential for bias, framing the data provided accordingly.

Although Page (1994) makes a number of strong points in her criticism of Fine's research, the conversation evoked by *Framing Dropouts* is a powerful one that brings into question historical and current practices in educating urban adolescents. Fine (1991) effectively exposes the story of one urban educational setting, providing insight into the realities of many urban educational institutions and the students who attend them, thus helping to frame questions and inspiring others to seek answers. Even though her research can be considered a case study of one school, the implications are far-reaching, strongly justifying a closer look at how we educate youth today.

Relevance to Today's Educators

Fine (1991) considered the institution of the public school to be the last hope for many families in poverty and urban communities, but she feared they had been betrayed by the very system designed to support them. She provided a meaningful critique of the ways in which hierarchies are supported and inequalities are perpetuated in the public school system, exposing efforts to maintain a hegemony of knowledge, power, and privilege under the guise of democratic practices. Her concerns remain relevant, as there has been little change in the dropout trends she highlighted in the mid-1980s and early 1990s.

The Trends Continue

Fine's (1991) research focused on one particular school community in the heart of New York City, but her research has ramifications for many urban school systems, especially given the increasingly diverse student populations we are experiencing today. Since Fine's intensive research, the trends in school completion rates have not fluctuated very much, with students of minority status continually overrepresented in the dropout statistics, with no evidence of a convergence in Black-White graduation ratios over the past 35 years (Heckman & LaFontaine, 2010).

Dropout rates continue to be high for students living in lower socioeconomic environments—specifically, those who are from Native American, African American, or Hispanic backgrounds, and who reside in urban settings (National Center for Educational Statistics, 2002). Research conducted by the Schott Foundation (2012) consistently demonstrates that Black males remain at greatest risk for dropping out over any other race, ethnic, or gender group. According to the foundation's research, only 10% of Black male eighth-graders are deemed proficient in eighth-grade reading; and only 52% are graduating from high school within a traditional 4-year period. Although the 52% represents an increase of 10% since 2001, the data still leave little to cheer about. At this rate, the Schott Foundation researchers (2012) predict it would take 50 years for the graduation rates of Black males to catch up to their White peers. We simply do not have that kind of time. The need for reform is urgent.

Balfanz and Legters (2004) report that there are approximately 900–1,000 high schools in the United States that graduate only 50% of the student population, and in 2,000 high schools across the country, the freshman class typically shrinks by 40% or more by the time students reach their senior year. "Nearly half of our nation's African American students, nearly 40% of Latino students, and only 11% of White students attend high schools in which graduation is not the norm" (Balfanz & Legters, 2004, p. v).

A population not mentioned by Fine, but for whom awareness has grown, is students with disabilities, whose graduation outcomes mirror the appalling outcomes of their socioeconomically disadvantaged peers. Students with disabilities remain much more likely to drop out of school than their peers without disabilities (Christenson & Thurlow, 2004), and of that population, students who have an emotional disturbance or behavioral disability have the greatest risk of dropping out (U.S. Department of Education, 2001). Students with the most significant disadvantages entering school, with arguably the greatest stake in obtaining an education, ultimately receive the least amount of schooling today.

A note concerning retention. Sixty percent of American public high schools with the lowest promotion rates are found in large and medium-sized cities, illustrating the profound predicament of students in urban schools. Poverty proves to be the key ingredient for retention, with schools that have a majority of minority students five times more likely to retain 50% or more of their students by the time they reach their senior year. These statistics have devastating consequences, since retention remains one of the most powerful predictors of dropout rates among students (Jimerson, Anderson, & Whipple, 2002).

Ignoring the Call

A flurry of failed urban school reforms inundated urban school settings in the late 1980s and early 1990s (Miron & St. John, 2003), perhaps ignited by Fine's (1991) groundbreaking research. Unfortunately, most focused on piecemeal approaches that neglected the central themes described in her study. The research in *Framing Dropouts* unveiled a plethora of processes and traditions that encouraged students to leave school before graduation, opening the door to new perspectives and foci for future research to better understand the complicity of the educational system in failing students. Yet many contemporary researchers have reverted to a focus on student characteristics instead of school policies and practices, such as the study conducted by America's Promise Alliance (2014). Reform efforts of the 1980s and 1990s failed to raise the consciousness of educators concerning the needs and perceptions of students (Clark, Hero, Sidney, Fraga, & Erlichson, 2006). The failure of educators to recognize their complicity in student dropout rates can perpetuate a "blame the victim" mentality in education. As statistics show, this has not been a productive focus of study or reform, as dropout rates for minority students in urban settings remain unacceptable.

Support for looking inward in research. Although there remains a research focus on identifying student characteristics related to school exodus, there is evidence that this locus of study is not productive. Bowers, Sprott, and Taff (2013) unveil the difficulty in determining predictors of dropout characteristics when the focus remains on the student. However, Balfanz and Legters (2004) have little difficulty determining predictors when the focus is on the characteristics of the school environment, much as Fine (1991) suggested. Bridgeland, Dilulio, and Morison (2006) identify six reasons for students dropping out: a lack of connectedness to school, uninteresting lessons, unmotivating or uninspiring teachers, personal issues, academic challenges and failing in school, and retention. With the exception of *personal reasons*, the predictors can be directly related to policies and educational practices in schools. "Dropping out of high school is not a sudden act, but a gradual process of disengagement" (Bridgeland, Dilulio, & Morison, 2006, p. iv) caused primarily by ineffective educational practices, and not student attributes.

Persisting ineffective practices. As Christenson and Thurlow (2004) explain, many who stress national reform for achieving high academic standards, reducing social promotion practices, and focusing on educational accountability remain blind to the realities of students who are at risk of school failure and dropping out. Although state exit exams are intended to encourage rigor and a quality education, "a potential unintended consequence is increases in the number of students who drop out" (Christenson & Thurlow, 2004, p. 36) as we move away from critical discourse in the classroom and connecting content with the lives of our students and toward rote memory, repetition, and teaching to the test.

GED and the military. Although Fine exposes ineffective alternative routes to graduation, these practices persist in urban schools, as well as schools whose students' families are economically disadvantaged. GED testing continues to be considered a viable alternative by educators for students to complete high school, and the military continues to be touted as a bridge to valuable careers and postsecondary education.

A quick search on the Internet demonstrates the plethora of sexy sites offering information on the GED, including official GED test sites ("GED Testing Service," n.d.), practice tests ("4 Tests," n.d.; "GED Practice Test," n.d.), and classes for test preparation ("Best Online High School Diploma," n.d.; "Life Skills High School," n.d.; "Best GED Classes," n.d.). Students continue to be enticed to drop out of school by a promise of future success (Heckman, Humphries, LaFontaine, & Rodriguez, 2012), even though recent reforms in the GED test have increased online media chatter about concerns for students taking the GED (Chandler, 2013; Hanford, Smith, & Stern, n.d.; Kourkounis, 2015; Smith, 2014).

Heckman and LaFontaine (2006, 2009) found that, despite comparable ability, GED recipients fared significantly worse on measures of economic and social outcomes than their peers of equal ability who received a diploma but did not attend college. In fact, GED recipients had outcomes that were more similar to those of their peers who dropped out than those who received a high school diploma. Although GED attainment theoretically provides vocational and educational opportunities, GED recipients more rarely reap the benefits.

The same is true for enticement into the military. Although most branches of the military require a high school diploma or GED to enlist ("Today's Military," n.d.), the draw for gaining skills and an education to advance an individual's career is front and center. The week after I re-read (for the purposes of this chapter) Fine's (1991) critique of the military's false promises, I witnessed an example of the same practices of student enticement as viewed by Fine—nearly 25 years after the publication of her research. While conducting an observation of a pre-service teacher in a high school that serves students from low-income families in a small urban community, I nearly ran into a life-size cutout of a young, attractive minority female dressed in army fatigues beckoning students to join the military as a way to earn money for college. By contrast, in the more affluent high schools I had visited that semester, there was little or no indication that students were being courted for military service. I was struck by the audacity of the open solicitation of students from low-income communities and the schools' open support of this practice.

Today's Educators Learning from the Past

Relevance in the classroom. As noted in *Framing Dropouts*, teachers who rose above the muck and mire of top-down edicts, overpopulated classrooms, and silencing practices found ways to make the curriculum relevant to students. Today, educators are gaining an appreciation for a relevant curriculum that makes connections for students between content and real-life experiences. Service learning, project-based learning, and problem-based learning all have a foundation in hands-on, collaborative learning approaches that weave authentic lessons within the curriculum. Successful teachers in Fine's (1991) study were able to cross the great cultural divide between the middle-class White teacher and the diverse students who lived very differently than their instructors. The teachers did this by asking questions and provoking critical conversations about current events that had a direct impact on students and their negotiations within their communities.

    Creating safe spaces. Over the last several decades, the processes and policies for education in low-income urban settings have changed little. The implications of Fine's work remain just as cogent in today's schools as when her research was originally introduced. We can learn from the small spaces of community uncovered in *Framing Dropouts*. Fine (1991) stumbled upon the safe spaces in single classrooms with teachers willing to embrace the lived experiences of students to better understand their cultures and daily existence. By allowing personal vulnerability and demonstrating a willingness to learn from students, teachers can help students find success in the classroom regardless of ability, background, home, or community environment and circumstances. We can learn from the echoes of history if we turn an ear toward them and listen. Generating ways to improve student retention in urban settings is not so much about adopting an effective program as it is about creating safe spaces in which students can learn and connect the curriculum to their lives, making meaning of the content in significant ways.

    Fine (1991) referred to public schools as the only hope for some low-income families and their children. As such, we have an obligation to dispose of those practices that promote ineffective teaching and learning resulting in dismal outcomes. Instead, we can relish in the promising practices unveiled by Fine and others. We need to improve education in public schools to make learning more relevant to students; improve supports for students who struggle; foster academic progress; build strong, positive relationships with students; improve communication with parents; and value student voices and perspectives (Bridgeland, Dilulio, & Morison, 2006).

As Fine (1991) revealed, teachers make the difference in the lives of students—not programs and initiatives, and certainly not test scores and curricula. Aspiring and veteran teachers should read this research in teacher preparation and graduate-level programs as a means of recognizing their potential for either perpetuating harm or generating good. Fine introduced, described, analyzed, and extrapolated from her research examples of phenomena that remain in present-day urban high schools—practices that marginalize and oppress students who live in poverty and who represent minority populations. Her powerful prose enlightens, challenges, promotes dialogue, and has relevance across the decades. Her in-depth analysis of the vital experiences of students, their families, teachers, and administrators continues to evoke critical questions of power and pedagogy, democracy and silencing.

References

America's Promise Alliance. (2014). *Don't call them dropouts: Understanding the experiences of young people who leave high school before graduation*. A Report from America's Promise Alliance and the Center for Promise. Medford, MA: Tufts University.

Balfanz, R., & Legters, N. (2004). *Locating the dropout crisis: Which high schools produce the nation's dropouts? Where are they located? Who attends them?* Report 70, Center for Research on the Education of Students Placed at Risk, Johns Hopkins University.

Best GED Classes. (n.d.). *Free online GED practice tests*. Retrieved from http://bestgedclasses.com/free-practice-tests2014/?gclid=CIzt9of468MCFQ6MaQodrk0AyA

Best Online High School Diploma. (n.d.). *Earn an accredited high school diploma online*. Retrieved from http://www.bestonlinehighschooldiploma.com/

Bowers, A.J., Sprott, R., & Taff, S.A. (2013). Do we know who will drop out? A review of predictors of dropping out of high school: Precision, sensitivity, and specificity. *High School Journal, 96*(2), 77–100.

Bridgeland, J.M., Dilulio, J.J., & Morison, K.B. (2006). *The silent epidemic: Perspectives of high school dropouts*. A report by Civic Enterprises in association with Peter D. Hart Research Associates for the Bill & Melinda Gates Foundation. Retrieved from http://files.eric.ed.gov/fulltext/ED513444.pdf

Chandler, M.A. (2013, April 20). GED high school equivalency test to get major overhaul, become more difficult. *The Washington Post*. Retrieved from http://www.washingtonpost.com/local/education/ged-high-school-equivalency-test-to-get-major-overhaul-become-more-difficult/2013/04/20/a2427996-a126-11e2-82bc-511538ae90a4_story.html

Christenson, S.L., & Thurlow, M.L. (2004). School dropouts: Prevention considerations, interventions and challenges. *Current Directions in Psychological Science, 13*(1), 36–69.

Clark, S.E., Hero, R.E., Sidney, M.S., Fraga, L.R., & Erlichson, B.A. (2006). *Multiethnic moments: The politics of urban education reform*. Philadelphia, PA: Temple University Press.

Dickinson, A.C. (2013, March 20). Re-imagining the comprehensive high school. *Edutopia*. Retrieved from http://www.edutopia.org/blog/sammamish-1-comprehensive-high-school-adrienne-curtis

Ellis, C., & Bochner, A.P. (2000). Autoethnography, personal narrative, reflexivity: Researcher as subject. In N.K. Denzin & Y.L. Lincoln (Eds.), *Handbook of qualitative research* (2nd ed., pp. 733–768). Thousand Oaks, CA: Sage Publications.

Fine, M. (1991). *Framing dropouts: Notes on the politics of an urban public high school*. Albany: State University of New York Press. 4 Tests. (n.d.). *Your free practice exam site*. Retrieved from http://www.4tests.com/ged

GED Practice Test. (n.d.). *For the educators*. Retrieved from http://www.gedtestingservice.com/educators/freepracticetest

GED Testing Service. (n.d.). Retrieved from http://www.gedtestingservice.com/ged-testing-service

Good Reads. (n.d.). Review of *Framing dropouts: Notes on the politics of an urban high school*, by Michelle Fine. Retrieved from http://www.goodreads.com/book/show/380026.Framing_Dropouts#other_reviews

Grannis, J.C. (1992). Dropping out and the reproduction of American society. *Educational Researcher, 21*(3), 31–32. doi: 10:3102/0013189X021003031

Hanford, E., Smith, S., & Stern, L. (n.d.). *Second chance diploma: Examining the GED*. American Radio Works. Retrieved from http://americanradioworks.publicradio.org/features/ged/

Heckman, J.J., Humphries, J.E., LaFontaine, P.A., & Rodriguez, P.L. Taking the easy way out: How the GED testing program induces students to drop out. *Journal of Labor Economics, 30*(3), 495–520.

Heckman, J.J., & LaFontaine, P.A. (2006). Bias corrected estimates of GED returns. *Journal of Labor Economics,* *24*(3), 661–700.

Heckman, J.J., & LaFontaine, P.A. (2009). *The GED and the problem of noncognitive skills in America.* Chicago, IL: University of Chicago Press.

Heckman, J.J., & LaFontaine, P.A. (2010). The American high school graduation rate: Trends and levels. *Review of Economic Statistics, 92*(2), 244–262. doi:10.1162/rest.2010.12366

Hemmings, A. (2003). Fighting for respect in urban high schools. *Teacher's College Record, 105*(3), 416–437.

Jimerson, S.R., Anderson, G.E., & Whipple, A.D. (2002). Winning the battle and losing the war: Examining the relation between grade retention and dropping out of high school. *Psychology in the Schools, 39*(4), 441–457. doi: 10.1002/pits.10046

Kourkounis, E. (2015, February 15). *Tougher GED means fewer earn equivalency diploma. TBO: The Tampa Tribune.* Retrieved from http://tbo.com/news/education/tougher-ged-means-fewer-earn-equivalency-diploma-20150215/

Life Skills High School. (n.d.). Free high school diploma. Retrieved from http://www.lifeskillshs.com/What-You-Get/Free-High-School-Diploma?refad=GEDMain&gclid=CImSgO_368MCFYI6aQod108AxQ

Miron, L.F., & St. John, E.P. (Eds.). (2003). *Reinterpreting urban school reform: Have urban schools failed, or has the reform movement failed urban schools?* Albany: State University of New York Press.

National Center for Educational Statistics. (2002). *The condition of education 2002* (NCES 2002–025). Washington, DC: U.S. Department of Education, Office of Educational Research and Improvement.

Page, R. (1994). Do-good ethnography: A review of *Framing Dropouts. Curriculum Inquiry, 24*(4), 479–502.

Schott Foundation for Public Education. (2012). *The urgency of now: The Schott 50 state report on public education and black males.* Cambridge, MA: The Schott Foundation for Public Education. Retrieved from http://www.schottfoundation.org/urgency-of-now.pdf

Smith, A.A. (2014, May 9). Tougher GED test means fewer take exam, pass. *USA Today.* Retrieved from http://www.usatoday.com/story/news/nation/2014/05/08/fewer-ged-test-takers/8847163/

Today's Military. (n.d.). *Review military entrance requirements.* Retrieved from http://todaysmilitary.com/joining/entrance-requirements

U.S. Department of Education. (2001). *Twenty-third annual report to Congress on the implementation of the Individuals with Disabilities Education Act.* Washington, DC: Author.

TWENTY-THREE

Nel Noddings, *The Challenge to Care in Schools: An Alternative Approach to Education* (1992)

Lynda Stone

Introduction

Nel Noddings's *The Challenge to Care in Schools*, first published in 1992, is an early example of her extensive writings that combine theory and practice for schooling and societal reform. It has a unique place in her work, having introduced the interaction of the major strands of ethics and curriculum change in a text aimed at practitioners through ideas that would mold her illustrious career as a philosopher and educator. It also demonstrates the significance of Noddings's theoretical style, what I want to call a "personable philosophy." This has made her work understood, recognized, and very much appreciated by a widely diverse audience worldwide.

This chapter incorporates key elements from *Challenge* (Noddings, 1992) organized to replicate categories for review found in other chapters in this reader: cultural and educational context, book synopsis, strengths and weaknesses, and influence and relevance. Given her own orientation toward education as a philosopher and within a personable philosophy, I have slightly re-cast the sections, entitling them: first, "Persistent Present"; second, "Text Organization and Content"; third, "Unique Contribution and Critique"; and fourth, "Personable Philosophy." While the final section briefly draws together Noddings's singular philosophical style, each section is theorized and presented as a representation of a personable philosophy. "Personable," of course, is typically applied to persons who are attractive, pleasant, and nice to be around—people with whom one wants to engage. While unusual and in no way trivializing of Noddings's work, there seems no reason why writing style cannot also be personable: hopeful and accessible, even when dealing with complex, sophisticated topics of serious societal and educational issues. A brief introduction to Nel

Noddings precedes an in-depth examination of her work. Noddings, currently in her middle eighties, is and remains a matriarch, teacher, and scholar. She was educated in public schools in the northeast United States and was a teacher and administrator before becoming an academic. Her degrees in higher education are from Montclair State, Rutgers, and Stanford Universities. She was on the faculties of Pennsylvania State University and the The University of Chicago before beginning her long tenure at Stanford. To date, Noddings has published nearly 20 books that have been translated into something like a dozen languages and has delivered lectures all over the world. She has also served as president of the John Dewey Society, the Philosophy of Education Society (North America), and the very prestigious National Academy of Education. She maintains a family home in a vacation community in New Jersey, writing daily and continuing to promote innovative ideas—usually a book a year or more—for educational reform as a philosopher and theorist.

Persistent Present

The Challenge to Care in Schools, from its first publication to today, has been very significantly tied to context, to what seems a persistent present. Noddings provides her own contextual statement in the book's first chapter, "Shallow Educational Response to Deep Social Change." With a long view since World War II, she identifies "enormous" changes in families, their work and living arrangements, their lifestyles, and in schooling (p. 1). Before turning to schools and classrooms, she has more to say about societal change and continuity, perhaps best stated as continuities within changes. Of the latter, in the United States, the national context in which she has been writing since the 1940s, the population has become significantly larger and resides in a vast and varied area. Economic improvement has come for some who have entered and remained in the middle class. More have earned college degrees, even in times of tenuous economic stability. The population is also more and newly diverse, a contested change with regard to "American" culture. It is, at its best, different and arguably more interesting today than a half century ago. One indication, of course, is the constant addition of new elements in the popular lifestyle, such as social media and music, not to mention seemingly "always new" technology. If some aspects of American life are positive changes, others continue to be negative. Even with national federal attention through legislative and executive action to welfare needs in the Great Depression and the late 1960s and early 1970s, the poor stay poor and the richest get richer. Discrimination that indicates that a nation "just does not care" continues to occur in employment, housing, transportation, and in a general lack of concern for everyone's welfare (Anyon, 2005). Poverty is affected by race, gender, and residence. The news is replete with reports that range from impoverished general conditions such as the school-to-prison pipeline, to especially horrendous events such as the shootings of young African American men. A persistent present changes and continues. One wonders if things are better now than before.

In *Challenge*, Noddings's emphasis on context connects changes in home life to classrooms, the experiences that students come from, and the schools' responses. She writes:

> On any given day, most students in any class have watched murder, assault, love-making, war-making, and/or competitive sports on television the previous night.... They feel alienated from their schoolwork, separated from the adults who try to teach them, and adrift in a world perceived as baffling and hostile. (p. 2)

In the 1990s, when the book was written, the schools typically revised the standard curriculum, emphasized objectives-based learning, relied on method as the research-based answer to problems of teaching and learning, and managed through a "pervasive goal…[of] control—of teachers, of students, of content" (p. 9). All of this was practiced in the name of achievement.

A contextual note can be added since the book's first publication. Significantly, two very "recent" events in U.S. history had not yet occurred. The first was the attacks of September 11, 2001, that shattered the general belief in safety at home. The second was the largest single decline in Wall Street's history on September 29, 2008, that signaled severe economic recession and loss of financial security (Clarke, 2014; see also Packer, 2013). The point is that the 1990s, the "high-tech" decade, was a boom time in which the general wealth and well-being should have been shared by all. It was not, and when "disasters" occurred, generosity was lost.

Text Organization and Content

Noddings's style as a philosopher and theorist was described above as "personable." This unique way of doing philosophy is captured in the content and form of her writing. In this section, the organization of the book's content is overviewed. At the outset, this must be made clear: Noddings's work is philosophy, and it is radical. She takes on controversial issues and does not shy away from strong opinions. While reading as "personal" in content, this is not her own story; however, she does draw on her own experiences for illustration and argument. Indeed, readers are invited into the text, as if she were speaking directly to them. This philosophical approach is uniquely her own and is one that readers can identify and "identify with."

Central to organization, Noddings begins the book with this statement of purpose:12

I will argue that the first job of the schools is to care for our children. We should educate all our children not only for competence but also for caring. Our aim should be to encourage the growth of competent, caring, loving and lovable people. This book describes education as such an endeavor. (p. xiv)

And here is its personal situating:

We will pretend that we have a large heterogeneous family to raise and educate. Our children have different ethnic heritages, widely different intellectual capacities…different interests. We want to respect their legitimate differences…[and] we think there are some things that they all should learn…[and] be exposed to. (p. xiii)

The introduction and the first three chapters of the book establish the context just briefly described, a founding critique through attention to liberal education, and an overview of Noddings's ethics of care. It is important to remember that *Challenge* is the first book for educators, other practitioners, and the public, following on the heels of her innovation for Western ethics *Caring: A Feminine Approach to Ethics and Moral Education* (1984; subtitle changed to *A Relational Approach to Ethics and Moral Education*" in the 2013 edition). The next two chapters overview an "alternative vision" that sets up the material on centers of caring—within a general theme of continuity. In the latter, a second "vision" chapter, Noddings offers some general suggestions for school change with regard to purpose, place, people, and curriculum. The six middle chapters depict different forms of "caring for": self, the inner circle, strangers and distant others, animals, plants and the earth, the human-made world, and ideas. The book closes with specific suggestions for "getting started."

Across the text, educational themes appear that Noddings carried over to many subsequent books and articles. In this as other works, and given centrality in philosophy of education, aims figure centrally. In addition to ethical life and moral education, Noddings most often focuses on reform in curriculum, as she does in this book. Examples are offered to emphasize the connections between home life and parenting, to posit the value for all persons from the lives of women, and to encourage attention to civic life through education. Never does one size fit all in education or in life.

Before we discuss exemplars of content, something needs to be said about Noddings's philosophical roots and influences. Care theory in *Challenge* and elsewhere owes much to the existentialist philosophy of Martin Buber and others of that tradition. John Dewey's writings also appear and generally influence all of Noddings's work. She is widely read in the educational classics and broad contemporary writings of her own training, and from teaching practice at all levels of education. Following from *Women and Evil* (1989), in which she first identifies as a feminist, her books contain references to historic women writers and feminist philosophical peers. Noddings is indeed a "cross-over" philosopher, very well regarded by diverse theorists in the parent discipline and beyond.

Thus far the book's organization in terms of purpose, structure, and general themes— here and in Noddings's other writings—has been overviewed. In *Challenge,* as elsewhere, her genius in curriculum theorizing is characterized by proposed changes in schooling organization that blur traditional academic disciplines and suggest new interdisciplinary structures. Importantly, a stepping-off point that leads to reform involves the school maintaining the traditional liberal arts curriculum but only for a half day, while incorporating her "alternative" for the other half. Another key is extending what curriculum means in more personalized examples from the categories listed above. One of Noddings's favorite activities is to propose that children and adults frequently engage in informal conversation, especially at mealtimes. A final example concerns changing the "boundaries" of school itself. In creating organizational forms in which schools include social and business groups such as child care associations and flower shops, she writes:

> The basic guiding idea is to make the school into a family-like center of care. We must stop moving children from place to place…[merely] to solve social problems or "satisfy their developmental needs." One of the greatest needs is stability—a sense of belonging. (p. 67)

Belonging is a key premise in the book's principal alternative of establishing curricular centers of care. This structural change is significant because they variously meet children's needs and emphasize interests. Two brief examples demonstrate not only the content of centers but also, by implication, what is missing in the traditional curriculum. "Caring in the Inner Circle" (Chapter 7) builds on Noddings's conception of relation and extends her ideas about "caring for self" from the previous chapter. Here, relations are characterized as equal and unequal: the first include mates and lovers, friends, colleagues, and neighbors; the second includes children and students. Consider one aspect of relations with mates and lovers: that of the role of fantasy in interpersonal relations. Discussion about its significance is important, Noddings asserts, but disclosure should be discouraged. Students should know that it is natural to fantasize, and "they need information and criteria by which to judge the health of their own fantasies" (p. 97).

A chapter that stands in contrast to those about human caring is "Caring for the Human-Made World" (Chapter 10). Noddings argues that caring for objects and instruments differs because "There" has no immediate moral impact (p. 139). However, there does exist a kind of moral sense in that treatment may affect lives. Think, for instance, of over-consumption of natural resources. A contributing factor for children to learn is that most often in life, objects assume order or arrangement. This arrangement, then, is part of their utility and hopefully contributes to persons' health and aesthetic sense. Care for objects further consists of maintaining and conserving, making and repairing, and understanding and appreciating. Again, a favorite example is that both girls and boys should "learn around a well-outfitted kitchen.... They should learn how to use mixers, blenders, processors, whisks, paring knives and potato peelers" (p. 146). Noddings, by the way, has a favorite little knife that she has used daily for over 50 years.

Unique Contribution and Critique

Challenge offers a unique contribution to the philosophy of education through practice and prefigures the several decades of such contributions from Noddings that followed this volume. First, in the 2005 second edition, she writes: "In the 1992 Introduction...I argued against an education system that puts too much emphasis on academic achievement defined in terms of test scores and the acquisition of information" (Noddings, 2005, p. xiii). Unlike others who continue to search for an answer through achievement to discrimination and inequality, she asserts, then and now, that ethical life and caring should be at the center of societal and school life. As stated earlier, *Challenge* presents this view for the first time for educators. Second, Noddings's challenges are radical because they are "truly" alternatives to both traditional and, in some respects, progressive curriculum and schooling. An example is the idea of centers itself, at one time found in many elementary classrooms but always about standard curriculum content. Third, the volume brings together what will become two major strands of her work: philosophical development of the ethic of care and schooling reform, particularly through curriculum. These appear variously together and separate in subsequent books.

At the time of its publication, *Challenge* was reviewed in such journals as *The Harvard Educational Review, Teachers College Record, The Journal of Moral Education*, and *Educational Studies* (Noddings's files, personal communication, 2015). Every review lauded Noddings's project and the need for it in schools. Many reviewers mentioned the personal quality of her writing, and some included exemplary illustrations that stood out such as those cited in this chapter. While not from the time of the book's publication, a useful recent analysis of Noddings's philosophical and educational project centered on caring is from Bergman (2004).

In general, three criticisms were offered. One concerned the practicality of butting up against the traditional disciplines (see Noblit, 1993). Two aspects were mentioned: the maintenance of supremacy of secondary teacher "favorites" given the interdisciplinary centers, and the general difficulties of substantive curriculum change in combatting tradition.

A second critique mentioned in several texts queried the relative importance of the school to family and community in the educational and moral lives of children (Kane, 1993). This criticism seems odd, given Noddings's elaborations on her own family life and—in the years since—her particular advocacy for teaching parenting in schools. Indeed, her Deweyan background would never have countenanced a dualism separating the school from society. A third issue raised difficulties of instantiating caring curriculum in schools, given the power press of larger political structures and institutions (e.g., Hindmarsh, 1994). Interestingly, in the mid-1990s, this reviewer referred to Noddings as "naïve" (p. 93). Humanist and pragmatist that she is, Noddings does not advocate utopias as answers to societal and educational problems (personal communication, 2015) and, her practical realism surely is not naïve. Perhaps more careful reading and decades of additional writings have clarified this impression. Additionally, some feminist philosophers early on did challenge her description of male/female relations and their history of power differentials. Noddings's feminism has acknowledged this history and calls for both men and women to care and for society to recognize the cultural contributions of women's lives for all persons.

Finally, in light of *Challenge*'s advocacy for an interdisciplinary curriculum and the passage of several decades, it does seem important to mention Noddings's recent view:

> I want to make clear that I do not foresee dramatic changes in the basic structure of curriculum in America. Sadly, I think we will go right on with...[the basic liberal arts curriculum]. Indeed if we continue in the direction we are now headed, the curriculum will become even more isolated from real life and its subjects more carefully separated. (Noddings, 2013, p. 11)

In the book cited, *Education and Democracy*, her reform strategy, in addition to continuing a re-thinking of traditional subject content, is to prepare youth for twenty-first-century thinking and life through broad curricular processes of "collaboration, critical thinking, and creativity" (p. 11).

Personable Philosophy

In the introduction to this chapter, the concept of personable philosophy was introduced as a frame for reviewing *The Challenge to Care in Schools* and Nel Noddings's unique theoretical style. This conclusion turns briefly to its form. Throughout the text of *Challenge* and the many books that have followed, readers are drawn into content through a form that is at once engaging, as an invitation to share an inquiry, and a project. Unmentioned previously, an initial observation about form is her general analytic approach: issues are raised, questions are asked, positions are presented, and queries are always open to continued conversation and deliberation. Never is a topic foreclosed, even with a radical commitment to reform.

In *Challenge*, additional elements of stylistic form are manifest. The first is what is often called "phenomenological" description: concrete, accessible points and illustrations. As described above, many ideas are based on Noddings's personal and comprehensive professional experience, as well as through references that range from literature to current events. Second, related to the central element of context, *Challenge* as well as Noddings's subsequent texts are always situated both in a societal and educational past and present. Reading this particular volume today—30 years after its initial publication—seems so very current. Finally, this personable philosophy suggests, even anticipates—possibility and potential. This is the case even in the direst of moments and times. This may be especially important today in an educational climate that seems unrelentingly constrained and less than hopeful of substantive change that would benefit all. In sum, Noddings's personable philosophy, even with her own realistic appraisal, reads as a hopeful beacon for positive change. This volume, like her writings overall, challenges all of us to envision society and education anew.

References

Anyon, J. (2005). *Radical possibilities: Public policy, urban education, and a new social movement.* New York and London: Routledge.

Bergman, R. (2004). Caring for the ethical ideal: Nel Noddings on moral education. *Journal of Moral Education, 33*(2), 149–162.

Clarke, T. (2014, February 13). Stock market crash history: The Dow's 10 biggest one-day plunges. *Money Morning.* Retrieved from http://moneymorning.com/2014/02/13/stock-market-crash-history-dows-10-biggest-one-day-plunges/

Hindmarsh, J. (1994). Review of *The challenge to care in schools: An alternative approach to education. Journal of Moral Education, 23*(1), 91–93.

Kane, P.R. (1993). Review of *The challenge to care in schools: An alternative approach to education. Teachers College Record, 95*(2), 294–297.

Noblit, G. (1993). Review of *The challenge to care in schools: An alternative approach to education. Educational Studies, 24*, 369–372.

Noddings, N. (1984). *Caring: A feminine approach to ethics & moral education.* Berkeley and Los Angeles: University of California Press.

Noddings, N. (1989). *Women and evil.* Berkeley and Los Angeles: University of California Press.

Noddings, N. (1992). *The challenge to care in schools: An alternative approach to education.* New York and London: Teachers College Press.

Noddings, N. (2003). *Caring: A relational approach to ethics and moral education* (2nd ed., updated). Berkeley and Los Angeles: University of California Press.

Noddings, N. (2005). *The challenge to care in schools: An alternative approach to education* (2nd ed. with new introduction). New York and London: Teachers College Press.

Noddings, N. (2013). *Education and democracy in the 21st century.* New York and London: Teachers College Press.

Packer, G. (2013). *The unwinding: The inner history of the new America.* New York: Farrar, Straus and Giroux.

TWENTY-FOUR

Jane Roland Martin, *The Schoolhome: Rethinking Schools for Changing Families* (1992)[1]

D.G. Mulcahy

Introduction

In *The Schoolhome,*[2] as in many of her writings, Jane Roland Martin employs a distinction between what she refers to as the public world of work outside the home and the private world of home. While she has elaborated on limitations of this two-sphere analysis in her more recent book, *Education Reconfigured,*[3] in general terms one may say that, for her, the distinguishing feature of the public world is its preoccupation with production: largely with industry and commerce, the professions, and governing. This world has historically been dominated by men and is considered the domain of men. By contrast, the private world—the domain of women—is centered on reproduction, that is, on what Martin labels the 3Cs of care, concern, and connection. Here the focus is on attending to family and relationships, nurturing the young, and tending to the sick and the elderly. Men are not drawn to the public world and women to the private by any difference in their natures. This is a function of culture, and men and women need to be educated to perform well in both domains.

As viewed in *The Schoolhome*, schooling has historically emphasized the values of the public world. It displays a bias favoring males and prejudicing females, a point highlighted by Martin in her critique of R.S. Peters's concept of the educated man.[4] By placing undue emphasis on academic attainments, with little or no attention given to educating the young for active engagement in the world, it places a premium on preparing students for observing the world as opposed to participating in it. Schooling is also shaped by social and economic factors of which, for Martin, two are especially important. First, because we live in a world that can be violent and disproportionally so toward females, schools are often places of violence and, additionally, disproportionately sites of harassment of females. Second, women are increasingly leaving home to join men in the public world, a matter that leads Martin to reveal early on the focus of attention in *The Schoolhome*: in the prologue, she asks poignantly, "what are we as a nation, a culture, a society going to do about the children who are being left behind?" (p. 4). An important accomplishment of *The Schoolhome* and its idealization of the schoolhome itself is the manner in which its answer to this question lays bare the implications for homes, society, and policymakers as much as for schools.

Synopsis

So what, then, is the schoolhome? What are the values upon which it is founded, and what are its guiding principles? How are these translated into practice, and what are the implications for homes, society, policymakers, and schools? Structurally, *The Schoolhome* is composed of a prologue, five chapters, and an epilogue. Given her concern regarding the tendency toward violence in our midst, the mistreatment of females even in educational settings, and the question of what is to become of children when parents leave home to work in the public world, Martin turns for inspiration to Maria Montessori and her work in Casa dei Bambini. As viewed by Martin, Casa dei Bambini was a home as much as a school, with all of the affective, moral, nurturing, educative, and positive connotations of home (pp. 9–11). The lessons taught there contrast with the martial virtues of obedience and contempt for softness, protection from harm, connectedness to one another, and harmony with nature admired by William James (pp. 17–24). These lessons also reclaim elements of child rearing rejected by some as not rising to the level of education (pp. 27–28) and for whom "the main activities on behalf of children are so effortless and so lacking in direction and purpose that they do not constitute teaching..." (p. 140).

It is the position of *The Schoolhome* that we need to teach children human activities, for they are not born with them. Boys, for example, need to learn to be caring and non-violent and girls to look out for themselves as well as others. But gender sensitivity is not sufficient. There must also be sensitivity to "race, class, ethnicity, religion, physical abilities, sexual orientation, and the other salient dimensions of American children's lives" (p. 118). In addressing education in activities and sensitivity to issues of gender, Martin introduces the notion of domesticity. For her, both John Dewey and William Heard Kilpatrick lacked "a concept of school as a domestic environment permeated by a family affection" (pp. 132–133). But Dewey and Kilpatrick are not considered to be alone in this: American literary classics depict home as a place to escape from. They have kept its positive contribution a secret, teaching us "to forget what is necessary to remember" (p. 149).

Because collective amnesia about domesticity places a stranglehold on educational thought, Martin argues that we need a transformative conception of the American schoolhouse that is "premised on the remembrance of domesticity" (p. 160). Herein lies a challenge, however: How can we introduce into the school the kind of care for all that can be found in the private world of the home if this is out of step with the priorities and values of the public world? And how can we justify it in school programs? Turning to them for answers, in *The Schoolhome* Martin introduces an innovative interpretation of the U.S. Constitution and of the nation's past. The Constitution, she argues, provides the necessary basis on which to establish and justify this new order. If we are to bring about a caring society, a fundamental restructuring of the social and political order is required. In such a caring society, the values of the private world of home become the foundational values of a new political order and of the public world. We can establish this new order by embracing the notion of the school as a moral equivalent of the home and by "a remapping of the logical geography of education as well as a revisioning of the public world" (p. 203). The schoolhome can help bring the values of the home, the school, and the world into alignment "by deriving its overarching aim from a rewritten domestic tranquility clause" (p. 203).

Although the schoolhome cannot fully replace the home, it can take on some of its roles while also transmitting to the young the full sweep of our heritage. This means being committed to education for living together and, as we have seen, replacing "training in spectatorship" with "an education for *living*" and working through with children "the cultural resistances to domesticity" (p. 203). Additional dimensions of the contribution of the schoolhome are highlighted in *Education Reconfigured*, where Martin revisits *The Schoolhome*. These include an emphasis on education for democratic citizenship and the importance of pedagogy,[5] the latter point so often bypassed in educational policymaking.[6] Moreover, it is made clear in *The Schoolhome* that Martin wants to see not just the nation but all the world as a home. In this new configuration of world, nation, school, and home, the schoolhome is seen as "the innermost point in a set of concentric circles, each one of which is a moral equivalent of the home" (p. 204).

Context

As is already evident in *The Schoolhome* (as in her work in general), Martin is keenly aware of the social and political movements of her day. This is seen in her perceptions of the relations between school and society and her concern for the disregard shown in official policies and pronouncements for educational needs of the young other than those pertaining to the public sphere. She is especially attuned to developments in the philosophy of education and feminist thought. It was her responsiveness to developments in feminism that heightened her awareness in the late 1970s and early 1980s of its potential for a reconceptualization of both education and the relationship between school and society. To this she first gave expression in a range of highly original writings leading up to *The Schoolhome* in which feminist thought was introduced with force and scholarly precision into the discussion of education and schooling.

In concepts and arguments central to *The Schoolhome* that took shape in writings dating back to the late 1960s, Martin lays out key components of her epistemological and gender critiques of the dominant orientation of philosophizing about education over the centuries.[7] These reflect a characteristic theme that has been present in her thinking ever since: a consideration of what happens to educational theory and practice once the contributions of women are brought into the conversation. Much of this earlier work is critical of prevailing views that influence thinking about education in general, the school curriculum, and the practice of schooling. One positive outcome of this is a broadening of the idea of what constitutes a worthwhile education. In this there is an emphasis on the place of caring in education and schooling combined with the emphasis on education for participation already referred to. In *The Schoolhome*, in short, while there remains some critique of long-standing educational thought and practice, the primary focus is on a consideration of alternatives. Somewhat excluded from these alternatives, however, is the consideration of an issue around which Martin's earlier work, *Reclaiming a Conversation*,[8] was constructed—namely, what constitutes an appropriate education for females. In *The Schoolhome*, as was ultimately the case also in *Reclaiming a Conversation*, Martin backs off from addressing that question. In its place she turns her attention to what is clearly considered a more pertinent project: a consideration of an entirely new ideal of the educated person and, more specifically, how we might educate both men and women for carrying out the productive and reproductive processes in society and for living well in both the public and private worlds.[9]

Strengths and Weaknesses

Those enamored of neoliberal conceptions of education that now saturate the legislative and governmental policy spheres would likely be critical of perspectives found in *The Schoolhome*.[10] While not dismissing these and their implicit criticism of *The Schoolhome*, scholarly critiques have been more specifically focused. For example, questions raised regarding Martin's writings in general, which also apply to *The Schoolhome*, point to the problematic nature of claims made for educational caring.[11] The matter of implementation is also a concern, with one sympathetic commentator asking how the concept of schoolhome is to be realized.[12] While not wishing to diminish the contribution of *The Schoolhome*, to which further attention will be given presently, here I shall address some additional concerns.

By Martin's own account of domesticity repressed, schools are unlikely candidates for housing the kind of education represented by the schoolhome. They put proficiency in the 3Rs before the 3Cs. They ignore the home in the push to prepare the young for the public world. Nor is it merely that skills associated with home are not taught in school: the school is expected to assist in casting off the attitudes of domesticity associated with the home. Sadly, too, schools can also be sites of misogynist messages and violence (see, for example, pp. 101–107). Given Martin's own strong reservations regarding the pronounced historical disinclination of schools to concern themselves with the affairs of the home,[13] and given her accounts in *The Schoolhome* of the insensitivity shown toward females in schools—even occasional disdain and harassment of them (see, for example, pp. 98–111)—one may reasonably ask if it is realistic to expect schools to replicate the values of Martin's idealized home. Following the lead of the schoolhome, can they become surrogate homes and capture "the intimacy and affection of family relationships and the shared day-to-day living that constitutes domesticity?" (p. 126).[14] Although it looks like a stretch, even if it is granted that the schoolhome and those following its lead will overcome the difficulties they face and strike out in a bold new direction by resembling homes that are "ideal, not dysfunctional" and that are "warm and loving and neither physically nor psychologically abusive" (p. 46), we are not yet out of the woods. The question remains as to what is to be done not just about negligent schools but about homes that do not meet the requirements of the idealized home. That is to say, how does one deal with homes considered inadequate, which in large part occasion the need for the schoolhome in the first place. Even if peace and tranquility were to be realized in society and support structures promoting civility instituted, presumably there would still be a need for "good" homes and "competent" parents in order to fulfill their roles in meeting the educational needs of the young. After all, it would be to actual homes—including those that may be dysfunctional and both physically and psychologically abusive—that some children return every day from the schoolhome. And it has not been shown in *The Schoolhome* how this challenge is to be met.

Beyond the question of feasibility there is also the question of desirability. Even if there is a role for the school in teaching the 3Cs and in sharing with the home "the labor of transmitting the culture's domestic curriculum"[15] to the young, tough questions remain. True, Martin does say she wishes for the values of an ideal, not dysfunctional home, one characterized by love and respect and sustained and justified by the appeal to peace and tranquility. She even gives the impression that we all know what we mean by this in "The Radical Future of Gender Enrichment" when elaborating on themes in *The Schoolhome*. There she writes that it is important for boys and girls alike to learn "to exercise the virtues which our culture thinks of as housed in our private homes."[16] But do we really know what we mean by these virtues? How culturally specific are our interpretations of them? Do we even agree about them? And so one may still ask: What is the "ideal, not dysfunctional home" and what versions or manifestations of the virtues in question are acceptable?[17]

Concepts alone seemingly fail to convey adequately what is meant by the 3Cs, the ideal home, love and respect, and the virtues our culture thinks of as housed in our private homes. If, as Nel Noddings suggests, there is no recipe for caring and that "cultural and personal differences will result in different manifestations of care,"[18] maybe we need a better way to convey what is intended. While recognizing that they will likely not capture all possible manifestations, perhaps it is necessary to present exemplars of the 3Cs, of the ideal home, of love and respect, and of the virtues housed in private homes everywhere. Accomplishing this, however, would be no small task.

Influence and Relevance

These questions notwithstanding, it is because of its innovative thrust and the possibilities it offers in addressing them that *The Schoolhome* makes an enduring contribution. In reflecting on the influence of *The Schoolhome* and its continuing relevance for today's educational landscape, several of its contributions justify its being thought of as an American educational classic. The alternative conceptualization of what constitutes a worthwhile education articulated in *The Schoolhome* expresses many of the elements in Martin's thought that represent a unique contribution to the philosophy of education. Of these elements, none is more original and far-reaching in its suggestive potential for schools and society than the ideal of a gender-sensitive education.

Gender-sensitive education reflects Martin's commitment to including the views of women in the debate on what represents a worthwhile education. This means educating boys and men as well as girls and women to participate in the full range of human activities in both the private and public spheres. At the same time, it means taking into account in the design of educational programs gender differences that may necessitate different approaches to ensure equality for all. This being so, it would appear that the values to which *The Schoolhome* and a gender-sensitive education are committed call for a radical departure from the norm. They lay down a sobering challenge for policymakers addicted to the prevailing corporate philosophy of education of our day and to the kind of educational practices it dictates, of which more recently both Martha Nussbaum and Diane Ravitch are so critical.[19]

Values inherent in the ideal of a gender-sensitive education may have greater implications for the education of boys and men than it does for females. This ideal has never enjoyed the kind of crusade led by Mary Wollstonecraft on behalf of the academic education of women, for few—if any—have argued as Martin has to augment the academic education of boys and men (as well as girls and women) with an education in the 3Cs. As Martin is well aware, such an education is likely to encounter opposition for no other reason than it requires that the education of the "softer" side of human nature that society associates with girls and women be extended to boys and men. It is a further measure of the challenge posed by the ideal of a gender-sensitive education that implementing the kind of education envisioned for the schoolhome disturbs what Martin claims the history of education itself has portrayed as proper.[20]

Historically, the dominant view of a worthwhile education—for which the terms "liberal education" and "general education'" are often used as shorthand—was that it consisted largely of a study of core academic disciplines. This ideal reflected Plato's belief that, in the education of the philosopher king, an emphasis ought to be placed on the pursuit of theoretical knowledge, including philosophy, mathematics, and the sciences. This view gained further support from the curriculum ideal of the liberal arts and sciences as it rose to prominence in the Middle Ages and shaped the academic requirements laid down by universities as they, too, came into existence at the time. While competing philosophical justifications have been offered on its behalf over time, ever since then it has been recognized as an appropriate form of curriculum for schools and colleges alike.

While not rejecting this view in its entirety, *The Schoolhome* highlights some of its limitations and presents an alternative ideal of a worthwhile education. It does so by adding to the range of normally accepted goals of education the development of each person as a member of a home and family.[21] When it comes to the specifics of her alternative ideal, Martin elaborates in *The Schoolhome* and elsewhere on what she had proposed in less developed form in her earlier seminal piece, "Needed: A New Paradigm for Liberal Education…,"[22] which foreshadowed the direction in which her thinking would move. It is not economic competitiveness so beloved of policymakers in the wake of *A Nation at Risk*, or cognitive growth, or liberal education as traditionally understood that receives sustained attention. Instead the focus is largely on domesticity and its associated values of care, concern, and connection to others; inclusion in regard to gender, race, ethnicity, religion, sexual orientation, class, and socioeconomic status; the integration of the productive and reproductive processes in the formation of boys and girls; and education for action—that is, for participation and not mere observation.[23]

Showing how they reach well beyond the traditional idea of a liberal education, essential features of the new, alternative theory on which Martin is insistent are spelled out by her in *The Schoolhome*. This sees academic education as but one part of a person's overall education. It is for this reason that Martin writes in *The Schoolhome* that children must be educated in ways of living in the world as well as knowing about it, in action as well as thought (pp. 85–91). This point—one on which Martin later took issue with Martha Nussbaum's plan for the reform of liberal education[24]—is reasserted in "Women, Schools, and Cultural Wealth" and in *Cultural Miseducation*. Underlining further the distinctive contribution of *The Schoolhome*, this is of such concern to Martin that, for her, any successful new conceptualization of liberal education must come to terms with it. It is a view now shared by others as they attempt to reconceptualize the role and form of liberal education in the university and in schools.[25]

Conclusion

Whether schools should or could provide education for the 3Cs, for family living, and for domesticity remains a matter for debate. Whether the general education of the young should aim to do so is a different question. *The Schoolhome* has made a powerful argument that it should, even if—as Martin maintains—this view is not reflected in the goals commonly adopted for schooling.[26] In making its argument, *The Schoolhome* considers the place of emotional growth as well as growth in practical knowledge and understanding alongside so-called intellectual formation. In doing so it widens the range of conventional values and often outdated discussions of general education by maintaining that these dimensions ought to be considered central to any such discussion.

Even if, as suggested earlier, there is a need for greater specificity on the question of the values to be taught in the schoolhome, Martin has successfully argued the case for a broader conceptualization of a worthwhile education by calling in her ideal of a gender-sensitive education for commitment to a wider range of educational values. It challenges us to work toward a more specific articulation of such values while recognizing that this may need to accommodate various interpretations and provide concrete examples of their accompanying behaviors. These would include, for example, behaviors that exhibit in various forms the kinds of care, concern, and connection that might be found in an ideal, not dysfunctional home, one characterized by love and respect.

Notes

1   Page numbers in the text refer to *The Schoolhome*. Writings by Martin in which she first introduced or developed themes found in *The Schoolhome* have also been published as a collection of essays to which, for convenience, I shall refer here when citing these: Jane Roland Martin, *Changing the Educational Landscape: Philosophy, Women, and Curriculum* (New York: Routledge, 1994).

2   Jane Roland Martin, *The Schoolhome: Rethinking Schools for Changing Families* (Cambridge, MA: Harvard University Press, 1992).

3   Jane Roland Martin, *Education Reconfigured: Culture, Encounter, and Change* (New York: Routledge, 2011), 30–32. See also Martin, *Changing the Educational Landscape*, 13–14.

4   Martin, *Changing the Educational Landscape*, 70–87.

5   Martin, *Education Reconfigured*, 190–195.

6   On this, see C.M. Mulcahy, D.E. Mulcahy, and D.G. Mulcahy, *Pedagogy, Praxis and Purpose in Education* (New York: Routledge, 2015) and Chapter Four of this volume by Barbara Thayer-Bacon.

7   See D.G. Mulcahy, *Knowledge, Gender, and Schooling: The Feminist Educational Thought of Jane Roland Martin* (Westport, CT: Bergin & Garvey, 2002), esp. 1–75, and D.G. Mulcahy, *The Educated Person: Toward a New Paradigm for Liberal Education* (Lanham, MD: Rowman and Littlefield, 2008), 109–126.

8   Jane Roland Martin, *Reclaiming a Conversation: The Ideal of the Educated Woman* (New Haven, CT: Yale University Press, 1985).

9   See esp. Martin, *Reclaiming a Conversation*, 193–199. Martin's movement in this direction is also evident earlier in her incisive critique of Paul Hirst's theory of a liberal education. For this, see Martin, *Changing the Educational Landscape*, 70–87.

10 For further discussion see, for example, Mulcahy, Mulcahy, and Mulcahy, *Pedagogy, Praxis and Purpose in Education*, 9–48, and Diane Ravitch, *Reign of Error: The Hoax of the Privatization Movement and the Danger to America's Public Schools*. (New York: Alfred A. Knopf, 2013).

11 See Audrey Thompson, "Caring in Context: Four Feminist Theories on Gender and Education," *Curriculum Inquiry* 33 no. 1 (Spring 2003): 9–65, and D.G. Mulcahy and Ronnie Casella, "Violence and Caring in School and Society," *Educational Studies* 37 no. 3 (June 2005): 244–255.

12 Benjamin Levin, "Review of *Changing the Educational Landscape*," *Journal of Educational Thought* 30 (April 1996): 79–81.

13 Martin, *Changing the Educational Landscape*, 228–241.

14 See also Jane Roland Martin, "Women, Schools, and Cultural Wealth," in *Women's Philosophies of Education*, ed. Connie Titone and Karen E. Moloney (Upper Saddle River, NJ: Merrill/Prentice Hall, 1999), 164.

15 Martin, *Education Reconfigured*, 190.

16 Martin, *Changing the Educational Landscape*, 233.

17 On this point see also Thompson, "Caring in Context," 26–28.

18 Nel Noddings, *Philosophy of Education* (Boulder, CO: Westview Press, 2012), 233; see also 231–245 for a discussion of complexities pertinent to these questions.

19 Martha Nussbaum, *Not for Profit: Why Democracy Needs the Humanities*. (Princeton, NJ: Princeton University Press, 2010); and Ravitch, *Reign of Error*. See also Mulcahy, Mulcahy, and Mulcahy, esp. 26–48.

20 See, for example, Martin, *Changing the Educational Landscape*, 53–69.

21 This point is directly addressed in Martin, *Changing the Educational Landscape*, 231–233.

22 Martin, *Changing the Educational Landscape*, 170–186.

23 Martin would later add to these: passing on a broader selection from our cultural wealth. See esp. Jane Roland Martin, *Cultural Miseducation: In Search of a Democratic Solution* (New York: Teachers College Press, 2002).

24 Jane Roland Martin, *Coming of Age in Academe: Rekindling Women's Hopes and Reforming the Academy* (New York: Routledge, 2000), 138; and Martin, *The Schoolhome*, 85–87.

25 See, for example, Association of American Colleges and Universities (AAC&U), *Greater Expectations: A New Vision for Learning as a Nation Goes to College* (Washington, DC: Association of American Colleges and Universities, 2002); Ivan Marquez, "Knowledge of Being v. Practice of Becoming in Higher Education: Overcoming the Dichotomy in the Humanities," *Arts and Humanities in Higher Education* 5, no. 2 (June 2006): 147–161; and William M. Sullivan and Matthew S. Rosin, *A New Agenda for Higher Education* (San Francisco, CA: Jossey-Bass, 2008). See also Mulcahy, *The Educated Person*.

26 See Martin, *Changing the Educational Landscape*, 231–233.

TWENTY-FIVE

Gloria Ladson-Billings, *The Dreamkeepers: Successful Teachers of African American Children* (1994)

J.B. Mayo, Jr.

Gloria Ladson-Billings (born 1947) received her K–12 education in the Philadelphia public school system. Remembering her early days in school, Ladson-Billings describes a setting where "everyone there was black," where "several of [her] classmates were children [she] knew from [her] neighborhood," and where "school…was safe and clean, with people who cared about you, a lot like home" (Ladson-Billings, 1994, pp. 3–4). In sharp contrast to her elementary school years, Ladson-Billings attended "integrated" junior high and high schools characterized by competition and tracked classes, where there were only a handful of African American students, none of whom she knew (p. 12). After high school, Ladson-Billings attended Morgan State University, a historically Black college in Baltimore, where she received a B.A. degree in education in 1968. For 10 years (from 1968 to 1978), Ladson-Billings taught and served as a supervisor in the Philadelphia Public Schools, along the way obtaining an M.A. (1972) in education from the University of Washington. She earned her Ph.D. (1984) in curriculum and teacher education from Stanford University. In 1989 the National Academy of Education's Spencer Foundation awarded Ladson-Billings a post-doctoral fellowship that funded the research that led to *The Dreamkeepers*. The research was conducted over the course of 3 consecutive school years: 1988–1989, 1989–1990, and 1990–1991. *The Dreamkeepers* is based on Ladson-Billings's observations, conversations, and reflections from those 3 years in the classroom. The book also represents the collaborative work of Ladson-Billings and the teachers with whom she worked and is peppered with memories from her own school experiences.

The Three Components of Culturally Relevant Teaching

In *The Dreamkeepers*, Ladson-Billings lays out her case for culturally relevant teaching, a pedagogy characterized by teachers' conceptions of themselves and others, the ways in which teachers facilitate social interactions in the classroom, and teachers' understanding that knowledge goes far beyond district-mandated curriculum. Significantly, Ladson-Billings focuses on her selected individuals' *teaching characteristics* and not the *individual teachers' personalities,* because she hopes to drive home the point that culturally relevant teaching can be learned by others and is not solely reliant upon a cult of personality that one either possesses or does not.

Utilizing a series of vignettes to exemplify her major points, Ladson-Billings describes in great detail the aforementioned components of culturally relevant teaching. In an attempt to honor this methodological move, I will include—in italics—a series of thoughts, memories, and reflections about my late maternal grandmother, Celestine V. Jordan (1919–2011), who, according to Ladson-Billings's descriptions, practiced culturally relevant teaching long before it was a recognized practice. Jordan was a long-time teacher (over 40 years) in the rural Virginia community where I grew up and attended school from kindergarten through twelfth grade in the 1970s and 1980s (Mayo, 2007).

Teachers' Conceptions of Self and Others

The first component of culturally relevant teaching centers on teachers' conceptions of self and others and is in direct contrast to what Ladson-Billings labels *assimilationist* teaching, a form of teaching that demands that both instructor and student conform to a predetermined and scripted mode of teaching and learning that may only be effective for certain students. Teachers who practice culturally relevant teaching view teaching as a form of art and themselves as artists who are fully integrated into, and give back to, the communities in which they teach. Further, these teachers encourage their students to find ways to contribute to their communities as well.

Though the term "community service" was not in vogue at the time, I clearly remember my grandmother being involved in many kinds of service to the community (most often using the local church as a vehicle to serve others) when she was teaching. She taught classes in Sunday school, played piano for the adult choir, directed the Christmas pageant, and baked countless sweet potato pies for various events like the church homecoming during the first week of August or funerals throughout the year. Her acts of service carried over into school as well because she insisted that students participate in an event called the Christmas Mother. Students would bring in non-perishable food items to be hand-delivered to area residents in need. I remember walking alongside several classmates with several bags of food to the home of an elderly woman named Mrs. Walker. Her house was very small, and she sat in a chair next to the window. We handed her the bags, wished her a Merry Christmas, and went along our way. The look of gratitude on her face stuck with me for many years, and to this day I think about that moment when I drive by the school and the site where Mrs. Walker's house once stood. My grandmother's example lives on.

In contrast, assimilationist teachers view themselves as technicians who simply perform a series of tasks in order to get the (teaching) job done. Being part of the community is not a priority for assimilationist teachers, and they send the message that students should aspire to achieve in school so that they can escape their community, rather than giving something back in order to make it better for others.

Just as teachers who practice culturally relevant teaching view themselves differently from those teachers who engage assimilationist pedagogies, Ladson-Billings reports similar differences in how these two groups of teachers view others. Teachers who practice culturally relevant teaching believe that all students can succeed in the classroom and that students have pre-existing knowledge that teachers must "pull out" and apply to current lessons being taught (Ladson-Billings, 1994, p. 34). Assimilationist teachers, conversely, think that failure is inevitable for some students and that knowledge comes from teachers and must be drilled into students' heads. In fact, these teachers appear to embrace this mentality, given the competitive, individualistic nature of learning that they endorse. Finally, teachers who practice culturally relevant teaching honor the differences found among their students but help them make connections between their community, national, or global identities and the dominant identity that surrounds them. In this context, dominant equals the homogenized "American" identity that is supported by assimilationist teachers (Ladson-Billings, 1994).

As an example, Ladson-Billings highlights an activity that one of her selected teachers engages in with her sixth-grade students. She recalls: "In the current-events lesson, [the teacher] insists that the students be able to make pertinent connections between the news items they select and themselves" (Ladson-Billings, 1994, p. 49). At the time, before the start of the Gulf War, tensions ran high in the Middle East and many students brought in articles about the impending conflict. When the teacher pushed the students to think deeply about what these tensions in the Middle East had to do with them, one student replied,

> Well, I think it affects us because you have to have people to fight a war, and since they don't have no draft, the people who volunteer will be the people who don't have any jobs, and a lot of people in our community need work, so they might be the first ones to go. (Ladson-Billings, 1994, p. 50)

Following this comment, another student shared that his dad told him the same thing had happened in Vietnam, when Blacks and Mexicans were the first ones drafted into service. The teacher's culturally relevant practice in this example allowed the students to examine how current events directly affected their lives, but it also gave them an opportunity to reflect upon the impact and consequences of their specific ethnic or cultural identities within the larger national (American) context.

Teachers' Construction of Social Relations in the Classroom

The second component of culturally relevant teaching focuses on how teachers create social relations in the classroom and extends them into the community. Again, Ladson-Billings creates a comparison between culturally relevant practices and assimilationist practices to make her points clear. In the culturally relevant classroom, for example, the relationship between teachers and their students is "fluid, humanely equitable, and extends to interactions beyond the classroom and into the community" (p. 55). As one teacher notes, "You've got to realize that being with the children for five or six hours a day is just not enough for the kind of impact you want to have on them" (p. 63). Therefore, Ladson-Billings's selected teachers extend open invitations to students to attend Sunday school, to join outside organizations like the Girl Scouts, or simply invite students to their homes for dinner or Saturday lunches.

In the assimilationist classroom, however, the relationship between teachers and their students is based upon a hierarchical, teacher-as-boss mentality that is strictly limited to more formalized roles in the classroom. In this scenario, teachers teach, students learn…period. The teacher who practices culturally relevant methods is able to connect with all of the students in the classroom and encourages a "community of learners" among them. One teacher comments: "I try to find out as much as I can about the students early in the school year so I can plan an instructional program that motivates them and meets their needs" (p. 67). Simply acknowledging students' birthdays or decorating the classroom with posters of students' favorite sports heroes or movie stars and then using these items as writing signals to students that teachers care about them as individuals. Meanwhile, they are still maintaining an academic purpose to the chosen room décor. In sharp contrast, the teacher who engages assimilationist practices will make connections with only a select group of students (such as those who behave well and who perform at a high academic level) and encourages achievement through competition between students.

Finally, teachers who employ culturally relevant practices facilitate collaborative learning, a style of learning that encourages students to teach each other, taking responsibility for each other's comprehension. As one teacher puts it, "Those that are helping [others] are really helping themselves" (p. 72). Teachers who utilize assimilationist methods encourage only individual learning and in isolation from their peers, helping only themselves to excel in the classroom.

> My grandmother shared with me how when she first started teaching in the late 1930s, she worked in a one-room schoolhouse where she taught students in grades 1–6—all at the same time. She had 6 year-olds and students as old as 12 in the same classroom. She would have the older ones help out with the younger ones usually with their spelling and that let her know that they truly knew how to spell their words. Years later when the one-room schools consolidated into one school, the Pocahontas School, Jordan used similar practices with students who were the same age but who worked from different ability levels.

To summarize, Ladson-Billings reminds us that culturally relevant teaching encourages social interactions in the classroom that support the individual within a group context. Individual students and the entire group make similar, collective gains when teachers employ this form of teaching, which creates a "we're all in this together" mentality—a form of family.

Teachers' Understanding of Knowledge

The third component of culturally relevant teaching discusses teachers' understanding of knowledge, how students make sense of and confront it, and how knowledge may be co-created in an ongoing cycle. Indeed, culturally relevant teaching supports the idea that knowledge continuously changes, is re-created and shared among teachers and students. From this perspective, knowledge is viewed critically and understood to be imperfect. Ladson-Billings highlights an example in which one of her chosen teachers helps students take a critical look at the language they use. Lamenting that some teachers would have her students believe the language commonly heard in their neighborhoods will be *all* they need, this teacher encourages them to use both forms of language—the language from home and the more formalized language taught in schools. This teacher comments:

My job is to make sure they understand that their language is valid but that the demands placed upon them by others mean that they will constantly have to prove their worth. We spend a lot of time talking about language, what it means, how you can use it, and how it can be used against you. (Ladson-Billings, 1994, p. 82)

Helping children understand that how they use language often results in judgments made by others exemplifies a critical understanding of knowledge. Teachers who come from an assimilationist perspective view knowledge as traveling in one direction: from teacher to student. They understand knowledge as being unchangeable and infallible (p. 81). Using the language example, assimilationist teachers would reinforce the idea that only "proper" language is appropriate in school without any recognition or validation of the language that students use at home and in their communities.

Teachers who use culturally relevant practices are not only keen to the critical use of language; they are also passionate about content, while at the same time helping their students develop necessary skills. According to Ladson-Billings, the assimilationist teacher is viewed as "detached," or neutral, about content, and expects students to demonstrate certain prerequisite skills, rather than having them develop skills that are needed in the moment. The assimilationist teacher may also make assumptions about what skills are unattainable, given her predetermined ideas about what students can and cannot achieve.

My grandmother never used the term "co-created knowledge" in my many conversations with her, but she certainly understood that knowledge comes from a variety of places and that students' [and Black teachers'] prior experiences contributed to its formation. During her second year teaching in the desegregated schools of Powhatan, Virginia, my grandmother suggested that the first graders should participate in an "operetta program." Though given the green light to move forward with the program, few white teachers supported the idea because they believed the students were too young to perform and learn their lines. But my grandmother knew her students were capable given her previous experiences directing elementary school performances at the all-Black Pocahontas School and at the Little Zion Baptist Church. Though few in number in 1968, some of Jordan's [Black] students had also performed at church, and they were able to bring that experience to the school play. In the end, my grandmother coached her first grade class to a show that went on "without a hitch." Her knowledge about what young students could do combined with the students' previous experiences in a different setting helped create a new standard for the first graders that would remain in place well after my grandmother's retirement in 1979. (Mayo, 2007, p. 24)

Low expectations on the part of teachers often hinder students' academic growth and place false ceilings on what they are able to achieve in and out of the classroom. Teachers who engage culturally relevant pedagogy push their students to maximize their potential instead of focusing on their students' limitations.

Finally, culturally relevant teachers view excellence broadly and take into account students' diversity and individual differences. Too often students are rewarded for mediocrity because what counts as "excellence" is so narrowly conceived. This scenario, in combination with a sense of pity from assimilationist teachers, leads to students being rewarded for substandard performance. According to one of the teachers highlighted by Ladson-Billings,

Some teachers come into this district and think they're doing the children a favor by sticking a star on everything. They don't care that they're rewarding mediocrity. But in doing so, they're really just setting the kids up for failure because somewhere down the road they're [the students] going to learn that that A was really a C or a D. (Ladson-Billings, 1994, p. 99)

In contrast, teachers who practice culturally relevant pedagogy view excellence from a broader perspective, an approach that allows them to reward students within areas where they truly excel. This requires teachers to know about their students' activities outside of the classroom, as in participating in team sports or singing in the church choir. Once the teacher has legitimately rewarded her students for true excellence, their self-esteem is improved, their confidence is increased, and, over time, they may feel "a stronger connection between home and school" (p. 99). The teacher can then acknowledge the students' efforts in an area of needs improvement and encourage them to do better without falsely labeling every effort as a "good job" and worthy of a reward. At the same time, when students see that their teacher "makes a fuss" about what they enjoy outside of school, they will seek out similar attention and recognition in the classroom.

A Note on Methodology: Teachers' Selection and Maintenance of Voice

The Dreamkeepers is significant not only in that it lays out Ladson-Billings's concept of culturally relevant teaching, but also because it embodies a spirit of collaboration in the manner in which the featured teachers were selected. The collaborative method of teacher selection complements the overall purpose of the book, given its reliance on multiple sources. Once selected, these teachers were heavily consulted on how data were collected and analyzed, which gives the book its high level of validity. In essence, the reader truly senses the authenticity with which Ladson-Billings writes. I will now briefly introduce the selected teachers—the dreamkeepers—and examine how they were selected and how their voices were maintained throughout the re-telling of their stories.

Ladson-Billings began the task of selecting teachers for her study through a process that Michele Foster (1991) calls "community nomination." In this process, researchers rely on members of the community, local organizations, newspapers, and so forth to judge whether or not a person (in this case, a teacher for Ladson-Billings's study) meets the established criteria. Ladson-Billings met with African American mothers of school-aged children after church services in the local community to receive their input on which teachers had been effective at teaching their children. This process resulted in 17 names that were then cross-checked with the principals and teaching colleagues of the persons suggested by the community members. The school personnel suggested 22 teachers, 9 of whom were selected by the community members as well. One member of the group declined to be in the study, citing a lack of time, which narrowed the group to the 8 dreamkeepers Ladson-Billings consulted in the course of the 3-year project. All eight of the selected teachers were women who taught in elementary school—three identified as White, five identified as Black, and their years of teaching experience ranged from 12 to 40 years. What they had in common—as perceived by community members and school officials alike—was the ability to manage a class and improve student attendance, a willingness to include parents without being patronizing, and an approach that demanded academic excellence (Ladson-Billings, 1994, p. 148).

Once selected, these teachers were interviewed and observed in the classroom multiple times. Their class sessions were videotaped, and each agreed to participate in a research collaborative where they "analyzed and interpreted collected data and their work together in order to better understand their collective expertise" (p. 145). Ladson-Billings reports that each interview was transcribed and then given back to the individual who had been interviewed to check for mistakes or to give them an opportunity to clarify or add any additional information. Interview scripts were then re-typed and later handed out to each of the eight selected teachers during their first group meeting to serve as a starting point for the collective's work. Segments of classroom videotapes were also shared with the collective so that each individual could comment on, and learn from, the actions taken by fellow group members. Given this process, teachers' voices and intentions were maintained throughout the re-telling of their stories in *The Dreamkeepers*.

Students "At Risk" or Students' Culture Denied?

The 1983 publication of *A Nation at Risk: The Imperative for Educational Reform* marked the beginning of a new way of categorizing certain children. For decades, African American children had been described as "culturally deprived" or "disadvantaged," but following this often-cited report, the new descriptor became "at-risk," and, though this marked a change in the earlier "language of deprivation, the [same] negative connotations remained" (Ladson-Billings, 1994, p. 9). Indeed, the problem of low academic achievement among at-risk students was most often understood as originating within the students themselves or in their families—classic blame-the-victim terminology.

This sets the backdrop for *The Dreamkeepers* as Ladson-Billings endeavored to uncover methods to successfully teach African American children. Frustrated by the lack of literature that specifically addressed the needs of these children, Ladson-Billings offers an explanation for the dearth of writing on a topic that has plagued the United States for decades. She posits that while U.S. educators understand that African Americans are a distinct *racial* group, they refuse to recognize African Americans as a distinct *cultural* group. Ladson-Billings writes:

> It is presumed that African American children are exactly like white children but just need a little extra help. Rarely investigated are the possibilities of distinct cultural characteristics (requiring some specific attention) or the detrimental impact of systemic racism. Thus the reasons for their academic failure continue to be seen as wholly environmental and social. (p. 9)

Given this limited perspective, past research often cited poverty and lack of opportunity as the *only* plausible reasons for African American children's poor performance in schools. As a result, any suggested interventions and/or remedies were designed to compensate for these "deficiencies," a clear example of a deficit-model-mentality at play. African American students needed to be "fixed" so that they could succeed at school.

Despite this less-than-ideal context, Ladson-Billings cites several programs and strategies that demonstrated at least some level of effectiveness for African American students. She groups these programs into three broad categories:

1.	Programs designed to remediate or accelerate without attending to the students' social or cultural needs;
2.	Programs designed to resocialize African American students to mainstream behaviors, values, and attitudes at the same time that they teach basic skills;
3.	Programs designed to facilitate student learning by capitalizing on the students' own social and cultural backgrounds. (Ladson-Billings, 1994, p. 10)

Ladson-Billings gives examples of each and suggests that, even in the more advanced category where African American students' cultural backgrounds are taken into account, they suffer some degree of "psychic cost" when they attempt to achieve academically in school. She writes: "Somehow many have come to equate exemplary performance in school with a loss of their African American identity...doing well in school is seen as 'acting white'" (p. 11). I can personally relate to this scenario, having been accused by a handful of African American peers over several years in school of "talking too proper" or, more blatantly, being called an Oreo—Black on the outside, White on the inside. As this logic dictates, students who don't want to "act white" have no choice but to purposefully perform poorly in school. *The Dreamkeepers* examines teaching for African American students that combats this vicious cycle because it highlights teaching that has helped them achieve academic success "while maintaining a positive identity as African Americans" (p. 13). When the teaching methods described by the dreamkeepers are enacted, African American students understand that academic excellence is not solely for White, middle-class students, but for them as well.

Concluding Thoughts: *The Dreamkeepers* Still Relevant 20 Years Later

Though it was published over 20 years ago, *The Dreamkeepers: Successful Teachers of African American Children* remains relevant because the challenges it addresses remain unresolved. In fact, some would argue that finding and engaging teaching strategies that will enable African American students to achieve academic success is even more important than ever. Whereas many students in schools across the United States continue to do well—as measured by grades and standardized test scores—several groups of children, including African American and other students of color—continue to lag behind middle-class White students. And the numbers of these diverse students is steadily growing. The oft-mentioned "achievement gap" persists and continues to widen between various groups of students in school districts across the United States. An enduring strength of *The Dreamkeepers* is that the teaching methods described within its pages can be applied to multiple groups of students. Culturally relevant pedagogies may be learned by teachers who are willing to put forth the effort and applied to their lessons and daily classroom practice, which will enable *all* students in the classroom to achieve academic success.

The timelessness of the lessons learned from *The Dreamkeepers* is also apparent, given the way culturally relevant pedagogies have adapted to fit within a modern-day teaching context. In teacher preparation programs throughout the nation, cultural competence is viewed as a requisite foundational quality if one hopes to be successful in the classroom. And how one understands cultural competence is changing. In fact, Ladson-Billings now talks about *culturally sustaining pedagogy* as a way of helping teachers to better understand how to reach their African American students and other students of color. She believes that today's students are more open to boundary crossing, shifting identities, and less structure. Indeed, she refers to them as "shape shifters" (Ladson-Billings, 2015) capable of multitasking and assuming multiple identities.

Given this new breed of students, Ladson-Billings makes connections between the culturally relevant pedagogy laid out in *The Dreamkeepers* and modern-day hip-hop pedagogy. Defined as a "pedagogical approach that alters the top-down power relationship in teaching and learning between teachers and students," hip-hop pedagogy stresses that teachers and other adults in school are no longer viewed as the only knowledge producers in the classroom (Prier, 2012, p. 191). Prier goes on to say:

> Urban youth are not objects who simply receive knowledge from teachers, but have the capacity to construct their own forms of knowledge in hip-hop [music] that [teachers] can learn from as well. Subsequently, there is much they can teach us about the society in which they live, and what young people are learning from this society, as expressed through culture and music. (Prier, 2012, p. 191)

Ladson-Billings views this kind of pedagogy as complementary to culturally relevant pedagogy and makes her case in an academic talk she gives entitled "Hip Hop, Hip Hope: (R)Evolution of Culturally Relevant Pedagogy." In the presentation, she aligns the three major tenets of culturally relevant pedagogy with hip hop pedagogy, suggesting that through a greater understanding and appreciation for hip hop culture, teachers will better relate to their "new-generation" urban students and the multiple, often untapped, talents they possess. That these three major themes of culturally relevant pedagogy—academic achievement/student learning, cultural competence, and sociopolitical consciousness—are compatible with a reputable, present-day teaching framework such as hip-hop pedagogy indicates that *The Dreamkeepers* is still relevant. It contains foundational knowledge for today's educators based on the classroom experiences and expertise of teachers sincerely invested in their African American students.

References

Delpit, L.D. (1996). Review of *The dreamkeepers. Contemporary Sociology, 25*(2), 240–241. Foster, M. (1991). Constancy, connectedness, and constraints in the lives of African American women teachers. *National Association of Women's Studies Journal, 3*(2), 233–261.

Ladson-Billings, G. (1994). *The dreamkeepers: Successful teachers of African American children.* San Francisco, CA: Jossey-Bass.

Ladson-Billings, G. (2009). *The dreamkeepers: Successful teachers of African American children* (2nd ed.). San Francisco, CA: Jossey-Bass.

Ladson-Billings, G. (2015). *Hip hop, hip hope: (R)evolution of culturally relevant pedagogy.* Retrieved from https://www.youtube.com/watch?v=o61GS3LPObE

Mayo, J.B. (2007). Quiet warriors: Black teachers' memories of integration in two Virginia localities. *Multicultural Perspectives, 9*(2), 17–25.

Prier, D.D. (2012). *Culturally relevant teaching: Hip-hop pedagogy in urban schools.* New York: Peter Lang.

TWENTY-SIX

Lisa Delpit, *Other People's Children: Cultural Conflict in the Classroom* (1995)

Kal Alston

As a parent, teacher, and researcher, Lisa Delpit repeatedly encountered profound disconnection between the experiences of children who brought racial/class/linguistic differences to their classrooms and their (often) well-intentioned teachers. Her 1995 book, *Other People's Children: Cultural Conflict in the Classroom*,[1] was published as a fiercely personal and political account of her own journey of understanding how schooling can consistently fail some students despite good-faith work to help them.

The book comprises nine essays grouped into three sections. The first section includes two essays originally published in the *Harvard Educational Review* that pose a challenge to popular strategies of teaching literacy skills to children, and a third that responds to some criticisms leveled at those essays. In the second section, Delpit takes up literacy, orality, and culture in Alaska and Papua New Guinea. In these essays she engages in a close analysis of teacher education and the challenges faced by teachers who are "native" to the communities in which they teach. In the third section, Delpit specifically calls for a reexamination of teacher assessments and standards as they were being developed at the time. She issues a call to educators to reconsider their practice in light of reflective self-knowledge, humility, and cross-cultural understanding.

Literacy and Teaching More Than Words

Delpit prefaces each section of the book with a "cover essay" that provides the context surrounding the original production of the pieces and how she conceives of them hanging together in this volume. She titles her first section preface, "Controversies Revisited," and leads with a narrative of how she came to write the two most widely-read articles in the volume, "Skills and Other Dilemmas of a Progressive Black Educator" and "The Silenced Dialogue: Power and Pedagogy in Educating Other People's Children." In the former, which Delpit wrote while a professor at the University of Alaska—and was experiencing the divide she talks about in the article in the White/Native context—she weaves a narrative that is personal and politically charged at the same time. She recounts her own childhood experiences with the skill-based literacy demands of the Black nuns who taught her in Louisiana, as well as the lessons she learned as an undergraduate and graduate student. Those lessons, she recounts, moved her away from her own experiences as a child, *and*, when successfully learned, connected her to her White peers in the classroom. The so-called process approach to the teaching of writing de-emphasizes the teaching of skills and emphasizes process, fluency, and context. Delpit is careful to articulate what she appreciates about this approach:

> [S]kills are a necessary but insufficient aspect of black and minority students' education. Students need technical skills to open doors, but they need to be able to think critically and creatively to participate in meaningful and potentially liberating work inside those doors.[2]

While the advocates of the process approach defended the value of their work, my suspicion is that it is the other descriptors that Delpit employs in fleshing out this divide—which she contends disadvantages poor and minority children—that really fuel the controversies that erupted. That is, Delpit gives voice to the Black and minority teachers who have rejected this approach as ineffective at best, and flat-out racist at worst; those teachers she highlights use explicitly racialized language. They, and Delpit, criticize White liberals as the perpetrators of this ultimately disabling strategy and assert that they will not participate in it. The race of the proponents of the two paths is always mentioned and always "at stake." Delpit's intentions are to seek a better set of educational outcomes for Black and minority children *and* to lift up those teachers whose shared cultural experiences with those children and consequent expertise have been forgotten or ignored. It is not unreasonable that some educators who supported these strategies would feel that they were defending themselves against charges of racism.

Delpit suggests that the White progressive teachers cannot see that their students are already bringing fluency into the classroom and may not have the cultural tools that "native" teachers have to recognize those skills. The former are essentially starting in the wrong place with those students, and the insistence that this method is the best for all children is misplaced arrogance. Delpit's tone throughout reflects how she begins the essay: "Why do the refrains of progressive educational movements seem lacking in the diverse harmonies, the variegated rhythms, and the shades of tone expected in a truly heterogeneous chorus?"

In the aftermath of the "controversy" stirred up by the skills article, Delpit gave a talk at the University of Pennsylvania that became "The Silenced Dialogue." Delpit reports that at the talk she was verbally challenged by audience members, including one White woman who suggested that Delpit was stirring up racial divisions where none existed. Delpit's stated aim for the essay is to highlight *both* sets of concerns raised by her previous article: one primarily raised by White educators who wanted to debate the value of skills-based literacy approaches, and the other raised by non-White educators who responded passionately to Delpit's acknowledgement of their voices. Her bridge between the two perspectives lay in ethnographic analysis and development of a theoretical connector—the "culture of power."

In the early 1990s this article was a syllabus standard in educational foundations courses, and many students were challenged by her formulation of the "culture of power." As she points out,[3] the first three postulates were established core tenets of sociology of education:

(1) Issues of power are enacted in classrooms.
(2) There are codes or rules for participating in power; that is, there is a "culture of power."
(3) The rules of the culture of power are a reflection of the rules of the culture of those who have power.

Delpit was looking to extend this logic of culture to explain how different participants in any culture of power (in this case, the classroom) come to understand where and who they are. The premises she adds to fuel her extended argument address those who are and who are not already in the culture of power:

(1) If you are not already a participant in the culture of power, being told explicitly the rules of that culture makes acquiring power easier.
(2) Those with power are frequently least aware of—or least willing to acknowledge—its existence. Those with less power are often most aware of its existence.

Delpit pivots quickly from this second set of premises to her main focus for this essay: that while teachers who are fully immersed in the culture of power believe that what they are doing is being egalitarian by doing for other people's children what they would do for their own, in fact those "other" children are disadvantaged by not being inculcated into the culture of power. Delpit is careful to be clear that those children have various languages and lenses through which they may fully understand their own cultures of home and community, but they do not necessarily come to the classroom fluent in the language of power assumed by their teachers.

Further, Delpit's experience is that those teachers, insofar as they are natives in the culture of power, are unaware of the ways in which the rules themselves are unavailable to those 'others' without being made explicit. This lack of awareness leads to further misapprehension of the skills children bring to the classroom, as well as a misunderstanding about what failures on the part of those children possibly mean. She analyzes literacy instruction as a site where the testimony from students and teachers who are "outside" the culture of power converges around a narrative suggesting that the progressive strategies for empowering students are read by many of those students as teachers breaking the teacher-student covenant.

Delpit's critics often misread her challenges to the process-based literacy program as her promotion of rote and drill-based methods. However, she writes:

> I do not advocate a simplistic "basic skills" approach for children outside of the culture of power. It would be (and has been) tragic to operate as if these children were incapable of critical and higher-order thinking and reasoning.... [This means] ensuring that each classroom incorporate strategies appropriate for all the children in its confines.[4]

She advocates for contextual and "real-audience" features of the method and rejects the idea that these approaches to teaching literacy are automatically opposed. However, the codes affiliated with the culture of power in the classroom are differentially available to students, advantaging those whose family life and culture operate on the same codes. For students without that background, Delpit states affirmatively that those codes need to be made explicit—not because they are *better*, but because they form the operating system on which performance and success will be judged. Failures of cultural communication underlie much of what appears as educational failure and cultural deficits. Delpit holds teachers responsible for that disconnect and argues that they must first acknowledge how their understanding of teaching and classroom communication styles must be made explicit. Further, she maintains, if they are going to enforce those understandings, they must assess the extent to which all students are prepared to participate fully.

Finally, Delpit argues with critics who accuse her of validating the culture of power and being conservative in her analysis. She asserts instead that her analysis is focused on what is and not on what should or could be. In her view, it is the blinkered vision of the distance between those two that keeps progressive White teachers separated from both the successes of their non-privileged students and full relationships with their non-privileged colleagues.

In the third article in this section, Delpit emphasizes the extent to which different language proficiencies can be re-purposed to support student learning in a multicultural and multilinguistic context. She demonstrates the weaknesses of the traditional approach in which the teacher focuses on correcting any dialectical differences from the "standard."[5] This piece provides real classroom examples of the importance of acknowledging the gaps in cultural-linguistic experience and of looking for materials and classroom methods to build bridges. Some of that bridge building is skill oriented; some of it is broadening perspectives about knowledge and knowers; some is being open to membership in multiple communities in a single classroom. Delpit ends the essay by proposing that this openness may become an asset for those seeking to be part of the global economy, which requires the ability to communicate in local and non-local language and cultural styles.

The Power of the Word: Transmitting, Decolonizing, Continuing Culture

In Section Two, Delpit shores up her arguments from the previous section by supplying rich data from New Guinea, Alaska, and various teacher education settings. Her work here seems impelled by a desire to get all educators (and parents and communities) to take up the particularities and importance of their culture of origin; to be able to acknowledge that that knowledge and way of being is not "natural" but is specific to the cultural setting; and to forge connections across differences that will enrich the educational experience of all children.

For Delpit, there is value in bringing illustrative cases from outside the traditional racial binary of U.S.-based schooling to pull U.S.-based educators out of their tired, comfortable positions. Finding ways to render the familiar strange and the strange familiar, as has been embraced as a means to spur creative thinking,[6] is a useful and strategic move on Delpit's part. By the time she returns to the "Black-White problem" as the main course in the third essay, she has been able—both rhetorically and affectively—to advance the reader's understanding of "the sort of thing" she is seeking to problematize in contexts that are doubtless not native to the majority of her readers.

The Papua New Guinea story of linguistic diversity and conflict is directly attributable to a post-colonial situation in which a simple "return" to a romanticized pre-English life is no longer achievable, much less desirable, even for those most alienated by that colonial history. As Delpit describes her own experience of being dropped into a culture very unlike her own—both to study the effects of a "mother-tongue-medium" instruction program and to conduct a government-sponsored evaluation of same—she acknowledges that travelling afar helped her to decouple her own story from the meanings of literacy and schooling.

After facing the tragic consequences of enforced English instruction and Western schooling on village life, the government sponsored work with a different approach. In the early 1980s the approach was adopted in the region in which Delpit studied, with the stated goals of sequentially teaching reading, writing, and basic numeracy in the native language; imparting the basic cultural understanding and expectations of that home culture; and transferring that expertise into the setting of the English language classroom. The purpose was to create students who were bilingual and bicultural and would not contribute to the further erosion of the traditional world of New Guinea.

Delpit discovered that the adults in the communities in which she studied had strong feelings about the local language and the importance of achieving literacy in that language. They were aware that putting all the eggs in the basket of English literacy could leave their children unable to operate in the local context and/or not well prepared in English. They understood (and Delpit supported) the need for their children to have access to the pathways of modernity, but also to be comfortable in their (native) authenticity, so that they were not "homeless" and disconnected, but rather could be flexible. Delpit's research at the time indicated that this approach was working for all the involved parties (students, families, educators, governmental planners) to accomplish the stated goals.

As an assistant professor in Alaska, Delpit continued her quest to understand how literacy works in and through various cultural contexts. She seemingly remains open to that exploration beyond what she has been taught in her own schooling—that is, she does not rely on a technologically limited definition of "successful" literacy. She is attuned to differences among and between communities and to the differences between parsing text and pushing text through context. The second piece in the section examines the challenges to connection between school and life. Delpit, with help from her Native Alaskan interlocutors, enumerates multiple instances in which Western schooling (and parenting) insists on listening to words as the primary arbiter of meaning—"say what you mean and mean what you say." Words expressed orally and in writing are the carriers of meaning and convey the extent to which the knowledge is "known." Delpit, in the memory of her own life and in her research with teachers, understands that words lack meaning without context, and that it is difficult to know what young "knowers" know without enhancing their use of language inside the contexts with which they are most familiar.

She offers the example of the roll call as an empty, decontextualizing ritual—asking students to verbalize their presence when they are physically in view of the teacher. The Native Alaskan teacher uses the ritual instead as an opportunity to inquire of students what they observed on their way to school—to connect them to the education of their senses and their environs. She quips that by engaging in a quick exchange with each student each morning, she sees that they are learning to be more observant—and she can also mark each "present" without asking a self-evident and useless question over and over.

Delpit further argues that the ways we value words and specific literacies provide instruction to children about what knowledge and expressions of knowledge matter in the adult world. They learn whether knowledge is the property of the individual or of the collective. They learn whether knowledge is externally or internally constituted. Delpit's view, as clearly articulated, is that leaving the door open to multiple understandings of literacy leads to a more broadly satisfying life that connects school to life outside of the classroom.

In the final essay of this section, Delpit returns to the more familiar world of the racial divide in (continental) U.S. classrooms. She begins the essay with the prediction (more than fulfilled) that K–12 students will become more than half minority (by 2014 the percentage of White students dipped below 50% for the first time) and a prediction about the racial demographics of K–12 teachers, a forecast that thankfully was not fulfilled (the percentages of non-White teachers increased by about 10% between 1986 and 2011). At the time, however, there were increasing numbers of non-White teachers who, although certified, were not entering or were exiting the profession. Delpit invoked their voices to explain their disaffection, even while they were passionate about supporting non-White students' academic success. In this essay, Delpit gives life to the consequences of the "silenced dialogue"—that is, when these teachers feel their experience is ignored in the university classroom and their insights into diverse students discounted. Their counter-narratives against the stereotypes that dominate the educational discourse are repressed when they are not expressed in the language of theory and do not match accepted historical texts. Their accounts of the educational problems to be solved are not included in the lessons that are required of teachers.

Delpit posits that this silenced dialogue makes both university and K–12 classrooms places that do not interrogate the ways in which difference is allowed to become discrimination and exclusion. She suggests that we need to diversify university education faculties, create conditions for majority faculty to serve as encouraging and inclusive mentors for diverse students, and organize university pre-service students into cohorts and teams that understand that their success is dependent on a broad understanding of difference. This is not meant to be a "feel-good" celebration of difference but an undergirding of critical examination of experience and knowledge.

Reading Truth in Power

In Section Three, Delpit examines several tensions implicit in her analysis of the culture of power. On the one hand, the same concerns about the cultural biases in standardized testing for students carry over into attempts at teacher assessment. On the other, Delpit wants to challenge the idea that members of minority communities cannot or should not learn the cultural language of the majority. How, then, are learning environments, goals, and methods to be properly balanced between the need to challenge the hegemony of a particularly valued mode of literacy and the demand that no one be excluded from the opportunity to understand and learn the rules of the culture of power? Despite understanding the challenge of reconciling this duality, Delpit remains optimistic that educational processes and institutions can move forward for teachers and learners. When she talks to teachers and others who care passionately about teaching, she hears snippets of consciousness and unconsciousness that offer strong clues as to what is missing from broader educational conversations. She clearly believes that closer attention to those clues can change our practices.

In the first essay of this final section, Delpit evaluates practices of teacher assessment, the development of which was at a fever pitch during the late 1980s. Groups all over the country were attempting to formalize and standardize instruments to shape and define teacher knowledge and to assess teacher competence in that knowledge. Delpit offers the insight that, rather than creating a gatekeeping exam like the bar exam for law school graduates or medical board exams for med school graduates, teachers need standards that are, in fact, less standard and more responsive to the conditions of practice. Not surprisingly for a scholar who is fascinated by language and linguistically driven culture, Delpit suggests that teaching is less like those traditional professions than like preaching. Preachers and teachers see their "clients" in groups and need to use language to reach those clients in the particular social context in which they live. Great teachers and great preachers make sense inside their context, although there are certainly shared values across contexts. It would seem odd, for example, to find a great teacher who didn't in some way evince caring for her students. That caring might be manifest in very different styles of interaction, from "tough love," to confidence building, to complete determination to impart a concept, to genuine warmth and affection.

Delpit's not-unreasonable concern is that the instruments that we tend to develop to assess professional competence—even if we move away from multiple choice, paper-and-pencil tests—do little to map conditions of knowledge and practice. However, she acknowledges that we do need to assess teacher performance, and she recommends that the standards be broadened and that performances required by the standards be made explicit to all candidates.[7] She encourages the use of "authentic assessment" that takes account of real settings in which teachers practice and calibrate the assessment location and construction beyond the university setting.

In the second essay in this final section, Delpit walks a very thin line as she addresses colleagues who are committed to social justice and empowerment of students who have been perceived as educationally and culturally deficient. The teachers she writes about here are very conscious of the ways in which language can be employed as a tool of oppression, and they have eschewed linguistic imposition. That is, their approach is at the opposite end of the continuum from those teachers referenced earlier who rely on constant dialect correction—that is, they emphasize the complete validation of the students' native idioms in the classroom. These teachers are critiquing classroom practices that, from their perspectives, buttress institutional racism by devaluing home culture. That perspective is clearly aligned with much of the work presented in this volume. Delpit, however, contends that the way these teachers run out this approach leads to paralysis at the point where Delpit wants them to teach the rules of the culture of power. This perspective instead advances a view that teaching the dominant discourses inevitably also teaches the superiority of those discourses. Further, Delpit asserts that despite their political commitments, many of these teachers do not genuinely believe that their students can successfully make use of dominant culture skills and rules.

Her critique of this progressive political stance and what follows from it is entirely consistent with Delpit's analysis of power. Her examples of overcoming the barriers of the culture of power, while powerful biographically, are grounded in the pre–Civil Rights Era. These biographies of successful code switchers do not acknowledge the fundamental changes that have taken place in the United States—the distribution of poverty, the effects of secondary segregation, and the demographics of teachers—all of which are central to bridging the gaps that she has so ably described throughout her book. She enjoins teachers to continue to pursue anti-racist, anti-oppressive practices in the classroom, but also to be conscious of how they are (partially) responsible for making genuine interventions in the conditions of unjust power in their communities, including in their classrooms. It is perhaps a necessary limitation of this volume that there can be no "rules" for dismantling the culture of power. Delpit is, instead, engaged in interventions intended to raise consciousness and encourage teachers and teacher educators to consider their practices anew and with a view of the "other," who is outside of their native worldview. They need to teach "more"[8] rather than less, more consciously rather than less, more openly rather than less.

It would be easy—and many of Delpit's critics certainly have found it so—to accuse Delpit of gross racial generalization[9] such as "all Black children" act this way or need this kind of instruction; "only Native teachers" can properly assess the needs of their children; "all White teachers" are part of and carriers of the culture of power. While many of the examples she employs in the essays that comprise the volume rely on racial differences, Delpit is clear that her first concern is the extent to which different voices (from whatever sources) have been silenced, ignored, or denigrated, and that these voices often carry the wisdom of excluded cultures. She wants to validate those experiences and those cultural voices, but she recognizes that any future advancement cannot rely solely on those who are "native" to minority cultures. Instead, those voices, perspectives, and cultural markers must be connected to dominant cultural forms in ways that are transformative for all students—and in those connective practices teachers at all levels must participate and expand their range of understanding.

Delpit's unflinching, direct discussion of a complex dynamic that exists in multiple cultural and educational settings has been widely adopted, criticized, incorporated, and challenged in higher education classrooms as well as in teachers' bibliographies. In addition to her introduction to the 2006 edition, which was written in the immediate aftermath of Hurricane Katrina, Delpit has written several other books since *Other People's Children*. "*Multiplication Is for White People*"[10] takes its title from the utterance of a frustrated African American boy. It is not focused on math skills as much as on the continued (and arguably increased) reliance on standardized testing in schools in the era of No Child Left Behind when, as Delpit and others argue, more and more children are in fact left behind. In this book, she extends her argument from the earlier volume that all children need to learn skills in ways that acknowledge social context and build critical thinking. Delpit's perspective continues to be needed in a time of increasing poverty, loss of resources in public schools, reliance on high-stakes testing,[11] and high-stakes racial and class divisions in the American social fabric—conditions that militate against high-quality schooling experiences for our (and other people's) children.

Notes

1   Originally published in 1995 by The New Press (New York). The New Press published a new edition in 2006, with a new introductory essay by Dr. Delpit and reflective essays by Herbert Kohl, Charles Payne, and Patricia Lesesne. Page references in this chapter are to the 2006 edition.
2   Delpit, 19.
3   Delpit, 24.
4   Delpit, 30.
5   Delpit cites Patricia M. Cunningham from her article "Teachers' Correction Responses to Black-Dialect Miscues Which Are Non-Meaning Changing," *Reading Research Quarterly* 12 (1976–1977), in which she tells the story of how the strategy of constant dialect correction of her own teacher-educator students sent them into a tailspin of frustration, shutting down, and tears. The story serves as a great example of how the experience of correction rather than instruction is a deterrent to learning.
6   This phrase has been variously attributed—I heard it as a tenet of sociology in the 1980s, most recently from C.W. Mills—but seems to have been first cited among the Romantic poets, probably the eighteenth-century German poet Novalis. http://alistair.cockburn.us/Making+the+strange+familiar,+and+the+familiar+strange (accessed April 3, 2015).

7   Delpit, 149.

8   Delpit, 173–175.

9   Joseph Check, "Book Review: *Other People's Children: Cultural Conflict in the Classroom*," *The Quarterly*, 18 no. 2 (1996): 29–35."

10 Lisa Delpit, *"Multiplication Is for White People": Raising Expectations for Other People's Children* (New York: The New Press, 2012).

11 Alan Blinder, "Atlanta Educators Convicted in School Cheating Scandal," *The New York Times*, April 1, 2015, http://www.nytimes.com/2015/04/02/us/verdict-reached-in-atlanta-school-testing-trial.html?_r=0, (accessed April 4, 2015).

TWENTY-SEVEN

David C. Berliner and Bruce J. Biddle, *The Manufactured Crisis: Myths, Fraud, and the Attack on America's Public Schools* (1995)

Mark Garrison

Introduction

Berliner and Biddle's *The Manufactured Crisis* (1995) was published during a critical point in the contemporary battle over how problems of public education are framed, understood and addressed in both public and academic discourse. Central to this turning point was not simply a continuation of the historic debate over the proper organizing focus of public education—vocational, college preparation, or comprehensive—or the connection of this focus to forms of inequality, but whether public schools *should continue to be public*. By the mid-1990s the now-dominant tendency of policy elites framing education narrowly in service of economic ends was also in full swing, with test scores and related data becoming prominent in discussions about the nature and functioning of American education. This chapter summarizes *The Manufactured Crisis* (TMC), understanding it as a response to this state of affairs, and examines its significance since its first publication 20 years ago.

While much of the critical narrative surrounding TMC focused on the efficacy of its claims—is there really no achievement crisis?—less attention has been paid to the significance of the thesis of a *manufactured crisis*, and how this thesis portends limited understanding of the objective nature of institutional *failure*. While the accuracy of the authors' claims about student achievement are reviewed, a key problem inherent in this debate is the tendency to uncritically attribute test score trends solely to public schools, and hitch uncritical notions of crisis to otherwise sophisticated analyses of data. *Crisis* is presented as a sociological reality not originating in the nonetheless real machinations of elites emanating from corporate, government, and philanthropic foundation offices. This perspective is offered to answer the question: What is the origin of the attack on public education by a class that historically fought for public school-ing as essential to the social order it once defended? In this way, the influence of Berliner and Biddle's work might be understood and used to evaluate current texts drawing on this now classic model.

An Overview of *The Manufactured Crisis*

The book's title readily suggests what the authors aimed to prove: disinformation about and misunderstandings of public schools have been consciously and systematically promoted to serve right-wing agendas. In this sense, TMC aimed for both a partisan and objective analy-sis, setting the record straight about public education while advocating for more politically progressive policy alternatives. Berliner and Biddle themselves (1996), in an effort to counter what they argued were misrepresentations of their work, presented a summary of TMC, also acknowledging that it had indeed become controversial (p. 10). They write:

> We began our book by noting that throughout most of the Reagan and Bush years, the White House led an unprecedented and energetic attack on America's public schools, making ex-travagant and false claims about the supposed failures of those schools, and arguing that those claims were backed by "evidence." (p. 2)

The book labeled this attack the manufactured crisis, and aimed to present, in Berliner and Biddle's words:

- the abundant evidence that contradicts its major myths;
- the likely reasons for its appearance in the Reagan and Bush years;
- the ways in which the "reform" proposals associated with this attack would be likely to damage America's public schools;
- the real and escalating social problems faced by our country and its schools, that lead-ers of the attack had but little interest in solving; and
- what can be done today to help solve the real problems of our schools. (Berliner & Biddle, 1996, p. 2)

Major Myths
The first 60 pages of TMC are focused on challenging popular presentations of what trends in standardized test scores revealed about public schools. But achievement, the authors claimed, was in fact not a problem. Student achievement, as assessed by standardized tests, did not de-cline sharply. American students did not "lag behind students in other Western countries" and America was not in danger of "falling into the ash can of history." These claims, the authors argued, are "nonsense" (p. 13; also see Berliner & Biddle, 1996).

Published criticisms of the TMC's handling of test data offer a good summary of both its arguments about student achievement and what key critics found problematic. Stedman, who self-identified as a progressive educator and who acknowledged agreement with the reform agenda promoted by Berliner and Biddle, produced a series of extensive and harsh criticisms of the interpretations of standardized test score data presented in TMC (Stedman, 1996a; Stedman, 1996b; also see Stedman, 1997). Stedman concluded that, while Berliner and Biddle "are generally right that achievement has been stable, they ignored important contradictory evidence and the 1970s decline" (1996a, p. 1). Stedman argued that TMC's authors errone-ously claimed that the SAT was the only test that showed decline.

> This is remarkable. High school students' NAEP civics scores, for example, dropped substan-tially between 1969 and 1976 and have been slipping ever since. Their science scores also fell during the 1970s and have only partly rebounded. In the late 1980s, younger students' NAEP reading and writing performance slipped. (pp. 1–2)

Berliner and Biddle (1996) countered, and presented NAEP data for civics, science, and reading, which supported TMC's claim of "general stability of scores over time" and thus no decline (p. 4; cf. Stedman, 1996a).

Stedman argued that while Berliner and Biddle attributed the SAT decline to demographic changes in test takers, they "never reviewed the evidence which shows this explains much, but not all, of the decline" (p. 2; also see Koretz, 2008). While average SAT scores suggested minor-ity gains, this "masked minority verbal [score] declines in the late 1970s and late 1980s" (p. 2). Again, Berliner and Biddle (1996) countered that these declines in minority verbal scores were not substantive nor was this conclusion of verbal decline supported by evidence from NAEP reading tests (p. 5).

Stedman also went to great lengths to argue that American students performed poorly rela-tive to students in other countries, especially in science and math. He argued that these results cannot be attributed to differences in curriculum, sampling or student demographics (1996b, pp. 4–5; 15–17; cf. Berliner & Biddle, 1996). Simply put, while Berliner and Biddle argued that the evidence does not support the conclusions that the United States faces an achievement crisis, Stedman (1996b) was steadfast in asserting, "the achievement crisis is real."

Berliner and Biddle (1995) also spent time countering other common myths about pub-lic education (pp. 65–125). This portion of the book, while equally important, received less critical attention. Over the span of another 60 pages, Berliner and Biddle marshaled evidence to disprove a variety of commonly repeated but false or misleading claims. For example, they showed that school textbooks were not amoral. Importantly, they also showed that school funding was related to academic achievement and that the United States did not overspend on schooling compared to other countries (for a primer on funding equity and how money mat-ters, see Baker [2015]). For example, using United Nations data, the authors showed that the United States ranked in the middle of 16 industrialized countries on K–12 per-pupil expendi-tures; disaggregated data revealed that the United States had a relatively high level of funding inequality compared to these Western countries (pp. 67–68). Private schools were not better than public schools, according to the authors (see Lubienski & Lubienski, 2014), nor did they find support for claims that there was a shortage of scientists to serve a high-tech economy. Many of these false claims are nonetheless constantly repeated in both public and academic forums.

One area in this section that received critical attention dealt with how TMC reported and interpreted survey data regarding public perceptions of public and private schools. Again, these criticisms came from Stedman, who worked to make the case that Berliner and Biddle's analyses were not to be trusted.

Berliner and Biddle used Gallup and Phi Delta Kappa survey data to claim that public school parents were "well satisfied with their schools" and "rate[ed] them highly" (p. 114). Stedman (1996a), in responding to Berliner and Biddle's response (1996) to his initial review

(1996a), pointed to what he saw as two problems—the first was conceptual, the second was empirical. First, Stedman questioned the value of parental opinion data. Few parents, he claimed, observe what goes on inside schools and have few if any indicators of the school's academic performance; if they did, he predicted, their opinion might be far more critical than it presently was (p. 19). Second, Stedman called Berliner and Biddle to task for the manner in which they reported the Gallup data. By combining ratings categories and eliminating the middle category, Stedman argued, positive ratings became inflated in the graph they presented. His own presentation of the same data showed, for example, that almost half the public school parents in 1993 expressed some displeasure with their community's schools, rating them a C or less (p. 20).

In the end, reading Berliner and Biddle (1995, 1996) and Stedman (1996a; 1996b) yields me to conclude this: student achievement is generally stable, and there is a tendency to overemphasize negative evidence and ignore positive trends in achievement and what this achievement might suggest about the relative (historically) positive effect of public schools. Yet it is hard to argue with Stedman's insistence that achievement levels should have been higher, and in some cases, then current performance levels were embarrassing. While the authors of TMC traced the "scores must be higher" logic to conservatives (p. 27), the demand is nonetheless compelling in light of the aim of a well-educated and active citizenry—a goal that few would argue has been fully realized. But while Berliner and Biddle may have overstated the case to make their point, Stedman's insistence on the existence of an "achievement crisis" relied on an unarticulated and seemingly common sense understanding of and standard for *crisis identification* (see Berliner & Biddle, 1996, p. 9), raising a whole host of new problems.

One problem is attribution. While one cannot help but appreciate efforts to set the record straight, the emphasis on test scores in particular has resulted in a significant problem that is especially evident with current policy, namely the use of student test scores to draw inferences about the quality of teachers (see Baker et al., 2013). Both TMC and Stedman sometimes stumbled in distinguishing between accurately discerning trends in test scores, and the validity of inferences about public school performance based on those test score trends. For example, quoting his earlier work, Stedman (1996b) reported that functional-literacy tests showed that between 20% and 30% of the population had difficulty with common reading materials, and he then stated that, "Even if schools are performing about as well as they have in the past ..." (p. 11), suggesting that tested literacy rates measured school quality. While literacy is obviously a desired outcome of schooling, trends in test scores vary with many out-of-school factors (Berliner, 2014).

Another good example of this problem can be found with Stedman's (1996b) discussion of NAEP civics, geography, and history exam trends. He presented self-evidently low levels of achievement to falsify TMC claims about student achievement: for example, following the Persian Gulf War, students had trouble identifying the Persian Gulf on a map. But schools are not the only—or even the main—source of information about civics or geography; neither are they the only social force to influence knowledge acquisition in those domains. Trends in these scores may have been related to the relatively large amount of time students spent watching TV (which Stedman documents: 1996a, p. 8), with half of those surveyed reporting that they watched three or more hours of TV each day in 1990. Berliner and Biddle (1996) suggested that mass media play an important role in informing and framing what knowledge is important and worth remembering, and, I would argue, often emphasized skills and content counter to what is presented and valued in schools. Thus, trends in scores, for better or worse, and whatever their inherent value, cannot be solely attributed to schools without empirical evidence and logical argument to support such attribution.

Thus, this debate, focused on test scores, seemed to inevitably bring along with it a logic that assumed student performance on any test was, *ipso facto,* a measure of public school quality. Many feel that in order to defend public schools, they must show positive test scores or dismiss low ones. But there is no necessary link between documenting problems with public schools and a rejection of the principle of public education or even the adoption of a particular reform idea. Score declines could easily be cited as a reason to call for increased funding for public schools (something, in fact, that TMC strongly advocated). Score declines could easily be used to justify calls to abandon the old, inherited methods that many students find unengaging. Again, TMC made these recommendations as well. But TMC assumed a necessary link between the myths and the policies advocated by the mythmakers *that does not in fact exist.* As I argue below, this is really a problem of values, one that is veiled by debates about data.

Origins of the Manufactured Crisis

Berliner and Biddle began this section of TMC by outlining a range of social factors that created the conditions for the public to be open to critiques of public education. The authors suggested a variety of important changes, including an aging population and a stagnating economy during the 1970s. As public education enrollment expanded to historic levels, so did education budgets. But not only were more students attending public schools; it was also increasingly expected that these schools would equally serve not only minority students, but also those with special needs as well. In fact, schools became the one social institution that was looked to for solutions to almost all social problems. This simultaneous increase in size, responsibility and expectation tensely coexisted with concerns about the economy and levels of taxation. Under these circumstances, it is not shocking that education became the subject of increased public scrutiny.

While Berliner and Biddle likened education bashing to a national sport, offering examples throughout American history, they contended that the election of Ronald Reagan signaled a turn to bring unprecedented support from government and industry to attack public schools. This political turn consisted of distinct political factions: the religious right, the new right, and neoconservatives (cf. Apple, 2001), and increasingly relied on private foundations (see Saltman, 2010) to launch a campaign against public education to either promote conservative reform ideas (excellence over equity) or the outright dismantling of public schools (e.g., vouchers). Again attempting to correct misconceptions regarding the aims of TMC, Berliner wrote (1996):

> This attack was led by specific persons—whom we named in our book—and created myths about education that were sometimes backed by no evidence at all, sometimes supported by misleading analyses of inappropriate data, and sometimes aided by the deliberate suppression of contradicting information. No such White House attack on public education had ever before appeared in American history—indeed, even in the depths of the Nixon years the White House had not told such lies about our schools. Since the attack was well organized and was led by such powerful persons—and since its charges were shortly to be echoed in other broadsides by leading industrialists and media pundits—its false claims have been accepted by many, many Americans. And these falsehoods have since generated a host of poor policy decisions that have damaged the lives of hard-working educators and innocent students. (p. 2)

While there is no doubt that these political factions acted as Berliner and Biddle suggested, and while the White House had not in the past acted as they describe, leading political figures, including the first Massachusetts Secretary of Education, Horace Mann, acted similarly during the Common School crusade in the mid-nineteenth century. There is in fact a very long history in the United States of assuming that public schools are failing and then working to find data that will support the favored reform agenda (Garrison, 2009).

What Is Wrong with American Education?
Berliner and Biddle had no illusions that public schools were perfect, or that they served all who attended them equally. They write:

> By now you may be convinced that American public schools had no problems, and that all concerns about the present state of American education is without merit.... Unfortunately, American schools face serious and real problems. Indeed, many of these problems are worse today than they were in earlier years, and many are more serious here than in other Western countries. (p. 215)

These problems were rooted in the social context of education, and TMC's authors assumed that understanding this social context was key to understanding what steps would actually help improve schools. For over 60 pages, TMC analyzed how social and economic inequality, economic stagnation and the restructuring of work constituted the "real problems of American education." Drugs, violence, discrimination, segregation, and the growth of suburbs, along with an aging population and competition for public funds, all created significant challenges for schools. Yet, these real social problems were rarely examined let alone taken into account when analyzing the performance of public schools or suggesting methods for school improvement (cf. Berliner, 2006). Although rather meekly, Berliner and Biddle recognized that racism has also been a feature of public schools themselves. For example, they report research that documented some school districts used "racially loaded procedures for sorting and disciplining students" (p. 230).

It might appear, then, that Berliner and Biddle asserted that what was wrong with public education was simply what was wrong with the United States. But this was not the case. The authors spent about 20 pages critiquing common features of American education.

> Real problems for schools are also generated by some of the everyday features of American education, but when distorted pictures of those features are painted, the public is likely to misunderstand these problems. It may be difficult to think about everyday features of education as a source of problems simply because they are familiar and are not normally examined closely. And yet, if we compare education in different countries, we discover that American education often has features that don't appear elsewhere. Moreover, it requires a historical perspective to understand some of the common, everyday features now found in American education and their consequences. (p. 241)

These features included such staples as the age-graded classroom, academic tracking, and ability grouping—all of which Berliner and Biddle contended contribute to a rigid curriculum. They also lamented an unhealthy emphasis on competition in schools and how this worked against the cultivation of social responsibility. Importantly, TMC also featured a section on the feminization of teaching, its relationship to a lack of role models for boys in the early grades and unequal employment status for women in the workforce. The authors also opposed bureaucratic structures for their role in limiting professional autonomy. Note, however, that while Berliner and Biddle decried oppressive bureaucracies, they nonetheless provided data in an earlier section of TMC challenging the view that education was top-heavy with administration (1995, pp. 79–81). The authors also saw the all-too-prevalent behaviorist assumptions governing public school practice, and linked those ideas to a reliance on standardized tests as key problems. In short, they oppose the "banking concept of education" (Freire, 2000), that is, that students should merely receive and regurgitate whatever knowledge teachers transmit to them.

A key problem faced by schools concerns the increasingly complex and varied types of achievement that have come to be expected of them (pp. 261–263). This point was especially important in light of efforts by school reformers to further narrow the purpose of education to the acquisition of workplace-related skills, and little else. Unrealistic expectations for schools helped create the conditions for a narrower focus as, somehow, a solution.

While many will agree with TMC's identification of key problems, one problem raised by the authors is less likely to be broadly accepted today: local control. While the authors noted that state and federal authorities had already increased their level of control over local school authorities (Conley, 2003; cf. Dorn, 2007), TMC presented an argument for further limiting the power of local school boards (pp. 259–261). Indeed, such limitation has occurred since 1995. With the rise of Common Core, Race to the Top, value-added models of teacher evaluation, along with a host of other federal and philanthropic initiatives, the power of local school boards has been effectively neutered without the predicted benefits of cost-reduction or wiser policy decisions (Garrison, 2015a, 2015b).

What Reforms?

A key aim of TMC is to link promotion of myths about public schools to a particular reform agenda. For example, claims that public school spending is unrelated to student outcomes, or that the United States spends too much money on education compared to other countries, are used to draw attention away from inequitable funding systems and toward an emphasis on accountability by way of high-stakes standardized testing. Not suppressing, TMC made a case against reforms promoted by the mythmakers and offered support for a range of alternative ideas for improving public education, generally understood as "progressive" in both political and educational terms. Unequal funding was to be corrected, and funding for schools, especially in high-needs districts, was to be increased. Vouchers are opposed, as are immersion language programs for students who do not speak English. While charter schools were not then the center of the education reform debate, the authors did support parental choice within a district, a practice that has yielded to, according to some observers, more inequality and no improvement (Glass, 2008). Berliner and Biddle also supported "small schools." Curriculum and teaching were conceived of as active, or "project based," and the authors recommended reducing the link between education and workplace skills, in favor of placing instead a greater emphasis on social goals, including the development of compassion. Finally, TMC called on educators to rethink how public schools assess achievement, advocating for "authentic" and "performance-based" approaches. As one example, Berliner and Biddle suggested a presentation of a "year-long project in social studies on the oral histories of local female senior citizens" to explore the changing role of women over time (p. 319). After all, these approaches are better suited to the curricular and pedagogical vision that TMC advanced.

Contexts and Crisis

The publication of TMC reflected the growing prominence of education as a political symbol (McGuinn, 2006), the politicization of education research and research reporting (Henig, 2008), and the foreshadowing of a new genre of public education advocacy literature targeted to broad albeit educated audiences (see Bracey, 1995, 2002; Berliner & Glass, 2014; Horn & Wilburn, 2013; Saltman, 2007, 2012). This new genre of literature defending public education is a historically important response to an odd feature of the American educational system that has existed at least since the Common School Movement of the nineteenth century (Bracey, 1995; Garrison, 2009; Tyack & Cuban, 1995). Tremendous faith is placed in public schools to solve an amazing array of complex social, economic, political and cultural problems, yet public schools have always been subjected to intense criticism that almost certainly seemed aimed at shaking public confidence in the very idea of this democratic endeavor.

The Manufactured Crisis also emerged from critical scholarship that emphasized the role of public schools in social reproduction, that is, in maintaining racist, sexist, and classist institutions (MacLeod, 2009). Suggesting their frustration with this literature, Berliner and Biddle cite the revisionist historian Joel Spring as someone who contributes to a "distorted picture of the history and current organization of American schooling," likening him to a "school basher" (p. 241). I think Berliner and Biddle saw this intellectual trend as creating doubts about the possibility of a truly public and democratic school system. Recalling my own doctoral studies, I can think of few (any?) positive portrayals of public education. I believe that TMC reflected the challenges many academics (especially liberal) faced at that time, and this reaction has resulted in a genre of literature defending public education and the democratic ideals it is to serve. Once the domain of leftist academics and radical community activists, social reproduction narratives started to be mobilized by right-wing forces to justify market-based and corporate inspired reforms. What was so good about "public" schools if they led to tracking, segregation, and the reproduction of social inequality (e.g., Hess, 2006)? This turn was especially evident among Third Way political forces that ascended to power with the Clinton administration following Reagan's battering ram against public schools, *A Nation at Risk* (Bracey, 1995).

But much of this debate in fact revolves around values and visions; it will not be sorted out empirically. A politically conservative push to back-to-basics might be justified on the basis of tested achievement, but what matters most is that back-to-basics is an expression of a desired social order conservative forces wished schools to contribute to bringing about (Apple, 2001). It is very important to understand that standardized testing was much more of a tool to bring this vision about than it was a tool for determining whether or not that vision had been realized.

An example from TMC can be used to highlight this point about vision. Berliner and Biddle correctly attribute a cause of increasing costs to an increase in services to students with special needs. And while the authors highlight that much of this increased cost was not due to waste, they fail to highlight that the enactment of special education laws reflected changing social expectations and values. Thus, interpretations of school performance are relative to school *purposes*, which in turn are relative to a society's level of social development and the aims that guide its educational initiatives, however conflict ridden they might be. Without an explicit set of goals, it is impossible to determine whether a test score decline or even test score increase means anything beyond the documented trend itself. Readers can imagine a situation where there is a documented increase in some skill or ability among young people, but that such an increase is insufficient for some purpose. But in place of explicit goals and democratically agreed upon means for assessing them, standardized tests sneak in a view of teaching and learning that serves certain interests, and not others (Garrison, 2009).

Thus, while TMC offers an analysis of the social circumstances that created the conditions for promotion of crisis rhetoric, neither TMC nor its critics offers a standard for answering the question: How do we know when an institution is in crisis? The use of the word becomes little more than rhetorical play. But institutions do face crises. My work suggests that the rhetorical crisis does in fact reflect a serious social crisis, one that is not manufactured (Garrison, 2009, 2015b)

A Crisis of Purpose, A Crisis of Politics

Education in the United States has been asked to serve a variety of purposes, and these purposes are in important ways competing (Labaree, 1997). While it was true that public schools were charged with developing citizens for the new republic, they were to serve other functions as well. One key role has been sorting out various types of social conflict and in administering and justifying an unequal distribution of various types of social benefits. According to Horace Mann, that famous nineteenth-century Common School crusader, the aim was to replace class struggle with the struggle for education. With this thesis, Mann placed at the schoolhouse door the task of meting out rewards and denying privileges, sorting out conflicts and establishing commonly accepted norms. As this process increasingly worked through schools' administration of credentials essential to the new industrial order then emerging, the role of standardized tests of ability and achievement increased (Garrison, 2009). Thus, public schools functioned to produce and justify certain types of equality (a certain kind of fairness) and certain types of inequality as well (high and low achievers, etc.).

The crisis that does exist, and the reason that elites whose social class once defended public education now attack it, is that schools are no longer serving as a viable means to administer inequality (Garrison, 2015b). They are failing in this respect, and this failure is a crisis of the social system. Public schools as historically organized are not capable of producing the extreme inequality that the emerging neoliberal austerity regime demands (e.g., Saltman, 2014). This neoliberal social order demands far greater inequality than that required by the liberal democratic order from which it emerged (see Brown, 2005). Thus the crisis is this: traditional public schools, even with their competing purposes, and even with admissions of lackluster performance, and even with their botched forms of community control, stand as a block to neoliberal reconstructions of the social world. The current *skillsification* of education and its logic of human capital evidence a crisis of purpose and a crisis of politics, and the elimination of public education is a means of resolving that crisis in favor of a section of the capitalist class. We are living through a turning point—indeed, a crisis—and it does not emerge from achievement tests or graduation rates. Targeting myths about public education without a clear standard regarding its purposes—those not narrowly inherited from the past but renewed for the future—will not serve to resolve the crisis from which the myths originate. This crisis emerges out of a historic battle over what should be the purpose of education and who decides.

References

Apple, M.W. (2001). *Educating the "right" way: Markets, standards, God, and inequality*. New York: Routledge.

Baker, B.D. (2015). On school finance equity & money matters: A primer. Retrieved from https://schoolfinance101. wordpress.com/2015/03/01/on-school-finance-equity-money-matters-a-primer/

Baker, B.D., Oluwole, J.O., & Green, P.C. III (2013). The legal consequences of mandating high stakes decisions based on low quality information: Teacher evaluation in the Race-to-the-Top era. *Education Policy Analysis Archives, 21*(5), 1–71. Retrieved from http://epaa.asu.edu/ojs/article/view/1298

Berliner, D.C. (2006). Our impoverished view of educational reform. *Teachers College Record, 108*, 949–995.

Berliner, D.C. (2014). Effects of inequality and poverty vs. teachers and schooling on America's youth. *Teachers College Record, 115*(12). Retrieved from http://www.tcrecord.org

Berliner, D.C., & Biddle, B.J. (1995). *The manufactured crisis: Myths, fraud, and the attack on America's public schools*. New York: Longman.

Berliner, D.C. & Biddle, B.J. (1996). Making molehills out of molehills: Reply to Lawrence Stedman's review of *The Manufactured Crisis*. *Education Policy Analysis Archive, 4*(3), 1–14.

Berliner, D.C., & Glass, G.V. (Eds.). (2014). *50 myths & lies that threaten America's public schools: The real crisis in education*. New York: Teachers College Press.

Bracey, G. (2002). *The war against America's public schools: Privatizing schools, commercializing education*. New York: Allyn & Bacon.

Bracey, G.W. (1995). *Final exam: A study of the perpetual scrutiny of American education: Historical perspectives on assessment, standards, outcomes, and criticism of U.S. public schools*. Bloomington, IN: Technos Press.

Brown, W. (2005). *Edgework: Critical essays on knowledge and politics*. Princeton, NJ: Princeton University Press.

Conley, D.T. (2003). *Who governs our schools? Changing roles and responsibilities*. New York: Teachers College Press.

Dorn, S. (2007). *Accountability Frankenstein: Understanding and taming the monster*. Charlotte, NC: Information Age.

Freire, P. (2000). *Pedagogy of the oppressed*. New York: Continuum.

Garrison, M.J. (2009). *A measure of failure: The political origins of standardized testing*. Albany, NY: SUNY Press.

Garrison, M.J. (2015a). Measurement as politics by other means: The case of test-based teacher evaluation. In K. E. O'Hare (Ed.), *Teacher Evaluation: The Charge and the Challenges*. New York: Peter Lang.

Garrison, M.J. (2015b). Value-added measures and the rise of anti-public schooling: The political, economic and ideological origins of test-based teacher evaluation. In P. Carr & B. Porfilio (Eds.), *The phenomenon of Obama and the agenda for education: Can hope audaciously trump neoliberalism?* Charlotte, NC: Information Age.

Glass, G.V. (2008). *Fertilizers, pills, and magnetic strips: The fate of public education in America*. Charlotte, NC: Information Age.

Henig, J.R. (2008). *Spin cycle: How research is used in policy debates: The case of charter schools*. New York: Russell Sage Foundation.

Hess, F.M. (2006). *Tough love for schools: Essays on competition, accountability, and excellence*. Washington, DC: AEI Press.

Horn, J., & Wilburn, D. (2013). *The mismeasure of education*. Charlotte, NC: Information Age.

Koretz, D.M. (2008). *Measuring up: What educational testing really tells us*. Cambridge, MA: Harvard University Press.

Labaree, D.F. (1997). Public goods, private goods: The American struggle over educational goals. *American Educational Research Journal, 34*(1), 39–81.

Lubienski, C., & Lubienski, S. T. (2014). *The public school advantage: Why public schools outperform private schools*. Chicago: University of Chicago Press.

MacLeod, J. (2009). *Ain't no makin' it: Aspirations & attainment in a low-income neighborhood* (3rd ed.). Boulder, CO: Westview Press.

McGuinn, P.J. (2006). *No Child Left Behind and the transformation of federal education policy, 1965–2005*. Lawrence: University Press of Kansas.

Saltman, K.J. (2007). *Capitalizing on disaster: Taking and breaking public schools*. Boulder, CO: Paradigm Publishers.

Saltman, K.J. (2010). *The gift of education: Public education and venture philanthropy*. New York: Palgrave Macmillan.

Saltman, K.J. (2012). *The failure of corporate school reform*. Boulder, CO: Paradigm Publishers.

Saltman, K.J. (2014). The austerity school: Grit, character, and the privatization of public education. *Symploke, 22*(1–2), 41–57.

Stedman, L.C. (1996a). Respecting the evidence: The achievement crisis remains real. *Education Policy Analysis Archives, 4*(7). Retrieved from http://epaa.asu.edu/ojs/article/view/630/

Stedman, L.C. (1996b). The achievement crisis is real: A review of the manufactured crisis. *Educational Policy Analysis Archives, 4*(1), 1–31. Retrieve from http://epaa.asu.edu/ojs/article/view/624

Stedman, L.C. (1997). Response: Deep achievement problems: The case for reform still stands. *Educational Researcher, 26*(3), 27–29.

Tyack, D.B., & Cuban, L. (1995). *Tinkering toward utopia: A century of public school reform.* Cambridge, MA: Harvard University Press.

Twenty-Eight

David Tyack and Larry Cuban, *Tinkering Toward Utopia: A Century of Public School Reform* (1995)

John L. Rury

Historians typically deal with change, or at least with changing circumstances, from one moment or period to another. For educational historians interested in schooling, these interests often find expression in the study of school reform—efforts to alter or modify institutions for the better. And it has a lengthy history. As long as schools have been linked to the peculiar American ideology of improvement through education, it seems someone has been trying to invent a better school. As students of history know, major periods in the development of American education are identified in terms of such change: common school reform, progressive reform, and equal rights reform are perhaps the most prominent examples. In each of these instances, along with innumerable others, schools responded to new ideas and changing social, economic, and political conditions. Whether they did so successfully, of course, is another question.

In this now-classic historical account, David Tyack and Larry Cuban examined the course of educational reform over the previous century, with a view toward informing current and future reform efforts.[1] Few history books have been as influential, at least judging from the number of citations it has accumulated in two decades. According to Google Scholar, *Tinkering* has been cited more than 3,500 times, easily eclipsing such older classic historical works as Lawrence Cremin's *Transformation of the School* (about 2,200) or *American Education: The Colonial Experience* (about 1,600), or even Tyack's earlier book, *The One Best System* (about 2,800 citations).[2] Rarely have works about educational reform been as widely cited, apart from those by luminaries such as Lee Shulman or Michael Fullan, least of all the contributions of historians.[3] *Tinkering* clearly resonated with a wide readership, extending far beyond the usual consumers of works in educational history and other foundational disciplines. It spoke to the much larger audience interested in educational reform: those wanting to change schools for the better.

This is a bit surprising, for *Tinkering* is hardly an exhaustive treatment of the topic; indeed, as a work of historical scholarship it is largely a sketch of selected themes. But more important, Tyack and Cuban offer a framework for interpreting reform, past and present, that draws heavily upon the work of certain sociologists, particularly those known widely as "neo-institutionalists." It is scarcely a coincidence, it seems, that the most prominent proponents of this perspective also work at Tyack and Cuban's institutional home, Stanford University. What is more, Tyack had been a coauthor with the doyen of neo-institutionalism, John W. Meyer, along with several of his prominent students.[4] Much of the success that *Tinkering* enjoyed stems from this line of influence; it is a historical account informed by sociological theory and research of a particular stripe. The book's most telling insights flow from an understanding of institutions gained from organizational analysis as well as historical research. The genius of Tyack and Cuban's contribution is that they marry these perspectives so successfully.

A Brief Introduction to Neo-Institutionalism

Institutions abound in modern society, and sociologists and other social scientists have long studied their behavior and interaction, along with their impact on individuals and society writ large. Perhaps the most basic definition of an institution is "stable, valued, recurring patterns of behavior," as postulated by Samuel Huntington some 50 years ago.[5] Some institutions are relatively informal, such as a family or a long-running weekly poker game, while others are bound by law, operated by means of formal rules and regulations, and often governed by bureaucratic systems of control. All are guided by a social purpose, whether implicitly or explicitly. Collectively, institutions shape and govern the behavior of individuals within a specific social setting, and today's society is densely populated with them. In this historical context, institutions interact with and influence one another, evolving in concert. Neo-institutionalism takes this process as its starting point.

In a classic statement of this perspective, John W. Meyer and Brian Rowan argued that organizations succeed when "institutional rules function as myths," which serve to legitimate their behavior, regardless of whether such rules or policies are rational or technically required to meet their goals.[6] Meyer and Rowan suggested that such features of organizational life are more than just norms, and indeed become the grounds for achieving legitimacy in a larger institutional field. This is critically important, because public acceptance or rejection of organizational behavior is often governed by prevailing mythologies regarding the sources of institutional success, whether it is utilizing appropriate expertise, following familiar patterns of conduct, or interacting with other legitimate organizations. Organizations that operate in fields with inherently ambiguous outcomes, such as schools and other educational institutions, are especially sensitive to these conditions. They are highly dependent upon popular impressions or tradition as a source of acceptability, and often utilize ritual and ceremony to assure constituents that they are indeed authentic purveyors of the products associated with their institutional purposes.

One consequence of this, although Meyer and Rowan did not dwell on it, is that institutions are typically slow to change, especially when their conduct is firmly associated with myth, ritual, and ceremony. Under these conditions, abandoning any prevailing mythology is a very risky business, as it potentially puts institutional legitimacy at peril. The stability of educational institutions has long been a complaint of would-be reformers, but too often such prospective change-agents forget that the organizational features they have targeted are embedded in a web of legitimizing ideas and practices, upheld by public perceptions with deep historical roots. Everybody has been to school, after all, and consequently most have a clear idea of how they think it is supposed to work. This informs the public's judgment, often making change quite difficult.

Meyer and his colleagues and students have studied the development of educational institutions and the expansion of schooling world wide to document the spread of these principles in recent history.[7] Isomorphic pressures prod schools everywhere along common pathways to growth. Another tenet of neo-institutionalism is that enrollments have expanded somewhat independently of economic and political developments, surging forward of their own momentum in a familiar S-shaped curve of contagion processes. This is taken as additional evidence of the mythical quality of institutional logic that informs popular behavior, regardless of technical requirements of the economy or political demands for conformity. Mass schooling developed largely because people everywhere held it to be good, enhancing future prospects both for individuals and communities.[8]

In the end, the neo-institutionalist perspective suggests that organizations such as schools, along with most other institutions in modern civilization, operate as belief systems that guide behavior and inform judgment in society at large. In the case of education, clearly a central institution in today's social structure, Meyer has even gone as far as to describe it as a secular type of religion, offering a form of transcendence that promises to mitigate uncertainty and insecurity about the future, while affirming social status and moral rectitude.[9] In order for particular institutions to benefit from these beliefs, however, they must conform to the expectations that sanction their status as legitimate purveyors of educational activities. This, of course, makes reform a very tricky proposition. It is this insight that informed much of Tyack and Cuban's analytical project in *Tinkering*, and accounts for much of its unique appeal.

A Sociologically Informed History

Tyack and Cuban readily acknowledged the influence of John Meyer on their thinking in this book, and cite the Meyer and Rowan article in particular. But they did not directly employ its sociological frame of reference or terminology in *Tinkering*. Rather, sociology operated in the background, shaping their analysis but seldom intruding or impinging upon the narrative. The book is written in the conversational tone characteristic of the best historical prose, but it is far from a conventional historical narrative. This, it turns out, is one of its principal strengths. It is fundamentally a book about ideas, many of them rooted in neo-institutional theory, but presented in engaging accounts of various reform experiments in the past. It is in these tales that the insights to be gained from sociological theory and research are shared. And since most people enjoy a good story, especially told by such skilled narrators, it has proven quite engaging.

If there is a dominant idea in *Tinkering* that can be linked to its sociological underpinnings, it is the suggestion that schools are fundamentally stable institutions. Yes, historians can readily point to periods of relatively rapid change in formal education, mostly during system-building moments of expansion. Sometimes schools are affected by large-scale cultural change, when prevailing organizational myths shift in one direction or another. Perhaps the 1960s and 1980s can be seen as examples of such periods in the United States. But the project that *Tinkering* undertakes is one of explaining the *absence* of change, a somewhat more challenging proposition than identifying shifts from one time to another. Accomplishing this with wit and aplomb, as Tyack and Cuban have, adds to the book's distinctiveness.

Two chapters in particular stand out with respect to the theme of stability. The first focuses on how schools change (or rather resist) reforms, and the other describes what Tyack labeled in an earlier article, "The 'Grammar' of Schooling."[10] With respect to neo-institutionalism, the latter is especially noteworthy. The term grammar, of course, is taken from linguistics, where it connotes a set of structural rules for composition of sentences, phrases, clauses, and other elements of language. As Tyack and Cuban suggest, these rules are rarely made explicit in everyday conversation or writing; instead they typically are learned in practice and are sustained by habit and familiarity. Observing them helps make communication clear and effective, reducing ambiguity and enhancing efficiency in speech and writing. While it may be easy to take such rules for granted, their transgression can prove quite disconcerting. Good grammar can enhance the acceptance or legitimacy of a speaker; bad grammar can have the opposite effect.

With reference to schooling, Tyack and Cuban use the metaphor of grammar to represent "organizational regularities" that include the age grading of students, ordering curricula into discrete subjects, and arranging classrooms with teachers at front and students sitting theater-style as audience.[11] Schools are structured as "egg-crate" shells of classrooms lining central hallways for batch processing of students, creating efficiencies in delivery of instruction and maintaining order.[12] Tyack and Cuban note that these features of schooling evolved as institutions adapted to changing conditions, particularly rising demand for education as the country grew and underwent urbanization.

At the same time that these and other features of organizational life made the task of serving large numbers of children more manageable, they also became associated in the public mind with the very meaning of schooling. Put into neo-institutionalist terms, the organizational mythology of schooling came to conform to this institutional structure. Consequently, certain beliefs became dominant: the authority of teachers is paramount, imparting order and discipline are essential tasks, and knowledge is best gained in disciplinary units conforming to such traditional subjects as reading, writing, mathematics, science, and history, along with vocational instruction. Institutions that deviated from these agreed-upon myths risked a loss of legitimacy, as was the case with progressive schooling in the mid-twentieth century. Tyack and Cuban do utilize this well-known example but focus on the fate of specific reform measures rather than the movement as a whole, befitting a book aimed at contemporary reformers.

As Tyack and Cuban observe, other institutional regularities became the stuff of normative isomorphism, even if they do not use the term. This was clearly evident in the case of the Carnegie unit, a measure of instructional time that established a common reference point for secondary schools.[13] This contributed to a mythology of uniformity as a desirable quality in schooling, underpinning the idea that course units and diplomas were interchangeable. Schools that ignored such measures potentially placed a burden on students, raising questions about their legitimacy as educational organizations. These were powerful incentives for schools to conform to prevailing views of what the public believed to be good educational practice. Given this, it is little wonder that American schools developed in a broadly similar fashion, despite a governance structure rooted in thousands of small, locally controlled districts. A shared educational mythology and institutional features such as the Carnegie unit, a broadly similar curriculum, and the ubiquity of age grading helped to define a national school "system" in the absence of practically any role for the federal government.

To a large extent, would-be reformers were compelled to offer a competing mythology in efforts to change the school. Tyack and Cuban note that progressive educators challenged the conventional wisdom in schooling, arguing that the practices and policies that comprised the familiar grammar of institutions were constricting and repressive. They offered new myths about the virtue of freedom and spontaneity in learning, the importance of play in personal growth, and the cultivation of creativity in openness. Helen Parkhurst's Dalton School called for a somewhat clear break with the past, as did the secondary institutions involved in the Eight-Year Study during the 1930s. As Tyack and Cuban point out, moreover, there is little evidence that students in these schools learned less than their peers in more conventional institutions. But prevailing beliefs and practices proved resistant to change. Teachers complained about the extra effort these schools entailed, and much of the public wondered about standards and discipline in such non-conforming settings.[14] In short, these progressive experiments were judged to be problematic, not due to educational failings but rather because they fell outside the prevailing mythology of what real or good schools were supposed to do.

Reconsidering the Nature of Reform

Ever responsible historians, Tyack and Cuban point out that schools have indeed changed in dramatic ways over the past century, and that much "reform" has worked to create the multi-faceted yet highly standardized educational system we have today. Along the way a great many alternative visions were offered, and a few novel ideas actually found their way into practice. For the most part, however, the tale that Tyack and Cuban tell is not a happy one for would-be reformers. Once the basic elements of the present system were in place, schools proved remarkably impervious to wholesale change. When changes did occur, they tended to be incremental, adding to the existing mode of schooling rather than dramatically altering it.

In the book's chapter on how schools change reforms, Tyack and Cuban consider the kindergarten and the junior high school, large-scale augmentations to the existing system of schools that began as reform proposals.[15] In both cases, advocates had high hopes that adding new steps or features to existing school structures would aid students at key developmental stages, just before they started elementary school and during the transition to secondary school or to work. Both were associated with a progressive outlook on schooling, offering a considerably more open or flexible approach to curriculum and learning, especially in the kindergarten. The junior high was meant to help students prepare for high school, but also to assist those who did not plan to attend beyond grade eight. Since both were new, they seemed to offer reformers a blank canvas upon which to imagine new possibilities for teaching and learning.

In a telling commentary on the fate of such educational reforms, however, Tyack and Cuban argue that the mythology of the larger school structure was too powerful to resist. Most such innovations become integrated into the existing system, usually without effecting dramatic changes. In the cases of the kindergarten and the junior high, both were considered fundamental reforms when first implemented. In time, however, each came to be seen as largely routine steps in the larger educational system. While it is true that the kindergarten and junior high have retained something of their distinctive identities, both were modified to better serve the grades above them. In this respect, it is possible to say that they, too, were compelled to conform to dominant organizational beliefs about public schooling. Tyack and Cuban cite these cases in suggesting that schools change reforms.[16] Without altering the larger system and its traditions, partial alterations such as these are not likely to retain whatever radical flavor they started with. In school reform, it seems, there has long been a grand regression toward the mean.

Of course, there has been much talk in the past century about educational reform, but Tyack and Cuban suggest that it has borne rather little on what actually happens in schools. Indeed, their distinction between "policy talk" and actual policymaking in schools is an important theme in the book (and one reflected in the earlier work of both authors).[17] It is not clear, for instance, whether the intense debates between progressive educators and their conservative opponents really affected the classrooms of most American teachers, as Cuban has shown in his seminal work *How Teachers Taught*.[18] Elsewhere Cuban has suggested that educational practice, the work of teachers in the "black box" of classrooms, has been largely unaffected by the stormy debates of policy advocates on the national stage.[19] As noted in *Tinkering*, educational technologies such as motion pictures, radios, and even computers have not altered the basic shape of the educational enterprise, despite the occasionally grandiose claims made by their promoters.[20] Tyack and Cuban suggest that much policy talk about schools often seems to lack appreciation for the historical processes that created the existing educational system, and hence ultimately proves ineffectual.

It is important to consider the sources of resistance to reforms that attempted to offer new ideas for organizing the entire system of instruction. Here, too, policy advocates fought an uphill battle; and few of these efforts appear to have exerted lasting influence. A telling example was the Dalton Plan, which attempted to offer high school students greater freedom and individual choice in designing curricula. As noted earlier, difficulties arose, however, when students transferred to other schools or applied to colleges. The existence of a larger system within which all schools must function proved to be a debilitating condition that ultimately hobbled even the most promising policy initiatives at the school level. Prevailing conceptions of education and organizational myths that guide public thinking were critical sources of stability, but hardly the only ones.

Tyack and Cuban argue that more was at work in these cases than simply the logic of systemic resistance to change. They also point to the teachers who worked in these schools. Allowing (indeed, encouraging) greater curricular freedom in the Dalton schools meant more work for teachers, as did such other innovations as open classrooms and the "new" math in the 1960s. Tyack and Cuban maintain that this is perhaps the biggest stumbling block to school reform. Without changes in the ways teachers work or are compensated, many reforms place great burdens on the very people who are responsible for making innovation successful: educators. Here is where the divide between policy talk and classroom practice is probably widest. While policymakers are free to speculate about ways to improve the system, teachers must contend with the daily task of controlling and motivating scores of students, many of whom would rather not cooperate. This makes their interest in reform quite different from the grand designs favored by many policy advocates. Teachers generally would rather have practical ideas, easy to utilize in their everyday work settings.

The reforms that teachers favor tend not to entail changes to the entire system. Instead, they represent alterations that modify things in a manageable way, without adding appreciably to the work of instruction. Recognizing this led Tyack and Cuban to advocate a reform strategy that would "graft thoughtful reforms onto what is healthy in the present system."[21] They were dubious about measures to privatize schools or employ competition, technology, and testing to foster greater attention to outcomes. Rather, they looked to promising programs to improve instruction and help struggling schools in an incremental rather than a revolutionary manner. This way, the involvement and commitment of educators arguably can be best realized. In the end Tyack and Cuban tell a cautionary tale. School reform is unlikely to succeed without involving educators. When the present educational system was in its formative stages at the end of the nineteenth century, massive systemic reform was possible. Belief systems and mythology about schooling were still somewhat malleable at that time. The authors of *Tinkering* suggest such change is far more difficult today.

A Prescription for the Future?

Obviously, the Tyack and Cuban thesis about the effect of the larger educational system, public expectations, and the influence of educators on school reform will have to be tested by further research on the history of reform—and by experience. Their book provides a rich agenda for scholars interested in reform issues, although it also focuses them on a particular conceptual frame of analysis. In the meantime, prospective school reformers would be well advised to consult it. The history of failure in school reform is perhaps more important in this respect than the record of success. This probably was *Tinkering*'s most unique contribution. But it was published two decades ago, and it is now possible to ask just how its arguments have held up over time.

In the book's prologue, Tyack and Cuban expressed hope that their discussion of past school improvement efforts would "contribute to the broader conversation about educational reform today." They noted that "in the last generation, reforms have come thick and fast, as educators can testify."[22] But they apparently did not anticipate the major reform initiatives that lay just around the corner, temporally speaking. The most important, of course, was No Child Left Behind (NCLB), which transformed the federal role in education dramatically. It was a large-scale reform effort, conducted on a national stage, precisely of the sort that Tyack and Cuban had cautioned against, and thus provides an interesting case to examine in light of the book's prescriptions.[23] This points to some of the limitations of their analysis, and to some of their insights as well.

NCLB represented a massive effort to reform schooling in a particular manner, largely from the top down. Such an approach, of course, was *not* focused on identifying the interests or needs of educators, as *Tinkering* had prescribed. In fact, NCLB quickly came to be quite unpopular among teachers—along with much of the public—fostering a good deal of resentment and resistance to the very idea of reform.[24] While the course of national school reform may not have followed the path that Tyack and Cuban had hoped for, it likely contributed to the popularity of *Tinkering* as a commentary on reform—at least among educators dissatisfied with national policy initiatives. The idea that reform should take teachers' ideas into consideration resonated strongly with critics of NCLB.

In many respects, however, the direction of school reform following George W. Bush's election in 2000 could hardly have been a big surprise to Tyack and Cuban, especially given their neo-institutionalist frame of reference in *Tinkering*. Education had become an important political issue in the wake of liberal reforms during the 1960s and 1970s, amid popular perceptions that academic and disciplinary standards had declined significantly. The critical national commission report *A Nation at Risk* had set the stage for this in 1983 and led to widespread use of standardized assessments to gauge curricular alignment and school-level outcomes. This helped to focus public attention on academic achievement as a reflection of school effectiveness.[25] In short, the prevailing myths about good schooling had shifted decisively in the direction of greater fidelity to traditional conceptions of school discipline and to public education's academic purposes. Reflecting this, test scores became an unavoidable source of legitimacy and status for schools and districts.

This call for change was somewhat different from those considered by Tyack and Cuban in *Tinkering*. Rather than adding to the tasks of schooling or changing its structure, this reform demanded that educators perform the core duty of academic instruction more effectively, at least as measured by standardized tests. The robust technology of standardized assessment became the mechanism by which reform was imposed on schools. Institutions were compelled to respond, largely because of federal dollars they could forfeit, but also because few were willing to defy the imperative to improve achievement. Academic instruction had long been a central rationale for the existence of schools, so it was virtually impossible for educators to resist the call for its enhancement, at least publically. The imposition of reform, and the threat of sanctions for non-compliance, did lead many to suggest that standardized tests were poor reflections of achievement.[26] But these arguments were often met with indifference, if not hostility, as they inevitably appeared to be defeatist, despairing, or self-serving. As one scholar put it, the American public supported testing and accountability.[27] This was a national reform measure like no other in American history, and it demanded changes that could not be accommodated within the existing system or with relatively little effort, at least in many schools.

There were other dimensions to NCLB, of course, particularly a requirement that historically under-achieving subgroups be tested for achievement. This was linked to an expectation that their progress would be a critical criterion in determining a school's success. This was a historic measure aimed at reducing or eliminating achievement gaps, but it became a source of consternation for many educators who had long ignored the academic performance of minority students. Now they were compelled to address the problems these students faced and focus on raising their achievement. This, too, became a source of anxiety for many educators, but not one that could be easily addressed within the prevailing structure of public schooling in the United States. This was not a problem that could be addressed by simply modifying existing school structures.

The problems that NCLB posed for educators highlighted some features of prior reforms that made them more amenable to change by the schools. Perhaps the most basic concerned the specificity of outcomes. Reforms such as the kindergarten, junior high schools, the Dalton plan, and the Eight-Year Study did not entail precise measurement of results. Indeed, each of them involved outcomes that were rather vague or ambiguous: healthier child development, greater freedom in learning, more creativity in teaching, or a better balanced, well-rounded education. While hard to argue with, goals such as these were difficult to ascertain with exactitude, making it relatively easy to modify reform measures to fit existing models of schooling. Reforms with ambiguous or uncertain outcomes, it seems, were more amenable to being changed by the schools.

Yet another feature of these past reforms is that they promised changes in aspects of school life that were somewhat ancillary to the central task of instruction. Even the Dalton plan, which proposed to give students a more central role in shaping their studies, was primarily a curricular reform rather than a change in teaching. The same might be said of reform measures undertaken by schools in the Eight-Year Study. This limited their potential impact. Since the focal point of most educators' work is instruction, reforms that do not directly affect it are unlikely to persist in any meaningful way. This, of course, echoes Tyack and Cuban's point about teacher resistance to reform. Changes that occur outside the classroom and that do not involve teachers in their formulation and development are unlikely to have a lasting effect. NCLB, on the other hand, posed a direct challenge to teaching without mandating any specific changes to it. In this respect it was perhaps the first major reform effort to finally breach the classroom door, or at least to attempt it. In this respect, it was unlike the other reforms discussed in *Tinkering*.

In other respects, however, Tyack and Cuban did indeed anticipate many aspects of school reform that would emerge in light of the new focus on instructional enhancement fostered by NCLB. Thoughtful reformers sought to help teachers collaborate on improved teaching, developing professional learning communities, and other means to assist one another in focusing on higher achievement. Researchers identified leadership roles for teachers and principals that contributed to improved academic performance, even in schools that were historically low-achieving.[28] Just as Tyack and Cuban suggested, studies found that involving teachers directly in the process of school improvement often resulted in significant progress. And the process of change was gradual, often proceeding by trial and error and advancing in increments. This was reform by success at tinkering. Good teaching, it turns out, was a major contributor to realizing the gains that NCLB called for, but it was not achieved by a dramatic reinvention of schooling. It put teachers and instructional improvement right at the center of change, finding a way to move ahead that prior reform efforts had not offered. This, too, was quite consistent with the reform model suggested in *Tinkering*.

NCLB, of course, also became associated with a number of problems in the schools, not least among them cheating by teachers and administrators to misrepresent achievement scores. Preoccupation with standardized assessments led to an inordinate level of attention to test preparation, a certain amount of outright cheating, and a narrowing of the curriculum, along with heightened anxiety for students and teachers alike. But it did focus attention on instruction in a way that earlier reforms had not. This, as suggested above, opened the door to yet other reform measures that promise to improve schooling in ways that hardly seemed possible in earlier times.

In light of research conducted in the past decade or so, it appears that one of the key points to instructional improvement is helping teachers to work together, collaborating on common instructional problems and learning from one another as they deepen their competence. Teachers assuming leadership roles has also taken on new significance in light of these developments, along with administrators serving as instructional leaders. In short, key changes in the schools have focused less on curricular or structural change than on modifying the roles of educators to focus more resolutely on the improvement of student learning. This is very much in line with what Tyack and Cuban recommended in *Tinkering*, even if its genesis may have been somewhat different from what they imagined as a reform agenda. In the end, they appear to have been correct about the prospects for success in reforming the schools: without the collaboration of educators on the ground, meaningful educational reform is not possible. That insight may well be an enduring contribution to the field of educational research.

Notes

1   David B. Tyack and Larry Cuban, *Tinkering Toward Utopia: A Century of Public School Reform* (Cambridge, MA: Harvard University Press, 1995).

2   Lawrence Cremin, *Transformation of the School: Progressivism in American Education, 1876–1957* (New York: Alfred A. Knopf, 1961); Cremin, *American Education: The Colonial Experience* (New York: Harper & Row, 1970); David B. Tyack, *The One Best System: A History of American Urban Education* (Cambridge, MA: Harvard University Press, 1974).

3   See Lee S. Shulman, "Knowledge and Teaching: Foundations of the New Reform," *Harvard Educational Review* 57 no. 1 (Spring 1987): 1–23, cited more than 11,000 times; or Michael Fullan, *The New Meaning of Educational Change* (New York: Teachers College Press, 2007), cited more than 15,000 times.

4   John W. Meyer, David B. Tyack, Joanne Nagel, and Audri Gordon, "Public Education as Nation-Building in America: Enrollments and Bureaucratization in the American States, 1870–1930," *American Journal of Sociology* 85 no. 3 (November 1979): 591–613; David Tyack and Aaron Benavot, "Courts and Public Schools: Educational Litigation in Historical Perspective," *Law & Society Review* 19 no. 3 (1985): 339–380.

5   Samuel P. Huntington, "Political Development and Political Decay," *World Politics* 17 no. 3 (1965): 394.

6   John W. Meyer and Brian Rowan, "Institutionalized Organizations: Formal Structure as Myth and Ceremony," *American Journal of Sociology* 83 no. 2 (September 1977): 340–363.

7   John W. Meyer, Francisco O. Ramirez, and Yasemin Nuhoğlu Soysal, "World Expansion of Mass Education, 1870–1980," *Sociology of Education* 65 no. 2 (April 1992): 128–149; Evan Schofer and John W. Meyer, "The Worldwide Expansion of Higher Education in the Twentieth Century," *American Sociological Review* 70 no. 5 (December 2005): 898–920.

8   For discussion of this, see John L. Rury, Argun Saatcioglu, and William Skorupsky, "Expanding Secondary Attainment in the United States, 1940–1980: A Fixed Effects Panel Regression Model," *Historical Methods*, 43, no. 3 (July 2010): 139–152.

9   John Meyer, "Reflections on Education as Transcendence," in *Reconstructing the Common Good: Coping with Intractable American Dilemmas*, ed. Larry Cuban and Dorothy Shipps (Stanford, CA: Stanford University Press, 2000), 209–221.

10   David Tyack and William Tobin, "The 'Grammar' of Schooling: Why Has It Been So Hard to Change?" *American Educational Research Journal* 31 no. 3 (September 1994): 453–479.

11   Tyack and Cuban, *Tinkering Toward Utopia*, 9.

12   Ibid., 164.

13   Ibid., 86.

14   Ibid., 87–97.

15   Ibid., Chapter 3.

16   Ibid., 83.

17   This term appeared in Larry Cuban, *How Teachers Taught: Constancy and Change in American Classrooms, 1880–1990*, 2nd ed. (New York: Teachers College Press, 1993), 276; also see David Tyack, "Public School Reform: Policy Talk and Institutional Practice," *American Journal of Education* 100 no. 1 (November 1991): 1–19.

18   Cuban, *How Teachers Taught*, Chapter 8.

19   Larry Cuban, *Inside the Black Box of Classroom Practice: Change Without Reform in American Education* (Cambridge, MA: Harvard Education Press, 2013), Part 1.

20   Tyack and Cuban, *Tinkering Toward Utopia*, Chapter 5; also see Larry Cuban, *Oversold and Underused: Computers in the Classroom* (Cambridge, MA: Harvard University Press, 2001), passim.

21   Tyack and Cuban, *Tinkering Toward Utopia*, 133.

22   Ibid., 4, 6.

23   On the genesis of NCLB, see Maris Vinovskis, *From A Nation at Risk to No Child Left Behind: National Education Goals and the Creation of Federal Education Policy* (New York: Teachers College Press, 2008), Chapter 7; and Patrick J. McGuinn, *No Child Left Behind and the Transformation of Federal Education Policy, 1965–2005* (Lawrence: University Press of Kansas), passim.

24   "No Child Left Behind Worsened Education, 48 Percent of Americans 'Very Familiar' with the Law Say in Gallup Poll," *Huffington Post Education*, August 21, 2012, http://www.huffingtonpost.com/2012/08/21/no-child-left-behind-wors_n_1819877.html (accessed April 3, 2015).

25   Vinovskis, *From A Nation at Risk to No Child Left Behind*, passim.

26   Alfie Kohn and Lois Bridges, *The Case Against Standardized Testing: Raising the Scores, Ruing the Schools* (Portsmouth, NH: Heinemann, 2000), passim.

27   McGuinn, *No Child Left Behind and the Transformation of Federal Education Policy*, 192.

28   On this point see Anthony S. Bryk, Penny Bender Sebring, Elaine Allensworth, Stuart Luppescu, and John Q. Easton, *Organizing Schools for Improvement: Lessons from Chicago* (Chicago: University of Chicago Press, 2010), 73, 239; and Richard Elmore, *School Reform from the Inside Out: Policy, Practice, and Performance* (Cambridge, MA: Harvard Education Press, 2004), passim.

TWENTY-NINE

Jean Anyon, *Ghetto Schooling: A Political Economy of Urban Educational Reform* (1997)

Aaron M. Kuntz

"If I had a gun I'd kill you. You're all hoodlums." (White fifth-grade teacher)[1]

The above epigraph, in all its starkness, is perhaps the most cited of Anyon's seminal text on urban schooling and educational reform in the later decades of the twentieth century. It is referenced in a host of reviews, educational and political commentaries, journal articles, and books. It was also the lead-in that *The New York Times* used to begin Jean Anyon's obituary two years ago.[2] In many ways the quote epitomizes the layered problems that Anyon's text addresses: historically embedded violence, racism, power disparities, stereotyping, and the inability to enact educational reform in contextual isolation.

That these two sentences were uttered by a White teacher to a fifth-grade class of predominantly poor, urban, African American students highlights the many ways in which problems of education are entangled in power-laden histories that exceed individual attention—isolate one element and you lose sight of a host of additional factors, all equally heavy with the weight of systemic inequality. This, then, might be the force that propelled Anyon's *Ghetto Schooling* into the realm of "classic" texts on education: a stringent determination to recognize the macro-level implications of poverty, racism, and ghettoization (to name but a few) on more localized educational reforms, policies, and practices, even as such micro-level enactments are shown to reinforce larger social trends.

Anyon's work remains remarkable today because of its impact on how we think about education, reform, and the complex inter-layers of social inequity. Beyond the content of the text, *Ghetto Schooling* serves as a methodological reminder of how to interrogate select social issues (often distinguished for the benefit of conceptual clarity) without losing sight of their intersection—the many ways in which they fold back upon themselves for explanatory power and self-sustaining reason. In this way, Anyon offers an extended case study of urban educational reform as a social skein—an entangled mass of intersecting social (dis)orders that finds meaning through its intersections. Rather than unwind the tangle and risk simplification, Anyon points to where connections occur, asking reformers and researchers alike to take critical aim at the density where points meet, where layer becomes fold, and where more than superficial reform is warranted if productive social change is to occur in any sustained way.

If I had a gun, I'd kill you. The promise of violence in urban educational contexts brings with it an anxious fear, one that often extends from anxieties that the uneducated (uneducable?) are inherently violent. Of course, this utterance was perhaps particularly jarring in that it was spoken by a White teacher to a classroom of ten- and eleven-year-old African American children. And yet, housed within this promise of violence is an enduring impotence: *I have no gun, I cannot kill you.* This doubleness—of violence, of impotence—is perhaps what made this quotation stand in for the entirety of the text in so many reviews of this book specifically, and Anyon's work on educational reform more generally. What are we to do with the threats inherent in the urban school context when we feel that the problems escape us, when trying to solve one problem inevitably leads us to a host of others? What are we to do when the fabrics of the skein fold back on themselves?

You're all hoodlums. Extending such anxieties is the social premise that some children simply cannot learn—they are stereotyped as beyond the reach of education. Further, there lies a historical (and, in the specific context of this book, this history is classist, racist, and geographically situated) stereotype that this deficiency is ultimately the responsibility of the individual in question. The educational system generally (and the teacher in the book, in particular) remains helpless against the perceived classroom of self-determined hoodlums. This is a violent helplessness, one that turns the frustration of immediate context back on the very students who, as Anyon shows, remain caught up in a complex history of social injustice. Thus, the stereotyped assertion (we might today substitute the term "thugs" for "hoodlums" in order to convey a similarly racialized identity) justifies the violent articulation even as it removes the responsibility for change from the social arena and places it on the individual in question.

When the two sentences come together, they seem to articulate and stand in for a sense of violent helplessness, one that seeks to strike out at the perceived products of social undoing. *If I had a gun I'd kill you. You're all hoodlums.* It is thus easy to become disheartened—even depressed—by the vast expanses of historical inequity that are detailed throughout *Ghetto Schooling,* as there seems to be no apparent entry point through which one might instigate positive change. These are the dangers, perhaps, of texts that demonstrate the destructive powers of social reproduction: incessant reproduction of structural inequality inevitably leads to apathy or dystopic visions of any effective change. And yet, when considered in the light of the dialectical qualities inherent in materialist analysis, Anyon might be read to provide a vast map of the educational terrain—one that does not prescribe specific changes for specific effects, but rather supports areas for intervention. Such intervention necessarily involves social institutions that overlap with (indeed, from Anyon's perspective, envelop) education: poverty reform, a revolution in class structure, and a determination to take seriously the implications of urban decay in all its many manifestations.

As a consequence, Anyon begins from the premise that if true educational change is to occur, it must extend from a systematic change to the larger economic structures that so dominate our contemporary society. We cannot talk about any social institution in isolation. Reform begins with the critical act of interrogating the multiple historical intersections that draw together political, economic, and educational structures into patterned ways of knowing, coming to know, and living.

With these issues in mind, I use this chapter to consider *Ghetto Schooling* within a critical framework, one that engages assertions of isolated "reform" with suspicion. After reviewing what the text *does*—that is, what it has to say about educational reform, suburban elitism, and everyday educational practice—I turn to how Anyon *does it*, paying particular attention to the Marxist engagements of this work and the means by which Anyon engages in a type of critical geographical analysis that has endured to classic status. Reading *Ghetto Schooling* as part of a critical geographical tradition allows us to understand why the text remains so powerful even with the passage of time. Though situations and contexts have perhaps changed, the fundamental elements of inequality remain strikingly visible within the field of education, indeed even amplified and accelerated given the globalized neoliberal values that predominate our contemporary moment. As such, Anyon's poignant critique becomes all the more relevant and essential today than it was nearly 20 years ago.

Organizational Overview of the Text

Ghetto Schooling is divided into three sections: "The Present," "The Past," and "Learning from the Past." Part I, "The Present," offers a contextual overview of schools in Newark, New Jersey, positing the overarching arguments that carry Anyon's text: one cannot understand school reform efforts in isolation but must instead recognize the ongoing effects of poverty and racism on schooling; conceiving of school reform in isolation risks perpetuating the very overarching biases that maintain large-scale educational inequity in our society. Importantly, Anyon establishes class and racial isolation as historical, noting the many ways in which a legacy of exploitation manifests in present-day educational reform and practice. As Anyon notes, "For schools—like people—are products of their past as well as of their present."[3]

As such, Anyon offers a compelling argument for reading the case of Marcy Elementary School (a pseudonym for the school at the center of Anyon's study) not simply in isolation but according to the geographical and historical contexts in which it is situated. To understand Marcy Elementary School, one must consider the urban context of Newark. To understand Newark, one must delve into the historical development of the region. To understand the historical development of the region, one must understand the social discourses (of race, class, and education) that extend across time and space (and, of course, in which we participate in the present day). In this way, Anyon builds a case for understanding the shocking inequalities she witnesses throughout her time at Marcy Elementary not as isolated instances bound by the walls of the school itself, but as a product of a distinct and patterned history of classism and racism that all too often results in overwhelming tragedy and shocking violence.

In this sense, Anyon's presentation of what otherwise might be understood as localized or immediate circumstance (a teacher threatening a student, an administrator screaming at a teacher) reverberates across time and space. These are the effects of social circumstances that we, ourselves, play a part in each and every day as we make our way within an increasingly hyper-capitalistic and racist society. In short, Marcy Elementary's "present" is our own. Implied in such an assertion is that in order to truly reform Marcy, we will need to simultaneously challenge our own ways of thinking, knowing, and being; educational reform can only happen within large-scale social reform, never without.

Part II of Anyon's book, "The Past," is its longest and most central. Here Anyon offers a detailed historical account of educational, political, economic, and geographic trends throughout the country and links their intersection to the incessant failure of school reform measures to bring about any sense of real educational or social change. If Marcy Elementary is situated as a case study for "failing" urban school reforms in Part I, Newark, New Jersey, serves as a case study in Part II for the economic and social devastation brought about by the political isolation of American cities that took place in the latter decades of the twentieth century. Anyon's detailed historical analysis reveals what she terms the "gradual ghettoization and stigmatization over time of the city's minority poor," a result of the economic disenfranchisement of urban areas, a revamping of educational policy to protect suburban norms, and daily educational practices that draw upon a building legacy of race and class inequality for their implied rationale.[4] Anyon thus launches her case to understand the many ways in which geographical formations reveal underlying fears, anxieties, and inequities of our shared society.

The explication of a historical political economy throughout Part II is perhaps what *Ghetto Schooling* has become most known for in education policy circles. As such, Anyon's text provided the long-sought-after evidence for more theoretical claims regarding social injustice and schooling that stem from Marxist interrogations of educational systems in the United States throughout history. Indeed, in her later text, *Marx and Education*,[5] Anyon notes that *Ghetto Schooling* remained part of a larger project to provide empirical evidence for Samuel Bowles and Herbert Gintis's[6] theoretical assertions regarding the intimate connection between the educational system and the needs of the larger socioeconomic system.

Thus, *Ghetto Schooling* extends the Marxist "correspondence theory"—linking educational processes and practices with continuing social and economic inequality—through tracing its empirical realities over time and across space. In this way, Anyon's pivotal historical work links theory with practice, giving her critiques all the more power and, even more important, her calls for radical change all the more urgency. As a result, a host of educational theorists who employ theories of social reproduction and/or some variant of historical materialism owe a debt to Anyon's evidence for structural inequality across multiple social institutions.

Perhaps less recognized—though no less a feature in Part II—is Anyon's keen use of geographic and social relationality to demonstrate the far-reaching effects of race and class bias in our culture on educational policy, practice, and (failed) attempts at reform. In this instance, we might rightly place Anyon's work within the aligned (and similarly Marxist-influenced) field of *critical geography*. Most notably, critical geographers such as David Harvey,[7] Doreen Massey,[8] and Edward Soja[9] remain concerned with the intersections and relationships of space, power, identity, and social inequality. From this perspective, geography is not simply an empty backdrop upon which meaning is made, but a contributing factor to meaning-making itself. For example, conceptions of the *city*—or, more precisely, *inner-city schools*—are rife with assumptions about who inhabits such places, what educational practices are enabled by such a location, and what possibilities exist for some sort of enacted reform within such a context.

As more contemporary educational scholars such as Robert Helfenbein[10] have noted, present-day formations of critical geography seek to map the multiple and overlapping power relations that extend from the globalized contexts of neoliberalism and manifest in select practices in localized places. Within the realm of education, neoliberal values of efficiency and productivity map on to educational practices that seek "successful" school graduates who possess the necessary skills to become economically productive and, as a consequence, useful citizens in our increasingly globalized era. Failure to generate such skills is, according to the predominant values of our times, interpreted as a deficiency. Further still, an inability to produce students as docile citizens—individuals malleable to the political needs of the economic market—is similarly negative, perhaps read as an inability to control or otherwise discipline the unruly.

In this sense, there lies an implicit assumption that any form of student resistance that takes place within the inner-city school is necessarily violent and must be met with equally violent forms of correction. That this scenario plays out in circular fashion within Anyon's case study of urban school reform is no accident: place matters. In many ways, then, *Ghetto Schooling* might be seen as an early example of critical geography scholarship in that Anyon recognizes the dynamic intersections of place (of Marcy Elementary and Newark concretely; of "the school," the urban ghetto, and rural elitism more generally, though no less materially) with the sociohistorical discourses that give such geographical alignments their "place."

The interrogative approach of critical geography may be most concretely located in Anyon's pointed analysis that historical formations of race and class intersect in Newark and Marcy Elementary to produce a type of "social distance" that constrains any attempts at economic, political, or educational reform.[11] Distance, in this instance, is both literal and metaphorical, emphasizing changing geographic placement and the varying experiences of differentiated class. Through her concept of "social distance," Anyon points to geographic changes to the city of Newark that result in rampant inner-city poverty and ghettoization that is ultimately overseen by an increasingly rural and/or suburban elite. This material realignment is met by a similarly material shift in the experiences of those social groups that are positioned within the ghettoized urban city or the privileged suburban/rural space respectively (or, of course, in the borderlands of such differentiation).

"Social distance" thus disconnects the economically well-off from the oppressed in simultaneously social and geographic terms; they fail to share similar spaces and can no longer identify shared connective experiences. In such contexts, geographical shifts in population intersect with historical biases and prejudices to promote select social identities and educational practices. The vagaries of "social distance" force a reliance on historically normed stereotypes of the mis-known *other*. Hence, the development of an intensified violent relation—the impotent rage noted earlier that stymies any attempt at isolated reform: *If I had a gun I'd kill you. You're all hoodlums.* How to imagine any semblance of sustaining reform within such circumstances?

In the face of such challenges, Anyon maintains a steadfast dedication toward envisioning some element of reform that is not bound by a historical adherence to small-scale change efforts that pay little attention to the socioeconomic conditions in which schools must operate. In order to enact sustaining reform, we must close the gaps of social distance, but doing so requires a deeply structural realignment of socioeconomic processes and practices. This move toward long-lasting and systemic reform is the basis for Part III of the book and remains an important reminder to critics of our educational system that we must extend our analyses toward visions for a possible—and more socially just—future.

In her concluding section, Anyon runs the risk of idealism, a charge that often extends from two elements: (1) that, in attempts to point a way forward, the critic demonstrates theoretical inconsistency, never fully integrating the complex relations of macro-level discourse with micro-level practice into concrete assertions of next steps; (2) that recommendations for reform are idealistically unattainable, not practical given the present-day circumstances. In the face of such challenges, Anyon uses her historical analysis to reconsider reform that begins at the starting point of the "destructive results of urban history" and the "overwhelming destitution [found] in city environments."[12]

Anyon thus begins with the premise that all reforms must be deeply structural, taking into account the economic, social, and educational inequalities that are built into our contemporary realities. Reform for Anyon extends from a stance for economic social justice: "We must ultimately...eliminate poverty; we must eliminate the ghetto school by eliminating the underlying causes of ghettoization."[13] By agitating for reforms that disrupt those processes that maintain the structures of poverty and ghettoization, Anyon points a way forward—a means to productively engage the historical patterns of social distancing. It is the promise implied in Section III that I wish to focus on throughout the rest of this chapter, as it demonstrates Anyon's dedication to aligning sustained critique with the promise of what has yet to be: critique in the name of renewal.

Affective Responses

Anyon's empirical work on the impact of oppressive social contexts on educational practice leads her to conclude that, beyond the statistical representations of educational "success" or "failure," extends an ongoing affective context. It links immediate, local contexts with larger-order considerations for the possibility of productive educational reform. For Anyon, the pressures of social inequality result in a systemic affect of lost hope. This hopelessness manifests as a collective sense of futility within, and anger directed toward, educators and educational institutions.

This perspective aligns with the concerns of Max van Manen, who offers a similar critique regarding how oppressive social systems infiltrate the very language of educational policy and practice with an insidious effect on a collectively felt sense of (im)possibility:

> The language of objectives, aims, teacher expectations, intended learning outcomes, goals, or ends in view is a language of hope out of which hope itself has been systematically purged. The language of aims and objectives, therefore, is a language of hopeless hope. It is an impatient language that neither bears nor truly awakens.[14]

Indeed, van Manen's words parallel those found in *Ghetto Schooling*, both pulling from an affective state of hopelessness that permeated North American schooling in the 1990s. Van Manen criticizes the language of educational policy as simultaneously contributing to and revealing a "hopeless hope"—a sensibility that certainly permeates the experiences of students, teachers, administrators, and community members alike who have been ghettoized by political and educational policies bent on maintaining—or even accelerating—the status quo.

Whereas van Manen points to the sterile language through which education and pedagogical practice are rendered, Anyon's work provides the empirical and theoretical backdrop that informs such "impatient language." When educational reform is enacted in isolation—as though it might be understood unto itself and outside the larger social processes of economic development, urban displacement, and racial hierarchies—it loses the possibility of contributing to productive social change on any deep level. The stripped-down, hopeless language of educational reform can only act upon itself; it loses any touchstone to those interconnective social issues of which it is a part.

Feelings of hopelessness are multiple here: there is the hopelessness of the teacher set up against an overwhelming context of inequity, the hopeless student who recognizes the futility of working within an educational institution that seeks to discipline him/her, the hopeless community member who sees educational systems as inevitably broken, and so much more. And, of course, though the language of educational reform might be stripped down to the point of social sterility—commenting only upon itself—the lost hope depicted in *Ghetto Schooling* manifests in anxiety, anger, and violence. Thus it is that Anyon's text offers example after example of the affective consequences of ghetto schooling. More than the statistical rendition of population change and failed test scores, Anyon's deeply ethnographic approach calls forth the material pain, rage, and anxiety that such circumstances produce. Both the sadness of context and possibilities for future change are deeply felt by her readers.

Engaging Structural Analysis: A Continued Influence

Anyon's productive structural analyses provide a useful entry point into overlapping and entangled oppressive systems. In line with her Marxist perspective, Anyon finds promise in revolutionary changes to the dominating systems of capitalism. If sustained change is to occur at the structural level, it must begin with a radical rethinking of our economic system: eradicate poverty and promote class equality for families regardless of geographical locale and/or race.

And yet, particularly in the third section of her book ("Learning from the Past"), Anyon softens her structural critique through a desire to make visible viable alternatives to the current system—though her critique perhaps calls for revolutionary change, her proposed solutions tend toward more reformist measures of practical change. This is not, of course, to criticize the latter portions of Anyon's text, many of which seek to point a way forward out of the morass of large-scale historical social inequality that is exemplified at the local level of Newark, New Jersey. Rather, Anyon's work might be read as a pragmatic engagement with structural inequality—one that refuses the ease of critique without response.

In this way, Anyon enacts an ethic of engagement that she perhaps sought to see in the very teachers, students, administrators, and community members that are depicted throughout her text. It is far too easy to look at the crumbling infrastructure of Newark, the ghettoization of its urban citizenry, the ongoing class and racial inequality that contributes to alarming incidents of violence, and shrug one's shoulders in overwhelmed disbelief. *What is to be done?* Anyon refuses the position of "social distance" in her critique and response (much as her methodological practices exchange distance for an engaged closeness that is not often seen in academic texts), intending instead to produce a critical commentary that is simultaneously local and global and addresses issues on the micro level of the school and the more macro consideration of social, economic, and educational policy.

And yet, despite the dangers of being overwhelmed by the enormity of inequality that Anyon's analyses provide—both historical in origin and manifesting in particularly insidious ways in our contemporary context—she does offer a sense of hopeful change. In keeping with the layered structural analysis that is the bulk of her critique, Anyon notes that any productive responses must also attend to the overarching problems of historical racism, poverty, and ghettoization of urban students. Anyon writes: "Not only the diagnosis, but our prescriptions also must be deep-structural."[15]

Consequently, Anyon's sociopolitical critique leads to the conclusion that if, indeed, socioeconomic status is a close corollary to academic achievement (and it is[16]), we must attend to both school-based reforms *and* address students' "social and economic well-being and status before and while they are students. We must ultimately, therefore, eliminate poverty; we must eliminate the ghetto school by eliminating the underlying causes of ghettoization."[17] It is through this doubled (both/and) approach to change that Anyon finds hope: simultaneously linking social *and* economic statuses of student well-being before *and* while they are in our schools; insisting on complementary changes at the local level of the school *and* the larger social systems that sustain poverty and racially driven policies of ghettoization. Through such critical analyses, Anyon refutes van Manen's "hopeless hope"; hers is a *determined hope* for radical change that rightly links education to the multiple social institutions that have a hand in social inequity and, as such, might be avenues for large-scale change in the name of social justice.

Further still, before offering strategies for productive change that extend from her critical analyses, Anyon puts forward a challenge to those who might otherwise remain immobilized by the force of her structural critique: "To believe that fundamental social change is impossible, is to be overly oppressed by the parameters of the present. Are we unwilling to reach beyond the surface structure of our lives for new ideas?"[18] In this way, Anyon asks her readers to remain true to the fundamentals of deeply structural critique: one cannot point to the multiplicity of injustices that maintain social inequity and offer only surface-level responses (or, worse yet, no response at all).

This is a reminder to all of us whose critical engagement with social institutions seeks sustained social change not easily appropriated by the oppressive "parameters of the present." "New ideas" necessarily interrupt and intervene within the systemic processes that maintain the status quo; this element of intervention remains a key component of any critical work. As the writer John Edgar Wideman has noted, "Our power lies in our capacity to imagine ourselves as other than we are."[19] Anyon's is a similarly productive vision of an ability to step outside the prevailing ways of thinking, being, and practicing everyday life that have so easily come to oppressively impact our educational systems. Her critique of deeply ensconced social structures provides a productive entry point, an avenue of hope through which progressive social and economic change might occur. To return to Max van Manen for a moment, we must recall that "to hope is to believe in possibilities. Therefore hope strengthens and builds."[20]

And it is with this notion of hope that Anyon concludes *Ghetto Schooling* as a strong text—not a hope of overly idealistic expectation that some semblance of humanity will bring us to our senses and cause us to collectively refuse the seductions of our classist, racist, and ghettoizing social systems, but instead a hope drawn from grim determination. This is a hope based in possibility, a product of engaged critical work that draws from "the outrage, the combativeness, and the courage that will transform our inner cities, and our inner city schools."[21] It is a materialist hope, a fully embodied refusal to either sustain systems of inequality or be deterministically frozen by them. It is a hope that offers critical intervention—one that has sustained a series of important critiques of social inequality generally and an oppressive educational system more specifically. That engaged hope might just be the enduring legacy of this text.

Notes

1 Jean Anyon, *Ghetto Schooling: A Political Economy of Urban Educational Reform* (New York: Teachers College Press, 1997), 30.
2 Margalit Fox, "Jean Anyon Dies at 72; Wrote 'Ghetto Schooling,'" *The New York Times*, September 29, 2013.
3 Anyon, *Ghetto Schooling*, xv.
4 Ibid.
5 Jean Anyon, *Marx and Education* (New York: Routledge, 2011).
6 Samuel Bowles and Herbert Gintis, *Schooling in Capitalist America: Education Reform and the Contradictions of Economic Life* (New York: Basic Books, 1976).
7 David Harvey, *Spaces of Capital: Towards a Critical Geography* (New York: Routledge, 2001).
8 Doreen B. Massey, *For Space* (Thousand Oaks, CA: Sage, 2010).
9 Edward W. Soja, *Postmodern Geographies: The Reassertion of Space in Critical Social Theory* (New York: Verso, 2011).
10 Rob Helfenbein, "Thinking Through Scale: Critical Geography and Curriculum Spaces." In *Curriculum Studies Handbook: The Next Moment*, ed. E. Malewski (New York: Routledge, 2010), 304–317.
11 Anyon, *Ghetto Schooling*, 23.
12 Ibid., 155.
13 Ibid., 164.
14 Max van Manen, *Researching Lived Experience: Human Science for an Action Sensitive Pedagogy* (Albany: State University of New York Press, 1990), 122–123.
15 Anyon, *Ghetto Schooling*, 164.
16 See, for example: Amy Orr, "Black-White Differences in Achievement: The Importance of Wealth," *Sociology of Education* 76 no. 4 (2003): 281–304; P. Boxer, S.E. Goldstein, T. DeLorenzo, S. Savoy, and I. Mercato, "Educational Aspiration-Expectation Discrepancies: Relation to Socioeconomic and Academic Risk-Related Factors," *Journal of Adolescence* 34 no. 4 (1971): 609–617.
17 Anyon, *Ghetto Schooling*, 164.
18 Ibid., 164–165.
19 John Edgar Wideman, *Fatheralong* (New York: Vintage Books, 1994), xxii.
20 Van Manen, *Researching Lived Experience*, 123.
21 Anyon, *Ghetto Schooling*, 186.

THIRTY

Alfie Kohn, *The Schools Our Children Deserve: Moving Beyond Traditional Classrooms and "Tougher Standards"* (1999)

Tian Yu

No one writes like Alfie Kohn. The freelance author of more than a dozen books about education and human behavior has certainly made his voice heard across an unusually wide spectrum. Not many academics have been profiled by newspapers such as *The New York Times* and *USA Today*, or featured on TV and radio programs such as *Oprah*. The "public intellectual" orientation of his work may be responsible for the very accessible and engaging style of his writing, which is evident in the book we will discuss in this chapter. To add one more testimonial to his appeal as a major critic of American education, *Time* recently described him as "perhaps the country's most outspoken critic of education's fixation on grade [and] test scores."

Grade-oriented traditional pedagogy and the test-driven standards movement are the two powerful forces shaping American education, according to Kohn, and he puts both under scrutiny in *The Schools Our Children Deserve: Moving Beyond Traditional Classrooms and "Tougher Standards"* (1999). But before we introduce the main themes and arguments of the book, let's say a little bit about the last several decades of the twentieth century in the United States and the state of its educational system during that time. This contextual analysis may help us to better understand Kohn's purpose in writing the book and his overall point of view.

American capitalism seemed to have worked well for the two decades following World War II. However, beginning in the 1960s, America's dominance in international economic, political, and military matters was challenged. As Shea, Kahane, and Sola (1989) note, the U.S. economic "stagflation" largely resulted from an emerging global economy and, particularly, a new international division of labor. The United States had lost its competitive advantage in labor-intensive industries. The capital flight to Third World countries and high-tech mechanization of the workplace had a dramatic impact on the workforce. In addition, the United States was facing strong competition from other capitalist economies such as Japan and West Germany. (China was still a sleeping giant at the time, yet to awaken.) Economic and social lives were greatly affected by the new technologies and demographics. Higher-level skills were demanded of workers, but rapidly changing demographics challenged such demand. Students of the 1980s would come from vastly different family structures, economic conditions, and cultural backgrounds.

A particular portrait of America revealed a bleak landscape: America was more illiterate, more hungry, more homeless, more unemployed, more alienated, and more hopeless. It was strongly argued that there was a mismatch between employer demands of an emerging high-tech, high-skill economy and an increasingly ill-prepared personnel supply from largely poor, minority, and single-parent households. Thus, schools naturally became the focus of the debate. As Bowles and Gintis (1976) point out, the evidently critical relationship between education and the economy re-emerged, and the use of education as a tool of social policy was emphasized. Corporate leaders, mainstream politicians, and many educators joined the chorus to advocate for schooling as the solution to the all-too-evident social ills. They initiated a new educational reform movement, starting with assigning blame to current schools:

> American workers are making substandard contributions to economic productivity. Schools are indicted for undermining the nation's industrial, commercial, technological, and military supremacy and in the world economy by turning out students who have antiquated personality habits and deficient academic skills. In order to restore military supremacy and economic predominance in the international economy, a more direct link is called for between a reformed educational system and a more productive economy. (Shea, Kahane, & Sola, 1989, p. 12)

There was a bipartisan campaign to link the United States' deteriorating economy with the so-called failure of public education. The criticism of public schools in the early 1980s was that they failed to serve the public because educational standards were too low, students were not learning enough to compete in the world market, and American children were shamefully lagging behind their counterparts in other industrialized nations in mathematics, science, and other key academic subjects. These are the all-too-familiar conclusions of the now-famous 1983 National Commission on Excellence in Education report, *A Nation at Risk*. The new reform agenda, therefore, called for higher standards for schools, a national curriculum and assessment system, and a return to traditional schooling represented by training in the basics (the 3 Rs, for example).

This standards-driven reform movement was entangled with a call for systemic cultural reform—a struggle for "common culture." This cultural struggle was best reflected in the controversy surrounding multiculturalism and the resurgence of the character education movement in schools. A popular discourse of moral decline was used to justify the teaching of traditional and "common" values, which were thought to have been eroded by the rise of multiculturalism and moral relativism in American society and schools. Thus, a marriage of standards and values was arranged in schools. Reformers such as William Bennett (1992) targeted the "entire mediocre education enterprise in America" (p. 47) and prescribed a return to basics and tradition. As Secretary of Education in the Reagan administration, Bennett consistently talked about "three C's"—content, character, and choice—and urged schools to teach a "sound common curriculum" emphasizing traditional academic subjects in liberal arts, moral character, and standards of right and wrong. He contended that "improving American education requires not doing new things but doing (and remembering) some good old things" (p. 56).

This school reform agenda, along with its rationale and basis, has been under serious challenge by thoughtful critics since its origin. Among early critical works (see Apple, 1996; Berliner & Biddle, 1995; Ohanian, 1999; Stedman, 1987, for example), *The Schools Our Children Deserve* represents a strong and influential example of such criticism.

Kohn opens the book with Chapter 1, entitled "Forward…Into the Past." He explains what traditional schooling is and makes the case that it is still the dominant model in American education. He then turns to the more recent, and closely related, phenomenon: the standards movement that has come to dominate discussions about school reform. Kohn compares the "two modes of schooling"—that is, traditional education versus progressive education. Never trying to hide his disdain for the Old School, he joins the ranks of John Dewey and Jean Piaget in defending progressive schooling, thus establishing a clear philosophical orientation for his overall argument.

The book continues with two well-put-together major parts. Part One, "Tougher Standards versus Better Education," offers a blistering critique of the standards movement. Each of the five chapters in this part takes on one of the five "shaky foundations" of the move toward tougher standards. Chapter 2 challenges the overemphasis on achievement and the widely shared and largely taken-for-granted belief in improving performance. The focus on results, Kohn argues, often turns out to be simplistic, and "a preoccupation with achievement is not only different from, but often detrimental to, a focus on learning" (p. 21). Chapter 3 targets the Old-School pedagogy that the standards movement tends to favor. "Holding schools 'accountable' for meeting 'standards' usually means requiring them to live up to conventional measures of student performance, and traditional kinds of instruction are most closely geared to—and thus perpetuated by—these measures" (p. 16).

In the Old School framework, teachers rely on lectures, textbooks, worksheets, and grades to transmit a series of isolated facts and skills to their students. Rebutting those who call for getting "back to basics," Kohn makes a persuasive case that the majority of schools never left them behind. Further, history and research both show that the Old School approach to teaching never even worked that well. In Chapter 4, Kohn reveals how the standards movement relies on standardized testing for the purpose of evaluation and how such reliance is both unreasonable and unjustified and leads to disastrous outcomes in American schools. He points out that high scores often signify relatively superficial thinking and that tests measure the least interesting and least significant aspects of learning. The teaching-to-the-test mania has essentially narrowed the whole conversation about improving education in this country. Chapter 5 takes on the top-down emphasis in the Old School standards-driven reform movement. By imposing tougher standards and accountability, using standardized and high-stakes tests, and manipulating teachers and students to raise scores, the movement is essentially mandating a particular kind of education. In Chapter 6, Kohn attacks an assumption about school improvement that is implicitly driving the movement, something he calls the "harder is better" confusion. It is the mindless idea that if something isn't working very well, you need to work harder on it. For Kohn, this is exactly why we don't see schools improve.

After Part One's devastating critique of the Old-School reform movement, Kohn brings hope in Part Two, presenting his case for progressive education in practice. In four chapters, he discusses what can replace the Old School as well as how we might rethink the whole idea of education. Chapter 7 refreshes readers with the author's progressive understanding of education and situates his specific reform ideas that are enlarged in chapters to follow. The chapter represents an urgent call to bring back the humanistic and democratic vision of schooling to the national conversation and offers a strong rebuttal to the economic justification for education that is trumpeted in all the talk about tougher standards and accountability.

In Chapter 8 Kohn provides a detailed, robust description of progressive education at work. Drawing on a remarkable body of research and using stories from real classrooms, he helps readers understand the need to move beyond a "bunch o' facts" model of teaching by showing how this can be done. He proposes multiage, interdisciplinary classrooms where students work cooperatively on projects and actively construct their own knowledge. In a democratic form of pedagogy, student voices are valued and teachers act as facilitators. For evaluation and assessment, traditional grades give way to performance-based qualitative methods. To support this progressive vision of schooling described in Chapter 8, Kohn uses two more chapters to expand and deepen his argument. Chapter 9 contests the backlash against the whole-language approach to reading instruction and reiterates his claim that "back-to-basics" types of training cannot work. Chapter 10 discusses the understandable barriers and obstacles in the progressive approach to education (both real and imagined) and challenges educators to re-envision education in alternative ways. After providing concrete ideas to replace traditional grades and standardized tests, he concludes the chapter with a call for political action to resist the current approach to education and demand the more progressive and democratic schools that our children deserve.

It is almost certain that a book with such contentious arguments will stir up strong reactions: "Amens" and cheers from the progressive enthusiasts, and frowning faces and gasps of displeasure from others. It is predictable that Kohn's progressive comrades such as Jonathan Kozol and Theodore Sizer highly praise the book. Some of their endorsements appear on its front pages. Positive reviews of the book have also been shared and published by a number of leading publishers and media outlets. For example, Jodi Mailander Farrell (1999), writing on Amazon.com, says, "Kohn has written a detailed, methodical treatise," and he "backs up his argument with research and observations." Farrell believes "the overall message of *The Schools Our Children Deserve* is a valid cautionary tale about the future of American education that deserves to be heard out by teachers, policymakers, and parents." Similarly, Kim Witherspoon (1999), writing for *Publishers Weekly*, also recognizes Kohn's use of current research in his analysis. "Kohn advances a series of well-reasoned arguments against traditional education without the usual storm of tree-shaking and excessive rhetoric. This is another balanced effort from an advocate who believes that taking our youth seriously and honoring their abilities and potential may be the first major step toward reform."

In the same fashion, in *Library Journal*, Samuel T. Huang (1999) writes that Kohn's book illustrates how each of the traditional methods "reflects a fundamental lack of understanding about how and why children learn." Huang also appreciates that Kohn provided solutions to the problem—in particular, his descriptions of "how the best teachers help students become critical, creative thinkers rather than filling them with forgettable facts or preparing them to take standardized tests." Huang urges parents as well as educators to "read this remarkable book and rethink our most basic assumptions about the nature of learning and the possibilities of education in the 21st century." Writing in *Booklist*, Vanessa Bush (1999) echoes Kohn's judgment about American education at the current historical moment: "The pendulum in educational trends is currently at a decidedly conservative, 'even reactionary,' cycle." She especially notes Kohn's appraisal that "urban schools and minority students are most scrutinized, most tested, and most vulnerable to the politics of school reform."

Of course, Kohn's critics also speak out. Mark Goldblatt (2000), writing in *Commentary*, complains that "Ideology animates Kohn's critique [of traditional education and the standards movement]." He accuses Kohn of providing an analysis "marred by pointless, ideological asides—as when he notes that the Christian Coalition supports direct phonics instruction, and that 'right wing' journals have published 'wildly enthusiastic articles' on the phonics method." In addition, he points to a presumed "reality problem" in Kohn's thinking. Goldblatt asks: "Would there be a back-to-basics movement in the first place if parents sensed that American schools were doing a good job?" Kohn's purported skirmish with reality also emerges with the question of teacher competence, he argues; and Kohn romanticizes teachers' potential ability for effecting progressive education. Most of all, Goldblatt is unhappy with Kohn's treatment of the traditionalist opposition, accusing him of setting up "false dichotomies" when he writes about the Old School versus the New School in education. Kohn is "especially unfair to Hirsch," Goldblatt declares, because Hirsch's position "is not, as Kohn would have it, that knowing a certain set of facts renders a person automatically 'educated' but rather that knowing a certain set of facts is a prerequisite for the kind of active intellectual engagements typical of educated people."

In a more balanced, but still quite critical, piece in *The New York Times*, James Traub (1999) acknowledges the strong research basis of Kohn's critical claims and arguments about homework, grades, and rote learning. He recognizes that Kohn "supplies a thorough and thoughtful, if hyperbolic, defense of that embattled fortress of progressivism known as whole-language instruction, in which children learn to read through immersion in written texts rather than through phonics." However, like Goldblatt, Traub seems to frown at a so-called ideological bias in Kohn's thinking and a seemingly simplistic treatment of the complex real world of education. He chastens Kohn for drawing "an absolute line" between progressive and conservative ways of schooling. Traub insists that, in reality, such an absolute line does not exist. Even E.D. Hirsch's Core Knowledge curriculum, Traub says, has been found by "the most comprehensive study" to utilize progressive techniques that Kohn advocates. In Traub's view, Kohn's problems are derived from "a sharp distinction between understanding and mere knowledge." He argues: "It seems paradoxical to slight domain-specific knowledge and yet advocate an ambitious pedagogy in which teachers range over many different disciplines and explore the most serious ideas." He calls this a "prejudice, shared by many progressive thinkers."

A *Kirkus Review* piece (1999) calls Kohn's book "another blistering critique of traditional public schooling by a progressive who displays the same intellectual rigidity he abhors in others." Even though the reviewer acknowledges Kohn for making "a persuasive case" about the prevalence of the old-style and transmission education in American schools (the review, however, falls short of rejecting this approach), he dismisses Kohn's solution as "just another brand of educational orthodoxy, the progressive version of the one-size-fits-all that currently afflicts the public schools." Echoing other critics, the author also accuses Kohn of "simplistic thinking" when framing the education debate in a divisive way ("education for profit" vs. "education for democracy," for example). Not surprisingly, the review concludes: "Though Kohn's zeal for reform is undeniable, in this book he seems content to preach to the progressive choir rather than persuade others to adopt his cause."

Since the publication of Kohn's book 16 years ago, little has changed in American education—or it might be argued that things have gotten worse. When politicians from both dominant political parties talk about education today, we hear essentially the same rhetoric we were bombarded with in the 1980s: preparing our young for global competition, setting up world-class standards for schools, teaching children more respect and responsibility, and demanding that teachers be more accountable.

We also continue to witness similar trends in national policies on education today. Despite Obama's occasional and fragmented critique of the Bush-era education legislation No Child Left Behind (2001), which pushed the standards movement to its peak, the Obama administration has, in effect, extended the neoliberal educational policy of his predecessor, notably with his Race to the Top initiative. Race to the Top encourages states to compete with each other for federal funding, and it awards them for developing or adopting common curricular standards and assessments, promoting charter schools, and using merit pay to ensure teacher accountability. Thus, public schools today are still caught up in a high-speed accountability race: rushing to meet Adequate Yearly Progress (AYP) or facing punitive school-choice mechanisms (school closure or restructuring) aimed at the privatization of public education. The assessment of schools relies on standardized tests based on uniform academic standards. To pass the tests and meet the standards, schools fall prey to the "teaching to the test" mania. In addition to the competition-driven choice programs, virtue-centered character education has been promoted to restore traditional morality in schools—imposing discipline, order, and a religiously oriented work ethic on students. In short, the Old-School plus Tougher Standards nightmare Alfie Kohn warned us about over 15 years ago is still alive and haunting us every day.

Ample research, both theoretical and empirical, provides convincing evidence that standards-driven, accountability-based school reform has failed (see Darling-Hammond, 2010; McGill, 2015; Meier & Woods, 2004; Noddings, 2007; and Ravitch, 2010). As Stedman (2014) writes:

> Beyond failing to improve achievement, standards-based accountability systems have constricted curricula and warped school culture. A new Taylorism and a ritualistic compliance with mandates are undermining learning and the development of civic literacy. Testing and grades, not learning, drive instruction. School climates have worsened, with the effects stratified by race and class. During most of the standards era, dropout rates grew and reading of all types declined—NCLB has made things worse, not better…. Proficiency-based curricula and bureaucratic schooling are devastating the quality of life inside schools. Teachers have joined students in leaving schools and are now dropping out at alarming rates. (p. 45)

Such criticism shares the spirit of Kohn's preceding work.

In concluding this review, I would like to add a strong moral critique of the accountability/standards-based school reform movement. Kohn and others have alluded to such a moral critique but have not fully expanded or substantiated it. It must be pointed out that the dominant school reform movement characterized by accountability, standards, and testing has eroded the moral mission of schooling. As economic objectives increasingly drive that movement, the moral purpose of education is increasingly forsaken. Forced into a uniform, standardized curriculum and an assessment system that evaluates learning according to high-stakes tests, students are denied their right to a well-rounded education that should necessarily address their moral development and character formation.

As a teacher with 40 years of classroom experience observes, the public school today is "gripped by a testing mandate that is literally choking life out of our classrooms" (Bruni, 2004, p. 153). This is happening because rigid emphasis on testing makes rich and stimulating curriculum disappear and hands-on, authentic instruction practically impossible. Such egregious narrowing of the curriculum and watering down of teaching and learning will inevitably result in a short-changed, impoverished education for generations of children. If this is not a moral problem, I don't know what it is. In addition to its academic and intellectual defects, the testing mania harms children physically and psychologically in a bluntly direct way. It is common knowledge that testing anxiety, the pressure to perform, and the fear of failure can cause serious damage to a tender young child. Stories of our children having sick stomachs, trembling hands, and wet pants during tests; developing worrisome behavioral patterns; or indeed becoming dreadful of schools—these narrative accounts should arouse moral outrage in us.

What about the fact that many schools and teachers engage in score-boosting activities that are downright dishonest and immoral in the race for accountability? "During recent years, the increasing prevalence of teachers' unethical score-raising tactics has forced almost all states to issue a list of verboten test-preparation and test-administration rules—along with the associated rule-violating penalties such as the loss of the teacher's job or license" (Popham, 2004, p. 168). Speaking of unethical practices, the once nationally acclaimed "Texas Miracle," a springboard for the country's mad march toward the testing movement, is a classic example. In July 2003 *The New York Times* reported that the turnaround of a poorly performing Texas school system, which was originally credited to higher academic standards and close monitoring of performance on high-stakes tests, turned out to be flawed. The reality pointed instead to the district's Enron-style accounting of the students who left the system (Bruni, 2004, p. 157). According to Bruni (2004), "Since the advent of TAAS [Texas Assessment of Academic Skills], the number of children excused from taking the TAAS test on the grounds of a Special Education Exemption has increased sharply—nearly doubling from 1994 [to] 1998. In fact, the number of youngsters being identified as special education students is, in some Texas communities, more than double the national norm" (pp. 154–155).

Another cheating scandal became national news just as I was about to complete this chapter. According to a CNN story on April 1, 2015, 11 public school educators in Atlanta charged with racketeering and other crimes were convicted of intentionally mishandling standardized tests. About 180 teachers at 44 schools were implicated initially, and 35 educators—including principals, teachers, and testing coordinators—were indicted. A state review had determined that some cheating had occurred in more than half the district's elementary and middle schools. The cheating is believed to date back to early 2001. For at least 4 years (between 2005 and 2009), students' answers on statewide skills tests were altered, fabricated, and falsely certified. Investigators found that educators cheated out of pride, to earn bonuses, to enhance their careers, or to keep their jobs.

As shown in the above examples, a moral irony can transpire as a result of the deadly drama of excessive testing. Well-intentioned but ill-informed people may be drawn to the claim of objectivity and fairness in a movement characterized by standards and standardized tests, yet the processes of test making, test preparation, test administration, and utilization of test results in high-stakes decisions are loaded with biases, prejudice, and injustice. These tests measure, for the most part, family income and socioeconomic status (Apple, 2001; Rothstein, 2004).

Test scores correlate most strongly with the relative privileges of social stratifications. They reflect—and amplify—the existing social inequalities in our society.

Truth be told, we need to face this reality: standardization and test-driven school reform further marginalizes poor children and children of color—the very students whom some reformers may have intended to help in the first place. Any top-down and one-size-fits-all approach to schooling would seem to sacrifice or undermine, by design or in effect, cultural diversity, individual rights, educational equality, and social justice. All these are at the heart of any educational system that can be viewed as moral. As Apple (1996) predicted: "behind the educational justifications for a national curriculum and national testing is an ideological attack that is very dangerous. Its effects will be truly damaging to those who already have the most to lose in this society" (p. 24). Now, NCLB has brought us exactly what Apple warned about: "The vast majority of poor children in our country are still denied access to an education that would help them to escape poverty and open doors of opportunity" (Noguera, 2004, p. 177). Noguera wrote these words in 2004; his observation about educational inequalities remains the same today (see Fergus, Noguera, & Martin, 2014).

The NCLB-guided and Race to the Top–aided school reform fails to recognize the fundamental issue in American schools. The most basic problem is educational inequality—reflective of larger social inequality, inequality not of hard work or intelligence, but of resources and opportunities. Unwilling to tackle this inequality, but continuing to starve schools of needed resources while blaming teachers, their unions, and students for the achievement gap, the extant reform movement can only exacerbate existing "savage inequalities" (Kozol, 1992) in American schools and contribute to the growing "educational debt" (Ladson-Billings, 2007) the nation owes to countless disadvantaged children in communities historically segregated, underfunded, and underserved.

That inequality and debt represent a grave moral conundrum that the reform movement continues to produce and perpetuate. As No Child Left Behind leaves more and more children behind, and Race to the Top tramples the human spirit of not only the "losers" but also the "winners," we see soul-losing and moral trembling in education. Recognizing this moral conundrum and tackling it head-on is perhaps the very first step we must take toward building the good schools that *all* of our children deserve.

References

Apple, M. (1996). *Cultural politics and education*. New York: Teachers College Press.

Apple, M. (2001). *Educating the "right" way: Markets, standards, God, and inequality*. New York: RoutledgeFalmer.

Bennett, W.J. (1992). *The de-valuing of America: The fight for our culture and our children*. New York: Summit Books.

Berliner, D.C., & Biddle, B.J. (1995). *The manufactured crisis: Myths, fraud, and the attack on America's public schools*. Reading, MA: Addison-Wesley.

Bowles, S., & Gintis, H. (1976). *Schooling in capitalist America: Educational reform and the contradictions of economic life*. New York: Basic Books.

Bruni, S. (2004). Choking the life out of classrooms. In C. Glickman (Ed.), *Letters to the next president: What we can do about the real crisis in public education* (pp. 151–157). New York: Teachers College Press.

Bush, V. (1999). Review. *Booklist*. Retrieved April 5, 2015, from booklistonline.com.

Darling-Hammond, L. (2010). *The flat world and education: How America's commitment to equity will determine our future*. New York: Teachers College Press.

Farrell, J.M. (1999). Review. Retrieved April 5, 2015, from http://www.amazon.com/The-Schools-Our-Children-Deserve/dp/B004Z4M1JU

Fergus, E., Noguera, P., & Martin, M. (2014). *Schooling for resilience: Improving the life trajectory of Black and Latino boys*. Cambridge, MA: Harvard Education Press.

Goldblatt, M. (2000). Review. Retrieved April 5, 2015, from http://www.markgoldblatt.com/2011/09/commentary-normal.html

Huang, S.T. (1999). Review. Retrieved April 5, 2015, from http://www.barnesandnoble.com/w/the-schools-our-children-deserve-alfie-kohn/1116855090?ean=9780547630663

Kirkus Review. (1999). Retrieved April 5, 2015, from https://www.kirkusreviews.com/book-reviews/alfie-kohn/the-schools-our-children-deserve/

Kohn, A. (1999). *The schools our children deserve: Moving beyond traditional classroom and "tougher standards."* Boston, MA: Houghton Mifflin.

Kozol, J. (1992). *Savage inequalities: Children in America's schools*. New York: HarperPerennial.

Ladson-Billings, G. (2007). From the achievement gap to the education debt: Understanding achievement in U.S. schools. *Educational Researcher, 35*(7), 3–12.

McGill, M.V. (2015). *Race to the bottom: Corporate school reform and the future of public education*. New York: Teachers College Press.

Meier, D., & Woods, G. (Eds.). (2004). *Many children left behind*. Boston, MA: Beacon Press.

National Commission on Excellence in Education. (1983). *A nation at risk*. Washington, DC: U.S. Government Printing Office.

No Child Left Behind Act. (2001). Public Law 107–110, 2002.

Noddings, N. (2007). *When school reform goes wrong*. New York: Teachers College Press.

Noguera, P. (2004). Going beyond the slogans and rhetoric. In C. Glickman (Ed.), *Letters to the next president: What we can do about the real crisis in public education* (pp. 174–183). New York: Teachers College Press.

Ohanian, S. (1999). *One size fits few: The folly of educational standards*. Portsmouth, NH: Heinemann.

Popham, W.J. (2004). The no-win accountability game. In C. Glickman (Ed.), *Letters to the next president: What we can do about the real crisis in public education* (pp. 166–173). New York: Teachers College Press.

Ravitch, D. (2010). *The death and life of the American school system: How testing and choice are undermining education*. New York: Basic Books.

Rothstein, R. (2004). *Class and schools*. Washington, DC: Economic Policy Institute.

Shea, C.M., Kahane, E., & Sola, P. (Eds.). (1989). *The new servants of power: A critique of the 1980s school reform movement*. Westport, CT: Greenwood Press.

Stedman, L. (1987). The political economy of recent educational reform reports. *Educational Theory, 37*(1), 69–76.

Stedman, L. (2014). Subverting learning and undermining democracy: A structural and political economy analysis of the standards movement. In J.L. DeVitis & K. Teitelbaum (Eds.), *School reform critics: The struggle for democratic schooling* (pp. 45–57). New York: Peter Lang.

Traub, J. (1999, September 19). Back to school. *The New York Times*. Retrieved April 5, 2015, from https://www.nytimes.com/books/99/09/19/reviews/990919.19traubt.html

Witherspoon, K. (1999). Review. *Publishers Weekly*. Retrieved April 5, 2015, from http://www.publishersweekly.com/978-0-395-94039-6

PART FIVE

The 2000s

THIRTY-ONE

C.A. Bowers, *Educating for Eco-Justice and Community* (2001)

Michael P. Mueller

This chapter analyzes Chet Bowers's book *Educating for Eco-Justice and Community* (2001). Bowers is a retired professor of environmental studies who formerly taught at the University of Oregon. He was very prolific during his career, writing many books and papers on a wide variety of topics, but was most importantly focused on analyzing the cultural patterns of thinking that are associated with behaviors that contribute to the rates and scales of ecological decline. His first book, published in 1974, was entitled *Cultural Literacy for Freedom* and emphasized the significance of the cultural aspects of ecological literacy in public schools and universities. At that time he used an emancipatory liberal framework as the basis for promoting the importance of cultural and ecological sustainability (Bowers, 1996). However, shortly thereafter he noticed how various environmental groups misused the environment for short-term economic gains and realized that liberalism actually justified, through the root metaphors of individualism and technological progress, the further degradation of the environment. Bowers carefully developed his critique of emancipatory and neoliberal frameworks for the next 35 years. He used Gregory Bateson (Bowers, 1990) and many others' works to articulate ecojustice theory.

Bowers's most influential books have been *Education, Cultural Myths, and the Ecological Crisis: Towards Deep Changes* (1993) and *Educating for Eco-Justice and Community*, which I explore here. Bowers has had a significant impact on educational philosophy and cultural studies, with ecojustice philosophy comprising a large part of his body of scholarship. One of the reasons why his book *Educating for Eco-Justice* was so influential is that it was published right at the turn of the century, when climate change began receiving more attention in the media and in the sciences. This also marked a time when theorists in education began taking Bowers's work more seriously, and some significant differences within eco justice theory began to emerge within the educational literature.

These differences are most notable with regard to how ecojustice theory is used. There is very little disagreement about the need to address neoliberal ideologies that have a heightened disregard for the integrity of the natural world. Indeed, these ideologies have been associated with cultural and environmental degradation. However, there is still some disagreement among theorists about whether the concept of "ecological crisis" serves ecojustice well. There is disagreement about whether place-based education and other educational theories that have as their primary purpose the protection of the Earth work in concert with ecojustice education—which I will describe later in this chapter. There is disagreement about whether the emancipatory liberal theories of Paulo Freire, John Dewey, and others contribute to living a life that sustains the natural world. Finally, there is disagreement about whether ecojustice can effectively change educational policy.

Nonetheless, eco justice theory has been used effectively to legitimize some really important studies in education, programs, and projects that contribute to the well-being of diverse communities and the natural world. Here I will describe Bowers's early influence in ecojustice, specifically articulated in *Educating for Eco-Justice and Community*. As I describe Bowers's ecojustice theory, I will offer some ways to think about his work with guiding questions. The intention is that these questions might be used to study *Educating for Eco-Justice* in more depth on one's own. Let's begin with Bowers's critique of social justice reforms.

The Failure of Social Justice Reforms

Bowers recognizes that there are many well-intentioned educators who have articulated educational reforms that are based on the need to be more aware of the disparities between people and to promote equity and fairness in the educational pursuits of children. These intentions have been largely focused on social justice, an approach that fails to take into account the characteristics and needs of nonhuman animals and geophysical habitats. Bowers also points out that many of these educational reforms are also based on the same cultural assumptions that have allowed corporations to exploit and destroy anything that gets in the way of capital gain—people and natural places alike. He demonstrates how many of the popular ideas in education stem from the emancipation traditions of John Dewey and Paulo Freire. Bowers shows how these ideas gained traction and co-evolved with the same cultural assumptions that stem from the Industrial Revolution. He argues that advocates of emancipatory learning who promoted social justice agendas fail to recognize that "any definition of social justice that does not take account of how human demands on the natural environment are affecting the lives of future generations is fundamentally flawed" (2001, p. 3). Social justice educators "fail to recognize that addressing the cultural basis of the deepening ecological crisis is fundamental to any vision of social justice" (p. 4).

In contrast, Bowers articulates a more encompassing ecojustice philosophy that takes seriously the concerns of extreme weather patterns associated with climate change, fossil fuel dependency, human illness and death associated with synthetic chemicals, the loss of jobs and the ocean's fisheries because of marine ecosystem declines, the loss of tens of thousands of species, and the annual loss of twenty billion tons of topsoil. Further, ecojustice takes seriously the increasingly consumer-dependent lifestyle adopted at the expense of traditional, cultural, and ecological knowledge. Ecojustice emphasizes indigenous ways of knowing and practices that are more ecologically aligned. Ecojustice points out the deep cultural assumptions carried forward in language stemming from the Industrial Revolution, the double binds of a progressive demeanor, and the commodification of many aspects of culture. Ecojustice addresses poverty at a local level, the resistance of environmental injustices by the marginalized, the need for intergenerational knowledge, the value of fostering marginalized talents and skills in higher education, and the interdependence of the family, community, and environment.

The Mantra of Ecological Crisis

While Bowers's ecojustice theory presumes the unchallenged notion of "ecological crisis" in education, I have argued that this presupposition fails to account for the exclusive anthropocentric rationality for addressing environmental degradation (Mueller, 2009a). This is not to deny the significant impacts of human-driven activities on the environment, but only to ask what purpose the mantra of ecological crisis serves in Bowers's ecojustice theory. In Alaska, for example, there are certainly visible changes in the rapidly melting permafrost and tundra ecosystems that can be linked to black coal energy emissions. To what extent are these changes associated with a universal ecological crisis rather than an opportunity to become more informed and learn to mitigate these changes and adapt? Which is more sustainable—a theory based on the shock doctrine of ecological crisis or a theory that promotes the value and worth of becoming informed and acting more responsibly? In Bowers's original notions of ecojustice, he never analyzed whether there was a danger in using the concept of ecological crisis to provoke thinking about rates and scales of Earth changes. This was the same mistake made by Al Gore, David Orr, and others in promoting eco-social change, but it has largely failed educational theorists as they realize the transitory effectiveness of using this term to promote learning about eco-degradation and the cultural ways of thinking that may be associated with it. Rejecting the ecological crisis, then, was a major modification to Bowers's original ecojustice theory that had to be made before it could be used more widely across educational domains—in particular, science education (Mueller, 2009a). For Bowers, then, the term *ecological crisis* used throughout his book is more accurately associated with the *human crisis* inherent in blindly contributing to both cultural and ecological changes, while acknowledging our ecological interdependence.

The Failure of Emancipatory Liberal Theories

Bowers notes how Hannah Arendt described that the cultural influences of tradition are much different from the authoritarianism of external control embraced by emancipatory thinkers for development or modernization. For emancipatory liberal thinkers, tradition had to be viewed as simplistic and backward in light of the autonomous individual who could advance knowledge through science. We see this notion in how some cultures are described as traditional versus modern and underdeveloped versus developed, and how the happiness of individuals is often equated with leaving behind the old and welcoming the new. Today this process of industrialization has become all-encompassing and includes the commodification of all aspects of everyday life—to free the consciousness of "traditional values and ways of thinking that foreground the reciprocal nature of communal relationships and responsibilities" (2001, p. 38). Bowers cites Susan Bordo, Vandana Shiva, and Andrew Kimbrell's essays that contribute to the idea that the industrial culture advances by marginalizing the traditions of cultures that represent alternate knowledge. He does not advocate that industrialization destroys all traditions—rather, only those traditions that are in the way. He notes how emancipation theorists strive through critical reflection to progress through continuous change, which is a different position than renewing traditions that have been helpful in sustaining ecological and non-commodified communities' ways of knowing. Traditions, therefore, can be equated with the deeply constructed and modified expressions of culture that go far into the past. Thus, to reject culture is impossible, since we are embedded in culture as human beings.

More specific to critical theory, Bowers discusses how Peter McLaren and Henry Giroux have perpetuated the emancipatory view that ignores ecological degradation while at the same time addressing social justice issues. According to Bowers, McLaren writes for the progressive elites in education and to indoctrinate graduate students into the language of neo-Marxism. Bowers questions whether McLaren's emphasis on the continuous critical inquiry of emancipation can ever be translated into pedagogy or curriculum. He notes that even though McLaren mentions ecological disasters, he does not pay enough attention to more ecologically aligned and less consumer-dependent cultures. Bowers's main concern is that McLaren advocates critical inquiry "as the *only* valid source of knowledge and the right of expert theorists to dismiss the practices and values of different cultural groups as expressions of false [political] consciousness that hide the real history of class and gender oppression" (p. 47; emphasis in original). Bowers believes that McLaren promotes a similar way of thinking about traditions-as-oppression that stems from the Industrial Revolution. Despite that advocacy, McLaren validates cultural knowledge traditions. His enlightenment view of emancipation through critical inquiry may threaten or even make more vulnerable the traditions that are associated with protecting the Earth, because they could be seen as oppressive in light of achieving social justice for people. While some might argue that Bowers is being overly critical of McLaren and other critical theorists, there is a key point in showing the limitations of any theory focused on resolving human disparities without also considering the ways in which these disparities are embedded in the tensions that exist between human-cultural and environmental systems.

Likewise, Bowers shows the limits of Henry Giroux's emancipatory perspective. Giroux recommends that teachers embrace critical pedagogy as a way to interrogate tradition. Bowers points out that Giroux does not establish any guidelines as to how teachers are supposed to distinguish between the traditions that "should *not* be politicized or reconstructed" (p. 51). Bowers explains that Giroux deemphasizes the crucial role of parents and other citizens in the process of emancipatory education because, for Giroux, teachers simply serve as the administrators of critical inquiry. An important point is that emancipatory theorists such as McLaren and Giroux advocate for dialogue and, at the same time, reject customs as problematic; yet they dismember anyone who disagrees with their universal emancipatory approach—even labeling them "fascists," according to Bowers (p. 53). The key point for Bowers is that emancipation scholars tend to represent cultural customs as oppressive, or mindless, habits that cannot contribute to social justice.

Bowers notes that McLaren, Giroux, and others use the term "conservatism" to represent the educators who want to transmit knowledge and ideas of economic development to further exploit the working class and those who embrace racism, sexism, and non-democratic decision making. In contrast, Bowers argues that conservatism can be found in the nature of biological processes, the ways in which cultural patterns are repeated, the linguistic systems necessary to culture/identity and relationships, the political language that emphasizes the work to regenerate eco-conscious communities, the philosophy of change and mutual obligation to the community/bioregion, and the knowledge that empowers indigenous cultures to live in concert with their environment.

Similar to McLaren and Giroux, Michael Apple and Jean Anyon also ignore the natural systems in their social justice work, according to Bowers. Bowers questions why theorists who advocate social justice fail to include the destruction and contamination of the environment. He suggests that these theorists are heavily influenced by anthropocentrism, which views nature as insignificant in the discussion of human issues. Bowers concludes that "Arne Ness, Edward Goldsmith, Wolfgang Sachs, and Helena Norberg-Hodge do address these issues, but they are not mentioned in the writings of McLaren, Giroux, Apple, Shor, and others" (p. 67). It might be argued, however, that Bowers does not recognize the contributions that these critical theorists have made to alleviating the oppressive social conditions that Bowers would argue were wrongly construed in the first place and should have been interrogated, rejected, and changed.

Bowers is less critical of John Dewey, and he discusses several important contributions that Dewey provides for educational reform. However, Bowers notes the influence of science in Dewey's scholarship and his pragmatism and process-oriented approach that significantly limits Dewey's ideas for ecojustice. Bowers also mentions Richard Rorty's inability to recognize the cultural assumptions that underlie Dewey's work as problematic. The key points are that Dewey's ideas led to homogenization and modern progress that undermines ecological integrity. Especially problematic is Dewey's process-oriented approach to social action. Dewey claimed that all community traditions and values are relative and thus open to continuous reconstruction. Bowers notes that Dewey's ideas are inconsistent with social justice because they do not account for cultural groups that do not view their traditions and values as in need of reconstruction.

Bowers contends that many of the criticisms of Dewey also apply to Paulo Freire. While he points out several important contributions that Freire makes to educational theory, such as critical reflection and dialogue, he suggests that Martin Buber has a more adequate and complex approach to dialogue. While Freire includes a place for diverse ways of knowing in his universal theory of critical consciousness, he places a strong emphasis on rationality. According to Bowers, Freire's ideas (individualism, self-determination, and progressive change, to name a few) stem from the Enlightenment. Like Dewey, Freire does not recognize that people are embedded in a set of taken-for-granted cultural traditions that are tied to the planet. Freire fails to sufficiently challenge the underlying assumptions that perpetuate anthropocentrism, and he promotes the "rootless individual" centered in a world of constant change (p. 74). Specifically, Freire emphasizes a universal Western notion of critical thinking that perpetuates anthropocentrism and ignores traditional ecological knowledge and intergenerational communication. Bowers notes that Freire's emphasis on critical consciousness fails to consider "which traditions of a cultural group need to be renewed and strengthened and which are morally problematic and thus in need of being reformed or entirely abandoned" (p. 75). For Bowers, ecojustice theory requires a greater sensitivity to cultural traditions.

As we will eventually see, Bowers draws on some of the fundamental ideas that also support emancipation theories, such as the emphasis on analyzing cultural language to decipher which traditions, if any, are more aligned with ecological integrity. In this way, I would say that he resonates with emancipatory liberal theorists while also offering some important distinctions that limit emancipation theories to deciphering ecojustice. In short, the most egregious charges have to do with the universalizing pedagogy described by critical theorists, or Gods-eye view (which is a common concern for critical theory), and the anthropocentrism inherent in emancipation theories that limits any role for the Earth. While emancipation theories have been used to alleviate tensions for oppressed indigenous communities, there is the risk that without the more encompassing analysis of what is renewed and what is lost, then communities of people historically dwelling well with their environment might not take forward the patterns of thinking needed to continue to live in ecologically viable ways or act in concert with the harmony of their environments.

The Failure of Educational Science and Theories of Evolution

Education and school research have been patterned after Western science for many years. Bowers notes that, while science makes important contributions to our understanding of the natural world and increases the conveniences of daily life, it also plays a significant role in "shaping the direction of the world's cultures" (p. 78). For a long time now, educationalists have upheld the merits of science to address problems in education. Bowers argues that there is a long history of educational psychologists trying to quantify the human brain and defending the genetic inheritance of intelligence. He cites the racist musings of educational theorists who were intent on providing a scientific basis for intelligence. He claims that "the inability of science to account for (indeed, its indifference toward) cultural differences in ways of knowing is one of the chief reasons why it is difficult to identify a scientific approach to teaching and learning that different cultural groups can agree on" (p. 80).

Bowers shows how the science-transferred-to-education approach remains central to the discussion of increasing efficiency and measurable educational outcomes. In teacher preparation, for example, he highlights how "educational theorists' insistence that theories of learning meet the scientific criteria of objective measurement and replicability has led to a huge literature and endless hours of required courses in educational psychology" (p. 80). Indeed, much of the research in educational psychology rests on the notion that knowledge lies within the autonomous individual, and there is no doubt that educational psychology has played a large role in education today. Yet we know that not all educational psychology need be construed this way.

Providing more holistic understandings of education, Bowers narrows his focus to the more recent theories of Lev Vygotsky and Jerome Bruner. According to Bowers, Vygotsky's very influential approach was not reliant on scientific reductionism, but rather on the interconnections "between language and cognition in social settings that opened the door to understanding the multiple ways in which the languaging processes of a cultural group carry forward the taken-for-granted thought patterns that are the basis of the group's form of intelligence" (p. 80). It is here that Bowers praises McLaren, Giroux, and Apple for their criticisms of science-infused approaches to school research, teaching, and learning. His main objective is to show how educational reformers in the science tradition have created a workforce of scholars and teachers who fail to recognize their own cultural embeddedness, that is, a rootless student population that easily succumbs to pressures of the consumer culture and a curriculum that does not teach about the cultural ideas that contribute to ecological degradation. Bowers does not lump all science knowledge into the categories he has designated, but suggests there are recent developments in science—such as in the field of quantum mechanics—that are challenging the traditional mechanistic view of science he critiques. He acknowledges that a few educational reformers are taking notice and aligning these recent scientific theories with their educational goals.

Bowers provides a lengthy analysis of Chaos Theory, but I do not take up his argument here because his thoughts are not well developed and are largely misleading. It does not characterize the way science has been theorized by others (Longino, 1990). In this regard, Bowers reiterates a concern that most philosophers of science, scientists, and educators have raised about the idea that science deemphasizes, or neglects, the role of culture in the further refinement and modern growth of scientific knowledge. According to Bowers, basing educational reforms on the ideas implicit in science and theories of evolution is short-sighted. He believes that Charles Darwin's theory of evolution has become an overarching and exclusive force in Western society. Now, many of the academic domains use the concept of evolution to describe progressive change through natural selection. Essentially, evolutionary development is equated with progress and closely aligned with Western ways of knowing that are implied to be better and more complex than indigenous ways of knowing. Bowers explains that it is surprising that educational reformers have not yet turned to an exclusive use of natural selection to justify "why certain classes, cultures, technologies, and ideas succeed while others fail" (p. 113). He notes that the influence of scientists who make daily discoveries linking genes to illnesses and traits will be hard to ignore. He explains how Darwin's theory of evolution is a simplistic explanation that reinforces the Western myth of progress and how evolution is now being used to explain how technology progresses (such as with genetically modified plants).

Bowers continues with a critique of how Carl Sagan and E.O. Wilson grant science too much superiority, legitimacy, and exclusivity. He believes this is an epistemological stance that is used to judge what counts (not just in science but in all domains outside of science). While Bowers acknowledges the many contributions of scientific knowledge to our understanding of the natural world, he sees a danger in using science to explain culture. He points out that Wilson has been primarily responsible for promoting the view that genes and culture co-evolved through epigenesis—that is, genes determine culture and account for a bias in ways of knowing. While Bowers acknowledges the successes of science that contribute to our well-being and daily conveniences, he charges that the underlying assumptions of scientific knowledge often neglect the traditions and ways of life that work to protect the natural world. The paradox that Bowers is concerned with is the way in which scientists investigate the natural environment, that is, using a legitimized scientific process that exacerbates the degradation of the natural world in the values, beliefs, and knowledge it carries forward.

While I appreciate Bowers's generalized critique of science, the question arises as to whether he has adequately consulted the philosophers of science who have rigorously contested the way in which he has aligned science with Wilson, Sagan, and others. He builds his arguments on scientists such as Wilson and Richard Dawkins, who tend to cast out a net of provocative statements about epistemology to ruffle feathers with floppy defenses. Generally, most scientists, philosophers, and educators will disagree with the way in which Bowers sets up the scientific endeavor; and he does not spend much time analyzing the merits of scientific knowledge, even when it is inseparable from the traditional ecological knowledge of indigenous peoples (Tippins, Mueller, van Eijck, & Adams, 2010).

It is true that educational systems have moved toward "scientifically based educational research" as the gold standard. And the ways that science research is conflated with educational research and the manner in which the National Science Foundation and U.S. Department of Education now constrain studies that fit neatly in a narrowly defined box of what counts is indeed concerning. Bowers's critiques of the root metaphors that undergird these developments in education are significant, but the historical characteristics of science that fail to contribute to ecological well-being and cultural integrity do not have as much influence as they once did. Perhaps it is through Bowers's ideas that we are reminded how easy it is to slip back into the root metaphors that drive patterns of thinking and action that work against the preservation of the Earth. Lest we forget how science gained legitimacy, superiority, and exclusivity in the Western world though a long history of personal gain, subject mistreatment, and fraud, Bowers could have delved further into this androcentric story by examining the history of science.

Withstanding the deeply embedded root metaphors of individualism, progressivism, and scientism that Bowers wrestles with, the ethnoscience of indigenous people is significant and appropriate for analyzing global ecojustice tensions such as the harms to farm workers that come from the herbicide Atrazine, which is applied to conventionally grown food (Mueller, 2009b), or the erosion of the environment through resource extraction and mining (Mueller, 2015). Unfortunately, Bowers takes too hard a stance on science, emancipation scholars, and computer technologies in his book, without acknowledging their important role in analyzing the tensions situated in neoliberal education that largely drive the patterns of thinking and ways that people treat animals and the physical world. It is also important to keep in mind, with respect to Bowers's theorizing, that ecojustice is a highly contextualized concept and pedagogy, and this is what Bowers intended for ecojustice theory. Over the last 15 years, this notion has been supported by the tremendous number of projects and papers that have emerged since Bowers's book. Ecojustice theory has emerged very differently in different locations of the world and is served best by an ontology of difference that creates and increases the opportunity to dissolve the situated tensions between people and the planet. An important question, then, is whether there can be one way of enacting ecojustice curriculum. Therefore, I delve into the next section of Bowers's book with some trepidation in that, while Bowers describes elements of what ecojustice curriculum might look like, he never meant them to be taken exclusively as ecojustice education.

Elements of Ecojustice Curriculum

Bowers recommends the development of an ecojustice curriculum that includes the marginalizing effects of technology in undermining cultural diversity and the environment. He believes that an ecojustice curriculum will empower marginalized cultural groups through the democratic decision-making process of their local communities. By democracy that is strengthened by ecojustice pedagogy, Bowers means democracy "that recognizes individualized perspectives and talents as being embedded in distinct cultural approaches to community" (p. 150). Bowers explains that the overarching goal will be to include all social groups affected by any decision. Interestingly, he says that Dewey and Freire cannot be viewed as early exponents of ecojustice pedagogy because the former promoted a "community-centered process of participatory decision making" (that is, all traditions being subject to change [p. 151]) and the latter promoted an emancipation pedagogy founded on anthropocentrism and universalism. He defines *understanding* not to mean "a purely cognitive grasp of abstract relationships and issues," but rather to "encompass an explicit understanding of relationships and the ecology of place, and an awareness of the layered nature of the interdependencies of life-sustaining processes" (p. 152). He notes that these ideas are endorsed by the American Association for the Advancement of Science (AAAS) and often called community-based research in science and education, which reifies the way that I've addressed Bowers's critiques above.

An ecojustice curriculum can start with what students already know about their interdependent communities and the impact of these communities in relation to the environment. Bowers suggests that teachers might ask their students to identify mentors and elders in the community and why they are important. They might examine the networks of mutual aid, characteristics of a lifestyle based on the principles of voluntary simplicity, and intergenerational skills that represent an alternative to meeting personal needs through consumerism. They might examine bartering systems, sources of fresh water and waste, patterns of animal migrations, native plants and animals, and features of the land that are most affected by extreme weather conditions. Finally, they might analyze whether there are narratives that contain wisdom about culture-nature relationships that were not understood by previous generations, and how place has influenced their self and identity.

Bowers explains that students' responses "need to be considered in relation to how the distinction between high- and low-status knowledge affects racial, gender, and class relationships" (p. 153). These analyses reveal the double blinds associated with how social and environmental justice studies may inadvertently perpetuate the modern ideologies that tend to degrade culture and the environment. They foster an understanding of how cultural patterns of domination privilege certain groups over others and how human changes to the environment affect human life. These analyses can help students participate in the renewal of intergenerational knowledge and revitalization of the community. Specifically, Bowers contends that ecojustice can serve as a cultural studies curriculum through comparative studies of high- and low-status knowledge: examining the cultural patterns associated with encoding print-based media, objectivity, autonomous individualism, cognitive constructivism, and consumerism. He describes the many cultural patterns that work against valuing everyday experiences, and he suggests that the "success of an eco-justice curriculum will thus depend on the willingness of classroom teachers and university professors to use the patterns reenacted in daily experience as a basis for raising awareness of what is ecologically problematic in the high-status knowledge that constitutes the curriculum" (p. 156). Bowers believes that an ecojustice curriculum will address many of the social issues that cut across cultural groups and social class. Thus, integral parts of an ecojustice curriculum will include the cultural resources available from within the local community.

Bowers posits several themes for an ecojustice curriculum, including commodification, traditions, technology, science, and language. The overarching construct is that contextually embedded, or taken-for-granted, assumptions will be made explicit through an ecojustice curriculum. He notes how this reflective, or *naming*, process is much different from what Freire sought for progressive change: "namely, the need for intergenerational accountability that renews the genuine achievements of the past in ways that do not diminish the prospects of future generations" (p. 158). Intergenerational accountability differs among various cultural groups. Bowers shows how teaching students "different explanatory frameworks, the history of ideas, and how different cultures developed" provides a new lens through the ecojustice pedagogy. He explains that, as students explore consumerism and comparative cultures, they can effectively learn how to renew the activities of the less consumer-dependent cultures.

Next, Bowers describes how an exploration of traditions can be emphasized by focusing on students' daily lives. By traditions, he "designates the entire scope and continuity of cultural practices" (p. 165). An examination of traditions includes what it would be like to live without traditions (what Bowers argues has been advocated by critical pedagogy theorists). Bowers explains that, without traditions, "there would be no community—just individuals engaged in critical reflection and an endless search for new forms of creative expression" (p. 165). Bowers suggests a cultural survey of the local community that can be used in the early grades to examine the forms of media that promote continuous change and innovation as expressions of progress. Students should understand their community traditions, the nature of traditions, the difference between traditions and fads, and how traditions do not stifle change and innovation. Further, Bowers illustrates how students can be engaged in the traditions of communities that are aligned with the environment (i.e., gardening, sports, craft knowledge, and volunteerism).

Technology amplifies and reduces certain aspects of cultural life. For students, Bowers emphasizes how technology has become the primary context for their experiences. Modern technology is now the greatest impediment to ecological ways of living. Those who do not have access to, or do not embrace, technological advancement continue to be marginalized. Bowers believes that the curriculum should incorporate an analysis of technology and ecojustice issues. Young children can be introduced to the culturally mediating impact of technology. They can learn how technology is not culturally neutral and how technology is interwoven in their everyday experiences. He argues that modern technology issues can be examined in every aspect of the curriculum—the arts, sciences, social studies, humanities, and others. He provides several questions that can be analyzed with older students: how technology has affected thought through language, impacted students' developmental skills, influenced relationships between cultures and people, and incorporated industrial revolution thinking or ecological design principles.

Bowers stresses that an ecojustice curriculum should provide a balanced view of science—its achievements and inappropriate uses—in an effort to democratize the use of science. Younger students can be taught that science is not culturally neutral and that "scientists share a linear view of progress with the dominant culture, emphasize the separation of objective knowledge from moral values, and too often disregard how the cultural language processes in which they are embedded organize their thought processes" (p. 174). He suggests that examples of indigenous practices and traditional ecological knowledge can be woven into the curriculum to reinforce this central point. Older students can learn about the history of scientific thought (p. 174). In addition to the disparities often associated with pursuing a career in science, science teaching can be expanded to encompass the situated tensions of ecojustice that illuminate the nature of science and the ways it reinforces the taken-for-granted ideologies in Western language.

Bowers further discusses language as the last component of an ecojustice curriculum. Students can analyze the language that carries forward taken-for-granted patterns of thinking through the socialization process of local communities. Even teachers ought to be continuously aware of their patterns of thinking that are reinforced by the language used in the curriculum. Bowers points out that language carries forward the experiences of cultures of the past and may include patterns of thinking—deep cultural assumptions—about ecological sustainability. He notes how cultural languages transmit geographic knowledge of place (local knowledge about biodiversity and natural systems). He contends that an ecojustice curriculum should make explicit the cultural assumptions passed on through language. Equally, if not more importantly, an ecojustice curriculum should foster a sense of awareness about the print-based messages that "exert a powerful influence in shaping the students' identity, expectations, and values" (p. 179). Bowers notes that "eco-justice pedagogy cannot be turned into a rigid set of prescriptions—no matter how well intended" (p. 186), and it must consider the prospects of future people.

Coda

Since *Educating for Eco-Justice and Community*, there have been hundreds of articles and books written that take seriously the ideas that were originally written in Bowers's book. While at its foundation Bowers has raised some heightened awareness around ecojustice, and curriculum and instruction around ecojustice, there is still much work to do for ecojustice to become more of a priority in the educational literature. Even with some common threads between scholars' ecojustice research, there are some major differences in how ecojustice has been further theorized and incorporated into teacher education. Most of the commonalities exist around locally centered projects where evidence for ecojustice theory and pedagogy can be gathered around the globe. The most visible of these projects has been around school gardens and food security, which is now a major concern for most people. Climate change, adaption, and mitigation strategies have also taken on a heightened emphasis for ecojustice scholars.

It is important that new scholars read the foundational literature that has emerged from Bowers's writings and form their own ideas for ecojustice theory and pedagogy, using the work of specific scholarship that matches their interests. Differences exist—for example, some scholars still privilege the "ecological crisis" narrative to do their work. It is crucial to understand how the crisis limits ecojustice. Other scholars have recovered Dewey and Freire to do their work. Still others have emphasized the significant role of science and technology (even STEM) to cultivate a citizenry focused on navigating science media (O'Connor, Fidler, Custer, Beckendorf-Edou, Stewart, & Mueller, 2013), citizen science (Mueller, Tippins, & Bryan, 2012), plant rights (Mueller, Patillo, Luther, & Mitchell, 2011), and organic market farming (Mueller, 2014).

The key point is that there are some notable differences with regard to how ecojustice theory has been advanced, and those distinctions are important to note as one develops her own sense of ecojustice to do important work. While there is still some disagreement about whether place-based philosophy and other ecologically centered education theories align well with ecojustice theory and pedagogy, there have been some recent developments in ecological mindfulness and cross-hybrid learning that have created a heightened confluence for ecojustice and place-based theory. (For a special journal issue on these topics, see Mueller & Greenwood, 2015.) Most important, we have yet to see whether ecojustice theory has changed the neoliberal system of education that has taken such a stronghold in our society and now worldwide. In the end, as educators and citizens, we must emphasize a form of education that dissolves tensions between people and places.

References

Bowers, C.A. (1990). Implications of Gregory Bateson's ideas for a semiotic of art education. *Studies in Art Education, 31*(2), 69–77.

Bowers, C.A. (1996). The cultural dimensions of ecological literacy. *Journal of Environmental Education, 27*, 5–10.

Bowers, C.A. (2001). *Educating for eco-justice and community.* Athens: University of Georgia Press.

Longino, H. (1990). *Science as social knowledge: Values and objectivity in scientific inquiry.* Princeton, NJ: Princeton University Press.

Mueller, M.P. (2009a). Educational reflections on the "ecological crisis": Ecojustice, environmentalism, and sustainability. *Science & Education, 18*(8), 1031–1055.

Mueller, M.P. (2009b). On ecological reflection: The tensions of cultivating ecojustice and youth environmentalism. *Cultural Studies of Science Education, 4*(4), 999–1012.

Mueller, M.P. (2014). A theory of socioecological characteristics for food mindfulness. *Brazilian Journal of Research in Science Education, 14*(2), 315–329.

Mueller, M.P. (2015). Alaskan salmon and Gen R: Hunting, fishing to cultivate ecological mindfulness. *Cultural Studies of Science Education, 10*(1), 109–119.

Mueller, M.P., & Greenwood, D.A. (2015). Special issue on ecological mindfulness and cross-hybrid learning. *Cultural Studies of Science Education, 10*(1).

Mueller, M.P., Patillo, K.K., Luther, R.A., & Mitchell, D.B. (2011). Lessons from the tree that owns itself: Implications for education. *International Journal of Environmental and Science Education, 6*(3), 293–314.

Mueller, M.P., Tippins, D.J., & Bryan, L.A. (2012). The future of citizen science. *Democracy & Education, 20*(1), 1–12.

O'Connor, L.M., Fidler, J.L., Custer, E., Beckendorf-Edou, T.L., Stewart, A.J., & Mueller, M.P. (2013). Breaking science news for encouraging science literacy in high school science students. *ORN Journal of Educational Research, 1*(1), 1–31.

Tippins, D.J., Mueller, M.P., van Eijck, M., & Adams, J.D. (Eds.). (2010). *Cultural studies and environmentalism: The confluence of ecojustice, place-based (science) education, and indigenous knowledge systems.* Dordrecht: Springer.

THIRTY-TWO

John Ogbu, *Black American Students in an Affluent Suburb: A Study of Academic Disengagement* (2003)

Jan Armstrong and Tryphenia B. Peele-Eady

What accounts for the difficulties some groups face in attaining high levels of academic achievement in public schools? Why do the children of some families enroll in more demanding courses, earn higher grades, garner higher scores on standardized tests of academic achievement, and gain admission to better colleges than others? And why do students display such a wide range of attitudes toward school?

In his 8-month ethnographic study of racial disparities in academic achievement in a middle-class school district, *Black American Students in an Affluent Suburb: A Study of Academic Disengagement*, John Ogbu (2003) addresses some of these questions. As many chapters in this volume illustrate, issues of fairness, equality, and justice in schooling have long concerned American educational analysts. Since the 1960s, a number of scholars and researchers have held that racial discrimination and economic stratification produce educational disparities. Although he acknowledges that the system (social structure) played a part in creating the academic performance gap, Ogbu focuses on social processes that might help to account for racial disparities in educational attainment, even when ample financial resources are available. He concludes "that the Black community and the school system were both responsible for the academic disengagement of Black students" (2003, p. 274), and he makes several recommendations for changes in policy and practice for the community, schools, and parents to discuss and consider (pp. 274–289).

Using empirical data and theoretical reasoning, Ogbu argues that neither systemic forces (discrimination, racism, and class differences), patterns of differential success in school, nor differences in economic class alone (a position held by many authorities at the time of the book's publication) are the sole causes of the "performance gap" and thus could not account for differential academic outcomes between White and minority-group students. Ogbu's argument contradicts popular academic assumptions. Specifically, his "cultural ecological theory" of minority education (what some now refer to as Ogbuian theory) is the culmination of a 30-year period of research examining patterns of educational achievement observed in many parts of the world.

We will begin by outlining Ogbu's major theoretical ideas before turning to the book, its strengths and weaknesses, and impact. Ogbu begins with a global observation that minority groups were adversely affected by their "caste-like" position in communities and schools. He argues that minority groups form "collective identities" that reflect their histories and influence how group members view schooling. Hence, Asians and minorities of African descent (e.g., from the Caribbean and Africa) do better in school than groups that have been in the United States for generations (e.g., African Americans and American Indians). Ogbu observes that many first-generation immigrant families began their lives in their host countries at or near the bottom of the economic hierarchy. They immigrated voluntarily and were willing to do jobs that others did not want—jobs that were difficult, unpleasant, and low paying. Yet the children of these immigrants tended to do better in school than other minority groups. Ogbu claims that "voluntary immigrants" see school as a means to an end—for them, going to school has instrumental value: it provides a pathway to better job opportunities. "Voluntary immigrants" form their collective identities before they leave their home countries, and this makes it easier for them to conform to the demands of formal schooling and embrace education for its instrumental or "pragmatic" value.

In contrast, in the United States, the collective identities of African American and American Indian groups are formed in response to their experience of White domination (slavery, conquest, and discrimination). As a consequence, members of these groups—the "involuntary minorities"—remain wary of the educational enterprise, interpreting the school curriculum as a malevolent force aimed at further subjugation (and/or cultural extermination). Due to their historical relationship with institutions largely run by White people, involuntary minorities tend to form "oppositional identities" and believe that the dominant class considers them inferior. They are also less optimistic about the link between schooling and workplace success and keenly sensitized to the historical injustices that have negatively shaped their collective identities.

Synopsis

In 1997 Ogbu received a call from Black community leaders in Shaker Heights, Ohio (an affluent suburb of Cleveland), who were concerned about an article published in the school newspaper that described the school district's "Black-white academic performance gap." The Shaker Heights community was known for its first-rate schools and commitment to voluntary desegregation at a time when racial tensions in the United States were at a peak and many communities resisted integration. Shaker Heights was home to Black and White middle-class and professional workers who had chosen to live in the suburb so that their children would benefit from its well-regarded school system. About one-third of the community's 30,000 residents were African American, 10% of families were poor, and many others were working class.

Ogbu, an educational anthropologist and University of California, Berkeley, professor, was born in Nigeria in 1939 to parents who were farmers and was a respected authority on minority education. By invitation, Ogbu visited Shaker Heights, talked with school and community leaders, and developed a proposal for research that the school district funded. The Shaker Heights study presented Ogbu with a unique opportunity to investigate the social processes at work in a community where most (though not all) residents were middle class. The school district and community members gave Ogbu full access to documents, records, classrooms, and public events. Although he received a strong welcome from the community, his visit was met with some controversy. Due to limited housing alternatives, Ogbu stayed with two community members, and some in the Black community felt that his relationship with his hosts undermined his objectivity and caused his interpretations to be biased. Ogbu concluded that this was not the case, noting that the community's response reflected a widespread mistrust of (primarily White) school authorities.

In keeping with the ethnographic tradition, Ogbu used a descriptive and holistic approach. He interviewed teachers, students, parents, school counselors, administrators, and members of the community. He attended meetings, read documents, studied demographics and economic data, investigated the history of the community, and conducted 110 observations of elementary, middle school, and high school classrooms. Comprised of 13 chapters and three sections, *Black American Students in an Affluent Suburb: A Study of Academic Disengagement*, was published in January 2003. In the volume, Ogbu reviewed current theories of minority education, summarized his cultural-ecological theory, reported his controversial findings, and offered recommendations to the community and school district.

Focusing on "community forces" that might help to account for the performance gap, Ogbu and his research assistant, Astrid Davis, detailed a number of interrelated patterns. To support their assertions, they used direct quotations from interviews and notes taken during classroom observations. They found differences in the content of classes taught at different levels—college prep, honors, and advanced placement. For instance, lower-level classes focused on reading comprehension, vocabulary building, and making connections to personal experiences, while the AP and honors classes required more homework and provided opportunities for more engaging and rigorous discussion of reading assignments. Few classes utilized materials relevant to the Black experience.

Ogbu noted that neither working-class nor middle-class Black parents seemed to understand how placement in classes affected their children's future prospects. School authorities struggled to find ways to engage Black parents in workshops and school events intended to benefit their children, with limited success. Across income levels, parents seemed to subscribe to the idea that their children's academic performance was the responsibility of the school district and teachers. They did not monitor homework or engage with teachers on behalf of their children (for example, regarding placement in more advanced classes), and students did not see the benefit of taking more difficult classes and getting good grades. Ogbu reported that students did not see or value their teachers as content experts and strongly preferred teachers who showed that they cared about them. Students reported that they did not work hard on their coursework, did not pay attention in class, and admitted that they could have done better had they done so. In keeping with major tenets of the cultural ecological theory, Ogbu argued that students did not hold a "pragmatic" view of the link between school success and the opportunity structure (employment opportunities). Instead, students chose role models in fields such as sports and entertainment industries that did not require educational success. While students viewed their parents as role models of social activism, they did not understand how their parents transitioned from high school to college to career. High school students were keenly aware that racism and discrimination limited their chances in the opportunity structure. A common belief among students was that Black people had to work twice as hard as Whites to attain the same level of reward in the workplace. They believed, for example, that White people considered Black people inferior and that teachers generally held low expectations for them.

Although he employed it only in part, Ogbu's field research in Shaker Heights seemed to confirm several premises of his cultural ecological theory. Black students appeared to have adopted attitudes and behaviors distinct from, and "oppositional to," those they associated with the dominant White culture, whose members maintained power within the educational and employment sectors at the time (at both local and national levels).

Cultural and Educational Context

Ogbu's early career was influenced by the continuing impact of the 1960s Civil Rights Movement and changes in the 1965 Immigration Act and subsequent amendments, which had made it possible for people from all over the world to immigrate to the United States. Schools began to see large numbers of immigrant children and families from "undeveloped" nations. By the 1970s schools had largely been desegregated and educational resources were distributed more equally across communities. Yet too many youth still struggled in school and a "performance gap" between White students and students of color remained. Social scientists rejected biological explanations for racial differences in intelligence (Henry, 1960) and proposed that cultural differences between dominant and marginalized groups provided a more plausible explanation. Ogbu was one of a number of anthropologists of education who investigated the relationship between "structural factors" (race, class, gender, and ability) and educational achievement beginning in the late 1960s.

Ogbu's trajectory of work long grappled with why children from historically underrepresented populations underperform in school and was largely influenced by his own migration to the United States in 1961 when, at the age of 22, he went on to study theology at Princeton and later transferred to the University of California, Berkeley, to study anthropology. There he continued researching and teaching until his death in 2003. Ogbu's work has been translated into Croatian, French, Italian, Japanese, Mandarin, and Spanish (Maclay, 2003), a testament to its impact. Prior to his work in Shaker Heights, Ogbu was well known for his California studies in Stockton and Oakland. *Black American Students in an Affluent Suburb* provides a synthesis of the central ideas that define his life's work.

Ogbu may be best known for his collaborative work on "acting White" with Signithia Fordham (Fordham & Ogbu, 1986; Fordham, 2014). Based on interviews with Washington, D.C., high school students, Fordham and Ogbu proposed that Black students feel peer pressure that compels them to avoid "acting White" (speaking a standard variety of English and appearing to work hard in school). A flurry of media attention latched onto the idea that students of color have "oppositional identities" and are therefore implicitly responsible for not achieving their academic potential, thus perpetuating the idea that in order for Black youth to succeed academically, they must adopt ideals of Whiteness. As is often the case, however, contemporary media reports paid little attention to the complex empirical and intellectual foundations that led to the researchers' conclusions. In much the same way, media responses to the Shaker Heights study highlighted only some aspects of Ogbu's findings while neglecting others. He reiterated the "acting White" theory in the Shaker Heights study, which generated controversy that continues even today.

Strengths and Weaknesses

Ogbu was among the first anthropologists to focus on the nature and complexity of structuralized racism and its role in the achievement gap. His work shed new light on the social processes that influenced minority students' school performance and their relationship to the system. Berube (2000) considered Ogbu one of four "eminent educators" of the twentieth century. He was a prolific author and an active researcher who was willing to take a stand on public debates about controversial issues. To illustrate, Ogbu was deeply engaged with the debates of the 1990s about whether African American vernacular English (AAVE), or "Ebonics," should be considered a legitimate language—different, but not inferior to standard American English. A gifted social scientist, Ogbu collected and reported data with meticulous care. He separated what people said from what they actually did—distinguishing between what people said in interviews and what he observed in the classroom and in community meetings.

Yet as an ethnographic study, *Black American Students in an Affluent Suburb* has been criticized on several grounds. Ogbu's interpretations might have relied too heavily on what interviewees told him. For example, he found *no* instances of a Black student indicating that she could not master a subject because she was taught in a European American manner. However, students' failure to make this connection for themselves does not mean that the curriculum content (and the way it was taught) had *no impact* on learning outcomes and attitudes. And while Ogbu himself noted that his constructs were "ideal types," some of his interview questions might be considered "etic"—focusing on particular terms and concepts derived from his model—and, in some instances, leading (that is, less open than they could have been). There is also less reflexivity (critical self-reflection) in this book than would be expected in similar ethnographic work today. Ogbu did not "put himself into the text." He did not give the reader access to his emotional reactions to the field experience or his sense of how his own status as a voluntary immigrant and a Berkeley professor affected the research process and his interpretations.

Critics have argued that Ogbu's conceptions of culture and oppositional culture are static and overly simplistic. Contemporary notions of culture emphasize complexity, dynamic change, and "intersectionality." Regardless of the group investigated, researchers today

> must acknowledge intragroup differences across multiple lines of difference, such as class, religion, gender, phenotype, and geographic location…[and] these intersectionalities need not only apply to involuntary and voluntary minority groups, but should inform the experiences of the dominant culture [as well]. (Rodriguez, 2014, p. 297)

For example, the term "acting White" implies the existence of a homogeneous White culture and a questionable Black/White binary. Studies that have countered Ogbu's arguments not only debunk the "acting White" framework; they also show how it wrongfully suggests that, in order for Black youth to be smart, they must assimilate to White ways of being (see Tyson, Darity, & Castellino, 2005). Ogbu places too much emphasis on what minority groups lack (their deficiencies) and does not attend to the strengths these groups bring to the educational enterprise. Moreover, attributing differences in school performance to the internalization of Whiteness entails a theoretical clash between psychological and anthropological understandings of achievement. There is a pervasive assumption on Ogbu's part that we can somehow disentangle societal problems from what is happening in schools, but anthropologists do not agree that these elements can be treated as separate entities.

Influence at the Time and Relevance for Today

Black American Students in an Affluent Suburb was controversial even before its publication and continues to evoke academic debate. Before the release of the book, a *New York Times* article illuminated the controversy surrounding Ogbu's claims (Lee, 2002). Conservative scholars and columnists such as Thomas Sowell and Clarence Page embraced Ogbu's notion that Black students were disengaged academically because they were more interested in athletics, friends, and entertainment than in schoolwork. Sowell, Page and others supported the idea that minority group members were wary of public institutions and formed oppositional identities, but they deemphasized the link to "caste" and its relationship to immigration status and historical oppression. At the same time, Ogbu reported that Black members of the Shaker Heights community questioned the veracity of his interpretations, arguing that school district people had undermined his objectivity.

Controversy notwithstanding, Ogbu was among the earliest scholars to consider the role of race as a factor in the educational achievement and life outcomes of Black Americans. He sought to articulate a holistic view grounded in empirical evidence—a view that drew upon detailed and comprehensive analysis of global and local contexts of schooling and the experiences of those involved in the process. At the time of his death, he was the most widely cited anthropologist in his university (Maclay, 2003). His cultural-ecological theory provided a new way to think about the multi-layered nature of the academic performance gap.

While Americans espouse ideals of equal opportunity and meritocracy, Ogbu's research provides extensive evidence for the persistence of racial inequality in U.S. schools. His focus on community forces and social processes illuminates how students' attitudes and behaviors reflect collective identities shaped by group-specific histories. Ogbu believed that minority group members had agency; and this being the case, they had the capacity to orchestrate alternative pathways for the future.

Across disciplines, scholars have expanded on the ideas Ogbu presented in the Shaker Heights study, pursuing the question of why some students succeed and others do not, and how and to what extent race matters. Researchers who have written about the intersections between race and achievement credit Ogbu for taking on the difficult task of providing a framework for understanding academic (dis)engagement and the performance gap (Foley, 2004; Lewis-McCoy, 2014). In addition to debunking theories of inherent deficit, Ogbu's work has influenced recent work that looks at the relationship among culture, race, and schooling (Howard, 2010; Nasir, 2012).

Since the publication of *Black American Students in an Affluent Suburb*, researchers have begun to examine Black student learning in contexts *outside* of school (e.g., Barron, Gomez, Pinkard, & Martin, 2014; Peele-Eady, 2011; Taylor, 2009). Recent studies describe conditions that support Black students' development as learners and explore the intersections of race, class, gender, and racial micro aggressions and the ways Black and White students engage culturally and socially with various aspects of schooling (Allen, 2010; Carter, 2005; Lewis, 2003).

Scholars have also used Ogbu's theory to shed light on the experiences of new immigrants to the United States (Gibson, 1988; Suárez-Orozco, Suárez-Orozco, & Todorova, 2010), demonstrating that students retain their cultural ways of life, yet selectively adopt the host nation's values. Work has also been done on culturally responsive pedagogies that support ethnic, racial, and learner identity development (Delpit, 2012; Ladson-Billings, 2009). In other words, researchers have shifted their focus to exploring the conditions that support African American students' successes rather than their failures.

Now, in the context of the recent killings of 17-year-old Trayvon Martin in Sanford, Florida, and 18-year-old Michael Brown in Ferguson, Missouri, and the subsequent public outcry for justice from a mixed-race public, we have seen an upsurge in discussions about the collective identities of Black youth and explorations of how racial, ethnic, and racialized identities inform school success and adult outcomes (Howard, 2010; Nasir, 2012). Access, equity, achievement, and internalized beliefs are now areas of research specialization in their own right. Ogbu's work has influenced new generations of social scientists who have tested and refined his ideas and proposed alternative frameworks of their own (e.g., Dumas, 2014; Foster, 2004; Lewis-McCoy, 2014). Although his arguments were controversial at the time, and some scholars continue to question the accuracy of his interpretations, Ogbu's legacy and his study of Shaker Heights offer a framework that invites readers to consider Black student achievement in more nuanced and productive ways. For this, John Ogbu remains a respected theorist and ethnographer.

References

Allen, Q. (2010). Racial microaggressions: The schooling experiences of Black middle-class males in Arizona's secondary schools. *Journal of African American Males in Education, 1*(2), 125–143.

Barron, B., Gomez, K., Pinkard, N., & Martin, C.K. (2014). *The digital youth network: Cultivating digital media citizenship in urban communities.* Cambridge, MA: MIT Press.

Berube, M.R. (2000). *Eminent educators: Studies in intellectual influence.* Westport, CT: Greenwood Press.

Carter, P. (2005). *Keepin' it real: School success beyond Black and White.* New York: Oxford University Press.

Delpit, L. (2012). *"Multiplication is for White people": Raising expectations for other people's children.* New York: The New Press.

Dumas, M.J. (2014). "Losing an arm": Schooling as a site of Black suffering. *Race Ethnicity and Education, 17*(1), 1–29.

Foley, D.E. (2004). Ogbu's theory of academic disengagement: Its evolution and its critics. *Intercultural Education, 15*(4), 389–397.

Fordham, S. (2014, August 16). Race and beyond: Are (Black) female academics ignored? Center for American Progress (blog). https://www.americanprogress.org/issues/race/news/2014/08/06/95248/race-and-beyond-are-black-female-academics-ignored/

Fordham, S., & Ogbu, J. (1986). Black students' school success: Coping with the burden of "acting White." *Urban Review, 18*(3), 176–206.

Foster, K.M. (2004). Coming to terms: A discussion of John Ogbu's cultural-ecological theory of minority educational achievement. *Intercultural Education, 15*(4), 369–384.

Gibson, M.A. (1988). *Accommodation without assimilation: Sikh immigrants in an American high school.* Ithaca, NY: Cornell University Press.

Henry, J. (1960). A cross-cultural outline of education. *Current Anthropology, 1*(4), 267–305.

Howard, T.C. (2010). *Why race and culture matter in schools: Closing the achievement gap in America's classrooms.* New York: Teachers College Press.

Ladson-Billings, G. (2009). *The dreamkeepers: Successful teachers of African American children* (2nd ed.). San Francisco, CA: Jossey-Bass.

Lee, F.R. (2002, November 30). Why are Black students lagging? *The New York Times,* sec. B, p. 9.

Lewis, A. (2003). *Race in the schoolyard: Negotiating the color line in classrooms and communities.* Piscataway, NJ: Rutgers University Press.

Lewis-McCoy, R.L. (2014). *Inequality in the promised land: Race, resources, and suburban schooling.* Stanford, CA: Stanford University Press.

Maclay, K. (2003, August 26). Anthropology professor John Ogbu dies at age 64. *UC Berkeley News*.

Nasir, N.S. (2012). *Racialized identities: Race and achievement among African American youth*. Stanford, CA: Stanford University Press.

Ogbu, J. (2003). *Black American students in an affluent suburb: A study of academic disengagement*. Mahwah, NJ: Lawrence Erlbaum.

Peele-Eady, T.B. (2011). Constructing membership identity through language and social interaction: The case of African American children at Faith Missionary Baptist Church. *Anthropology & Education Quarterly, 42*(1), 54–75.

Rodriguez, P.J. (2014). Review of *minority status, oppositional culture and schooling*. *Educational Studies, 50*, 294–298.

Suárez-Orozco, C., Suárez-Orozco, M.M., & Todorova, I.I. (2010). *Learning in a new land: Immigrant students in American society*. Cambridge, MA: Belknap Press of Harvard University Press.

Taylor, E.V. (2009). The purchasing practice of low-income students: The relationship to mathematical development. *Journal of the Learning Sciences, 18*, 370–415.

Tyson, K., Darity, Jr., W.A., & Castellino, D.R. (2005). It's not "a Black thing": Understanding the burden of acting White and other dilemmas of high achievement. *American Sociological Review, 70*(4), 582–605.

THIRTY-THREE

Richard Rothstein, *Class and Schools: Using Social, Economic, and Educational Reform to Close the Black-White Achievement Gap* (2004)

Leslie S. Kaplan and William A. Owings

Richard Rothstein is a research associate of the Economic Policy Institute (EPI) and senior fellow of the Chief Justice Earl Warren Institute on Law and Social Policy at the University of California (Berkeley) School of Law. He is one of the nation's leading authorities on the impact of socioeconomic factors on disparities in student achievement. From 1999 to 2002, he was the national education columnist for *The New York Times,* and he has written extensively on student achievement and school reform. The book that is the subject of this chapter originated in Rothstein's lectures in 2003–2004 at Teachers College, Columbia University, although some chapters expand work done at EPI or published elsewhere.

Synopsis

Since our nation's inception, public schools have been America's chosen means of preparing its children for civic responsibility, economic advancement, and social mobility. In the nineteenth century, Horace Mann called public schools "the great equalizer of the conditions of men—the balance-wheel in the social machinery" (Mann, 1848). For many, however, this has been more the ideal than reality.

Today's policymakers, education reformers, and the general public assume that the persistent achievement gaps between children of color and White students results from "failing public schools." They argue that a combination of wrong-headed policies, low teacher expectations, unfocused leadership, poorly designed curricula, too-large classes, and disruptive school climates—among other factors—are to blame for the persistent disparities in student outcomes. Generally speaking, middle-class and affluent students tend to achieve well in school; low-income and minority students do not.

In *Class and Schools* (2004), Richard Rothstein asserts that if we genuinely want all children to leave school with equal potential for civic, economic, and social advancement, we must reform social and economic institutions *beyond* the schools—as well as improve schools. He uses logical reasoning and data to explain how social class differences are likely to affect children's academic performance and offers recommendations to help overcome them.

Rothstein's Main Themes and Arguments

Rothstein advances his argument with three major themes and three recommendations.

Rothstein's Themes

- **Children's social class contributes to the achievement gap.**

  The combined effects of social class differences between middle-class and lower-class students are probably too powerful for even the best schools to overcome.

Americans don't like to think about social class. Seeing ourselves as democratic and meritocratic, we prefer to use euphemisms such as "disadvantaged" or "high-risk" to describe children of "low socioeconomic status." Eschewing such "political correctness," Rothstein deliberately uses the term "lower-class" to refer to families of children whose achievement will be, on average, predictably lower than that of middle-class children. By "lower-class" he means "a collection of occupational, psychological, personality, health, and economic traits that interact, predicting performance not only in schools but in other institutions as well that, on average, differs from the performance of families from higher social classes" (Rothstein, 2004, p. 4). "Lower-class" encompasses more meaning than "low-income."

As Rothstein observes, the characteristics that define differences in social class inevitably influence the average tendencies of students' academic achievement. These traits include parenting styles (childrearing, discipline, communication, reading to children); health differences (vision, oral hygiene, asthma, nutrition, pediatric care); housing (affordability and adequacy); and parental wealth (available resources and opportunities). Cultural characteristics originating in social and economic conditions may also contribute to the Black-White achievement gap.

- **The achievement gap extends to non-cognitive skills.**

  Education's goals include academic and character outcomes.

Personal character traits, or non-cognitive skills (including perseverance, self-confidence, self-discipline, punctuality, communication and organizational skills, social responsibility, and the ability to work well with others and solve conflicts), are also important public school goals. Non-cognitive gaps that may exist between children of different social classes are just as important as the academic and cognitive gaps. But because accountability requirements don't include them, teachers tend to ignore them.

Public opinion surveys consistently show that Americans want schools to produce good citizens and "socially responsible adults first and high academic proficiency second" (Rothstein,

2004, p, 7). Rothstein notes: "Econometric studies show that non-cognitive skills are a stronger predictor of future earnings than are test scores" (Rothstein, 2004, p. 7). If employers are going to assess integrity and other non-cognitive skills, he contends, schools should develop them and expect satisfactory group performance on their assessments as well as on academic tests.

- **School reform is not enough; we must also reform our social and economic institutions.**

    Because enormous disparities in family income and socioeconomic circumstance create enormous disparities in children's school readiness and educational outcomes, reforms need to narrow these background gaps between children who come to school.

Parents' income, health, home, and community profoundly impact children's academic performance. Even in "super schools," children's poverty matters. Schools and programs that trumpet their ability to close the achievement gap between low-income and middle-class children—such as the Heritage Foundation's "No Excuses" schools, the Education Trust's "high flying" schools, KIPP (Knowledge Is Power Program) schools, Pentagon schools, and "Success for All"—all present incomplete and misleading information. Rather than close the racial or social class achievement gaps, these schools misinterpret their test scores and/or "select" their successful student body. These schools, Rothstein concludes, are working with above-average children and using instructional approaches that would not close average students' achievement gaps. His "goal…is to direct attention to reforms that are less-often promoted but that are at least as important, if not more so" than strictly school reform (Rothstein, 2004, p. 132).

Rothstein's Recommendations

Rothstein proposes three recommendations in education and economic arenas for moving forward.

- **Expand the definition of "schooling."**

    "Schooling" should include important out-of-school hours, and we should provide programs for children during these times.

For infants and toddlers, Rothstein suggests comprehensive, high-quality early childhood programs using professional caregivers and low child-to-adult ratios. For instance, the successful Perry Preschool, Head Start, and Project STAR programs, over time, resulted in students with fewer special education referrals, fewer discipline problems, more high school graduates, higher adult earnings, fewer arrests, and fewer needing government support, on average, than their peers without these preschool experiences. Additionally, he recommends after-school and summer programs containing academics, supervised recreation, and other activities to reinforce educational gains and develop curiosity, creativity, self-discipline, and organizational skills. These varied learning experiences build the cultural and social capital that middle-class and affluent students receive from home. Lastly, Rothstein recommends school-community clinics that serve lower-class children and their parents in order to address health problems that impede learning.

Rothstein attaches a dollar amount to the costs for these educational and health reforms: an additional $12,500 per student per year over and above the $8,000 average per child per year already being spent—for a total of $156 billion a year. Adding perspective to this "down payment on the achievement gap," Rothstein calculates, "The average annual spending increase of $156 billion is only about two-thirds of the average annual cost of federal tax cuts enacted between 2001 and 2004" (Rothstein, 2004, p. 145).

- **Stop relying on standardized tests and statistical methodology for school accountability.**

  Limitations of standardized tests and statistical methodology often produce incomplete, inaccurate, and misleading results.

Rothstein contends that although standardized tests can indicate whether students have mastered basic skills (measuring basic recall, recognition, and low-level reasoning), they do little to assess other important academic skills (such as creativity, abstract reasoning, applying knowledge in new situations) or good citizenship that cannot be easily evaluated in standardized formats. Plus, their results may be misleading and not fully reliable, especially for small schools.

Moreover, Rothstein explains how *proficiency* is a subjective judgment, not an objective fact. Cut scores can be "manipulated" for political ends, for example, lowered to allow many children to appear proficient without improving teaching, curriculum, or learning. For example, when 85% of Texas fourth-graders score "proficient" on the state's reading test, while only 27% of them are "proficient" in reading on NAEP, both results cannot be accurate (Rothstein, 2004, p. 89).

Finally, Rothstein criticizes value-added assessments' statistical and methodological shortcomings. Although they can probably accurately identify more or less effective teaching, they do not indicate what practices effective teachers use. And even if the "best" teachers could be identified, political, parental, and fiscal issues would prevent assigning them to lower-class students if it meant taking them away from middle-class students.

- **Improve economic policy to reduce income inequality.**

  Better economic policies would benefit lower-class children's school achievement.

Rothstein recommends supporting minimum wage increases, permitting collective bargaining rights, expanding earned income tax credits, and endorsing policies that reduce unemployment. Similarly, supporting programs that provide stable and adequate housing would help low-income families reduce transient home life and maintain children's continuous school attendance without interrupting their (or their classmates') learning.

Climate of the Times

Throughout our nation's history, poverty was not destiny. Education could change life outcomes. Yet since the mid-twentieth century, American education has been buffeted by a confluence of cultural, economic, social, political, educational, and international factors. The result has been increasing politicization of American education that is undermining its effectiveness. *Politicization* is a process of giving an otherwise neutral issue a particular political, ideological, or emotional character in a way that makes people less likely to agree about it.

The selected events described below reflect 60+ years of interacting influences on American society that mirror the milieu in which Rothstein wrote. None, however, can be separated from the *political*—competition between opposing interest groups or individuals for power and leadership.

Key Cultural, Economic, Social, and Educational Influences

Post–World War II Western economies began shifting from the industrial to the informational. Machines now perform many repetitive jobs once available to less educated workers, while Web-networked professionals overseas work many jobs formerly held by U.S. college graduates—for a fraction of U.S. salaries. This new economy requires all high school graduates to have increased knowledge and skills if they are to become employable at living wages.

Likewise, changing American and worker demographics pose serious implications for education and our national well-being. The 2010 U.S. Census predicts that Latinos, African Americans, and other minority groups will collectively become the United States' majority population by 2043. By 2018 minorities will constitute more than half the children under 18 (Yen, 2013). Over time, the American workforce will shift from a majority of White workers to include more people of color. Children from these same groups are those whom our public schools traditionally have underserved.

In a related demographic shift, 2006 saw the first Baby Boomers (1946–1964) turn 60 years old and begin retiring in large numbers, drawing on Medicare and Social Security. Declining birth rates and increasing numbers of retirees mean fewer workers paying taxes to support retirees' benefits than in years past. For instance, the 2012 Social Security Trustees Report finds that in 1945, 41.9 workers supported each Social Security beneficiary; in 2011 only 2.9 workers sustained each beneficiary. The number of workers per retiree is expected to drop to 2:1 by 2030, "an unsustainable ratio" (de Rugy, 2012).

The implication is that, unless the upcoming workforce has the high-quality education and skills necessary to secure adequately compensated employment, buy goods and services, pay taxes, and exercise responsible citizenship, our social safety networks may not be able to meet our obligations.

In the education arena, 1954's *Brown v. Board of Education*, a unanimous U.S. Supreme Court ruling, prohibited states from segregating schools by race. Focusing the nation's attention on how Blacks were systematically denied equal rights, the *Brown* decision helped fuel a wave of freedom rides, lunch counter sit-ins, and voter registration drives, leading ultimately to civil rights legislation in the late 1950s and 1960s and presumably ending "separate and un-equal" public schools.

The Elementary and Secondary Education Act (ESEA) in 1965 and the 1964 Civil Rights Act rapidly expanded the federal role in education. Designed in part to equalize educational opportunity for poor and minority students (and close achievement gaps), ESEA provided additional funding to schools that enrolled large numbers of low-income students.

In 1966, in response to the U.S. Congress's desire to assess diverse children's equal educational opportunities, the Coleman Report appeared to show that family backgrounds, rather than school factors, were the primary influence on student achievement (Coleman et al., 1966). It also revealed that the schools' quality explained about one-third of the variation in student achievement, with the other two-thirds attributable to non-school factors (Rothstein, 2010).

In the 1970s educational equity became a widespread concern. School finance litigation in 45 of the 50 states from the 1970s onward challenged state school funding formulas to provide low-income and minority children with the fiscal resources to afford them an "adequate" education (Berry & Wysong, 2010).

Meanwhile, retreating from *Brown*, the U.S. Supreme Court in *Dowell*, 489, U.S. 237 (1991) began ruling that once-segregated Southern schools could be declared "unitary" and removed from U.S. federal oversight to keep them integrated. Being *unitary* meant that a school district complied with desegregation orders for a reasonable period of time, ended all vestiges of past discrimination to the extent practical, and demonstrated a good-faith commitment to the constitutional rights that led to the judicial intervention in the first place. Two similar court rulings followed.[1]

In their attention-grabbing 1994 book, *The Bell Curve*, Richard Herrnstein and Charles Murray argued that the Black-White achievement gap resulted, in large measure, from genetic differences between the races. Critics challenged the authors' oversimplifications that considered only current income and parental education, not the multitude of socioeconomic differences that undermine children's health, stability, and cognitive readiness for school learning (Rothstein, 2004).

Economically, the labor market recessions of the early 1980s, early 1990s, and 2001 increased many families' financial insecurity. The downturns fueled unemployment, reduced family incomes (because of layoffs, reduced hours, or job losses), cut the number of families with health insurance, and increased the number of people living in poverty. African Americans were especially harmed, with 4.3, 2.0, and 3.5 percentage-point employment declines, respectively, in those years (Schmitt & Baker, 2008).

Although not meant to be all-inclusive, these events suggest the tenor of the times. They—and other more overtly political occurrences (discussed below)—have led to education becoming politicized.

Politicization of American Education

Since the 1980s an array of factors has helped imbue education as a partisan—rather than an impartial—concern. In this context, liberal and conservative advocates have interpreted the achievement gaps—and offered recommendations—according to their own viewpoints.

Generally speaking, liberals value public education and some forms of school reform. They hold that more effective teaching, a rigorous curriculum, better leadership, extra support for struggling students, and positive learning climates—along with needed government resources (tax dollars)—can make a meaningful difference in low-income and minority students' achievement. They connect equity and excellence. They also believe that socioeconomic reforms would allow low-income and minority children to perform as well as white children in school, but this is not their primary focus (Kaplan & Owings, 2015).

In contrast, conservatives, in general, believe that minority underachievement has cultural (and, perhaps, genetic) roots, and moral behavior and self-help are the best ways to remedy their underachievement; economic reforms are relatively unimportant. Conservatives believe that schools can close the achievement gap with a "back to basics" curriculum, accountability, and current (or even reduced) funding levels. Meanwhile, they encourage parents to exert more choice in how they educate their children and seek "alternate" educational venues by using "free-market mechanisms"—including vouchers, tax credits, "opportunity scholarship" and publicly funded charter schools—and to improve "failing" public schools through competition (Kaplan & Owings, 2015).

Overtly political events have also played roles. In 1983 President Ronald Reagan's Secretary of Education, Terrel Bell, commissioned a report on American education, *A Nation at Risk,* that sharply criticized public schools. Our nation's education foundation, it concluded, was "presently being eroded by a rising tide of mediocrity that threatens our very future as a Nation and as a people." Most states adopted the report's agenda and increased their standardized testing for accountability. Also in response, David Berliner and Bruce Biddle's *The Manufactured Crisis* challenged the report's statistics and conclusions, alleging that it was an example of how political leaders were misleading the nation about our public schools' quality (Berliner & Biddle, 1995).

In 1991 Minnesota enacted the nation's first charter school legislation. Funded largely by public tax dollars and promoted as a parent-choice alternative to traditional public schools, charters were excused from certain state or local rules and regulations in exchange for delivering acceptable student performance. In 2013 more than 2.3 million public school students attended nearly 6,000 public charter schools in 42 states and the District of Columbia (Center for Research on Education Outcomes, 2013) despite their widely varying effectiveness (CREDO, 2009, 2013).[2]

In 2002 standards-based, test-driven accountability became law. With bipartisan congressional support, No Child Left Behind (NCLB), the renewed ESEA, attempted to close achievement gaps by requiring reading and math achievement testing in specified grades and disaggregated test results by demographic subgroups. Schools that did not meet annual performance expectations for each identified subgroup were subject to penalties. NCLB's authors assumed that school effectiveness and rigorous standards—not poverty or its related ills—were the primary drivers of student learning and achievement, and high-stakes accountability could equalize schooling for diverse students (Orfield & Frankenberg, 2014).

The entertainment culture also weighed in. In *Waiting for Superman*, his 2010 documentary, Davis Guggenheim presented what a *Washington Post* reviewer called a "scathing, moving critique of American public education" (O'Sullivan, 2010). The film examined teachers' unions, challenged teacher tenure laws, questioned teaching standards, and made heroes of education reformers who defied teachers' unions and encouraged low-income families who entered charter school lotteries to remove their children from the "failing public schools."

Around the same time, state-driven political and judicial decisions began placing teachers' collective bargaining rights and tenure protections at risk. In 2011 Governor Scott Walker led Wisconsin's legislature to end nearly all collective bargaining rights for most state public employees, including teachers. Several other states also moved to end teacher tenure protections (Education Week, 2014).

In a concluding example, the Common Core State Standards are caught in political crosshairs. The Common Core is a National Governors Association–initiated set of nation-wide college and workforce readiness curriculum standards in English and math that states and localities develop into teaching curricula. Benchmarked to international criteria, they claim to foster depth of knowledge and critical thinking for American students wherever they live. Nonetheless, detractors call them "ObamaCore" (Grace, 2014) and a "federal takeover" of local education authority. Teachers worry that students' scores from Common Core–aligned assessments will be used prematurely as part of teacher evaluations; New York City parents are upset that their children are being assessed on difficult content they were never taught (Mulgrew, 2013). Education scholars call them cases of excessive and inappropriate corporate influence on public education (Ravitch, 2013; Schneider, 2014) and part of a concerted effort to destroy public schools (Ravitch, 2013). While these standards were initially adopted by 45 states and the District of Columbia, several states have since withdrawn or are considering withdrawing from them (Kardish, 2014).

Strengths and Weaknesses of *Class and Schools*

Many of Rothstein's contemporary reviewers agree that *Class and Schools* makes major contributions to education reform and social policy. Ten years later, it still does.

To begin, Rothstein's clear, direct, and readable writing style, his lack of educational jargon, his logical presentation, and his extensive data and endnotes make his argument logical, persuasive, and readable for a wide audience (Hatheway, 2006; Strike, 2005).

Reviewers concur that *Class and Schools* comprehensively examines the relationship between social class and education and credibly identifies how children's socioeconomic status influences their readiness to succeed in school (Baskin, n.d.; Greene, 2007; Hatheway, 2006; Noguera & Wells, 2011; Romero, 2007; Strike, 2005). They also laud Rothstein for debunking the education reform myth that good schooling *alone* is enough to reduce the achievement gaps (Baskin, n.d.; Greene, 2007; O'Brien, 2006; Romero, 2007; Strike, 2005).

Next, critics appreciate Rothstein's encouraging schools to value and teach non-cognitive skills that contribute importantly to adult success (FairTest, n.d.) They applaud his recommendations that educators look more broadly toward educational and social policy reforms for potential solutions, including high-quality early childhood education, after-school programs, and summer school—as well as higher minimum wages and earned income tax credits (Baskin, n.d.; O'Brien, 2006; Noguera & Wells, 2011).

Additionally, reviewers applaud Rothstein's insight that many reform beliefs are not only incorrect, but ideological (Baskin, n.d.; FairTest, n.d.; Strike, 2005). Strike (2005) asserts that maintaining the notion that *schools alone* can reduce or close the achievement gaps—in the face of 50 years of evidence that they cannot (rather than recognize the need to improve lower-class students' achievement by improving their social and economic conditions)—must be satisfying people's interests or prejudices. Likewise, FairTest (n.d.) notes that even Rothstein's discussion of standardized testing's limitations for school accountability—namely, the inaccurate, misleading, and incomplete information they generate, the ability to "game" the system, and NCLB's 50 different ways to define "proficiency"—opens education policy to "almost endless political manipulation." Similarly, several agree with Rothstein that slogans such as "All children can learn" and "no excuses" can create unrealistic outlooks, incorrectly assign blame to schools and teachers, erode teachers' morale, and provide ideological respectability to those politicians and policymakers seeking to hold public schools accountable for their inevitable failure (FairTest, n.d.; Noguera & Wells, 2011).

At the same time, reviewers find certain weaknesses in Rothstein's argument. O'Brien (2006) and Romero (2007) protest that Rothstein does not adequately explain or define "lower class" as a distinct socioeconomic group in a theoretically rigorous way, accusing him of conflating the social concepts of race and class and using them interchangeably. O'Brien (2006) also believes that Rothstein relies on lower-class stereotypes without using data or evaluation to support their existence and risks perpetuating them, thereby increasing negative attitudes toward poor people.

O'Brien (2006) and Romero (2007) fault Rothstein for his focus on the Black-White achievement gap, ignoring other racial and ethnic groups—including Hispanics, Native Americans, Appalachian, and others—who also come to school with poverty-driven educational deficits (O'Brien, 2006; Romero, 2007). Nor does Rothstein consider gender and achievement (Romero, 2007).

Critics also lament Rothstein's "defeatist attitude" (Greene, 2007) or "pessimism" (O'Brien, 2006) about education reform's potential to improve learning outcomes for diverse children. Not championing educational reform, they contend, is a "recipe for inaction," gives comfort to those who keep the educational status quo, and rationalizes away school systems' shortcomings (Greene, 2007; O'Brien, 2006). Likewise, Greene (2007) claims that Rothstein does not explain how named reforms are ineffective; nor does he cite successful large-scale reform efforts.

In another vein, Baskin (n.d.) and Romero (2007) chide Rothstein for ignoring the critical theory perspective. Rothstein does not discuss how schools, as societal institutions, serve to advance the majority's interests at the minority's expense, how they reflect power arrangements in the larger society, or how they seek to reinforce the political, economic, and social status quo. Similarly, Romero (2007) derides Rothstein's "uncritical celebration of white middle class cultural forms."

Also taking him to task for what he did not say, Strike (2005) challenges Rothstein's failure to discuss the roots of the American public's "denial" of—and refusal to address—the socioeconomic factors that undermine lower-class children's school success. Strike (2005) suggests that Rothstein strengthen this aspect of his argument if he is to gain the political support needed to make the necessary social policy changes. Rothstein doesn't consider education's larger goals (for example, the "examined life," including the arts that help students enhance the quality of their experiences) beyond the subjects tested for accountability. Nor does he fully explore the limitations of standards-based education reform or challenge the ethos underlying the constant achievement testing that implies, "We don't trust; therefore, we must verify" (Strike, 2005).

Finally, in an arcane turn, Strike (2005) scolds Rothstein for using the term "*non-cognitive*" when describing non-academic skills, calling it "inaccurate and suspect," and referring to its early twentieth-century philosophical meaning as "beyond reason."

Many of these critiques have merit. Others reflect the authors' specialized professional knowledge in related fields, but do not actually address Rothstein's argument. What no critic noted, however, is Rothstein's use of *cognitive dissonance*—the mental discomfort that an individual experiences when trying to hold two or more contradictory beliefs at the same time or who acts in ways inconsistent with held beliefs. Rothstein's logical argument and supportive evidence attempt to make educators and policymakers uncomfortable with their established views about how to close the achievement gaps—in the hope that this discomfort will motivate constructive action in both school and socioeconomic contexts.

Rothstein considers himself an honest broker. He understands the achievement gaps holistically, logically presents his argument, supports it with substantial data, and offers clear recommendations. He asks us to recognize the reality: not all children begin kindergarten with the cognitive and experiential skills needed to succeed with schools' academic and social curricula—and the implications for policy.

Likewise, Rothstein discards the polite euphemisms and addresses social class straight on. On average, the children on the losing side of the achievement gaps tend to be *lower class*—a convergence of powerful occupational, psychological, economic, and health influences that affect their growth and learning. For Rothstein, education occurs 24/7, occurring both where students live and where they go to school. Accordingly, expecting schools, by themselves, to close the achievement gaps is naïve and harmful. Instead, Rothstein wants educators to continue increasing their own and their schools' capacities as well as become active citizens who support educational and fiscal policies that effectively address their students' socioeconomic conditions.

Moreover, Rothstein wants to move the education debate beyond its current politicization. Speaking as a public intellectual, his tone is matter of fact and not adversarial. At the same time, he doesn't let educators "off the hook" by saying that "family trumps school" in its influence on children's learning and achievement. School reform should continue apace, and teachers should have high expectations and increased instructional effectiveness so all children can move forward academically. Likewise, Rothstein doesn't let conservatives "off the hook" by allowing them to place all the responsibility for children's learning on the schools, declare schools as "failures" if they cannot, and then legislate "free market remedies" that remove public money from "government" schools.

Rothstein stresses that public schooling is an important—but perhaps not the *only* important—part of children's educational experiences. Those across the education debate spectrum need to understand the situation in its totality and act appropriately.

Significance and Influence When Written and Its Relevance Today

Upon its publication, *Class and Schools* was considered an astute and persuasive "must read" that might not have gone far enough. Determining *Class and Schools'* relevance today requires considering several key factors—student achievement and attainment, poverty, income inequality, segregated schools, and per-pupil spending—and assessing how they compare with 2004. Do Rothstein's arguments still have merit?

Educational Achievement and Attainment. At present, the racial achievement gaps are narrowing while the income achievement gaps are widening. Over the past 40 years, the Black-White and White-Hispanic achievement gaps in reading and math have narrowed by about 40% (Reardon, 2014). But the gaps remain very large, and progress across the country is uneven. In contrast, the achievement gaps between children from high- and low-income families has widened by about 40% over the past 30 years (Reardon, 2014). Achievement gaps are still with us.

Regarding students' educational attainment, recent evidence suggests that the "graduation gap" between Black and White students has declined sharply in the last decade; it is now half the size of 4 decades ago. Nonetheless, Black and Hispanic students are less likely to earn a B.A. degree or to enroll in a highly selective college than are White students—at a higher rate than 30 years ago. These higher education attainment gaps have changed little over the past few decades (Reardon, 2014).

The Stanford Center on Poverty and Inequality's study of achievement and attainment draws several conclusions (Reardon, 2014). First, the narrowing in racial/ethnic-White achievement gaps coincides with the onset of the educational accountability movement, but most of the NAEP-narrowed racial gaps may reflect pre-kindergarten trends rather than K–12 educational improvements (or NCLB). This conclusion supports Rothstein's view about "testing for accountability" and "50 varieties of proficiency cut scores" (and the teaching and learning practices that accompany them). Second, both racial and economic achievement gaps appear to contract during the school months and then widen again during the summer. This has not changed since Rothstein's 2004 observations. And third, states where the Black-White income and parental education gaps are larger and where school segregation is higher have much larger Black-White achievement gaps than states where income, education, and segregation disparities are smaller (Reardon, 2014). Again, these data support Rothstein's premise that children's family and economic circumstances—their out-of-school time—continue to be a major factor in their educational achievement and attainment. Inequality of educational outcomes by race and social class background in the United States remains very high (Reardon, 2014).

Poverty and Income Inequality. The nation's poverty rate is rising and, with it, other forms of social and economic disadvantage that affect children's educational and life outcomes. From 2007 to 2012, the official poverty rate increased from 12.5% to 15%, and the child poverty rate increased from 18% in 2007 to 21.8% in 2012 (Wolff, 2014). At least one out of every three African American (39%), Latino (34%), and American Indian (37%) children in the United States live in a household with an income below the poverty line (Annie E. Casey Foundation, 2013). And the Great Recession of 2007–2009 reduced Blacks' and Hispanics' net worth much more than it reduced Whites' net worth (Wolff, 2014), affecting the resources available for health care, housing, and other extras that keep children in school, healthy, and learning.

Additionally, income inequality is receiving policy, media, and public attention. Most workers no longer share economic growth's benefits as they did in the quarter-century after World War II (Danziger & Wimer, 2014). The failure of wages to grow for the vast majority is the leading reason why progress in reducing poverty has stalled over the last 35 years (Bivens, Gould, Mishel, & Shierholz, 2014). Except for the years between 1995 and 2000, salaries for most American workers have either stagnated or declined since 1979. Gaps between hourly wages of Black and Hispanic workers relative to White workers remain essentially unchanged at the low end of wage distribution and widening at higher levels (Desilver, 2014). The Black-White income and wealth gaps in the United States persist.

And as the numbers of low-income children keep growing, the gap between their well-being and that of their middle-class and affluent peers keeps widening. According to the Pew Research Center (2014), U.S. pretax income inequality is at the highest level it has been since 1928, more unequal than most of its peers in the developed world (Desilver, 2014). Between 1979 and 2007, the top 1% of U.S. taxpayers took home more than half (53.9%) of the total increase in U.S. income; its income grew by 200.5% (or 10 times as much as the average income for the bottom 99%, which increased by 18.9%). Between 2009 and 2012, the top 1% took 95% of the total income growth (Sommeiller & Price, 2014).

To an increasing degree, one's economic position in childhood determines one's position in adulthood, and this is more true in the United States than in many other advanced countries (Bivens et al., 2014). In light of Rothstein's suggestion that schools also perform a social service function, such as providing for health services, today's increased poverty and income inequality make his recommendations even more urgent than in 2004.

Segregated Schools. Since the *Brown* decision, student enrollment percentages nationally have shifted dramatically—an almost 30% drop in White students and close to a quintupling of Latino students. The South and West, regions with the most population growth, are now "minority-majority" areas (60% and 55%, respectively), with Latinos outnumbering Blacks in the South. And poor and minority children are no longer largely confined to inner cities; suburbs, metropolitan areas, and entire regions are also experiencing this complex educational reality (Orfield & Frankenberg, 2014).

Despite *Brown*, today's schools are becoming more segregated by race, ethnicity, and family income. Black and Latino students tend to attend schools with a substantial majority of poor children. Today's typical Black student attends a school where only 29% of his or her fellow students are White, down from 40% in 1980 (Siegel-Hawley & Frankenberg, 2012, p. 4, fig. 3). Latino students are the nation's most segregated (Orfield & Frankenberg, 2014). Further, in 2011–2012, 45.8% of all public school students were classified as low-income. Many schools are doubly segregated—by race and class (income)—isolating students from White, Asian, and middle-class peers (Orfield & Frankenberg, 2014). A well-received study of Chicago school reform found that concentrating students with social and economic disadvantages in low-income, racially homogenous schools—despite noteworthy improvements in teaching, curriculum, and leadership—made little or no difference in their school achievement (Bryk, Sebring, Allensworth, Luppescu, & Easton, 2010). Measured by these data, school segregation by race and income is worse today than in 2004.

Per-pupil spending on Black and White students in 2014 was about equal (compared with the wide discrepancies of 60 years ago). But students who come to school with lower social-class status and its attendant influences need many more resources than those enjoyed by White, middle-class students to catch up and keep up (Rothstein, 2013). What may be equal may also be inequitable.

Additionally, the Great Recession (2007–2009) brought increased unemployment, homelessness, poverty, and reduced tax revenues that fund schools. The school year 2013–2014 saw at least 35 states providing less funding per student than before the recession. From 2008 to August 2013, school districts cut 324,000 jobs. These cuts undermine school reform and hinder school districts' ability to deliver high-quality education, with negative consequences for national economic competitiveness (Leachman & Mal, 2014).

Recent Education Politicization. Since 2004 American education has become even more politicized. In addition to the examples above, a very brief list of high-profile education politicization would include: a 2012 presidential candidate who referred to "government-run schools" rather than "public schools" and called for their elimination (Benen, 2011); at least eight states grading schools on an A-to-F scale—each using a different methodology—for making decisions about funding, closure, and state takeovers (Layton, 2013); a state education commissioner who resigned his job amid disclosures that he instructed his staff to change the "C" grade assigned to a charter school founded by a million-dollar campaign donor when he was education chief in his previous state (Layton, 2013); and a *Los Angeles Times* columnist who asked, "Why have public schools at all?" (Goldberg, 2007).

If anything, the political clamor around education has grown shriller.

Conclusion

Rothstein's call to improve lower-class children's achievement by addressing the socioeconomic conditions that undermine their school and life success remains relevant. Unless we as a society can find the political will to focus policy attention and resources on both the school *and* the economic conditions that jeopardize our children's academic success, the goal of a twenty-first-century education for all children will continue to be elusive. And the fact that millions of American children are losing the possibility of economic security and social mobility due to inadequate education—in large measure because of poverty and economic inequality—places us all at risk.

Notes

1   *Freeman v. Pitts,* 503 U.S. 467 (1992); *Missouri v. Jenkins,* 515 U.S. 70 (1995).
2   The 2009 CREDO charter school study of 16 states, more than 2,400 charter schools, and 70% of the U.S. charter school students found that 17% of charter schools were better, 37% were worse, and 46% were comparable in math achievement to traditional public schools. The 2013 CREDO charter school study in 27 states covering over 5,200 schools and over 95% of all charter students shows some learning gains, in part because states closed more than 10% of "severely underperforming" charters; but charter school quality remains uneven.

References

Annie E. Casey Foundation. (2013). *2013 Kids Count data book: State trends in child well-being.* Baltimore, MD: Author. Retrieved from http://www.aecf.org/m/resourcedoc/AECF-2013KIDSCOUNTDataBook-2013.pdf

Baskin, R.S., Sr. (n.d.). Review of *Class and schools: Pressures on American education.* George Mason University, Fairfax, VA. Retrieved from http://www.google.com/url?sa=t&rct=j&q=&esrc=s&source=web&cd=7&ved= 0CFIQFjAG&url=http%3A%2F%2Fmason.gmu.edu%2F~rbaskin%2FClass%2520and%2520Schools%25 20Book%2520Review.doc&ei=qzeOU4O1F4eEogT8yIHABg&usg=AFQjCNFlz11XX6KE4x4kRaAyXKE EKhcCCw

Benen, S. (2011, March 25). When the GOP's hostility towards public schools becomes more overt…. Political Animal. *Washington Monthly.* Retrieved from http://www.washingtonmonthly.com/archives/individual/ 2011_03/028621.php

Berliner, D.C., & Biddle, B.J. (1995). *The manufactured crisis: Myths, fraud, and the attack on America's public schools.* Reading, MA: Addison-Wesley.

Berry, C., & Wysong, C. (2010, Summer). School-finance reform in red and blue. *Educationnext, 10*(3). Retrieved from http://educationnext.org/school-finance-reform-in-red-and-blue/

Bivens, J., Gould, E., Mishel, L., & Shierholz, H. (2014, June 4). *Raising America's pay: Why it's our central economic policy challenge.* Briefing Paper #378. Washington, DC: Economic Policy Institute. Retrieved from http:// www.epi.org/publication/raising-americas-pay/

Bryk, A.S., Sebring, P.B., Allensworth, E., Luppescu, S., & Easton, J.O. (2010). *Organizing schools for improvement: Lessons from Chicago.* Chicago: University of Chicago Press.

Coleman, J.S., Campbell, E.Q., Hobson, C.J., McPartland, J., Mood, A.M., Weinfeld, F.D, & York, R.L. (1966). *Equality of educational opportunity.* U.S. Department of Health, Education, and Welfare. Washington, DC: Government Printing Office.

Center for Research on Education Outcomes (CREDO). (2009). *Multiple choice: Charter school performance in 16 states.* Stanford, CA: Stanford University. Retrieved from http://credo.stanford.edu/reports/MULTIPLE_ CHOICE_CREDO.pdf

CREDO. (2013). *National charter school study 2013.* Stanford, CA: Author. Retrieved from http://credo.stanford. edu/documents/NCSS%202013%20Final%20Draft.pdf

Danziger, S., & Wimer, C. (2014). Poverty. National report card. In *The poverty and inequality report 2014* (pp. 15–20). Stanford, CA: The Stanford Center on Poverty & Inequality. Retrieved from http://web.stanford. edu/group/scspi/sotu/SOTU_2014_CPI.pdf

De Rugy, V. (2012, May 22). *How many workers support one social security retiree?* Arlington, VA: Mercatus Center, George Mason University. Retrieved from http://mercatus.org/sites/default/files/worker-per-beneficiary-analysis-pdf.pdf

Desilver, D. (2014, January 7). *5 Facts about economic inequality.* The Pew Research Center. Retrieved from http://www.pewresearch.org/fact-tank/2014/01/07/5-facts-about-economic-inequality/

Education Week (2014, June 12). Some states roll back teacher tenure protections. Langhorne, PA: Author. Retrieved from http://www.edweek.org/ew/articles/2014/06/12/some-states-roll-back-teacher-tenure-1.html

FairTest (n.d.). *Class and schools looks beyond classroom for learning gap solutions.* Jamaica Plain, MA: Author. Retrieved from http://www.fairtest.org/class-and-schools-looks-beyond-classroom-learning-gap-solutions

Goldberg, J. (2007, June 12). Do away with public schools. *Los Angeles Times.* Retrieved from http://www.latimes. com/la-oe-goldberg12jun12-column.html

Grace, S. (2014, July 11). Forget Obamacare. Common Core is the Republicans' new big enemy. *The Washington Post.* Retrieved from http://www.washingtonpost.com/posteverything/wp/2014/07/11/forget-obamacare-common-core-is-the-republicans-new-big-enemy/

Greene, J.P. (2007, Fall). The odd couple: Murray and Rothstein find some unexpected common ground. *Educationnext, 7*(4). Retrieved from http://educationnext.org/the-odd-couple/

Hatheway, S. (2006). Review of *Class and schools: Using social, economic, and educational reform to close the Black-White achievement gap. American Secondary Education, 34*(2), 85–88.

Herrnstein, R.J., & Murray, C. (1994). *The bell curve: Intelligence and class structure in American life.* New York: Free Press.

Kaplan, L.S., & Owings, W.A. (2015). *Educational foundations* (2nd ed.). Stamford, CT: Cengage Learning.

Kardish, C. (2014, January). Will the common core backlash return in 2014? *Governing.* Washington, DC: Governing the States and Localities. Retrieved from http://www.governing.com/topics/education/gov-common-core-backlash-comeback.html

Layton, L. (2013, August 3). A-to-F systems for grading public schools get new scrutiny. *The Washington Post.* Retrieved from http://www.washingtonpost.com/local/education/a-to-f-grading-systems-for-public-schools-get-new-scrutiny/2013/08/03/03533aa2-fbab-11e2-a369-d1954abcb7e3_story.html

Leachman, M., & Mal, C. (2014, May 20). *Most states funding schools less than before the recession.* Washington, DC: Center on Budget and Policy Priorities. Retrieved from http://www.cbpp.org/cms/?fa=view&id=4011

Mann, H. (1848). *Report No. 12 of the Massachusetts Board of Education.* Retrieved from http://www.tncrimlaw. com/civil_bible/horace_mann.htm

Mulgrew, M. (2013, April 28). Common Core is a wake-up call. *New York Daily News.* Retrieved from http://www. nydailynews.com/opinion/common-core-wake-up-call-article-1.1328565

Noguera, P.A., & Wells, L. (2011). The politics of school reform: A broader and bolder approach for Newark. *Berkeley Review of Education, 2*(1). Retrieved from http://steinhardt.nyu.edu/scmsAdmin/media/users/zs374/PDFs/eScholarship_UC_item_9mj097nv.pdf

O'Brien, M.T. (2006). Book review. *Educational Studies: A Journal of the American Education Studies Association, 40*(1), 87–93.

Orfield, G., & Frankenberg, E., with Jongyeon, E., & Kuscera, J. (2014, May 15). *Brown at 60: Great progress, a long retreat and an uncertain future.* Los Angeles, CA: The Civil Rights Project/Proyecto Derechos Civiles. Retrieved from http://civilrightsproject.ucla.edu/research/k-12-education/integration-and-diversity/brown-at-60-great-progress-a-long-retreat-and-an-uncertain-future/Brown-at-60-051814.pdf

O'Sullivan, M. (2010, October 1). Emotional lessons about our public schools. *The Washington Post.* Retrieved from http://www.washingtonpost.com/gog/movies/waiting-for-superman,1160154.html

Ravitch, D. (2013). *Reign of error: The hoax of the privatization movement and the danger to America's public schools.* New York: Knopf.

Reardon, S.F. (2014). *The Policy and Inequality report 2014.* Education. National Report Card (pp. 53–59). Stanford, CA: The Stanford Center on Poverty and Inequality. Retrieved from http://web.stanford.edu/group/scspi/sotu/SOTU_2014_CPI.pdf

Romero, M. (2007, Summer). Social class and schools: Using social, economic, and educational reform to close the Black-White achievement gap. Book Review. *Journal of Negro Education, 76*(3), 517–518.

Rothstein, R. (2010, October 14). *How to fix our schools.* Washington, DC: Economic Policy Institute. Retrieved from http://www.epi.org/publication/ib286/

Rothstein, R. (2013). Racial segregation and black student achievement. In D. Allen & R. Reich (Eds.), *Education, justice, and democracy* (pp. 173–195). Chicago: University of Chicago Press. Retrieved from http://s1.epi.org/files/2013/Seg%20and%20Student%20Ach%20%20IAS%20Volume%2013.pdf

Schmitt, J., & Baker, D. (2008, January). *What we're in for: Projected economic impact of the next recession.* Washington, DC: Center for Economic and Policy Research. Retrieved from http://www.cepr.net/documents/publications/JSDB_08recession.pdf

Schneider, M. (2014). *Chronicle of echoes: Who's who in the implosion of public education.* Charlotte, NC: Information Age.

Siegel-Hawley, G., & Frankenberg, E. (2012, October 18). *Southern slippage: Growing school segregation in the most desegregated region of the country.* Los Angeles: University of Southern California at Los Angeles, The Civil Rights Project, September 2012. Retrieved from http://civilrightsproject.ucla.edu/research/k-12-education/integration-and-diversity/mlk-national/southern-slippage-growing-school-segregation-in-the-most-desegregated-region-of-the-country/hawley-MLK-South-2012.pdf

Sommeiller, E., & Price, M. (2014, February 19). *The increasingly unequal states of America: Income inequality by state, 1917 to 2011.* Washington, DC: Economic Analysis and Research Network. Retrieved from http://www.epi.org/publication/unequal-states/

Strike, K.A. (2005). Class and schools: Using social, economic, and educational reform to close the Black-White achievement gap. Book Review. *American Journal of Education, 111*(3), 414–422.

Wolff, E.N. (2014). Wealth inequality: National report card. In *The poverty and inequality report 2014* (pp. 36–43). Stanford, CA: The Stanford Center on Poverty & Inequality. Retrieved from http://web.stanford.edu/group/scspi/sotu/SOTU_2014_CPI.pdf

Yen, H. (2013, June 13). Census: White majority in U.S. gone by 2043. *NBC News.* Retrieved from http://usnews.nbcnews.com/_news/2013/06/13/18934111-census-white-majority-in-us-gone-by-2043?lite

Linda Darling-Hammond, *The Flat World and Education: How America's Commitment to Equity Will Determine Our Future* (2010)

John Smyth

The Author

Linda Darling-Hammond is the Charles E. Ducommun Professor of Education at Stanford University. After completing her doctoral studies at Temple University in 1978, she worked as a social scientist for the RAND Corporation, becoming Director of Education and Human Resources. From 1989 to 1998 she was a professor of education at Teachers College, Columbia University, and, while William F. Russell Professor, co-founded the National Center for Restructuring Education, Schools and Teaching (NCREST). From 1994 to 2001 she was the executive director of the National Commission on Teaching and America's Future. She was education advisor to Barack Obama's presidential campaign. She holds honorary doctorates from a number of universities and was named in 2006 by *Education Week* as one of America's most influential people on education policy in the last decade. Her research and policy interests focus on issues of school restructuring, teacher quality, and educational equity.

Synopsis

This book positions itself as a "wake-up call" regarding the condition of American education as compared to that of educationally high-performing countries. The report card provided is not good, and the purpose of the book is to provide a "roadmap" for what needs to be done to organize schools for successful teaching and learning and the policies needed to support them. The essence of the book can be summarized in the underlying argument that "America is losing ground" educationally because of a number of major "failings":

[It has] failed to maintain focused investments in a stable, well-prepared teaching force; has allowed the direction of learning to be whipsawed by unproductive "curriculum wars"; and has spent millions creating innovative schools that, although promising, remain at the margins of a system that has not been redesigned to support a 21st-century schooling enterprise. (pp. 8–9)

Darling-Hammond draws on very extensive statistical material to make her case. Her title is borrowed from Thomas Friedman's *The World Is Flat: A Brief History of the Twenty-First Century* (2005), which argues that the forces of globalization are "flattening" the globe in previously unimaginable ways that are producing forces of competition for natural, physical, and human resources. That is to say, future successes, whether economic or educational, can no longer be guaranteed on the basis of historical hegemony, privileged status, or strategies that might have worked in the past. Darling-Hammond argues that facing this challenge will require confronting one of the most entrenched features of the American education system— that "the greatest resources [are] being spent on children from the wealthiest communities" (p. 12). Her argument is compelling: "if [the United States] is to survive and prosper as a First World nation in the 21st century," then it will have to desist from "squandering much of its human capital" and begin to address "structural inequalities in accesses to knowledge" and the "persistent and profound barriers to educational opportunity for large numbers of our citizens" (p. 25).

What becomes somewhat more controversial is what to do about this worrisome situation—but more about the contestation shortly. For the moment, Darling-Hammond leads us through the success stories of a number of other countries, and from them draws out a compendium of directions for change, among them:

- learning that is meaningful to students;
- better teacher education;
- school choice;
- smaller schools;
- targeting funding according to instructional needs;
- standards and forms of assessment that are relevant to students;
- schools organized for student and teacher learning.

These combine to form an eminently sensible ensemble that is not especially controversial. But, on their own (and I will come to this point later), there are also some major silences.

Darling-Hammond's Main Themes and Arguments

My reading of Darling-Hammond's book is that when we get beyond the incredible amount of detail presented, it coalesces around six main themes as they relate to American education:

(1) That we can learn and benefit from *international comparisons*, and that embedded within them are approaches and ideas that *can be appropriated*.

From what she describes as the crisis of confidence confronting the United States, which is educationally and economically "losing ground," Darling-Hammond describes the specific ways in which the education system is not up to the task because of its "inertia" and excess of "high-blown rhetoric" (p. 9). Moving beyond what I would call a massive case of "policy blindness," Darling-Hammond's strategy is to point to the enchanted educational wonderlands of countries that have pursued very different educational policy trajectories, including Finland, South Korea, and Singapore.

From the panoply of statistics, tables, and international comparisons, the features that can be distilled from Darling-Hammond's quest for an alternative to America's dysfunctional schools can be highlighted from the experiences of countries that have built strong teaching and learning systems.

Thus, *Finland* is often referred to as the educational "miracle" case, and Darling-Hammond points to successful school completion as a key indicator: "More than 99% of students now complete compulsory basic education, and about 90% complete upper secondary school" (p. 165), with the majority of the resources provided by the government rather than private sources. There are also high levels of cultural diversity in some Finnish schools in which there is up to "50% [of students]…whose mother tongue is not Finnish" (Sahlberg, 2009, p. 49). The five core underlying principles to which Darling-Hammond attributes the success in Finland are: (1) "resources for those who need them most" (p. 171); (2) "high standards and support for special needs" (p. 171); (3) highly "qualified" teachers (with master's degrees) who are publicly respected (p. 171); (4) "evaluation of education" using action research approaches; and (5) "balancing decentralization and centralization" (p. 171). Notably absent from this list, Darling-Hammond states, is the neoliberal canon of any "highly regulated system of curriculum management" (p. 169) bolstered by "external standardized tests used to rank [or compare] students or schools" (p. 169). These simply do not exist in Finland; in their place, the emphasis is on teachers creating a "challenging curriculum" (p. 171) for students through joint planning and curriculum development, resulting in "teaching students to think creatively and manage their own learning" (p. 169), in which classroom evaluation is through "open-ended assessment" (p. 169), with "teacher feedback to students…in narrative form" (p. 169)—all of which are made possible through a strong investment in teachers' autonomy "to make their own decisions about what and how to teach" (pp. 168–169), with cross-school sharing in which teachers learn laterally from colleagues.

South Korea is highlighted by Darling-Hammond as being illustrative of an instance of a country that has demonstrated a "climb to extraordinary educational attainment" (p. 173). This "stunning" climb to educational success, which started from a very low base and against a history of rote learning and "exam cramming" that they called "exam hell" (p. 173), was made possible because of investment in, and a "respect" for, knowledge and teachers (pp. 173, 179), with teachers being highly qualified, paid as well as doctors are, and heavily influenced by Confucian ideals (p. 179). Once certified, well-qualified South Korean teachers have a job for life (p. 180). Surprisingly, Korean educators have been heavily influenced by the ideas of John Dewey (p. 175)—hence their commitment to inquiry/discovery approaches and higher-order thinking skills. As Darling-Hammond concludes, in South Korea (as in Finland) there is "no individual-level external testing of students before the end of high school" (p. 177). Within this kind of context of a "highly qualified, experienced and stable teaching force in all schools" (p. 181), with an emphasis on curriculum for solving problems of daily life, it is not surprising to hear that teacher induction and professional development are well funded (p. 180), that promotion is based on "length of service, performance, and research achievements" (p. 181), and that a high priority has been accorded to investing heavily in teachers, buildings, and facilities.

The third international exemplary educational success story described by Darling-Hammond is *Singapore*, where the shorthand explanation given is in terms of "thinking schools, learning nation"—a reference to an initiative that began in 1997 (p. 182) and that is still in place. The stellar Singapore performance has occurred in a context where the earlier emphasis has shifted from "rote learning to thinking schools" (p. 184), with a strong emphasis on "merit, competition, technology, and international standards" (p. 184). The alleged success has been due in no small measure to the pursuit of an explicit focus on the development of "a creative and critical thinking culture" (p. 182) that broke with an earlier "reputation for being rote-oriented" (p. 185), and in regard to which Darling-Hammond claims to have been profoundly "struck by how much of this vision had been actualized" (p. 186) during what she says she witnessed in visits to school (something I will return to later). There has been a very heavy national investment in education in general of around 5% of GDP (with a goal of 6% to match other countries such as Japan) (p. 183) and specifically in teacher education, an approach that has made teaching a much more lucrative profession in Singapore than medicine, law, or engineering (p. 189). Darling-Hammond applauds the official intent to "give students…room to exercise initiative and to shape their own learning" (p. 186). As she summarizes: "At every school, an emphasis on holistic education to develop well-rounded human beings was evident" (p. 186), with students being encouraged to become innovative entrepreneurs of their learning and themselves in their schools (p. 186). What follows are forms of assessment that are "much more open-ended" and that "require critical thinking and reasoning" (p. 188). There is in Singapore lots of support for teachers' ongoing professional development, teachers' learning networks, co-learners/critical friends, coaching by "master" teachers (p. 191), and other forms of leadership. Nervous parents who might be skeptical of this seemingly humanistic turn are given reassurance through endorsements from prestigious international universities such as Yale, Harvard, Princeton, and the London School of Economics (p. 188).

These dazzling standout cases that have performed so stunningly on international-league ladders of measured educational performance, and which are sufficient to put the politics of envy into overdrive for readers in Anglo countries, constitute the essence of the book. They quite justifiably leave the indelible impression of nirvana. Explaining how this "educational leap frog" (p. 192) has been possible, Darling-Hammond offers six themes:

- schools are funded equitably;
- there is an elimination of examination systems;
- standards and curriculum are organized around higher-order thinking;
- strong national policies exist that are committed to supporting the status of teaching;
- there is ongoing support for teacher learning; and
- reforms are consistent and long-term, not faddish. (pp. 192–193)

Moving beyond this overarching theme, which really has to do with lessons that can be learned from these "leap froggers," as Darling-Hammond calls them, we need to dig back into them in a way that surfaces some of the sub-themes embedded within them—and my comments here will be more of a commentary upon, rather than a summary of, her ideas.

(2)   That the *required changes* are, by and large, *school/classroom focused.*

As we step back and look across the various elements that Darling-Hammond isolates from the experiences of countries that have gotten their acts together, it becomes clear that there is a strong, almost overwhelming focus on teaching and learning. This is a refreshing departure from the stifling and moribund decades-long policy onslaught that has been promulgated on schools around notions of administration, management, leadership, and governance—none of which have any demonstrable evidentiary connection to improved student learning. For example, the focus in her recommendations on supporting teachers stands out as a sensible and long-overdue position. "What matters" is said to be consistent policies around teaching; giving teachers a "strong" beginning through rigorous teacher education programs; support for collaborative and collegial inquiry; providing time in the course of the day for teachers to share and learn from colleagues; systematic dissemination of "best practices" among teachers through intensive paid professional development; and, overall, a commitment to "enabling teachers to continue to improve" (p. 226). We see all of this coming together around a class-room focus on students. Overall, the message is one of sensibly "designing schools for teaching and learning" (p. 240) around

- small school units (p. 245);
- structures for personalization (p. 246);
- intellectually challenging and relevant instruction (p. 250);
- performance-based assessment (p. 257); and
- professional learning and collaboration (p. 260).

I have no argument with any of this, although there is no indication of how we will develop the crucial political resolve to break away from the current infatuation with managerialist approaches.

(3)   That we should place our *faith in the capacity of educational policy and educational policy-makers* to "get the mix" right.

Coursing through Darling-Hammond's very sensible set of suggestions for a classroom/school-led renaissance is a sense of unreality that the impetus will somehow come from the already heavily compromised policy elite, and that the mechanism for re-invigoration will take the form of policy proclamation from "on high." On a practical level it is hard to see how this might work, given the deeply held and long-term, unswerving commitment of this cadre of people to notions of control, command, accountability, punishment, and retribution, and for whom ideas of empathy, understanding, encouragement, support, and reward would present as a completely foreign language. We can see the evidence of this, for example, when Darling-Hammond's so-far convincing ideas collapse down to rhetorical epithets and empty-sounding phrases such as:

- supporting successful innovation;
- sustaining change;
- building professional capacity;
- deregulating strategically;

- changing contracts (away from a factory model);
- rethinking accountability (pp. 264–277).

It is not that these fine-sounding ideas are totally unworthy, though they might make the eyes water a little and glaze over somewhat; rather, it is hard to see how they might be given life in the current hostile climate—even more so when we hear about the need for an unproblematic, enforced cohabitation of a concern for "quality" with "equality" (p. 278).

(4) Following on from this is the underlying theme that the *people who "know best"* about what is required are distant and *removed from schools/classrooms.*
The kind of omnibus lists of categories and recommendations that Darling-Hammond provides throughout the book seem to come from everywhere and nowhere. By that I mean, in the absence of any indicators to the contrary, they seem to have their genesis in Darling-Hammond's perusal of the literature and the policies and the practices of the places to which she has some obvious affection and attraction. That's fine. But what we don't hear anything about is which of these policies/practices/dispositions, if any, have their legacies in the indigenous theorizing, thinking, and practices of teachers. Or, are they artifacts of what well-meaning policymakers think *might be good* for schools, teachers, and students, and that have been, however benevolently, imposed upon them? They may well have a democratic and enlightened hue about them, and they may well resonate with the views of teachers, but what is not obvious in the way they are presented is how they came to be, and whose interests they really serve. (More about this later.)

(5) That in many cases, *what is required* is qualitatively "*more of the same,*" what is *already known* and has *been tried*, rather than moving in a *radically different direction.*
It is a little hard to see what is radically different in what is being suggested in this book, despite its focus on some seemingly radically different ideas from other parts of the world. The question to be posed is: Do the recommended actions constitute a sharp break with the past as experienced by educators in the United States, or are there still vestiges of the control-and-command ideology hidden within? In other words, is there some shop-fronting going on here in which some of the old players are still very much present, but behind new facades? My guess is that there is an element of this, and my reason for saying so is that there are some strong veins running through this text about accountability, standards, evaluation, policies, and testing that in many ways do not sound that different from the status quo. What is being spoken about in a fashion that we have not had much mention of hitherto (except in hushed tones in the context of harsh policies that have been relentlessly bearing down on teachers and schools) are the new kids on the block in the form of the language of equity, authentic learning, innovative teaching, strategically building strong forms of teaching, and the like. The question really is, what is figure and what is ground here?

(6) That what is required is to *make schools more responsible* for what transpires, by giving them an *agenda developed by outsiders.*
The sense I get of what Darling-Hammond is proposing is that schools should dutifully exist as "implementers" of ideas rather than as their "initiators or developers." In other words, there remains a sharp distinction in her book between conception and execution—and teachers and

schools would, in her view, reside very much in the latter category. It is as if the underlying theme is that it is legitimate that schools should have, and be given, autonomy, but only within the limits of implementing the agenda set by others. This is very much the neoliberal agenda whereby schools are accorded a modicum of self-responsibility but are held to account for the delivery of targets set by others, and for which promised resources never actually eventuate. This is a model where teachers are considered to be technicians, not intellectuals.

Strengths and Weaknesses

There is a logic to this book that has a certain degree of appeal. First, it starts out by establishing, through some rigorous empirical evidence, the crucial importance of a commitment to equity through the fact that the United States is demonstrably ill-equipped to compete globally as a nation largely because of its inequitable treatment of students. As one reviewer put it, "the most alarming news is that most Americans, who live in middle-class suburban areas, believe that the schools their children attend are the norm everywhere else" (Walker, 2012, p. 275). As another reviewer put it, "gut-wrenching realities of inequity lie at the heart of [this] book… [that] illustrate the degree to which America's schools have become palaces or prisons of the haves and have-nots" (Jean, 2010, p. 2). Second, Darling-Hammond lays out the obstacles confronting marginalized students—"ration[ing] the best education to the most advantaged" (Walker, 2012, p. 275); the continuing tradition of labelling these student as if they were deficits; a failure of high-stakes testing to deliver anything; and a situation in which teachers and schools are besmirched. Third, there are references to instances in which progress has been made, in the United States (in New Jersey) and in other countries such as Finland, South Korea, and Singapore. Finally, there is a turn to what needs to be done to have well-functioning schools. So, what we have in terms of the overt strengths of the book is a persistent focus on inequality and an insistence on the need to move policy attention away from the "destructive effects of…anti-teacher policies" (Saltman, 2011, p. xvii) to the point where the "classroom teacher is [the] key" (Berry, 2012, p. 1).

The major weaknesses of this book reside in its blind spots, of which there are several, and they are major ones. Where the book fell apart for me was in its unfortunate decision to associate itself with the work of Thomas Friedman and his *The World Is Flat: A Brief History of the Twenty-First Century* (2005). While this might be seen as a clever ploy to make a connection with a high-profile Pulitzer Prize winner, there were always bound to be dangers in endorsing, through association, his glib assertion that globalization is "flattening" the playing field. As he puts it, people "from more…corners of the planet [are] on a more equal footing than at any previous time in the history of the world" (p. 8). This is demonstrably not the case, and there is an array of people more qualified in this domain than Friedman who have shown otherwise. See, for example, Thomas Piketty's *Capital in the Twenty-First Century* (2014), Joseph Stiglitz's *The Price of Inequality* (2013), and Wilkinson and Pickett's *The Spirit Level: Why More Equal Societies Almost Always Do Better* (2009). The truth is that the playing field is tilted more unevenly in favor of the advantaged than at any other point in history—the gap between rich and poor is widening within as well as between countries. So, while Darling-Hammond seems to have had a predilection in the direction of doing something about redressing inequity in education in her book, her political naïveté in associating her title with someone who is an avowed denier is a damning indictment that is hard to recover from. Here is a taste of what Friedman

(1999) has to say from his *The Lexus and the Olive Tree: Understanding Globalization*, in which he makes clear what he sees as a crucial set of connections:

> The hidden hand of the market will never work without the hidden fist. McDonald's cannot flourish without McDonnell Douglas, the designer of the …F15. And the hidden fist that keeps the world safe for Silicon Valley's technologies to flourish is called the U.S. Army, Air Force, Navy and Marine Corps. (p. 373)

I am not alone in my concern. In a review that is generally supportive of Darling-Hammond's book, Christina Jean (2010) says that "Ironically, the use of the 'flat world' metaphor has the least resonance for me" (p. 4). Deeply insinuated in the book is the view that education must be the savior of U.S. global dominance. As Saltman (2012) puts it, it is implicitly sustaining the assumption "that America is an empire that needs to be maintained…[and an acceptance] of public schooling as principally serving the end of global economic competition" (p. 168). Saltman goes on:

> Here we find that one of the leading liberal policy thinkers wraps her calls for equalized educational resources, investment in teacher work, and desegregation in a set of rightist assumptions: education is for competition in a corporate-dominated capitalist system; the goal of schools is to include more students into the existing social order, not to produce critical citizens who can challenge and transform that order; and what goes on in schools has nothing to do with the political and ethical values behind the maintenance of an imperial military complex. (p. 681)

Significance and Influence Then and Now

It is hard to accurately judge the significance, influence, and impact of this book without knowing something more about what its real purpose was. One thing we do know is that Darling-Hammond was well connected to the educational thinking as an advisor in the campaign of Barack Obama. *The New York Times* reported that she was "being considered for Education Secretary" (Dillon, 2008), so we can imagine that much of the mammoth work that went into producing the book was going on at this time, and that it filtered through to some of Obama's "ambitious educational program" (Dillon, 2008). If it was indeed intended as a blueprint, then it would have to be said, with the benefit of hindsight, that it might be a case of a classic testimony that never quite came to be—or, at least, that has yet to be seriously engaged with by U.S. education authorities.

Perhaps we can push this impact issue a little further, in which case we can see the beginnings of the possible seeds of its demise in the comment by Jean (2010) that

> After having outlined her quarrels with the inadequacy of American education…[the difficulties begin to appear in her] suggested courses of action [that] include…requiring that federal and state governments redistribute money and resources equitably and with a focus on classroom instruction, and insisting on standards and assessment that have meaning for students. (pp. 3–4)

Not a bad idea, but it flies in the face of the powerful educational and business lobbying groups with huge vested interests in keeping things the way they are.

But, more significantly, there is an even deeper nationalistic and psychic reason as to why Darling-Hammond's ideas were unlikely to gel and gain the widespread acceptance necessary to underpin radical change. It has to do with the underlying way in which the United States conceives of itself as a world superpower. There is something essentially demeaning in having to fess up to the fact that such a global behemoth is severely lagging behind the educational performance of some late-starter, small Asian nations, and a relatively minor European player (Finland). Jean (2010) states that, for her, "Using the education systems of other countries as a model for US reform was a tactic that didn't have as profound an effect on me as it probably should have" (p. 4). As she tellingly goes on to say,

> the fact of the matter is that comparing these countries with America is like comparing apples and herring, or chicken rice, or kimchi. For all of its many amazing features, the Finnish education has little to do with the current realities faced by American schools. Rather than proving to motivate and inspire me…comparing and contrasting America to these other progressive nations *left me feeling bitter and wistful.* (p. 4; emphasis added)

At another fundamental level, what would have to be seriously confronted is the real elephant in the room, which is acknowledging the inherently racist and classist nature of U.S. education, and it is hard to see that kind of strident naming in Darling-Hammond's treatise. It seems to back off at precisely the point where it needs to become deeply indignant.

An illustration may serve to underscore my point. If we look seriously at the case of Singapore's "thinking schools" initiative, it is here that questions arise as to what Darling-Hammond witnessed, what she was shown, or what kind of lens she brought to her observations. There is ample evidence in the literature to show that "critical thinking" in Singapore has a particular, limited interpretation in the Singaporean context (see Lee, 2010; Yao, 2006; Koh, 2002, 2008, 2010, 2011; Lim, 2013, 2014). As Saltman (2012) comments, "critical thinking" in Singapore means pursuing "problem solving approaches while eschewing critical pedagogy's understanding of teachers' work, curriculum and pedagogy as political, as part of broader social movement, and theoretical, and as inextricably linked with individual, community and social transformation" (p. 678). There is no sense in Darling-Hammond's writing of tangling with equity issues by "encouraging students to comprehend" (p. 678) underlying interests, or how power works and for whom. Missing also are "the voices from below, the perspectives of the oppressed, and how the knowledge learned is struggled over by classes and cultural groups and…the agency of students to work collectively to transform oppressive structures of power" (Saltman, 2012, p. 678). All this leads to the fundamental problem that thinkers like Saltman (2012) and myself have and that Darling-Hammond denies: the politics of education, implicitly conveying the message (which is itself highly political) that it is "the goal of schools to include more students into the existing social order, not to produce critical citizens who can challenge that order" (p. 681; see also Smyth, Down, & McInerney, 2014; Smyth, Down, McInerney, & Hattam, 2014).

Conclusion

This book is clearly an important work by a very high-profile scholar. It tackles a topic that is very difficult to confront, and it pulls no punches. After all, who wants to openly admit that her national educational system is failing, especially for those groups who are already being demonstrably marginalized and excluded on a number of fronts? As I have argued in this review, the book is hard-hitting in its analysis and comes up with an extensive array of suggestions, even though there might be questions about how the lessons from other countries might be acted upon. There is much in *The Flat World of Education* that is hard to disagree with. What is a little harder to ascertain (beyond the fact that the book has attracted some 900 Google Scholar citations) is where the book has been able to make real inroads into changing mind-sets and bringing about dramatic changes in policy thinking and practice.

The major shortcoming of the book—and the one that proved most difficult for me personally—was its naïveté. First, I point to the over-romanticizing of what is actually happening in other countries, especially the cases of Asian countries such as Singapore and South Korea. The reality is that the education systems of these countries (despite what they might say and what is selectively shown to international visitors) are still fiercely competitive, even to the point where suicide is endemic among young people who fail to succeed (see Nguyen, 2013). Second, these are also countries that demonstrably advance the interests of the already advantaged, as indicated earlier in the example of Singapore. This is something that severely undermines Darling-Hammond's equity claim that emulating them will somehow alleviate what is already a deeply mired, inequitable U.S. education system. It will produce the opposite. Third, education systems are deeply embedded cultural and historical entities, as the Finnish system shows so well (see, for example, Simola, 2005; Sahlberg, 2011) and are not amenable to simple forms of copying or transplantation. There are quite profound sociological reasons that militate against this—among them, what we are not being told in *The Flat World of Education* about profoundly racist, classist, sexist, and patriarchal systems in some of these countries— and Darling-Hammond is silent on how such issues would be addressed in any attempt to borrow educational reforms from these places.

In the end, attending to these shortcomings requires an incredible amount of courage, and there is little in the book that would really embolden educators and activists to confront these deeply embedded norms and shibboleths. It just may be the case, as Saltman (2012) argues, that books like this "are making things worse" (p. 674), and perhaps the focus needs to be more directly on the kind of issues and arguments rehearsed in books like *School Reform Critics: The Struggle for Democratic Schooling* (DeVitis & Teitelbaum, 2014).

References

Berry, S. (2012, December). Book review of *The flat world and education: How America's commitment to equity will determine our future*, by Linda Darling-Hammond. *Northeast Indiana Friends of Public Education*, *27*. Retrieved September 10, 2014, from http://neifpe.blogspot.com.au/2012/12/book-review-flat-world-and-education.html

De Vitis, J., & Teitelbaum, K. (Eds.). (2014). *School reform critics: The struggle for democratic schooling*. New York: Peter Lang.

Dillon, S. (2008, December 2). The new team: Linda Darling-Hammond. *The New York Times*. Retrieved October 13, 2014, from http://www.nytimes.com/2008/12/02/us/politics/02web-darlinghammond.html?_r=0

Friedman, T. (1999). *The lexus and the olive tree*. New York: HarperCollins.

Friedman, T. (2005). *The world is flat: A brief history of the twenty-first century*. New York: Farrar, Straus & Giroux.

Jean, C. (2010, November 20). Review of *The flat world and education: How America's commitment to equity will determine our future*, by Linda Darling-Hammond. *Education Review*, 1–5. Retrieved September 10, 2014, from http://edrev.info/reviews/rev996.pdf

Koh, A. (2002). Towards a critical pedagogy: Creating "thinking schools" in Singapore. *Journal of Curriculum Studies*, *34*(3), 255–264.

Koh, A. (2008). On Singaporean authoritarianism: Critical discourse analysis and contextual dissonance. *Pedagogy, Culture and Society*, *16*(3), 303–314.

Koh, A. (2010). *Tactical globalization: Learning from the Singaporean experiment*. New York: Peter Lang.

Koh, A. (2011). Singapore's "global assemblage": Digging into the culture of education policy making. *Critical Studies in Education, 52*(3), 267–278.

Lee, T. (2010). *The media, cultural control, and government in Singapore*. London: Routledge.

Lim, L. (2013). Meritocracy, elitism and egalitarianism: A preliminary and provisional assessment of Singapore's primary education review. *Asia Pacific Journal of Education, 33*(1), 1–14.

Lim, L. (2014). Critical thinking and the anti-liberal state: The politics of pedagogic recontextualization in Singapore. *Discourse: Studies in the Cultural Politics of Education, 35*(5), 692–704.

Nguyen, K. (2013, October 21). *Rising youth suicide rates in South Korea*. University College Maastricht, Netherlands. Retrieved October 20, 2014, from http:///www.kvnjacobs.files.wordpress.com/2013/10/srinsk-kimberly.pdf

Piketty, T. (2014). *Capital in the twenty-first century*. Boston, MA: Harvard University Press.

Sahlberg, P. (2009). Educational change in Finland. In A. Hargreaves, M. Fullan, A. Lieberman, & D. Hopkins (Eds.), *International handbook of educational change* (pp. 1–28). Dordrecht, The Netherlands: Kluwer Academic Publishers.

Sahlberg, P. (2011). *Finnish lessons: What can the world learn from educational change in Finland?* New York: Teachers College Press.

Saltman, K. (2011). *The failure of corporate school reform: Toward a new common school movement*. National Education Policy Center. Retrieved September 20, 2014, from http://nepc.colorado.edu/blog/failure-corporate-school-reform-toward-new-common-school-movement

Saltman, K. (2012). Why Henry Giroux's democratic pedagogy is crucial for confronting failed corporate school reform and how liberals like Ravitch and Darling-Hammond are making things worse. *Policy Futures in Education, 10*(6), 674–687.

Simola, H. (2005). The Finnish miracle of PISA: Historical and sociological remarks on teaching and teacher education. *Comparative Education, 41*(4), 455–470.

Smyth, J., Down, B., & McInerney, P. (2014). *The socially just school: Making space for youth to speak back*. Dordrecht, The Netherlands: Springer.

Smyth, J., Down, B., McInerney, P., & Hattam, R. (2014). *Doing critical educational research: A conversation with the research of John Smyth*. New York: Peter Lang.

Stiglitz, J. (2013). *The price of inequality: How today's divided society endangers our future*. New York: Penguin Books.

Walker, B. (2012). Book review of *The flat world and education: How America's commitment to equity will determine our future*, by Linda Darling-Hammond. *Journal of Education Policy, 27*(2), 275–278.

Wilkinson, R., & Pickett, K. (2009). *The spirit level: Why more equal societies almost always do better*. London: Allen Lane.

Yao, S. (2006). *Singapore: The state and culture of excess*. London and New York: Routledge.

THIRTY-FIVE

Henry A. Giroux, *Youth in a Suspect Society: Democracy or Disposability?* (2010)

Sheila L. Macrine

Like the canary in the coal mine who alerted miners to poisonous air, Henry Giroux's book serves as a bellwether, warning its readers that we ignore the plight of youth at our own peril. Giroux proposes a dramatic and hopeful shift in how we think about youth and schooling and places them in political and ideological perspectives.

Scholar, educator, and cultural critic, Giroux engages in a passionate take-down of the practices associated with a negative form of globalization (Giroux, 2006), including biopolitics and neoliberalism, by exposing their punishing effects on today's youth and the poor. He critically analyzes the deployment of, as well as, the real and symbolic effects of neoliberalism on youth. Recognizing this new type of imperialism as a more powerful, pernicious, and perilous state, Giroux makes explicit the importance of a renewed cultural dynamics and the need to make pedagogy and hope central to any viable form of politics engaged in the process of creating alternative public spheres and forms of collective resistance.

Neoliberalism has become the "planetary vulgate" of modern capitalism, one that relies upon, and resides in, the socialization of uncritical citizens (Bourdieu, 2000, p. 541). Further, its dominant framework of individualism, self-responsibility, and symbolic violence often leads people to (unjustly) blame individuals for their own suffering while simultaneously obscuring the role of society. Within the current radical free-market culture, Giroux elegantly elaborates that "the conditions produced by the financial crisis have resulted in not only the foreclosure of millions of family homes but also the foreclosure of the future of our young people as the prospects of the unborn are mortgaged off in the interests of corporate power and profits" (p. x).

Likewise, such neoliberal policies of economic deregulation and social-welfare retrenchment have contributed to the generalized increase of carceral populations and the growing reliance upon the penal system to serve as an instrument for managing social insecurity by containing social disorders created at the bottom of the class structure. Responding to the rapid rise of neoliberal ideologies that are decimating the economic state, dismantling the social state, and strengthening the penal state, Giroux emphatically highlights their negative impact on young people by adding that "hope is precariously bound to commodities and a corrupt financial system, [where] young people are no longer at risk they are the risk" (2009, p. x).

Giroux cautions that the world is blindly marching toward a dark political and economic future with the intensification of neoliberalism and the influence of an ideological fundamentalism that both seizes absolute control of fundamental resources and that destitutes everyone it excludes (Monbiot, 2000). Here, Giroux mirrors Žižek (2007), reaffirming that the world is entering an age of totalitarian capitalism that renders the state moribund, thus decimating the dynamics of hope and possibility by targeting the weakest and most vulnerable members of our society. Giroux (2009) adds that "the havoc wreaked by neoliberal economic policies can be seen in the hard currency of human suffering such policies have imposed on children, readily evident in some astounding statistics that suggest a profound, moral and political contradiction at the heart of one of the richest democracies in the world" (p. 3). Symptomatic of this fundamental collapse in society, argues Giroux (2009), is the impending subjugation of humanity's progeny that demonizes the young through a "war on youth."

Giroux's deeply researched indictment demonstrates how the "war on youth" has gained currency within a wide array of neoliberal institutional and cultural practices and has been energized through lethal alliances with religious fundamentalism. Neoliberalism is, quite literally, a crusade against youth—one Giroux aptly theorizes as a "politics of disposability" and is largely the result of how biopolitical formations of self-regulation (the organized practices, mentalities, rationalities, and techniques through which market conforming subjects are governed) have become the essential normalizing function in strengthening the current neoliberal global hegemonic. In this "biological century" neoliberal biopolitics feeds on proliferating fears, anxieties, and hopes at a time when such basic concepts as scientific truth, race and gender identity, and the human being itself are destabilized in the public eye and in public practices (De Costa & Philip, 2010, p. 1). Further, neoliberal states have withdrawn from their democratic roles as guarantors of minimal social and economic protections, and safety nets, i.e., they have abdicated their responsibility to its citizens and youth.

Perhaps most disturbing about the relationship between neoliberal biopolitics and the current global crisis is that those entities have become both their own ends as well as the means to those ends. That relationship is the totalizing regime of truth in the 21st century, as it has captured the discourse/knowledge/power dialectic so productively for its own purposes that not only does it destabilize democratic institutions, it also effectively camouflages itself behind a mask of democracy.

The five major sections of the book serve as windows into the construction of a global social order that increasingly demonizes, dehumanizes, and criminalizes youth and the poor. Giroux's comprehensive empirical record enhances our critical understanding of how the pathologization, victimization, and infantilization of young people have developed into essential components of neoliberal market logic invested in new forms of biopolitical (re)production. The book's analysis of neoliberal politics and the key role education plays in realizing its policies is situated politically and ideologically within the current historical moment, which is precisely the thread that connects Giroux's work dating back to the late 1970s.

Neoliberal Biopolitics

Giroux foregrounds his argument by exposing the crude disciplinary forms of control exercised upon today's youth under the biopolitics of neoliberalism, and he illustrates how the conditions that have been created yield little moral responsibility and a politics that no longer advocates for compassion, social justice, or the fundamental provisions necessary for a decent life (p. 11). Unwitting young people have inherited a world marred by uncertainty, instability, volatility, and war (Searls-Giroux, 2008). Youths now represent the greatest challenge to adult society because "they have become disposable in a neoliberal world and a militarized state in which instrumental reason, finance capital, market rationality, instant gratification, deregulation and a contempt for all things public, including public values, have reigned supreme for the last thirty years" (Giroux, 2009, p. 17).

What's more, he argues, these representations disregard the reality that the lives, experiences, and environments of young people are entirely different from that of previous generations and that underlying these differences are various political, cultural, and social forces in which they are considered unworthy of care, targeted and relegated to a biopolitics of neoliberalism that privatizes reason and exhibits a disdain for all collective undertakings, especially those that address social responsibility and solidarity (p. 17).

Such dehumanization has become possible not just because of the privatization of reason, goods, and democratic participation. It has become possible because those who support neoliberalism have also been able to effectively reshape the historical narrative regarding the power of the market as a democratic institution.

Neoliberal policies and practices of privatization and deregulation have acted to reconstitute both the public and the private sphere, and have de-politicized the way in which we think and understand societal issues, social justice, equality, democracy, freedom, and education. This process has diminished public power and compromised democratic agency. As a result, the world is witnessing a historical transition into a new phase of capitalism, with new forms of power, resistance, and a globalization that shifts societies' center of gravity away from politics and toward corporate prominence (Robinson, 2004).

Giroux's discussion of biopolitics builds upon a foundation of theory across multiple disciplines. Michel Foucault (1979) first introduced the concept of biopolitics to describe how neoliberal governments engaged in a transformation wherein the body-politic—society in its social, cultural, economic, and political dimensions, as well as the physical biomass of society's constituents—becomes the primary object of intervention. In this way, biopolitics becomes a form of governmentality that is "premised on the active consent and subjugation of subjects, rather than their oppression, domination or external control" (Clegg et al., 2002, p. 320). Thus, "neoliberal forms of government feature not only direct intervention by means of empowered and specialized state apparatuses, but also characteristically develop indirect techniques for leading and controlling individuals without at the same time being responsible for them" (Lemke, 2001, p. 201). Giroux's body of work is a genealogical analysis of the inner workings of power and the challenge to democratic practices over the last three decades, and *Youth in a Suspect Society* adds to his corpus by engaging the reader to consider the impact of neoliberalism on those who will have the future in their hands.

Giroux explicates the amplification of neoliberal biopolitics as it affects the world's youth, which in turn works well within Bauman's equation of glocalization: the "globalization for some/localization for others" or that "some inhabit the globe/others are chained to place." At the core of Bauman's (1989, 1998) approach to glocalization is a worldwide re-ordering of society and the collapse of the public sphere. Along with this re-ordering of society, we are witnessing the removal of the public sphere from social consideration. Further, notions of the public good are replaced by an utterly privatized political culture that is celebrated by neoliberal warriors rather than perceived as a dangerous state of affairs that all Americans should be both contemptuous of, and ashamed, to support (Giroux, 2001, p. 3).

According to Bauman (1989) the "public" has been emptied of its own separate contents; it has been left with no agenda of its own—it is now but an agglomeration of private troubles, worries, and problems (p. 65). Complicating this is the threat that, under the control of a neoliberal ideology, the state is increasingly transformed into a repressive apparatus aimed at those individuals and groups who are caught in its ever-expanding policing interventions (Giroux, 2001, p. 56). For Giroux, the ultimate victims of the newly conceptualized state apparatus are not simply those who turn to government for assistance. Anyone who cannot contribute to the economic state is a drain on society, and are therefore victims of their own making.

Youth and Democracy at Risk

In the present global moment, neoliberalism has entered a New Gilded Age in the United States, which Giroux describes as even more savage and anti-democratic than its predecessor. The current form of market fundamentalism demands new critical approaches that use, construct, and edify different conceptual and analytical tools that not only frame neoliberalism through an economic optic but also through cultural projects such as modes of rationality, governmentality, and critical public pedagogy. He further develops the biopolitics of neoliberalism by exploring how it uses market values as a template for realigning corporate power and the state, one in which the state paves the way for the market, while simultaneously producing modes of consent that are vital to the construction of a neoliberal subject and a more ruthless politics of disposability (Giroux, 2008).

Within this new form of neoliberal rationality and biopolitics—a political system actively involved in the management of the politics of life and death—new modes of individual and collective suffering emerge around the modalities and intersections of race, class, and gender (p. 1). Biopolitics, as Giroux helps us understand, deals with conflicts and intricate social articulations and re-articulations that frame and determine human life as well as its political implications. At the same time, such social articulations and re-articulations, as Bauman (2008) claims, are determined by a liquid dynamics that forces and pushes critical theorists to advance their own analyses in order to deconstruct reality as a social construction (Berger and Luckmann, 1976). By winning the battle over common sense, neoliberalism has been able to extend a set of policies and practices (i.e., No Child Left Behind) that not only push youth into a risk category, but also put the whole democratic architecture into jeopardy.

Youth and the Pedagogy of Commodification

Giroux describes how today's youth have become "market conformed subjects" groomed as consumers and caught between a dialectic of consumption and commodification within neoliberal biopolitics. By reducing citizens to pale commodities, and consequently students to clients, negative globalism has been able to produce a generation that is entirely at odds with the notable pillars of a true democratic society and citizenship. For this generation, concepts such as freedom, solidarity, and equality are totally twisted or non-existent. As odd as it might seem, young people are actually facing modern problems without modern solutions (Sousa Santos, 2007). Meanwhile, neoliberalism pushes values, morals, and social relations toward a "neutral" path (that is anything but neutral) that threatens any possibility for youths' social existence outside of this path, thus making it almost impossible to imagine a more democratic and just global world.

Furthermore, Giroux (2002) conceives neoliberalism as the most dangerous ideology in the present historical moment. He argues that, within such a corporate culture, citizenship is portrayed as an utterly privatized affair that produces self-interested individuals. For him, "corporate culture ignores social injustices by overriding the democratic impulses and practices of civil society through an emphasis put on the unbridled workings of market relations" (pp. 425–464). Giroux adds that these trends favor social Darwinism; that is, they value one's ability to compete and win. These values, ideologies, social relations, and practices of commerce mark a hazardous turn in U.S. society—one that also threatens our basic understanding of democracy. So within this cult of corporatization and individualism, it becomes difficult for young people to imagine a future in which the self becomes more than a self-promoting commodity (p. 17).

One cannot ignore the role that schooling and teachers play in such strategies and how Giroux (2009) describes consumption beyond the pedagogy of commodification. Despite the fact that commodification can be seen as a form of social death, youth who are marginalized by virtue of their race, gender, and class bear the burdens of not only the implacable impositions of a de-humanized market-driven culture, but also the harsh experiences of disposability that make them disposable and redundant populations (p. 24).

Today, social and daily life has been so de-politicized that people do not even realize that they are engaged in a politics of consumption. This dynamic equation of consumption and commodification demonstrates how neoliberalism can sustain and evolve in the form of an empire and ultimately result in the complete withering of civil society (Hardt & Negri, 2000).

The neoliberal ethos of consumption has penetrated every sphere of our lives. As a result, culture, leisure, sex, politics, and even death turn into commodities; and consumption increasingly constructs the way we see the world (Crawford, 1992). Giroux (2009) argues that in order to challenge this market mentality and neoliberal sovereignty, we need to recognize the need for a new politics in which matters of education, power, and governance are mutually determined. Such a challenge rests on a politics that seeks to understand how governmentality and the pedagogy of commodification are produced and circulated through new modes of market sovereignty (p. 65).

What must be emphasized in a democracy, Giroux argues, is that there is no room for a politics animated by a rationality of maximizing profit and the construction of a society free from the burden of mutual responsibility—that is, a society whose essence is captured in the faces of children facing the terror of a future with no hope of survival (p. 67).

Education and the Youth Crime Complex

Giroux makes visible the harshest elements of the punishing neoliberal state and exposes the egregious policies it enacts. It reinforces a set of oppressive and coercive policies to dehumanize poor, disposable, and politically powerless youth. Here, Giroux shifts beyond the dialectic of "consumption versus commodification" and posits how the sovereignty of the market impacts differently on poor youth of color who have been systematically excluded from participation in its diverse pleasures and seductions and who, as a result, are defined through the registers of disposability and social death (Giroux, 2004, 2009). In fact, his analysis allows us to see how disposability is not a consequence of a capitalist system. It is rather its tonic. That is, those who enact neoliberalism have figured out how to make balances out of the imbalances (Jessop, 2002). This imbalance of disposability and social death is made possible by totalitarian capital-ism's continued disequilibrium.

Giroux's (2009) term the "politics of disposability" is a fitting descriptor for the attacks on poor young people and the powerless; at the same time, it graphically describes the daily lives of a huge majority of the population around the globe. He describes it as a politics in which the unproductive (the poor, weak, and racially marginalized) are considered useless and therefore expendable. It is a politics in which entire populations are considered disposable, unnecessary burdens on state coffers and consigned to fend for themselves (ibid., 2006). These policies and practices re-highlight the Freirean dialogic of the oppressor and the oppressed (Freire, 1999) as binary frameworks in the service of domination; and they are used to distinguish the privileged from the dispossessed and the powerful from the powerless.

No longer simply a dream of some conservative economists, neoliberalism has become a commonsense of the times (Brenner & Theodore, 2002). It has maintained control not through violence and political and economic coercion, but ideologically, through a hegemon-ic culture in which the values of the bourgeoisie become the "common sense" values of all. Gramsci (Hall, 1986) described a type of "common sense" that emerges from such a hegemon-ic culture. The creation of this "common sense" helps to maintain the status quo, often to the detriment of the poor and working class (Ives, 2007). Similarly, as Giroux has documented, the current neoliberal hegemonic has been able to naturalize and domesticate, through the politics of common sense, a set of crucial concepts that pull them from the social and political sphere into a reductive economic equation that trivializes them. In so doing, concepts such as poverty, democracy, social justice, freedom, and education are seen as individual currencies totally de-tached from a collective engagement. This has lethal implications within identity politics and practices. Not only is it appropriate to blame the victims (for example, poor people who are shut out by society's institutions are later described as being abandoned because they just won't work harder), it is also acceptable that there are winners and losers in the global marketplace.

This neoliberal hegemony that Callewaert (2006, p. 127) recently characterized as "the tragedy of our time, [includes among other reconfigurations] the radical change from educa-tion by educationalists to education by neo-liberal management" and has affected living and working conditions globally for all, including educators in schools or universities, through acts of surveillance, the introduction of different forms of privatization, intensification of all types of educational work, and the general demand to follow market practices.

In other words, those who have the least are expected to take most of the blame and should receive no assistance as they attempt to put their lives back together. Giroux writes elegantly about this lynchpin of neoliberal policy, i.e., eliminating the concept of the "public good" of community and the "public sphere" and replacing it with a demand for "individual responsibility." It pressures the poorest people in a society to find their own solutions to the lack of health care, education, and social security—and then blaming them, if they fail, for being "lazy." Although many mainstream and liberal scholars have neglected the politics of blaming the victim, it remains fully ideological. The very strategy to de-ideologicize the "politics of disposability" is, by definition, inherently ideological, something that Giroux's work overtly demonstrates.

Under fully established negative globalization, we find neoliberalism in the eye of the hurricane, where it has been engaged in a kind of "welfare-a-cide" that has been responsible for the dismantling of the working and middle classes and the war on youth. They have been defined and understood within a war on terror that provides an expansive anti-democratic framework for referencing how they are portrayed, talked about, and inserted within a growing network of disciplinary relations. The latter respond to the problems they face by criminalizing their behaviors and subjecting them to punitive modes of conduct (Giroux, 2009).

Giroux contends that youth in America (and arguably in the rest of the Western society) have increasingly been criminalized and dehumanized to the point of invisibility while being blindly robbed of a future. Their crippled lives have been mortgaged to a hobbled future that is largely invisible in terms of their own needs. As the social state is reconfigured as a punishing state, youth become the enemy. They have been forced into assuming a different subjective position—that of a burden to society, which is much different from being the promise of the future of society. Giroux (2009) accurately claims that youth embody an ethical referent that *should* require adults to question the prevailing economic Darwinism and the future it emphatically denies in favor of an eternal present subject only to the market-driven laws of capital accumulation (p. 72). It is undeniable that global neoliberalism has been capable of transforming youth into characters of a story that they do not want to be part of—and they should not have been subjected to.

Accordingly, Giroux (2009) writes, the language of democracy is divested of concern for the future, adult obligations, and social responsibility in general; complex and productive representations of young people have gradually disappeared from public discourse only to reappear within the demonizing and punishing rhetoric of fear and crime (p. 72). Giroux adds, "Youth are no longer inscribed in the metaphors of hope, especially those marginalized by race and class and gender, have now been cast into an ever growing circle of groups targeted through the rhetoric of war and terrorism. In reality, youth now occupy the status of what Bill Owens the former conservative governor of Colorado referred to as 'a virus…let loose upon society'" (p. xx). In fact, the criminalization of youth needs to be seen as a political and ideological strategy among other issues to justify a set of policies that are claiming the needlessness of public education, and consequently the reinforcement of a privatized penal system, because today's youth are not seen as part of the solution to tomorrow's problems. They are the problem. To paraphrase Mark Twain, when you open a school, you close the doors of a prison. Here, however, the reverse is true. When you close a school, you will need to open a prison. And if you open a prison, there is profit to be made.

Giroux explores the logic of disposability as the underside of commodification—the fate of those considered flawed consumers, unworthy of social protections because they are considered a liability and utterly disposable in a market-driven world whose anthem is the survival of the fittest. In fact, this Darwinian equation reveals a much darker side by subjecting poor youth and youth of color to the harshest elements, values, and dictates of neoliberal ideology. White, wealthy young people may labor under the narrow dictates of a commodity culture; but they are not incarcerated in record numbers, placed in schools that merely serve to warehouse the refuse of global capitalism, or subjected to a life of misery and impoverishment. Many actually benefit in the long run from the transfer of public funds into private hands. For those disposable populations of young people who are poor (especially Black and Latino youth), neoliberal politics governs them through an analytic of punishment, surveillance, and control. As mentioned above, we are in the face of a panopticon (Foucault, 1977) that actually puts the oppressed in the position of creating and sustaining their own oppression (Freire, 2006). Indeed, one cannot fully understand the politics and practices of disposability if one denies the need to understand how such policies clash between the oppressed and oppressor dynamics, i.e., the oppressor will always be oppressed as long as he/she refuses to engage radically in transforming his/her subject position. As Hannah Arendt has shown us, making human beings superfluous is not a trivial pursuit; it is an illustration of democracy and the antidote is in urgent need of being reclaimed. For that reason, Giroux urges us to confront the "biopolitics of disposability" and to recognize these dark and dangerous times in which we live. He offers up a vision of hope and possibility.

Locked Out: Youth and Academic Unfreedom

Next, Giroux considers the role that academic institutions may take in addressing the crisis of youth and its relationship to politics and critical education. Here Giroux analyzes the multifaceted attacks conducted by various conservative groups against youth and those who are most likely to support them by undermining academic freedom and the conditions that make critical teaching and learning possible. At issue is how the role of the university might be defined as a democratic, if not defiant, public sphere even as it is subjected to both a ruthless corporate logic that confuses training and patriotic correctness with education and to a right-wing attack on any vestige of critical thought (p. 25). Giroux takes up this right-wing assault on higher education and points to an ominous future for critically engaged intellectuals. The influence of the religious right, along with conservative and corporate-minded policies, are suppressing academic freedom, silencing political views, and reducing the professoriate to detached professionals and their teaching to vocational exercises (p. 111). Just as a powerful cadre of conservative interests are coming together to redefine and shape political discourse through the deployment of massive amounts of money, they are using the same tactics to limit the scope of academic research to meet their own political ends.

At a time when young people are increasingly constructed as disposable, redundant, and expendable, Giroux calls for universities to step up and play a significant role in the future of youth so that they may become active and critically minded citizens. Higher education has become part of a neoliberal, market-driven logic that eliminates spaces to think critically while undermining substantive dialogue and restricting students from thinking outside of established expectations. Giroux rightly argues that, as higher education becomes more corporatized, it addresses mainly the needs of the privileged few. We will thus see insurmountable chasms in educational and personal wealth; and the future of the working class and poor youth will indeed be grim, with little chances for higher education. The result is that those in higher education have, wittingly or not, become parts of the web of commodification and dehumanization that will eventually solidify the redundancy and expendability of young people (p. 110).

Students also face a variety of challenges to their civil liberties through censorship; thought and behavior codes; private and arbitrary disciplinary procedures; and the release of records to governmental authorities, the military, and corporations (Weisman, 2002). Giroux's predictions about the disposability of youth presage future happenings as he warns us that, if we do not protect the rights of youth, there will be dire consequences.

Just months after the book was published, the FBI charged one of Philadelphia's wealthiest suburban school districts with spying on their high-school students in their own homes and in their own bedrooms with the video cameras attached to the laptops that the school district provided their students. The school district said that they activated the spy-ware unbeknownst to the students in an effort to prevent theft and to retrieve stolen laptops. However, the school administrators underwent a legal battle, defending numerous videos and pictures of students in their bedrooms (whom they suggested were engaged in problem behaviors). This panopticonic abuse of power, invasion of privacy, and victimization of youth is a clear example of the biopolitics of disposability. In fact, this is far more complex than a category of lost privacy by being surveilled, but rather the destruction of identity and the mutilation of agency, a reality that Giroux helps us understand.

This type of policing mechanism against young people again brings to mind Foucault's interpretation of British philosopher Jeremy Bentham's (1748–1832) panopticon, which demonstrates the transformative and disciplinary potential of surveillance as a means of extracting knowledge. It is the power inherent in such acts of information collection and analysis that is acquired through the towering specter of Orwell's Big Brother.

Such continued chipping away of the civil liberties of youth and the poor has been made possible through the policies and practices inherent in biopolitical neoliberalism, where one is presumed guilty. One example is the Arizona Immigration Bill SB 1070, which ex-Arizona governor Jan Brewer signed into law. It (1) bans the state's schools from teaching ethnic studies classes; (2) builds barriers to keep people out; (3) dismantles schools of education (e.g., Arizona State University); (4) institutes current neoliberal school reform efforts (i.e., vouchers, charter schools, high-stakes standardized testing, and tuition tax credits); and (5) systematically discriminates against minorities in U.S. schools that are more segregated today than before *Brown v Board of Education* (1954). The absurdity of Arizona's "Paper Please" law is that it makes it a state misdemeanor for a foreigner to be on Arizona's territory without carrying "acceptable" legal documents and cracks down on all those who might shelter immigrants.

Clearly, the world and the United States, in particular, have entered a period in which the war against youth and the poor offers no apologies because it is too arrogant and ruthless to imagine any resistance, argues Giroux (2009). He adds that, in order to confront the biopolitics of disposability and the war against young people, we need to create conditions for multiple collective and global struggles that refuse to use politics as an act of war and markets as a measure of democracy (p. 142). Giroux urges us to take the challenge of reimagining both civic engagement and social transformation.

In the Shadow of the Gilded Age: Biopolitics in the Age of Disposability

In his final section, Giroux provides a broader theoretical analysis of what he calls the bio-politics of neoliberalism. He examines it not just as an economic discourse but also as an educational, cultural, and political discourse that has gutted the notion of the social state and produced a set of policies which lay the groundwork for a politics of disposability—one with dire consequences for society at large, and especially for young people. He contends that only by understanding the pervasive and all-embracing reach of neoliberalism and its new mode of bio politics does it become possible to grasp the contours of the present historical period in which a war is being waged against youth (p. 142). Conversely, by drawing attention to the particular effects of neoliberalism on the lives of young people, Giroux puts a face on the rav-aged victims of a morally bankrupt and pernicious neoliberal doctrine that is spreading like a pestilence and infecting democracy in the United States and around the globe (p. 25). As a result, the victims are no longer abstract "others." They are our brothers, sisters, sons, and daughters.

Most crucial, Giroux writes, is the gap in the various theories, discourses, and critiques that try to counter the impact of the current financial and economic crisis facing young people, labor, and others who are marginalized because they are poor, old, sick, brown, Black, or sim-ply left on their own to deal with the savagery of the free-market fall-out (p. 25). He suggests that, while there is a great deal of discussion among progressives about inequality generated by economic institutions, finance capital, and the legacy of historical imbalances in resources, power, and wealth, there is very little talk about creating the conditions for individual and col-lective agency as a fundamental basis for building social movements (p. 141). That is, Giroux argues that we must imagine the ways and means that make it possible for people to believe that their participation in political life matters, that they have voices that count, that they can make history. He posits that the task of a reinvigorated Left is in large part to foreground consistently and imaginatively the question of justice in ways that translate private issues into public concerns. He thus urges us to break open "common sense" in the interests of critical and reflective sense, and struggle to bring into being the conditions that enable people to use their power responsibly to control and shape the basic forces that shape their lives. Giroux is adamant in declaring that this is not merely a theoretical issue, but rather a preeminently edu-cational issue that is at the heart of any viable notion of politics and central to addressing the related crisis of youth and democracy (p. 25).

He punctures the complacency of these times when he turns the tables and applies the label of "politics of disposability" to the idea of biopolitical neoliberal progress. This idea of progress is, in Giroux's approach, intrinsically connected with a radical transformative disposition. And this is not a minor issue in an era fashioned by the "fetish belief that there is a technological fix for each and every problem" (Harvey, 2005, p. 68). *Youth in a Suspect Society: Democracy or Disposability?* underscores the reemergence of the "Gilded Age" mentality that viscerally chal-lenges us to confront the neglect and abuse of youth in our society. This book steers the reader to unfamiliar places—such as a restricted prison cell—to allow individual contemplation and the hopeful possibility of a collective conversation about the underlying politics of a justice system that boasts the world's largest penal system with over two million prisoners.

In order to confront the biopolitics of disposability, Giroux (2006) says we need to recognize these dark times and offer up a vision of hope. We need to work to create the conditions for collective and global struggles that refuse to use war as an act of politics and markets as the measure of democracy. Giroux (1994) argues that we need a public pedagogy to confront history as more than simulacrum and to view ethics as something other than the casualty of incommensurable language games. Postmodern educators need to take a stand without standing still, to engage their own politics as public intellectuals without essentializing the ethical referents to address human suffering.

Therefore, a people's democracy is in urgent need of being reclaimed (p. 2), and Giroux's work makes a laudable call for a re-democratized democracy. It is also a crucial analysis for and of the left. As one gathers from Giroux's approach, the left political praxis cannot surrender to the theoretical cynicism visible in many academic corridors, but is rather one in need of a new vocabulary—new coherent phraseology, one that is deeply political. Giroux diligently argues that the social and economic policies of this new millennium have worked to destroy the bedrock of our future by punishing and blaming our youth as a risk to be reckoned with and selling the public on the idea that policing and punishment are the solution to all social and economic problems. Giroux helps us to become witnesses as critical spectators, to experience primeval tragedy. He asks us to respond to the tragedy depicted in his work, but also to extend beyond its confines in order to alert the public to the plight of youth worldwide.

Conclusion

This book asserts that, with the continued and aggressive rise of market fundamentalism and its subsequent economic and financial disasters, young people are facing a crisis unlike that of any other generation. Exacerbated by the collapse of the welfare state, youth are no longer seen as a social investment but as troubled and, in some cases, disposable, especially poor minority youth. Caught between the discourses of consumerism and a powerful crime control-complex, they are increasingly viewed as commodities or subjected to the dictates of an ever-expanding criminal justice system.

Giroux's critical enterprise is predicated on Edward Said's (1994) prescription of the public intellectual as an oppositional figure who revels in transgressing the official lines of power—someone whose whole being is staked on a critical stance, a sense of being unwilling to accept easy formulas or ready-made clichés, or the smooth, ever-so-accommodating confirmations of what the powerful or conventional have to say, and do (p. 23). As a public intellectual, Giroux continues to present us with clear, deeply researched analytical and literary accounts of political and social injustices. He alerts us to the oppressive walls rising around us that are beginning to look impregnable. But before we can decide how they might best be demolished, we must first recognize that the "disposability of youth" is yet another brick in the wall that the neoliberal regime has built.

References

Agamben, G. (2005). *State exception by Giorgio Agamben*, trans. K. Attell. Chicago: University of Chicago Press.
Bauman, Z. (1998). *Globalization: The human consequences*. New York: Columbia University Press.
Bauman, Z. (1999). *In search of politics*. Stanford, CA: Stanford University Press.

Bauman, Z. (2001). *The individualized society*. London: Polity Press.

Bauman, Z. (2003). *Liquid love*. London: Polity Press.

Bauman, Z. (2004). *Wasted lives*. London: Polity Press.

Bauman, Z. (2005). *Liquid life*. London: Polity Press.

Bauman, Z. (2006). *Liquid fear*. London: Polity Press.

Bauman, Z. (2007). *Liquid times: Living in an age of uncertainty*. London: Polity Press.

Bentham, J. (1995). Panopticon; or the house-inspection. In his *The Pantopticon Writings* (pp. 29–114). London: Verso.

Berger, P.L., & T. Luckmann. (1966). *The social construction of reality: A treatise in the sociology of knowledge*. Garden City, NY: Anchor Books.

Bourdieu, P. (2000). For a scholarship of commitment. *Profession*, 42–43.

Bourdieu, P., & Wacquant, L. (2001, January). Neoliberal Newspeak: Notes on the new planetary vulgate. *Radical Philosophy*, 108, 2.

Brenner, N., & Theodore, N. (2002). *Spaces of neoliberalism: Urban restructuring in North America and Western Europe*. New York: Wiley-Blackwell.

Burke, L. (2008). Environmental disposability: Populations and the ideology of scarcity. Paper presented at the annual meeting of the American Political Science Association,

Boston, August 28, 2008. Retrieved July 3, 2010 from

http://www.allacademic.com/meta/p278 068_index.html

Callewaert, S. (2006). Looking back, but not in anger. In L. Dahlström & J. Mannberg (Eds.), *Critical educational visions and practices in neo-liberal times* (pp. 127–132). Umeå, Sweden: Umeå University, Global South Publishers.

Clegg, S. R., Pitsis, T.S., Rura-Polley, T.,& Marosszeky, M. (2002). Governmentality matters: Designing an alliance culture of interorganizational collaboration for managing projects. *Organizational Studies*, 23(3), 317–337.

Crawford, M. (1992). The world in a shopping mall. In M. Sorkin (Ed.), *Variations on a theme park: The new American city and the end of public space*. New York: Macmillan.

Da Costa, B., & Philip, K. (2010). *Tactical biopolitics: Art, activism, and technoscience*. Cambridge, MA: MIT Press.

Eid, H., & Ghazel, K. (2008). Edward Said: Agent provocateur. *Nebula*, 5(3), 111–120.

Foster, J.B. (2007). The financialization of capitalism. *Monthly Review*, 58(11), 1–14.

Foucault, M. (1980). The eye of power. In his *Power and Knowledge: Selected interviews and other writings, 1972–1977*. New York: Pantheon.

Foucault, M. (1995). *Discipline and punish: The birth of the prison*. New York: Vintage.

Giroux, H.A. (1994). Slacking off: Border youth and postmodern education. *Journal of Advanced Composition*, 14 (2), 347–366.

Giroux, H.A. (2002). Neoliberalism, corporate culture, and the promise of higher education: The university as a democratic public sphere. *Harvard Educational Review*, 72(4), 425–465.

Giroux, H.A. (2006). *Stormy weather: Katrina and the politics of disposability*. Boulder, CO: Paradigm.

Gramsci, A. (1971). *Selections from the prison notebooks*. London: Lawrence and Wishart.

Gray, M. (2003). Urban surveillance and panopticism: Will we recognize the facial recognition society? *Surveillance and Society*, 1(3), 314–330. Retrieved from http://www.surveillance-and-society.org

Hall, S. (1986). The problem of ideology: Marxism without guarantees. *Journal of Communication Inquiry*, 10, 28–44.

Harvey, D. (2005). *A brief history of neoliberalism*. Oxford, UK: Oxford University Press.

Ives, S. (2007). *Mediating the neoliberal nation: Television in post-apartheid South Africa*. ACME Online: Editorial Collective.

Lyon, D. (2002). Surveillance studies: Understanding visibility, mobility and the phenetic fix. *Surveillance and Society*, 1 (1), 1–7 Retrieved November 15, 2015, from http://www.surveillance-and-society.org/articles1/editorial.pdf

Mathiesen, T. (1997).The viewer society: Michel Foucault's panopticon revisited. *Theoretical Criminology*, 215–234.

Monbiot, G. (2000, June 29). Totalitarian capitalism. *Guardian*. http://www.monbiot.com/archives/2000/ 06/29/ totalitarian-capitalism/ Paraskeva, J. (2010). Hijacking public schooling: The epicentre of neo-radical centrism. In S. Macrine, P. McLaren, & D. Hill, *Revolutionizing pedagogy: Education for social justice within and beyond global neo-liberalism*. New York: Palgrave Macmillan.

Peck, J., & Tickell, A. (2002). Neoliberalizing space. *Antipode*, 380–404.

Penna, S. (2009). Children and the "new biopolitics of control": Identification, identity and social order. *Youth Justice: An International Journal*, 9(2).

Rai, A. (2006, January 31). Power, process, and panopticon: An introduction. ETALKING HEAD. Retrieved from http://www.etalkinghead.com/archives/power-process-and-panopticon-2006–01– 31.html

Rancere, J. (2006). *The politics of aesthetics*. New York: Continuum.

Robinson, W.L. (2004). *A theory of global capitalism: Production, class and state in a transnational world*. Baltimore, MD: Johns Hopkins University Press.

Said, E. W. (1984). *The world, the text and the critics*. Cambridge, MA: Harvard University Press.

Said, E. W. (1994). *Representations of the intellectual: The 1993 Reith Lectures*. New York: Vintage.

Searls-Giroux, S. (2008). Generation kill: Nietzschean meditations on the university, war, youth and guns. *Works and Days, 51/52*(1 & 2), 24.

Silva, M. (2009). *Classes sociais. Condicao objectiva. Identidada e accao colectiva*. Lisbon, Portugal: Humus.

Somers, M. R. (2008). *Genealogies of citizenship: Markets, statelessness, and the right to have rights*. Cambridge, UK: Cambridge University Press.

Vatter, M. (2006). Natality and biopolitics. In H. Arendt (Ed.), *Natality and biopolitics: Revistade coevcia politica, 26*(2), 137–159. Retrieved from www.scielo.cl/pdf/revcipol/v26n2/art08.pdf

Watson, S. (2008, April 2). Programs Spy on Americans Panopticon society in full swing. Infowars.net. Retrieved from http://www.sodahead.com/living/programs-spy-on-americans-panopticon-society-in-full-swing/blog-111609/

Weisman, D. (2002). Civil liberties of students in higher education. *Issues in Teaching and Learning, 1*(1). Retrieved from http://www.ric.edu/itl/volume-01-weisman.php

Welsh, S. (1990). *A feminist ethic of risk (other feminist voices)*. Minneapolis, MN: Augsburg Fortress.

Žižek. S. (2007). Afterword: With defenders like these who needs attackers? In P. Bowman & R. Stamp, *The truth of Zizek*. London: Continuum.

THIRTY-SIX

David F. Labaree, *Someone Has to Fail: The Zero-Sum Game of Public Schooling* (2010)

Wayne J. Urban

The Author

David Labaree is Professor of Education at Stanford University, where he has held that position and a variety of administrative posts since 2003. Prior to that he spent 18 years on the faculty at Michigan State University, moving through the ranks from assistant professor to associate professor to professor before he left for Stanford. He received a master's and a Ph.D., both in the field of sociology, from the University of Pennsylvania, the latter degree in 1983. He also earned a B.A. in Social Relations from Harvard in 1970.[1] Labaree's doctoral dissertation was written under the supervision of Michael Katz, a renowned scholar in the history of American education, as well as in the larger fields of history and sociology. It was published in 1988 by Yale University Press, titled *The Making of an American High School: The Credentials Market and the Central High School of Philadelphia, 1839–1939*. This volume received an Outstanding Book Award from both the American Educational Research Association and the History of Education Society in 1989. It was a pathbreaking monograph on the development of the first public high school in the city of Philadelphia, dealing imaginatively and convincingly with that school and its relation to issues of social class and status.

The influence of Michael Katz accounts in large part for both Labaree's sociological orientation and his rigorous historical dissertation. Labaree's subsequent books, however, differ significantly from his work on Central High School. *How to Succeed in School Without Really Learning: The Credential Race in American Education* (1997), *The Trouble with Ed Schools* (2004), and *Education, Markets, and the Public Good: Selected Works of David F. Labaree* (2007) represent a different species of historical work from the monographs that most scholars, including Labaree, produced to obtain their doctoral degrees. These later Labaree works all reveal a scholar seeking to raise big questions about big topics that are of significant importance to an audience far beyond that for most historical treatises. They are in the tradition of the scholar as a public intellectual, speaking to audiences far beyond his or her colleagues in an effort to contribute to the larger social and political dialogue about society, education, and educational policy. They are reminiscent of the approach to intellectual history taken long ago by Crane Brinton in *The Shaping of the Modern Mind* (1953) and by C. Wright Mills to sociological study in all of his works and, especially as discussed at length, in his *The Sociological Imagination* (1959). Michael Katz is also a model for Labaree's work, in his reach for the current implications of his historical studies and his emphasis on studying people and institutions from the bottom up. Katz's rigorous quantitative methods, however, on display in many of his works, are not evident in Labaree's work. More similar to Labaree, perhaps, is the work of Diane Ravitch, who has written for a larger public than educational historians throughout her illustrious career.

Two other historians deserve mention for their influence on Labaree and, particularly, the work that is the subject of this chapter, *Someone Has to Fail: The Zero-Sum Game of Public Schooling*. They are David Tyack and Larry Cuban. In his acknowledgments section, Labaree mentions the presence of Tyack and Cuban at Stanford as an important factor that led him to take a position there.[2] He adds that his book *Someone Has to Fail* was developed in large part through his teaching a course in the History of School Reform at Stanford, a course that he inherited from Tyack and Cuban and one that they used in the development of their book *Tinkering Toward Utopia* (1995). One might conclude from the inclusion of Callahan, Labaree, Ravitch, and Tyack and Cuban in this volume that historical works that address big questions—such as how to explain the failure of school reform—stand a good chance of becoming "classics." I will have more to say about this subject at the conclusion to this chapter. For now, let us now turn to the pages of *Someone Has to Fail*.

The Argument

After a few introductory pages on the history of school reform in the United States, a topic developed in greater detail in later chapters, Labaree states his primary thesis in *Someone Has to Fail* as follows:

> My argument is that schooling in America has emerged…as a bad way to fix social problems, but as a good way to express (if not realize) personal dreams. The problem is that these dreams are deeply conflicted and thus the school system is conflicted as well. We want it to meet the ambitions of our children and to protect them from the ambitions of other people's children.[3]

To reach these conclusions Labaree produces three chapters on the history of school reform, followed by two chapters on the structure of American education, focusing on the organizational forms of public schooling and the structure of the teaching profession. After that, he spends three chapters on the interaction of school reform and reformers, particularly late twentieth-century reformers, with the structure and institutions of public education in this country. In one he notes the inability of reformers to penetrate the structure to effect meaningful change; in another he describes the feeble, and largely misguided, attempt to achieve socially productive economic outcomes through public schooling, especially the recent, largely ineffective calls for workforce development. In still another chapter he tries to understand why, in the midst of all of these failures, the public school edifice has continued to maintain itself largely, though not completely, while impervious to the efforts of reformers to alter the enterprise. Labaree's explanation for the failure is based mainly on the disconnect between the social or economic objectives pursued by reformers and the individual betterment motives of parents and students to achieve upward mobility—or prevent downward mobility—through school success.

The title of the book refers to Labaree's argument that, though some persons may be gaining social status, economic improvement, or other advantages through the schools, other persons lose status and relative position. "Someone Has to Fail" is the embodiment of this argument, that if taken on an individual level, would mean that for every winner there is a loser. This is a slightly exaggerated version of Labaree's argument, for he never actually puts it in quite these exact words. What he does say, however, is that the devotion to individual improvement through education in the American educational experience is a frustratingly evident illustration of the zero-sum game of schooling in the United States. He adds, further, that the evolution, mainly though not only in the twentieth century, of a change in the ideological basis for schooling toward a consumer orientation that privileges individual mobility and status is characteristic of the contemporary educational experience, as well as of many of its predecessor experiences. Further, it is the devotion to this consumer orientation that has frustrated both mainstream educators and educational reformers for different reasons.

Educators, who teach primarily for content or intellectual objectives, must deal with students and parents who value these, if at all, for what they can achieve in the larger society, not for any intrinsic intellectual purpose. Reformers, on the other hand, have sought to achieve a variety of social, economic, or political purposes over the years, but have been continually frustrated by the fundamentally individualistic orientation of students and parents—both groups of which see the school as a vehicle for individual advancement rather than for larger social, political, or economic goals.

In pursuit of his argument, Labaree discusses a variety of school reform efforts, including the common school crusade of the early nineteenth century, the Progressive Era of the late nineteenth and early twentieth centuries, the Civil Rights Movement of the mid-twentieth century, the more recent educational standards movement signaled by the publication of *A Nation at Risk* in the 1980s and intensified by passage of the No Child Left Behind Act of 2002, and the equally recent school choice movement represented today by the popularity of vouchers and charter schools. Of all these reform movements, Labaree maintains that only the common school crusade was successful. It achieved the implementation of a republican ethos in the public school, a rough-and-ready social equality within the institution that helped students adapt to the economic changes of the first half of the nineteenth century. The common school sought to treat and to train all students for citizenship in the republican society of the early nineteenth-century United States. None of the successor reform efforts—progressivism, civil rights, standards, or choice—succeeded in their goals, however different each was, and is, from the others. The reason for the lack of success in subsequent reforms had to do, for Labaree, with the structure of the schools, the structure of the teaching force, and, most important, the continuing desire of parents and students, the consumers of the education proffered through the schools, to use the schools to pursue individual mobility, social status, and economic welfare through the educational system.

Labaree presents anything but a pleasant picture of the evolution of the American educational enterprise, but also acknowledges the formidable accomplishment of that enterprise in achieving not educational or social or political goals, but in maintaining the belief in the users of the system that it worked for individual betterment. Before evaluating Labaree's argument and its conclusion, it seems appropriate to look at several of the pieces of the argument that led up to it.

The first thing that strikes this reader of Labaree is that his argument is unique, at least in my experience. The failure of educational reform is not the unique aspect, however. Rather, Labaree is alone, at least among the educational historians that I know, in attributing substantial and lasting success to the common school movement. The origins and objectives of that movement have been a signature issue in American educational historiography with revisionist historians, beginning with Labaree's mentor Michael Katz questioning the value of the common school to the very segments of the population designated to benefit from it, that is, the non-elite members of the society.[4] Labaree ignores the debate sparked by Katz's questioning of the common school as a legitimate social mobility device, concentrating instead on the social, cultural, and political commonality that he thinks was brought about by the institution. It is also the case that Labaree makes this point more by assertion than by any rigorous analysis of the common school and those who proposed—and opposed—it.

Labaree continually contrasts the success of the common school movement with the failure of all successor movements. The argument is not the same in every case, but the judgment of a mature public school system impervious to reform is. Progressives, at least child-centered progressives, failed to turn the tide in American pedagogy in a direction that valued real student learning and innovative teaching to achieve that learning. Their more successful counterparts, the administrative progressives, succeeded in establishing a structure of public education sufficiently complex, inefficiently loosely coupled, and rigid enough to frustrate the child-centered progressives as well as all subsequent reformers. The institutional embodiment of that movement was the comprehensive high school, an institution seeking to enroll all students but also making sure to sort those students into groups taking the distinct tracks of a newly differentiated curriculum. The comprehensive high school invited newer groups of students to attend in order to better themselves but succeeded in influencing most of those students toward newer, less academic curricula than traditional college preparatory studies—curricula that seemed to promise occupational relevance at the same time they were geared to inhibiting, or at least not toward enhancing, equality among students.

Later groups of reformers, profiled in the latter chapters of the book, all adopted approaches to reform that sought concrete betterment for students that would yield both individual and social amelioration. The civil rights-oriented desegregationists of the mid-twentieth century achieved a legal, but pyrrhic, victory in their attempt to attain racial justice in the schools. Using an argument that rhetorically invoked democratic equality as the basis for change, they sought a fairer chance at success for their children through enrollment of minority children in schools from which they had previously been excluded. They gained at best a token level of racial mixing of student bodies that, when it threatened to go beyond tokenism, resulted in White flight from the public schools and a resulting resegregation of non-White students in those schools.

The standards reformers are the only group of reformers discussed by Labaree that can be seen as addressing subject matter in the schools. To do this, however, they used a fundamentally political argument to justify their changes that saw the United States as enmeshed in competition with other nations for world dominance or influence. Their most stated goal was to improve what they considered to be deplorable American results in international tests of educational achievement. To accomplish this objective, students at all levels of the educational system needed to experience a rigorous curriculum that would yield collective, as well as individual, improvement. The measurement of that improvement, however, took on a life of its own. Tests and test scores became more important to many than the educational content that they were supposed to measure. Standards reformers also floundered against the opposition of teachers who, intuitively and often viscerally, detested the standardization, particularly the standardized testing, that typified that reform. Especially repulsive was the anti-intellectualism embodied by most parents and students who failed to appreciate the intrinsic value of subject matter and academic achievement, preferring instead to follow the allure of a credentialing system that thrived on objective tests and any allied measures that allowed students to be ranked and rated in relation to each other.

Finally, the choice reformers who have become increasingly vocal and politically organized in the last decade or so have sought to defeat traditional education at its common school roots, that is, at the level of a publicly supported, locally managed, and professionally staffed educational system. The system is the problem for choice reformers, who argue that its complex bureaucratic organization and political governance mandate a rigidity that makes it impossible to meet the needs of students and parents who desire different versions of individual service from a system that offers one version to all comers. In a way not really noticed by Labaree, the choice reformers strike at the very heart of the public school system much more so than their predecessors. In a volume that provided the intellectual foundations of the choice movement, two political scientists argued that the very basis of the public schools—their locally elected management by boards of education—was the problem. For these scholars, school boards were frighteningly political, concentrating on many things, including being reelected, in place of a concern for educational accomplishment.[5] Choice, then, in addition to its rhetorical invocation of a market approach to education in a society that, rhetorically at least, idealized the market as the solution to all problems, struck directly at the political bases of American public schools, their management by local board members, and their statutory status as instruments of state government.

Strengths and Weaknesses

There is much to admire in this volume. As already mentioned, it is a bold effort to synthesize the American experience with educational reform, and to account for the failure of most reform efforts, the success of the institutional edifice that is American public education, and the interaction between those two phenomena. This purpose is evident throughout the volume, especially in the final chapter. A review of the various section headings in that chapter reveals where the author has taken the reader and what the journey might mean in the final analysis. The last chapter is entitled "Living with the School Syndrome." The sections of the chapter include discussions of "The Modest Impact of School Reformers," "Why We Persist in School Reform Despite Its Repeated Failures," "The Immodest Impact of School Consumers," "Is the School Syndrome Curable?," "Unusable Lessons for School Reformers," and "The Resilience of the School System." These sections summarize much of the content of the volume and indicate the conversational, informal language that Labaree often adopts and how that language can attract a reader's attention and provoke reader reaction to the argument.

Additionally, there is plenty of good writing in the book, especially some attractive passages that reveal the author as a committed teacher, as well as an accomplished scholar. For example, he leads off his acknowledgments section by describing how the book has resulted from his teaching the course in the history of school reform at Stanford. He mentions that he tried out various arguments in class and that student reaction often led to modification of the arguments. He then notes the finality of publishing an argument in contrast to the fluidity inherent in teaching it. He remarks that he tells his students that "talking about ideas in the classroom is like singing in the shower; it may sound good there but the real test comes in the recording studio."[6] As one who has also tried out ideas in class that eventually found their way into print, I concur that this is an exceedingly vivid and revealing description of the two stages of that process.

Labaree also often crystallizes his larger argument by highlighting how it is illustrated by a typical institutional development. We have already discussed the salience of the common school movement as an example of a successful reform. Not so successful as a reform, but enormously successful as an institution, was the comprehensive high school of the twentieth century. The institution itself was an enormous success, but Labaree indicates the qualified nature of that success when he notes that the comprehensive high school served the purpose of accommodating new groups of students, but did so with a tracking system that almost immediately put those students on a different, and inferior, footing from traditional high school students. I am familiar with both parts of this argument through my recent work on James Bryant Conant, perhaps the most famous advocate of the comprehensive high school in the middle of the twentieth century. Conant, however, had such a powerful belief in the validity of standardized testing that he ignored the paradox or contradiction implicit in the tracking that accompanied the comprehensive high school and its differentiated curriculum. He believed instead that standardized tests mitigated the negative consequences of tracking, separating students on the basis of intellectual accomplishments and not on social or economic background. Labaree is not seduced by the devotion to testing that captured Conant, which allows him (Labaree) to see how the comprehensive high school both promised equity through making the high school curriculum available to newer groups of students and, unfortunately, delivered inequity in the differentiation of that curriculum.

Another attractive quality of Labaree's account is that it spends a significant amount of time on teachers, and on students and parents. He shows how both groups interacted with reform and reformers in ways that interfered with, or simply frustrated, reform. Teachers are discussed more often as opponents than as supporters of reform. The discussion, however, is sympathetic to teachers' allegiance to content and learning in their classrooms. Curriculum, pedagogy, and learning were seldom the concerns of reformers, and teachers' interaction with reform more often than not stressed these educational concerns over the larger objectives of reformers. Labaree is sympathetic to the opposition, noting that it may be beneficial for both school and society as a bulwark against impractical reform (p. 161) and that it also may have been, and may be, effective at promoting learning in school (p. 192). Parents and students, on the other hand, often frustrate teachers' intellectual objectives as well as the organizational, political, or social objectives of school reformers through their devotion to individual advancement through the schools. The consumer orientation of parents and students stands in stark contrast to that of teachers or reformers, and the power of the consumer approach puts a largely effective damper on the other actors in the school drama.

While there is much to appreciate in Labaree's volume, there are also several things that seem to me to be puzzling or problematic in the argument. I have already noted his unusual attribution of complete success to the common school reformers, a judgment that is controversial for many educational historians. On this issue, as on most issues in this book, Labaree relies almost completely on secondary sources in supporting his arguments. In and of itself, this is not a fatal flaw, except if Labaree were doing a historical or empirical work on a distinct and discrete problem or issue. Secondary sources are often used in constructing large arguments like the one Labaree makes about the failure of school reform. A problem, however, is that he sometimes seems to use his sources idiosyncratically. For example, as noted in a review of the book by an accomplished quantitative educational historian, Labaree interprets evidence on educational achievement and social mobility in a way distinctly different from the interpretation of the authors he cites.[7] What Labaree owes his readers, and does not deliver to them, is an acknowledgment that his interpretation differs from that of the source he himself cites in support of his interpretation. Quantitative evidence is exceedingly complex and open to interpretation, but differences in interpretation deserve acknowledgment and discussion, especially when the source appears to question, if not contradict, Labaree's own conclusions.

Additionally, there is a problem—or at least an issue—in Labaree's explanation of his own stance on the topic of school reform. He refers to himself often as a pessimist and uses that stance to applaud teacher opposition to reform as well as to question the consequences if reform were to succeed. In the last chapter of the book, he describes schooling as an American syndrome, implying thereby some sort of near-pathological compulsion on the part of our citizens about schools, a stance surely compatible with his stated pessimism. This introduction of a medical dimension, if only metaphorically, to the inquiry in the closing stages of the book, however, leaves a reader confused, since medicine does not come under any description of work in social science that I am familiar with, and it is not a concern in any of the earlier chapters. My discomfort is enhanced when Labaree, in deference to those who would state that critics of a phenomenon offer some suggestion to address the phenomenon productively, asks if the school syndrome is curable (p. 243). He argues that it isn't and then proceeds to offer some lessons that can be drawn from his analysis, not because they will have any productive impact, but because he is "quite confident that no one will follow them" (p. 245). There is a seeming disingenuousness here, or at least an aspect that bothers this reader of Labaree's work. How can recommendations that the recommender does not expect to be taken seriously be taken seriously?

Finally, I think that Labaree's need to encompass all school reforms within his analysis causes him to slight significant differences among the reforms. Particularly, the two most recent reforms he discusses, standards-based education and school choice, are recent enough that it seems presumptuous to include them in the larger category of ineffective attempts at change. Standards are becoming more and more prominent in federal educational policy, and the increasing power of the federal government, as evidenced in No Child Left Behind's mandates for accountability based on student test scores and Race to the Top's carrots-and-sticks approach to achieving both that accountability and a common core curriculum, seems unprecedented in the history of American school reform. Similarly, the school choice movement seems to have found a way around opposition to it based on a fear of privatization by focusing on low-income students in failing schools and public charter schools as a remedy for their plight. Charters, to me, seem like vouchers lite, but they are a formidable challenge—really a significant threat—to the American public school as we know it. This is not necessarily to say that either of these reforms will succeed in the long run but, rather, that they are at a relatively early stage in their development and their future is, at the moment, not clearly known.

Despite these reservations, I return to my initial judgment of *Someone Has to Fail.* It is a bold volume dealing with education in its largest sense and presenting a compelling, if not completely convincing, argument about the failure of school reform. It deserves to be read and discussed by all those interested in the future of American education, especially those who envision a future unlike the past. Labaree's argument that reform has failed, and his implication that it will continue to fail, challenges reformers as well as supporters of American public education. Both groups have visions of school improvement, though they are very different from each other. Whether either vision can result in success is a doubtful, though not impossible, premise.

Notes

1   http://www.stanford.edu/~dlabaree (accessed February 6, 2015).
2   David F. Labaree, *Someone Has to Fail: The Zero-Sum Game of Public Schooling* (Cambridge, MA: Harvard University Press, 2010), 281.
3   Ibid., 6.
4   Michael B. Katz, *The Irony of Early School Reform: Educational Innovation in Mid-Nineteenth Century Massachusetts* (Cambridge, MA: Harvard University Press, 1968).
5   John E. Chubb and Terry M. Moe, *Politics, Markets, and America's Schools* (Washington, DC: The Brookings Institution, 1990).
6   Labaree, 279.
7   John Rury, Review of *Someone Has to Fail. History of Education Quarterly* 51 (August 2011): 419–421.

THIRTY-SEVEN

Diane Ravitch, *The Death and Life of the Great American School System: How Testing and Choice Are Undermining Education* (2010) and *Reign of Error: The Hoax of the Privatization Movement and the Danger to America's Public Schools* (2013)

Marcia Peck

I left the Western United States and my 22 years as a public school teacher 6 years ago to become an education professor in the South. While I was excited to begin a new career and elated at the lack of snow in winter, I was quite puzzled by what I observed in classrooms and heard from my students. Everything I knew about the characteristics of quality education seemed to have been co-opted by draconian measures of control. This was especially evident in schools with mostly poor children of color. I observed children standing silently in line on the "third tile from the wall" and being screamed at if they moved or talked. I saw high school students only allowed bathroom privileges when they were escorted en masse to the locked restrooms during class. I heard about silent lunch, no recess, and 7 weeks of test preparation followed by a month of testing. I was confused by such happenings, since most of the recipients of this inhumane treatment were the very children most in need of quality pedagogy and a supportive school climate.

In frustration, I asked one class of practicing teachers, "How can you allow a child to go to middle school unable to read? What are you doing wrong?" I was informed that they knew what to do, but were not allowed to do it. I was skeptical. Then I was shown a pacing guide that all geometry teachers had to follow and could not deviate from, even if the students didn't understand. I heard about a teacher being reprimanded because she allowed an elementary student to share a rock brought from home. She was informed, "Rocks are not part of today's standard." A pre school teacher described being visited by the district "SWAT" team, while a high school instructor was scolded for not having students recite the standard at the beginning of class.

Teachers told me how they would lose their jobs if students didn't perform well on *the Test*; how their school was a failing school and was monitored by the state; how they were forced to support what they knew to be poor pedagogy; and how they feared what they were becoming. I began to believe them but was still confused that any administration charged with educating children, many of whom were poor and Black, would order teachers to conduct their classes in such a fashion. But then I found Diane Ravitch, and it all started to make sense.

Ravitch, an educational historian, served as assistant secretary of education under President George W. Bush. She helped to craft and was a supporter of the federal government's No Child Left Behind (NCLB) policy, believing it could improve education for all children, but especially for those historically underserved by the public schools—poor children and children of color. After implementation of NCLB, though, she began to alter her opinion of the legislation and became an ardent critic of the culture spawned by its implementation. According to Ravitch, such federal accountability programs created a culture of fear and mistrust among all educational stakeholders, which research demonstrates leads to demoralized schools and low academic achievement (Johnson, Kraft, & Papay, 2012; Payne, 2008). In addition, such policies encouraged cheating, a narrowing of the curriculum, over-reliance on test scores in determining quality, and huge amounts of funds earmarked for education spent instead on training teachers and students to achieve higher test scores (Ravitch, 2013, p. 13). In fact, NCLB, and later the Obama administration's Race to the Top initiative, were actually hurting the very students she had hoped would be helped by such legislation.

Ravitch's work therefore became the voice of reason for me and many of my students. Her critiques of misplaced accountability measures and the standardized testing debacle were clearly evident in the schools in which my college students (both pre-service and practicing teachers) attempted to engage their students. They were being stymied at every turn. I would often hear my students state, after reading Ravitch or hearing one of her speeches, "Oh, finally someone gets what we are going through. It makes me feel hopeful that someone really understands." Indeed, Ravitch herself seemed to appear somewhat hopeful that public schools could get back on track in her text, *The Death and Life of the Great American School* (2010).

Ravitch was advocating for the education of humans in the face of a strong societal push to apply mechanistic, corporate reform principles used to increase efficiency and productivity in neighborhood public schools. The false assumption was that standardization of the means of production would lead to improvement in the creation of an educated mind just as it did in the creation of an electric motor in the factory. If a school didn't improve—in other words, raise its test scores—then even more standardization and control must be exerted to bring it into line, a dubious market principle illustrated within the schools my teachers inhabited. When production still failed, the school could be closed, all faculty fired, or students provided the choice to go elsewhere for their education. Hence, the public was saturated by the movement toward vouchers, online academies, and charters—in other words, privatization of a public responsibility and public good.

With the publication in 2013 of *Reign of Error: The Hoax of the Privatization Movement and the Danger to America's Public Schools*, Ravitch seemed to signal an end to a hopeful outcome for public schools. Instead, she raised a forceful voice of warning by indicating that the current privatization movement, fueled by the national meta-narrative of the failure of public schools, could effectively signal the death of American public education. In essence, she urged a stay of execution. According to Ravitch, the failure of public education was a fictional story incited by corporate reformers, as well as media hysteria sparked by special reports from television reporters and the major motion picture *Waiting for Superman*.

In *Reign of Error,* she sought to provide the facts of what was actually going on in public schools as well as offer solutions that, if implemented, would improve educational attainment.

Her text effectively established her as a "voice crying in the wilderness" of the educational debate. The question remained, though, whether that voice would be heeded.

The importance of a publicly funded education system has been a topic of national and local discussion that dates from the beginnings of this country. Thomas Jefferson advocated for state public schools to provide 3 years of free education to all White, non-slave youth as a means of preparing children to become productive American citizens (Huerta, 2007, p. 10). In the early 1800s Horace Mann pushed for publicly supported common schools that would serve all children, reasoning that such schools would equalize opportunity, increase the economic strength of the nation, and prepare children for citizenship (Huerta, 2007, p. 12). "Schools became the arenas where…collisions of culture, language, traditions and religions would take place" (Huerta, 2001, p. 12).

The public good of education was continually reaffirmed in modern times. For example, The Bilingual Education Act of 1968 established that English Language Learners (ELL) had special educational needs, while *Lau v. Nichols* (1974) established that schools must provide an equal education to ELLs (Huerta, 2007, p. 246). These past and present educational debates and policies were based on the belief that an educated citizenry was essential for an effective, functioning republic; therefore, it was in America's best interest to provide a free public education to all young citizens. While addressing a variety of issues, such discussions focused on reforming or improving the current system of public education.

The current reform debate addressed by Ravitch in her recent texts should create some alarm, as it differs from those of the past in an important way. The "reform" movement she opposes is not focused on ways to improve public education, but instead on dismantling it in favor of privatization. Ravitch intended *Reign of Error* to stimulate a national dialogue around this issue, as it has the potential to drastically alter the landscape not only of education, but the fabric of the nation as well.

Ravitch built her case against the proponents of privatization by first noting that corporate reformers such the Gates Foundation and the Walton Family Foundation needed to create a narrative concerning the wholesale failure of American public education in order to pave the way for the dismantling and privatization of a societal institution common to most citizens— the public school. Ravitch denounced this stand:

> Public education is not broken. It is not failing or declining. The diagnosis is wrong and the solutions of the corporate reformers are wrong. Our urban schools are in trouble because of concentrated poverty and racial segregation. But public education is not "broken." Public education is in crisis only so far as society is and only so far as the new narrative of crisis has destabilized it. (Ravitch, 2013, p. 4)

She then dedicates the first half of her text to debunking this lie by providing the "facts" about national and international test scores, high school and college graduation rates, poverty, and teachers. To illustrate her claim, Ravitch addresses the facts of national test scores by referencing the only "authoritative" measure of academic performance over time, the National Assessment of Educational Progress (NAEP), an assessment of learning conducted by the U.S. Department of Education. According to this measure, the NAEP scores of almost every group of students have improved "slowly, steadily and significantly since 1992" (Ravitch, 2013, p. 49). For example, "the proportion of fourth-grade students who were 'below basic' declined from 50% in 1990 to an astonishingly low 18% in 2011" (Ravitch, 2013, p. 50).

Additionally, she notes that international test scores are not as dismal as reported. "American students in schools with low poverty—the schools where less than 10 percent of the students were poor—had scores that were equal to those of Shanghai and significantly better than those of high-scoring Finland, the Republic of Korea, Canada, New Zealand, Japan and Australia" (Ravitch, 2013, p. 64). Ravitch elaborates: "It is important to recognize that the scores of students in low-poverty schools in the United States are far higher than the international average…and the scores decline as poverty levels increase, as they do in all nations" (Ravitch, 2013, p. 65).

The "fact" is that the public schools work for a large portion of students; the population not faring well in public schools today are poor children and children of color in segregated communities—the very same group that has historically not thrived in the system at any time. Ravitch contends: "Yes, we have problems, but those problems are concentrated where poverty and racial segregation are concentrated. The reformers say they care about poverty, but they do not address it other than to insist upon private management of the schools in urban districts; the reformers ignore racial segregation altogether. Thus, they leave the root causes of low academic performance undisturbed" (Ravitch, 2013, p. 6).

Along with debunking the failure of public schools for the nation's children who do not attended segregated schools in poor neighborhoods, Ravitch analyzes the rhetoric used to justify privatizing education. Reformers emphasize that the solution to failure is not systemic improvement efforts, but rather the need for jettisoning the public nature of schooling. They propose a business model of market reforms that would turn education into a private business run by private individuals or corporations. Doing so, they argue, would provide parents with choice while at the same time improving education by imposing successful business practices on a failing public enterprise.

While giving a nod to corporate reformers who may actually believe they are helping schools, Ravitch notes that privatizing education has created an economic bonanza for private speculators looking to make a substantial amount of money from a continuous funding source—the taxpayer-supported public school system. According to Ravitch (2013), "'Reform' is really a misnomer, because the advocates for this cause seek not to reform public education but to transform it into an entrepreneurial sector of the economy" (p. 19). For example, she details how Andre Agassi formed a partnership with an equity investing firm to raise $750 million in capital to build charter schools for 40,000 or more students. "This was not philanthropy; it was a profit-making venture. Investors quickly figured out that there was money to be made in the purchase, leasing, and rental of space to charter schools" (Ravitch, 2013, p. 17).

School districts spent huge sums of tax dollars on consultants and professional grant writers, while charter school executives received salaries of $300,000 or more. All of these funds could have been used to educate the country's children but were diverted instead to private, for-profit entities. Ravitch claims: "The privatization movement masks its underlying goal to replace public education with a system in which public funds are withdrawn from public oversight to subsidize privately managed charter schools, voucher schools, online academies, for-profit schools and private vendors" (Ravitch, 2013, p. 31).

For the first time in history, "the U.S. Department of Education designed programs with the intent of stimulating private sector investors to create for-profit ventures in American education" (Ravitch, 2013, p. 17). Ravitch warns that a move to such a system is quite dangerous. Not only is there little oversight over public funds, but the historical purpose of public education—to create educated citizens for a pluralistic society and to equalize opportunity—would be lost as well. "When public education is in danger, democracy is jeopardized. We cannot afford the risk" (Ravitch, 2013, p. 324).

Instead of selling the education of the nation's children to the highest bidder, Ravitch postulates that a better solution is to acknowledge that public schools do work for a particular group of children, and then seek to determine how to improve educational and life opportunities for the groups not well served—namely, poor children and children of color. It is to this end that she dedicates the final chapters of *Reign of Error*. She advocates for universal pre natal care and pre school, smaller class sizes, and a well-rounded education with physical and mental health clinics available to children while at school. "Unfortunately, many people are unwilling to address the root causes of poor school outcomes, because doing so is either too politically difficult or too costly. They believe it is faster, simpler and less expensive to privatize the public schools than do anything substantive to reduce poverty" (Ravitch, 2013, p. 37). She also recommends using testing with care, strengthening the teaching profession, and maintaining local, democratic control of schools.

For Ravitch, though, the most important school reform should deal with what she refers to as the "toxic mix": schools that are highly segregated and located in high-poverty areas. She emphasizes this notion as follows:

> When students go to school with others who are highly motivated, it lifts their performance as well. Schools attended by affluent and academically successful students not only tend to have a richer curriculum and smaller classes but also have the benefit of better school climate and positive peer effects. The schools for the poor are likeliest to sacrifice time for the arts and other studies to make more time for standardized testing and test prep, for fear that if the scores don't improve the staff will be fired and the school closed. (Ravitch, 2013, p. 295)

While a few politicians—for example, Secretary of Education Arne Duncan—have spoken out against Ravitch's work, far more educational reviewers and professionals find her message to be refreshing, powerful, and accessible. It is not that she is saying anything really new. Numerous recent studies concerning school improvement and reform have offered similar critiques and solutions (Darling-Hammond, 2010; Cassanova, 2010; Kozol, 2005; Payne, 2008). But the tone of her recent books is different; instead of the usual academic nod to fairness and objectivity, the texts present a strongly worded denunciation of current reform efforts and the reformers behind them. From her perspective, public education—and therefore the nature of our society—is at a crossroads, and she is not going to sugar-coat the truth to appease anyone. Ravitch reminds readers of the importance of her message by stating, "Genuine school reform must be built on hope, not fear; on encouragement, not threats; on inspiration, not compulsion; …on belief in the dignity of the human person, not a slavish devotion to data" (Ravitch, 2013, p. 325).

This morning in class, my graduate students and I were discussing Kozol's *The Shame of the Nation* (2005). One student commented that she couldn't believe that the depressed, segregated schools Kozol described can still be found today. "I thought we did away with these types of schools a long time ago," she said in exasperation. Another student, a pre school teacher, chimed in: "It's like we are going backwards. We desegregated schools and insisted on a quality education for all kids, but now we are going back to the way it used to be." A quiet student raised her hand and plaintively commented: "I read this book and suddenly understood why my school is the way it is. I'm living this every day. My school is a science and technology magnet school, but we don't have any technology." Another student added, with a noticeable touch of anger: "I'm taking my child out of public school because of the testing. He has a disability and doesn't test well. I'm tired of him getting the message that he is dumb and worthless every month. I'm a teacher and want to support the public schools, but he's going to a private school because of the testing." As I listened to the thoughtful and passionate discussion, I thought Diane Ravitch would be both saddened and elated by my students' grasp of the current realities of public education.

References

Cassanova, U. (2010). *Si se puede: Learning from a high school that beats the odds.* New York: Teachers College Press.

Darling-Hammond, L. (2010). *The flat world and education: How America's commitment to equity will determine our future.* New York: Teachers College Press.

Huerta, G. (2007). *Educational foundations: Diverse histories, diverse perspectives.* New York: Houghton Mifflin.

Johnson, S., Kraft, M., & Papay, J. (2012). How context matters in high-need schools: The effects of teachers' working conditions on their professional satisfaction and their students' achievement. *Teachers College Record, 114*(10), 1–39.

Kozol, J. (2005). *The shame of the nation: The restoration of apartheid schooling in America.* New York: Crown.

Kozol, J. (2013, September 26). This is only a test. *New York Times Book Review.* Retrieved March 9, 2015, from http://www.nytimes.com/2013/09/29/books/review/reign-of-error-by-diane-ravitch.html?_r=0

Payne, C. (2008). *So much reform, so little change: The persistence of failure in urban schools.* Cambridge, MA: Harvard Education Press.

Ravitch, D. (2011). *The death and life of the great American school system: How testing and choice are undermining education.* New York: Basic Books.

Ravitch, D. (2013). *Reign of error: The hoax of the privatization movement and the danger to America's public schools.* New York: Knopf.

THIRTY-EIGHT

Yong Zhao, *World Class Learners: Educating Creative and Entrepreneurial Students* (2012)

Alison LaGarry and George W. Noblit

Introduction

There are epochs to ideas. In that sense, context shapes what is possible to image, to do. In the current neoliberal global economic context, the knowledge economy has given way to the creative economy (Florida, 2002). In this epoch, ideas and images are a currency, symbols are to be managed, and design becomes the fundamental work process. There are other tropes of the epoch as well. Creativity becomes a watchword and entrepreneurship the vehicle to new economic opportunities. Many find these two tropes to be linked directly—entrepreneurship is in some ways creativity. This is a mantra increasingly common in business circles, one that reproduces the education/economy linkage that has defined schooling at least since industrialization, even if the industrial order is no longer the defining aspect of economic growth.

Education is definitely out of sync with this economic shift, bound as it is to increasing control as the mechanism for increasing learning. Politics and policy are still heavily invested in standardizing curriculum and learning—a model of education tied to the now-moribund industrial economy. Politicians and policymakers seemingly cannot imagine schools that would enable people to work in the newer knowledge and creative economies, but one does wonder if this is a lack of imagination or purposeful stratification. In any case, creativity is everywhere if limited to experimental moments, local constructions, and hopeful proposals (Sefton-Green, Thomson, Jones, & Bresler, 2011). Yet in the creativity/entrepreneurship epoch, it may be that possibility is more powerful than ever in history, more able to produce the *new*.

Yong Zhao has provided an account of possibility for what education would be—could be—in a neoliberal economy. He draws the equation: entrepreneurship is creativity, at least in some important ways. They are linked by the imperative of innovation.

In what follows, we provide a synopsis of Zhao's book *World Class Learners* and a summary of its main arguments. The author has addressed much of the important educational, economic, and political context and climate of the time when the book was written, and this sets up his main argument that entrepreneurship and creativity are inextricably linked. Also, we examine his contributions to our current understanding of entrepreneurship and creativity in a neoliberal epoch and explore possibilities not yet realized in the wider discourse on entrepreneurship and creativity.

The Wrong Bet

In Chapter 1, Zhao first describes the current "bet" being made by politicians and educational policymakers. With the ultimate aim of global competition, the Common Core State Standards (CCSS) were launched on June 2, 2010. These standards have been widely implemented; at the time of *World Class Learning*'s publication, Zhao stated that 45 states and the District of Columbia had adopted them. In this case, the wager relies on a centralized, prescribed model of education that highlights specific subject areas, and is evidence of "an increasing trend toward homogenization of student learning in the world" (p. 27).

The trend toward homogenization that Zhao identifies is justified by educational policymakers and politicians as a method to increase U.S. performance on internationally benchmarked assessments such as the Programme for International Student Assessment (PISA) developed by the Organisation for Economic Co-operation (OECD), and the Trends in International Mathematics and Science Study (TIMSS). Zhao outlines three necessary steps in the process of curricular homogenization,

1. The identification of core subjects;
2. The development of centralized curriculum standards; and
3. The use of high-stakes testing to enforce standards of core academic subjects. (p. 27)

In the case of the CCSS, the subjects of mathematics, literacy/reading, and science have been centered as the core of the curriculum. This centering implies that "core" subjects receive heightened attention from educators and administrators, often at the cost of subjects now located outside this core. Zhao explains: "When all energy and resources are poured into defining and enforcing the common curriculum and standards, nothing is left to pursue anything else" (p. 35). This results in curriculum narrowing that, in effect, de-emphasizes disciplines that may hold promise for development of creativity and innovation. In addition, employing high-stakes testing to assess these narrowed standards shifts curricular focus to preparation for testing in the form of memorization and recall and de-emphasizes such activities as inquiry and exploration that might build students' capacity to innovate.

Zhao concludes the first chapter by stating that the "bet" made on standard, centralized curriculum is the wrong bet and is, in fact, antithetical to his aims of fostering creativity and entrepreneurship. He notes that standardization is a trope that is no longer relevant in a global economy. He states that "the dominant paradigm of modern mass education has been about producing employees with similar skills to meet the demand of local economy and a common citizenry with similar values compatible with local society" (p. 42). The outcome of a central-ized and homogenized curriculum is that it produces a workforce with a unilateral set of skills. In other words, "the outcomes are precisely the opposite of the talents we need for the new era" (p. 45).

The Changed World

Zhao then outlines the need for entrepreneurship as a way to address the lack of available jobs. The take-away point from this chapter is that, in a global economy, we must shift our mind-set from *finding* jobs to *creating* job opportunities through innovative entrepreneurship. As reasons for the barren job market, Zhao describes the recent realities of youth unemployment, increased individual productivity, longer life expectancies and longer work lives, and the global redistribution of jobs. Despite each of these factors, Zhao proposes that the global redistribu-tion of jobs is not necessarily a zero-sum game. "The number of jobs is not finite, carved in stone at one time. It is not about keeping jobs home and preventing others from taking the jobs away, rather, it is about creating new jobs" (p. 59). It is upon this assumption that Zhao builds his argument for creating new jobs through innovation and entrepreneurship.

Zhao credits technology and shifting methods of doing business as the sources of unem-ployment and also believes (he says: paradoxically) that these are the very sources that will open up opportunities for entrepreneurs to create new jobs. Four areas are presented as holding the potential for job creation: previously unmet or unrecognized human needs, emerging needs, a global customer base, crowdfunding as a global capital pool, and crowdsourcing as a global workforce. Embracing these will require a significant shift in mind-set from finding to creat-ing jobs, and Zhao posits that the heretofore "missing link" in this equation is entrepreneurial spirit. He believes this entrepreneurial spirit is lacking due to an outdated system of education that "has been focused on producing employees who are taught to look for jobs and wait for orders" (p. 70). In order to combat this, Zhao suggests a keen focus on fostering the skills and qualities necessary for entrepreneurship.

The Entrepreneurial Spirit

Zhao elaborates on his vision of entrepreneurship by unpacking historical definitions of entre-preneurship and entrepreneurs. In the initial usage of the word, an entrepreneur is "someone who undertakes a significant project or activity" (p. 76). The connotation of the term has evolved and today is generally used "to refer to individuals who organize, manage, and assume the risks of a business or enterprise" (p. 76). Acknowledging the evolution of entrepreneurship based on the emerging global context, Zhao also discusses different types of entrepreneurs, including social entrepreneurs, intrapreneurs, and policy entrepreneurs. Social entrepreneurs are those whose work is aimed at creating "social values, benefits to the society, rather than fi-nancial values" (p. 77). Intrapraneurs are entrepreneurs who work within a corporation and are tasked with "assertive" approaches toward innovation that help the company to turn a profit. Policy entrepreneurs use their creative and innovative talents to inform and create policy in the name of public service. In 2011 the World Economic Forum released a global report on youth entrepreneurship that contained the following statement:

> Entrepreneurship is about growth, creativity, and innovation. Innovative entrepreneurs come in all shapes and forms and their impact is not limited to start-ups—they also innovate in the public, private, and academic and non-profit sectors. Entrepreneurship refers to an individual's

ability to turn ideas into action and is therefore a key competence for all, helping young people to be more creative and self-confident in whatever they undertake. (World Economic Forum, 2011, p. 5)

This paragraph seems to be the base of Zhao's entire argument throughout the book, in that it suggests a direct link between entrepreneurship and creativity. The report also highlights diversity of thought as beneficial to innovation and situates entrepreneurship as a "competence" that can be scaffolded and taught to students in schools.

The Myth of Education Giants

Returning to education, Zhao highlights stories of several countries (China, Singapore, Korea, and Japan) that have experienced high levels of academic success but have not produced entrepreneurs the likes of Steve Jobs. Jobs is heralded throughout the book as the ultimate innovator and entrepreneur, and Zhao describes two hypothetical scenarios of how Jobs and his company might have fared in the educational climates of China and Singapore. These scenarios drive the argument that there is an inverse relationship between test scores and entrepreneurial activities. In other words, students in countries that employ centralized and homogenized approaches to education *do* produce higher test scores. However, the statistics presented by Zhao show that these same students are engaging in very little entrepreneurial activity. Two potential conclusions are derived from the data, he explains. "First, in countries where fewer entrepreneurial activities exist, students have higher academic achievement.... The second interpretation is that efforts to pursue academic achievement may come at the cost of entrepreneurial activities" (p. 110). Another possible reason for this failure to engage in entrepreneurial activities, Zhao posits, is a lack of confidence consequent to the intense pressure placed on students to perform academically. The "press" for achievement, then, not only narrows curricula; it also suppresses the entrepreneurial spirit.

China vs. the United States

Zhao then juxtaposes the educational approaches of China and the United States in a comparison that highlights the *unintended* effects of each approach. In the case of China, education is intensely focused on performance on high-stakes assessments such as the *gaokao* college entrance exam. Book-reading (*dushu*) or book-learning is given the highest value in Chinese society, and a focus on achievement places significant pressure on Chinese students from a very young age. Zhao offers the criticism that this "laser focus" on education may limit China's ability to produce a creative and entrepreneurial workforce (p. 126). He positions this critique based on six observations. First, because of the focus on and value of academic excellence, ventures outside of this are not valued; students have little opportunity to discover creative talents. Second, success is defined as the ability to perform well on tests, and potential entrepreneurial talent may be sorted out early. Third, the type of education promoted in China may actually work to remove and stifle dispositions that contribute to innovative talent. Fourth, so much time is spent studying that students have little time to socialize, work in teams, or experience failure. Fifth, Zhao states, "when children follow such a prescribed path, there is little chance of a detour" (p. 129). Sixth, pressure to succeed in academics internalizes a sense of inferiority that inhibits the confidence that Zhao believes to be necessary for entrepreneurial ventures. Chinese citizens and policymakers see the limitations of the current system and have been working to transform Chinese education for decades. Interestingly, they seek to emulate the

American educational system: "What the Chinese find valuable in American education is a decentralized, autonomous system that does not have standards, uses multiple criteria for judging the value of talents, and celebrates individual differences" (p. 133). The paradox, of course, is that American educational policymakers and politicians have been undercutting this type of system for at least 35 years in order to emulate the focus on high achievement sought by the Chinese (and earlier Japanese) educational policy and culture.

In emulating the Chinese system of education, Americans policymakers and reformers see solutions to the problems that arise *because* of a decentralized, autonomous system. "The American education reformers view the aspects of its education admired by the Chinese as an indication of a broken and obsolete system that is considered responsible for the lackluster academic performance and the persistent achievement gap" (p. 133). Despite this "broken system," America is able to create enterprises that produce goods and services that are in demand worldwide and "has not been as good as the Chinese at killing creativity and the entrepreneurial spirit" (p. 134). Zhao uses a slightly disturbing analogy of a sausage maker to illustrate his point, describing Chinese education as taking in diverse talents and knowledge and producing consistently uniform "sausages" of its students. The imperfect model of American education, he suggests, produces some imperfect "sausages," but also produces "bacon"—creative and entrepreneurial talents—as an unintended byproduct. He explains further: "The features of American education that have been much criticized by American education reformers for ruining the sausage are what allow the bacon to emerge" (p. 135).

These features are centered on the idea that American children are given more time outside of studying to develop interests and dispositions that will serve them well as future entrepreneurs. There are more opportunities to uncover talents and areas of personal interest, and teachers are afforded more autonomy for relevant curricular planning due to the lack of a national high-stakes test. For better or worse, students may have differing educational experiences based on their geographic location and context. More free time allows American children the luxury of play, where they have the opportunity to build and manage social relationships and practice independence. There is less competition in American classrooms due to a lack of rigor, which—according to Zhao—allows teachers to pay attention to students' enjoyment of academics, thus preserving student confidence. Finally, the general availability of extracurricular activities allows students to see and explore other choices and options that may inspire them to pursue other careers. In sum, Zhao suggests, "the strengths of American education are not so much in its deliberate design to cultivate creative and entrepreneurial talents as in its 'poor' execution as a designed school system" (p. 138). Slippage is our greatest asset for the creative economy.

From Accident to Design

In Chapter 6, Zhao describes the dominant paradigm of education that is prevalent in educational systems around the world and also proposes an alternative paradigm that would encourage creativity and entrepreneurship. The dominant, or traditional, paradigm is aimed at preparing employees and has involved prescribed learning and consistent execution of a common curriculum. The effect of this paradigm is to narrow human diversity, and it was originally conceived with the aim of producing employees in support of mass production and standardization. Under this model, individual, cultural, and economic differences are funneled down through schooling in order to produce a set of standard desirable skills. This paradigm has worked well historically in societies where "knowledge was not easily accessible and a few experts monopolized all of the skills" (p. 150). In an expanding global economy, societies are now able to access information through technology, and local communities are more open to outside influence. Because of this rapidly changing context, it is more difficult to predict what jobs might look like in the future, and how individuals will obtain these jobs. Following this, there is no longer a set of predictable skills that will prepare students for the workforce.

In order to prepare students to be creative and innovative, Zhao believes that an alternative paradigm is necessary such that entrepreneurship is the result of careful and deliberate design rather than an accidental byproduct. It is not enough to simply "fix" the traditional paradigm; promoting entrepreneurship will involve a total paradigm shift. In this alternative paradigm, educators should be encouraged to follow the interests and curiosity of the child in order to expand their existing human talents. Here, schooling serves an expansive purpose, building on human diversity in order to enhance expanded talents. The idea that schooling should center on the child is not new. Despite evidence that children thrive in environments where their interests and talents are valued, authoritarian and dictatorial models of education still reign internationally. In support of this paradigm shift, Zhao uses the remainder of the book to outline possibilities and provide examples of the alternative paradigm he suggests.

Creating a World-Class Education

Chapters 7, 8, and 9 are case studies of schools that exemplify particular pedagogical approaches that Zhao believes will encourage the development of entrepreneurs, including student autonomy and leadership, product-oriented learning, and a vision of the globe as the school campus. Each of these approaches is detailed in the final chapter, in which Zhao lays out his re-imagined framework for education in the service of growing and educating entrepreneurs: the *Triad Model of Education for Global Creative Entrepreneurs*. First, students must be granted autonomy in the learning process; they must be given the freedom to pursue lines of inquiry that are interesting and meaningful to them. This will help students develop "unique and diverse talents" rather than standardized skills that have been the aim of education in previous epochs. In leveraging student curiosity and creativity, students will be inspired to push past "adequate" to heightened achievement.

Second, product-oriented learning positions learners as the creators and providers of knowledge, and positions them as a source of knowledge with some autonomy over their learning ventures. In this case, the teacher abdicates the traditional position of power in favor of a position as "a motivator, a reviewer, a facilitator, and an organizer" (p. 240). Under this conception of learning, problems are conceived as opportunities for action that challenge the status quo. Students can be asked to examine other people's needs, with an eye toward seeking innovative solutions and suggestions. Asking students to complete projects aimed at production also allows them to discover their own strengths and weaknesses, which Zhao positions as vital knowledge for future success.

Third, schools must create an atmosphere that allows students to feel that they are part of a global campus. Zhao suggests that educators help students develop a global perspective and work with global partners on the projects described above. He explains that there is promise in encouraging students' capacity to help and collaborate with others rather than compete. Finally, Zhao suggests a set of indicators for identifying world-class schools, including student voice, student choice, authentic products, sustained and disciplined processes, a strengths-based approach, a global orientation, and global competence. There is also a brief discussion of how the "basics" of learning might be approached under this model.

Summarizing this project, Zhao suggests that we must attempt to remove the obstacles that prevent a re-envisioning of the purposes of schooling. We must challenge traditional conceptions of academic achievement in order to disrupt the status quo, and we must train teachers who are willing to engage in leadership that promotes expansive globalized thinking. Additionally, we must take advantage of the new opportunities presented by technology and globalization in order to connect students and teachers with their peers on a global campus. Overlying each of these opportunities, however, is the directive that we must place value on and encourage student interest, engagement, and talent in order for the project to succeed. Zhao states that "[this project] is about respecting children as human beings and about supporting, not suppressing, their passion, curiosity, and talent. If schools can just do that, our children will become global, creative, and entrepreneurial" (p. 256).

At the close of the book, Zhao describes rumblings of discontent surrounding CCSS and what that might mean for the type of education that he proposes. Since the time of the book's publication, criticism of the CCSS has grown on several fronts. For an initiative that was launched with little public notice, implementation has sparked intense criticism from students, parents, and educators alike. While Zhao may well have predicted the effects of the CCSS, he also would recognize this "problem" as an *opportunity* to encourage a broadening of curriculum and a shift in educational aims toward creativity, innovation, and entrepreneurship.

Contributions and Possibilities

There is much in this book that deserves more public and policy attention. It is important to recognize the disjuncture between the current policies of standardization and accountability and developing workers who can thrive in the creative economy. The former does not serve the latter. While Zhao notes this disjuncture, he does provide an analysis of why we are pursuing the "wrong bet." Nevertheless, for education and the economy to move forward, this analysis and critique seems necessary. There are other tensions as well. Creativity is not the same thing as entrepreneurship, for example. There are tensions between globalization and democracy that also seem to demand consideration, as do the tensions between the pursuit of the new (creativity, entrepreneurship) and the importance of tradition and some level of social stability. Lest these seem all too negative, we will approach our discussion from the perspective of contributions and possibilities.

As above, a major contribution of Zhao's book is a critical analysis of the standards movement. Unlike critiques from the political left, where power, ideology, and oppression are seen as exacerbated by the standards and testing regimes, Zhao highlights the fact that the U.S. system was formed in the industrial era, when control was already seen as required. Certainly he notes that the recent policies are going in the wrong direction, but his point is that as far as creativity is concerned, the U.S. *system* of education never was able to systematically produce this. Instead, creativity came about because of slippage in the system, rather than by an intention to foster creative ideas and production. His proposals of learner autonomy, product-oriented learning, collaboration, global competence, and so on are all reasonable, but how to get to them is not his key concern. Thus there are many possibilities for work to be done.

First, an analysis and critique of the current system is sorely needed. This critique must be less about the structures and more about what allows the structures to be taken for granted. Why is it that control is so attractive to adults and system-thinkers alike? Why cannot we embrace an "investment in process" that Zhao proposes? The "power over" concept of structure no doubt springs from the colonial origins of mass education (Willinsky, 1998), but its intractable nature needs careful deliberation. Thus there is a set of possibilities for unpacking structures and of deep understanding that Zhao provides.

There are more possibilities as well. Zhao offers a set of cases that demonstrate his point, but there is clearly the possibility of more alternatives—outside of mainline educational institutions—that offer possibilities. Museum education seems to have a role that could be exploited in terms of developing creative people. Conceptualizing work in terms of apprenticeships may also lead to direct involvement in the creative process. There are many other venues, including local arts organizations and cultural agencies, that may find creativity more central to their processes. Finally, given that creativity lies between educational structures, there is the possibility that some of us can create new forms beyond what Zhao or other educational theorists have imagined. New assumptions may generate creative places yet to be imagined— contexts that invite the entrepreneurial activity.

Zhao's equation of creativity and entrepreneurship is a valuable contribution. This equation leads to questions about why we think business and art are separate spheres of activity. Many years ago, G.L.S. Shackle (1966) drew a distinction between truth seeking and truth making. Truth seeking is in the language of science—discovering what is there and discerning its nature and disposition. In truth seeking, truth is already in existence, and the task, then, is to search it out. Truth making, in contrast, sees the world as that yet to be imagined, yet to be produced. For Shackle, truth making was the language of business, which he saw as a form of poetry. Zhao speaks to this distinction in his contribution, and in doing so marks off much of what is taught in business schools—planning, a reliance on data, a view of organization as a fixed system to be administered, and so forth. For Zhao, jobs are now less in existing organizations and more to be made by individuals and collectives. Entrepreneurship is this creative urge—the urge to poetry—and for this contribution Zhao should be remembered.

There are possibilities other than that creativity and entrepreneurship are in a direct, one-to-one relationship. Equations are funny things—they often contain unknowns. There is the possibility that the unknown in Zhao's equation is in fact about the difference between the process he identifies as essential and the goal of a return based on one's creation. This is not to say that artists should not be paid for what they produce, but rather that this may be a form of goal displacement—from creating something yet unimagined to something that is sufficiently recognizable to be desired by a clientele. Entrepreneurship may lean toward the latter, while creativity may lean toward the former. The unknown in all this is how much creating the new is based in what is already in play, and how much is based in novelty. Put another way, how much is innovation on that which exists and how much is invention of the new? This distinction offers a host of possibilities; any *differences* between creativity and entrepreneurship may lead to conceptions of more possibilities than reducing each to the other allows.

Zhao also contributes to our understanding of globalization both through a set of international comparisons and by emphasizing how much of education and the economy are globally situated. This has been true for centuries, but technologies of travel, shipping, production, and information have made it fully evident. Globalization, of course, is often seen as opposed to democratization. Zhao, though, seems to suggest that these are not fully opposed forces. Information access and social media may feed democratization, but the Arab Spring teaches contradictory lessons on these counts. Creativity and entrepreneurship seem to celebrate individual liberty in Zhao's formulation, but none of these insure a democratic political system, even if much of the rhetoric over liberation and transformation of well-being is caught up in escaping a hidebound past—as Zhao depicts schools geared for academic achievement.

There are possibilities yet unrealized here as well. Creativity is certainly necessary if an economic process of globalization is to be linked to the political process of democratization. We say this because so many see globalization as the economy outstripping democratically elected governments and reducing citizens to consumers. Zhao points to the many forms of entrepreneurship, including social entrepreneurship, that seek to create a better world. It may be that there are possibilities for other forms of entrepreneurship yet to be imagined. We may need, for example, creative forms of government, and creative ways of reining in the economy in service of people rather than growth. Some recent work suggests that economic growth is not sustainable and "that a pro-poor approach to growth can make a positive impact without proportionate GDP growth" (Heffernan, 2014, p. 302). This model, of course, is less interesting to global capitalists, but it holds out the possibility that we can build creative economies beyond the one that drives us today, and to which Zhao is uncritically linked.

References

Florida, R. (2002). *The rise of the creative class.* New York: Basic Books.

Heffernan, M. (2014). *A bigger prize.* New York: Public Affairs.

Sefton-Green, J., Thomson, P., Jones, K., & Bresler, L. (Eds.). (2011). *The Routledge international handbook of creative learning.* New York: Routledge.

Shackle, G.L.S. (1966, December). Policy, poetry and success. *The Economic Journal,* 755–767.

Willinsky, J. (1998). *Learning to divide the world.* Minneapolis: University of Minnesota Press.

World Economic Forum. (2011). *Unlocking entrepreneur capabilities to meet the global challenges of the 21st century: Final report on the entrepreneurship education work stream.* Geneva, Switzerland: World Economic Forum.

Zhao, Y. (2012). *World class learners: Educating creative and entrepreneurial students.* Thousand Oaks, CA: Corwin.

THIRTY-NINE

David L. Kirp, *Improbable Scholars: The Rebirth of a Great American School System and a Strategy for America's Schools* (2013)

Linda Irwin-DeVitis

Improbable Scholars (2013), by David L. Kirp, is an accessible, engaging, and thorough case study (Whitehurst, 2013) of continuing and successful education reform in Union City, New Jersey. To be sure, Union City has all the myriad problems that confront many urban schools: poverty, drugs, violence, less-than-satisfactory facilities, transient students, large numbers of English language learners (many of whom do not have legal status), parents who are often barely literate in their first language, and health (hunger, vision, and dental) problems (Kirp, 2013, pp. 17–19). Union City Schools are in many ways typical of the urban miasma that creates chronic low achievement, high dropout rates, and grist for the demands for a revolution in American public education. It is rare to locate an urban district with these problems that is successful, and even more unusual to find a system where that success is maintained over the long term. David Kirp spent 2 years and innumerable hours in his case study of this rare urban district success story. *Improbable Scholars* (2013) is the outcome of his in-depth exploration.

There are few novel or breakthrough ideas in *Improbable Scholars*. Instead, Kirp celebrates the "ordinariness" of the major ideas and principles he documents. His analogy is evolution, not revolution. Kirp's metaphor for writing this case study is that he plays the role of the watchmaker examining a "Swiss watch," a system of many parts working together, finely balanced and focused, and completely ordinary. He documents the evolving, never-ending process of shaping a district grounded in community at all levels and committed to students and families. Kirp provides a rich portrait of a district fully engaged in the continuous work of building a culture of success based on the best research and professional practice and a deep respect for all constituents.

Should *Improbable Scholars* be included in this volume? It is not a theoretical tour de force, as are the seminal books authored by Freire (2000) and a number of others listed here. It is not a call for revolution based on a well-developed ideology, as are books by Michael Apple (2004), Henry

Giroux (1992), and Peter McLaren (2014). It is not a policy analysis in the mode of Ravitch (2011), Boyer (1985), or Zhao (2009), nor is it a polemic like Kozol's emotionally charged books and the new genre of agenda-driven movies—*Waiting for Superman* (2011), *Won't Back Down* (2012), and *The Lottery* (2010). It is not a "teacher/leader as super-hero" tale like the popular works about/by Geoffrey Canada, Joe Clark, Erin Gruwell, or Jaime Escalante. Rather, *Improbable Scholars* is a well-told case study that provides hope and a vision of building success in a low-income, urban school district without silver bullets, overheated rhetoric, or a rescue by edu-philanthropic, top-down reform.

In the growing divide between the educational research community and policymakers and practitioners, Kirp's stance (as is true of several others whose books are reviewed in this volume) is that of a public intellectual who chooses to write for a general audience. His purpose is to go beyond abstract theory and make education research, theory, and practice both concrete and accessible. Kirp paints a lively and textured portrait of theory in practice, and he largely succeeds in his chosen stance as watchmaker: he details the urban education in the Union City district, describes many of its complex interrelationships, its intersecting and multiple variables, and the often politically charged and chaotic environment in which it occurs. In this age of cynicism, when educators and education watchers wince at the appearance of yet another fad and its accompanying jargon, Kirp shares a well-crafted and engaging portrait of hard-won success.

Improbable Scholars is much needed today. Kirp's book provides a potent antidote to the tropes emanating from think tanks and corporate boardrooms that dominate the discourse of current education reform in both the popular media and in federal and state legislatures. It is my sincere hope that the education reform principles identified in *Improbable Scholars* will become so mainstream that Union City's ongoing evolution is no longer considered visionary or noteworthy—that is, when *Improbable Scholars* will be cited only for its role in illustrating complex and successful educational transformation built on solid research and grounded theory.

This essay review will look at several topics, including Kirp's rationale for the book within the context of current educational reform discourse; his criteria for defining educational success; his portraits of educators and their work; the principles he cites based on this case study to guide urban educational reform; and his efforts to go beyond Union City to find support for his conclusions. Finally, the review will return to situate *Improbable Scholars* and its place in this volume of influential books in the last half-century of American education.

How Does Kirp Situate the Union City Case Study in the Discourse of Current Urban Educational Reform?

Without inflammatory rhetoric or bombast, Kirp provides a critique of the current education reform agenda: the misplaced faith in school closings and mass firings as "turn-around" strategies; the largely unregulated expansion of charter schools; the overemphasis on high-stakes tests and *Teach for America*; and the imposition of often outdated business models for educational administration. He is clear and unequivocal in his concern about the hyperbolic *U.S. Education Reform and National Security* report (2012); the involvement of edu-preneurs, including Bill Gates, Oprah Winfrey, and David Brooks; and propaganda films such as *Waiting for Superman* (2011) and *Won't Back Down* (2012). Kirp exposes the short-term public relations hype of President Obama's touted 2011 visit to Central High School in Miami, where the president celebrated its "amazing" improvement in test scores by noting that the "progress" still left the school among the worst in the state of Florida. Its ranking for 2012–2013 indicates that, even now, only 19% of its students are proficient in reading, while 44% remain below the basic level. In addition, 30% of Miami Central students don't complete high school. The Florida Department of Education (2015a, 2015b) grades Miami Central (after adjustments) with a D overall. It is one of the three lowest-performing high schools among the 51 rated high schools in Dade County. So much for "high expectations" for all of our children! Like many others (Rothstein, 2004; Allington & Walmsley, 2007; Ravitch, 2011), Kirp concludes that there are "no quick fixes" for the problems in American urban education.

Kirp (p. 5) clearly identifies the real problem in American K–12 education: the miseducation of low-income and minority children. He chronicles state disinvestment in K–12 public schools, rising child poverty, and the exponential increase in numbers of English language learners. Using California as an example (now ranked 43rd in the nation, according to Wallethub, as reported in the *Huffington Post* [Klein, 2015], and earning a D+ from the Quality Counts 2015 analysis as a poster child for these policies), Kirp notes the disastrous decline of California schools. California's decline continues, even as the disinvestment in its teachers and schools has finally been halted by Governor Jerry Brown. Kirp cites what he sees as outstanding charter schools (e.g., KIPP and Green Dot), yet he is clear, if not enthusiastic, in his assertion that "it is in nearly 100,000 ordinary public schools that most of our 55.5 million schoolchildren will be educated" (p. 5).

Kirp's analysis is not exempt from ubiquitous assumptions that are part of the national discourse and are often accepted as commonsense, though they are lacking in empirical evidence. Many of the assumptions of the reform agenda Kirp criticizes are, nevertheless, taken for granted in his book. He uses the language of "college and career ready" without critique or caution. The mantra of "college and career ready" can be traced to Achieve, Inc. "College and career ready," the new de facto goal for American education, was endorsed by "leading" governors and business leaders at an education summit. There Achieve, Inc., joined other think tanks in sidelining the work of educators and educational researchers (other than a select few) and instead created national standards and assessments under the guise of state-driven policy— a bait and switch that did not pass muster. By 2008 Achieve had begun development on the common core and made it clear that the Common Core State Standards, when completed, would be inextricably linked to common assessments.

Kirp also uses the alarmist reformer rhetoric of international comparisons so common in the report he derided, *U.S. Education Reform and National Security* (2012):

> *The only chance we have to maintain our competitive position in the global economy is by doubling down on our investment in education and boosting the number of well-trained college graduates.* (p. 7)

Current international comparisons have been widely challenged and critiqued (Zhao, 2009; Berliner, Glass, & Associates, 2014; Loveless, 2012). While this section is contextual and not central to the story of Union City that Kirp tells, it is disconcerting to see these unquestioned assumptions in his contextual scan of the state of American public education. In addition, as we all do, Kirp uses test score performance as the ultimate evidence of success:

> Here's the reason to stand up and take notice—*from third grade through high school Union City students' scores on the state's achievement tests approximate New Jersey's averages.* You read that right—*these youngsters, despite their hard-knocks lives, compete with their suburban cousins in reading, writing and math.* (p. 8)

Yet he acknowledges in his introductory chapter that

> Union City's schools are constantly struggling to balance this command against all other priorities—sparking students' creativity, responding to the health problems and emotional baggage that many of these youngsters bring with them, generating a sense of community within the school house. Sometimes these schools succeed in maintaining that balance, always they try. What's more, those dazzling test scores don't depend on drill-and-kill instruction—the schools aim to turn kids into thinkers, not memorizers. (p. 8)

In his closing chapter, Kirp relies on test score performance, quantitative data, and quantitative benchmarks almost exclusively in his attempts to broaden his argument by looking at other successful urban districts. For each of the three districts (Montgomery County, Maryland; Sanger Unified in California; and Aldine, Texas) Kirp provides a one- or two-page overview:

Montgomery County, Maryland

> *In 2003, only half of the district's [Montgomery County] black and Hispanic fifth graders passed the state's reading test; by 2011, 90% did. Fewer than half the district's kindergartners could read in 2003; by 2011, more than 90% could read.... In 2011, 62% of Montgomery County eighth graders passed algebra, one of the benchmarks on the... "roadmap to college."* (p. 200)

Aldine School District, Texas

> *In the mid 1990's Aldine's schools were a disaster area. State achievement tests showed that many high school students could barely read or write.... Achievement scores have been steadily climbing ever since and now exceed the state average.* (p. 201)

Sanger, California

> *In 2003, Sanger was labeled a "failing" school system...but what a difference a decade can make. Sanger now ranks among the top half of California districts in reading and mathematics.*

To be fair, Kirp does mention the graduation rate for Latino students—a number that places Sanger in the top 10% of high schools nationwide (p. 204).

Kirp attributes these changes in Montgomery County, Sanger, and Aldine to the principles he extrapolates from Union City's success: (1) motivated leadership; (2) evolutionary change from within, relying on internal expertise; (3) use of data; (4) standardized curriculum, scope, and sequence, constructed by the teachers; and (5) continuing and intensive district-shaped professional development for teachers. However, he neglects one of the most striking factors in his case study of Union City's transformation: the role of the culture of caring (*abrazos*) that permeates so much of his inquiry. Each reader's perspective is shaped by his/her own worldview, experience, and values. But it is clear that *abrazos* in Union City is a fundamental piece of the transformational change that Kirp documents—from the decision to look to early childhood education as a model for curriculum change and to George Washington Elementary School as the finest exemplar of the Union City way:

At Washington, however, the teachers who have been on the job the longest are those who have con-tributed the most to making this such a fine school.... Nowhere at Washington are the virtues of col-legiality and collaboration more visible.... The culture of abrazos, of love and caring, at Washington School is rooted in close relationships of long standing between Les [the principal] and the teachers, among the teachers, and between school and the families. (pp. 60–62)

Kirp goes on to note the importance of conscious planning to make sure teachers have time to work with and learn from one another: "the class schedule gives teachers in each grade forty-five minutes a week for brainstorming, and the Dream Team uses this time to tackle the questions that arise in the practice of their craft" (p. 65). This caring is manifested most clearly in the first semester, but after the Christmas holidays, Kirp notes, "the challenge is to maintain Washington School's culture of abrazos" amid the harsh climate of high-stakes exams (p. 73). While this notion of caring and family is not the only factor that Kirp highlights, he gives it significant emphasis in his discussion of Union City. He also documents the "mostly" single-minded and unifying goal of Union City's teachers, administrators, political and civic leaders, parents, and the community to provide success for the young people—all the young people—who attend Union City Schools (p. 62).

In Kirp's presentation, the respect for students and their families is clear, authentic, and individualized. Students (and teachers) are valued as unique and worthy people. This is so un-like the reform language of NCLB and the prescriptions of Common Core. Just to document how different this attitude is, one need look no further than the words of David Coleman, principal architect of the Common Core in reading and currently president and CEO of the College Board. In his stump speech to local education leaders ("David Coleman's Global Re-venge," 2012) to drum up support for Common Core, Coleman had this to say about high school students' personal narratives: "as you grow up in this world, you realize people don't really give a sh*t about what you feel or think. What they instead care about is, 'can you make an argument with evidence...' or 'what is the difference between a fable, a myth, a tale and a legend?' The only problem with that question is that no one knows what the difference is and no one cares" (p. 2).

It is hard to imagine anyone saying or thinking those words in Union City. While Union City teachers want critical and high-level thinking—and yes, evidence to support assertions—they also value the personal narratives of their students. There is a respect for the cultural context and the personal voice of each student. There is an understanding of the centrality of narrative to humanity, collectively and individually. That vital theme has been argued by scholars from Plato, Nietzsche, and Bettelheim to Lev Vygotsky. While Union City's teachers may not cite those towering thinkers, they live this respect for individual and personal narratives in the attention and care they provide for their students. As one of the newer teachers puts it:

Of course I want them to become better readers, writers and mathematicians, but in the long run I really want them to become good people, respectful and responsible for themselves.

Another teacher notes that she chooses stories thusly:

Great author, great situation.... Those stories teach the students about character, about the impor-tance of respect and the need to talk things through. (p. 66)

While talking about these personal traits and social-emotional learning can quickly become a recipe and simply a fad, there is little doubt that such attention to each student and her story (whether told, written, or as the context for shaping effective instruction) is a critical factor in student success (Payton et al., 2008).

Kirp notes the historical tensions, the problematic policies and leadership, and the sad comparison to wealthier Orange, New Jersey, in maintaining this focus. It is this context of *abrazos* that is most salient in Kirp's description of George Washington Elementary School and the visionary leaders of the Union City District. The drive to create an integrated and caring school system and to eschew the "principal as savior" approach is all the more amazing given the pressure of an impending state takeover. Rather than have big-bucks consultants come in, Union City found strong leaders who worked with teachers to follow a sturdy path based on their own reading of the research. The district focused on a strong and uniform scope and sequence and charged the teachers with "unearthing strategies that the research had shown to work and then matching them with materials that sharpened the skills of thinking, reasoning, and collaborating, not rote learning." According to Diane Capizzi, a member of the committee shaping curriculum, "We had to know the theory behind what we were talking about and the evidence to back it up" (p. 79). Capizzi and her fellow teachers were clear: "the time they spent sitting around the cramped conference table and hitting the books opened their eyes to new ways of educating children" (p. 80).

There were some basic principles that the teachers agreed upon. All students would be on the same academic path. They were no longer "pulled out" for special services, since specialists came in to support students in the regular classroom. Learning centers and group projects all revolved around teaching students how to read. Literature pervaded all classrooms, and books were provided in English and Spanish. For the first year, the focus was on K–3. In addition, further monies came from the state, including $500,000 to create mini-libraries in each classroom. Many other grants were obtained, and most were used to increase the number of computers and augment teaching materials. Other districts (e.g., Trenton) that received additional monies chose to follow the "Great Leader" approach, hiring superstar principals and allowing them the freedom to do as they chose. The results are manifest: the Union City grow-your-own model, a district-wide approach, was far more successful than Trenton's hire-a-superman/woman approach. Kirp cites Max Weber, the influential nineteenth-century political theorist who warned of the lack of continuity in the charismatic leader approach, and he quotes today's Malcolm Gladwell: "The organizations that are most successful are the ones where the system is the star" (p. 89).

What Are the Major Principles Kirp Cites as Crucial to Union City's Success?

These are the criteria that Kirp extrapolates from the educational success of Union City:

1. *High-quality, full-day preschool for all children starts at age three.*
2. *Word-soaked classrooms give youngsters a rich feel for language.*
3. *Immigrant kids become fluent first in their native language and then in English.*

4. *The curriculum is challenging, consistent from school to school, and tied together from one grade to the next.*

5. *Close-grained analyses of students' test scores are used to diagnose and address problems.*

6. *Teachers and students get hands-on help to improve their performance.*

7. *The schools reach out to parents, enlisting them as partners in their children's education.*

8. *The school system sets high expectations for all and maintains a culture of* abrazos—*caring—which generates trust.* (p. 9)

Kirp also talks about another criterion related to the seventh and eighth characteristics mentioned above: "Based on these initial impressions, Union City readily passed my 'Golden Rule' test—I'd be happy if my own child went to school here" (p. 10).

It is the trust among constituencies (hard-won and very much a focus) of Union City that may well be the foundational principle for transformational change. In a recent summary (2012) of research on school climate, Thapa and colleagues describe the work of Bryk and his colleagues in a multi-year study of Chicago schools:

> Bryk and his colleagues found evidence that schools with high relational trust (good social relationships among members of the school community) are more likely to make changes that improve student achievement (Bryk & Schneider, 2004). In their most recent summary of this work, Bryk, Sebring, Allensworth, Luppescu and Easton (2010) detail how the following four systems interact in ways that support or undermine school improvement efforts: (i) professional capacity (e.g., teachers' knowledge and skills; support for teaching learning; and school-based learning communities); (ii) order, safety and norms (labeled as "school learning climate"); (iii) parent-school-community ties; and (iv) instructional guidance (e.g., curriculum alignment and the nature of academic demands). The authors underscore how their research has shown relational trust is the "glue" or the essential element that coordinates and supports these four processes, which are essential to effective school climate improvement (Bryk, Sebring, Allensworth, Luppescu, & Easton, 2010). (Thapa, Cohen, Higgins-D'Alessandro, & Guffey, p. 10)

The research summaries on school climate are congruent with Kirp's principles and foreground the notion of relational trust. Kirp cites Bryk's work, and he documents the unusually strong relational trust in Union City at most levels of the community and within most schools. The most detailed and engaging descriptions come from George Washington Elementary:

1. Kirp notes that, on Parents' Night at the school, despite a downpour, the gym is full of families (p. 43).

2. The principal "did whatever she could to alter the atmosphere" by thanking teachers and staff constantly, providing an inviting teachers' lounge, and being "supportive but demanding" (p. 45). Les (the school liaison) works to find staff who share her values and who always put the kids' needs above their own (p. 50). She manages this for the most part, although she does not have total control of who will be assigned to her school.

3. The school and district have a dynamic school liaison who works for the families but is also relentless in contacting parents when students are late or absent. She is the "go-to" person when parents need assistance, have questions, or just need an ear.

4. Les is first and foremost an instructional leader—a job far more difficult than simply managing a building. As one of the teachers says, "I want to knock on your door and not be intimidated. I want to talk with someone who knows about education, not just discipline" (p. 52).

5. Finally, and perhaps most telling, Kirp documents the respect and trust (sometimes slow in coming) among the teachers. He points out that these teachers are distinctly different in their personalities and teaching styles, and yet they are effective, caring, and collegial teachers. While a few are superstars, many are "just" good teachers who work together and continually improve their practice. As Kirp notes, this is truly a faculty dedicated to kids and to continuous improvement.

The relational trust does not stop with George Washington. Kirp underscores the relationships among the district staff and their trust in their own teachers. Asked to describe his proudest achievements, the superintendent highlights the homegrown assessments of student performance and the system's blueprint for running an effective school, which is gleaned from the best practices of the district's highest-achieving schools (p. 91). When there were major funding cutbacks, Union City, unlike other districts faced with budget challenges, chose to abstain from layoffs, to outsource non-educational activities, and to do more of its special education in-house (p. 99).

Finally, relational trust goes all the way to the city's leadership. Kirp portrays the city's mayor, Brian Stack, as inspirational. Mayoral control of urban schools is dicey and has proven unsuccessful in many districts. However, when the mayor is dedicated to the city's young people, is committed to strong public education, and is a talented workaholic, the result is amazing. Kirp notes that this mayor is "part Boss Daley, part Mother Teresa" and documents his passion for "his kids" and his commitment to fulfilling the aspirations that Union City parents have for their children. From finding funding for a new high school (with significant help from the state) to being available to parents who have concerns, the mayor is a constant presence and partner of Union City's educators—demanding and supportive.

Despite this emphasis in the Union City case study, Kirp does not make relational trust a foundational issue in his principles. Relational trust cannot be lumped together as just a strategic, concrete educational process or policy (vertical and horizontal curriculum alignment; teacher planning time; learning centers; universal early childhood education beginning at age 3; data collection, analysis, and use; and a word-rich environment). Rather, relational trust is central to this portrait of the Union City School District's success and allows the implementation of the more concrete educational processes and strategies that Kirp identifies.

How Does *Improbable Scholars* Portray Educators and Their Work?

Kirp's up-close observations of educators, both individually and in teams, is one of the most important aspects of his book. While he does not shy away from noting some of the issues and problems with individual educators and the difficulties in mounting cohesive, strong teams, he generally paints a picture of committed, hard-working professionals who may not all be destined to fame like Escalante, Gruwell, and Esquith, but who nevertheless are doing admirable work. Kirp not only finds the heroic in the daily lives of these professionals; he also celebrates their differences. Unlike the scripted curriculum that attempts to be teacher-proof, and unlike the celebration of young, smart, mostly temporary, and largely unprepared missionaries of Teach for America, Kirp documents the lives of teachers who often grew up in the district and who are frequently first-generation college students, most of whom attended state colleges that are unlikely to be at the top of the *Forbes* or *U.S. News & World Report* rankings.

Does *Improbable Scholars* Provide an Adequate Research Basis for Kirp's "Core Principles" in Urban District Reform?

In trying to make the case for generalization, Kirp cites the Broad Prize winners as examples of outstanding urban districts. He chooses to do brief profiles on three districts: Aldine, Texas; Montgomery County, Maryland; and Sanger, California. He cites these districts as additional examples of whole-district reform that bolster his analysis and conclusions in Union City. This attempt to generalize is questionable, given the track record of districts cited as Broad winners and finalists. Of the 27 districts, 12 (41%) have been the target of allegations of cheating on standardized tests based on unexplainable anomalies uncovered by statistical analysis (Perry, Judd, & Pell, 2012) and/or documented cases of cheating on achievement tests (Vegh, 2010; Spencer, 2004). Included in this questionable group of award winners are Aldine (Texas) and Montgomery County's (Maryland) Highland Elementary School, which won a national Blue Ribbon Award and a visit from Arne Duncan in 2009 (Judd, Perry, & Vogell, 2012).

There are myriad other ways in which districts can improve their statistical profile to win awards or assuage policymakers and parents—strategies that are much more difficult to document. For example, Fairtest has identified the following manipulations in urban districts: having teachers view tests before they are administered, excluding low scorers from enrolling or attending school on the day of the tests, using signals to alert students to wrong answers, and correcting erroneous answers prior to turning in answer sheets.

In addition to the cheating concerns associated with Broad Prize winners, it is not clear how much, if any, real time Kirp spent on site in these districts. Certainly, the districts are not studied in the depth and breadth of Union City, where Kirp documents his lengthy and repeated visits and observations. This is the weakest section of *Improbable Scholars* for several reasons. First, the evidence is not strong enough to shape reliable generalizations of what should happen in urban districts. Second, only the Union City case is a documented, in-depth case study, and the inclusion of other districts weakens an otherwise commendable case study. Finally, the stretch to find "common ground" restricts the otherwise rich qualitative portrait and relies too much on student test scores as the only arbiter of a good school district.

Kirp provides a list of "common factors" or "core principles" in successful urban districts. They are districts committed to:

- *Putting the needs of students, not the preferences of staff, at the center of decision making*
- *Providing quality pre-school*
- *Relying on rigorous, consistent, and integrated curriculum*
- *Using data to diagnose problems and pinpoint solutions*
- *Building a culture that combines high expectations with respect and a "can do" emphasis on the positive*

- *Stability and avoiding political drama*
- *Continuously improving—planning, doing, reviewing—building a true system not a collection of schools.* (p. 209)

Can the Successes in *Improbable Scholars* Be Replicated Beyond Union City?

This is the question that Kirp answers, if somewhat perfunctorily, in his last chapter. Forestalling critics such as Russ Whitehurst, Kirp begins his last chapter with the words "What works there can't work here—we're different because [fill in the blank]." Although he aims these words at "leery practitioners," it is, in fact, Russ Whitehurst (2013) who takes him to task in his review for the Brown Center Chalkboard, funded by the Brookings Institution. It is rare that I find myself agreeing with Mr. Whitehurst, but he has a point regarding Union City. It has any number of factors going for it (in addition to all the negatives in the demographics), including the tight-knit, largely Hispanic community; its amazing mayor; and the timing of the evolution to coincide with a court decision that meant significant investment in the district. There is much to be learned from Union City, and unlike Mr. Whitehurst, I do think *Improbable Scholars* has much value for practitioners and policymakers.

Yet Kirp's attempts to beef up his analysis using three other exemplars is much less convincing than his in-depth case study of Union City. There are ample additional case studies that point to greater successes by immigrant communities than America's multi-generational, low-income minority communities. There are multiple theories that attribute this performance to stronger and more intact families, the immigrant culture, and less cynical views of the value of education and the American Dream. With Sanger, Aldine, and Montgomery counties, there are gains in test scores similar to those in Union City. The decision to go "in-house" for expertise and investment in long-term teaching professionals is shared to some degree. Another striking consistency is the quality and commitment of district leadership in all four districts. While Kirp consistently eschews the "super-hero" leader, he also paints portraits of leaders who in many ways meet that criterion. Even as Kirp argues for stability, for continuous improvement, and professional community and collegiality, he describes many leaders in these districts who are exceptional—although their focus is aimed at collective impact and how to get there, rather than relying on individual charisma alone.

What Is the Possible/Probable Impact of *Improbable Scholars*?

Scholars and activists who advocate revolution will not be altogether happy with the stance of *Improbable Scholars*. While Kirp recognizes the problems inherent in high-stakes testing, the political realities of mandates, inadequate budgets, and, most glaringly, the realities of impoverished students, families, and communities, his work captures a school system that works within the constraints of these realities and still largely succeeds in its mission. The school leaders are pragmatic and persistent. The teachers are committed and hard-working, but their activism is largely confined to the school buildings in which they work. The politicians are realistic and creative—they are not revolutionaries. The people of *Improbable Scholars* are not super-heroes. To call them incrementalists would be generally correct, yet incomplete. Perhaps the most accurate way to describe them would be to characterize them as talented and committed professionals who share a common purpose.

A teacher or leader reading this book will be inspired and intimidated by many of the educators Kirp describes. Yet each of the educators whose stories and lives are part of this book is distinctly individual and decidedly human—no super-heroes here. The teachers and leaders who read this text will recognize the tensions, realities, struggles, successes, compromises, failures, and overall "messiness" they experience every day in their own districts and schools. Many teachers and leaders will find guidance and comfort in the ordinariness of the problems, the districts, and the people. They will find guideposts and, most important, hope and inspiration. *Improbable Scholars* is not easily dismissed as impractical or impossible—although it will be dismissed by some educators who will find reasons to doubt its lessons: *It's not possible here because…; we don't have any leaders like those; our students are too…; our resources are not…* (p. 112).

Education scholars will quibble with Kirp's wording, the consistency of his analysis, and the generalizability of any case study (it's their job and professional inclination to do so). Most of these scholars will also value *Improbable Scholars* for the depth of its analysis and will recognize the need for case studies to illuminate and "make real" the intersection of theory and practice.

However, the key to the book's ultimate impact will be the general reader—whether parent, community member, voter, school board member, or legislator. It challenges the dominant discourse of high-stakes accountability, teacher incompetence, teacher unions' intractability, student apathy, and the failure of urban public education. *Improbable Scholars* eschews the silver bullets of charter schools, state takeovers, Teach for America's short-term missionaries, highly paid outside consultants, and commercially boxed panaceas. Union City has no edu-philanthropist providing guidance, money, or personnel. Instead, *Improbable Scholars* is a potent example of how a real district—with real teachers and leaders, families, and politicians—can pool its resources to create a stable and successful school system where we would all be happy to send our children. The message of *Improbable Scholars* is important. Only time will tell whether the message reaches its most important audience and succeeds as a counter-narrative to the flawed popular discourse of urban education reform.

References

Allington, R., & Walmsley, S.A. (2007). *No quick fix: Rethinking literacy programs in America's elementary schools* (RTI ed.). New York: Teachers College Press.

Apple, M. (2004). *Ideology and curriculum.* New York: Taylor & Francis.

Berliner, D.C., Glass, G.V., & Associates. (2014). *50 myths and lies that threaten America's public schools: The real crisis in education.* New York: Teachers College Press.

Boyer, E. (1985). *High school: A report on secondary education in America.* New York: HarperCollins.

Bryk, A.S. (2003). Trust in schools: A core resource for school reform. *Educational Leadership, 60*(6), 4–45.

Bryk, A., & Schneider, B. (2004). *Trust in schools: A core resource for improvement.* New York: Russell Sage.

David Coleman's global revenge and the common core. (2012). *Schools Matter Blog.* Retrieved from http://www.schoolsmatter.info/2012/04/david-colemans-global-revenge-and.html

Fairtest. (2013). [Website]. Retrieved from http://www.fairtest.org/k-12/accountability/html

Florida Department of Education. (2015a). [Website]. Retrieved from http://schoolgrades.fldoe.org/pdf/1011/HighSchoolGradesPressPacket.pdf

Florida Department of Education. (2015b). [Website]. Retrieved from http://schoolgrades.fldoe.org/default.asp

Freire, P. (2000). *Pedagogy of the oppressed.* New York: Bloomsbury Press.

Judd, A., Perry, J., & Vogell, H. (2012). Cheating our children: Suspect scores put award's integrity in question. *Atlanta Journal Constitution.* Retrieved from http://www.myajc.com/news/local/cheating-our- children-suspect-scores-put-awards-in-nQtpy/

Kirp, D.L. (2013). *Improbable scholars: The rebirth of a great American school system and a strategy for America's schools.* New York: Oxford University Press.

Klein, R. (2015). These are the states with the best and worst school systems, according to new rankings. [Blogpost]. *Huffington Post.* Retrieved from http://www.huffingtonpost.com/2014/08/04/wallethub-education-rankings_n_5648067.html

Loveless, T. (2012). *How well are American students learning?* Washington, DC: Brookings Institution.

McClaren, P. (2014). *Life in schools: An introduction to critical pedagogy in the foundations of education* (6th ed.). New York: Paradigm.

Mellon, E. (2014). HISD cheating scandal escalates as 5 more teachers face firing. *Houston Chronicle.* Retrieved from http://www.houstonchronicle.com/news/education/article/HISD-cheating-scandal-escalates-as-5-more-5461503.php

Payton, J., Weissberg, R.P., Durlak, J.A., Dymnicki, A.B., Taylor, R.D., & Pachan, M. (2008). *The positive impact of social and emotional learning for kindergarten to eighth grade students: Findings from three scientific reviews.* Chicago: Collaborative for Academic, Social, and Emotional Learning (CASEL).

Perry, J., Judd, A., & Pell, M.B. (2012). Cheating our children: Suspicious school test scores across the nation. *Atlanta Journal Constitution.* Retrieved from http://www.ajc.com/news/cheating-our-children-suspicious-school-test-sco1/nQSTS/

Quality Counts 2015: State report cards map. (2015). Retrieved from http://www.edweek.org/ew/qc/2015/2015-state-report-cards-map.html

Ravitch, D. (2011). *The death and life of the great American school system: How testing and choice are undermining education.* New York: Basic Books.

Rothstein, R. (2004). *Class and schools: Using social, economic, and educational reform to close the Black-White achievement gap.* New York: Economic Policy Institute and Teachers College Press.

Spencer, J. (2004). 3 Acres Homes schools accused of cheating. *Houston Chronicle.* Retrieved from http://www.chron.com/news/houston-texas/article/3-Acres-Homes-schools-accused-of-cheating-1634150.php

Thapa, A., Cohen, J., Higgins-D'Alessandro, A., & Guffey, S. (2012). *School climate research summary: August 2012.* New York: National School Climate Center.

Vegh, S.G. (2010). Report: Norfolk students were shown answers during test. *The Virginian Pilot.* Retrieved from http://hamptonroads.com/2010/03/report-norfolk-students-were-shown-answers-during-test?cid=amc

Whitehurst, G.J.R. (2013). Deconstructing Union City. *The Brown Center Chalkboard.* Washington, DC: Brookings Institution.

Zhao, Y. (2009). *Catching up or leading the way: American education in the age of globalization.* Alexandria, VA: Association for Supervision and Curriculum Development.

Contributors

Kal Alston is a professor of cultural foundations of education and of gender and women's studies at Syracuse University.

Jan Armstrong is a professor in the Department of Individual, Family and Community Education at the University of New Mexico.

Roberto H. Bahruth is a professor of literacy, applied linguistics, and bilingual education and coordinator of the master's program at Boise State University, Idaho.

John A. Beineke is Distinguished Professor of Educational Leadership and also a professor of history at Arkansas State University.

Brett Elizabeth Blake is a professor of curriculum and instruction at St. John's University in Queens, New York, where she is also a senior research fellow in the Vincentian Center for Social Justice and Poverty.

Robert W. Blake, Jr., is a professor and chair of Elementary Education at Towson University in Towson, Maryland. While he was an MAT student at Brown University, Ted Sizer was the professor who most shaped his beliefs on teaching and learning.

Sue Books is a professor of education at the State University of New York, New Paltz.

Steven P. Camicia is an associate professor of social studies education in the School of Teacher Education and Leadership, Emma Eccles Jones College of Education at Utah State University.

Gary K. Clabaugh is a professor of education emeritus at La Salle University in Philadelphia, Pennsylvania; a founding partner of newfoundations.com; and managing editor of the policy-related journal *New Educational Foundations*.

John F. Covaleskie is a professor in the Department of Educational Leadership and Policy Studies at the University of Oklahoma, with appointments to the faculty of the Women and Gender Studies Program and the Center for Social Justice.

Joseph L. DeVitis has taught social foundations of education and higher education at five universities in his 43-year career.

Jean Ann Foley is an associate professor in the Department of Teaching and Learning at Northern Arizona University.

Barry M. Franklin is a professor of education emeritus in the School of Teacher Education and Leadership, Emma Eccles Jones College of Education and Human Services, Utah State University.

David Gabbard is a professor in the Department of Curriculum, Instruction and Foundations at Boise State University, Idaho.

Mark Garrison is a professor of educational policy and research in the Educational Leadership Program at D'Youville College, Buffalo, New York.

James M. Giarelli is a professor of education and philosophy in the Department of Educational Theory, Policy, and Administration in the Graduate School of Education at Rutgers, The State University of New Jersey.

Timothy Glander is a professor of social and psychological foundations at Nazareth College in Rochester, New York.

Karen Graves is a professor of education at Denison University, Granville, Ohio.

Jessica A. Heybach is an associate professor of education at Aurora University, Aurora, Illinois.

David Hursh is a professor of teaching and curriculum in the Warner Graduate School of Education and Human Development at the University of Rochester.

Linda Irwin-DeVitis is a professor of literacy education in the Department of Teaching & Learning at Old Dominion University, Norfolk, Virginia.

Melissa J. Jones is a professor of special education at Northern Kentucky University.

Leslie S. Kaplan, a retired school administrator with the Newport News, Virginia, public schools, is an education researcher and writer and an adjunct research professor at the Old Dominion University Research Foundation, Norfolk, Virginia.

Wendy Kohli is a professor of educational studies emerita in the Graduate School of Education and Allied Professions at Fairfield University, Fairfield, Connecticut.

Aaron M. Kuntz is an associate professor of educational research and department head, Educational Studies in Psychology, Research Methodology, and Counseling at the University of Alabama.

Alison LaGarry is a doctoral candidate who is completing a dissertation in the areas of music education, social foundations of education, and social justice education, at the University of North Carolina at Chapel Hill.

Donaldo Macedo is Distinguished Professor of Liberal Arts and Education at the University of Massachusetts, Boston.

Sheila L. Macrine is an associate professor of education at the University of Massachusetts Dartmouth.

J.B. Mayo, Jr., is an associate professor of social studies education at the University of Minnesota.

Michael P. Mueller is a professor and chair of Secondary Education with expertise in environmental and science education in the Department of Teaching and Learning at the University of Alaska, Anchorage.

D.G. Mulcahy is CSU Professor in the School of Education and Professional Studies at Central Connecticut State University.

Emily Nemeth is an assistant professor of education at Denison University, Granville, Ohio.

George W. Noblit is the Joseph R. Neikirk Distinguished Professor of Sociology of Education at the University of North Carolina at Chapel Hill.

Richard Ognibene, formerly a professor and dean of the College of Education at Seton Hall University, South Orange, New Jersey, recently retired from Siena College in Loudonville, New York, where he is a professor of education emeritus.

William A. Owings is a professor of educational leadership at Old Dominion University, Norfolk, Virginia.

Marcia Peck is an associate professor of educational foundations at Georgia College & State University.

Tryphenia B. Peele-Eady is an associate professor of educational thought and sociocultural studies in the Department of Language, Literacy, and Sociocultural Studies at the University of New Mexico.

William M. Reynolds is an associate professor in the Department of Curriculum, Foundations, and Reading at Georgia Southern University.

E. Wayne Ross is a professor in the Department of Curriculum and Pedagogy and co-director of the Institute for Critical Education Studies at the University of British Columbia in Vancouver, Canada.

John L. Rury is a professor of education and (by courtesy) history at the University of Kansas.

Susan Schramm-Pate is an associate professor of curriculum studies in the Department of Instruction and Teacher Education at the University of South Carolina.

John Smyth is a visiting professor of education and social justice at the University of Huddersfield in Yorkshire, England.

Lynda Stone is the Samuel M. Holton Distinguished Professor and Professor, Philosophy of Education at the University of North Carolina at Chapel Hill.

Barbara J. Thayer-Bacon is a professor of philosophy of education at the University of Tennessee, Knoxville.

Wayne J. Urban is a professor of higher education and associate director of the Education Policy Center in the Department of Educational Leadership, Policy, and Technology at the University of Alabama.

Kenneth Vogler is an associate professor in the Department of Instruction and Teacher Education at the University of South Carolina.

Joseph Watras is a professor in the Department of Teacher Education at the University of Dayton.

Joseph C. Wegwert is an associate professor in the Department of Teaching and Learning at Northern Arizona University.

Tian Yu is an associate professor of education at Southern Illinois University Edwardsville.